The E-Mail Frontier
Emerging Markets and Evolving Technologies

Daniel J. Blum
David M. Litwack

Addison-Wesley Publishing Company
Reading, Massachusetts • Menlo Park, California • New York
Don Mills, Ontario • Wokingham, England • Amsterdam • Bonn
Sydney • Singapore • Tokyo • Madrid • San Juan • Milan • Paris

To Ginny, Jack, Scott, Carolyn, and Jessica

Many of the designations used by manufacturers and sellers to distinguish their products are claimed as trademarks. Where those designations appear in this book, and Addison-Wesley was aware of a trademark claim, the designations have been printed in caps or initial caps.

Texts extracted from the International Telecommunication Union (ITU) have been reproduced with the prior authorization of the Union as copyright holder. Selection of extracts and modifications thereof lies with the authors and can in no way be attributed to the ITU. Complete volumes of the ITU material, from which the tests reproduced are extracted, can be obtained from: International Telecommunication Union, General Secretariat-Sales Section, Place des Nations, CH-1211 Geneva 20 (Switzerland).

Acquisitions Editor: Thomas E. Stone
Sponsoring Editor: Deborah Lafferty
Marketing Manager: Robert Donegan
Production Supervisor: Mona Zeftel
Text Designer: C. J. Petlick
Cover Designer: Diana C. Coe
Illustrator: George Nichols
Compositor: Publishers' Design & Production Services, Inc.
Manufacturing Coordinator: Evelyn Beaton

Library of Congress Cataloging-in-Publication Data
Blum, Daniel J.
    The e-mail frontier: emerging markets and evolving technologies /
  Daniel J. Blum, David M. Litwack.
        p.   cm.
    Includes bibliographical references and index.
    ISBN 0-201-56860-8
    1. Electronic mail systems—United States.   I. Litwack, David M.
    II. Title.
    HE6239.E54B58   1994
    384.3'4'0973—dc20   94-2513
                                                                  CIP

1 2 3 4 5 6 7 8 9 10   MA   98 97 96 95 94

P R E F A C E

The writing of this book has taken the kind of exciting turns and twists that resemble the exploration of a new frontier. Five years ago, we originally undertook to write a book about an international Message Handling System standard called X.400. Times change, markets change, and perceptions change. After several false starts and restarts, we realized that electronic mail in all its magnificent variations was the subject we were most interested in writing about, and we agreed that X.400 and its X.500 Directory Services companion were but some of the threads (albeit important ones) in the tapestry of global electronic messaging. We decided that this book would present that entire tapestry.

It has not been an easy task. But after three years of intensive research, we believe that this book now represents a snapshot of the state of e-mail in the mid-1990s. It is a state that truly resembles a new frontier—roughshod yet full of promise, chaotic yet full of opportunities that we can only partially imagine. The world has over 50 million e-mail users. This book is for those among them who want either to delve into the technology or to understand the market challenges and opportunities that lie ahead. It is intended especially for e-mail industry practitioners—investors, regulators, executives, managers, marketers, analysts, writers, and engineers—for whom, we dare hope, it will prove an invaluable reference text.

ORGANIZATION

In this book e-mail is covered from a number of points of view for a wide variety of practitioners and current and prospective users. These points of view include

- An overview introducing an e-mail vision, reviewing concepts and technology, and outlining the issues that will be addressed throughout *The E-mail Frontier.*
- A description of the private messaging, public messaging, and EDI messaging markets to assist decisionmakers in supporting their current and future e-mail requirements.

- A description and analysis of both proprietary and standards-based e-mail technologies that should prove of benefit to all levels of our readership.
- A vision supported by recommendations on e-mail planning and implementation for users, vendors, service providers, and public policy developers.

Chapters 1 and 2 present today's issues and tomorrow's challenges for e-mail by (1) tracing the evolution of e-mail and electronic commerce, (2) introducing key standards and technologies, and (3) developing a vision of the opportunities that e-mail offers for controlling and dominating the information glut that has become a ubiquitous attribute of our society and economy.

In Chapters 3 and 4 we describe and analyze private messaging facilities and public messaging markets with a view to identifying the important trends and obstacles to be overcome. In Chapter 5, we describe the architecture of host and LAN-based e-mail systems, gateways, and e-mail integration servers, also discussing how they function and how they interconnect to each other, and concluding with case studies of current products from selected market leaders. Chapter 9 discusses leading edge uses of e-mail for mail-enabled applications, electronic commerce, and workflow automation.

Chapter 6 describes how the X.400 standard works in considerable detail and analyzes its benefits and shortcomings, and its successes and failures. Chapter 7 provides a similar discussion and analysis of Internet Mail which, coupled with the TCP/IP suite of communications protocols, is enjoying great success positioning itself to assume the mantle of a worldwide e-mail architecture. (We also provide information in Appendix A on the major standards groups and consortia, including how they work and how to receive information from them.) Chapter 8 delves into directories to underscore their importance to the success of an e-mail infrastructure. Chapter 9 covers the intersection of messaging and electronic commerce technologies including EDI, mail-enabled applications, and workflow.

Chapter 10 revisits the e-mail vision first broached in Chapter 1 as we attempt to assemble and give coherence to the plethora of issues that have surfaced in this book. We do so by recommending factors that users should consider in using or implementing e-mail; and we also consider the issues from the perspectives of vendors, service providers, and public policy developers. In conclusion, we assess how far the e-mail industry has come, how far it has yet to go, and what barriers it must yet overcome in order to achieve the e-mail vision and to pacify the e-mail frontier.

ROADMAP

We have organized this book so that it can be read in a number of ways:

- For those readers who are new to the field of electronic messaging and commerce, Chapters 1 and 2 should serve as a useful and necessary introduction and overview.
- For those readers who want to know more about emerging e-mail markets and trends, Chapters 3 and 4 will be of special interest.

- Chapter 9 also addresses the emerging markets for EDI messaging, mail-enabled applications, and workflow automation using an e-mail infrastructure.

- Those readers with a primary interest in technology may first want to read Chapters 5–9 (where the architectures and functions of the major e-mail, directory, and electronic commerce technologies are described in detail) before moving on to market trends.

- Appendix A provides an introduction to the de jure and de facto standards and standards bodies as well as technical detail on what the standards cover. Readers may want to browse through the Appendix before attacking the technologies in Chapters 5–9.

- Chapter 10 provides recommendations on what to consider for those readers poised to deploy or to expand an e-mail system. This chapter is written with the assumption that readers have read the previous chapters.

Figure P.1 visually illustrates how *The E-mail Frontier* is organized and the relationships between the chapter groups described above.

To assist in making your reading as efficient as possible, each chapter ends with a summary which reviews the thesis of the chapter and its key points.

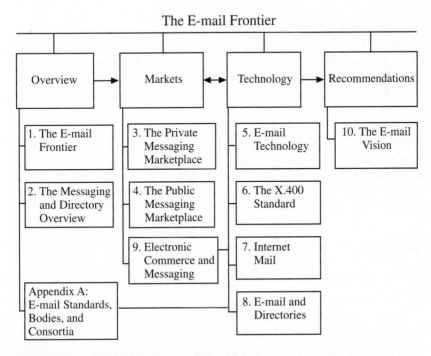

Figure P.1   Roadmap to *The E-mail Frontier.*

SUMMARY CROSS-REFERENCING GUIDE

Table P.1 shows where information on certain major topics can be found in this book. This table is intended to serve as a quick reference guide for the reader eager to pursue a specific topic.

Topic	Chapter or section reference	
APIs	Chapter 5	Technology: 5.3
		Case study: 5.6.2
Directories	Chapter 2	Overview: 2.4, 2.5
	Chapter 3	Market: 3.8
	Chapter 4	Public services: 4.8
	Chapter 5	Features: 5.2.8
	Chapter 6	X.400 use of: 6.10
	Chapter 8	Comprehensive tutorial
EDI/Electronic Commerce	Chapter 2	Overview: 2.6
	Chapter 4	Public service: 4.9
	Chapter 9	Comprehensive tutorial: 9.2–9.5
Internet Mail	Chapter 2	Overview: 2.5
	Chapter 3	Private market: 3.7
	Chapter 4	Public service: 4.4
	Chapter 7	Comprehensive tutorial
LAN E-mail	Chapter 2	Overview: 2.3
	Chapter 3	Market: 3.3
	Chapter 5	Comprehensive tutorial
	Chapter 9	Workflow considerations
Mail-enabled Applications	Chapter 5	Features: 5.2
	Chapter 9	Comprehensive tutorial
Security	Chapter 6	X.400 security: 6.13
	Chapter 7	Privacy enhanced mail: 7.6
	Chapter 8	X.500 security: 8.3.6
	Chapter 9	Electronic document authorization: 9.6
Workflow	Chapter 3	Market: 3.3
	Chapter 9	Comprehensive tutorial
X.400	Chapter 2	Overview: 2.5
	Chapter 3	Market: 3.6
	Chapter 4	Public service: 4.3, 4.7
	Chapter 6	Comprehensive tutorial
	Chapter 7	Internet interworking: 7.10
	Chapter 9	EDI over X.400: 9.3
X.500	Chapter 2	Overview: 2.5
	Chapter 3	Market: 3.8
	Chapter 4	Public services: 4.8
	Chapter 8	Comprehensive tutorial

Table P.1 Cross-referencing guide.

ACKNOWLEDGMENTS

We are grateful to many people for their contributions to *The E-mail Frontier,* including those who have given us moral encouragement and those who have diligently reviewed our manuscripts and offered us astute and trenchant commentary. They include

- Harald Alvestrand of Norwegian Telecom for his insistence on precision and accuracy and for his care in giving us a European point of view.
- Richard Ankney of Fischer International Systems Corporation
- Dave Crocker of Silicon Graphics and the IETF for his diligence in assuring that we provide an accurate and objective view of Internet Mail capabilities and initiatives.
- Rik Drummond of the Drummond Group
- Ted Myer and Gary Rowe of Rapport Communication for their support, review, commentary, and provision of Rapport Communication written and illustrative material
- Anthony Rutkowski of Sprint International
- Michael Ransom and Steve Trus of the National Institute for Standards and Technology
- Michael Zisman, President of Soft*Switch, Inc.
- All the users, vendors, and professional associates who have taken the time to provide us with background material and comment on sections of our manuscript.

We would like to thank and commend those individuals in voluntary standards work—through organizations both accredited de jure and de facto—for their devotion to the cause of standards and their dedication to the ideal of worldwide, ubiquitous e-mail and electronic commerce.

We must also thank our editor, Tom Stone, for his unflagging patience and encouragement; our associate editor, Debbie Lafferty, for her perseverance in the face of what, at times, must have seemed like incipient authorial grouchiness; and our production supervisor, Mona Zeftel, for her efforts to give aesthetic harmony to our work.

Finally, we thank our beloved wives and children who endured our virtual if not physical absences while we toiled at our workstations. Their love and support have brought us to this pass.

Daniel J. Blum
David M. Litwack

F O R E W O R D

The term "electronic mail" originated more than twenty-five years ago when the users of the first time-shared mainframe systems discovered the value of interpersonal communication by computer as an informal adjunct to the exchange of computer files. The term is an example of what my colleague Jacques Vallee used to call "the horseless carriage syndrome"—using the terminology and concepts of a previous generation's technology to describe a new technology. In the years following the first electronic mail systems using data networks and distributed computing systems, a search began for more generic, less confining terms. Terms like "computer-based messaging," "computer-mediated interaction," and "message handling" were all tried out, and the community now seems to have settled on "electronic messaging" as the term of choice in the scientific and technical literature.

But the term electronic mail remains most comfortable. E-mail evokes the image of a general-purpose conveyance system, equally capable of transporting the electronic postcard and the data equivalent of a large, heavy parcel. We conceive of e-mail as a means of improving the communication among people, organizations, and increasingly automated processes that comprise today's enterprise. This term serves as both an analogy and a metaphor for those who have designed and deployed the e-mail systems and services now in widespread use.

In their preface, Dan Blum and David Litwack describe the writing of this book as resembling the exploration of a new frontier, complete with the investigations and explorations that both led them astray and led them to insights. The term "frontier" implies a boundary between the known or the familiar, and the unknown. Their use of frontier correctly implies both the excitement and the risk of today's e-mail technology.

The beginnings of an electronic mail industry—the emergence of computer-mediated communication from the realms of universities and research institutes—has no clear historical milepost. But many would agree the e-mail industry began about fifteen years ago, in the late 1970's, with the effort to create the TCP/IP suite of protocols and the Open Systems Interconnection (OSI) family of data communication standards for services and systems. At about the same time, the pragmatists of electronic data interchange (EDI) were starting to consolidate what had been independently developed approaches to electronic commerce. As the TCP/IP suite of protocols emerged and the CCITT and ISO began their work on what was to become X.400, the key issues that arose were ones of fundamentals.

At issue was the creation of compatible messaging systems without jeopardizing their usefulness or ability to meet new unpredictable demands. What was sought might best be described as standards for e-mail "plumbing" and assurances that services and private systems could interoperate. The industry's successful effort to address these primarily technical issues is measured by the commercial success and growth of e-mail since 1980. Furthermore, the success of the industry in developing a technical infrastructure malleable enough for use in novel and unanticipated ways can be observed by considering the range of applications to which e-mail is now put. Blum and Litwack have done an admirable job of consolidating the knowledge and decisions of the industry, providing the reader with the insight and ability to consider his or her options in progressing with the creation of a private e-mail infrastructure and the use of e-mail services.

In the past fifteen years, many of the initial objectives established by the e-mail industry have been met, successfully defined, and implemented. Others have remained unsolved and persist in troubling the industry. Perhaps the two greatest problem areas recognized since the outset are those of addressing and naming conventions, and the creation of a complementary infrastructure to e-mail that provides distributed, interoperating directory services. We also face "success problems," the ones that few of us considered at the outset of the industry, and which have become more troublesome as e-mail becomes widely adopted. These issues often cannot be addressed by elegant technological solutions. Or they defy technology altogether because they are social issues. The examples of each type of problem concerning today's pioneer in his or her investigation are e-mail system management in multivendor environments (a technological problem that has defied clear solutions) and the dual issues of e-mail user security and privacy (a social, regulatory, and legal set of issues). In addition to these longstanding issues, Blum and Litwack point to a few themes for the next decade of e-mail which bear repeating and which the reader should keep in mind.

The addition of "intelligence" to e-mail is one of the most interesting challenges facing the e-mail industry. For some years we have heard about filters on mailboxes and customizable user interfaces. But the issue of e-mail intelligence goes further to include questions of how to place machine intelligence at the mailbox, in the envelope, in the message content, and in the directory. Another way of describing the objective of the investigation is the question: How does one "program" the entire e-mail system to behave in a way that is individually personalized, but which guarantees compatibility and interoperability among all users and their various e-mail systems?

Until recently, the use of e-mail as a basis for formal business transactions has focused (correctly) on EDI. All indicators point to EDI as one of the most explosive growth areas in commercial data communication and transaction processing. However, with the rapid deployment of devices and services targeting the individual consumer, electronic mail as the conduit for electronic commerce to the retail customer is becoming more realistic in the minds of providers. The question is whether the services can be as compelling for the end user as they are to the technology and service providers. Perhaps more than any single area of application, the extension of e-mail to incorporate more of the business-to-business and more customer-to-supplier transactions will be the focus of the next decade. It is likely to be a very wild territory, complete with spectacular attempts (and failures) and significant, novel insights into the deployment of messaging technology.

In any treatment of e-mail, the questions of privacy and security will undoubtedly surface. The issue is not only the pursuit of protection and assurances for our financial and business transactions. As important, and even more fundamental, are assurances that our individual rights and those of the businesses that provide messaging systems and services are respected and preserved.

If one point can be made by this introduction, it is this: The future of e-mail is not pre-determined, but rather it has a crafted future. Unlike a geographical frontier, the e-mail frontier does not separate the "known" from the "yet-to-be-discovered." Rather, what lies beyond the frontier of e-mail is yet to be created and managed by the explorers. Whereas a geographical frontier is usually investigated, mapped, and thereafter "civilized," the territory beyond the e-mail frontier is unformed and plastic. This factor makes it all the more important to understand the nature of today's frontier and to focus attention on those aspects which permit us to make a significant impact on the future of the industry.

Like most frontiers, the e-mail frontier has been and continues to be a line of demarcation in constant flux. E-mail is a communication medium which requires redefinition and creation of new technologies as well as new business practices, legal guidelines, and standards of etiquette. Because, like all pioneers, we rely on the experience of our predecessors and our contemporaries, books like *The E-mail Frontier* are increasingly valuable. Blum and Litwack have done us all a great service by succinctly mapping a large part of the "known world" of e-mail, and providing insights, lore, and guidance to that part of the e-mail world that is still in the process of formation and open to exploration by the reader.

Rich Miller
Menlo Park, California

CONTENTS

C H A P T E R   1

The E-mail Frontier

E-mail, currently the computer industry's fastest growing corporate application and an indispensable productivity aid to millions of individuals, represents a new frontier in the world of communications. Although a relatively old technology, e-mail today wears many new faces. We will explore both traditional e-mail and its new faces in this book. First, we will define our use of the word e-mail.

Any technology enabling the non-interactive exchange of electronic messages between e-mail users is called e-mail. An electronic message is any digitized object (or collection of objects) with a sender, a recipient list, a routing envelope, and various optional formatted fields. An e-mail user may be a person or a mail-enabled application, that is, a word processor or an advanced electronic bulletin board system that uses e-mail as a means of transporting information. We use the term e-mail in its broadest sense of person-to-person, person-to-application, application-to-person, and application-to-application communication.[1] Synonyms for this use of the word e-mail are electronic mail, electronic messaging, integrated messaging, or just messaging.[2] We use these terms more or less interchangeably in this book.

---

1. This categorization was coined by Mike Zisman, president of Soft*Switch, Inc. [SOFT89]

2. As the concept of e-mail broadens to encompass workflow and EDI, the influential Electronic *Mail* Association (EMA) recently went so far as to change its name to the Electronic *Messaging* Association.

As e-mail users, we can send messages directly from our desktop computers, portable computers, or personal communicators to other people or to computer applications. The same message that appears on our own computer screen also appears on the computer screen of our correspondent. Moreover, messages received electronically not only can be read, but also be stored, revised, answered, forwarded to interested parties, and otherwise processed by both the recipient and by computer programs in myriad ways. Just as face-to-face is the best way to communicate interactively (because there is no information loss), e-mail is often the best way to communicate information non-interactively. Our vision statement for e-mail is as follows:

> E-mail is a key communications application of the information age. It enables people or mail-enabled applications to exchange revisable multimedia information, workflow, and electronic data interchange transactions. This exchange can occur with anyone, anytime, anywhere with speed, ease of use, intelligence, security, and at low cost.

This vision statement stretches the definition of what can be accomplished with e-mail today, but it represents a worthy target for the messaging industry to achieve by or before the end of the decade. Chapter 1 discusses the socioeconomic factors that make e-mail both natural and inevitable, the uses and benefits of e-mail, and the ways in which e-mail is changing in response to global megatrends (some industry professionals among our readership may already take this for granted). Chapters 2–9 will cover e-mail's evolving markets and emerging technologies in considerable depth. Chapter 10 will help readers integrate the many concepts discussed in this book and closes with an assessment of e-mail's current progress toward achieving this target vision.

1.1   MEGATRENDS AND BUSINESS REQUIREMENTS: THE DRIVING FORCE

The business and personal technological requirements of our faster, more flexible information age are the driving forces along the e-mail frontier. At the macro level, key business trends impacting e-mail are the emergence of an information economy, globalization, and social change.[3] These trends need review in order to make the connection between the larger forces shaping our lives, the ways in which organizations at the micro level are adjusting to those forces, and how e-mail fits onto the global canvas more clear.

- **Information economy emergence:** More and more, services and other industries are based on information. Even in traditional industries, the timely and efficient capture of information becomes the key to success. The compa-

---

3. We are grateful to Debra Schofield of AT&T, whose presentations on industry megatrends inspired this coverage.

nies that succeed in the information economy will be those who can increase the timeliness of information distribution to their customers, trading partners, and suppliers and those who can build information refineries to manage the information glut. In this regard, Richard Miller, President of Telematica, and co-founder of messaging industry think tank Rapport Communication, said at the Electronic Mail Association (EMA) conference in June 1993 that "[t]he information age will truly have arrived when individuals and companies *never* complain that they are getting too much information." E-mail is already a convenient method for distributing information; more significantly, e-mail developers are also mindful of *filtering* the information as it is delivered.

• **Globalization:** Continued growth in the trade of goods and services and increased trans-border capital flows act to shrink the globe daily. More and more companies are operating in a multinational context. Japanese auto plants are setting up shop in the United States. IBM moved its communications division headquarters to Europe. The use of inexpensive labor in the developing countries for tasks as diverse as parts assembly in Mauritius, data entry for credit card receipts in Mexico, and software development in India is on the rise. The sun never sets on the modern multinational enterprise. Global teams must work together to solve problems rapidly. Global e-mail networks are needed to assist such communications without regard for time zones or national boundaries. These networks are emerging today.

• **Social trends:** Democratization proceeds at both organizational and national levels. Facsimile (e-mail's elder cousin) was a factor in thwarting the 1991 coup in Moscow. The workforce grows increasingly mobile and more independent. Environmental concerns press for the paperless office and telecommuting. The American Disabilities Act demands access to information for those who cannot travel or cannot see. The emergence of the virtual office makes e-mail an indispensable tool for many. By enabling open communication, e-mail not only promotes democracy, but can be an essential tool for personal, professional, and environmental liberation.[4]

If the changes on the macro level increase the importance of e-mail, so do the ripple-down effects occurring at the micro level in response to the larger forces. These ripple-down effects include organizational decentralization, the emergence of the "virtual enterprise," outsourcing, consolidation, mergers and acquisition, and rightsizing the computing platform base.

All of these ripple-down effects further emphasize the importance of networked communication and therefore e-mail. As indicated below, these organizational

---

4. Jerry Berman, executive director of the Electronic Frontier Foundation said at the EMA conference in June 1993: "The advent of information superhighways (of which messaging is a part) promises to be one of the greatest advances in free speech ever. Anyone can be an information receiver or information provider. We need to assure that the highway is affordable and accessible to all."

trends both fuel the already roaring e-mail market and drive the technology in new directions.

- **Organizational decentralization:** Economic forces (e.g., ever-increasing overhead costs and a need for the flexibility to respond to ever-decreasing windows of opportunity) are driving organizations toward decentralization. This paradigm promotes empowerment of employees via increased information flow, increasing use of consortiums and other organizational partnerships, and increasing use of "agile" consultants with specific expertise. Large organizations are being reinvented. Our reliance on middle management as an information load-bearing structure is reduced; networks and e-mail step in to assume more of the burden. For example, products such as Lotus Notes (a mail-enabled application supporting workflow and document filing/distribution capabilities) thrive in the flattened organization, and help to accelerate the decentralization process.

- **Virtual enterprise:** If the large, hierarchical organization is on its way out, the virtual enterprise is on its way in. The virtual enterprise is organizationally decentralized and geographically distributed. Yet it works because its parts are better coordinated than the parts of the older enterprises ever were. Virtual offices empower networked workgroups. Open standards and interoperable communications enable integration between the arms of the organization. Tightly linked webs of trading partners, customers, and suppliers replace vertical integration and enhance the division of labor. Networks for e-mail and electronic commerce can become the circulatory system that enables the virtual enterprise organism to thrive. As an example consider the portrait in Chapter 2 of a vast virtual automobile enterprise spanning engineering plants, assembly lines, parts suppliers, and dealerships (see Section 2.6). In *Paradigm Shift* [TAPS93], the authors describe a virtual enterprise as existing on three levels—the workgroup, integrated organization, and extended enterprise level—and they cite networks and e-mail as key enabling technologies. Figure 1.1 diagrams the elements, or levels, of the virtual enterprise, and the importance of e-mail at each level.

- **Outsourcing, consolidation, mergers, and acquisition:** Outsourcing is a result of the two previous business trends toward decentralization and emergence of the virtual enterprise. Few enterprises install a messaging network, or any other commodity product, without posing the buy/lease question. As we shall see in later chapters, outsourcing has major implications for public messaging services. Moreover, the consolidation of industries through corporate acquisitions spotlights the criticality of e-mail standards that will ensure users with different products can communicate when suddenly thrown together.

- **Rightsizing the computing platform base:** As a consequence of business decentralization trends and the evolution of microcomputer technology, computing power during late 1980s and early 1990s began migrating from mainframe hosts and onto desktop workstations. As one of many computer

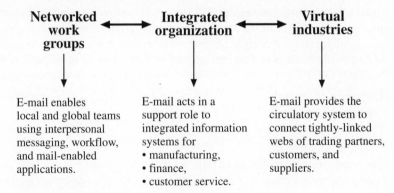

Figure 1.1   E-mail and the virtual enterprise.

applications, e-mail follows changes to the platform base. Thus e-mail is also migrating from a departmental to a desktop application.

1.2   THE USE OF E-MAIL

In response to these megatrends, individuals and organizations both large and small are using e-mail networks that enable people to send anything from a short note to a long word-processing file, to one recipient or many recipients, over land-based or wireless data links, regardless of whether or not the sender and receiver use the same data communications network, computer platform, or e-mail system. These networks are becoming basic to achieving organizational or individual goals.

The day will come when a doctor in New York can receive critical life-saving information from a doctor in San Francisco because medical e-mail networks enable prompt and secure communications. World hunger will be reduced when relief agencies in remote areas of the world are in e-mail communication with grain elevator operators carrying surpluses and shipping companies with excess capacity. Law enforcement professionals will be more productive when a Miami policeman, a litigator in Washington, the state police in Texas, and an FBI agent in California can cooperate closely in tracking a criminal because their very different computer systems are able to exchange mail. More and more, these scenarios are not science fiction—they are fact.

Improved communications through e-mail empowers rank-and-file employees at all levels of the enterprise. Even CEOs and other high-level managers have been known to sing the praises of electronic mail for its ability to give them a view into the workings of their own organization. Uses of e-mail include[5]

5. Some of the listed material was adapted from the Electronic Messaging Association's "A White Paper on 1988 X.400 Migration." [BLUM92] The EMA's support for that work is gratefully acknowledged.

- **Basic interpersonal messaging:** Day-to-day communication between people whether they are in the office, telecommuting from home, or on business travel. Interpersonal messages can be casual or formal. Time savings resulting from e-mail are estimated on the order of one half hour or more per day per worker.

- **Exchange of revisable files:** Word processing, graphics, and spreadsheet applications can be mail-enabled or programmed to use the e-mail system. This eliminates the need for rekeying or reformatting information, speeds collaborative work cycles, and boosts the quality of office output.

- **Electronic data interchange (EDI):** Exchange of formatted trade data containing quotes, purchase orders, shipping notices, invoices and other business documents can achieve dramatic savings and productivity improvements.

- **Workflow:** Electronic forms (or other information) routing and approval technology can be used to automate internal business processes, such as purchase requisitions, expense reporting, sales leading tracking, and a myriad of others.

The confluence of interpersonal messaging, EDI, and workflow over a single, secure messaging network enables *electronic commerce*. For example, consider the ways in which e-mail could improve quality and production in the automobile industry. Dealerships could submit trouble reports via e-mail. Engineers could route, process, and resolve the trouble reports with the aid of workflow management systems. Factories could order new parts using EDI purchase orders; EDI invoices could be sent to a billing facility. Chapter 2 will take these ideas and expand them into a scenario. The important point to note is that all the electronic commerce activities just mentioned can take place over a robust messaging infrastructure.

These benefits indicate that e-mail and electronic commerce translate into competitive advantage for all types of business by helping them produce higher quality products, improve customer satisfaction, reduce costs, and improve communications within the company as follows:

- **Higher quality products:** In the global information economy, organizations must be prepared to create and change plans rapidly and flexibly. E-mail allows employees of an enterprise to remain in better communication with other employees, with associates, with allies, with strategic partners, and even with customers. EDI offers improved interfaces with both suppliers and purchasers. Businesses can shift production or delivery schedules more rapidly to respond to changing market demands and product revisions.

- **Higher level of customer service:** E-mail can help businesses to provide a higher level of customer service. Customer access to the appropriate goods, services, and staff assistance can be streamlined and improved. Trouble reporting can be centralized in an electronic mailbox or a help desk to which customers can send messages around the clock. The customer is put on hold less frequently and for shorter intervals. Problems are sorted and prioritized offline. Customer orders, trouble reports, and other information received via e-mail can be stored automatically in corporate databases, providing a customer profile for future marketing and service efforts.

- **Reduced costs / hard dollar savings:** Hard dollar savings[6] are easy to quantify. With a relatively paperless office, less floor space is needed for file cabinets and archives. Clerical staff can be reallocated to other functions. Errors that previously occurred during manual paperwork processing are drastically reduced or eliminated. Inventory carrying and remaindering costs fall as businesses move to quick-response strategies at the point of sale and just-in-time inventory strategies at the warehouse. Retail outlets can fill customer needs more rapidly, leading to increased sales. Overall expenses of accounting and auditing fall as well with the use of online databases fed from EDI and workflow processes.

- **Reduced costs / soft dollars savings:** These savings can only be estimated but should not be ignored. The general benefits of e-mail include improved communication flow and information sharing within the business. Various functional groups in the company are more aware of each other's work, resulting in increased interaction between engineering, marketing, sales, operations, and other departments. These interactions lead to unexpected innovations and synergies, as well as the reduction of redundant efforts.

These benefits are translatable to government or public service institutions as well. In addition to these generic benefits of messaging, some of the ways in which government agencies will utilize messaging to positive effect within agencies, between agencies, and with outside organizations include automated collection and distribution of survey information from individuals, corporations, or local government organizations; electronic collection of tax forms; electronic distribution of publications; Freedom of Information notifications; and EDI, Electronic Funds Transfer, and Continuous Acquisition and Life-cycle Support

The areas where government can benefit from messaging networks are thus many and diverse. For example, the cc:Mail product was used to good effect in the Persian Gulf War to send messages back to the United States concerning sealift logistics. On the environmental front, millions of tons of paper can be saved by increased government use of electronic publishing. Increased telecommuting leads to decreased fossil fuel usage. There are many ways to increase productivity so that, even with the same operating budget, e-mail and electronic commerce can make government users more effective. In recognition of this, the Clinton administration issued an Executive Order [EXEC93] on 26 October 1993, mandating that the government move to an electronic commerce system for exchanging acquisition information with the private sector.

---

6. Hard dollar savings are those that can be readily measured and reported.

1.3   THE NEW FACES OF E-MAIL

Increasingly, e-mail is mission-critical to the modern virtual enterprise. Yet in terms of global messaging infrastructures today, we are running expensive cars over dirt roads, the signs are missing or misleading, and the maps are nonexistent. The goals articulated in our vision statement remain elusive.

Still solutions are at hand. An ongoing feedback loop exists between business and technology trends. Requirements generate technology, technology creates new paradigms, new paradigms create new requirements. Consider that, to manage our affairs in the information age, we needed more efficient means of communication—one of these was e-mail. So we got e-mail, but too much of it, and too many different flavors. To illustrate, as we were writing this chapter, one of our colleagues returned from a week's absence to find over a *thousand* waiting messages in his mailbox. A large oil company counts eighty-seven different (largely incompatible) mail systems in use corporatewide.

So the requirements change. We still want e-mail, but with a few twists. Now it must conform to certain standards so that it can interoperate with our neighbors' e-mail systems. And it must come with smart messaging and smart mailbox capabilities to help us filter and file our e-mail.

This feedback loop, or spiral, drives e-mail evolution. Today, e-mail markets and technologies are advancing along three trends, or wavefronts: multimedia messaging, unparalleled connectivity, and electronic commerce and electronic communities. These wavefronts are discussed next.

1.3.1   Multimedia Messaging

What if you could send sound or video information in e-mail messages? What if you could send compound documents? You can. Both business needs and burgeoning technological opportunities (both in the bandwidth and interface areas) are driving a key multimedia messaging trend. As we shall see, current messaging standards, as well as local messaging solutions such as Microsoft Mail and cc:Mail, are all now positioned in one way or another to better accommodate multimedia messaging. But what *is* multimedia messaging?

The term multimedia messaging has been used often, but sometimes in an unclear manner. We clarify it here by defining it along a two-dimensional axis in Fig. 1.2.

Multimedia message content, of course, is what a user puts in the message. Regarding content, the transition of e-mail from a simple, line-oriented medium for exchanging textual information to a grass roots groupware medium for exchanging revisable files is well underway. The next stage—e-mail's transition to a medium for exchanging sound and video information—has barely begun. This transition will be driven by the proliferation of optical character recognition, scanning, and imaging technology; speech recognition, voice annotation, voice synthesis, voice response systems and subsystems; and desktop video capabilities.

Multimedia message conveyance, on the other hand, concerns how the message travels. An e-mail message that originates in a desktop PC or departmental minicom-

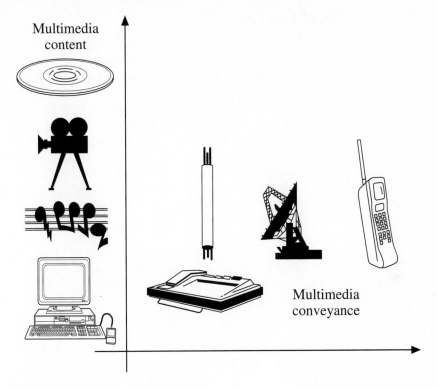

Figure 1.2   Multimedia messaging.

puter may travel to a similar system, or be sent to a fax machine; it may be printed, wrapped in a postal envelope and paper mailed; it may be broadcasted over satellite networks to users with personal wireless communicators; or it may be switched through telex or teletex. E-mail should flow to its recipients by whatever path (or medium) is available or preferred by the recipient at a moment in time.

But multimedia mail content and multimedia conveyance are orthogonal to one another, as Fig. 1.2 suggests. That is, not all contents are suitable over all conveyance mechanisms. Short video clips can turn into massive messages, making them ill-suited for wireless transmission, bandwidth-limited land lines, or even conventional local messaging infrastructures.[7] This paradox creates confusion about multimedia mail and poses a technology challenge that will be resolved through an eventual network bandwidth explosion and increased routing/processing intelligence in messaging infrastructures, yet another developing trend.

---

7. An employee of a U.S.-based Fortune 100 corporation cited a stark internal risk assessment for their 6000 user network: If a single originator packaged a five-minute video clip as an e-mail message to all employees it would bring the network down for five to seven days.

1.3.2   Unparalleled Connectivity

E-mail today offers unparalleled connectivity between users employing fundamentally different computing platforms, including PCs, mainframes, and minicomputers. These users reside on fundamentally different networks, such as Local
Area Networks (LANs), Wide Area Networks (WANs), and even POTS (plain old
telephone system) networks, but can communicate because of e-mail's *store and
forward* architecture. Here message switches can transfer messages between different platforms connected over incompatible, intermittently connected networks.
This development should be old news but is not because unparalleled connectivity
requires full interoperability between different kinds of mail systems. Only when
full interoperability (and thus connectivity) is achieved can new paradigms (e.g.,
the convergence of e-mail, groupware, and electronic commerce) be realized. This
section will discuss first the challenge of interoperability, then the opportunities
that lie ahead.

   During the 1970s and 1980s, many organizations installed e-mail as a workgroup or departmental-level solution without regard to its strategic implications
for the whole organization. Consequently, not only do different organizations use
different e-mail systems, but often different departments within the same organization use different e-mail systems as well. As e-mail came to be considered a
strategic application, a strong requirement emerged for e-mail integration and
e-mail interoperability. Users of different e-mail systems, suddenly thrown together on new projects, found they could not send each other e-mail or could only
exchange messages imperfectly.

   So, Bob can't send mail to Alice, but Alice can send mail to John, and John
might be able to send mail to Bob . . . is this communication? Faced with such
problems, organizations demanded e-mail standards for message formats and for
the means of message exchange. Standards emerged and products began to support the standards. Chapter 2 will introduce two major e-mail standards families:
X.400 and Internet Mail. These families, together with a collection of de facto
standards promoted by vendors, have begun to halt the slide toward an e-mail
Tower of Babel. Though the coexistence of e-mail standards remains imperfect
and uneasy, standards and technology seem to be converging toward a common
set of capabilities. These capabilities include the ability to exchange identified
binary file types, place multiple attachments in messages, use globally recogniz-
able addresses, and use directories in support of e-mail.

   Even as standards emerged, so did e-mail integration products that offered
gateways between incompatible e-mail products, or between e-mail products and
standard protocols. E-mail integration products, such as Soft*Switch Central with
gateways to over 50 environments, offered the means for organizations to interconnect their e-mail systems into enterprise messaging networks. Once interconnected, privately operated enterprise messaging networks could communicate
with one another and with the outside world at large through public messaging
services, such as the Internet, MCIMail, and ATTMail. With greater interoperability during the late 1980s, e-mail began to trickle down to the masses. As a

sign of the times, the White House opened the electronic floodgates in 1993 with its own Internet connection.

For e-mail to become truly ubiquitous, and to realize fully the potential articulated in our vision statement, however, the interoperability situation must improve still more. One of the major remaining blocking factors to e-mail is the relative difficulty users face in specifying address information for a message. We call this the *Rolodex Problem*.[8] Because there is no single universally accepted standard for how e-mail addresses are written or entered into an e-mail system, it is impossible to print an e-mail address on a business card in the correct syntax for every potential correspondent with every potential e-mail system. The Internet e-mail address (see Chapters 2 and 7) is the closest thing we have to a universally-accepted, easy-to-use addressing standard. But until this (or some other) standard is universally agreed, fax (with the familiar telephone number) will remain easier to use than e-mail despite its disadvantages in other respects.

Our hope is that the messaging industry can continue moving along the wave front toward greater interoperability, surpassing today's addressing dilemmas and uneasy X.400/Internet coexistence. A need for more flexible standards exists to cover not only interoperability issues between multiple systems, but also the portability of mail-enabled applications, operation of e-mail over telephone lines as well as leased lines, the use of international character sets, infrastructure support for electronic commerce, and so on. To make e-mail ever more ubiquitous and easy to use, the interoperability imperative demands the ability to run *anything over anything*.

1.3.3   Electronic Commerce and Electronic Communities

E-mail is becoming more than a form of casual interpersonal messaging. E-mail promises to become *integrated messaging*, and now encompasses the beginnings of an infrastructure with the ability to carry interpersonal messages, EDI, and workflow messages. With the advent of integrated messaging, e-mail has become a form of *electronic commerce* between organizations. Enterprises will eventually be able to use a messaging infrastructure for external trading that is more secure than paper media are today, and infinitely more productive and responsive. Within their internal office environs, they will be able to create white collar assembly lines through workflow technology based on messaging and distributed databases.

Electronic commerce technologies can also potentially engage a vast user base for consumer messaging. The vision of an *electronic community* first began to gel in early 1994. With the formation of the Commerce Net consortium in the Internet environment, and the announcment of AT&T's PersonaLink service and General Magic's Magic Cap™ software platform and Telescript™ communication technology, the first ground was broken in combining intelligent, or smart,

---

8. We are indebted to Martin Schmidt, International Trade Commission, United States Government, for this insightful phrase.

Figure 1.3   Downtown.   *Taken from Magic Cap software platform, developed by General Magic, Inc.*

messaging and electronic marketplaces. *Smart messaging* and *smart mailboxes* are technologies that enable increased intelligence to be built into messaging platforms, so that they may better support group collaboration within enterprises (or virtual enterprises) or a diverse array of consumer messaging services. These services function, in effect, like an object-oriented electronic marketplace. Figure 1.3 depicts an actual screenshot of the Magic Cap software's "downtown scene" as it might be displayed on a Personal Intelligent communicator (portable hand-held device). In a production environment, the downtown scene would represent the actual electronic community within PersonaLink, populated with electronic shops and services that users could enter with a push of a button.

We highlight the General Magic Initiative not because we can be certain it will succeed, but because it is the outgrowth of a bold vision: the creation of electronic communities and marketplaces using advanced technologies (in which e-mail prominently figures). Today's e-mail networks—including millions of Internet Mail users, X.400 users, and users of other systems—are already creating electronic communities. But they have yet to create electronic marketplaces within such communities. We salute those in the industry who dare to dream and put their dreams into action.

The e-mail infrastructure, consisting of enterprise messaging networks and public messaging networks, is only just beginning to catch up with the age of electronic commerce and electronic communities. The wavefront of infrastructure change encompasses the following:

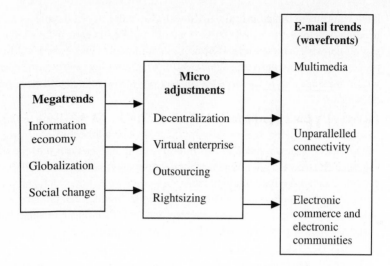

Figure 1.4   Summary of E-mail and E-mail relevant trends.

1.4   SUMMARY

E-mail is changing in response to emerging socioeconomic paradigms, and in re-sponse to the opportunities and problems generated by its own roaring technologi-cal engine. The relationship between the new faces of e-mail and global trends is summarized in Fig. 1.4 on page 14.

The e-mail frontier itself is too wide to permit its complete description in any one volume. However, in this book, we will be covering the topics that we feel are the most important to readers attempting to grasp the nature of the e-mail market, e-mail technologies, and e-mail industry trends. We hope that you will follow our roadmap along the e-mail frontier and benefit from this book, and that the e-mail vision statement at the beginning of this chapter will become a reality for you and your organization.

- **New standards:** Standards already developed, currently in developme needing development include those standards tailored to carry EDI over saging networks and to support group scheduling and rules-based workl processing. Also included are standards for programming instructions carr within messages and standards for storing workflow-related information directories.

- **Increased e-mail platform intelligence:** Why build the same complex workflow routing machinery into application after application and process after process? Instead, much of this intelligence should be built into the messaging infrastructure. A number of innovative approaches are available to provide increased e-mail intelligence in support of workflow, electronic shopping, and other applications. Smart messaging techniques can be used to enable the messaging platform to perform intelligent routing and other tasks based on rules or programs defined by a user or an application.

- **Security:** As e-mail becomes intrinsic to business processes that must be controlled, as decisionmakers depend on interpersonal messaging for communication, and as the messaging network itself becomes a bearer of transactions with legal and financial value, security must be increased. Users must be able to encrypt messages quickly and easily, to bulletproof them against any modification, and to prove that they have been delivered to the desired recipient. Within three to ten years, messages that do *not* bear an advanced form of protection known as the *digital signature* will become the exception in e-mail.

With the advent of next generation operating systems based on object-oriented, distributed file-system technology, local messaging infrastructures will merge seamlessly with other groupware systems. In a sense, e-mail will become one of many front-end views into a vast enterprise database consisting of public, workgroup, and private information. Messages will exist as rich structured forms as well as textual objects. They will increasingly be exchanged between and among mail-enabled applications and they will be sent to shared databases as well as to individual mailboxes.

As the waters of the information flood climb relentlessly, e-mail and the larger database information delivery system must become smarter. Today's increased e-mail platform intelligence, provided through rules-based processing of messages as they enter a mailbox, is only the edge of a trend that goes even beyond our already ambitious vision: the convergence of e-mail and artificial intelligence technology. We cannot fully imagine the effects of this post-vision convergence, other than to hypothesize that much of the traffic conducted by people and mail enabled applications today will be filtered through agent programs (our electronic doppelgängers[9]) capable not only of being programmed, but also of learning (or even anticipating) what information we want to see and how we want to handle it.

---

9. We borrow this phrase from Paul A. Strassman, who spoke on the convergence of e-mail and artificial intelligence at the E-mail World conference in November 1993.

The Messaging and Directory Overview

2.1   The Concept of E-mail

2.2   E-mail History

2.3   E-mail Infrastructures

2.4   Directory Infrastructure Considerations

2.5   Strategic Standards—the Infrastructure Enablers

2.6   Electronic Commerce and Smart Messaging Systems

2.7   Pulling It All Together

2.8   Summary

This chapter presents a high-level, wide-angle overview of key messaging concepts. A technical baseline is provided that enables the reader to proceed comfortably to the more specific and in-depth market and technology discussions and analyses in later chapters.

E-mail has reached a critical juncture in terms of both technological advancement and dramatic changes in the marketplace. Changes in the global information economy have driven enterprises to realize that they face a strategic imperative to maximize the use of their information resources by implementing integrated messaging throughout their organizations. Enterprises are also beginning to realize the potential of smart electronic messaging as a workflow process reengineering tool, and providers are recognizing the importance of smart messaging as a way of stimulating what is eventually expected to become a vast consumer messaging market.

These complementary organizational and market-driven opportunities for electronic messaging can only be realized through the development of an infrastructure. Such an infrastructure will include private, public, local, and global components. It is developing today, based on technological advances in the messaging industry, open architectures in products, and standards for use between components. However, significant obstacles remain. In this chapter, we trace the evolution of the e-mail infrastructure, the standards upon which it is based, its future prospects, and obstacles which must be overcome. First, however, a more complete definition of the term e-mail is needed.

2.1   THE CONCEPT OF E-MAIL

E-mail is introduced in Chapter 1 as any technology enabling the non-interactive exchange of electronic messages between e-mail users. An electronic message is any digitized object (or collection of objects) with a sender, a recipient list, a routing envelope, and various optional formatted fields. An e-mail user may be a person or an application.

This is e-mail today. It evolved from earlier electronic messaging technologies, such as the telegraph and telex. In the broadest sense, the definition of e-mail encompasses computer-based messaging, facsimile, and voice mail systems. However, this book focuses primarily on computer-based messaging while acknowledging the coexistence and convergence of computer-based messaging with other media. For example, coexistence and convergence with facsimile is especially important given facsimile's huge installed base and recent technology developments.

Only one of several computer communications technologies, e-mail is logically separate from real-time transaction processing, direct client-server database access, printing, and interactive file transfer. However, e-mail historically has had several great strengths that have distinguished it as a communications medium and made it one of the most popular computer applications in the world. Its fundamental strengths are its use of a familiar office memorandum metaphor (for interpersonal communications), dynamic replying/forwarding to enable many-to-many communication, and the ability to transfer information between people or applications on unconnected or intermittently connected networks. In the paragraphs below, we will explain the basic e-mail concept primarily from an interpersonal messaging perspective. Later we will discuss the evolution of an electronic commerce concept, where messaging infrastructures can be utilized to support other forms of messaging beyond interpersonal correspondence.

Most e-mail systems support the familiar office memorandum format with *To, From,* and *Subject* prompts, either text-oriented or graphical, for composing messages. They also provide access to a directory in order to simplify the selection of recipients (for the *To, cc,* or *bcc* fields) and ensure the accuracy of the information entered. Many systems now allow the attachment of files created in other applications. The recipient is given the possibility of answering or forwarding the message and detaching attachments for further work in the original application. In this way, entire conversations or work processes can be carried out between groups, regardless of geographic location, schedule, or time zone. Figure 2.1 illustrates an interpersonal e-mail conversation.

```
To: Parts Supply Manager
From: Engineering Design Manager
Subject: FWD: REPLY: Malfunctioning Part

COMMENTS:

FYI. Please note any impact this might have on your
inventory. We are full steam ahead on redesign.

FORWARDED MESSAGE:

   > To: Dealership Executive
   > From: Engineering Design Manager
   > Subject: REPLY: Malfunctioning Part
   >
   > OK. The teleconference is on.
   >
   > REPLIED TO MESSAGE:
   >
      >> To: Engineering Design Manager
      >> From: Dealership Executive
      >> Subject: Malfunctioning Part
      >>
      >> This is the 15th such part replacement (PT
      >> 1667F) we've experienced in the last month on
      >> the new Frontiers! If we don't get a handle on
      >> this, we're going to see a lot more!
      >> How about a teleconference on Tuesday at 2 p.m.?
      >>
      >> Vice President
```

Figure 2.1   An e-mail example.

This single message captures the dynamism of an e-mail conversation.[1] A message was sent from the automobile dealership executive to the engineering design manager requesting a teleconference. The engineering design manager replies to the dealership executive and forwards the reply message to a parts supply

---

1. Note that this example shows a simplified view of an e-mail message. Actual user interfaces might display elements of the messages' digital envelopes and/or other optional fields such as Message ID or Priority in addition to the key memo-style fields. For the sake of clarity, the example uses the organizational roles of the individuals involved in this mail exchange.

manager also expected to attend. All the messages are in a straightforward, easy-to-understand office memorandum format. But the medium is very dynamic. A user can carry on a dozen such conversations within the space of an hour. Nor is the e-mail concept limited to human users. Mail-enabled applications can participate in a primitive way (for example, the user can send mail from within a word processor) or in a sophisticated fashion, as in workflow routing systems.

2.2   E-MAIL HISTORY[2]

The e-mail concept is rooted in the early timesharing systems and research laboratories of the late 1960s. Throughout the 1970s and early 1980s, e-mail systems proliferated in both the Research and Development (R&D) and commercial environments. In the R&D environment, the ARPANET (created by Defense Department's Advanced Research Projects Agency), later to become the Internet, spread rapidly. In commercial environments, e-mail was a natural complement to host-based environments where hundreds of users were attached by terminals. Proprietary host e-mail systems such as IBM's Professional Office System (PROFS) or DIStributed Office Support System (DISOSS) and DEC's All-In-1 or VMSmail emerged as important productivity tools.

Also during the late 1970s and early 1980s, public messaging networks provided messaging to individuals and organizations who chose not to own and operate their own host-based mail systems.[3] Public services introduced in this period included AT&T Mail, MCI Mail, Dialcom, Telemail, CompuServe, and the IBM Information Network. The combination of public services and private messaging offerings served to establish electronic messaging rapidly in many organizations.

E-mail systems in the 1970s and 1980s were, by and large, deployed by enterprises in a *laissez-faire* fashion, department by department. They generally operated as separate islands of interoperability. Nevertheless, a growing awareness emerged in the industry that messaging islands would someday need to be connected into an infrastructure and that standards would be needed to foster that infrastructure.

Thus, the 1980s also witnessed the emergence of standards out of each of the two parallel universes of messaging—the commercial/public messaging and Internet communities. From the commercial community emerged the initial 1984 X.400 Message Handling System (MHS) international standard and the 1988 X.400 MHS and X.500 Directory Services standards. The Internet community developed the Simple Mail Transfer Protocol (SMTP), the Request for Comment (RFC) 822 message format, and Domain Name System routing in the early to mid 1980s.

But even as the standards were being formulated, whole new proprietary e-mail environments were being invented. In the mid to late 1980s, the advent of

---

2. Portions of this section were originally developed in the *Rapport Messaging Review,* Vol. 1, Issue 1, [RAPP93A], Copyright © Rapport Communication, 1993. They are reprinted here with the permission of Rapport Communication.

3. Chapter 3, "The Private Messaging Market," begins with a discussion of the differences between public and private messaging networks.

PCs gave users who were not attached to mainframes or minicomputers access to public e-mail systems. Then, as PCs began to attach to LANs and the installation of these LANs grew, the idea of bringing e-mail capability to these small groups of users took hold. This ushered in an era of explosive LAN e-mail growth. Early LAN e-mail implementations included cc:Mail, Microsoft Mail for the Macintosh, Network Courier, and The Coordinator (which was based on Action Technologies' Message Handling System later licensed by Novell).

In addition to the emergence of standards on the one hand and LAN e-mail on the other, the late 1980s and early 1990s witnessed substantially enhanced public service offerings, early standards implementations, and the rapid growth and commercialization of the Internet. Figure 2.2 highlights notable milestones and trends in the evolution of electronic messaging.

In the late 1980s and early 1990s, a groundswell in e-mail usage fostered dramatic growth in proprietary commercial messaging, Internet Mail, the X.400 environment, and emerging wireless e-mail. Host e-mail systems continued to grow, and the public messaging networks were interconnected via X.400. Internet

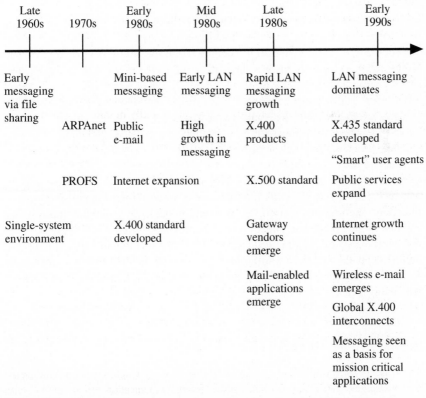

Figure 2.2   The evolution of messaging.   *Gary Rowe and Ted Myer, Rapport Communication. Reprinted with permission of Rapport Communication. Copyright © 1993.*

and LAN e-mail growth rates soared exponentially. E-mail integration products emerged, offering gateways to link e-mail islands into private enterprise or public messaging networks. Many of these gateways based their internal message formats on X.400, others on SMTP, and others on proprietary models. New standards emerged, including X.435 to carry EDI messages over an X.400 network and enhanced Internet standards for carrying binary data in message bodies.

In the early 1990s, as e-mail grew in importance to become a mission critical application and while revenue opportunities expanded, consolidation took place in both public and private messaging markets. This period saw AT&T acquire Western Union's EasyLink service, BT purchase Dialcom, Microsoft buy Network Courier, Novell acquire the MHS product from Action Technologies, and Lotus purchase cc:Mail. This consolidation has further strengthened the position of major product vendors and service providers such as Microsoft, Lotus, Novell, AT&T, and BT. However, the era of consolidation is now giving way to an era of partnerships. For example, in late 1993 e-mail integration market competitors Soft*Switch and Hewlett-Packard announced their intent to cooperate on some user contracts. Microsoft, Lotus, and other large LAN e-mail vendors continually seek to strengthen their position through partnerships with legions of Independent Software Vendors (ISVs).

In yet another development of the early 1990s, e-mail suddenly hit the big time, finally (at least in the U.S.) reaching the masses. In the public messaging environment, diverse organizations ranging from the White House, to news networks, to newspapers, to radio stations have joined the ranks of the e-mail aware. (This realization fully struck us when, while driving to a meeting, one of the authors heard a disk jockey at a rock and roll station announce the Internet Mail address through which one could request, via e-mail, that a specific song be played). In the private messaging environment, e-mail has for some time been shipping as a commodity desktop application for PC/LAN users. Massive growth ensued and seems certain to continue.

In the last decade, e-mail technology has also undergone dramatic change. It has evolved from being primarily a medium for text information exchange to an integrated messaging medium for multimedia mail, mail-enabled applications, and electronic commerce. However, it is important to grasp one critical fact: The historical legacy of e-mail is still with us. Without exception, the types of systems mentioned in this section are still in service. All of them (host e-mail, LAN e-mail, X.400, Internet Mail, old versions, and new versions) still have millions of users. And many of these systems are still growing!

2.3   E-MAIL INFRASTRUCTURES

The concept of e-mail rests on the availability of infrastructure to store and transport messages. Increasing sophistication in e-mail infrastructures is being driven by rising user expectations. By and large, users are no longer satisfied with simple text-based user interfaces and media support. They want e-mail to be so easy to use that messaging services are virtually invisible. They expect to be able to

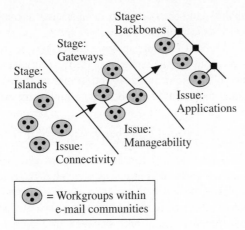

Figure 2.3 Evolution of a global infrastructure.
*Derived from and reproduced with
permission of Hewlett-Packard Company.*

choose a mail recipient from a directory list without having to know whether that
recipient is on their network or another one. They demand products that support
integrated messaging features such as enhanced fax (the ability to receive, send,
and broadcast faxes from e-mail stations) and mail-enabled applications.

Users also expect transparent operation between all their legacy systems. After experiencing rapid message transfer between mailboxes within the same local
messaging system, they sometimes expect the same rapid delivery to occur even
when messages must cross geographic boundaries and transit through gateways
into separate local messaging systems. Their expectations are relatively insensi-
tive to the increasing size of the multimedia packages they are sending. This level
of operation requires more powerful processors, more efficient designs, and fewer
protocol translations.

If we consider these user requirements and recall our history lesson, a pattern
emerges. The e-mail infrastructure has been evolving all along to meet user requirements, and, in that evolution, we can distinguish three identifiable stages.
These stages are shown in Fig. 2.3.

In the *island* stage, stand-alone hosts and LANs proliferated in isolated departments. They became islands of e-mail interoperability, among other things.
When departments like Finance realized the usefulness of interconnecting their
local e-mail system with other departmental systems, such as Human Resources or
Engineering, interconnectivity became an issue. Unfortunately, each department
had already procured its local environment and accompanying e-mail system to
support its particular function and need.

During the *gateway* stage, users and vendors began to develop gateways between disparate e-mail systems. These gateways evolved into hubs that performed
the interconnection of e-mail systems from a central host. But gateway/hubs often
transferred information with some loss of format and even data and presented
other problems of manageability. Thus arose the need for a more manageable and

performant backbone to connect LAN and departmental e-mail systems of all stripes in a robust, efficient topology.

The *backbone* stage will fully arrive when the messaging infrastructure enables the fulfillment of our e-mail vision statement from Chapter 1. Users and applications will be able to connect easily into a high-performance, distributed and ubiquitous, secure, manageable backbone with multimedia support.

2.3.1   Understanding and Categorizing Local Infrastructures

Unlike the telephone network, which today consists of a relatively few highly standardized components, the e-mail infrastructure is bewildering in its diversity. It consists of LAN e-mail, host e-mail, gateway, e-mail integration server, public e-mail, X.400, Internet Mail, and many other components. Collectively, they provide a polyglot environment somewhere between the gateway and backbone stages of evolution. The total messaging infrastructure can in fact be characterized as a *catanet*, or concatenated network of diverse components.[4]

In order to better understand how the various components of e-mail work together to provide a messaging infrastructure and what must happen to move that infrastructure forward, we distinguish and define two types: *local infrastructure* and *global infrastructure*. The conceptual relationship of these two infrastructures is shown in Fig. 2.4.

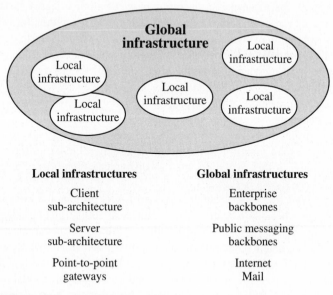

Local infrastructures	Global infrastructures
Client sub-architecture	Enterprise backbones
Server sub-architecture	Public messaging backbones
Point-to-point gateways	Internet Mail

Figure 2.4   E-mail infrastructures.

4. Einar Stefferud, President of Network Management Associates, suggested the use of the term "catanet" to describe the current state of global e-mail at the November 1993 E-mail World Conference.

Local infrastructures are the set of components necessary to provide a single local messaging system to a community of users. They are composed of a client sub-architecture (responsible for the user interface at the desktop and, often, access to mail-enabled applications) and a server sub-architecture (which stores and transports messages and provides the directory functionality that enables e-mail users to communicate with one another). Local infrastructures may overlap when two different types of systems are connected by a dedicated point-to-point gateway. Global infrastructures, on the other hand, are the facilities needed to bridge between local infrastructures.

The distinction between local and global infrastructures can also be categorized by reference to our e-mail scenario in Fig. 2.1. In that example, note that if the dealership executive, engineering design manager, and parts supply manager use the same LAN e-mail system, messages between them remain entirely within their local infrastructure. But if the three users reside on three different e-mail systems, global infrastructure interconnections will be required to forward messages to and from the parts supply manager and engineering design manager or between the parts supply manager and dealership executive. The forwarding could occur over an enterprise messaging network, a public messaging network, or the Internet.

Finally, note that recent developments in facsimile technology suggest the possibility of an infrastructure of fax and other office equipment running in parallel to local and global messaging infrastructures. Its implications are sketched in Section 2.3.3.

2.3.2   Local Infrastructures

A local infrastructure is the set of components, such as LAN e-mail clients and servers, providing desktop e-mail and directory access as well as mail transfer between a community of users. To meet this definition, these users must be found within the same organization, use the same vendor's equipment, and be located at a single site (or at multiple sites with adequate connectivity between them). Thus, an enterprise may have one local infrastructure or a number of different local infrastructures. If global messaging networks are analogous to the telephone system, then local infrastructure components are analogous to telephone equipment. As with telephone equipment, these components may be owned by the customer or rented from a public service provider. We provide a basic introduction to local messaging systems here and cover them fully in Chapter 5.

Background

Local infrastructures, or local messaging systems, fall into two broad categories: host (or departmental) e-mail systems and LANs. Host e-mail systems, such as PROFS or DEC All-In-1, run on departmental mainframes or minicomputers. LAN e-mail systems, such as cc:Mail or Microsoft Mail, run on LAN servers. Local messaging systems in both the host and LAN configurations typically utilize proprietary protocols. In such cases they require a gateway for interconnection to e-mail components from other vendors or to a messaging standard, such as X.400 or Internet Mail.

With host e-mail systems, users at terminals access the host over local or remote connections from which they log into the host's command line or menu-driven user interface. Host e-mail systems are often well integrated with a variety of other office automation capabilities such as calendaring and bulletin boards. However, they have never attained the response time and graphical capabilities of contemporary LAN-based e-mail.

LAN e-mail is at the cutting edge of both local infrastructure technology and private mailbox growth. LAN e-mail can be defined as systems implemented for distributed LANs consisting of DOS, Windows, Unix, or Apple operating environments. Unlike host systems where the entire process is in the host, with LAN e-mail systems the user interface portion of the system is in the user's PC or workstation.

Most LAN e-mail systems have been designed for early PC equipment possessing minimal disk, memory, and processor capabilities. In a LAN e-mail system, the user accesses a PC or workstation through a user interface which in turn accesses a message storage system or Post Office. As shown in Fig. 2.5, the Post Office is typically located on a file server, and the file server is typically connected to user client PCs via a LAN network operating system such as NetWare or LAN Manager. With this file server architecture, the desktop device acts as the client, and the file system as the server. The server provides mailbox storage and directory listing services. These implementations also provide a transport facility to other compatible Post Offices on remote file servers or gateways to other messaging infrastructures. In some cases, the transport facility is located on the file server; in others, on a separate PC.

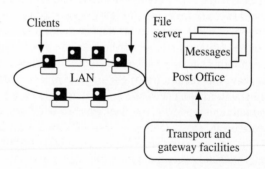

Figure 2.5 Basic LAN e-mail local infrastructures.

Evolutionary Direction

Driven by fierce competition, vendors have continually improved on both the architecture and functionality inherent in early local messaging implementations. Modern local infrastructures are evolving to a more powerful model in which file

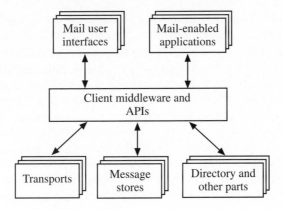

Figure 2.6   Modularized architectures.

server interfaces are replaced by client-server architectures with higher perfor-mance, higher reliability, and improved functionality. At the same time, the client and server components are becoming separate sub-architectures of the local infra-structure and are carving out separate niches in the local messaging market. This decoupling, or modularization, enables e-mail users to choose one vendor's client and another vendor's server much as in the stereo system marketplace where con-sumers are able to assemble speakers, CD players, and tape decks from different vendors to create a complete sound system.[5] Figure 2.6 illustrates how modular-ization of the client-server messaging infrastructure works.

As can be seen from the figure, the key component enabling modularization of local messaging components is a set of software utilities that expose application program interfaces (APIs) to both client applications and diverse "back-end" ser-vices. Examples of such enabling components are the Microsoft Messaging API (MAPI) and the Apple Computer Open Collaboration Environment (AOCE). By enabling the modularization of e-mail functionality, APIs allow a division of labor between vendors to take place. Vendors no longer need to tackle all the parts and pieces of an e-mail solution. Instead, they can focus on providing a particular set of specialized functions and rely on other vendors to provide the rest of the solu-tion. Customers are then able to choose and combine best-of-breed products.

As a result, e-mail clients have been imbued with more and more functional-ity, including the ability to interact with applications through attachment launch-ing and mail enabling. The beginnings of smart messaging capabilities are reflected in the development of mailbox intelligence or rules-based applications such as forms routing. Directories are becoming more sophisticated and better integrated with the LAN operating system and enterprise directories in surround-ing environments.

---

5. Dr. Michael Zisman originally coined the e-mail/stereo analogy.

A key local infrastructure trend will be the convergence of e-mail and group-ware systems. This development is already in its early stages with vendors bundling e-mail and group scheduling software—a combination that would have automated the process by which the engineering design manager, parts supply manager and dealership executive set up their meeting in Fig. 2.1. Advanced products, such as Lotus Notes and Microsoft Mail's next generation messaging server, already take e-mail and groupware convergence much further.

As part of this development, local messaging systems will be increasingly integrated into the distributed, object-oriented file systems,[6] such as the expected Apple/IBM's Taligent and Microsoft's Cairo offerings. Such integration will enable the user to perceive e-mail (with its conversational dynamism and convenient memo-like format) as one front-end view into a broader *enterprise database*. This enterprise database will encompass private (person-to-person) messages, public (person-to-group) messages posted on bulletin-board style objects, and multiple views of electronic forms. It will also include directory listings of users and other resources that exist as persistent queries (i.e., periodically refreshed surveys of actual objects resident in the network) and may require no special administration. Vendors will add value to this e-mail/database structure by devising increasingly creative ways of indexing, summarizing, and archiving e-mail, voice mail, fax messages, and other objects that reflect the enterprise memory or knowledge base.

Just beyond the convergence of e-mail and groupware lies the convergence of e-mail and artificial intelligence. This convergence is vital if e-mail is to remain a usable tool in a time of mounting message volumes and information glut. We are just starting to see the beginning of this convergence in products, notably Beyond Mail and General Magic's Telescript implementation. Smart messaging techniques that combine smart mailboxes (able to play rule sets against incoming or waiting messages) and smart messages (able to execute scripts or programs in the network) offer the promise of dramatic new ways of working. For example, a user could configure rules for a smart mailbox to file all messages from specific originators in specific folders. Or a user could send a smart message into a consumer information service with the mission of making airline, hotel, and rental car reservations for a business trip. Chapter 4 further discusses future services that will be based on smart messaging and Chapter 9 explores the theory of smart messaging technology in more detail.

2.3.3   Global Infrastructures

Global infrastructures can be defined as any facilities that bridge geographically separate or incompatible local infrastructures. Such bridging is vital to meeting users' expectations of transparent operation between e-mail systems. The nature

---

6. Object-oriented file systems are systems that allow users to manipulate computer files, file directories, user accounts, folders, mailboxes, application data elements, devices, programs, and other objects within the framework of a consistent file system name space and user interface. Distributed file systems are those that span multiple computers and Local Area Networks.

of global infrastructure components is highly technology-dependent. They may comprise gateways, standards-based message switching systems, or merely a set of standards, packet switching systems, and routing directory services that, between them, enable two local infrastructures to communicate directly (as is usually done with Internet Mail today). We have identified three current categories of global infrastructure that coexist uneasily: enterprise backbones based on e-mail integration servers, public messaging networks based on X.400, and Internet Mail.

Within an enterprise, global infrastructure components called *e-mail integration servers* or *enterprise messaging backbones* (from vendors such as DEC, HP, and Soft*Switch) provide store-and-forward connectivity between different mail systems. They may also provide directory synchronization and wide-area directory access. Public messaging networks (such as Advantis, AT&T Mail, or MCI Mail) are similar to enterprise messaging networks, except that they must provide connectivity worldwide. The Internet global infrastructure in its entirety provides global IP connectivity, global domain registration, and dynamic domain routing service. Of all the global infrastructures, Internet Mail is now the largest, and its addressing conventions are now dominant.

Global infrastructures are in the process of moving from the gateway stage toward the backbone stage. They will enter the backbone stage fully when they are pervasive, modular, flexible, scalable, intelligent, secure, and manageable. Another precondition is the emergence of a single global messaging standard, or at least a much higher degree of convergence among the global standards (X.400 and Internet Mail for messaging and X.500 for directories).

While users within some local infrastructures can attain a high degree of functionality, the great dilemma of e-mail (as of early 1994) is that as soon as users must communicate *across* local infrastructures, functionality deteriorates radically. In most cases, with a modicum of patience and familiarity with a variety of e-mail addressing conventions, a user can get a short text message to a very large population of other users that are connected to public messaging networks. Binary attachments can sometimes be sent with messages and the recipient can sometimes effect a reply to the originator. That, unfortunately, is about the extent of present capabilities when global infrastructures are taken as a whole.

Moreover, most local infrastructures do not implement the global X.400 and Internet Mail standards except through gateways. These gateways vary widely in their level of functionality. This results in the polyglot environment, a desultory mix of local and global infrastructures, depicted by Fig. 2.7. Imagine a message traveling from cc:Mail (in the "other" cloud on the bottom left of the figure), through an X.400 gateway, into an X.400 public network, across an Internet gateway, and into a NetWare MHS hub at the top right-hand side of the figure. It happens all too often. Though the industry as a whole is getting better at making concatenated messaging networks (or catanets) work, one has to wonder: Did our cc:Mail user need to type in an arcane address? How much of the message is left after all the transmutations? How many hoops do the administrators of the systems involved have to jump through to maintain connectivity? How much unimaginable effort (and sunk cost) goes into developing and maintaining so much protocol translation hardware and software?

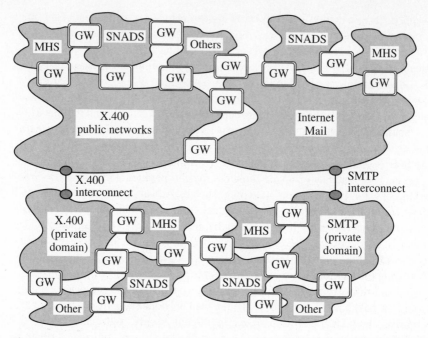

Figure 2.7   Present-day state of the e-mail infrastructure.

Successful infrastructure development must rest on a set of agreed standards that will enable components from multiple vendors to interwork. Many challenges lie ahead. Standards are still lacking in areas such as electronic forms for workflow. Multiple standards have proliferated in many facets of messaging functionality, including messaging protocols, APIs, and security capabilities. Many of these standards represent duplicate efforts. In some cases, standards can coexist; for example, gateways can be built between X.400 and Internet Mail. However, such coexistence is often uneasy and difficult, in part because of political and economic factors, and in part because of technical issues. Technical obstacles to coexistence tend to arise because e-mail is a dynamic, cooperative application, and it is difficult to construct gateway technology that solves every conceivable interworking scenario.

2.3.4   Facsimile Infrastructure

It is incumbent upon us to note that, while our focus is on e-mail, recent developments in fax communications could enable it to rival the efficiencies of its computer-based cousin. These developments hinge on LAN/fax developments and, in particular, on Microsoft Corporation's recent unveiling of Microsoft at Work (MAW) [MICR93] and its use of Binary File Transfer (BFT), an ITU standard for sending binary files through fax modems.

The MAW prospect of tying office equipment, including telephones, fax machines, copiers, printers, mobile devices, and video systems to computers has important implications. MAW can be thought of as an operating system for all those pieces of office equipment that are not PCs [EMMS93B, EMMS93D, EMMS93E]. MAW for fax is a proprietary Microsoft kernel, packaged with Microsoft's openly published Messaging Application Programming Interface (MAPI) and Telephony Application Programming Interface (TAPI). MAW for fax runs on top of Microsoft Mail via MAPI, and TAPI is used to control phone lines and distinguish between fax and voice calls.

The two major elements of MAW are printer rendering and BFT. Printer rendering is a page-description language that enables documents to be faxed at high resolution with fewer bits than would be required using the ITU Group 3 facsimile, thus resulting in reduced telephone time and cost. By using BFT in fax transmissions between two MAW devices, a document can be sent as a print file in a fraction of the time it would take to send a Group 3 bit-mapped image. Print rendering will ensure that anything faxed via BFT will be printable and viewable. In addition, revisable computer files can be sent for reprocessing by an appropriately enabled recipient.

In addition, MAW implements a sub-addressing scheme that will ensure that this new grade of fax is routed directly to MAW-enabled mailboxes. While the scheme is not conformant with the one under development by the ITU, Microsoft claims that it can be easily transitioned when appropriate. Microsoft has also built in extendibility in anticipation of a whole range of other future services.

It has been suggested that this incursion by Microsoft will drive the creation of computer fax standards as it transforms a fax-only vehicle into one for general purpose image, file, document transfer, and, yes, e-mail. More importantly, if costs, security, and ease-of-use can be validated, such faxing may become a sought-after alternative to e-mail. In this regard, the use of BFT offers cost reductions of as much as 25 percent between MAW-equipped systems. Security embracing encryption, authentication via public/private keys, and digital signing has been demonstrated and gives faxing potential commercial and legal validity. Finally and perhaps most importantly, the industry recognizes the ease-of-use of fax machines for walk-up users and the growing ease-of-access to fax for PC and LAN users.

Taken in its entirety, MAW and BFT could form the basis for a fax-based, e-mail–like infrastructure. Its success would depend on the willingness of large organizations to pioneer the infrastructure by building intracompany networks of such fax machines. The lack of a currently installed base and the cost of upgrading faxes and client/server software suggests that such an infrastructure will not fall into place in the immediate future. What MAW, BFT, and subaddressing *should* do in the near term is spur the messaging industry to solve its addressing and interconnection problems and to coexist with fax technologies as part of the overall messaging infrastructure.

2.4   DIRECTORY INFRASTRUCTURE CONSIDERATIONS

Directories complement the messaging infrastructures previously described. Given the huge number of e-mail addresses and the complexity of some address forms, users and both the local and global messaging infrastructures themselves require the use of a directory. Electronic directories enable users to obtain addressing information for correspondents while relieving the e-mail application of the burden of maintaining address information. Thus, the user addressing an e-mail message at the *To:* prompt of the mail user interface could type in a simple name (e.g., *David Litwack*), and the mail client would query the directory to substitute an address.

2.4.1   Advanced Directory Infrastructure Uses

Basic directory infrastructures provide the e-mail user with an easy way to look up the addresses of their prospective correspondents (even when correspondents are frequently reassigned and moved from office to office) and are an essential component of user-friendly message handling systems. Advanced directory infrastructures will someday not only assist the sender in determining recipient addresses, but will also contain information to support many other sophisticated functions, such as:

- **Mail routing, delivery, and conversion** by local and global messaging infrastructures
- **Address translation** by the global infrastructure from one local messaging format to another
- **Network topology information** for both messaging and non-messaging components
- **Secure messaging** services for both messaging and non-messaging components by listing user public cryptographic keys inside protected certificates
- **Electronic commerce capability profiling** by listing trading partner e-mail and connectivity profile information
- **Organizational role and authority determination** for workflow and smart messaging systems
- **Generalized White Pages or Yellow Pages lookup** for public messaging services, electronic shopping services, online telephone directories, and the intelligent networks of the future
- **Integrated information locator** for resources on the Internet (or other networks)
- **Integrated enterprise database** containing personnel listings, resource listings, and even pointer information into databases of photographs, service records, contracts, and other data—this goes beyond e-mail and into the realm of total enterprise information reengineering.

Directory infrastructures have the potential to become knowledge discovery systems enabling users and providers to navigate distributed information listings and promising the automation of a myriad of functions in both messaging and non-messaging environments.

However, despite their great potential usefulness, advanced directory infrastructures have been very slow to take hold. The global X.500 directory is only just coming into being in a production sense. In general, individual e-mail users have access only to their vendor's proprietary directory, which contains the names of the other employees in their division and a smattering of remote user names. Directories for EDI trading communities are even more primitive, taking the form of paper listings containing alphanumeric designations handed out off-line to participants by such registering organizations as Dun & Bradstreet.

2.4.2 Directory Synchronization

Directory synchronization could allow, for example, cc:Mail users to obtain information about PROFS users from their local cc:Mail directory. Since it would be difficult for PROFS and cc:Mail users to address mail to one another without such assistance, directory synchronization becomes critical to the larger goal of heterogeneous enterprise messaging integration.

Directory synchronization encompasses the software and procedures needed for keeping an electronic directory with the names and addresses of enterprise users accessible, consistent, and up-to-date across all participating e-mail platforms. Synchronization tools collect information from different directories, reformat the data, and ship updated information to each directory. They enable entries from different vendors' directories to be collected, updated, and displayed within a local directory service. These tools or procedures vary widely between implementations. They may be manual, semi-automated, or fully automated. They may involve the use of incremental updates or batch file processing.

Unfortunately, in the absence of a multivendor standard, synchronization mechanisms are complex, difficult to scale, and require significant maintenance because of the need for successive releases. Also, they do not provide a global infrastructure solution that solves the problem of directory access to actual or potential trading partners, customers, and suppliers existing beyond the enterprise perimeter.

Today, directory synchronization can only be accomplished on a large scale through proprietary techniques. For example, Soft*Switch provides a Names Directory that automatically accepts updates from supported mail systems such as cc:Mail. Thus when a new cc:Mail user is registered, the cc:Mail directory at a local cc:Mail Post Office is updated, and Soft*Switch software residing in a gateway transmits the update to Soft*Switch Central where it is made available to other directories.

2.5 STRATEGIC STANDARDS—THE INFRASTRUCTURE ENABLERS

Standards are essential to establish global infrastructures, to connect local infrastructures from different vendors, and to interface mail-enabled applications to local infrastructures. Given that so many legacy systems have been installed in the past and constant technological innovations often make emerging local e-mail features irresistibly attractive, few large enterprises have the luxury of operating with a single local messaging system. Yet, without standards, finding the gateway software to enable arbitrary pairings of incompatible local messaging systems to interoperate can be difficult.

Standards support becomes a way of protecting the user's investment in existing messaging systems and existing backbones. Standards are needed for specifying message envelope formats and for the format of text, voice, fax, telex, EDI, and other data which may be enclosed in messages. Standards are also needed for message acknowledgment procedures and directories.

Note that e-mail standards emanate from three major technology domains.[7]

1. The accredited international standards community represented by the International Organization for Standardization (ISO)[8] and the International Telecommunications Union (ITU).[9]

2. The Internet community represented by the Internet Engineering Task Force (IETF), the Internet Engineering Steering Group (IESG), and the Internet Architecture Board (IAB).

3. Various industry consortia, including vendor alliances.

Each standards technology domain addresses a slightly different set of problems and, in this respect, may complement the other two. However, the three domains also address similar problems in different ways, resulting in competition and confusion in the marketplace. In practice, the standards have come to have somewhat different applicability. Internet Mail provides inexpensive, worldwide interpersonal messaging (and thus has garnered the lion's share of the current explosion in the public mailbox population), but X.400 is preferred by many large organizations for high end "business class" messaging. We will briefly introduce these strategic standards here, with extensive coverage to come later.

2.5.1   Accredited International Standards: X.400, X.500, and Open Systems Interconnection

During the 1980s and early 1990s, CCITT and ISO rolled out an ambitious set of standards under the Open Systems Interconnection (OSI) umbrella. The most important of these—and the ones most directly relevant to e-mail—are the X.400 MHS and the X.500 Directory Services standards. Both were originally conceived as OSI application layer standards that utilize the lower-layer OSI transports.

---

7. Appendix A provides a comprehensive survey of the history of these standards, of the process for developing standards in each standards domain, and of the mission of the many standards consortia that have been organized in recent years.

8. ISO's full name is ISO/IEC. IEC stands for the International Electrotechnical Commission.

9. The branch of the ITU that handles telecommunications standards was formerly known as the International Consultative Committee on Telephony and Telegraphy (CCITT).

X.400 Message Handling Systems

X.400 [ITU84, ITU88] is the set of ITU/ISO standards for interconnecting messaging systems worldwide in a store-and-forward fashion. X.400 is intended to facilitate the exchange of all sorts of information between users including simple text, images such as facsimile and graphics, digital voice, or complete documents including complex objects such as spreadsheets and multimedia hypertext. The two main types of messages that are addressed in the 1988 series of standards (we will refer to the current X.400 specification as the 1988 standard since the 1992 version is compatible with the 1988 version) are interpersonal messages (IPM), and EDI messages between business applications.

X.400 is based on a simple functional model that consists of a few main components:

- *User Agents (UAs),* which are software components that create messages in standardized formats
- The *Message Store* (*MS* added in 1988), which holds messages until recipients choose to read them
- *Message Transfer Agents (MTAs),* which store and forward the messages within and between networks
- The *Message Transfer System (MTS),* which is the set of all the MTAs worldwide
- *Access Units,* which interface the message handling system to telematic and physical delivery services such as fax, Teletex, Telex, and the post office.

This model and the relationship of these parts are shown in Fig. 2.8.

(Note that the terms UA and MTA are often used for UAs and MTAs that support other protocols instead of or in addition to X.400. For example, Internet Mail documentation sometimes uses these terms. This book will take the same liberty at times.)

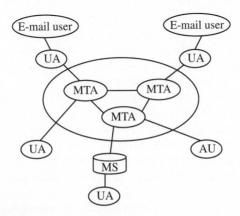

Figure 2.8   The X.400 message transfer system.

Other important aspects of X.400 include domain modeling, addressing, message structure, and rich functionality. The global MTS is modeled as a collection of management domains, or a collection of one or more MTAs and UAs, MSs, and AUs operated by a single organization or administration. Two basic classes of management domains are defined according to the type of organization operating it: administration management domains (ADMDs), run by public service providers; and private management domains (PRMDs), run by user organizations.

X.400 domain modelling determines the structure of X.400 addressing. X.400 provides a global addressing structure known as the originator/recipient (O/R) address. There are many options to the O/R address, but the most common form identifies the country, ADMD, PRMD, organization, organization units and personal name of the user. For example:

Given Name:	John
Surname:	Doe
Private Management Domain:	Widgets
Administration Management Domain:	Speedmail
Country:	US

This address would be written as: *G=John ; S=Doe ; P=Widgets ; A=Speedmail ; C=US*. X.400 addresses have been recognized as problematic because of their complexity and verbosity. Also, all components besides the ADMD and Country elements are optional, or can be used many different ways, leading to inconsistent representations.

X.400 messages are structured as an *envelope* and its *content*. Message envelopes contain addresses and various routing and handling options. The content contains the information desired by an X.400 application, such as an interpersonal message (IPM) or an EDI message (EDIM). The content can contain multipart attachments (called body parts) of any format.

Finally, X.400 supports a wide range of functions, including delivery and non-delivery reports, receipt and nonreceipt notifications, mail distribution list expansion, conversion of body parts into a recipient-specified format, facilities for interworking with physical delivery systems (such as postal mail), and security features for authentication, integrity, confidentiality, and nonrepudiation of messages.

X.400's strength lies in its rich functionality and its strong backing from the powerful Public Telecommunication Operators (PTOs) and large organizations that drive the ITU/ISO standards communities. Its problems lie with its complexity and with its origin as a top-down standard created by committees that could not and did not follow up on their standardization effort to create the conditions for its complete success. Some of the enabling conditions that were not initially available for X.400 in 1984 or 1988 included freely available electronic copies of the standards documents themselves, freely available source code reference implementations of the standard, and a free-of-charge, internationally accredited registration infrastructure for allocating user address domain names and other technical objects. Some of these enablers have finally become available in the early 1990s, but others have not.

X.400 does not dominate local infrastructures, as it was once intended to do. It has, however, had some considerable success in global infrastructures, with operating ADMDs in at least 60 countries, perhaps 100 or more different X.400 implementations, and X.400-capable backbones in many large organizational environments.

X.500 Directory Services

X.500 [ITU88A] defines a standard for a distributed directory system intended to support global access across organizational and geographical boundaries. It provides a standard method of representing and identifying users and resources across multivendor, heterogeneous systems. X.500 also defines how information stored in the directory can be accessed by client software. The directory is composed of four elements:

* *Directory System Agent (DSA)* servers, where each one holds a portion of the directory database
* *Directory User Agents (DUAs)*, clients that act on behalf of the user to access the directory
* The *Directory System Protocol (DSP)*, which enables the communication between DSAs
* The *Directory Access Protocol (DAP)*, which enables the DUA to communicate with DSAs.

In the directory model shown in Fig. 2.9, the DUA can be incorporated within a user interface or within an application entity as a collection of software services. The information incorporated in the DSAs is organized hierarchically and can include e-mail addresses, telephone numbers, names, titles, or arbitrary user-defined information items.

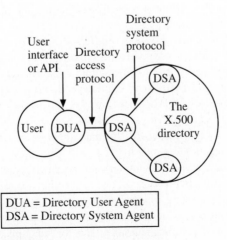

DUA = Directory User Agent
DSA = Directory System Agent

Figure 2.9   The X.500 directory.

X.500's strengths and weaknesses are similar to those of X.400. It has had the advantage of very significant support from both the international research and development community and from the public messaging service providers in North America. However, it also has an even more difficult problem to solve than X.400 in that distributed directories require much more coordination than messaging systems.

Use of X.500

Users of the 1988 X.400 systems (and other applications) can make use of the X.500 directory in many ways. X.500's naming capabilities identify X.400 users by their directory name without requiring the originator to know the details of that user's address or messaging capabilities (such as what types of documents the user can receive). Also, distribution lists can be stored as one name in the X.500 directory and can be expanded for the forwarding of messages by the responsible MTA. Finally, the X.500 directory can store certificates containing public cryptographic keys retrievable by any inquiring entity (MTA or UA) in order to authenticate another entity's identity. It can also store passwords and make them available for access control. In fact, tight integration with X.500 functionality is deemed an essential ingredient for delivering the robust, highly functional backbone features intended in 1988 X.400.

2.5.2   Internet Mail

The Internet, a collection of research, academic, and commercial networks whose origins are in the U.S. Department of Defense's Advanced Research Projects Agency (ARPA) network of the late sixties and seventies, has long utilized several e-mail standards. These standards, published in Requests For Comment (RFCs), are available in the public domain and enable systems from different vendors to interoperate. Internet Mail is based on various RFCs, including RFC 821 for the Simple Message Transfer protocol, RFC 822 for message format, and other RFCs for the Domain Name System.

The Simple Mail Transfer Protocol (SMTP) [POST82], is often distributed as a commodity product with Unix-based workstations and other equipment, and many vendors of either proprietary or X.400 messaging software support SMTP gateways.

SMTP is defined in RFC 821 and implemented over the Transmission Control Protocol/Internet Protocol (TCP/IP) in the Internet. It describes the sequence of control messages that are passed between computers to effect the transfer of a mail message. The memo-style format of the mail message is defined in RFC 822 [CROC82]. The interaction between a given system's mail preparation and examination program usually involves communication through a file system. SMTP and RFC 822, as originally defined, were limited to carrying text messages.

A technique for including arbitrary binary data in Internet Mail called Multipurpose Internet Mail Extensions (MIME) [MIME93 and MIME93A–B] was developed in 1992 for structuring messages and for carrying application-defined information as well as image, audio, and video data. Also, the Privacy Enhanced

Mail (PEM) [PEM93A–D] protocol was designed to provide such services as confidentiality, integrity, origin authentication, and nonrepudiation to RFC 822. Some parts of the Internet Mail environment now use these enhancements, other parts do not.

Some of the factors that made Internet Mail popular are the simplicity of its e-mail address form, the ease of worldwide user address domain registration, and the ease with which messages can be dynamically routed over the global IP network. This easy routing is facilitated through the use of a distributed directory called the Domain Name System (DNS) [MOCK87] for mapping (or translating) domain names embedded in the e-mail addresses into network IP addresses.

The Internet address is a simple text string of the form *someone@somewhere*; for example, *daniel_blum@rapport.com*. It is easily registered and remembered. It is also easily routed. In our example, the local SMTP component can simply cast a query into the global DNS and obtain forwarding information for the domain "Rapport."

Other Internet mail strengths include a workable standards process, an enormous supply of volunteer labor from the R&D community, and a practice of providing free electronic copies of RFCs and free source code implementations of RFCs. While SMTP is not as robust a backbone protocol as X.400 (as of early 1994, it lacked approved standards for message delivery status notification mechanisms and most implementations could not carry binary data), these deficiencies are being addressed in future RFCs.

Successive rollouts of enhanced SMTP functionality will likely be implemented in a piecemeal fashion throughout the Internet. Because Internet Mail is very much a global infrastructure in flux, it remains to be seen how well interoperability—using its more advanced functions—takes place in practice. But perhaps most significantly, it has proven enormously popular as an open, user-driven e-mail standard that has grown from the bottom up.

2.5.3   Major Consortia

While standards are key to defining the essential services of a messaging infrastructure, not all aspects of those services have been defined by the accredited or de facto standards-making bodies. Partly in response to the challenge of incompatibilities in electronic messaging standards and partly with the aim of implementing standards through the further refinement of profiles, industry consortia, joint ventures, and associations have been organized to grapple with a plethora of issues. These consortia and associations are important in both setting and defining infrastructures that make the standards workable. They also have the unenviable task of wrestling with the sometimes competing requirements emanating from the two standards communities and various vendor implementations. The most prominent consortia, associations, and joint ventures include the following:

- Aerospace Industries Association (AIA)
- Asynchronous Protocol Specification (APS) Alliance
- Corporation for Open System (COS)

- European Electronic Mail Association (EEMA)
- (North American) Electronic Mail Association (EMA)
- General Magic
- Japanese Electronic Mail Association (JEMA)
- Institute of Electrical and Electronics Engineers (IEEE)
- Manufacturing Automation Protocol/Technical and Office Protocol (MAP/TOP)
- MHS Alliance
- North American Directory Forum (NADF)
- Open Software Foundation (OSF)
- Utilities Communication Architecture (UCA)
- API Association (XAPIA)

These consortia and associations are described more fully in Appendix A. We summarize here the work being done by the XAPIA, MHS Alliance, NADF, and General Magic, because these organizations are especially active and influential in producing standards or infrastructure in today's messaging environment.

The X.400 Application Program Interface (API) Association (XAPIA)　was founded to develop consensus on how application programs (which cannot necessarily communicate with X.400 services provided by different vendors) can interface to network service providers. XAPIA has developed a set of APIs to enable implementations to interface directly to the software providing X.400 and X.500 functionality.

In 1992, the XAPIA expanded its scope beyond X.400, and set about developing specifications for a high-level, nonprotocol-specific API dubbed the "Common Mail Calls" (CMC) [DAWS93]. CMC contains a set of simple mail calls that are not tied to any e-mail system, operating system, messaging protocol, or hardware platform. The intent of CMC is to replace existing proprietary API calls with equivalent functionality (or to provide a portable subset of messaging functionality that vendors could implement on top of their APIs). The intent of establishing a simple, universal standard is to reduce sharply the effort required for developers to deploy mail-enabled desktop applications across platforms.

CMC provides consistent ways for application programs to accomplish such basic functions as simple send, fetch, and get. It specifies how a program builds, addresses, and sends a message even when the underlying message system is not known. Also, for developers who want to accommodate features specific to a given message system, XAPIA intends to specify API extensions. These extensions can be registered with the XAPIA as a way of encouraging consistent implementation across the industry.

The XAPIA has also taken on work to develop a standardized API for directory synchronization as well as a calendar and scheduling enabling API.

The MHS Alliance   consists of companies organized to foster and extend the Novell NetWare Message Handling System (MHS) de facto e-mail standard. It consists of Novell itself and various companies that have developed local e-mail systems that are based on an MHS infrastructure. The Alliance has recently released a specification that enables interoperability among MHS calendaring and scheduling packages. The specification calls out five key interoperability functions that allow users of a variety of packages to work together to find a common time for a meeting, to send a notice of the meeting to all participants, to modify meeting details including the time, place, or participants, to cancel a meeting, and to RSVP.

By developing such specifications through the Alliance, Novell ensures that Alliance members will rapidly release products that support them and thereby enhance the quality of features and performance of MHS.

The North American Directory Forum (NADF)   is an organization of telecommunications carriers and information service providers who have reached consensus on the fundamental shape of X.500 interconnections among directories in North America. Formed in 1990, the NADF was the first organization to address practical arrangements for public X.500 Directory interconnection.

The establishment of NADF has resulted in major agreements on billing, directory registration, and other practical matters. The NADF intends to ensure that public directory listings do not infringe on the privacy rights or expectations held by the owners of the listed information. Consequently the organization has developed a "User Bill of Rights," defining how and when information may be listed. NADF is also in the process of conducting an experimental pilot involving both public service providers and users.

General Magic   is not officially a standards body, but a private company created as a joint venture of a number of vendors, including Apple Computer, AT&T, Motorola, Phillips, and Sony. However, one of General Magic's principal activities is the development and publication of the Telescript distributed programming standard, which can be used in smart messaging technology. As we shall see in Chapter 4, Telescript technologies hold important implications for the future direction of public consumer information services. The technical workings of the Telescript language itself will be summarized later.

2.6   ELECTRONIC COMMERCE AND SMART MESSAGING SYSTEMS

Electronic commerce embraces EDI for external communications between enterprises and workflow messaging for automation within enterprises. While historically EDI has not been conducted over messaging infrastructures, EDI documents are today seen more frequently as yet another message content type. Likewise, workflow automation involves the use of messaging infrastructures to improve work processes and increase productivity. Workflow automation can be assisted by mail-enabled applications and smart messaging capabilities, both of which will be influential in opening a potentially vast consumer messaging marketplace.

The economic desirability of these umbrella concepts and the accompanying vision of a less paper-intensive enterprise make them very attractive to implementors as complementary features of electronic mail. This section provides an introduction to electronic commerce and workflow technologies and opportunities.

2.6.1   Electronic Data Interchange

EDI, or the exchange of structured business documents between organizations, is a major application that could benefit from the use of robust messaging infrastructures. Already, EDI and its financial counterpart, EFT, have been proven to reduce the cost of doing business for trading partners by ensuring the timely flow of proper parts or the more rapid payment of bills. For example, EDI increases the efficiency of interorganizational shipments and can decrease the number of times documents are processed by human beings. The use of messaging infrastructures for EDI communications should result in economies of scale and thereby provide the impetus for the acceleration of EDI solutions in the general marketplace.

The term EDI encompasses all forms of interactive, batch, or store-and-forward electronic interchange, but it has come to be more narrowly defined in practice as a set of standard structured formats for the electronic exchange of business information or trading data between computers. EDI is slowly replacing paper quotes, purchase orders, and invoices. It allows automated pricing, purchasing, ordering, and payment, and can also be used to replace such administrative transactions as import/export documentation.

EFT is a variation on EDI. It differs from EDI primarily in that issues surrounding security are paramount and standardization issues are worked through the banking community rather than through general industry standardization groups. While most payment systems are still dominated by paper media like cash and checks, a movement toward the use of electronic systems is underway for reasons of cost control, paperwork reduction, increased privacy, and better cash management. Currently deployed EFT systems include interbank transfer networks such as The Society for Worldwide Interbank Financial Telecommunications (SWIFT), payment networks such as the U.S.-based Bankwire and CHIPS, settlement systems such as Fedwire, automatic teller machine (ATM) networks, and stock or commodity exchange securities networks. Figure 2.10 illustrates EDI, EFT, and the business process in an electronic trading environment.

There are currently two format standards for EDI: the American National Standards Institute's X12, and the United Nations' Electronic Data Interchange for Administration, Commerce, and Transport (EDIFACT). X12 dominates in the U.S., and EDIFACT dominates outside the U.S. Standard utilities and procedures

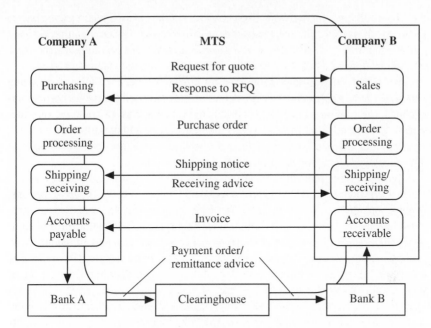

Figure 2.10 EDI, EFT, and the business process. *Ted Myer, Rapport Communication. Reprinted by permission of Rapport Communication. Copyright © 1991.*

exist to translate between the two formats. Both EDIFACT and X12 define a character-oriented format wherein each document is a sequence of codes.

While enterprises have favored EDI as a way of reducing costs, the communications aspects of EDI have been largely neglected. Often, communications have been handled by the EDI application itself—especially in the U.S. where EDI implementations proliferated much earlier than in the rest of the world. Until recently, EDI proponents have focused on developing industry-specific character set standards and relied exclusively on point-to-point connections over asynchronous telephone links, or over IBM remote job entry (RJE) and 2780/3780 binary synchronous links. The number of such directly connected links became so large that a demand emerged for value added networks (VANs), such as the Advantis joint venture between IBM and Sears, to supply EDI interconnection across their packet switching infrastructure. Most VANs now provide a range of complementary services including translation, transmission, and EDI mailboxes.

While most EDI is not yet based on store-and-forward messaging, scalability concerns are driving it in that direction. (EDI traffic is increasing by roughly 20 percent or more per year.) Most EDI connections are currently dial-and-dump (and pray) arrangements between trading partners. This means that the initiating network accumulates transactions for trading partners on a second network. Then at a scheduled time, the network dials out to a mailbox on the receiving network and dumps messages, which are subsequently distributed. The pray epithet derives from the fact that such network interconnections lack sufficient audit trails, often resulting in finger-pointing when problems occur on interconnected data links.

The use of general-purpose messaging infrastructures for EDI communications could have many salutary effects on the EDI industry. It could improve the reliability and timeliness of EDI communication, begin to drive down the costs of using VANs (since organizations could theoretically pay bulk mail rates without the additional charges for value added services), or facilitate the downsizing of EDI processing elements off of mainframes and on to PCs.

Figure 2.11 diagrams the concept of a messaging infrastructure used to facilitate EDI communications between PC-based EDI applications, external trading partners, and VANs.

While message-based EDI is only now beginning to take hold, this concept caught the imagination of standards developers early on and sparked the creation

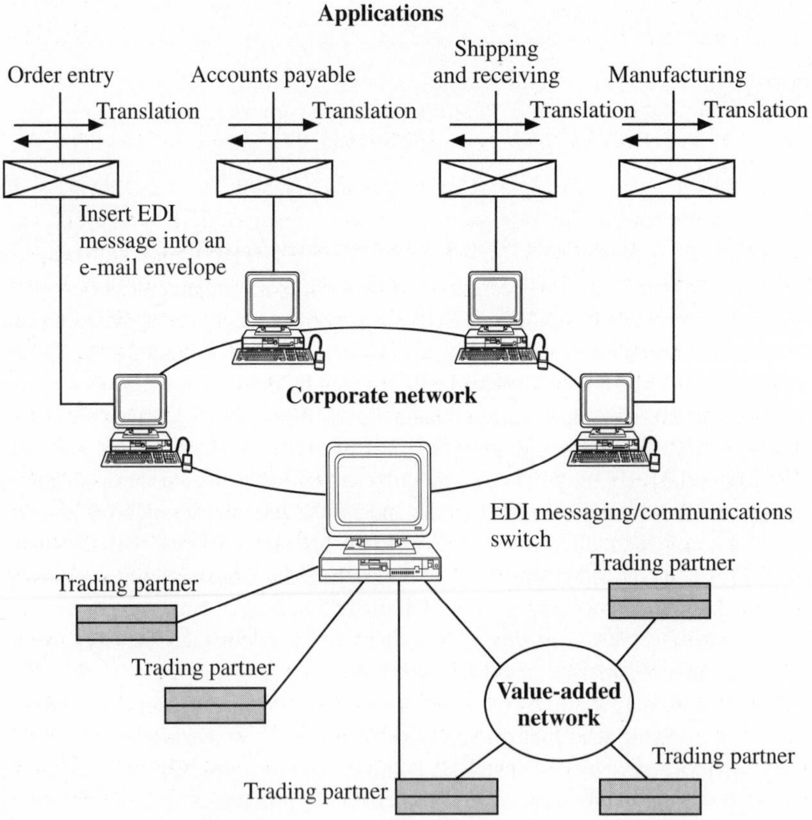

Figure 2.11   EDI applications and communications.

of the CCITT/ISO X.435 standard. X.435 is designed to provide an X.400-based alternative to the current dial-and-dump and leased-line solutions. The standard offers enhanced security, tracking, and audit features not currently available from most other solutions.

But while X.400 is seen by many as the long-term EDI messaging solution, other options have proliferated as well. The X12 community has shown a penchant for developing quick interim fixes; one of these was the ANSI Interconnect Mailbag Structure, which was rapidly deployed by EDI VANs in the U.S. The ANSI X12 Accredited Standards Committee (ASC) also developed the X12 841 transaction set to enable the encapsulation of binary files in X12. More recently, the IETF standards community signaled its interest in carrying EDI traffic by proposing a special MIME body part type for EDI.

The use of integrated messaging as a vehicle for carrying EDI interchanges will someday offer EDI and EFT ubiquitous connectivity. In the future, EDI messaging applications, whether enveloped by X12, X.435, or Internet Mail, will make use of encryption, digital signature, and nonrepudiation security techniques. Since digital signatures can ensure the end-to-end integrity of messages, their availability should add force to the argument that EDI and EFT messages can be accorded legal validity, an important consideration for the growth of computer trading.

2.6.2   Workflow Automation and Mail-Enabled Applications

Workflow solutions involve the use of automated applications, databases, and messaging infrastructures to improve internal enterprise work processes and increase productivity. Workflow can be assisted by both mail-enabled applications and by smart messaging techniques. The workflow market is still young, but early implementations are proliferating. These applications are precursors to powerful forms of automation that will be achieved when intelligent, distributed applications add store-and-forward messaging to their communications repertoire.

Intelligent distributed applications are not a new phenomenon. However, linking these applications to the messaging infrastructure is new. For some time, enterprises have been using internal forms of EDI to improve logistics. Communications techniques, however, were limited to asynchronous or bisynchronous connections linking intelligent mainframe applications. In this environment, much of an application's intelligence and processing power becomes absorbed in managing the communications burden.

Today, such functions as internal EDI can be conducted in near real time using store-and-forward messaging platforms. Such applications can offload the distributed communications burden to dedicated private or public messaging facilities. This capability allows developers of intelligent applications to focus on business issues instead of communications issues. It facilitates the development of highly automated systems capable of performing functions such as crossreferencing purchase orders with inventory and invoices and the deployment of expert systems able to maintain supplier/consumer profiles. It enables workflow applications to automate intra-organizational transaction flows, such as the movement of expense reports, timesheets, purchase requisitions, and human resource forms. These applications will then have two features in common: their facile and transparent link to an embedded messaging utility (through APIs or disk queues); and the integration of messaging and database resources, including directories.

Consider, for example, an automated procedure to facilitate the collection of timely employee performance reviews. A mainframe downloads via e-mail a list of employees due for performance reviews to an agent built especially for this purpose. The agent joins each employee's name with his or her manager's name and generates e-mail forms to each manager. The managers are thus prompted to conduct the reviews, fill out the forms, and reply. If a manager delays too long, the agent dispatches a reminder. The eventual reply (a completed form) does not go to another human user but back to the agent, who circulates it as an e-mail message to a chain of co-signers prior to feeding the approved information back into the database. Payroll and budgetary systems are subsequently activated to process any salary changes.

While messaging infrastructures are of critical importance in making this example viable, the performance review application has not yet been completely relieved of its communications burden. The application still has to organize the information into a visual object (the form). It still has to define rules and semantics for the routing and circulation of the message and for tracking the status of messages. Moreover, each intelligent distributed application dealing with that same workgroup, department, or enterprise must duplicate these remaining redundant communications chores. This situation serves to emphasize that even greater economies of scale can still be achieved by pushing more and more intelligence down into the messaging network through the use of smart messaging techniques, such as active mailboxes and active messages.

2.7   PULLING IT ALL TOGETHER

Integrated messaging holds great promise. Such facilities, when enhanced with smart messaging capabilities to support electronic shopping and information filtering, will not only make enterprises more productive, but will also eventually offer an infrastructure for personal liberation.[10] We have spent the bulk of this chapter explaining the basic technologies and the messaging infrastructure elements currently available. We will conclude by presenting a messaging enabled electronic commerce infrastructure scenario and by developing a high-level statement of infrastructure requirements that must be in place before such a scenario can become cost effective and commonplace.

---

10. This was the title of an address by Nathaniel Borenstein of Bellcore to the E-mail World Conference, November 1993.

2.7.1   An Electronic Commerce Scenario

Consider the ways in which electronic mail, EDI, and workflow products could combine to enable service bays in an automobile dealership to report customer problems with a new model. This scenario presents functionality that is several notches above that one shown in the e-mail interaction that took place among the dealership executive, the engineering design manager, and the parts supply manager in our Fig. 2.1 scenario. It can involve all the participants in providing more immediate and responsive product and service quality as follows.

1. First, the dealership dispatches an EDI parts trouble ticket to an engineering facility, where it is received by a state-of-the-art engineering lab featuring CAD/CAM systems.

2. The engineering unit acknowledges receipt of the trouble ticket. Internally to the engineering unit, workflow processes are engaged to assign the trouble ticket a number, queue it into a work management system, and route it together with appropriate information to the engineers assigned to resolve the problem.

3. Upon redesign, an engineering change order for the part in question is dispatched from the engineering lab by e-mail to the supplying parts factory.

4. Either the factory or, as in this case, the dealership, can also use EDI to order a replacement or a newly designed part from a supplier.

Figure 2.12 provides a visual aide to this example.

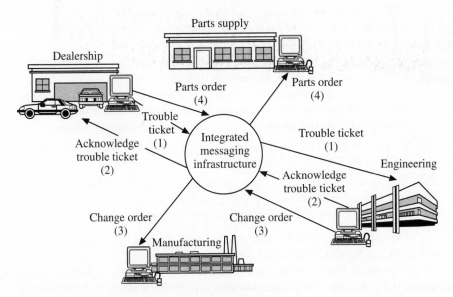

Figure 2.12   A dealership's messaging network.

This entire process appears as a coherent whole. These EDI, workflow, and electronic mail actions promise simultaneously to improve future versions of the car in question and to accelerate repairs of the current model. Also, the economic implications for similar mail-enabled models are dramatic, especially when compared with the costs and likely error and delay that occur as a result of our current paper-based processes.

2.7.2   The Infrastructure Imperative

The dream of "pulling it all together" suggests an infrastructure imperative. The combination of local and global infrastructures should comprise a facility that users can access through a public messaging service, through private facilities, or through a crafted mix of public and private messaging services. The essential point is that this infrastructure should be so ubiquitous that users will take it for granted. Users and applications simply plug in, and their messages should transit the infrastructure smoothly and at low cost.

The infrastructure, considered as the sum of its parts, should be

- **Pervasive:** It must be universally available, with its tentacles reaching everywhere. All local infrastructures should be connected through the global infrastructure. Local infrastructures should provide a consistent means of access by mail-enabled applications.

- **Modular and flexible:** It must be able both to work with standards-based components and to coexist with the installed base of legacy systems. It should contain modular components, enabling customers to mix and match solutions from multiple vendors.

- **Scalable:** It must be able to provide a range of price/performance features to satisfy various needs. It must also be able to handle a range of sizing requirements with respect to many different parameters, including the number of messages, domains, users, or addresses that it can support.

- **Intelligent:** It must be capable of interacting with directory systems and providing directory functionality. It must be capable of supporting emerging workflow and smart messaging capabilities in an appropriate manner.

- **Secure:** It must be capable of providing acceptable grades of security for different uses, from bulk mail to full electronic commerce.

- **Manageable:** It must provide sophisticated management capabilities to enable affordable operation, reliability, survivability, and lights-out management as a local or global infrastructure function where appropriate.

The implications of these infrastructure requirements juxtaposed against the infrastructure standards deficiencies discussed in Section 2.3 are myriad and will be addressed at various points throughout this book. However, there are many talented and dedicated individuals working through the standards process to create new standards and to help older standards converge.

It is not surprising that today's e-mail infrastructures present an unfinished agenda. The evolution of a messaging backbone can be thought of as analogous to the evolution of the telephone system where a user now has dialtone access to almost to any other user in the world. We are at that point in the evolutionary process where we have begun to install our gateways and we recognize the desirability of an integrated e-mail backbone. Our vision is that this backbone will provide universal service analogous to the telephone paradigm, in effect allowing any e-mail user who is connected to it access to any other e-mail user. Still, the telephone network took over fifty years to construct!

2.8 SUMMARY

The fundamental strength of e-mail lies in its use of the familiar office memorandum format, its dynamic replying/forwarding mechanism which enables many-to-many communication, and its ability to transfer information between people or applications on unconnected or intermittently connected networks. In order to derive maximum advantage from these capabilities, users have spurred the evolution of e-mail from islands of departmental interoperability (characterized by host-based and LAN-based e-mail systems) to enterprise-wide connectivity (often effected by e-mail integration servers) and ultimately to global connectivity. A global infrastructure is essential to attaining global connectivity. Universally accepted e-mail and directory standards are essential to establishing a global infrastructure.

At present, local infrastructure standards are being set by the dominant e-mail vendors, (often acting through consortia). For the global infrastructure, there are two sets of standards: one centered around the ITU/ISO X.400 and X.500 architecture, the other centered around Internet Mail. In addition, a number of user and vendor consortia have formed to develop specifications in areas where there are no official accredited standards (such as APIs) to further refine existing standards. However, the failure to achieve a single global infrastructure that is easily accessed and used could retard the development of e-mail and could thereby spur the development of such competitors as a fax-based infrastructure.

This would be an unfortunate outcome since global e-mail based on a set of comprehensive standards could provide the necessary infrastructure to support integrated messaging, which includes electronic commerce, smart messaging, and workflow automation. By harnessing the power of smart messaging and the efficiencies promised by workflow automation in conjunction with electronic commerce, enterprises will be able to reduce their costs and enhance their productivity dramatically.

The requisite infrastructure to support this vision of integrated messaging has yet to be attained. But the challenge of this vision and the opportunity to explore the ways by which it might be achieved are exactly what have inspired us to make this foray into the e-mail frontier.

KEY POINTS

- Store-and-forward messaging is a form of communication distinct from other types of networking, such as file transfer, transaction processing, and database access.

- E-mail has evolved through three stages: the island stage, the gateway stage, and the applications infrastructure stage. As e-mail moves into the infrastructure stage, standards such as X.400, X.500, and Internet Mail become increasingly important.

- Local infrastructures are the components enabling e-mail within a community of users. Global infrastructures—which include e-mail integration backbones, public messaging services, and Internet mail—are the facilities that bridge between local infrastructures.

- Electronic directories are essential to e-mail. Directory issues include standardization and the synchronization of disparate directories.

- Electronic Data Interchange (EDI) is a means of automated business transaction interchange which has not been based on store-and-forward messaging in the past, but is being driven in that direction by scalability concerns.

- E-mail with directories will provide a complete infrastructure for electronic commerce, mail-enabled applications, and workflow automation.

- Pulling it all together, however, requires an infrastructure which is pervasive, modular, flexible, scalable, intelligent, secure, and manageable.

C H A P T E R   3

The Private Messaging Marketplace

E-mail markets and technology are in transition, giving birth to a new, integrated messaging paradigm able to support the business drivers identified in Chapter 1. E-mail is evolving into a multimedia backbone for electronic commerce and workflow applications and into a carrier of revisable documents for both stationary and mobile users.

This evolution has many implications for the market, not the least of which is the strategic importance that messaging assumes for providers and users. Domination of the local messaging infrastructure and its means of access are coming to represent a key leverage point for desktop applications sales, almost all of which will be mail-enabled in the LAN e-mail environment. For micro- or midrange enterprise server vendors, the ability to provide e-mail client or e-mail integration services becomes a critical factor affecting their credibility. For public service

49

providers, e-mail comprises not only an increasing proportion of their traffic, but a chance for outsourcing business with large multinational accounts.

3.1   THE OVERALL MESSAGING MARKET

The overall e-mail market consists of both privately owned and operated messaging networks and publicly offered messaging services. This section will distinguish between public and private messaging services by providing a classic definition and example of each and by contrasting the attributes of classic public and private messaging services in a summary table. It will then discuss the three user communities served by both markets and characterize the status of the e-mail market as a whole.

3.1.1   Classic Definitions

A *public messaging service* is any offering involving the sale of messaging services to customers. In the pure classical configuration, the hardware and software providing e-mail functionality is owned, operated, and managed by the service provider.[1] For example, in the case of MCIMail or Prodigy, the customer pays ongoing fees (generally usage-based) for access to one or more mailboxes on the service provider's network. Chapter 4 will discuss such public messaging services and markets at length.

A *private messaging system*, on the other hand, comprises the hardware and software system (such as cc:Mail or Microsoft Mail) that is owned and operated by the customer. With private mail systems, the customer makes the capital investment required for initial installation and pays no ongoing usage fees thereafter. Table 3.1 compares and contrasts the classic public and the pure private messaging options.

Public services are a necessity for those users who lack a messaging infrastructure: residential subscribers, very small organizational subscribers, and traveling users. These services may also represent a limited capital investment or

Classic public mailbox service	Classic private messaging network
Owned by service provider	Owned by user
No capital investment by user	Upfront capital investment by user
Managed by service provider	Managed by user
User pays usage fees	No usage fees
Service provider handles upgrades	User handles upgrades

Table 3.1 Comparison of classic public and private messaging scenarios.

---

1. We call this the "classic definition" because there are numerous hybrid scenarios, about which more will be said in Chapter 4.

national standards organizations and minimal presence at EMA and EEMA. Although SMTP gateways to other environments were not uncommon, deployment of Internet Mail systems was largely confined to UNIX-based host systems. However, the massive growth and increasing commercialization of the Internet has enabled the Internet Mail user base to expand into the commercial backbone and LAN e-mail space. Organizationally, the Internet Mail community has not (as of early 1994) been absorbed into the international standards organizations or e-mail associations (especially in the U.S.). Rather, it has operated as a separate camp and today is dominated by a mix of researchers, users, and a budding vendor and service provider subculture. Because of the Internet's massive growth, many members of this community perceive themselves as possessing the "edge" or historical initiative. In 1991 the Internet community began developing MIME and PEM as separate, SMTP-based standards offering features competitive with X.400.

Although divergent e-mail standards and technology domains have evolved because of the existence of three distinct messaging communities, what is striking in the description of these three subcultures is the degree to which their user bases are converging. While the enterprise messaging backbone community remains a formidable presence with a massive user base, it is adapting to the pervasiveness of LAN e-mail and Internet Mail technology. At the same time, the LAN e-mail community is converging with the enterprise backbone community. Internet Mail remains somewhat apart, but its presence in the enterprise is expanding, its seminal public user base continues to grow, and its technology is beginning to spread from UNIX-based systems into Apple and DOS/Windows-based LANs.

3.1.3   Growth—The Market Driver

E-mail is being increasingly discovered, receiving an avalanche of attention in the trade press, newsletters, and other media organs since 1992. According to a late 1992 survey by Omnitech, Inc., of 150 senior Fortune 500 executives, e-mail is the number one work-related usage for PCs (42.4 percent) [EMN93F]. Over 95 percent of the executives interviewed felt that e-mail was very important or somewhat important to their company's success. Figure 3.3 depicts our notion that the messaging market is entering an "early majority" stage of development.

The rate of user deployment is accelerating, encouraging more providers, more research dollars, and more attention to the elimination of those blocking factors that might hold up the industry. With rapid growth underway, both desktop and integration-oriented products are improving rapidly. Like great tectonic plates grinding against one another in the earth, alternately discharging destructive earthquakes and healing lava, the tensions between incompatible e-mail markets and communities have generated protocol wars, API wars, and a symbiotic e-mail integration server market that acts as a palliative. Regarding the latter, a wave of enterprise e-mail integration server products (able to deliver "any-to-any" message translation) is emerging to fuse together today's existing messaging backbone and gateway implementations in both public and private environments.

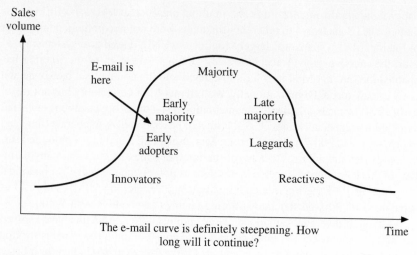

Figure 3.3   E-mail market stages.

This market will continue to evolve. E-mail access to the end user or mail-enabled application is being provided as a feature of LAN network operating systems. Office applications using e-mail as an accessory are another market megatrend, feeding massive growth as they spur usage and traffic to continually higher levels. E-mail and its workflow cousin are now recognized as key to office productivity. Users are becoming accustomed to mail-enabled applications, including word processors, forms generators, databases, spreadsheets, and groupware-oriented calendaring. Soon they will expect an integrated desktop environment where mail flows horizontally between both applications and workgroups and where access to the ubiquitous e-mail utility is as easy as picking the *Mail* option on any application's pull-down menu. Providers will scramble to offer increased applications integration, new workflow capabilities, additional security, smart messaging, and greater wireless "roaming" capabilities.

This evolution in products has spurred dramatic growth in e-mail usage. Exactly how much mailbox growth has and will take place is subject to different estimates. Our best indication is that the worldwide mailbox population will rise from a base of approximately 50 million in 1994 to approximately 100 million in 1997. (A 46.5 million year-end 1993 estimate is provided by the Electronic Mail and Messaging Systems (EMMS), and the 100 million estimate for 1997 by the International Data Corporation.)

To obtain a qualitative picture, note that earlier estimates from EMMS stated that overall mailboxes in the U.S. increased from 19 million to 25.9 million in 1992. At the time, LAN e-mail led the charge in the U.S. with a 42 percent rate of increase, the host-based market (including Internet mailboxes) followed with 38 percent, public e-mail grew at 36 percent, and the Internet had a 20 percent growth rate in the U.S., but higher rates abroad. Both LAN e-mail and Internet Mail rates

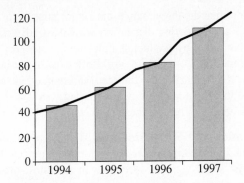

Figure 3.4   Mailbox population projections
(in millions of users).

of growth have since increased and will surely account for much of the climb towards the 100 million mailbox level.

Figure 3.4 displays what might happen to combined public and private mailboxes using the EMMS 1993 year-end figure and a (possibly conservative) 33 percent growth rate.

The quantitative aspects of growth are evident in Fig. 3.4. In qualitative terms, mailboxes and traffic, once almost entirely devoted to interpersonal mail, now include a healthy application component. Growth of electronic commerce and workflow will accelerate this trend. Also, the number of messages per user will increase by 10–20 percent per year. With multimedia mail, message sizes could rise from something in the 1 to 5,000 byte average size to a 50,000 byte (or more) average size in the latter half of the decade.

Although analysts agree that LAN e-mail is growing more rapidly than host-based mail, host-based mail nevertheless retains a very large market share. A 1993 Ferris Networks survey [FERR93] of 100 of U.S. Fortune 2000 organizations found that IBM/OfficeVision and IBM PROFS together controlled 35 percent of the installed Fortune 2000 mailbox base, cc:Mail controlled 10 percent, DEC All-In-One 9 percent, and Microsoft Mail 6 percent. Analysts differ on how rapidly LAN e-mail will eclipse host e-mail. Ferris shows LAN e-mail growing at 40 percent and host e-mail at (−4 percent), but EMMS, as we saw above in its 1992 survey, was much more bullish on host e-mail.

3.2   PRIVATE MESSAGING MARKET

This section describes the present day private messaging market as it exists in the early to mid 1990s. It characterizes the users and their needs, and it identifies the providers of e-mail products, including private dedicated backbone complexes, e-mail integration servers, and end user systems. It identifies blocking factors and the nature of their eventual resolution.

Earlier we identified the three main e-mail communities for background purposes. However, in the following discussion we will stratify the market, not by user community, but rather by product and technology category. Thus, our major categories will be the LAN e-mail and workflow market, the host and midrange e-mail market, the X.400 market, the Internet Mail market, the e-mail integration server market, and the directories and X.500 market.

Several trends tend to affect all these markets.

Vendor Stratification and Specialization: With local messaging infrastructures becoming modularized, products are becoming stratified by their architectural level. That is, some vendors specialize in infrastructure (server product, e-mail integration product, or backbone product) and others, in applications (e-mail clients or various mail-enabled application niches).

Shift from Monolithic to Value-Added Model: Only the largest vendors can afford to compete in more than one or two markets or architectures. The overall market is shifting from a cottage industry to a value-added cascade,[3] where vendors build on top of one another's functionality.

Partnerships: The trends toward stratification and value-added cascade are signs of a maturing industry. Complex messaging solutions can no longer be provided in a single monolithic product line. Partnerships are being formed at a dizzying rate between vendors who are at different stages of the value chain and have complementary offerings. Partnerships are also being formed between vendors and their users who act as service providers to their internal organizations and thus begin to accumulate expertise as well as software tools that may prove useful in the market. In a sense, the messaging industry is becoming a virtual industry composed of many interlocking partnerships.

We will cite examples of these trends in several areas of the market covered below.

3.3   THE LAN E-MAIL MARKET

Based primarily on Microsoft DOS/Windows platforms but also on the Macintosh, UNIX workstation, OS/2, and NT platforms, the LAN e-mail market is the locus of the most innovative office automation, e-mail, and desktop user interface software in the industry. In this fertile terrain, the mission of e-mail is rapidly broadening to encompass responsibility for carrying revisable word processed files, for integrating facsimile, voice, and e-mail, and for supporting an expanded set of office automation or groupware utilities. Such groupware utilities include scheduling or calendaring at the low end and increasingly sophisticated techniques for workflow or smart messaging at the high end. These new office productivity aids, which will soon be taken for granted much as the typewriter was

---

3. This theme was offered by Einar Stefferud of Network Management Associates, Inc. at a November 1993 E-mail World presentation.

in the mid-twentieth century and the fax machine is today, are not only offered by the large computer manufacturers, but also by third party developers.

The market is moving well into the early majority stage of its development. Small- to medium-sized business users deploy LAN e-mail everywhere. Large users have downsized or plan to downsize many of their midrange systems to LAN e-mail. Providers compete fiercely to dominate the market, going so far as to bundle LAN e-mail gratis with operating system software. In this market, LAN messaging market share can represent far more than the ability to sell an e-mail client package for $20 to $50 a desktop. To dominant vendors, such as Microsoft or Lotus, LAN e-mail represents the key to controlling a mail-enabled applications and workflow environment or platform, thereby leveraging sales[4] of various software packages.

To the user, LAN e-mail is a local messaging infrastructure with a hospitable graphical user interface and the promise of telephone-like ubiquity. However, even with gateway solutions, interconnection between LAN e-mail systems and other external systems remains problematic for small and large users alike.

Larger users face the additional challenge both of managing large multiple server, multiple site LAN e-mail installations and of integrating the LAN e-mail systems of their choice with host-based and other internal e-mail systems. To compete for such large installations, LAN e-mail vendors now offer increasingly comprehensive product sets, including directory synchronization, cross-server management and monitoring, and expanded installation and maintenance support. Because today's users are evaluating how well LAN e-mail systems will interoperate with host-based, UNIX, and public mail systems, LAN e-mail vendors offer their own gateway interconnections to other mail systems.[5] These offerings include X.400 and SMTP gateway services. Where the gateway offerings of LAN e-mail vendors do not suffice, a separate e-mail integration server market is thriving.

3.3.1 The Providers

During the early 1990s, the LAN e-mail market went through relentless consolidation. This consolidation trend began in 1991 with Lotus Development Corporation's acquisition of cc:Mail, Da Vinci Systems Corporation's acquisition of Action Technology's The Coordinator product, Novell's acquisition of the rights to Action Technology's MHS product, and Microsoft's acquisition of Consumer Software's Network Courier. More recently Novell bought out WordPerfect.

Today, Lotus, Microsoft, and Novell dominate the LAN e-mail market by virtue of their size, influence, and market share. Runners up include CE Software, Banyan Network Mail, Da Vinci E-mail, Notework, Higgins Group, Futurus

---

4. Microsoft obtained 51 percent of its gross sales from application packages in 1991 according to ValueLine figures. Yet a Microsoft employee indicated that there were more developers working on Microsoft Mail and related messaging products than there were on Microsoft Word, Powerpoint, Excel, and other desktop packages combined.

5. Interoperability with public messaging networks is important even to small user enterprises, who would otherwise need to maintain dual mailboxes.

Client package	Mailboxes (000)
cc:Mail	4,500
MS Mail	4,000
WP Office	2,200
Da Vinci	2,000
Banyan	1,200
CE Software	1,100
Lotus Notes	750
Futurus Team	400
Notework	400
BeyondMail	300
Higgins	250
Reach Software	100
Other	300
Total	17,500

Table 3.2 LAN e-mail clients, 1993.

Team, and BeyondMail. Table 3.2 shows LAN e-mail vendor market share, as estimated for the end of 1993 by [EMMS94], which also noted that IBM resells cc:Mail/Notes and that DEC's continuing efforts in the LAN e-mail client arena have yet to be rewarded with significant market share. As a further symbol of the market consolidation and top vendor dominance, e-mail client packages (but not the server software) are sometimes sold as a component of "software suites," such as Microsoft Office. Table 3.3 provides information on a representative sampling of LAN e-mail vendors.

Because LAN messaging is strategic to the dominance of both the DOS and Macintosh mail-enabled application and network operating systems environments, the heavyweights—Microsoft, Lotus, and Novell—are maneuvering to achieve market control. Each vendor has its own messaging architecture and product suite. New releases and new architectures from these vendors often become de facto market and technical standards, rallying legions of third party e-mail client, e-mail integration server, and mail-enabled application support while introducing new quirks for those who wish to attain interoperability. We provide a brief history of these three companies below and discuss their market drivers, similarly we offer a technical discussion of the dominant vendors' product offerings and architecture in Chapter 5.

Lotus Development Corporation

Lotus was founded in 1982 to develop applications for the then emerging personal computer market. Its first product, the Lotus 1-2-3 spreadsheet, was partially responsible for the overall success of personal computers. Throughout the 1980s, Lotus set about to deliver desktop productivity tools and to follow the trend to-

LAN vendor	Product	Platform	Remarks
Banyan	Banyan Mail	PC DOS with Banyan Vines NOS	E-mail component of Banyan NOS, 1,200,000+ installed base.
Beyond	BeyondMail	PC DOS and industry standard LANs	This NetWare MHS-based system was the first general purpose, rules-based e-mail system for inter-personal messaging and workgroup applications.
cc:Mail (a division of Lotus)	cc:Mail	PC DOS and Windows, Macintosh, UNIX, and wire-less platforms	The market leader. *See* detail on Lotus below.
CE Software	Quickmail 2.5	Macintosh, Appletalk LAN	Competes with Microsoft Mail for leadership on the MAC platform.
Da Vinci Systems Corporation	Da Vinci E-mail and Da Vinci Coordinator	PC Windows/ Major LANs	With its Coordinator and e-mail products combined, Da Vinci has the largest installed base of any of the NetWare MHS-based e-mail systems.
Enterprise Solutions	Enterprise Mail and Directory	PC DOS, Major LAN	Provides native X.400 client that works with various X.400 transport systems (Retix, NCR, and others). Claimed 100,000+ user installed base in late 1992.
Futurus	Team	PC DOS/ Major LANs	Another NetWare MHS-based system.
Microsoft	Microsoft Mail	Macintosh, PC/ Major LANs	*See* detail on Microsoft below.
Notework Corporation	Notework	PC DOS and Windows	NetWare MHS-based "pop-up" (under DOS) e-mail system. Runs in 5K of RAM.
Reach Software	Mailman and Workman	PC DOS/ Major LANs	E-mail and database integration for workflow messaging. Based on NetWare MHS or Banyan Mail.
WordPerfect Corporation	WordPerfect Office	PC DOS, Windows, MAC, UNIX	E-mail with office automation system.

Table 3.3 Summary information of representative LAN e-mail vendors.

ward graphical environments, network computing, and integrated application offerings. Such applications include continuing releases of 1-2-3, word processing (AmiPro), scheduling and calendaring (Organizer), databases (Approach), and graphics (Freelance).

In 1991, Lotus acquired cc:Mail, a leading LAN e-mail package. In 1993, Lotus sold 1.6 million cc:Mail "seats," an increase of 500,000 over 1992. Under

Lotus, cc:Mail has evolved into an enterprise-wide e-mail package that works across all major desktop operating systems and is up-to-date on most major features users seek in e-mail systems today. Users with cc:Mail LAN-based or remote clients access mailboxes and directory lists on cc:Mail Post Offices. Messages are transferred by cc:Mail Routers.

In 1990, Lotus released Notes, a distributed document database or knowledge-sharing system, with tools for building applications customized to a group's requirements. In 1993, Lotus sold 260,000 Notes seats compared with 133,000 in 1992. (Sales have doubled annually since 1990.) Like cc:Mail, Notes works across multiple networks and operating systems and supports remote users. It supports the storage of multiple data types—including text, graphics, images, and editable objects from other applications—in a single compound document. However, in contrast to cc:Mail, Notes supports a database as well as a messaging model of information access. It organizes information for group access (including document tracking, routing, and dissemination). The information is stored in databases on servers that sort and categorize documents to provide a common structure for the group. Also, Notes databases are distributed among multiple servers using replication technology to allow for the automatic synchronization and update of the databases. Notes has a messaging layer to support the movement of documents between databases.

Lotus has recognized that messaging and groupware applications will become the foundation for mission critical business solutions in the 1990s [LOTUS3a]. The company's strategy is to become the leading supplier of high performance, scalable, and reliable messaging services and messaging and groupware products. This approach includes crossplatform, crossnetwork message transports and message stores leveraging cc:Mail and Notes, directories, mail-enabled applications, systems management, and security. Applications are now able to interact directly with Notes via Notes/FX, an integrating technology that enables the application to save its output as a Notes document with all the integral Notes services, including field-based views, multi-user access, security, replication, and workflow process management.

A consequent challenge to Lotus is to integrate cc:Mail and Notes. In 1992, the company released Lotus Mail Exchange, a gateway that provides message transfer between the two products while preserving bitmaps, fonts, tables, and color. It also provides automatic directory synchronization. Furthermore, native Notes client mail functions could now be processed by cc:Mail, and the entire Notes Mail menu could be integrated with cc:Mail's user interface using a Lotus API.

Another challenge was to contest Microsoft's bid for mail-enabled application dominance through its messaging API (MAPI). With impetus from Lotus in collaboration with Apple Computer, Novell, and Borland International, the Vendor Independent Messaging (VIM) consortium was formed in early 1992. The consortium published the VIM programming interface to help software and corporate developers write crossplatform, mail-enabled applications. VIM is supported by cc:Mail and Lotus Notes, Novell's MHS, Apple's OCE, IBM's OS/2 Extended

Services, and other messaging products. However, Apple and Microsoft recently agreed to support one another's APIs (Apple Open Collaboration Environment [AOCE] and MAPI) in their respective cross platform developments. This decision and the emergence of XAPI's CMC suggests VIM's position has weakened.

More recently, Lotus has undertaken an across-the-board updating of its two-part messaging capability. First, the company has announced the development of the Lotus Communications Server (LCS) to provide message transport services for cc:Mail and Notes across multiple platforms including DOS, NetWare Loadable Modules (NLM), Unix, OS/2, and Windows NT. The LCS will provide connections for cc:Mail Post Offices, native support for cc:Mail, Notes, 1988 X.400, SMTP/MIME, and gateways to FAX, MHS, All-In-1, and PROFS as well as connectivity for wireline and wireless communications via cc:Mail Mobile.

This strategy calls for new cc:Mail and Notes clients that will incorporate the best of both technologies (the former optimized for client/server or "send" model, and the latter for file sharing) and a common user interface. Also, cc:Mail will use the Notes-based message store and directory (based on X.500 hierarchical naming) in a way that will permit the addition of full Notes capability should the user so desire it. Likewise, Notes users will have the option of accessing cc:Mail from within Notes for e-mail and mail-enabled applications.

Thus, Lotus positions its offerings based on the premise that desktop software is evolving into workgroup solutions. Its approach is to use the cc:Mail messaging infrastructure and the Notes groupware infrastructure to create a workgroup platform. To this end, the company announced its intention to mail-enable virtually all its applications (and, through VIM, other vendors' applications). In so doing, Lotus has the opportunity to capture a significant market share of desktop workgroup (and ultimately workflow) applications.

Microsoft

This company, which some call the new IBM of the computer industry, offers both hardware and software products. Its software products are centered around the Windows operating system and, more recently, the NT operating system. Products include the operating system itself and various desktop applications, such as Microsoft Word (a word processor) and Microsoft Excel (a spreadsheet). It also sells multimedia products, such as Sound and Video for Windows.

Microsoft's original e-mail product was Microsoft Mail for the Macintosh. In 1990, however, Microsoft acquired a Vancouver-based company called Consumer Software, Inc., which owned what was then the Network Courier mail system. With the stroke of a pen, Microsoft acquired a PC e-mail system to complement its Macintosh offering and a 1984 X.400 Message Transfer Agent capability as well. Since then, Microsoft and former Consumer Software developers have labored to integrate their respective MAC and PC mail systems, with mixed results.

At the same time, Microsoft licensed 1988 X.400 technology from Data Connections, Ltd., in the UK and commenced work on integrating an X.400 MTA into its NT-based Enterprise Messaging Server (EMS). In addition, Microsoft became increasingly visible as an X.400 player, both in terms of public support for the standard and by other actions, for example, by taking a leading role in the registration of document types to be carried in X.400 messages.

Microsoft's strategy of positioning messaging as a part of the operating system (OS) emerged in 1992. This strategy will support Microsoft's central objective to be an operating systems provider; it will also promote Windows sales and sales of desktop applications that might be more highly integrated (or might be perceived as so) with the Windows environment than those of the competition. (In the messaging as part of the OS model, messaging capabilities are considered analogous to printer drivers.)

The linchpin of Microsoft's messaging in the OS strategy [MICR93] is the Microsoft Messaging API (MAPI) [MAPI93, MAPI93a], which is part of a conglomerate of Windows Open Systems Architecture (WOSA) APIs. MAPI actually provides both high-level and low-level client API interfaces for mail-enabled applications, and a backend Service Provider Interface (SPI) that third party and e-mail integration server vendors can use to plug into what Microsoft hopes will become the Messaging OS.

Announced in late 1991, MAPI soon ran afoul of the rival VIM specification. At that time, many users became concerned about a proliferation of incompatible APIs. The trade press seized on the controversy dubbing it the "API Wars." In the end, Microsoft handled the situation rather adroitly, declining an invitation to join the VIM Consortium and instead requesting that a broader forum—the X.400 API Association—develop a set of simple standard procedure calls for simple mail-enabled applications. The XAPIA accepted this Microsoft gambit, and produced a simple API under the name of Common Mail Calls (CMC). Microsoft then began building in support for the CMC but has in no way reduced its commitment to MAPI.

Microsoft bundled Microsoft Mail and a companion scheduling product free with the Windows for Workgroups operating system released in late 1992. This electronic mail component provides MS Mail in the LAN environment but requires the Microsoft Mail server (a separate purchase) for dialup or other forms of remote e-mail transport. Initially perceived as a grave threat to Lotus and Novell because it offered "free" e-mail clients on the one hand and inexpensive peer-to-peer networking on the other, Windows for Workgroups has since proved to be a market nonstarter.

Yet another Microsoft strategy in 1992 was to bundle e-mail with its word processing (Word), graphics (Powerpoint), and spreadsheet (Excel) desktop applications. The entire package, dubbed Microsoft Office, sold for less than $500. Other vendors, such as Lotus and WordPerfect, followed suit, offering "desktop suites" of their own. (Lotus later removed cc:Mail from its SmartSuite package, however.)

Microsoft also entered the LAN e-mail/workflow market with its release of Workgroup Templates functionality (enabling administrators to install commonly used office forms in Microsoft Mail). A related offering, the Electronic Form Designer product, enables users to design their own forms.

The centerpiece of Microsoft's messaging activity in 1994 and 1995 will be its release of the Windows NT-operating system–based Touchdown Server. Formerly known as the Enterprise Messaging Server (or EMS), the Touchdown

Server will support 1988 X.400, SMTP/MIME, various gateways, an X.500 directory service, and the extensive administrative and instrumentation capabilities of Window NT. An advanced database capability will provide public folders that will support context sensitive views of electronic forms and rules processing.

While the Touchdown server supports a DCE-based client-server interface to mail clients, it will also continue to support older Microsoft Mail clients via a shared file server. Microsoft's goal is to provide an e-mail fax and voice client called Explorer with the "Chicago" release of Windows to as many as 40 million customers. Explorer will operate across supported platforms running over whichever server the customer selects.

Novell

From modest beginnings as a small startup that burst on the scene in the mid 1980s to pioneer the LAN network operating system market, Novell grew into a giant. Today it dominates over 70 percent of what has become the lucrative Network Operating System (NOS) business. As a result of this growth, Novell has also profoundly influenced the evolution of the LAN e-mail market.

If Microsoft has recently emerged as the pioneer of messaging in the OS, Novell has long been the pioneer of messaging in the NOS. In the late 1980s, realizing that a store-and-forward messaging engine for enterprises or distributed workgroups was an essential supplement to other NetWare services (such as file sharing and printing), Novell began to promote a product called the Messaging Handling System from Action Technologies. Eventually it purchased the product, and NetWare MHS[6] has remained the centerpiece of Novell's messaging strategy ever since. Over the years the product has grown, acquiring more features in successive releases while retaining its simple interface. That is, on submission, an MHS application, such as an e-mail client or mail-enabled application, needs to do no more than place a message arranged according to the precepts of Novell's Simple Message Format (SMF) into a disk directory.

Like Microsoft and cc:Mail/Lotus, Novell by the early 1990s had become too large to live in a proprietary world alone. The company added a 1984 X.400 gateway through XAPIA and Retix support. The company also built gateways to SMTP, PROFS, and SNADS. It joined the VIM Consortium but, always pragmatic, pledged MAPI and Apple Open Collaboration Environment (OCE) support as well. It augmented its directory capabilities and dubbed the entire product suite NetWare Global Messaging (NGM) in 1992. This appellation was later dropped. With NetWare 4.0, Novell rolled out its NetWare Directory Services, which has "X.500-like" hierarchy and object typing features. Novell is developing X.500 as well.

Historically, Novell itself never really entered the e-mail front end client or user interface business. It attracted a strong following of native MHS e-mail vendors who benefit from the ability to piggyback on a de facto standard, to leverage Novell's transport services, and to seed their e-mail directories with Novell's Bindery directory (which contains user account information). Leading native MHS e-mail

---

6. NetWare MHS should not be confused with X.400 MHS. The two are *not* the same.

vendors include Da Vinci E-mail, BeyondMail, and Futurus Team (formerly known as Right Hand Man). In February 1993, Novell founded the MHS Alliance of MHS vendors, which includes Beyond, Da Vinci, Futurus, and others.

However, with non-MHS products dominating LAN e-mail, Novell's strategy of treating MHS vendors in an even-handed manner may be changing. In early 1994, Da Vinci announced that its product would soon be offered as a Novell product with a Novell part number. This change in course may undercut the other MHS vendors, probably encouraging them to build toward newly opened Microsoft and Lotus server subarchitectures as well as MHS.

Another important development was Novell's 1992 purchase of Univel, formerly the UNIX arm of AT&T. This acquisition is a major area of expansion for Novell. It was occasioned, some analysts believe, by Microsoft's head on charge into Novell territory through its release of peer-to-peer networking (and free e-mail) with the Windows for Workgroups software. It remains to be seen whether greater NetWare integration with UNIX will lead to greater integration with TCP/IP, NetWare, MHS, and Internet Mail environments.

In early 1994, Novell's purchase of WordPerfect and of the Borland spreadsheet division catapulted it into direct competition with Microsoft and Lotus. Also, Novell suggests it may downgrade global MHS from a strategic product, increasingly blending it into NetWare 4.x.

3.3.2   LAN E-mail Market Blocking Factors

Several factors impeding the LAN e-mail market from attaining even more stellar growth rates include the following:

- Downsizing from host-based environments is not always as simple or cost-effective as it is advertised to be. As users move off the familiar mainframe environment into the turbulent world of LANs, they encounter new and unexpected training, management, and applications-related costs.

- Large organizations face some difficulty in centrally managing LAN e-mail systems, in some cases even to the point of being unable to dictate a single enterprise standard LAN e-mail system to be deployed by all departments.

- Interoperability on the messaging protocol level remains a problem. There are three significant de facto protocol standards (X.400, SMTP, and NetWare MHS), three significant connector standards (VIM, MAPI, and NetWare SMF), and mounting difficulties with making new technology (e.g., workflow messaging or Object Linking and Embedding [OLE]) fit into any interoperability model. However, there is some cause for optimism as Microsoft and Lotus open their architectures and, together with Novell, enhance their commitment to X.400 and SMTP/MIME.

While organizations will ultimately face the paradigm costs associated with downsizing, manageability and interoperability difficulties tend to delay the death of host mail and the full flowering of LAN e-mail technology in the large enterprise. At the same time, the e-mail integration server market is flourishing as organizations grapple with LAN e-mail interconnection, directory, and document transfer difficulties.

3.3.3 LAN E-mail and the Workflow Market

Users face a long-term need for total business automation based on distributable, multimedia, multiplatform, interoperable messaging, workflow, and EDI. They require a single, ubiquitous workflow platform that provides full integration with databases, e-mail systems, EDI, and other aspects of the automated enterprise. This platform must also operate within a context of full business audit, security, and control; must be flexible and easy to use; and must act as a development platform for electronic routing and approval applications.

The workflow market, an increasingly important subcategory of the LAN e-mail market,[7] is only beginning to scratch the surface of the formidable user requirements cited. At the low end, workflow products comprise calendaring or group scheduling software; at the high end, they comprise sophisticated electronic forms routing and approval systems. While the high end of the workflow market is still in the "innovator" stage of development, low-end calendaring and electronic forms software is quite common.

Workflow is currently dominated by LAN e-mail's major vendors: cc:Mail and Lotus Notes provide low-end and high-end workflow respectively; Microsoft provides scheduling software with Microsoft Mail; and Novell leads the MHS Alliance Consortium in an attempt to establish de facto forms and calendaring standards. Niche vendors, such as Beyond, Inc. and Reach Software, made their names with similarly innovative products. A number of vendors, such as Delrina and Perform Pro, built forms packages designed to be independent of the underlying mail system. Lotus Notes dominates the field of workflow application development platforms; it enjoys broad support from third party vendors, many of whom have integrated their mainstream database and desktop applications, or their niche specialty applications with Notes. Other products, particularly workflow development platforms from Borland, Microsoft, and Oracle will heavily impact the market by late 1994 and 1995.

The workflow market is a prime example of the industry's supply-side shift toward a value-added cascade. For example, Novell provides a message transfer server infrastructure; Reach Software's Mailman and Workman products provide an e-mail/workflow platform; imaging products such as Watermark provide specialized image handling software; and independent software vendors build specialized vertical industry (e.g., real estate, retail, or medical) applications.

The major blocking factors for workflow result from the immaturity of messaging security technology and conflicting standards (or lack of standards) for workflow processing. The Internet Mail community is dabbling with a scripting technology called the Tool Command Language (Tcl), the MHS Alliance is deliberating de facto forms and calendaring standards, and General Magic has pub-

---

7. Of course, workflow can also be part of the context of host, midrange, and public messaging environments.

lished a smart messaging standard called Telescript. It is too early to tell whether one approach or standard will come to dominate or how smooth the interworking between variants will prove to be.

3.4   THE HOST AND MIDRANGE E-MAIL MARKET

We can group both mainframe and midrange e-mail systems into the host e-mail category. The host e-mail market is comprised of e-mail system products from vendors such as IBM OfficeVision/VM, PROFS, DEC VMS-MAIL or ALL-IN-1, Wang Office Mail, Unisys OFIS, and Bull HN's Q-Office. While host mailbox populations are commonly thought to be in decline, by various estimates they may yet make up at least 50 percent of the installed mailbox base.

Much growth is coming from host-based Internet Mail users, especially outside the U.S. Traditionally the IBM mainframe has been a breeding ground for third-party–provided mail systems, such as Fischer International's EMC^2/TAO and Verimation's Memo. Table 3.4 provides a representative sampling of host and midrange e-mail products.

It is important to distinguish between host e-mail as a platform for user mailboxes and as a server platform for clients that are actually located on the LAN. Host e-mail is growing in both categories, but the bulk of new client or user interface sales will occur on workstations, not hosts. More and more enterprises are downsizing from mini- or mainframe departmental systems to LAN architectures. This movement sometimes assumes landslide proportions. A source from a major Fortune 500 company estimated that the charged-back monthly bill for mainframe

Departmental vendor	Platform	Mail system
Bull HN Information Systems, Inc.	DPX/2	Q-Office, ALIS
Data General	DG/UX	CEO Mail
Digital Equipment Corporation	ULTRIX, VMS	VMS Mail, All-In-1 Mail
Fisher International	IBM VM/MVS	EMC^2/TAO
Hewlett-Packard Ltd.	HP-UX, other UNIX	HP Desk, Openmail
International Business Machines Corp.	IBM VM, MVS, Other	PROFS, OfficeVision/ VM, OfficeVision/ MVS, Others
Siemens Nixdorf Information Systems AG	SINIX	OCIS Office Automation Package
Tandem Computers	Guardian, UNIX	PS Mail
Uniplex Integration Systems, Inc.	UNIX	onGO
Unisys Corporation	UNIX, Others	OFIS Mail, OFIS Link
Verimation	IBM	MEMO
Wang Laboratories	WANG/VS	Wang Office Mail

Table 3.4 Host and midrange e-mail systems.

PROFS users averaged between $300 and $400 per month and noted that, as department after department downsizes to its own LAN e-mail system, the rate for those departments still remaining on PROFS skyrockets. However, many users are loath to abandon PROFS, with its integrated calendaring and other reliable capabilities, for the new (and uncertain) world of LAN computing.

A bright spot for the host e-mail market stems from the growth in UNIX-based client offerings that can run on scalable UNIX platforms from low-end workstations to minicomputer systems. Examples are onGO from the Uniplex corporation (a native X.400 mail system), and Zmail from the Zsoft Corporation. These recent products take a page from the LAN e-mail book by concentrating heavily on multimedia features and mail-enabled applications support.

Converging from the opposite direction, some LAN e-mail vendors who attempt to provide crossplatform client support offer UNIX as well as DOS, Windows, MacIntosh, and OS/2 clients. Thus, for example, a user could run cc:Mail on a SUN workstation. (Microsoft has been notable for its lack of UNIX support; a Microsoft employee observed that "the revenues aren't there.") Those LAN e-mail client vendors that support UNIX have done so to differentiate themselves from Microsoft as well as to capitalize on an expanding UNIX-based workstation software market.

Midrange and mainframe platforms are also important in the server category. With modularization, major LAN e-mail vendors such as Microsoft and Lotus are decoupling LAN e-mail clients from message storage, transport, and directory functions. This is blurring the distinction between LAN e-mail and host e-mail by providing new opportunities for a midrange platform (likely to be based on UNIX or NT) to act as a server for LAN e-mail clients (i.e., handling the directory, message store, and message transfer—but not the user interface—functions). Section 3.5.3 discusses an early example of this development—the HP *clients of choice* offering.

3.5   THE E-MAIL INTEGRATION SERVER MARKET

With legacy midrange and mainframe e-mail systems remaining in the picture and with continued technological and market turbulence in the burgeoning LAN e-mail market, interoperability woes have not disappeared. As users come to regard e-mail as a mission critical application and interconnect their systems, the difficulty of getting messages across enterprises between trading partners, customers, and suppliers has led to a healthy market for e-mail integration server products that are able to perform message translation and associated services between incompatible local e-mail systems and act, in some cases, as a high performance backbone linking distributed e-mail sites.

Pioneered by companies such as Soft*Switch, which for years has provided a high-end IBM-based switch with over 50 gateways, and Retix, which provides low-end, PC-based LAN e-mail gateways, the e-mail integration server market is now nearing the end of its early adopter phase. It is experiencing a swelling of supplier ranks, reduced barriers to entry, and increased growth.

Table 3.5 identifies a representative sampling of 14 e-mail integration server vendors with 15 products, most of which support the X.400 and SMTP standards

E-mail integration vendor	Product	Platform	Features
Amadeus, Inc.	MBLink	Server: DEC VMS, PC Gateways: LAN-based, midrange, host.	Low-end product with some directory synchronization capabilities. Links to X.400 via DEC Message Router.
Alisa Systems, Inc.	AlisaMail	Server: DEC VMS Gateways: LAN-based, midrange, host	High-end switch offering X.400 and multiway gateways with features mapped via a relational database. One-way directory synchronization inward to AlisaMail directory.
Boston Software Works	Interoffice Message Exchange	Server: IBM, DEC/UNIX Gateways: LAN-based, midrange, host	Original equipment manufacture (OEM) product licensed to various backbone and platform vendors, such as HP and ISOCOR. Directory synchronization, document conversion, and other features.
Control Data Systems, Inc.	Mail*HUB	Server: UNIX Gateways: LAN based, midrange, host	Provides 1988 X.400 and X.500 directory. SMTP functionality leverages X.500 directory. Works with various gateways, and supports directory synchronization to some environments.
Digital Equipment Corp.	MAILbus	Server: DEC VMS, Ultrix Gateways: LAN-based, midrange, host	High-end Mailbus 400 product offers 1988 X.400 and X.500. Digital's older Mailbus product, Digital Directory Service, and Directory Synchronizer are required for various gateways.
Hewlett-Packard	HPX.400, HP Openmail	Server: HP / Unix Gateways: LAN-based, midrange, host	High-end product offers 1988 X.400 and X.500. Obtains gateway capabilities through partnerships with Boston Software Works, Worldtalk, and other vendors.
ISOCOR, Inc.	ISOPLEX Message Server Family	Server: HP / Unix, DOS Gateways: LAN-based, midrange, host	Offers crossplatform support and VIM, MAPI, OCE, and XAPIA API support. Also supports 1988 X.400, X.500, X.435, and security features.
NCR	StarPRO Enterprise Messaging	Server: NCR / Unix Gateways: LAN-based, host	Offers X.400, X.500, and integration with Retix gateways.

Vendor	Product	Server/Gateways	Description
Novell	NetWare Global MHS	Server: PC DOS Gateways: LAN-based, SNADS	A collection of gateways implemented as NetWare Loadable Modules (NLM) loosely architected around NetWare MHS and NetWare Directory Services (NDS). XAPIA-connected Retix OpenServer NLM offers X.400.
Retix	OpenServer	Server: PC DOS or Unix Gateways: LAN-based	Low-end PC-based switch with offboard XAPIA gateways in LAN e-mail systems. 1988 X.400 and Directory Exchange Server (DXS) offered on newer versions of OpenServer. Its gateway products are widely resold as "bootstrapping" technology by other vendors.
Soft*Switch	EMX: Enterprise Mail Exchange	Server: Data General/ Unix Gateways: LAN-based, midrange, host	Sold as turnkey hardware/software solution. Supports numerous gateways, advanced rules-based address mapping and advanced directory synchronization. Includes built-in 1988 X.400, SMTP, SNADS, and PROFS support.
Soft*Switch	Central	Server: VM or MVS (IBM) Gateways: LAN-based, midrange, host	Mainframe-based switch with world's largest collection of gateways. Offers directory synchronization and document conversion. X.400 is supported through a PC-based gateway.
Technology Development Systems, Inc.	NetSwitch	Server: PC DOS Gateways: LAN-based, midrange, host	Supports X.400 and numerous LAN-based, midrange, and host gateways.
Wingra Technologies, Inc.	Missive	Server: DEC VMS Gateways: LAN-based, midrange, host	Supports X.400 and numerous LAN-based, midrange, and host gateways.
Worldtalk	Worldtalk 400	Server: PC DOS or Unix Gateways: LAN-based	Low-end LAN e-mail gateway providers offers high-quality alias name mapping between supported mail systems and directory synchronization capabilities. Runs on various platforms (such as HP) where it is integrated with the X.400 capability of the platform vendor.

Table 3.5 Representative e-mail integration server vendors.

and between five and 50 gateways each to proprietary local messaging systems or protocols. At the beginning of 1992, perhaps half of these products existed. During 1993, existing e-mail integration servers broadened their range of gateway support and new players entered the market. In many cases, product enhancement will be accomplished via the value-added cascade as vendors license e-mail integration technology from one another. The Boston Software Works, for example, has licensed its Interoffice product to Hewlett-Packard and several other companies. Those vendors that provide or plan to provide document conversion in the e-mail integration server almost universally license a product called Keyword, from KeyPak, Inc. Retix has licensed source code for X.400 or gateway implementations to Soft*Switch, Digital, NCR, and others. Moreover, third party vendors, such as Control Data Systems, Digital, and ISOCOR work with the Retix X.400 gateway products[8] for connectivity to LAN e-mail systems.

New breeds of e-mail integration server products are emerging to meet increasingly sophisticated user demands. We noted earlier that global infrastructures are evolving from a gateway model to a backbone model. This affects e-mail integration server products, whether they are targeted to become the underlying technology within public messaging networks, within private messaging backbones (as we are discussing here), or within both. Figure 3.5 illustrates the difference between gateway model e-mail integration servers and backbone model servers.

In the gateway model, the e-mail integration server sits at the center of a web of onboard (i.e., coresident on the same platform with the server) or offboard gateway facilities. The server/gateways reformat and relay messages between proprietary local messaging systems and send them on their way without necessarily providing assistance in solving such other messaging problems as application access to the mail system or directory synchronization between diverse systems.

E-mail integration servers that fit our backbone model can interwork with local messaging systems at either the client level or at the server level. In client interworking mode, the e-mail integration product takes care of all the client's transport, storage, and directory needs in one of two ways. First, it may position a software driver component on the client platform; this driver component in turn communicates with the e-mail client via an API. Second, it may support a standardized access protocol, such as X.400's P7 or Internet Mail Post Office Protocol (POP). In server interworking mode, the backbone model e-mail integration product operates similarly to a gateway model e-mail integration product but provides more functionality. In addition to simple gateway interconnection, it performs functions such as directory synchronization, rules-based address mapping, and

---

8. The Retix gateway products, which run coresident with LAN e-mail server packages, have become a sort of industry de facto standard. They output an object formatted similarly to an X.400 message, and thus can be utilized to bootstrap third party X.400 products into the e-mail integration server market. For such configurations, the customer must buy both the X.400 product and the Retix gateway, which is either resold by the X.400 vendor or purchased directly from Retix. The Retix gateways do not themselves provide directory synchronization, rules-based address mapping, or other advanced interworking features.

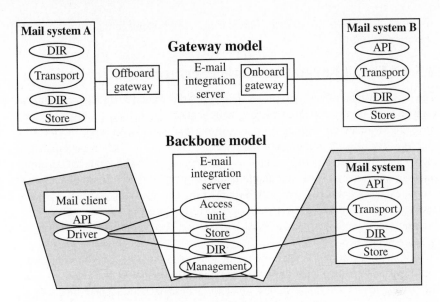

Figure 3.5   The gateway model versus the backbone model.

(possibly) operational health monitoring and control.[9] When multiple e-mail integration servers are deployed in large messaging networks, they form a dedicated messaging backbone, often with distributed management capabilities.

Another sign of the gateway-to-backbone paradigm shift is a change in the language used in e-mail integration product literature. As if the word *gateway* were becoming a pejorative, many vendors are naming their multiprotocol connectivity components *access units* instead. Thus, an e-mail integration server might support multiple access units, some standards-based, some not. The Soft*Switch EMX, for example, provides X.400, SMTP, PROFS, and SNADS connectivity components, which it calls access units. It also supports a special access unit called SNAPI to communicate with its offboard (PC-based) gateways to LAN e-mail and other systems.

Thus, today's e-mail integration products are in transition from the gateway to the backbone model, providing various gradations of functionality. Almost all e-mail integration products provide standards-based interconnection of some kind, especially X.400 and SMTP support. Some provide rules-based address mapping, enterprise directories, and directory synchronization. A few provide conversion of documents sent as e-mail attachments from one format to another.

---

9. Management of local e-mail products from the backbone will eventually be made possible through management standards; converging efforts toward defining e-mail management standards are underway in the IETF, the IFIP E-Mail Management Group, and the ITU.

Some provide health monitoring of local messaging systems, but none yet provide operational control.

3.5.1   E-mail Integration Market Segments and Trends

The overall e-mail integration server market divides roughly into two segments: a high end and a low end. High-end segment vendors typically offer high capacity message switches on midrange or mainframe platforms with large numbers of gateways for host, midrange, and PC systems. They also include robust management capabilities and feature extensive standards support. This segment currently includes computer and software manufacturers, such as Digital Equipment Corporation, Hewlett-Packard, and Soft*Switch, Inc. The low-end segment includes lower-priced, PC-based offerings supporting fewer gateways and a smaller number of users. Companies such as Novell, Retix, and The Worldtalk Corporation fall into this segment.

E-mail integration providers are racing to win the gateway sweepstakes by supporting as many e-mail interconnects as possible. Above and beyond gateways, they are striving to add additional value by including these backbone model functions. A relatively new trend, spearheaded by DEC, is for the vendor to offer facilities-managed turnkey backbone e-mail integration solutions. Their operations and consulting staff will customize, manage, and operate the product for use in the customer environment for an annual fee. In return, the customer receives unlimited messaging usage and is freed from the complex and expensive task of planning, designing, and operating a large multiprotocol messaging network for a large, geographically dispersed user enterprise. Such complexity has engendered the high-end outsourcing/systems integration niche. It has also led many vendors in the market to live and die by partnerships,[10] both with other vendors and with users.

Partnerships between vendors are necessary because monolithic product lines cannot keep up with the rapidly evolving technology and user requirements and the plethora of functional variations. Partnerships between vendors and users are needed because no large complex messaging network is exactly like any other, and all messaging networks exist in a state of rapid change. A system based on rigid requirements tends to require expensive custom components (e.g. , linkage to a home-grown directory) and sometimes difficult-to-integrate third party provided components (e.g., an obscure gateway) in addition to the less expensive, turnkey off-the-shelf components that users prize. Murphy's Law[11] suggests that by the

---

10. In a dramatic example, high-end e-mail integration competitors HP and Soft*Switch announced in November 1993 an agreement to provide joint messaging networks to some customers. This partnership would be particularly applicable where a customer required Soft*Switch components not available from HP, and extensive system integration services not available from Soft*Switch. HP and Soft*Switch will continue to compete for the customer base where the Soft*Switch component/HP systems integration requirements do not intersect. (Control Data Systems and the Worldtalk Corporation struck a similar agreement in early 1994.)

11. Murphy's Law: What *can* go wrong, *will* go wrong.

time the system is planned, specified, assembled, and rolled into production, the requirements will inevitably change even if they were accurately specified in the first place.

Thus complex messaging networks can only flourish where, through a flexible partnership, the vendor and the user work together in a win-win mode. Within the framework of such partnerships, both the vendor and user learn from one another. The vendor uses its accumulated knowledge and tools to solve customer problems, but components developed on a custom basis for the user may be reused in other environments or even in future off-the-shelf product releases.

3.5.2   E-mail Integration Market Opportunities—Thriving on Controlled Chaos

Widespread use of native X.400 or Internet Mail transport services in local messaging systems could theoretically replace gateways and render the e-mail integration server market, as it presently exists, obsolete. However, messaging standards in themselves do not resolve the terrible trio of directory interchange, document interchange, and e-mail management problems.

In a sense, the e-mail integration market thrives on the industry's misfortunes. The industry's blocking factors, which include a proliferation of message formats, service interpretations, and APIs, create much of the demand for e-mail integration in the first instance. To the extent that the e-mail integration environment becomes too chaotic, however, the overall market does not grow as rapidly, traffic does not increase as rapidly, and the growth rate of e-mail integration server sales languishes.

Cynics in the messaging industry might argue that the e-mail integration market thrives on carefully managed chaos. Overly successful standards might ultimately constitute a blocking factor for e-mail integration sales. However, total chaos and confusion are also blocking factors for the reasons discussed above. A balance must exist between standards and chaos. Such a balance certainly exists today.

In the long run, as standards-based local messaging systems become more widespread and as what we have been calling the backbone model of e-mail integration becomes more pervasive, the requirements set for the e-mail integration market will change. We believe that backbone e-mail integration opportunities will abound for the remainder of the decade. As old integration issues of lowest common denominator interconnectivity and directory synchronization are solved, new issues will surface. These issues will include support for workflow routing, any-to-any attachment conversion, highest common denominator, object-oriented X.500 directories, sound and video bearing megamessages, and lights out command and control of LAN e-mail components from the server to the desktop. Then, as in the meantime, a need will still exist in many enterprises for a high-performance, centrally managed backbone that handles external interconnections, directory services, health monitoring, and other management functions such as accounting. This need may exist even in environments using only a single local messaging system.

3.5.3   E-mail Integration Server Vendors

The remainder of this section discusses the three high-end e-mail integration server providers: DEC, HP, and Soft*Switch. Although not covered in this section, CDS' Mail*Hub product line (recently strengthened on the LAN gateway side by CDS' alliance with Worldtalk) is rapidly moving into the high-end e-mail integration space.

DEC

Digital Equipment Corporation (DEC) was once recognized as the leading challenger to IBM in the computer industry (second in total revenues) and remains a networking leader. DEC keeps abreast of new technologies and often turns out products that set industry standards as soon as such technologies become feasible. Of late, however, Digital's overall position has weakened primarily because of slumping minicomputer sales.

DEC characterizes itself as a leading supplier of networked computer systems and systems integration (initially in engineering and scientific environments, now in business environments as well). Since messaging is an important facet of networking, DEC has been involved in all aspects of the business by providing interpersonal messaging clients, workflow, and e-mail integration products. Its successive e-mail systems include VMSMail, ALL-IN-ONE, and Teamlinks. In addition, it has resold native XAPIA-capable X.400 e-mail clients such as Enterprise Mail from Enterprise Solutions and Poste from Alfalfa software. DEC's e-mail integration server product lines are Mailbus and Mailbus 400.

While DEC released Mailbus 400 with 1988 X.400 support in the summer of 1992, many DEC users still require elements of the older DEC Mailbus product line, which integrates a core Message Router (MR) component with All-In-One and VMSMail gateways, a 1984 X.400 (MR/X), SNADS gateway (MR/S), and a PROFS gateway (MR/P). During 1992 and early 1993, DEC resold various Retix LAN-based gateways to X.400 but gradually implemented its own version of these products.

On the directory front, DEC products during 1992 and 1993 consisted of the DEC X.500 product to complement Mailbus 400 and the older proprietary Digital Directory System (DDS). While accessories such as the DEC Synchronizer (for directory synchronization) still require DDS, DEC is integrating these products. Its X.500 implementation is advanced, even supporting some 1993 X.500 features such as simplified access control.

While DEC has not succeeded in all aspects of the messaging business (its Teamlinks client has yet to wrest a significant LAN e-mail market share from cc:Mail or Microsoft Mail), it has met success in the e-mail integration business via the Mailbus and Mailbus 400 product line. DEC provides a strong alternative to Soft*Switch, especially in installations where one or more processors from its VAX family were previously deployed. To the extent that Digital is able to integrate its old and new products and to the extent that X.400 and X.500 attain greater critical mass, DEC will be well positioned to expand this position.

One approach that may help differentiate DEC from the competition is its emphasis on service and facilities management. As noted above, DEC is spearheading an emerging trend towards facilities-managed, turnkey backbone e-mail integration solutions. DEC's operations and consulting staff will customize and operate the product for use in the customer environment for a fixed fee. DEC formally launched an "Open Talk" customized service and operation offering in early 1993 aimed at multinational companies. Earlier DEC landed the Pepsi Cola International account (spanning 165 companies) by offering this mix of products and services. With the Digital solution, a Pepsi spokeswoman indicated that the company expected to save $4.1 million of its previous $6 million annual messaging expenditures.

In early 1993, DEC took the astute step of providing direct support for its Teamlinks LAN e-mail clients on its ALL-IN-1 servers, thus eliminating a previously required intermediary server product called "Mailworks." There is some speculation that the ALL-IN-1 server may eventually support other e-mail clients from third party vendors, such as cc:Mail. This direction by DEC would be consistent with the backbone model, the rebirth of host e-mail systems as enterprise servers, and other trends noted in this chapter.

Hewlett-Packard

(HP) designs, manufactures, and markets more than 10,000 products in the areas of test and measurement instruments, integrated instrument and computer systems, medical electronic equipment and instrumentation, chemical analysis, and computer systems and peripherals.

In the mid-1970s, HP began providing networking tools as part of a strategy it dubbed AdvanceNet, which was recently dropped in favor of HP's "networking strategy." This strategy includes the HP product line that is intended to produce a family of scalable, fast machines, networking, PC integration, RISC (Reduced Instruction Set Computing architecture), networking, and standards-based, open systems architecture.

HP's major markets include telecommunications, aerospace, aircraft, electronics, the automotive industry, and medicine and scientific research. Nearly 50 percent of Hewlett-Packard's sales are outside the U.S., with Europe accounting for over 65 percent of that portion. Its other major markets include Japan, Canada, Australia, the Far East, and Latin America. HP sells its products through a network of direct sales personnel housed in over 500 sales and support offices worldwide.

HP offers a strong standards-based product line. It is a leading vendor in the areas of backbone messaging, standards-based technology, and network management. Its core offering consists of the HP OpenMail system, an SMTP gateway, a 1988 X.400 MTA, and an X.500 Directory. Based on UNIX, the HP software is sold on HP hardware platforms and sometimes ported or licensed to other platforms. Its 1988 X.400 implementation was released in late 1991 and the X.500 implementation has been in general availability since the beginning of 1992, making both products among the most long-lived of their kind in the industry.

HP rounds out its messaging product line with a series of third party offerings. The company currently offers LAN gateways based on an implementation of the Worldtalk 400 product family and midrange/host gateways from the Boston

Software Works product family. This strategy brings with it useful diversity but also the risk of structural weaknesses and lack of strategic control in the HP product line, particularly in the area of directory integration.

In mid-1993, HP began supporting native MS Mail and cc:Mail clients in OpenMail as part of a new OpenMail product strategy dubbed *clients of choice*. OpenMail acts as a back-end implementation, replacing the Microsoft and cc:Mail Post Offices. While this approach offers improved management and reduced support costs, the user must pay OpenMail as well as cc:Mail/Microsoft Mail client licenses. OpenMail and clients is expected to be particularly attractive to large users just beginning to migrate to the LAN e-mail environment and who have no current investment in a Lotus or Microsoft server infrastructure.

HP's greatest strength in the backbone messaging business lies in its appeal to user communities where advanced standards capabilities are highly prized or where cost advantages accrue from an installed base of HP hardware. HP's greatest weakness historically has been in the lack of integration among its product components. This manifests itself in several ways: HP OpenMail, HP X.500, Worldtalk, and Boston Software Works directories all require integration to operate as a seamless enterprise directory; also HP Openview is a state-of-the-art network; also management platform, but its capabilities are not as yet fully leveraged for use with HP's messaging and directory products.

While the clients of choice strategy again puts HP at the leading edge of e-mail integration technology (as it moves from the gateway to the backbone model), the short term success of this strategy is not guaranteed given that both Microsoft and cc:Mail are enhancing the price/performance, standards support, and manageability of their respective back ends. The future will tell whether OpenMail can seize market share by providing sufficient added value within its window of opportunity before the next generation Microsoft and cc:Mail back ends are up to full speed.

Soft*Switch

A privately held Wayne, Pennsylvania-based company, Soft*Switch began by selling document conversion software and has been a pioneer in electronic mail networking for over ten years. Founded in 1980, Soft*Switch introduced the first bridge to PROFS in 1983, the first bridge to DISOSS in 1985, the first non-IBM implementation of SNADS in 1986, and the first X.400 gateway with connectivity to multiple services in 1989. The firm's markets are comprised of large corporations and institutions that are setting up enterprise-wide messaging systems. Soft*Switch also licensed its products to various public messaging service providers, including Infonet, MCI, AT&T, and Sprint.

In 1990, Soft*Switch expanded its reach by acquiring Systems and Telecoms, PLC, a leading supplier of advanced fax and telex gateways in the United Kingdom. Soft*Switch also established a development facility in Reading, England, and sales and operations in Europe to support its international distributors.

Soft*Switch's strategy is to design, develop, market, and service electronic mail backbone components, including the world's largest collection of gateways with

X.400, SMTP, directory synchronization, and mail management and monitoring capabilities. With regard to standards, Soft*Switch is market driven, sometimes acting as a leader, sometimes as a follower. The company tends to make the investment in implementing standards, such as X.400 and X.500, when the market requirements and signals from its own customers clearly require such an investment.

Soft*Switch's Central product line has been the company's main offering since its introduction in 1985, and is one of the longest-lived e-mail integration server products on the market. The connectivity, management, directory services features of Central as well as its support for SMTP, 1984 X.400, and the world's collection of gateways enabled the product to maintain a leadership position in the Fortune 1000 market.

Central's initial strength lay in its ability to operate in an IBM Host (MVS or VM) environment native to most of the IBM-based Mail systems. However, with the emerging importance of LAN e-mail and UNIX environments, customers began demanding e-mail integration functionality on UNIX processors. Soft*Switch's strength was becoming a weakness.

In 1992, Soft*Switch branched out into scalable UNIX-based message switches. The company's flagship product entering the mid-1990s is the EMX, or Enterprise Mail Exchange. Soft*Switch now markets the EMX as a family of scalable turnkey hardware/software backbone messaging switches. The EMX operates as a 1988 X.400 messaging backbone MTA and includes gateways able to interoperate with a variety of e-mail systems using their existing protocols. As of late 1993, Soft*Switch planned to roll out additional functionality, such as X.500 support, MIME support, and enhanced management capabilities in the 1994 and 1995 timeframe.

Soft*Switch successfully positioned itself as the leading provider of electronic mail integration products to high-end (Fortune 500 and other similar-sized organizations) customers. It leads the industry in market share and in e-mail integration capabilities. However, high-end competitors, such as DEC and HP, are surpassing Soft*Switch in their implementation of international standards. At the same time, increasing pressure is being mounted from the low end as those vendors, such as the Worldtalk Corporation, Boston Software Works, ISOCOR, Lotus, Microsoft, and Novell, expand their e-mail integration capabilities and four synergistic alliances with other vendors. Over the next several years, Soft*Switch will need to maintain its e-mail integration edge and to tap new markets—markets such as store-and-forward EDI and direct back-end server support (based on VIM or MAPI) for popular e-mail front ends or mail-enabled applications—in order to retain its leadership position.

3.6 THE X.400 MARKET

The X.400 market comprises X.400 software for local e-mail and EDI messaging systems, mail system gateways, and e-mail integration servers. The success of computerized messaging generated a demand for X.400 interoperability, but the growth trend through 1991 was slow, leading many to give up on the standard. "OSI is dead!" trumpeted certain pundits and, with regard to the ill-starred OSI lower layers and Virtual Terminal efforts, they were correct. However, it is reasonable to separate X.400 from the less successful components of the OSI suite and to assert that, while X.400 may not have conquered the messaging world as the industry once assumed it would, the standard remains very much alive.

X.400's initial growth rate in the private e-mail environment from 1984 through 1991 was undeniably slow. Some of the reasons behind its initial slow growth rate include the following:

- Until 1990, products based on the 1984 standard were few, expensive, and short on quality or functional integration with other applications in their vendor's product line.

- Proprietary products with gateways to SNADS, MHS, or SMTP provided alternatives to X.400 and limited its growth, at least in the short term, in small or homogenous enterprise environments where such products can provide interoperability.

- Because the 1984 standard is limited, users began waiting for 1988 products—just as production-grade 1984 products arrived.

- The 1991 recession in the U.S. and parts of Europe tended to reduce capital expenditure budgets.

It is necessary to discuss user X.400 strategies to understand the dynamics of this market. These strategies run the gamut from the pioneering approach of installing X.400 early on, to the transitional approach of specifying X.400 in a five-year plan, and, finally, to the incremental approach of installing X.400 only if and when it can be justified by a pressing interconnection need. Most small- to mid-sized user enterprises fall into the incremental category, and many larger users fall into the transitional or incremental category. Thus, the demand for X.400 is driven by very large multinational corporations and public sector enterprises that instigate X.400 pilots or specify X.400 in transition plans because they have a pressing need for any-to-any interoperability. Examples of initiatives that have driven the messaging market toward X.400 are the U.S. GOSIP, the U.K. GOSIP, the EC Directive 87/95 requiring OSI for procurements greater than 100,000 European Currency Units (ECU), the U.S. Aerospace Industries Association (AIA) interconnection project, and the European Central Banks interconnection program.

X.400 has spread slowly in the U.S. because of the huge installed base of IBM/SNA equipment on the one hand and the rapidly growing Internet Mail and proprietary LAN e-mail markets on the other. In the U.S., installations of new equipment and software providing open standards are usually driven by the desire to save money. Saving money is a motivation in Europe as well, but Europeans have an additional motivation to move toward standards in order to break down trade and communications barriers. Cost is a primary factor in the slow growth of X.400 and OSI; also while SMTP (at least in the past) was often included gratis with UNIX workstation operating systems, low-end X.400 LAN e-mail switches cost $5,000 to $10,000 and midrange server implementations cost even more.

X.400 technology has taken hold in the backbone, e-mail integration market, where it provides a part of the total connectivity solution. Many e-mail integration systems not only offer X.400 connectivity, but also base their internal representation of messages, addresses, and other objects on X.400 formats. However, local messaging systems have been slow to implement native X.400 support either on the client or server side. Thus, while native X.400 software implementations are available from companies such as Enterprise Solutions, ISOCOR, and OSIWARE, the bulk of X.400 products are either part of an e-mail integration solution or exist as standalone gateways to proprietary mail systems. Such products are provided as add-ons to both departmental and distributed LAN messaging systems from system vendors, such as IBM and DEC, as well as from third party software providers.

Other indicators point to increased growth for X.400. By early 1994, implementations of 1988 X.400 products and services were increasingly prevalent and exhibited substantial improvements in price and performance. This 1988 X.400 trend began with the e-mail integration server vendors and spread to key LAN e-mail vendors. Several public service providers, notably GEIS and MCI, began converting their 1984 X.400 facilities to run the 1988 standard. Increases in the number of available OEM source code implementations drove down prices and improved overall quality, thus making X.400 software technology more accessible to system integrators, third party vendors, and end users.

Moreover, the incorporation of X.400 as an embedded messaging engine directly supported on Microsoft NT servers, NetWare servers, and Lotus Communication Servers will make the standard more accessible to users. Large, standards-based enterprise procurements or industry initiatives now in the planning, design, and pilot stages will begin deployment. For example, Walmart deployed a native X.400 internal messaging network based on the Enterprise Mail product from Enterprise Solutions, Ltd., and will ship the package to 2,000 suppliers currently connected to Walmart.

Although X.400 deployment seems to be picking up speed, a competitive global messaging infrastructure standard—enhanced Internet Mail with MIME, and PEM—took the stage in 1992. Its advocates herald MIME's new multimedia capabilities and boast of the standard's simplicity. (No one claims X.400 is simple.) While MIME does not in itself provide the feature-rich backbone capabilities of X.400, some hybrid implementations will encapsulate MIME-formatted message Body Parts in X.400 messages. Also, the Internet's Simple Mail Transfer Protocol (SMTP) is slowly being extended. Internet Mail has emerged as an alternate choice to X.400 for many, and, given the Internet's rapid expansion, will limit but perhaps not derail X.400's progress.

In late 1993, an interagency U.S. Federal Government committee was given the task of deciding how to adapt GOSIP (which was originally intended to intercept low-cost, widely available, standards-based solutions from vendors) to include TCP/IP.[12] GOSIP Version 3, the long-awaited government mandate for 1988 X.400 and X.500, was put on hold pending resolution of the TCP/IP Internet issue. Should the government back away from the standard, migration away from X.400 by other large organizations could be triggered. More likely, future versions of GOSIP will modify the X.400 mandate to address pragmatic concerns, essentially giving individual government agencies more flexibility to choose different messaging protocols for different situations and a license to operate X.400 and X.500 applications over TCP/IP networks.

Because X.400 products are complex and total messaging solutions based on X.400 are still more complex, there is a multi-tiered market for X.400 technology. In this market, equipment vendors or service providers may be the customers for X.400 sourcecode OEM implementations or, a few links further down the e-mail market food chain, for third party customized X.400 products, to which they add value before reselling the resulting product to end users. System integrators and end users may obtain products from any or all of the above sources. (Naturally, in some cases the equipment vendor is also the OEM developer or the system integrator.)

For example, the French company Marben sells its X.400 source code to the Worldtalk Corporation in the U.S. Worldtalk customizes that code and adds gateway LAN modules to produce the Worldtalk 400 product. Worldtalk 400 is sold directly to end users but parts of Worldtalk are resold to Sprint International and also to HP where they are bolted together with other components to produce new products. The London-based Data Connections, LTD's X.400 product has been licensed by both Lotus for its LCS implementations and by Microsoft for EMS. Figure 3.6 diagrams the complex heritage of many X.400 products.

In the X.400 market discussed above, fortunes will not necessarily be made by implementing X.400; but fortunes may be lost by not implementing it. OVUM, a U.K. consultancy, in "OSI-The Commercial Benefits," [OVUM93] notes that in

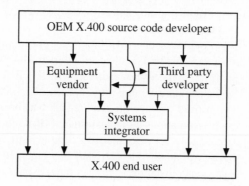

Figure 3.6 The X.400 product food chain.

---

12. Note that X.400 can operate over TCP/IP as well as OSI.

1988 30 percent of large information services contracts required X.25 support and projects that X.400 will be similarly required for 30 percent of such contracts in 1995. That is, public sector and industry procurement initiatives can have the effect of breaking the chicken and egg cycle that tends to bog down grand interoperability schemes requiring significant investment from both users and vendors. Vendors (particularly equipment vendors and systems integrators) have put X.400 in their product lines if for no other reason than to avoid being excluded from these lucrative markets.

3.7   THE INTERNET MAIL MARKET

Although Internet Mail is very widespread, the private premise-based market for Internet Mail software products (as distinct from Internet public services, which will be covered in Chapter 4) was virtually invisible until recently. Prior to the early 1990s, most Internet Mail software was generally provided free of charge by UNIX platform vendors and consequently its use was largely limited to the UNIX environment. However, with the success of Internet Mail as a public service and growing interest in its use as an internal enterprise connectivity option, new markets for the technology are beginning to emerge. Among them are the following:

- **Enhanced UNIX client offerings:** These include onGO and Zmail (discussed under host e-mail above), which offer LAN e-mail–like multimedia features and support the MIME format.

- **LAN client offerings:** A rapidly growing segment of the market comprises DOS or Windows-based Internet access software packages offering Internet Mail and a variety of other Internet information services. An example is NetManage's Chameleon product. NetManage claims to have sold the product to thousands of residential, mid-sized enterprise, and larger enterprise users. Frontier Technologies and FTP Software also compete in this market.

- **SMTP Gateways:** Most local messaging systems, third party gateway providers, and e-mail integration vendors offer an SMTP connectivity component. By late 1994 or 1995, many of these gateways will support MIME, improving Internet Mail viability as a backbone protocol.

PC-based Internet Mail clients are very attractive both to small organizations accessing the Internet via routers, and especially to residential users. The major blocking factor in the organizational sector of the private Internet Mail market is the entrenched position of the LAN e-mail vendors, whose high-powered offerings are increasingly integrated with desktop applications and tailored for enterprise-grade manageability. Internet Mail LAN client vendors will be hard pressed to compete against the likes of Lotus, Microsoft, and Novell. The true windfall may lie in software sales to the residential or consumer messaging market. Vendors such as Qualcomm (with its Eudora product) are offering user-friendly PC-based clients on shareware terms and pricing. Eudora users can access inexpensive Internet service providers via the POP 3 protocol (which is becoming widely supported) over a Serial Line IP (SLIP) telephone connection. However, as of early 1994, installing and configuring a SLIP-capable Internet access package was still no easy feat for the average home user. More coverage will be provided later on Internet Mail from the public messaging market perspective.

3.8   DIRECTORIES AND THE X.500 MARKET

At first glance, the directory is just one more component in an e-mail architecture. However, because of their complexity and their applicability to other applications besides e-mail, we consider directory products separately. Moreover, directories are one of the hottest issues in the minds of messaging system users and planners today. More and more users are becoming aware that messaging is a strategic resource and are beginning to think about interconnecting their existing e-mail systems and integrating e-mail with other applications. Such interconnection and integration, however, cannot be accomplished in a fully satisfactory fashion without enterprise directories based on a multivendor architecture.

One company's experience serves as an illustration of the importance of directories to interconnection and integration. In implementing a proprietary enterprise directory that spanned a handful of e-mail systems, the company in question noted that the number of interdepartmental e-mail messages crossing from one e-mail system to another shot up from 10 percent of total traffic to 30 percent. This startling statistic suggests that if e-mail end users can look up one another's addresses and thus have within their grasp the ability to correspond easily and rapidly, they will do so with an attendant increase in communication across the enterprise.

Some, but not all, of the benefit of enterprise directories can be achieved through directory synchronization technology. Directory synchronization involves automatically copying directory information between disparate mail systems. While synchronization does not solve the interenterprise directory problem and suffers from scalability and other limitations, a strong demand for the technology has sprung from the ranks of users. Most major e-mail integration products provide directory synchronization support, and there have even been instances of vendors providing standalone directory synchronization products. The X.400 API Association is deliberating directory synchronization standards, and directory synchronization is provided with most e-mail integration solutions, many gateways, and many local messaging systems.

The limitations of directory synchronization underscore the importance of the ITU/ISO X.500 directory standard. In brief, X.500 offers the promise of scalable, multivendor, public/private directories. A number of X.500 products have been released and others are expected shortly. Software vendors are currently motivated to develop directories in order to enhance current messaging or other products, to be positioned strategically for system integration contracts with X.500, or to develop standalone products.

Many X.500 vendors are providing the first wave of source code X.500 directory and departmental system X.500 products. Source code OEM vendors include the ISODE Consortium, Marben, and Retix. These OEM implementations served as the basis for numerous other products. NCR, CDSI, the ISODE Consortium, Wollongong, and Nexor all use as their source code base an X.500 product called QUIPU that was developed on a freely available basis for the research community. However, many of the existing X.500 implementations remain largely experimental products that are not highly integrated with third party applications or even with applications developed by the same vendor.

E-mail integration vendors such as Digital, HP, and Northern Telecom/ICL are leading a second wave of X.500 implementation. These vendors need to demonstrate both long-term and interim directory solutions, with X.500 filling the long-term role. Retix and ISOCOR, who are promoting the non-X.500 Directory Exchange Protocol as an interim multivendor directory synchronization solution, also offer X.500.

What has been disappointing about X.500's progress in products to date has been its lack of implementation in local messaging systems such as cc:Mail and Microsoft Mail. Recently, however, a number of network operating system vendors (such as Novell, Banyan, Microsoft, and the Open Software Foundation[13]) have begun building "X.500-like" directories. These directory products do not support the standard protocol but do support its fundamental information building blocks, such as hierarchical naming and object typing. We envision a blueprint for transition to X.500 as a mixed environment featuring directory synchronization, interworking between X.500 and X.500-like implementations, and the introduction of third party products that offer X.500 as an add on to popular e-mail systems. Third party X.500 client support would be enabled by the modularization of e-mail components (where a local messaging vendor's directory could be replaced by a third party product supporting the appropriate API) and is yet another manifestation of the value-added cascade effect in the overall market.

X.500 directory remains an innovator's market. The prize that most early adopters of X.500 envisage is an integrated enterprise directory serving multiple applications—not only e-mail but also network management, document indexing, secure applications, and others. A conceptual view of this prize—integrated enterprise directories—is illustrated in Fig. 3.7.

While some large enterprise users are interested in leveraging the benefits of integrated multipurpose directories, most are taking a cautious approach at present. Messaging will obviously be the first major directory application; general-purpose corporate directories will come later. There will be a shortage of X.500 pioneers among companies because the 1988 X.500 standard is incomplete, the 1993 standard is brand new, and the slow penetration of X.400 makes the business case for X.500 less pressing. Further, users perceive 1988 X.500 as coming with significant security risks, performance problems, and potential privacy issues. Widespread implementation of X.500 in private messaging networks may eventually be driven by the desire to interconnect with public directories. (Some encouraging signs for emerging public directories will be discussed in Chapter 4.)

---

13. OSF has both an X.500-like "local" directory and supports X.500 (via the Siemens/Nixdorf implementation) as its "global" directory.

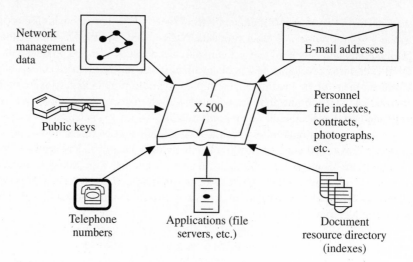

Figure 3.7   Integrated, multipurpose enterprise directories.

3.9 SUMMARY

The private messaging market, consisting of three major communities, is growing rapidly. While the enterprise backbone community is heavily invested in host-based, proprietary e-mail offerings, many users in this community are downsizing to LAN e-mail systems and interconnecting their heterogeneous internal messaging networks with a mix of e-mail integration server and X.400-based tools. This community also consists of e-mail service providers who offer and are interconnected by X.400 service. The Internet community is expanding from its origins as an R&D enclave to commercial ventures and LAN e-mail, offering interconnection services via enhanced SMTP and MIME. Interestingly, the LAN e-mail community is leading the charge in e-mail growth and innovation. The dominant vendors in this environment are Lotus, Microsoft, Novell, and WordPerfect, and their efforts to compete with one another shape much of the LAN e-mail market dynamics.

The most pronounced trends in this private messaging market center on the stratification or modularization of products, where various vendors supply different specialty elements and users can mix and match these elements to construct an integrated messaging infrastructure that meets their needs. Since no vendor can compete in all the submarkets and provide all the architectures, this stratification approach has created a value-added cascade where vendors build on top of one another's functionality. To this end, vendors are teaming with each other as well as forming strategic partnerships with users in order to derive maximum leverage for the submarkets in which they provide value.

Also as LAN e-mail becomes increasingly perceived as strategic to the enterprise, users have spurred LAN e-mail vendors to build support for X.400, SMTP, and API standards. Meanwhile, the UNIX/Internet Mail wing of what is otherwise a declining host e-mail market continues to thrive, while the distinction between DOS LANs, UNIX LANs, LAN e-mail, and Internet Mail slowly blurs.

As the LAN e-mail vendors jockey for position and as X.400 and SMTP/MIME contend for protocol dominance, e-mail integration vendors will enjoy a field day, rushing ever more sophisticated products to market. Also, as the rate of e-mail deployment accelerates, vendors and providers will commit more research dollars and products will exhibit dramatic improvements in their ability to interconnect and interoperate with competitor products. Therefore users can look forward to steadily improving interoperability and portability (although they may never attain the dream of a single protocol or API) and to the dramatically more interesting offerings that are just beginning to emerge in such areas as X.500 directories, smart messaging, and workflow.

KEY POINTS

- The overall e-mail market is divided between a private messaging marketplace and a public messaging marketplace.

- Companies and large organizations have determined that e-mail is mission critical and have set about to deploy and leverage it in a number of ways.

- The private messaging market is booming and fiercely competitive. Mailboxes are growing at a rate that has been estimated as high as 33 percent per year.

- The LAN e-mail environment is the focal point for innovative office automation. The LAN e-mail market is consolidating as major LAN e-mail products, such as cc:Mail, Microsoft Mail, and Novell Message Handling Systems (MHS) dominate. Workflow through e-mail is also emerging as a hot product area running on LANs. Blocking factors to the spread of LAN e-mail are the difficulty of administering large LAN e-mail networks and the incompatibilities between systems.

- E-mail integration servers of increasing flexibility are proliferating to interconnect disparate e-mail products and provide directory synchronization. Key vendors are Soft*Switch, DEC, and HP. In theory, e-mail integration servers could be rendered obsolete by the adoption of standards, but this day will be a long time coming, if it ever arrives.

- The market for X.400 and X.500 standards-based products is emerging and will continue to prosper if large users, such as the Fortune 500 companies, the U.S. government, and large European institutions stay the course.

- Internet Mail solutions are also increasingly penetrating private messaging environments. Residential users with Internet access can now buy e-mail packages on shareware terms and pricing.

C H A P T E R 4

The Public Messaging Marketplace

Public messaging networks today serve millions of users in the U.S. alone and provide fee-based switching services for thousands of organizations who also have their own premise-based electronic mail systems. The value-added networks of service providers, acting as third party clearing houses, are increasingly the preferred method of attaining EDI connectivity among thousands of companies moving in the direction of the paperless office. In short, public services occupy a key role in the world of e-mail and the broader electronic messaging marketplace.

4.1　WHAT IS A PUBLIC MESSAGING SERVICE?

The public messaging marketplace is the market for public messaging services, such as those offered by the traditional commercial messaging services (e.g., ATTMail and Sprint Mail), those offered by Internet Mail service providers, and those offered by EDI Value Added Network providers. In Chapter 3, we distinguished between public and private messaging services by providing a classic definition and example of each. It is important to note during this introductory discussion, however, that there exist many hybrid cases where the classic public-private models become somewhat muddied. In addition, we also note that public messaging services often function as a part of more generalized information service offerings.

4.1.1　Hybrid Public Messaging Services

At this point, we must leave the comfortable cocoon of the classic public/private e-mail model long enough to point out that the real-world messaging marketplace contains many more complex hybrid scenarios. Consider the following:

- A user with private mailboxes on a LAN e-mail system and a public X.400 message relay service to communicate with external correspondents.
- A user with an inhouse mail system employing an Internet access service to reach external correspondents.
- A user organization owning its own local messaging system but paying a service provider for facilities management of that service.
- A user employing both public and private mailboxes, owning a mix of self-managed and facilities managed components.

As e-mail technology becomes more complex, as the division of labor between vendors becomes more pronounced, and as services become more specialized, we can expect to see additional hybrid scenarios surface.

4.1.2　The Relationship of Messaging and Other Information Services

Public messaging services, both pure and hybrid, must also be seen in the context of the larger public information service marketplace. To most providers, e-mail is just one important offering among a collection of information services. For example, non–e-mail services such as file transfer comprise approximately half the traffic on the Internet. MCIMail and ATTMail (whose names reflect the fact that mail is their primary service orientation) also offer optional access to information services such as online news, stock quotes, and airline reservations. In addition, e-mail is often integrated with fax and postal mail; for example, a user creating a single message can dispatch it to fax, postal, and e-mail correspondents at the same time.

Despite its position as one of many information services, e-mail is strategic not only because of the volume of usage it generates, but also because it can serve

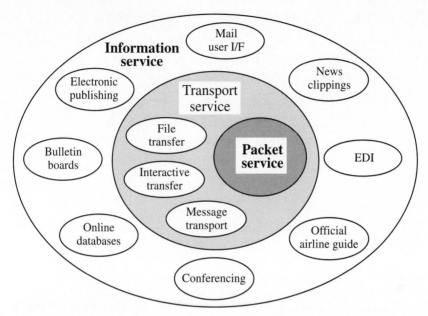

Figure 4.1   The relationship of e-mail, message transport, and information services.

as a transport mechanism for other services. For example, online news stories are often delivered by the provider to the user via e-mail. Messaging is useful as a transport vehicle in cases where the e-mail office memorandum metaphor is convenient for information retrieval functions, requested information is not required immediately by the user, or direct point-to-point connections to an information source are not possible or are impractical.

Figure 4.1 shows a conceptual relationship between mail user interfaces, potentially mail-enabled information services, transport (message, file transfer, and interactive connections), and a packet service underlying the transport.

The number of both mail-enabled and nonmail-enabled information services will increase, especially as smart messaging (or distributed programming) services such as Telescript turn consumer information services into object-oriented electronic shopping malls. In addition, some information services may make simultaneous use of multiple transport mechanisms; for example, multimedia applications may use e-mail as a means of signaling and coordinating, but employ a dedicated connection as the means to transfer bulky video information.

4.2   CATEGORIZING PUBLIC SERVICES

Now that we have defined the public messaging concept, the next step in our exploration of the market is to categorize public information services. This is no trivial task, for the 1990s is both the decade of partnerships and unparalleled

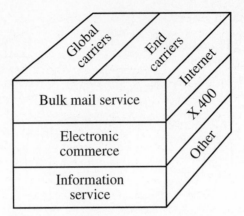

Figure 4.2 E-mail service provider
categorization cube.

connectivity. Analysts may classify service providers in terms of their national, regional, or global market potential. Users may classify an offering in terms of the services it provides or the protocols it supports. For the purposes of categorization, Fig. 4.2 defines a model that, though perhaps oversimplified, is sufficient to capture the major distinctions from both the user and the market analyst perspectives.

The e-mail service provider categorization cube model analyzes service providers along three dimensions: (1) Is the service provider a global carrier or an end (local) carrier? (2) Does the provider offer bulk mail, electronic commerce, or information services? (3) Does the provider support X.400, Internet, and/or other protocols?

Keep in mind that all offerings exist in all three dimensions and may or may not straddle multiple rows in each of the services and protocols dimensions. Thus, for example, SprintMail is a global messaging carrier which supports bulk mail, electronic commerce and general information services, Internet Mail, X.400, and other protocols. Performance Systems International, on the other hand, is a U.S.–based Internet access provider supporting Internet-based information services. Providers accomplish this "straddling" through partnerships and gateways as well as through direct offerings. More examples and nuances of support for the different public messaging services and protocols will become clearer as we proceed. First, we will focus on the carrier dimension of our e-mail service provider categorization cube.

4.2.1 Global Versus End Carriers

All users have a need for services that are adapted to their local environment providing, for example, software that displays (or speaks) the local language and displays the local character sets as well as offering access to local information services. But some users, such as multinational corporations or institutions, also require a consistent global public messaging service enabling the far-flung arms of their organization to communicate in a consistent manner. Hence, the public messaging market has a need of both global public services and locally adapted services. In other words, there will be a continuing need for both global carriers and end carriers.

The major global messaging service provider organizations operating today are Advantis IBM Mail Exchange, AT&T Easylink Services, British Telecom Messaging Services, GE Information Services, Infonet, MCI, Sprint, and Unisource Business Networks. In addition, other service providers, such as RAM Mobile Data and ARDIS are operating as global wireless service providers.

Global carriers typically support both bulk mail and electronic commerce services and both X.400 and Internet protocols. Their primary focus has historically been on the X.400 protocol. End carriers vary widely; some do not provide all the basic services and protocols. Some target horizontal markets and others provide services to vertical markets. (Horizontal markets are said to span multiple industries, whereas vertical markets address the needs of a single industry such as banking.) There are even multinational (global) carriers addressing the vertical needs of a single industry. The Society for Worldwide Interbank Financial Transaction (SWIFT), for example, coordinates interbank settlements internationally and handles messaging, electronic funds transfer (EFT), security, and management for 3,000 financial institutions worldwide. The network transfers messages in special SWIFT formats packaged in an X.400 envelope. Other vertical messaging networks include the Society for International Air Transport (SITA), which operates an aeronautical/customs network, and ARINC, the U.S. equivalent of SITA.

To the user, key differentiators among global carriers are its ability to provide global messaging access, the cost of the service, billing/control mechanisms, and functionality. Global access is provided on a world area by world area or country by country basis. It may be provided in a number of ways:

- **Global access, in-country messaging facility:** The service provider may operate messaging switches and facilities in a country. In the X.400 global network, it may be registered in multiple countries as an Administration Management Domain (ADMD). Of the global carriers, AT&T, Advantis, and GEIS had the greatest number of ADMD registrations in late 1993. The service provider may have extensive local connections in a country, as well as a local help desk and support facilities.

- **Global access, licensees:** The service provider may operate a messaging service in country indirectly through a licensee organization. In this case, it derives revenues from the sale of software, facilities, and support services to the licensee and may take a percentage of the licensee's revenues or profits. The global carrier may even hold an equity investment in the licensee organization; for example, Sprint owns a percentage in the Russia-based SOVMAIL service, and the local firm is named Sprint Networks. Licensee messaging networks are usually connected to the global carrier's major messaging networks, and services may (but need not) be tightly integrated.

- **Global access, point of presence:** Without owning or licensing messaging facilities in every country or world area, a service provider may operate or lease network points of presence (POP). Users place a local (or toll free) phone call and/or maintain dedicated circuits to the POP. Once through the POP, users can log in to their mailbox even though it actually resides on a host sited in another country.

- **Global access, interconnection arrangements:** In some cases, service providers do not own or lease messaging services or POPs in a country, but are still able to deliver the mail through interconnection arrangements with end carriers or other local services. Within Internet Mail, world areas and countries are connected through various backbone networks or interchanges, and the mail can be routed more or less seamlessly if the provider has access to one of the interchanges. In the X.400 messaging environment, ADMDs set up bilateral interconnection, routing, and settlement arrangements.

Global messaging carriers typically use all or most of these techniques in delivering service to users. Complex cost/quality of service equations result: more interconnections may be expensive to maintain, but may lower network costs and improve customer delivery times and reachability. Complex relationships result: one global carrier may lease bandwidth or POP facilities from a competitive carrier, or another carrier may facilitate the existence of a licensee organization (and derive pull-through revenues from it) and yet compete with the licensee for customers.

Regarding the remaining global carrier differentiators, functionality of public services in general will be treated throughout this chapter, and user evaluation factors will be dealt with later. Costs for different types of services will also be discussed in general terms here; typically small users obtain a standardized service package at a standardized rate structure, whereas larger users with worldwide traffic negotiate a custom contract. Billing and control mechanisms are important to larger organizations that may wish to obtain a single invoice with cost detail records itemizing costs by department or other categories.

4.2.2 Bulk Mail, Electronic Commerce, and Information Services

Users have a need for different kinds and grades of messaging service. They need an inexpensive, pervasive bulk mail capability and a highly reliable, secure electronic commerce (or business class) mail capability. To use a postal analogy, they need both third class mail and special delivery services (first class, overnight, business courier). In addition, users often employ information services that make use of e-mail for transport purposes. The message transport used for the information services may be either bulk mail or business class depending on the type and criticality of the service.

Table 4.1 compares and contrasts classic bulk mail and business class electronic commerce services.

Readers will note that this table oversimplifies some of the issues. It is only intended as a device to clarify certain pervasive service/protocol issues arising in this chapter. We must qualify this table in several ways. First, some of the at-

	Classic electronic commerce service
pidly	More expensive
	Moderate volume, growing at 20 percent or more per year
	Business transactions (commercial e-mail, EDI, EFT, EMC[1])
ation	Mostly on EDI VANs and X.400 networks
Open and pervasive	Strictly controlled
Delivery time/reliability guarantees less important	Firm delivery time/reliability guarantees required
Basic customer assistance available	Well staffed and equipped help desks expected
Not auditable	Auditable
No security guarantees	Relatively closed networks

1. EMC = Electronic medical claims

Table 4.1 Bulk mail and electronic commerce.

tributes of classic electronic commerce are more of a wish list than a reflection of actual offerings. Second, a great deal of mail traffic crosses these somewhat artificial boundaries. Some bulk mail traverses X.400 networks and EDI Value Added Networks (VANs). Electronic commerce traverses the Internet. Finally, some messaging services can or will offer both bulk mail and electronic commerce grades of service. The trend is toward service convergence and blurring of all public messaging boundaries.

Nevertheless, some real economic and cultural issues are associated with the customer's decision to use a service provider who is positioned as a bulk mail offering versus one that is positioned as an electronic commerce offering. To consider a postal analogy, in 1994 U.S. third class mail charges begin at 23¢ or less per item. Federal Express costs begin at $9.00 per item. Third class mail cannot be easily or conveniently traced, and there are no delivery guarantees. Federal Express mail can be traced and it will be delivered, or the user will get a phone call and/or the mail will be returned. Thus, some users make the business or personal decision to employ one or the other means of transport depending on their requirements.

Our belief is that public messaging services will stratify into at least two tiers, which loosely correspond to the bulk mail and electronic commerce grades of service previously discussed. Internet Mail will dominate the bulk mail tier, while electronic commerce messaging tier services will be provided by both X.400 and Internet Mail service providers, who provide security and delivery time/reliability guarantees. As was suggested by Peter Williams of Sterling Software at the April 1994 EMA conference, further stratification may introduce an additional official messaging tier, tailored to the more stringent messaging security needs existing for some national or local governments.

4.2.3   Global Messaging Network Protocols

There are now two major global messaging protocols; that is, protocols into w
one can dispatch an e-mail message (using the address of a new correspondent fo
the first time) and have a reasonable expectation of seeing that message delivered
almost anywhere in the industrialized world. These two networks consist of the
international X.400 network and the Internet. There are many other messaging
protocols, but only X.400 and Internet Mail have a global addressing scheme and
global reach. Other protocols can thus be said to mostly exist on the periphery of
the global messaging networks.

The X.400 global network is a collection of networks offered by X.400 service providers, such as PTTs and large public network operators. These same operators also often operate EDI VANs (nonmessaging services) and will gradually
integrate their X.400 and VAN services. The relatively closed and controlled
X.400 and EDI VAN networks are the preferred vehicle for the electronic commerce of many large organizations. Today, X.400 carries both bulk mail and electronic commerce. It can almost universally handle binary file transfer, supply
delivery or non-delivery reports when requested, and support large message sizes.
It is also growing rapidly, though not nearly as rapidly as Internet Mail.

The Internet is not a single network, organization, service, or protocol. It is
rather a vast collection of service providers utilizing a specific set of Internet protocols. Internet Mail is any mail carried over the Internet, and is usually of the
SMTP/RFC 822 text-only variety. When used in the Internet environment, this
type of mail essentially provides a bulk mail service. It is experiencing very rapid
growth worldwide today. SMTP-based Internet Mail is being enhanced on an ongoing basis to provide binary file transfer (MIME), security (PEM), larger message sizes, and other capabilities.

The following subsections compare and contrast the connectivity, architecture, addressing, functionality, and applicability of the two global networks.

Connectivity

Table 4.2 lists countries known in 1993 (from EEMA93B, EEMA93G, and
EMMS93F) to have either an Internet or an X.400 link (or both).

Architecture

X.400 and Internet mail networks are based on fundamentally different architectures. These differences must be understood because they form the basic differences
in resultant connectivity, administration, security, and pricing. Architecturally, the
X.400 global network provides a message relay service based on incremental routing at the message level by service providers. This type of service increases the
control, traceability, and auditability of mail, but raises costs. The Internet provides an IP packet relay service usually based on dynamic point to point message
routing (using the Domain Name Service or DNS) through the globally connected
IP network. This mechanism has proven tremendously scalable. Reliability varies

Country	Internet link	ADMD providers and service names
Antarctica	Yes	None
Argentina	Yes	Total-net–TOTALNET
Australia	Yes	Australia Telecom–TELMEMO OTC–OTC IBM International–IBMX400
Austria	Yes	Plus Communications–GmbH Radio Austria–ADA IBM International–IBMX400
Belarus	No	RTTE–BELPAK
Belgium	Yes	Regie van Telegraffe en Telephon–DCS 400 IBM International–IBMX400
Brazil	Yes	Embratel Brazil–EMBRATEL
Bulgaria	No	IICAS Bulgarien–BULMAIL
Canada	Yes	Telecom Canada–STENTOR CNM <Envoy> Teleglobe Canada–TELEGLOBE Canada Post–OMNIPOST and CPCMHS
Chile	Yes	VTR Telecommunicaciones–TOMMAIL
China	No	Telecoms General Directorate–CHINAMAILBJ (Beijing) or CHINAMAILSH (Shanghai)
Colombia	No	IBM International–IBMX400
Costa Rica	Yes	Radiographica Costaricense S.A.–RACSAMAIL
Croatia	Yes	Hrvatrska Posta i Telekom–CRO400
Cyprus	Yes	None
Czech Republic	Yes	None
Denmark	Yes	GEIS–MARK400 Post Og Telecoms Data–TELDK/DK400 SynergiData a/s–UMI-DK GEIS–MARK400 IBM International–IBMX400
Dominican	No	IBM International–IBMX400 Republic
Ecuador	Yes	IBM International–IBMX400
Estonia	Yes	None
Finland	Yes	Finnish University–FUMAIL Telecom Finland–MAILNET The Helsinki Telephone Company–ELISA
France	Yes	France Telecom (Transpac)–ATLAS GEIS–MARK400
Germany	Yes	Deutsche Bundespost–DBP <TeleboX400> GEIS–MARK400
Greece	Yes	None
Greenland	Yes	None
Hong Kong	Yes	AT&T–ATTMAIL Hutchison Inet–INET.HK IBM International–IBMX400

Table 4.2 International Internet and X.400 connectivity.

continued

Country	Internet link	ADMD providers and service names
Hungary	Yes	IBM International–IBMX400
Iceland	Yes	PTT Iceland–ISHOLF
India	Yes	Videsh Sanchar Nigam–VSNB

Ireland	Yes	Eiretrade LTD–EIRMAIL400
		    Inet Ltd–INET400
		    Postgem United–POSTGEM 400
		    IBM International–IBMX400

Israel	Yes	Israel Telecom–BEZEC

Italy	Yes	Italcable–OMEGA 400
		    Teleo–MASTER 400
		    Italian Postal Administration–PT POSTEL
		    IBM International–IBMX400

Japan	Yes	Ace Tele-mail International–ATI
		    AT&T–ATTMAIL
		    Kokusai Denshin Denwa–KDD
		    NTT–NTTPC
		    IBM International–IBMX400

Kuwait	Yes	None
Latvia	Yes	None
Luxembourg	Yes	Regie van Telegraffe en Telephon–DCS 400
Malaysia	Yes	Syarkiat Telekom Malaysia–STM.TELE-MAIL
Mexico	Yes	Telecom Mexico–TELEMENSAJE IBM International–IBMX400
Monaco		France Telecom (Transpac)–ATLAS

The Netherlands	Yes	GEIS–MARK400
		    IBM International–IBMX400
		    PTT Telecom/Unisource–400 NET

New Zealand	Yes	Netway Communications Ltd–STARNET
		    Synet Communications–SYNET
		    IBM International–IBMX400

Norway	Yes	Telepost–TELEMAX
		    Academic Research Network–UNINETT
		    IBM International–IBMX400

Poland	Yes	PTT Poska–POLECOM
Portugal	Yes	Sevatel–GOLDMAIL Marconi-SVA LDA–MARCONI-SVA
Puerto Rico	Yes	None
Russia	No	PTT Teleport–PTTNET Sovmail–SOVMAIL
Sierra Leone	No	IBM International–IBMX400
Singapore	Yes	Singapore Telecom–SGMHS
Slovakia	Yes	None
Slovenia	Yes	SP PTT Slovenia–MAIL
South Africa	Yes	Gentel/SAPT–TELKOM400
South Korea	Yes	Dacom Corp–DACOMMHS Korean Telecom–KT
Spain	Yes	Telefonica Servicos Avanzados Informacion– MENSATEX

Table 4.2 *continued*

Country	Internet link	ADMD providers and service names

Sweden	Yes	GEIS–MARK400
		    Scandinavian Info Link–SIL 400
		    TeleDelta–TEDE400
		    Unisource Business Networks–400NET

Switzerland	Yes	GEIS–MARK400
		    Swiss PTT–ARCOM
		    IBM International–IBMX400

Taiwan (ROC)	Yes	Taiwan Telecom–TTNMAIL and PIPMAIL
Thailand	Yes	Communications Authority of Thailand–CAT
Tunisia	Yes	None
Turkey	Yes	IBM International–IBMX400
United Arab Emirates	No	ETISALAT–EMNET

United Kingdom	Yes	AT&T–ATTMAIL
		    British Telecom Telecom–Gold
		    GEIS–MARK 400
		    Infonet–INFONET
		    Sprint International–SPRINTMAIL

USA	Yes	AT&T–ATTMAIL
		    Bell South–BELLSO. MESSAGE CENTRAL
		    British Telecom–BT TYMNET/DIALCOM
		    Compuserve–COMPUSERVE
		    GE Information Services–MARK400
		    IBM International–IBMX400
		    Infonet–INFONET NOTICE400
		    MCI–MCIMAIL
		    Motorola–EMBARC
		    Pacific Bell–PACBELL
		    Sprint–SPRINTMAIL <TELE-MAIL>

Venezuela	Yes	IBM International–IBMX400
Yugoslavia[1]	No	IBM International–IBMX400

1. While Yugoslavia is no longer a single nation state, the PTT managed from Belgrade is still listed by the EEMA *Briefing* as offering ADMD service, and we therefore feel obliged to include YUMAIL in our ADMD list.

Table 4.2 *continued*

widely in both networks. One could assert that, architecturally, message relay is more reliable than packet relay when the source and destination nodes are unavailable more than 50 percent of the time; otherwise packet relay service is equally or more reliable.[1]

Addressing

The Internet address is a simple text string of the form *someone@somewhere;* for example, *daniel_blum@rapport.com.* The X.400 address is a complex coded

---

1. This metric was suggested by Harald Alvestrand of Norwegian Telecom.

structure with many variations; for example, *G=Daniel ; S=Blum ; P=Rapport ; A=MCI ; C=US.*[2] The simpler Internet address is made possible by the DNS; having no DNS, X.400 instead embeds routing information (e.g., send this message to Rapport by way of MCI in the US) in the address. The Internet address is undoubtedly the more user friendly of the two, and this fact underlies the Internet's considerable success in providing bulk e-mail service to the general public.

Functionality

As codified in the standard, X.400 has much more functionality than the original Internet Mail RFC 822 (message content) and RFC 821 (SMTP). The 1988 version of X.400 includes delivery reports, receipt notifications, security, use of X.500 directory, distribution lists, conversions, labeled binary attachments, and much more. The original Internet Mail had only text messages, the Internet Mail address, and the DNS. The higher functionality level of X.400 has led many large organizations to back X.400 as their means of electronic commerce and often as their means of interconnecting local messaging systems. However, because of the complexity of X.400, some of its advanced features have been slow to reach the marketplace. Meanwhile, the IETF has been busy building additional functionality into enhanced SMTP and MIME.

Applicability

Both Internet Mail and X.400 carry both bulk mail and electronic commerce. The Internet carries the greatest volume of bulk mail today. However, while electronic commerce does traverse the Internet, some large organizations perceive security risks in sending electronic commerce traffic over this wide open network. In 1993, the U.S.-based Gartner Group cautioned corporations not to use the Internet for electronic commerce, but also projected a 60 percent probability that the Internet would obviate the need for educational and governmental institutions to use VANs for electronic commerce by 1997 [WHEA93D].

Global networks potentially assume great importance in the world of electronic commerce, particularly electronic commerce between governments, corporations, and even individuals.[3] Ultimately, electronic commerce between the government and corporations must be as legally valid as (or more so than) paper commerce. This requires statutory recognition of an entity that can provide both a certification infrastructure to help authenticate messages and messaging users and electronic postmarking capability to authenticate the time of message origination

---

2. In the example, "G" stands for given name, "S" for surname, "P" for private management domain, "A" for administration management domain, and "C" for country.

3. One of the most dramatic examples of electronic commerce is the U.S. Internal Revenue Service (IRS) tax modernization plan, which currently anticipates that individuals and corporations will file electronic tax returns via public service providers in the late 1990s. The level of traffic generated—especially around the time of the April 15 tax filing deadline—could be monumental. The security requirements for this messaging application are significant.

or receipt. In most countries, public sector organizations (such as the U.S. Post Office or PTTs in other parts of the world) would be the first candidates to assume a notary role, parts of which might be delegated to certified ADMDs. However, if standard certification and encryption mechanisms were developed and legitimized to certify information packages sent between two end users (regardless of the intervening network), much of the security gap between the wide open Internet environment and the relatively controlled X.400 environment could be narrowed.

The Internet and X.400 global networks are likely to coexist uneasily for an indefinite period of time. They will coexist because they must—users will tolerate nothing less—and because continually improving gateways will become increasingly adept at mapping messages between the two environments. The coexistence will be uneasy because the different architectures create an inherent *paradigm clash*[4] and because of a certain level of (deplorable) hostility between X.400 and Internet advocates, especially in the United States. Users can only hope that the distinction between X.400 and Internet Mail networks will slowly blur and, as far as commercial service is concerned, be eliminated as a user-visible issue within five years or less.

4.3   THE X.400 ADMINISTRATION MANAGEMENT DOMAIN (ADMD) PROVIDERS

The X.400 global network grew up around 1984 X.400-compliant services offered by the Postal Telephone and Telegraph (PTT) organizations. Later, as the regulatory ice of the worldwide PTT communications monopolies began to thaw in the late 1980s and early 1990s, many other companies entered the X.400 public service market. These included both indigenous national network operators (such as the U.S. domestic telephone companies) and the global carriers (such as British Telecom, AT&T, MCI, Sprint, and IBM). The X.400 global messaging network is primarily used by business subscribers for commercial messaging purposes.

According to the European EMA's August 1993 count, the X.400 global network encompasses 54 countries. The interconnect situation between those countries is spotty. The EEMA publishes a table of European providers that shows more and more interconnects with each revision. (We did not include this information because it changes too rapidly.)

In general, the X.400 global network is still based on the 1984 version of the protocol but is migrating to the 1988 version with the first 1988 implementations coming online in 1994 from carriers such as MCI, GEIS, Advantis, and AT&T. Both protocols support binary data and delivery and receipt notifications. The 1988 X.400 protocol will also support an X.435 content type for EDI.

We noted above that, architecturally, X.400 provides a message relay service based on incremental routing by service providers as shown in Fig. 4.3. In a message

---

4. This use of the term was suggested by Einar Stefferud of Network Management Associates, Inc.

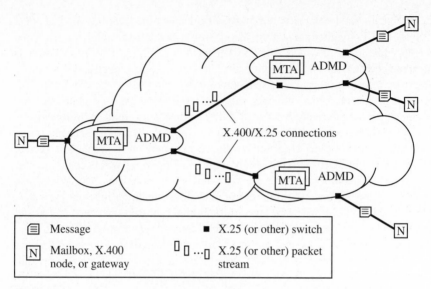

Figure 4.3   X.400 global network architecture.

relay or store-and-forward type of service, public mailboxes and private messaging nodes or gateways submit messages to an ADMD by X.400 or by another supported protocol. Once submitted, messages are safely stored, logged, routed based on static routing tables, and delivered to a local mailbox or relayed as messages to another private messaging domain or to another ADMD.[5] In the absence of a dynamic routing service that automatically provides them with the current network address of a correspondent's MTA, users have an incentive to use the ADMDs for X.400 because it becomes expensive for them to maintain the routing information for many trading partners themselves. The pricing of ADMD services in turn reflects the need to maintain message switching components and routing databases, help desks, and settlement/reconciliation systems for billing.

The major differentiators between individual public service providers offering X.400 lie in their basic messaging functionality, types of information services, alternate delivery methods (enhanced fax, postal), pricing, interconnectivity to other networks such as the Internet, and their means of access to services. Many of these differentiators are not specific to X.400 service providers, but apply to all service providers. Support for 1988 X.400, X.435, and X.500 directories will emerge as increasingly important differentiators once the X.400 global network begins its long-awaited transition to 1988 X.400 in 1994. Even X.400's static routing architecture may eventually change. Research is going on regarding the possi-

---

5. Only those messages that travel between ADMDs or between X.400-capable PRMDs actually travel via X.400, amounting to a small percentage of aggregate traffic.

bility of adding dynamic X.400 routing capabilities by storing information in the X.500 directory [ALVE93B].

Pricing in the ADMD services is generally handled on a usage-sensitive basis. There are per-message-sent or per-character-sent charges, and there may be connect time charges. User interfaces range from the simple character-oriented interfaces to full graphical interfaces, increasingly employing popular e-mail front ends, such as Microsoft Mail, which offer special driver options to access the service provider.

Large organizations access ADMDs via full X.400 over X.25 lines. For the small organization or individual, no generally viable standard access method for X.400 exists today, though the availability of X.400's access protocols over dial-up lines using a 1993 standard called the Asynchronous Protocol Specification (APS) could change that situation. In the meantime, ADMDs offer multiprotocol access support, enabling small organizations to access their services via protocols like cc:Mail and NetWare MHS.

The sections below will discuss X.400 commercial messaging services from the perspective of the North American, Western European, and Pacific Rim markets. We do not specifically cover other world areas, which now comprise only one percent of the world's mailbox population. However, it is anticipated that e-mail growth in developing world areas—including Eastern Europe—will be substantial in the future.

4.3.1   North American Public Messaging Market— ADMD Providers

The overall U.S. public messaging market is dominated by the "Big Six" providers (Advantis, AT&T Easylink, BT North America, GE Information Systems, MCI International, and U.S. Sprint), but this may change over time as more of the Regional Bell Operating Companies (RBOCs), recently released from regulatory restrictions on their ability to provide information services, enter the arena. Telecom Canada dominates the Canadian market. In general, most North American public services are operated by long-distance carriers and RBOCs, but because any company may enter the U.S. public messaging service market and become an ADMD, certain companies in the information services industry are represented as well. Figure 4.4 details mailbox demographics estimates [EMMS93H, EMMS94] for the major U.S. ADMD providers.

Note that the AT&T total is made up of AT&T Easylink and AT&T Mail users. The BT North America users are on the Tymnet–Dialcom mail system; BT's North American operation was acquired and may be merged with MCI. The mailboxes for consumer messaging services, such as America Online, CompuServe, and Prodigy, are shown separately later. (The mailboxes in Fig. 4.4 represent business users fairly heavily.)

It is noteworthy that the number of public messaging mailboxes for the global carriers is decreasing. However, mailbox numbers are only one reflection of a service provider's success; there is also message volume and messaging revenues.

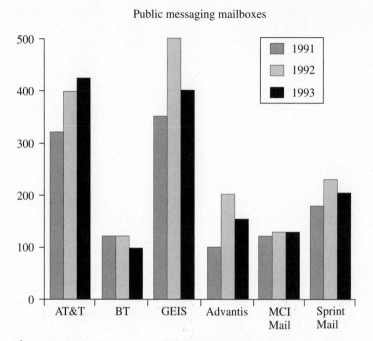

Figure 4.4 Public service mailbox demographics (in thousands of users).

The latter figures can increase even while mailbox counts are declining, since ADMDs also relay interenterprise traffic. Also, many business customers have a single mailbox that is heavily used as a gateway or by a mail-enabled application. In terms of message volume and revenues, AT&T led the pack in 1993 with 13.3 million messages per month and annual revenues of 140 million dollars (GEIS was next with 7.5 million messages per month and 100 million dollars annual revenues). AT&T cited healthy revenue and message volume growth in 1993.

ADMD Interconnection

X.400 ADMD interconnection is a key issue in the diverse public messaging environment. The Aerospace Industry Association's (AIA) 1989 X.400 pilot originally hastened interconnection in the U.S. The AIA member companies found that their employees had a need to communicate via electronic mail with employees of related firms using a variety of public messaging services. The initial AIA pilot provided a financial incentive for a number of major service providers to establish X.400 interconnection.

As a result, each of the Big Six providers active in North America today has a link to all of the others. Other public service providers, such as Infonet, Telecom Canada, Geonet, Bell Atlantic, Bell South, and Pacific Bell, all have links to one or more of the Big Six. AT&T and Sprint are currently approved providers on the U.S. Federal Government's FTS-2000 network, and other providers may be brought on board FTS-2000 in the future. Nationwide, X.400 traffic is on the increase; one ADMD service provider, GEIS, reported that its network was carrying 100,000 X.400 messages per month in early 1993 versus 25,000 a year before [EMN93E].

Over time, more and more subscribers of the public services will be able to exchange messages freely as the providers complete interoperability testing and, equally important, establish commercial billing and settlement arrangements among themselves.

A public service provider consortium recently established the U.S. National Message Transfer System (U.S. NMTS) Implementors Group to implement a U.S. national messaging network. The group includes Advantis, AT&T, BT North America, GEIS, Infonet, MCI, Pacific Bell, and Sprint. The objective of this group is to provide telephone-like ubiquity to X.400 messaging. It would do this by creating a message routing infrastructure where any private organization could interconnect to any ADMD and have its messages routed to any recipient. This ubiquitous routing capability will require nationwide registration of private messaging domain names. It will also require each ADMD to share with the other ADMDs the names of private domains registered exclusively with their service.

4.3.2   North American Public Messaging Market: Regional Bell Operating Companies (RBOCs)

The RBOCs, several of whom now provide X.400 service, could emerge as a major new presence in the U.S. public messaging market. Because of their anticipated ability to combine global messaging capabilities with local loop services (i.e., services based on intelligent Metropolitan Area Networks supporting the integration of fax, e-mail, voice-mail, wireless access, videoconferencing, and gateways to local bulletin boards and other information services) RBOCs may bring about profound changes in market share distribution among service providers and in the nature of the services offered.

The RBOCs are something of a dark horse in the messaging race. With their deep pockets, access to updated name, telephone number, and address listings, and control of existing and ubiquitous circulatory systems for information (the telephone network, and eventually, cable television networks), they have resources and capabilities beyond the reach of other information service providers. Because of these assets, they will be able to extend high-bandwidth multimedia messaging and information services to the small business and to the homes of individual consumers. If during the 1990s they enter the integrated messaging market with a vengeance, many analysts are concerned that the RBOCs may cause a shakeout among existing information service providers by taking advantage of their unique telephone database and line/switching resources. Others believe that increased competition will lead to better services over all and that alliances between RBOCs and existing providers will benefit the industry as a whole.

4.3.3   European Public Messaging Market

It is noteworthy that while the economies and populations of North America and western Europe are roughly equal, North America has nearly four times as many e-mail users as western Europe. As of the end of 1993, there were an estimated 31.6 million e-mail users in the U.S. [EMMS94]; the country with the next largest user population was Germany with 2.2 million. Possible reasons include the fact that most e-mail software is written by English and American vendors for English speakers. Also with regard to messaging networks, Europe has undertaken wider deployment of X.400, no doubt the result in part of tighter control of national telecommunications markets by PTTs who are strong advocates of CCITT standards. Perhaps because of such advocacy, Europe is about two years behind the U.S. in the growth of Internet services, where mailbox growth has been the most dramatic.

A recently published report by Ovum Ltd., a London-based consultancy, sheds additional light on the state of the European e-mail market [EMN93D]. Ovum reports that the highest levels of per capita e-mail usage are in the Netherlands, Sweden, Switzerland, and the UK while the lowest levels are in Germany, Italy, and Spain. While the latter two could be attributed to language or economics, Germany seems to be a unique case. In fact, German business communications demand greater formality than elsewhere such that interpersonal mail, which is best suited to short informal messaging, does not fit German business requirements. Also, the Deutsche Bundespost invested heavily in teletex (higher speed, higher quality telex) in the 1980s and thereby diverted user interest in e-mail. That situation is changing in favor of the increasing use of e-mail through the Deutsche Bundespost's ADMD, perhaps explaining why Germany's mailbox population is now estimated to be the largest in Europe.

European ADMDs are a mixture of PTT-operated public messaging networks, indigenous national public service providers, and pan-European services operated by the international service providers such as AT&T, British Telecom, GEIS, IBM, Infonet, MCI, and Sprint as well as the more aggressive PTTs such as Switzerland's ARCOM. According to a recent European Electronic Mail Association (EEMA) interconnectivity matrix, none of the pan-European services were complete as of late 1993. At that time, Germany's Deutsche Bundespost, the Swiss PTT's ARCOM, British Telecom's BT/GOLD 400, Unisource Business Network's 400NET, and MCI offered the broadest interconnectivity in Europe with nearly 30 interconnections each [EMN93D]. Unisource (a joint venture of Televerket Sweden, PTT Telecom Netherlands, and PTT Switzerland) calls itself the first truly pan-European supplier of corporate telecommunications services, and its announced goal is to become the leading service provider in Europe with global coverage.

The Unisource undertaking marks a gradual trend toward deregulation of the European telecommunications environment. To signal this trend, value-added services such as messaging were opened to competition continentwide in June 1990. On January 1, 1993, the market for data transport services including X.25 and frame relay was opened as well. However, countries without advanced public data networks can extend the deregulation deadline until 1996 and implementation of these deregulatory moves often falls short of announcements. Thus in many European countries, the PTTs still operate the only major ADMD.

Of the 22 European countries shown above in Table 4.2, nine have more than one national or regional provider (one of which is the national PTT or equivalent). In some cases, however, the companies have merely agreed to divide the market and do not really compete for e-mail market share.

Perhaps as a result of Europe's many nations and very heterogeneous environment, the continent's ADMDs are not yet as widely interconnected as those in North America. This situation is beginning to pose problems for multinational corporations and other international organizations operating throughout Europe. Thus during the early 1990s, large European users interconnecting their systems via multinational PRMD backbones pushed for better connectivity.

The goals of such users were later codified by the European Electronic Mail Association (EEMA) in a "Memorandum of Understanding for the Specification, Development, and Implementation of a Pan-European Electronic Messaging Infrastructure (MOU)" as follows:

• A single address for any user regardless of how many ADMDs are subscribed to

• The option to use a globally unique PRMD name

• The ability to connect to any ADMD in any country

• The right to route messages freely through private networks with or without entering the public domain

• A global ADMD backbone

• One stop billing, even if more than one ADMD was involved in the transmission and delivery of a message.

The EEMA has since continued to spur ADMD cooperation by sponsoring a European ADMD Operators Group (EAOG) subcommittee charged with resolving contractual issues and with establishing quality of service parameters. The EAOG will develop a European ADMD Charter casting the goals derived from the earlier MOU as requirements for accepted good practices for ADMDs. The EAOG will also develop a template for European ADMD agreements—heretofore bilateral—in order to accelerate interconnectivity. Once such a template has been devised, the EEMA will negotiate with its sister organizations in North America and Asia to have it applied worldwide.

In a corollary effort, the EEMA has undertaken to create a naming policy and simplify or codify a methodology for the complex business of X.400 naming and addressing in its community. The EEMA will organize to address such issues and harmonize the use of X.400 address components as yet another means of promoting ADMD interconnectivity.

Finally, the EEMA has recognized the need to address security and legal issues that go hand in hand with interconnectivity requirements. The chartered EEMA subcommittee will establish requirements for ADMDs in areas of substantial concern to electronic commerce including confidentiality, reliability, unauthorized use, audit capabilities, and management. It will also have to grapple with the plethora of legal issues that will inevitably surface in a multinational undertaking. This initiative is intended to drive efforts to ensure that, when interconnected, European ADMDs can provide each other trusted services.

With all these issues to address, we might conclude that the European public messaging market is in dire straits. On the contrary, European e-mail VANs earned a respectable $150 million during 1992. Currently, British Telecom holds a 13 percent market share followed by IBM with eight percent and Unisource and GEIS with seven percent each. Also, AT&T EasyLink, Saritel (Italy), Mercury (UK), France Telecom, Scandinavia InfoLink (Sweden), Sprint International, and GSI (France) earned at least $4 million from messaging services in 1992.

Ovum projects an increase in total European messaging revenues to $1.3 billion by 1997. Ovum notes that, while 88 percent of e-mail revenue comes from single terminals and PCs connected directly to public services at present, this proportion will drop to less than 50 percent by 1995 and even to 20 percent by 1997. The consultancy further projects that 20 percent of all mailboxes will have access to public services by 1995. The implications are that terminals, PCs, and workstations on private e-mail systems will generate a significantly greater portion of all e-mail traffic. In fact, Ovum projects that most revenue will come from private systems connected to public providers via gateways. Figure 4.5 shows growth projections from the Ovum forecast.

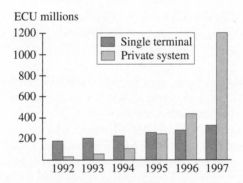

ECU: European Currency Units

Figure 4.5   European electronic mail network
service revenue forecast.

4.3.4   Pacific Rim Public Messaging Market

Public messaging is on the rise in the Pacific Rim, with X.400 services active in Australia, Hong Kong, Japan, Malaysia, Singapore, and Taiwan. EDI is beginning to spread and considerable standards activity is also going on under the auspices of the Asian Oceanic Workshop (AOW) and the Promotion Conference for OSI

(POSI), which are active in the work to define International Standard Profiles (ISP) for X.400 and X.500. However, mailbox population levels remain low, estimated at only 7.1 percent of the world's installed base for a region with 20.6 percent of the world's GNP.

Japan is the Pacific Rim's largest e-mail user, with an estimated 1.2 million users. (The fact that Japan also has 7 million fax machines to the U.S.'s 7.5 million suggests an enormous potential market for e-mail once better approaches are found to digitizing, displaying, and transferring pictorial character sets.) Important differences exist between the way e-mail is used in Japan and the way it is used in countries like the United States. In many Japanese companies, an entire department will share a public mailbox. The departmental secretary periodically prints out the correspondence for the group. Thus, the average mailbox in the United States might generate in $50 per month in revenues, but in Japan the figure would be $300 per month or more, although the number of mailboxes is fewer.

Although numerous Japanese firms and international service providers operate electronic mail or have plans to do so, the ones that have adopted an X.400 solution are Kokusai Denshin Denwa (KDD) and Ace Tele-mail International (ATI). KDD operates an X.400 mail service in Japan called Messavia that supports various features, including facsimile and telex delivery.

ATI began as a joint venture of Sprint and five Japanese firms: Intec, Sumitomo Corporation, Sumisho Computer Service Corporation, the Bank of Tokyo, and the Mitsubishi Bank. Full-scale electronic mail service began in 1986. By May 1988, ATI adopted the X.400 protocol and a facsimile delivery service. Today, ATI has interconnected its ACE Tele-mail service with the public carriers (X.400 ADMDs) from at least 22 countries. ATI also supports PRMD interconnects; one such interconnect links Japan's National Space Development Agency (NASDA) and the United States National Aeronautics and Space Administration (NASA), facilitating the exchange of technical correspondence among aerospace engineers. ATI supports both English language service for international correspondence and the Kanji and Katakana character sets for domestic Japanese correspondence.

To the east, South Korea's DACOM has developed a "Steel VAN" and a pilot air cargo customs clearance system allowing airlines, customs brokers, air freight forwarders, and warehouses to receive electronic documents like import/export declarations and manifests. Although the air cargo system will eventually migrate to utilize EDIFACT and will be generalized to cover other imports/exports, there have been numerous difficulties with large companies rolling out proprietary EDI formats and forcing their suppliers to adhere to these. DACOM also has an X.400 service.

Far to the south, Singapore has launched an Information Technology (IT2000) project whose ambitious aim is to computerize the entire nation. Not all of this bears on messaging (the project contemplates developing intelligent road systems and other futuristic applications), but of particular interest are its EDI applications. These include Tradenet which supports automated clearing of shipments through customs and Medinet which allows automated processing of medical insurance claims.

4.4   INTERNET MAIL

We noted above that Internet is not a single network, organization, service, or proto-col. Internet Mail is any mail carried over the Internet, and includes SMTP/RFC 822, Unix-to-Unix Copy Program (UUCP)/RFC 822, BITNET,[6] and even X.400. How-ever, RFC 822 is the common denominator message format, and SMTP the usual message transport. The Internet itself is a huge global internetwork loosely charac-terized as comprising all networks reachable via TCP/IP.

4.4.1   The Concept

David Crocker, the author of the original RFC 822 and currently an active IETF contributor, characterizes Internet Mail as shown in Fig. 4.6.

One can thus think of Internet Mail functionality as increasing rings of inclu-sive concentric circles, with the functionality being greatest at the inner level and least at the outer level. Hence, these rings can be characterized as follows:

- **Full Internet Mail:** At the core, native SMTP/RFC 822 and, increasingly, MIME.

- **Extended Internet Mail:** RFC 822 and MIME are supported, but a variety of relay protocols might be used; for example, UUCP, BITNET, or a LAN e-mail system with transparent Internet mail address and message content support.

- **Global Mail Connectivity:** Reachable via Internet Mail by means of low function Internet gateways, but only at the most basic level (only text bodies pass reliably).

Yet another view proposed by Crocker is to regard Internet Mail as both a technology and as a domain-based address space with connectivity. While the technology (SMTP/RFC 822/MIME) is important, the address factor ultimately makes the Internet the core of a global relaying service, sometimes using SMTP/RFC 822/MIME and sometimes not. It is the nature of Internet Mail's global ad-dress space and connectivity that represents the "keys to the kingdom."

Figure 4.6   Levels of Internet Mail.

---

6. BITNET is a large collection of cooperative systems based on IBM mainframes, which defines a batch version of SMTP (BSMTP) and uses a derivative of RFC 822.

4.4.2   The Architecture

While X.400 providers offer message relay service, most Internet Mail rides as packet streams on the Internet global network. This basic concept is illustrated in Fig. 4.7. Messages can be said to have entered the Internet (TCP/IP) via a mailbox or a gateway; they can be said to enter through an SMTP messaging node. The mail then is packetized and extruded through a router. The packets make their merry way through the global internetwork of routers and backbones until they emerge at the recipient's mailbox or gateway. This architecture enables Internet access providers to operate at a price advantage over X.400 providers. They can operate with a minimum of message switching, message tracing, and billing/settlement overhead.

Figure 4.7 represents the classic concept of Internet Mail, but there are also Internet Mail-based relay services, where many organizations desire access to the Internet but not at the cost of exposing their internal networks to hackers or other predators that might lurk within and beyond the edges of known cyberspace. Thus there are firewalls at both the Internet Mail and the Internet Router level. All mail (in packets) to such organizations is relayed through the firewall, which readdresses and forwards the information to internal recipients—perhaps still using SMTP/RFC 822/MIME, perhaps not.

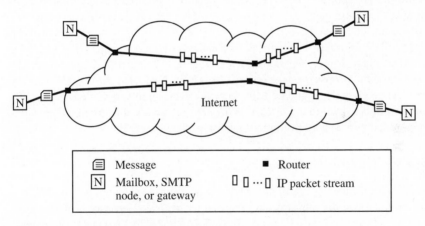

Figure 4.7   The architecture of Internet Mail.

4.4.3   The Extent of the Internet

The size of the Internet and of Internet Mail is a controversial subject. A Fall 1993 EMA Membership Meeting presentation [GUPT93][7] yielded the following international statistics (all are time stamped because the information changes rapidly):

---

7. The statistics in [GUPT93] were based on a parse of March 1993 InterNIC and NSF data, performed by Anthony Rutkowski, vice president of the Internet Society.

- 92 countries with registered IP addresses (9/93),
- E-mail and other gateways to 137 countries (8/93),
- 49,018 registered domains (9/7/93),
- Commercial packet traffic growth rates of 12 percent per month, research traffic growth at 7–8 percent per month (9/93),
- Commercial traffic at least 30 percent of total and growing (7/93), and
- Aggregate monthly traffic of 10 terrabytes counting the U.S.-based NSFNET backbone alone (9/93).

None of the above statistics translates directly into the number of mail users to whom Internet is the primary mail system, nor to the number of mail messages that traverse the Internet. In early 1993, the number of Internet Mail users was variously estimated as being between 3.5 million and 12 million [EMMS93J], with many more users indirectly reachable through gateways. Our spreadsheet tells us that if the number of Internet mail users were to grow from that base at the rate of 10 percent per month, we would have between 9 and 35 million mail users on the Internet by mid-1994.

Most growth statistics include those hosts directly connected to the Internet. However, the number of hosts not connected directly to Internet but running TCP/IP in LAN environments could be on the order of 10 times the directly connected host count. Increasingly, LAN operating systems, such as Windows NT, will be shipped TCP/IP-ready. These are all candidates for Internet connection! Anecdotal evidence suggests that the stratospheric estimates of Internet Mail growth may be real. The White House is on the Internet, as is NBC News, the Boston Globe, every university and college, and perhaps someday every high school. Internet Mail is bringing bulk e-mail to the masses. What are the roots of this promising technology, what are its regional variations, and where is it going?

4.4.4   The Roots of the Internet

Historically, the Internet has been a public research and development network that has grown up around the infrastructure provided by the U.S. Department of Defense's Advanced Research Projects Agency Network (ARPANET). During the 1980s, most of the academic and research community moved over to the U.S. National Science Foundation Network (NFSNET), the ARPANET was shut down, and the military community moved onto what became the Defense Data Network (DDN), whose unclassified portion is called the MILNET. The Internet has also acted as an unofficial commercial network for some time and is now in the process of transitioning to more formal modes of commercial operation and international service.

For the last decade, the registration and administrative hub of the network was provided by the Network Information Center (NIC) installation in the San Francisco area; however, the NIC was moved to Chantilly, Virginia in 1992. The political organ of the Internet, the Internet Society, now reflects the network's international scope (formerly the U.S.-based Internet Activities Board or IAB ran the Internet, or managed it by the consent of the governed, to be precise). The governing structure of the Internet and its key standards setting activities are described in Appendix A. The NIC currently houses the registration function for IP addresses and network numbers (on behalf of the Internet Registry) and names and numbers (on behalf of the Internet Assigned Numbers Authority or IANA) for diverse uses, such as MIME message body part identification information.

During the early 1990s, the Internet began to sprawl out of the U.S. into Europe and the Pacific Rim as well.[8] Internet interconnectivity among public services providers became as ubiquitous as X.400 connectivity. Growths rates of the Internet in Europe and the Pacific Rim are now exceeding those in the U.S.

4.4.5 North American Internet

The core of the Internet in North America is the NFSNET, a multiprotocol (TCP/IP and OSI) router backbone based on T3 links. The NFSNET was upgraded in 1991 and 1992 to support a T3 backbone by Merit, Inc., and Advanced Network Services (ANS), Inc. (ANS is a joint venture of MCI and IBM.) As of early 1994, the NFSNET was surrounded by a number of regional networks and commercial networks, but was slated to become wholly commercial later in the year. In addition, most X.400 public service providers and public information networks have Internet Mail gateways and some of them, notably Sprint, are themselves active Internet commercial service providers.

North American Internet service providers can be differentiated along several dimensions, as diagrammed in Fig. 4.8. On one dimension, we can distinguish between a service provider's realm of operation: either R&D or commercial. On

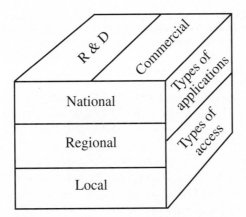

Figure 4.8 Differentiating Internet service providers.

---

8. The Internet Association of Japan was created in December, 1993 to interact with Japan's Ministry of Post and Telecommunications. Among the 41 members are Interop Japan, commercial IP service providers, Internet Initiative Japan (IIJ), and AT&T (Jens) Spin Project research and education providers WIDE and TISN, and several router vendors.

another, we can distinguish between their scope of coverage: national, regional, or local. Finally, we can distinguish qualitative factors, such as the type of applications offered and the type of Internet access offered.

Realm of Operation

A major distinguishing factor between Internet service providers is whether or not they promulgate any restrictions on the type of traffic (commercial or R&D) that they will carry. Because the Internet grew up as a government-subsidized network to encourage research and development, vast areas of the Internet are, in theory, off limits to commercial traffic. The archetypal restriction to commercial traffic is defined in the NSFNET's Acceptable Use Policy (AUP).[9] Other regional networks also have AUPs.

Thus, a major differentiator among service providers is whether or not they have AUPs. If a commercial organization interconnects to the Internet through a commercial service provider, AUP compliance then becomes the service provider's concern. Alternatively, a commercial customer can interconnect to the Internet via a quasipublic provider, but only at the inconvenience of assuming the AUP policing responsibility itself.

In an effort to promote a commercial Internet, a number of regional and commercial Internet access service providers have banded together as the Commercial Internet Exchange Association (CIX). The CIX providers form a matrix of interconnected commercial networks that bypass all AUPs. The major commercial Internet access services providers listed in a July 1993, *Buyer's Guide* from Network World [NETW93] include: Advanced Network and Services, Inc. (ANS), Performance Systems International, Inc., Sprint Corporation (SprintLink), and UUNET Technologies, Inc.

The commercial Internet is expanding both as the ANS begins selling off excess T3 capacity and as the Internet spreads further internationally.

Scope of Coverage

Another differentiator among the Internet service providers is their scope of coverage—national, regional, or local. National service providers tend to be commercial service providers who make Internet and Internet Mail access available via a dedicated line, local phone call, or 800 number nationwide. They feature unrestricted traffic, international connectivity, and enhanced applications and support services. They provide service to individuals, small organizations, and large organizational users. [NETW93] referenced the above listed ANS CO*RE services and SprintLink on its shortlist.

Regional providers were originally funded by the NSFNET, and many now receive commercial revenues as well. They generally offer direct access within a

---

9. This policy states: "NSFNET backbone services are provided to support open research and education in and among U.S. research and instructional institutions, plus research arms of for-profit firms when engaged in open scholarly communication and research. Use for other purposes is not acceptable."

few contiguous states and/or toll free access nationwide. Their clientele is weighted toward educational and research institutions.

Local providers operating in state and local areas constitute the low end of the market. They offer limited services, sometimes only e-mail, sometimes at reduced prices. Some, however, offer specialized application services that may not be available elsewhere.

Internet Access Methods

Other qualitative factors that differentiate Internet service providers are the type of access they provide and the type of applications. Types of Internet access include

- **Dedicated line access via a router:** This form of full Internet access is appropriate for large organizations or smaller entities that use the Internet heavily. An entire LAN community can be interconnected to Internet through the router in this way.

- **Dial-up access to a host-based account (terminal interface):** Many services support dial-up access to character-oriented mail user interfaces and perhaps other information services. The mailbox is on the host. If available, File Transfer Protocol (FTP) downloads must be done twice; once from the Internet to the host, and once over the dial-up line using an asynchronous modem protocol such as Kermit.

- **Dial-up access to a host-based account (client interface):** This is dial-up access to a host-based account. The mailbox is in the host, but a front end user interface is provided on the client. The package may also support single download FTP access from the Internet. Finally, the package may offer a graphical user interface.

- **Temporary Dial-up TCP/IP Connection:** This type of service enables a subscriber to act temporarily as a full Internet TCP/IP node, employing whatever applications (i.e., direct SMTP and others) are supported by the subscriber's software packages. This sleight of hand is accomplished through the use of Serial Line IP (SLIP) or the Point-to-Point (PPP) protocol, which effectively simulate TCP/IP connections to the Internet through the service provider's host. The subscriber is assigned a temporary or permanent IP address for use during the session. Mail is retrieved from the host and stored in a client mailbox using the Post Office Protocol Version 3 (POP 3) (or some other protocol, such as UUCP).

The temporary dial-up connection to the Internet offers the greatest flexibility for users. With a phone line and a POP 3 mailbox on their PC, residential users literally have e-mail (and many other applications) at their fingertips. No longer need they follow cumbersome host login procedures and grapple with command line interfaces. However, at prices ranging as high as $150 per month in early 1994, many of the SLIP or PPP connections are more expensive than host-based mail only accounts. Also in that early 1994 time frame, these connections were often difficult for the ordinary home user to configure or install. But should these cost/complexity barriers be removed (along with a few other blocking factors covered later) and should graphical user interfaces to Internet Mail continue to be available at shareware prices, few obstacles remain to deter virtually the entire residential population of Windows or Macintosh users in the developed world from (someday) riding the Internet information highway straight into the e-mail frontier.

Internet Applications

The pool of Internet applications is widening, summarized here because, although they are not strictly related to e-mail, they serve to illustrate the compelling attraction of the Internet to those who have access. Service providers can provide access to Internet applications directly by packaging them in client software, by implementing a host-based client to which the user must dial up, or simply by enabling the user to employ the TELNET terminal service to access a third party's host providing the desired applications. Internet applications (or services) available in early 1994 included

- **TELNET:** Telnet is a terminal service that enables a user to sign on to any host connected to the Internet and attempt access employing a user name and password. Once logged in, the user can interact with the computer using a shell program configured by the system administrator. Various services can be provided in this manner.

- **FTP:** FTP is a protocol enabling a subscriber to sign on to a computer on the Internet and copy specified public files from it. It is often used by sites to distribute software and various kinds of information. Some sites allow users to log in with the user name of "anonymous" and the password "guest."

- **USENET:** USENET is the bulletin board and news service of the Internet. It utilizes a variety of underlying networks for transport, including parts of the Internet, UUCP, BITNET, and others. USENET is not part of the Internet backbone and has no central administration. USENET software allows the subscriber to download a list of news groups, subscribe to groups and receive postings, and post items to the group. Topics (or groups) number in the hundreds or thousands.

- **Archie:** This system was created to track anonymous FTP archive sites automatically. It makes available the names and locations of several million files at more than 1000 archive sites. Its User Access component and "Whatis" database allow the subscriber to obtain lists, locations, and descriptions of archives and files.

- **Gopher:** Gopher is a menu-driven information browser. Gopher servers store a wide variety of information, such as phone books, recipes, weather reports, and news items.

- **Wide Area Information Service (WAIS):** WAIS is a distributed text-search system that allows the user to enter a sequence of words and then search archives for occurrences of those words.

- **WHOIS and WHOIS++:** WHOIS is a centralized database of Internet users that has long been available on a NIC host, and WHOIS++, a newly developed and distributed directory service.

More and more such applications are invented, it seems monthly. The ones listed above are already well-established; additional emerging services, such as the World Wide Web, are discussed shortly. In this environment, providers will best be able to differentiate themselves by putting together systems that can integrate information from many applications. Research is underway that may make this possible by employing a number of tools, including e-mail and directories.

4.4.6   The European Internet

While originally deprecated by Europeans as a U.S. Department of Defense (DoD) suite of protocols, the Internet began making inroads in Europe in the mid- to late 1980s. By all reports, Internet Mail usage is growing even more rapidly in Europe than in North America, and over 20% of all Internet hosts are now located in Europe. Accreditation of RARE as the European IETF secretariat is currently under discussion. Meanwhile, the Reseau IP Europeen (RIPE) provides registration and address allocation services for the European Internet and attempts to serve as the coordination center for routing issues.

At least two backbone services, EUROPAnet and EBONE, and several hubs were operating in late 1993. Neither of these can claim the mantle of backbone the way NSFNET does in the U.S. EUROPAnet is funded by the European Commission and offers IP connectivity up to two Mbps over a network that was originally designed for X.25 traffic. EUROPAnet has an acceptable use policy. It also buys its connectivity to the U.S. from EBONE, the other provider.

EBONE is a joint effort between academic and commercial IP networks operating a 256–512 kbps backbone between six large switching centers. One of the major hubs connected through EBONE is the CERN physics laboratory. CERN routes traffic including Internet Mail messages to hundreds of networks and provides much of the international network connectivity to southern and central Europe. EBONE operates three links to the U.S.—from CERN, London, and Stockholm—running up to one Mbps across transatlantic cable. EBONE does not have an acceptable use policy and therefore handles unrestricted commercial traffic.

It is noteworthy that Unipalm, Ltd (Cambridge, England) launched a commercial Internet service called Pipex (Public Internet Protocol Exchange), which is connected to the CIX in the U.S. Pipex provides service over 64 Kbps leased lines for a flat annual fee. It currently connects 200 blue-chip clients (including the British Library, ICL, the BBC, and Powergen) to the Internet and claims that connections are rising at the rate of 10 percent per month. Pipex also holds a 25 percent interest in Oleane, a French company providing Internet services to France and the U.K. Also EUnet, a Finnish venture, is offering commercial service throughout western Europe via dial-up and leased lines and is seeking partnerships in North America and Eastern Europe. Suffice it to note that the European Internet situation is undergoing rapid change, and we are best advised to underscore that the current options are subject to imminent revision and may even be supplanted by a more formal European Internet backbone that, like the NFSNET, would interconnect regional networks.

While Europeans have readily implemented and deployed ISO/CCITT standards-based ADMDs and PRMDs, they are also very conscious of the need to interconnect to the research and development (read Internet) world. Thus, R&D networks are widely interconnected to the X.400 world. Users can reach these Internet networks by subscribing to one of the ADMDs that provide such connections as shown in Table 4.3 or by subscribing to an ADMD that can reach one of those ADMDs shown.

These R&D networks are interconnected using SMTP. Many of these networks operate RFC 822 to X.400 gateways implementing RFC 1327, which is the specification for such gateways. In addition, there is a separate R&D X.400 backbone international service called COSINE MHS.

On the other hand, commercial use of the Internet in Europe is still hampered by a lack of agreements on charging and accounting models, of confidence that R&D-based service providers are not crosssubsidizing their commercial offerings, of guarantees of quality of service levels including notifications, and of coordination and integration of routing and gateway services to X.400 services. The fact

Country	R&D network	ADMD connection
Austria	ACONET	ADA 400
Belgium	BRNET	RTT
Denmark	DUNET	DK400
		TELDK
	DENET	DK400
		TELDK
Finland	FUNET	FUMAIL
		ELISA
		MAILNET 400
		IBMX400
France	RED	Atlas 400
Germany	DFN	DBP
Ireland	INCIP	EIRMAIL400
Italy	INFN	MASTER400
The Netherlands	SURFNET	400 NET
Norway	UNINETT	TELEMAX
Slovenia	ARNES	MAIL
Spain	RedIRIS	MENSATEX
Sweden	SUNET	SIL
Switzerland	SWITCH	ARCOM 400
United Kingdom	JANET	BT/GOLD400
		Interspan
		IBMX400
		TMAILUK

Table 4.3 Internet/ADMD interconnections in Europe.

that EEMA has commissioned a project to identify and explore such issues suggests a growing interest in using the Internet by a major European group—one which has been previously focused exclusively on X.400 services.

4.4.7   Emerging Internet Information Services

Emerging integrated Internet information services with diverse components are beginning to link together a number of the different applications and information services detailed earlier. The vision of an integrated Internet information architecture able to classify, move, and interchange information began from an initiative known as the World Wide Web (WWW or W3). World Wide Web is a *hypertext*[10] system spanning the Internet. As of late 1993, WWW consisted of

- A Hypertext Transfer Protocol (HTTP), a stateless, object-oriented protocol that supports remote navigation, or search, retrieval and manipulation of hypertext documents. It enables systems to negotiate the data representation to be used, allowing systems to be built independently of the development of new advanced representations.

- MIME with special heading fields, which is used by HTTP to move information.

- Hypertext Markup Language (HTML), a document type based on Standard Graphics Markup Language (SGML) interchanging basic hypertext documents (including graphics and links via Uniform Resource IDs).

- Uniform Resource Identifiers to classify information resources.

- A publicly available WEB client called Mosaic, with GUIs to WWW, GOPHER, X.500, and other services.

Additional work began in October 1993 when an IETF working group posted a draft document called "A Vision of an Integrated Internet Information Service [WEID93]." This paper notes that in the Internet and in the world at large, a number of large but autonomous regions of networked information are available through diverse tools, such as FTP, WAIS, and GOPHER. But just as the world now entering the Information Age needs interconnected networks, it also needs ways of publishing, classifying, correlating, and retrieving information in distributed environments so that information is at our fingertips or, better yet, proactively available from the computer.

How can this be done in an environment where, to paraphrase the authors of the paper, there is no unique information protocol that will provide the flexibility, scale, responsiveness, world view, and mix of services that every information consumer

---

10. Hypertext is a method of presenting information electronically whereby words in a text display can be expanded into pictures, sounds, files, or other objects. The words are, in effect, links to computer-based objects. For example, a reader might select the word "Argentina" to display a map of that country, from which he or she could select a city in order to request maps, graphics, and text information on the city.

wants, where distributed systems are a better solution to large-scale information systems than centralized systems, and where users don't want to be bothered with the details of the underlying protocols used to provide a given service?

The Integrated Internet Information Service (IIIS) paper proposes the use of Uniform Resource Name (URN) and Uniform Resource Locators (URLs) to help tag and locate information; transponders that emit URNs from resources as diverse as e-mail folders, Telnet sessions, GOPHER menus, and FTP archives; and resource (URN) discovery and locator (URN to URL) systems, perhaps based on X.500 and/or WHOIS++ directories. A publicly available WEB to X.500 gateway, released in early 1994 heralds an early trial of parts of the IIIS concept.

Another issue still to be addressed is the commercialization of Internet services as well as access. Internet applications work very well as long as information resources are being made available *gratis*. But what if a provider or publisher wishes to be paid each time a document or resource is accessed? Today, the only way to ensure such payment is for both the buyer and the seller to subscribe to the same access service provider. In early 1994, however, various service providers and organizations banded together in consortiums with the intent of bringing electronic commerce to the Internet. For example, CommerceNet (to be discussed further in Chapter 9) will leverage Privacy Enhanced Mail, Mosaic, and WWW technology to support secure electronic ordering.

These topics remain formative, but the great popularity of Mosaic and the widespread adoption of Internet Mail suggest that the Internet has the potential to become the world's ultimate consumer information service. Clearly, various ideas are coming together in the Internet environment and moving us forward into exciting and uncharted waters.

4.5   CONSUMER INFORMATION SERVICES

We have just spent considerable time discussing information services from the perspective of the Internet, but there are many other information services we should consider. These fall into a submarket that we will term consumer information services. Sometimes also called online services, they offer messaging, online news, stock quotes, electronic shopping, real-time chat, and other services. They draw much of their customer base from residential users. Many of these offerings grew up as islands but are being increasingly interconnected to global messaging networks via the Internet and via X.400.

Like the Internet, consumer messaging is growing rapidly, and in this market sector may lie the sleeping giant of public messaging. Figure 4.9 diagrams consumer information service mailbox growth to date [EMMS93H, EMMS94].

In October 1993, [EMMS93K] estimated that America Online (AOL), Compuserve, and Prodigy (plus GEIS' GENIE and a few other smaller providers) now have a total of 4.4 million subscribers, up 26 percent since the beginning of that year. Note that while consumer messaging mailbox populations are growing rapidly when compared to the declining public mailbox base, consumer mailboxes

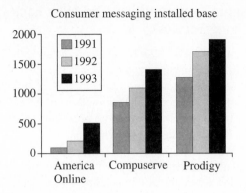

Figure 4.9   Consumer mail services.

do not generate anything close to the traffic levels of commercial mailboxes, and therefore larger numbers of mailboxes are required to achieve a substantial revenue base.

It is likely that larger companies, such as Microsoft, will eventually enter the online services market much as IBM and Sears launched the Prodigy service in the 1980s. Other possible entrants will come from the major media or telecommunications companies, such as Telecommunications, Inc., Time Warner, Inc., and AT&T. In 1993, Apple Computer announced it was entering the market with Apple Online Services.

Tomorrow's online services will be a far cry from today's PC and modem-accessed offerings. A dawning megatrend will rise out of the marriage between cable companies and local telephone access providers. It is projected that this marriage will take place within the next five years given that the Clinton administration signaled in 1993 its intent to remove regulatory barriers. Already merger activities, alliances, and other coexistence arrangements are in process between telephone and cable companies. By providing the ability for users to access consumer information services via ubiquitous devices (interactive TV and enhanced telephones), the cable TV and telephone access providers could revolutionize today's consumer information service marketplace. Consumer messaging will also be heavily impacted by CommerceNet and by the entree of breakthrough technology in the hands of a company called General Magic, and a new consumer messaging service called PersonaLink by AT&T.

For now, the e-mail component of online services accounts for roughly 15 percent (or one-seventh) of usage and revenue. As with commercial Internet services, users are generally billed a flat monthly rate, with additional per-message or connect time charges after a certain amount of usage. There may be additional charges for special services. For example, in 1993 AOL charged $9.95 per month for up to five hours, with additional hours billed at $3.50 each. Prodigy charged $14.95 per month for unlimited basic service, but posted additional charges for services such as the use of a message board.

4.5.1   Electronic Communities: The New Face of Consumer Messaging Services

In the very beginning of 1994, AT&T and a consortium called General Magic[11] went public with their announcement of a new consumer messaging service, a new operating system, and a new smart messaging/distributed programming language. Together, they claimed, these new technologies and services would make the much-touted information superhighway more accessible to millions of people.

The service is PersonaLink, the operating system is Magic Cap, and the smart messaging language is Telescript. PersonaLink is the first Telescript-based service; it acts as network platform for merchants providing electronic products and services. Magic Cap is the first Telescript-based operating system; initially running on personal communicators and Macintosh PCs (and later under Windows), Magic Cap comprises one possible graphical interface to PersonaLink. Telescript constitutes that vital component that embeds intelligence in the network platform. It is essentially a distributed programming language: Telescript programs can be sent as smart messages or over point-to-point connections. Once received, the programs are interpreted with security and integrity by a Telescript engine.

This Telescripted intelligence enables PersonaLink to serve as a host for electronic shops and services. With appropriate authorization and security, providers can configure and change Telescript places in the platform, which acts as the provider of connectivity, billing, and other services. Customers who possess Telescript-enabled mailboxes can work, shop, and play in the community with the aid of Telescript agents (sometimes called intelligent assistants). Through a gateway to AT&T Easylink, PersonaLink users can interact with the rest of the messaging world. Figure 1.2 diagrams one user view—the Magic Cap *downtown* display of PersonaLink.

Figure 4.10 diagrams the architecture of a Telescripted service. It shows users with personal computers or personal communicator devices sending and receiving Telescripted agent programs or other data to and from their mailboxes, which in turn dispatch agents into electronic places in the network platform. Merchants configure their electronic places via their own agents.

Using a Telescripted service, a user could send an agent into the network requesting[12]

- Travel arrangements for a trip to Disneyworld and the Florida Keys. The message could be automatically processed by competing travel agents with further smart messages being dispatched to confirm the most attractive prices and bookings for hotels, rental cars, airplane tickets, and event bookings.

- Front row seat concert tickets on any weekend night that they are available. And then, when the tickets are purchased for a specific night, the agent obtains restaurant reservations and visits a florist.

---

11. The General Magic consortium was established by Apple Computer, AT&T, Motorola, Sony, and other investors.

12. These examples were suggested to us by General Magic employees.

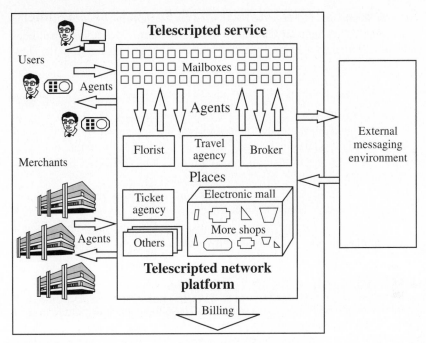

Figure 4.10   A Telescripted consumer information service.

- Relief—a harried executive juggling a busy schedule could be automatically notified by his or her agent of airline flight delays.
- Dinner menus from various sushi restaurants. The meal, ordered in advance, can be obtained at a discount and served more quickly to the customer.

Although electronic shopping is not new, Telescript-enabled services take the concept to new levels. First and foremost is the system's use of intelligent agents. Less obvious is the benefit conferred by the Magic Cap platform and Telescript Technology's object-oriented architecture. Telescript technology users not only can purchase physical goods and services, but they can purchase self-installing software capabilities, such as new Magic Cap software programs (which may show up as new desktop icons or new rooms in the Hallway), fonts, rubber stamps used to illustrate messages, mailbox rules, and other accessories. Thus Telescript technology providers can install the framework of a service on the network and customize it as it is used by sending out new programs. Of course, Telescript programming is not necessarily simple—one would not expect every electronic flower shop or restaurant operator to build their own implementation. More likely, a software vendor would create a general purpose flower shop package to be customized for individual operators.

A few words should be said regarding the Magic Cap platform, which provides the first user interface to Telescript technology and PersonaLink. While this user interface does not support pen-based computing (handwriting recognition technology is still somewhat inadequate), it is unique among GUIs in its top to bottom usage of *physical metaphors*. Observe the Magic Cap screen shots in Fig. 4.11, where the Magic Cap software user is first presented with a *Desk* scene. Messaging capabilities are obtained from the messaging package, and *rooms* can be visited from the *Hallway*. Beyond the Hallway, lies the *Downtown* scene where users can access services, products, and organizations in the electronic marketplace.

As noted earlier, Magic Cap will initially be shipped on personal intelligent communicators from vendors such as Sony and Motorola. During the briefing we received from General Magic on the technology, one trademark on a slide stood out: *Magic TV*. This interest in bringing their user interface to the ubiquitous interactive television devices of the future is no accident, but is reflective of the ambition that burns in the halls of this Silicon Valley start-up.

It will be interesting to see whether the competition allows Telescript technology to stand, or whether rival standards will emerge. As of early 1994, Microsoft's plans remain shrouded in mystery. It will also be interesting to see how long it takes to populate the electronic community once PersonaLink is in place.

4.6 PUBLIC MESSAGING TRENDS

All public networks will face the same trends. These trends include paradigm shift and transition from a public mailbox model, to a message relay model, to a facilities-oriented service; integration of e-mail, fax, and (longer-term) voice, video, and wire-

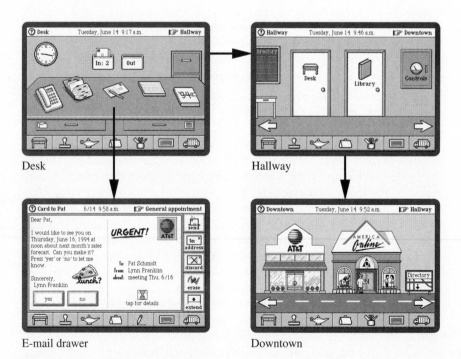

Desk   Hallway

E-mail drawer   Downtown

Figure 4.11 Magic Cap software.

less messaging services into a universal mailbox functionality; convergence of e-mail, integrated information services, and smart messaging capabilities; uneasy coexistence of X.400 and Internet Mail; long-term evolution of public directory services; and the growth of wireless services.

4.6.1   Shifting Paradigms in Service Orientation

The LAN e-mail explosion is the major force driving a paradigm shift from a mailbox, to a message, to a facilities-oriented service. With LAN e-mail initial purchase price coming down to the $30 (or lower) per desktop range while simultaneously offering creative, user friendly front ends that are highly integrated with mail-enabled applications, the demand for host-based public mailboxes has slackened. To a limited extent, public messaging providers have been able to stem the erosion of their commercial mailbox population by offering their own PC-based client implementations that mimic many of the functions of typical LAN e-mail products while using the public mailbox as a message store. Examples of such client front-end implementations are the BT North America Dialcom service's Upfront product and AT&T Mail's use of the Microsoft Mail front end.

The erosion of the commercial mailbox population does not imply, however, that public messaging services are on the wane. Small business and consumer demand remains strong, shoring up the revenues of Internet and consumer information service providers. All three forms of service—mailbox, message, and facilities management—will long be features of public messaging. Today, the growth in intra-enterprise e-mail traffic, in intra-enterprise traffic between distributed workgroups, and in site-to-headquarters enterprise traffic, as well as the rise of the virtual enterprise have accelerated the demand for public services providing wide area message transport capabilities based either on message relay (X.400 ADMD and/or Internet firewall model) or packet relay.

For a time, based on the rationale that users would not want to manage thousands of bilateral interconnects to their trading partners, the industry seemed to be moving in the direction of message relay via ADMD services. This development mirrored earlier developments in the EDI world when most EDI traffic began flowing over commercial public VANs during the late 1980s. However, the ability of trading partners to maintain bilateral interconnects is technology dependent[13] and Internet general connectivity/DNS capabilities have proven that letting the users maintain general purpose wide area messaging interconnects was not as unreasonable as it first seemed. It is likely that bulk mail (of both the X.400 and Internet variety) will switch over to the packet relay model, while at least a large percentage of electronic commerce will continue to be sent using the store-and-forward (message relay) model. This category of electronic commerce will include EDI traffic migrating off of non-messaging EDI VAN services into X.400 or Internet Mail.

---

13. We are grateful to Harald Alvestrand of Norwegian Telecom for convincing us of this concept.

With the message-oriented service paradigm, messages are prepared on the customer premises by customer-owned messaging equipment. The customer handles internal traffic locally but presents external traffic to the public messaging service. Large commercial organizations often collect messages at an X.400 gateway for delivery to an ADMD. Some of the same commercial organizations maintain Internet gateways (firewalls) to Internet service providers; another possible development would be for Internet service providers to themselves offer firewalls.

Smaller commercial organizations generally found early 1990 X.400 products too complex and expensive for practical ADMD interconnection. Thus, a demand for multiprotocol e-mail access to ADMDs was born. This demand led service providers, such as AT&T, Compuserve, GEIS, Infonet, and MCI, to offer gateways (usually with technology licensed from Soft*Switch, Retix or other e-mail integration server vendors) to proprietary e-mail systems, such as PROFS, DEC ALL-IN-1, cc:Mail, and Microsoft Mail. The ease-of-use, pricing, and accessibility of X.400 products improved and will continue to improve dramatically with standards breakthroughs (allowing X.400 to be used over telephone lines and with product releases from vendors, such as cc:Mail and Microsoft). Nevertheless, multiprotocol ADMD capabilities are still needed to facilitate the next wave of change in public messaging: a shift to a facilities management model.

With the facilities management model, the public messaging service provider allows a large customer to outsource the management of its e-mail backbone. Facilities management offerings are particularly applicable to large organizations with a complex fabric of multiple local e-mail environments. Managing an e-mail backbone, such as the Soft*Switch Central, is a major undertaking; some organizations would prefer to focus on their core business and leave their messaging infrastructure management up to professionals. In such cases, service provider operations and consulting staff will craft a solution able to accept all the native e-mail data streams in the customer environment and (as the technology develops) provide value-added services, such as message storage and directory synchronization, for an annual fee. In return, the customer receives unlimited (all you can eat) messaging usage, not only for their intra-enterprise, but also for their inter-enterprise mail.

Infonet and MCIMail have taken leadership positions in the public messaging facilities management arena. Infonet resells OSIWare, Retix, and Soft*Switch products and offers turnkey installation along with a variety of facilities management solutions and its Notice 400 service. Facilities managed offerings are not limited to public messaging providers; certain system vendors, such as Digital, seek such business, as do systems integrations firms. MCIMail launched its Enterprise Family offering in late 1992. We will summarize this offering since it may be precursor of others to come.

Enterprise Family has three components: Enterprise Connect, Enterprise Connect X.400, and Enterprise Partner—each targeted at successively larger companies with higher traffic volumes. With Enterprise Connect, MCIMail resells a Soft*Switch Central messaging switch to the customer with one gateway (regardless of number of users) thrown in free (all other Central accessories are based on

Soft*Switch prices and terms) along with a proprietary Mail Exchange Protocol (MEP) interface to access MCI Mail. Enterprise Connect X.400 (ECX) is an easy upgrade from Enterprise Connect on the same terms but adding a higher bandwidth link to MCIMail by using the Soft*Switch X.400 Gateway.

Note that, with both MCI's EC and ECX, the customer operates the equipment onsite at its facility. However, the final stage of Enterprise Family—Enterprise Partner (EP)—will be a true facilities managed solution. Based on technology still under wraps at MCI, the EP program purports to offer full facility managed PRMD support to customers, including enterprise directory services and messaging level network management.

Other service providers are also fishing in the facility management waters, even though they may not yet have announced an elaborate program. For example, AT&T will offer large customers facilities management based on a combination of technologies, including DEC, Retix, Worldtalk, Wang Office, Soft*Switch, and Microsoft Mail gateways. The challenge for AT&T (and other service providers) is to strike commercially advantageous arrangements with third party e-mail integration vendors, mixing and matching technologies and deals. The service provider must then leverage the various technologies and commercial arrangements, on a customer-by-customer basis, in order to attain profitable configurations while still managing to integrate the various components sufficiently so as to allow efficient operation with reliable directory synchronization and transparent gateway or X.400 mapping.

4.6.2   Universal Mailbox Services

One of the major added values that a service provider should offer via mailbox, message-oriented, or facilities managed service is the integration of various forms of messaging—e-mail, e-mail to fax, enhanced fax, e-mail to postal envelope, and e-mail to telex or telex to e-mail. These are basic bread-and-butter services provided by most public service providers.

Ultimately, public service providers will have revenue opportunities from integrating voice mail and e-mail, and e-mail and video services as well. Voice mail can be integrated with e-mail in various ways, for example, touchtone access to the mailbox and voice synthesis on the one hand, and notification through e-mail of newly arrived voice messages on the other. With public voice mail systems from telephone companies often competing with private voice mail switch solutions today, public service providers that are also telephone companies (such as the U.S. RBOCs) are well positioned to advance on this front.[14]

Thus, voice mail and e-mail integration is slowly approaching. And while no one would seriously advocate the use of store-and-forward messaging for live videoconferencing, messaging will be used for background mailing of video ex-

---

14. Bellcore tested the waters in 1993 with a Message Transport and Relay System (MTRS) that allowed users to address e-mail by phone number. The MTRS system would look up the recipient in the database and hand off the message using the appropriate medium.

cerpts to and from people, cable-based information services, applications, information kiosks, and databases of the future.

4.6.3   Convergence of Integrated Information Services and Smart Messaging

Smart messaging could open the door to much more intelligent workflow services for organizations and sophisticated electronic shopping capabilities for both organizations and individuals. It will take time for offerings, such as PersonaLink, based on such smart messaging technology and integrated information services, to permeate the market. However, Chapter 1 highlighted smart messaging as one wavefront of change in the messaging industry and forecasted the (distant) convergence of e-mail and artificial intelligence. This exciting trend is beginning to manifest itself now.

4.6.4   Uneasy Coexistence of the X.400 and Internet Global Networks

On the surface, the Internet and X.400 global networks are converging. Enhancements to Internet Mail, such as MIME and PEM, as well as recent moves to add structured delivery reports to Internet Mail are part of an industrywide trend toward implementing many of the 1988 X.400 services and semantics, even in mail systems that do not support the X.400 protocols directly (such as SMTP/RFC 822/MIME and later versions of NetWare MHS). With Internet Mail and X.400 supporting similar services, and with Internet RFCs that describe how X.400-to-RFC 822 and X.400-to-MIME gateways should work, convergence is underway. For it will be much easier for a gateway to map message formats between two mail systems that both support multipart binary message bodies than it is to map between a system that supports multipart binary and a system that supports only a single text message body part.

However, there are areas where X.400 and Internet Mail are *not* converging. The two environments do not use a common domain registration infrastructure, although there is no technical reason why they should not. They do not use the same address format, creating endless grief for users grappling with what we described as the Rolodex problem. Finally, Internet access is free (or almost free) to many R&D users and many commercial Internet users pay relatively low flat monthly charges. X.400 users, on the other hand, pay relatively higher per message charges. There have been abuses where users have taken advantage of these differences; for example, users in the R&D department of one corporation reportedly addressed internal messages so that they would be routed through the Internet, to an X.400 service provider, and back through the gateway to a non-Internet mail system in the same company—all at no charge.

There is also a disparity in traffic levels between X.400 and the Internet. ADMDs that have interconnected to the Internet have reported roughly 10 incoming Internet messages for every outgoing Internet message. This is a problem when ADMDs bill on the sender-keep-all basis, and thus do not get paid for incoming messages. Some service providers, such as Compuserve and AT&T, have taken to charging their users a postage-due fee for incoming Internet messages. Others have erected walls to chip away at the problem. For example, if we were to attempt to send a message from an MCIMail box to an address *john.doe@attmail.com* on ATTMail, we would receive an error report: "You cannot send a message to AT&TMail via the Internet." The message had to be readdressed for X.400 before it would pass. We also have occasionally sent messages to an Internet distribution list including many recipients on the Internet and a few recipients on MCIMail. When the distribution list is exploded on the Internet and copies of the message are routed back to the MCIMail recipients, they are rejected.

In Europe, X.400 and Internet advocates have worked more or less cooperatively through the European EMA to understand and resolve this problem. In [OPEN93], EEMA Executive Director Roger Dean was quoted as suggesting that the system must be organized so that service providers could make a reasonable profit; and that the Internet (or at least those parts of it that are subsidized) may need to introduce a dual charging scheme with one set of rules applying to internal messages and another for external ones. But some Internet advocates might balk at this and counter that they are happy to let the ADMDs sit behind their walls and lose their user base (or so the Internet advocates believe). In this case the users—who need choices—lose.[15]

Paradigm clashes, billing wars, address incompatibilities, and registration incompatibilities are some of the dilemmas discussed in Section 4.7 on blocking factors. We believe that the industry should work toward a truce in the billing war, a single address form, and one-stop international messaging domain registration. During late 1993, a proposal began circulating for adopting using the Internet address within X.400. But these proposals, at least initially, involved changes to the very Internet address they were seeking to employ because the proposals were designed to make this very traumatic change in addressing/routing functionality easier for X.400 implementations. Thus, if the current (late 1993) debates are any indication, convergence will not be easy.

4.6.5 The Growth of the Wireless E-mail Market

It will not be long before the personal communicator (*à la* Star Trek) becomes a common sight on the streets of international metropolises and rural byways alike. Field service or sales personnel soon will be able to answer questions or solve problems right before their customers' eyes. They can determine which items are in stock, perform credit checks, trace orders, and obtain dispatch instruction. Taxi

---

15. In the postal mail realm, users can employ Federal Express style services for some mailings and third class mail for others. This is their business decision and their ability to choose should be facilitated. Users should be able to make a similar business decision vis-a-vis X.400 or Internet (or however they care to conceptualize the world of e-mail). But e-mail messages are far more dynamic than their postal counterparts: they are copied, replied to, forwarded, and gatewayed. Partitions are intolerable. Users cannot make a high end electronic commerce decision in isolation of bulk mail considerations, or vice versa.

fleets, military, police, medical units, or any service that today depends on a voice dispatcher can improve its efficiency with radio messaging.

Such applications are enabled by a number of factors. Governments are in the process of releasing previously underutilized radio frequency spectrums. New technologies for infrared LAN data transmission and cellular digital packet distribution are in the making. Wireless technologies and services (of which e-mail is an application) are on the rise, and these days every respectable service provider has its wireless strategy or alliance.

Wireless e-mail allows users to be intermittently connected without the need for a modem; cellular, satellite, packet radio, or wireless LAN links provide such connectivity. The major users of wireless e-mail today are traveling executives or professionals and mobile service workers in business, such as parcel delivery, law enforcement, surveying, sales, and long haul trucking. These different types of users have varying requirements for service attributes, such as geographical coverage, throughput, and integration with other forms of messaging (desktop e-mail system or fax services). For example, while traveling in metropolitan areas, the professional may sometimes need to receive large binary files forwarded from his or her desktop mailbox. The country salesperson, however, may only need short price update messages from a transaction system.

Despite the current high cost of entry into the wireless service provision market, many players are emerging. A key success factor for the wireless service provider is the nature of the synergistic alliances and interconnections it can forge with ADMDs or with other wireless providers. In some cases, packet radio services and satellite services are natural allies whereas packet radio services and cellular data services are direct rivals. This is because both the packet radio and cellular media function best as a relatively high-bandwidth facility concentrated in metropolitan areas, while satellite services function best when serving low-bandwidth or broadcast applications, especially those that must operate with blanket coverage over rural areas.

All service providers face the imperative to interconnect to as many land-based public services as possible to maximize their accessibility to customers. On the e-mail front, this has driven most to seek ADMD status or partnerships with existing Internet or X.400 service providers. Wireless e-mail usage is projected to grow rapidly as the cost of handheld wireless messaging equipment falls[16] and as e-mail capabilities integrate with both pen-based equipment and wireless clients from e-mail vendors, such as cc:Mail.

The major wireless service providers in North America include RAM Mobile Data, ARDIS, and Embarc. RAM Mobile Data is now online in over 100 cities throughout the U.S. and other countries. The RAM Mobile Data Network is based on open protocols developed in cooperation with the Swedish PTT and endorsed by numerous countries represented in the Mobitex Operators Association. While this two-way radio packet service is not conducted in a store-and-forward fashion internally, e-mail is a major RAM application and Internet or X.400 gateways can

---

16. Consumer electronic manufacturers are investing heavily in the handheld communicator market. Both Sony and Motorola were among the principal investors in General Magic.

link RAM subscribers to the global messaging networks. RAM also offers a wireless fax service. ARDIS, a joint venture of IBM and Motorola, operates an infrastructure similar to RAM's.

In 1992, Motorola Inc. unveiled a new nationwide wireless e-mail service called Embarc. Embarc combines an e-mail front end with a paging back end. Unlike RAM's two-way radio mail, Embarc offers a one-way wireless broadcasting capability at a fixed price per message regardless of the quantity of recipients. Users send e-mail from any public or private mail system via X.400. Embarc's Tandem-based MTA then prioritizes, stores, encodes, and uplinks the information to the satellite. The satellite relays the messages to one or more regional transmission sites. A downlink station rebroadcasts the messages to special receivers that download the messages into computers running MS-DOS compatible e-mail software. Users wishing to reply to a broadcast message can do so via land links.

In general, although packet radio wireless networks can offer very high throughput, they suffer from limits on the amount of coverage they can provide to rural areas, and the current state-of-the-art radio transceivers make ARDIS and RAM handheld computers relatively expensive at over $1000 each. Interestingly, both RAM and ARDIS make use of the same wireless e-mail application: a product called RadioMail.

Portable wireless devices sporting the Magic Cap platform will be a major access component of the new AT&T PersonaLink consumer messaging service in 1994. The availability of this technology could galvanize the wireless and personal communications systems (PCS) industries. According to various estimates there may be as many as five million PCS units in deployment by 1996.[17] Even if, as some analysts believe, the market falls short of the mark in the near term due to blocking factors such as the current weakness of handwriting and speech recognition technology (General Magic did not even attempt handwriting recognition and Apple's Newton handwriting recognition capability has been criticized), substantial opportunities await the aggressive investor.

AT&T clearly believes that the wireless market could one day become almost as ubiquitous as the telephone system. The telephone giant's investments are massive, including a $12.6 billion acquisition of McCaw Cellular, earlier buyouts of NCR and of the former Western Union's Easylink division, its controlling interest in EO (pen-based computer and personal communicator manufacturer), and its interest in GO Corporation and General Magic.

4.7 PUBLIC MESSAGING BLOCKING FACTORS

The user's long-term strategic requirement is the ability to conduct reliable messaging and electronic commerce worldwide within the branches of the largest multinationals, between the decentralized offices of virtual enterprises, and between dispersed small businesses, residential users, academia, government, and

---

17. The 5 million PCS by 1996 figure was based on forecasts of Dataquest, BIS, and IDG as quoted in [SEYB93].

unrelated organizations of all kinds. Users want to be able to conduct global messaging over wireline or wireless links, between humans and applications, and with
or without any or all forms of multimedia content. They may wish relatively open
bulk mail service, or they may wish relatively controlled electronic commerce
supported by advanced cryptographic security mechanisms.

The user's rather formidable requirements cannot be fully met by today's patchwork of ADMDs and Internet service providers; they must be met by a global infrastructure (and therefore public messaging services) that is pervasive, modular,
flexible, scalable, intelligent, secure, and manageable. Here we will identify the
major blocking factors standing against public messaging's struggle to reach its full
potential and single out several that have not yet been explained for deeper coverage.

Major blocking factors include the lack of a single worldwide e-mail address
format. Earlier we discussed the critical importance of resolving this issue, perhaps
by universal adoption of the Internet address. The lack of a single messaging standard is also problematic. [RAPP93B] distinguishes two kinds of standards deficits:
those that exist in the absence of any reason not to standardize, and those that exist
for a good reason, such as in areas where the technology base is changing too rapidly. The former deficits must be rectified. Secure messaging remains paralyzed by
controversy over the development of statutory provisions, technology, and infrastructures to support security services based on scalable public key cryptographic
mechanisms. National and international norms must be developed to define the business obligations of parties engaged in sending and receiving messages bearing legal
and financial import. These issues are discussed in Chapters 6, 7, and 10. Multilateral billing problems are another factor, as are routing and registration problems.
Finally, there is a great need for knowledge discovery systems provided through
highly connected directories.

4.7.1   Multilateral Billing Problems

Without a charges settlement (or some other means of cost recovery) between
service providers, interconnection cannot occur over the long term. Thus, the inherent complexity of multilateral, or any-to-any billing, creates a potential brake
on the interconnectivity of public messaging networks. This section will first discuss the billing problem as it manifests itself in the X.400 environment and then
make note of the Internet method for solving it.

To understand the billing problem from the X.400 perspective, first note that
while the number of ADMD interconnects in the U.S. is impressive on the surface,
at present these interconnects are restricted to operating as direct bilateral links. In
Europe, ADMD interconnection is somewhat less advanced and also is undertaken
on a direct bilateral basis.

Limiting the paths along which X.400 messages can transit the public backbone to bilateral links restrains messaging connectivity between diverse subscribers. For example, suppose AT&T Easylink is connected to MCI Mail, and
ADMDX is connected to AT&T. MCI Mail customers can send messages to
AT&T customers and vice versa. ADMDX customers can also send mail to AT&T
customers and vice versa. However, if ADMDX is *only* connected to AT&T, MCI

Mail and ADMDX subscribers cannot communicate because AT&T will not relay the message through MCI even though the X.400 protocol would allow such relaying and is in fact designed for it.

The bilateral limitation is primarily a result of billing and service factors. While the International ADMD Operator's Group (IAOG) and the successor CCITT Recommendation D.36 both allow for reconciliation of charges in relaying scenarios, ADMDs today are settling on a sender-keep-all basis. The assumption is that e-mail is bidirectional and today's e-mail originator will be tomorrow's recipient. These simplifying assumptions, however, leave no way for an ADMD to make a profit by relaying messages. When even more sophisticated interactions are introduced (such as distribution list expansion in a service), the billing uncertainties grow even greater.

Long-term global interconnectivity cannot occur solely on a sender-keep-all/bilateral basis. There will be too many service providers, too many protocols and gateways, too many management domains; in short, too many links in the chain to ever hope to connect the mesh completely. Both the Commercial Internet and the ADMD worlds will have to solve the multilateral billing problem.

An alternative to any-to-any billing in the Internet environment is the use of interchanges. For example, the U.S.-based Federal Interchanges FIX-East and FIX-West connect NASA, NSFNET, and other federal agencies. The CIX connects most of the big commercial IP service providers. A recently established global IX (GIX) aims to establish global interconnect without an acceptable use policy. In the interchange model, all participants pay to connect to an IX, provide the necessary equipment and share routing information. No one charges the others for accepting traffic from an IX. The concept works because connectivity is the most important consideration for all partners.

4.7.2 Routing and Registration Problems

Global registration exists with Internet, but not in the X.400 global network. In the X.400 environment, bilateral interconnect limitations sometimes force users to subscribe to multiple ADMDs. In addition, multinational users often have no alternative other than to use different ADMDs in different countries. This need to use multiple ADMDs or to switch from one ADMD to another is a serious problem since current practice calls for all X.400 addresses to contain a specific single-valued ADMD field. Since the value of that ADMD field is generally hardcoded in the mail system directory entry for each user, the need to change ADMDs or use multiple ADMDs creates an administrative nightmare for whomever is maintaining the PRMD's directories.

While the addressing option of specifying a particular ADMD (e.g., a wireless service) for a given recipient has its uses, users should ideally also be able to use (and service providers to route) addresses that do not specify an ADMD. The nontechnical explanation is that, for nonservice provider specific addressing to work, every PRMD name in the nation has to be unique and each ADMD has to maintain directory/routing information identifying the supporting ADMD for each PRMD. A problem arises when each ADMD registers PRMD names without consulting other ADMDs. In the United States, the U.S. National Message Transfer System Consortium is working to establish a unique national registration of management domain (ADMD or PRMD) names, a function that will be performed by ANSI.[18] Free national PRMD Name registration is already in place in the United Kingdom, Norway, and other countries.

To complicate matters further, some multinational PRMD users are more concerned with having the ability to use a single ADMD across national borders (one-stop shopping) than they are with the ability to use multiple ADMDs (à la carte). Such users have surfaced the desire for a worldwide unique PRMD name registration and routing capability, but this remains at least several years away. Undaunted, some international ADMDs are catering to multinational customers by expanding their service into Europe and elsewhere.

However, as of early 1994 ADMDs had not put in place a global dynamic routing directory. All routes have to be configured statically and by bilateral agreement. This process is not only labor intensive, but anticompetitive as well. Suppose a service provider, such as the British BT ADMD, wishes to recruit customers in Germany. Suppose Herr Fritz Weber signs up and is told that his address will be *G=FRITZ ; S=WEBER ; A=BT ; C=GB.* "But why," he asks, "does my address not contain C=DE, for Deutschland?" He is told the problem is that the local German ADMDs will not route to *A=BT ; C=DE,* but only to *A=BT ; C=GB.* Thus, the workaround for static routes and administrative restrictions is for international ADMD users to employ the ADMD's home country code in their address. Do recipients want their e-mail address to list something other than their own home country? Not especially. Until dynamic routing mechanisms can be developed for X.400, a measure of a global carrier's influence is the number of static routes that they are able to get other ADMDs (end carriers or global carriers) to configure, which is then reflected in the quality of the addresses they are able to issue to their customers.

The Internet, by contrast, already has a worldwide system of registration and routing. Its users have neither the advantage of being able to specify a service provider in an address nor the administrative problem of maintaining addresses for multiple service providers. Instead, Internet address-to-route mapping is done dynamically through the DNS. While domain names are not yet a problem, ironically the Internet may soon become a victim of its own success. It is running out of class B IP addresses, and wrenching changes will be needed to expand its current 32-bit IP address.

4.7.3 Knowledge Discovery

The success of Internet Mail so far is largely due to the simplicity of its addressing/registration mechanisms and the availability of the DNS as a routing/knowledge discovery capability. Knowledge discovery will be similarly critical to the scala-

---

18. Unfortunately, as of late 1993, ANSI still insisted on charging $1500 to organizations for the privilege of registering a PRMD name.

bility of X.400 messaging networks once they move towards a flatter address space by eliminating the requirement to specify an ADMD field in every address and as the use of international ADMDs spreads.

For X.400 ADMDs, the knowledge discovery mechanism could be provided using conventions developed in the Long Bud pilot [ALVE93B] for storing X.400 message routing information in the X.500 Directory System. For example, a U.S. ADMD wishing to route a message to an African PRMD would look up the next hop in the X.500 Directory. X.500 systems will also provide for additional kinds of intelligence, including the ability of a service to determine whether to deliver a message to a recipient by fax, by wireline e-mail, by wireless e-mail, by postal mail, or by other means and into what format to convert message attachments (if necessary) like word processed files. Similar knowledge discovery mechanisms beyond routing would also be useful to Internet Mail and private local e-mail systems.

4.8 PUBLIC DIRECTORY SERVICES

Public directory services have been an important discussion topic ever since the 1984 X.400 standard emerged, leaving directories as a "for further study" item. Early on, it was realized that distributed directory standards were required to interconnect private e-mail directories, telephone directories, and public e-mail directories. In support of that goal, the 1988 and 1993 versions of the X.500 standard have been developed.

X.500 remains an emerging standard in its early stages of adoption. It was conceived as a top-down effort by the CCITT/ISO standards group, that is, it was thought that PTTs and public messaging service providers would build public X.500 messaging systems and local e-mail directory systems and that private domain users would fall in line. In practice, the public messaging community has only moved slowly, and the standard has not been implemented by local messaging vendors. This section presents a high-level discussion of the prospects for and progress toward global directories.

There were signs in 1993 that the X.500 stalemate might finally be ending and global public directories may be on the horizon. These signs included, on the public side, a worldwide X.500 R&D directory system edging closer toward commercial modes of operation; a consortium of public messaging service providers establishing a pilot service in North America and opening the pilot to users; and European PTTs and service providers preparing to launch a commercial European Directory Pilot.

On the private directory facility side, some users (albeit a minority) stepped forward as early adopters; these included numerous large corporations, multinational institutions, and government agencies. X.500 products became available from over a dozen vendors; and even those vendors who were not implementing X.500 protocols directly began implementing X.500-like information structures that can be more easily integrated with standards-based directories than earlier proprietary offerings. Modularization of local messaging products promises to eventually enable third party client implementation.

On the other hand, a cloud rose on X.500's horizon during 1993. Disenchanted with the standard's slow pace toward deployment, elements of the IETF research community launched a new distributed directory standards effort WHOIS++. WHOIS++ is an X.500-like directory with distributed processing and information templating capabilities. It is differentiated from X.500 primarily on the basis of claims to greater simplicity and freedom from hierarchical information structure constraints. If successful, WHOIS++ could invite the same uneasy coexistence to the world of directories that MIME and PEM have brought to the world of e-mail. As of early 1994, however, there were few signs that WHOIS++ proponents would be able to quickly and easily cut through the many complexity issues that bedevil distributed directories in general.

The global directory conundrum should not only be considered from the standards perspective, but from the perspective of other meta-issues. These include

- **Listing** Private users have an *inverted incentive structure*; they do not want to list their own information, but would like other users to do so.[19] Access control issues, privacy policies, and authentication techniques are thus important considerations in deploying any public directory service.

- **Billing** When are directory services separately billed, and when are they considered part of another service? Should a sender-keep-all, multilateral settlement, or an interchange model be used?

- **Regional variations** European public service providers are interested in developing national public directories.[20] The concerns of would-be U.S. Administrative Directory Management Domain (ADDMD) service providers for X.500 differ for two reasons: first, the concept of a national directory is much more difficult to implement in the highly deregulated U.S. telecommunications environment than in Europe; and, second, the public messaging environment in the U.S. is already characterized by a high degree of X.400 interconnectivity utilizing systems with proprietary directories that predate X.500.

Our current prognosis is that X.500 can succeed in becoming the global directory it was designed to be if current efforts to create a global infrastructure are vigorously pursued, if applications are developed to use the existing infrastruc-

---

19. The term "inverted incentive structure" was coined by Marshall Rose of Dover Beach Consulting.

20. France Telecom has been the most active European provider in the public directory arena. It supports Minitel, a French public network incorporating a national directory that can be accessed at cheap, government-subsidized rates through six million special Minitel terminals. The initial motivation for the Minitel directory was to replace paper directories for many users, boost telephone use, reduce operator assistance costs, provide another source for revenue from paid advertisements, and support over 13,000 online videotex services, including financial, mail order, and other information services. According to [OVUM93A], directory services now account for five percent of Minitel revenues. France Telecom has since added an X.500 gateway to Minitel. With pan-European telephone directory inquiry traffic growing 30 to 40 percent per year, France Telecom and other European service providers with X.500 under development may eventually see an economic motivation to push toward national directory interconnections using X.500.

ture, if local messaging systems accelerate their evolution in the X.500 direction, and if user interest heightens.

4.8.1   The PARADISE Directory

The Piloting A ReseArcher's DIrectory Service for Europe (PARADISE) project is significant because it has established and proved the concept of an actual world-wide X.500 Directory Information Tree (DIT) in the research community. Originally funded by the European COSINE organization and financed through the European Commission's VALUE program from 1993 through April 1994, the project grew out of earlier research efforts to interconnect ISODE Consortium QUIPU X.500 Directory System Agent implementations. These efforts began as early as 1988, and were formalized in the pilot beginning in November 1990.

The major activities of the pilot were to register country-level DSAs and to maintain a Root DSA, called Giant Tortoise, to link together the country DSAs. Administrators of the country DSAs were assigned on a first-come, first-served basis, then linked up to lower-level organizational DSAs within their country. By the end of the 1993, the PARADISE pilot database encompassed over 1.5 million listed entries (many of these are listed in the U.S. branch of the pilot, called the U.S. White Pages pilot), over 600 DSAs, over 2000 organizations involved, and over 35 countries.

These numbers, though impressive, still only represent a minuscule percentage of the user population. They indicate that the pilot has been successful in establishing an X.500 presence. The next steps for the project are to attempt to move it to some form of commercial (self-supporting) operation, to link in additional directory pilots sponsored by commercial public service provider organizations (such as the North American Directory Forum in North America and the European PTT association EURESCOM), and to utilize the infrastructure for additional applications. Moving toward self-supporting operation involves developing some revenue-generating applications and obtaining reliability guarantees from or replacing research organizations that currently operate national DSAs. Linking with other pilots could involve expanding the pilot concept to allow multiple country level DSAs in a single country. Additional applications utilizing the PARADISE infrastructure as of late 1993 included a pilot called PASSWORD for testing Secure X.400 and PEM utilizing the directory as a Certificate database, the Long Bud pilot, and a German pilot for storing topological network management information in the directory.

4.8.2   The North American Directory Forum

The North American Directory Forum (NADF) is a group of organizations that currently operate public services or have stated an intention to operate public X.500 services. An additional criterion for NADF membership is the willingness and intention on the part of the service provider to intercommunicate with other service providers. Table 4.4 provides a roster of NADF members.

While PARADISE created a research DIT within the constraints of the X.500 standard (which basically was only designed to support one DSA per country), the

Advantis	GSA
Allied Signal	GTE
AT&T	MCI Communications Corp.
Bell Canada	Pacific Bell (with Bellcore)
BT North America	Performance Systems International
Canada Post	Premenos Corp.
Digital Equipment Corp.	Sprint International
GE Information Services	U.S. Postal Service

Table 4.4 Roster of NADF members.

NADF attacked the more difficult issue of making X.500 work in a world of competitive commercial carrier interconnections. In order to achieve this goal, the NADF created a number of agreements codified in Standing Documents. These agreements address many directory issues, including the structure of the North American DIT, the means of registering organizational and geographical entries in the directory, and a "User Bill of Rights" that protects the privacy concerns of listed organizations and individuals. Further, to enable multiple competitive carriers to cooperate, agreements were struck on the means of maintaining a "virtual DSA" at the U.S. national level, in effect allowing each public service provider to operate a DSA. A Central Administration and Naming (CAN) infrastructure was established to exchange the necessary directory knowledge information to support the operation of multiple country level DSAs.

The NADF has been involved in testing its agreements and piloting the CAN infrastructure for some time. In 1993, the NADF opened its pilot to user organizations and was shortly joined by Allied Signal, Bellcore, and DEC. Plans were also laid for interconnecting the NADF portion of the DIT to the PARADISE pilot. The success of the NADF is critical to X.500 acceptance, both from the standpoint of "deepening" the DIT, and from the standpoint that NADF agreements can serve as a model for a European Directory Forum (or many national DFs in Europe) and for a Pacific Rim Directory Forum.

4.9   THE EDI MARKETPLACE

EDI is that type of public electronic commerce implemented to enable the exchange of trading data between computers, and it is conducted in the currency of a set of standardized structured formats called EDIFACT and X12. This form of interchange is generally used between different companies or organizations and referred to as external EDI (by far the largest use), but it can also be used within enterprises where it is termed internal EDI.

The method of external EDI communications is undergoing an evolution. Until now, most EDI has been conducted with the aid of direct (dial-up or bisync) connections between trading partners. This arrangement is often characterized by a hub and spoke configuration where the dominant enterprise, acting as a hub, provides EDI services to its trading partners which appear as spokes. (Some of these hub enterprises even charge their spoke trading partners extra to process paper.)

More and more, enterprises are recognizing the value of using a public provider as a Value-Added Network (VAN) service to support EDI, and VANs, supporting the next step in the evolution of EDI communications, now constitute a major EDI market. (There is also a private software and equipment market for customer-premises EDI translation equipment—equipment usually linked to other internal transaction systems and to communications systems for external, VAN connections.)

The last step in the evolution of EDI communications derives from the realization on the part of users that they have a long-term need for total business automation, automation based on distributable, multimedia, multiplatform, interoperable messaging, workflow, and EDI. As they build industrial strength messaging networks internally (or use the messaging networks of public service providers), users will increasingly encounter cost and productivity arguments for conducting non–real-time EDI over those same messaging networks. Thus, businesses will soon have an interest in conducting EDI and other forms of electronic commerce within a security and legal framework as robust as, or more robust than, today's paper-based models.

On the other hand, bridging the gap between such interests and today's realities is difficult. Messaging and EDI are plagued by the usual chicken and egg syndrome. First, users must reckon with their installed base and that of their customers. Users of EDI who are driven primarily by customer coercion are unlikely to move to store-and-forward EDI on their own, and the first big customer organizations that attempt to force X.435 or any other form of store-and-forward EDI on their suppliers are likely to face an uphill struggle.

North American Public Messaging Market—Electronic Data Interchange (EDI)

The success of EDI VANs from leading North American providers, such as the IBM Information Network/Sears Communications Network joint venture dubbed Advantis and Sterling Software's Commerce Connection, serve as key indicators for the growth of electronic commerce. (Note that there is a significant degree of overlap between EDI VAN and ADMD providers, including the obvious ones such as BT and AT&T, and the less well-known ones such as Harbinger, which supports Sprint's EDI service.) The IBM/Sears merger captured the trading partners of the two companies as well as a significant percentage (the Gartner Group estimates 40 percent) of internal accounts. General Electric Information Systems (GEIS) will manage the National Wholesale Druggist Association's Healthcom initiative to transmit pharmaceutical orders via EDI. Sterling Software acquired Control Data Corporation's Redinet in 1992 and has fully integrated that client base. BT will enable the transfer of student transcripts through EDI, and it has also been proactive in building toward the support of X.400 and X.435-based services. Such services as Railinc, operated by the American Association of Railroads, will continue to operate in vertical markets.

VAN	1992 growth percentage of U.S. dollars	1992 market share change	1992 market share
GEIS	+ 44 %	+ 5	30 %
Sterling	+ 21 %	0	17 %
Advantis	+ 88 %	NA	18 %
BT	− 33 %	− 4	5 %
Kleinschmidt	+ 18 %	0	8 %
Transnet	+ 10 %	− 1	6 %
Railinc	+ 12 %	0	6 %
Harbinger	+ 5 %	0	2 %
Transettlements	+ 32 %	0	3 %
AT&T	− 25 %	− 1	2 %
Others	+ 14 %	0	3 %
TOTAL	21 %		100 %

Note: Statistics are somewhat suspect since few vendors divulge accurate revenue figures which are sometimes buried in overall VAN figures.

Table 4.5 1992 EDI growth and market share. *Reprinted with permission from The Gartner Group. Copyright © 1993.*

As a group, these VANs experienced a 20 percent growth to $170 million in revenues in 1992. Table 4.5 shows this 1992 growth and the percentage of market share for the 11 largest EDI providers.

Also in June 1993, the Gartner Group released a report grouping and rating the various EDI vertical markets [WHEA93A]. According to their projections, the group composed of services including automobile repair, real estate, and lodging will experience the most dramatic growth—300 percent—in the use of EDI. Government, health and education facilities, and banking/finance and insurance will experience growth in the 125–150 percent range. Because health care reform is a burning issue in the U.S., we can also expect a dramatic rise in the use of electronic medical claims. Altogether, revenues for the North American market are projected by the Gartner Group to grow to $790 million for EDI, $925 million for e-mail, and $1 billion for integrated messaging by 1998.

Overall, both the public and private EDI markets are well into the early adopter stage in North America and the more advanced innovator stage in Europe. Growth factors will continue to make store-and-forward messaging (well suited for any-to-any intermittent communication) an attractive means of EDI conveyance. In anticipation of this trend, the CCITT produced Recommendation X.435 for carrying interchanges in X.400 messages. Also, an EDI Body Part was recently proposed for MIME. (This body part has fewer features than the X.435 content but would at least enable the specification of EDI types in messages.)

For now, the U.S. EDI environment is dominated by a very large installed base of IBM 2780/3780 and other link-level protocol users. While X.400 has a ready-made solution for EDI in the X.435 standard (allowing companies to integrate their e-mail and EDI infrastructures), X.435 adoption will be slow until large

DoD, IRS, and other government projects come online in the mid- to late 1990s and until users of conventional EDI gradually depreciate their obsolete equipment. In the meantime, to improve connectivity, VANs will support support the ANSI Mailbag Interconnect Structure and a transaction set called X12 841 that provides for carrying binary files.

Also, the Internet's rapid growth, ubiquity, and more attractive pricing make it a candidate as a supplier of electronic commerce services. The University of Southern California's FAST project uses the Internet to support electronic component procurements for researchers. Enterprise Integration Technologies is poised to become a value-added EDI Internet supplier through the addition of security and auditing services. However, the Gartner Group [WHEA93C] argues that the Internet has a reputation for easy accessibility to a constituency of hackers and that software for trusted and privacy enhanced mail is not yet widely deployed. The VANs, on the other hand, provide relatively tight, built-in security and auditability, especially under X.400. It is also worth noting that, while some Internet backbones offer high performance, many of the subnetworks through which messages might travel are not optimal. The results include unacknowledged, delayed, and even lost messages. Finally, in what might be viewed as an effort to retain EDI market control, most VANs offer ASCII messaging passthrough to Internet users but do not support the attachments, acknowledgments, or other X.400-type features essential for reliable electronic commerce.

EDI Messaging—Trends

The U.S. EDI environment is still primarily mainframe based and its mode of communication is dominated by a very large installed base of IBM 2780/3780 and other link level protocol users. According to one survey of EDI users in nine industries, only 25 percent of the users employed the same network for both EDI and e-mail, and 55 percent intended to continue to use these different e-mail and EDI networks [WHEA93A].

On the other hand, the number of European companies utilizing automated trading is expected to grow fivefold over the next three years. Because they had a later start than their U.S. counterparts, European companies will be able to leapfrog mainframe-based EDI in favor of more contemporary store-and-forward alternatives, especially X.435. For example, Transpac in France claims that about 40 percent of its X.400 traffic is carrying EDI. POSTGem in Ireland is handling X.435 traffic. BT's EDI-Net is offering a variety of economy and flat rate EDI prices as well as EDI-to-fax and EDI-to-postal delivery services. While a shakeout among European suppliers of EDI is likely, the market is expected to continue to support the existing set of pan-European EDI service providers—AT&T, Istel, BT, GEIS, IBM, and Infonet.

The worldwide movement toward EDI and messaging will gather steam slowly. Today, X.435 is a stable, workable standard. It is being pushed primarily by associations, such as the Aerospace Industry Association (AIA) and the American Petroleum Industry (API) association in the U.S. and Tedis (Trade Electronic Data Interchange System) and Cefic (Conseil Européen des Fedération de l'Industrie Chimique) in Europe, as well as by a few innovative companies. There are X.435

products on the market from vendors such as ISOCOR, DEC, Retix, Tandem and Control Data Systems. Additional products will follow, and VAN service plans for the standard have been announced. Another major driver will come when governments implement plans currently on the drawing boards for electronic commerce between industry and their regulatory or banking institutions.

While the user requirement and trend toward store-and-forward EDI is clear, legal, inertial, and cultural blocking factors are holding it back. Our prognosis is for gradual integration of EDI and messaging in the United States with perhaps more rapid growth in Europe. More than anything else, industry downsizing trends should drive EDI in the messaging direction. Increasingly, invoices, purchase orders, and other documents will be generated by PC-based software rather than by mainframe-based transaction systems. The same PC users filling in the invoice forms that become structured EDIFACT or X12 messages will also be using e-mail (e.g., to check on the prices or status of back orders). The more information that can be transparently passed between e-mail and EDI modes of operation, the greater the opportunities for cost saving at the desktop through automation and process reengineering.

EDI Messaging—Blocking Factors

Aside from the classic chicken-and-egg syndrome, where the existence of an EDI dial and dump installed base blocks forward movement, the state-of-the-art in EDI messaging today is blocked primarily by the relatively slow scaling of usage and by cultural factors. Until EDI scales from tens of thousands of users into hundreds of thousands, the cost savings from a store-and-forward mode of operation will not always justify the initial expense of conversion.

At the cultural level, we remain addicted to paper as a society. For example, as the U.S. Government continues to automate, its output of paper nevertheless continues to grow geometrically. Also, while the technical means of electronically notarizing, postmarking, and signing interchanges exist (although as an industry we insist on creating conflicting approaches), they have not been legitimized in national or international law.

Cultural factors surface within the MIS departments of corporations as well. In many cases, the e-mail infrastructure is run by a different group than the EDI infrastructure. The e-mail group may be in the midst of catering to a LAN e-mail revolution in the ranks, while the EDI group maintains a tightly controlled mainframe empire. These groups are not natural allies. Also, EDI implementation has been justified on the basis of customer coercion or cost reductions. In either case, the initial cost of messaging integration may be difficult to justify in the short term, and the integration may bring perceived security risks.

4.10 SUMMARY

Public messaging services will continue to play a crucial role in connecting individuals and organizations. However, the public messaging market currently consists of a patchwork of services and facilities offering a variety of related information services applications and interconnecting in various ways. The carriers who offer these services can be categorized as those providing global connectivity and those providing local or end carrier services. They can also be catego-rized by those carrying bulk mail, those carrying electronic commerce, those of-fering value-added information services, and those providing a mix. Finally, these service offerings have coalesced around two candidate protocols for the backbone infrastructure: X.400 and the Internet.

While these two protocols can coexist (albeit uneasily) through the use of gateways, their coexistence is really characterized by a paradigm clash. They dif-fer significantly in the way they handle addressing, billing, and registration. Also, the IETF standards body has developed MIME and PEM in an effort to emulate and sometimes surpass some of the features specified in X.400.

Furthermore, X.400 is to a great degree the product of the public carrier cul-ture whose thinking can be characterized as hierarchical and process-oriented with a focus on international consensus. The Internet was developed by the research and development community where protocols gain allegiance through proof of concept projects, testing, and deployment. X.400 offers a store-and-forward ser-vice, while Internet Mail is transported in packets whose contents are usually touched only by the originator and recipient. Thus, Internet Mail has been typi-cally successful at providing bulk mail services, while X.400 is more trusted for carrying electronic commerce over the messaging transport system.

Each world offers strengths that, if adopted by its counterpart, would nudge them further toward convergence. For example, X.400 is developing a flatter, and therefore easier to use, address space, and the Internet is adapting its mode of operation to accommodate commercial e-mail traffic. These efforts and others should accelerate true convergence, which in turn could lead to a formidable worldwide messaging backbone.

For users, convergence can come none too soon. Users want the relaying net-works and their protocols to be transparent and to have no discernible impact on performance. They want easy addressing using both automatic and manual direc-tories, understandable billing, and a common registration mechanism. They also want solid security for their electronic commerce messaging as well as legal recog-nition for e-mail business traffic such as contracts and purchase orders. Finally, they want notifications of message delivery or non-delivery and a modicum of assurance that their various types, sizes, and quantities of messages will be delivered.

Users have these requirements because they recognize that messaging could become a transport mechanism for a plethora of services. The Gartner Group re-cently projected North American five-year growth in e-mail services in terms of traditional e-mail, but also EDI, electronic medical claims (EMC, which is ex-pected to take a dramatic leap because of health care reform in the U.S.), and integrated messaging services which will embrace all forms of electronic messag-ing and all types of media. These projections are shown in Fig. 4.12.

The message from this forecast is clear. But if public messaging carriers are to meet user requirements, they will have to develop electronic communities, knowl-edge discovery systems, international domain name registration, and universal mail-boxes offering e-mail, electronic commerce, fax, postal, video, and voice services. They will also have to resolve their difference over protocols and architectures in order to provide what users demand—a ubiquitous, global messaging infrastructure.

U.S. dollars in millions

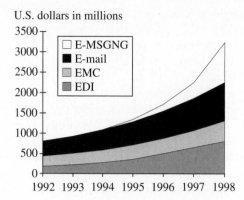

Figure 4.12   North American EDI, E-mail, EMC and
Integrated Messaging Services forecast.
*Reprinted with permission from The
Gartner Group. Copyright © 1993.*

KEY POINTS

- Public service provider offerings are an alternative for users that do not own
  private messaging networks and need global connectivity.

- Service providers can be categorized in terms of global or local coverage, the
  type of mail service they support (bulk mail or electronic commerce), and the
  type of protocols.

- A rapidly expanding Internet Mail infrastructure is bringing bulk e-mail to the
  millions of computer-literate users. Both Internet Mail and X.400 are becoming important bearer services for electronic commerce.

- New consumer messaging services promise to awaken a sleeping giant by
  making e-mail and other information services accessible to ordinary, less
  computer-literate consumers via electronic communities, personal communications systems, and interactive television.

- EDI will be an important service that will make use of the global e-mail infrastructure and in turn drive its evolution.

- Public messaging services will support mailbox-oriented services, message
  relay services, and facilities management services. While the evolutionary
  trend is from a mailbox-oriented model to a facilities management model, all
  three models will coexist.

- Formidable blocking factors to the global public e-mail networks involve billing, name and address registration, directories, and security. Some barriers
  can be resolved by the implementation of directory services. This chapter describes initiatives to implement such a directory based on the X.500 standard.

- Public messaging services are stratifying into two tiers based on these different
  types of traffic. A third tier, official messaging, may develop in some nations.

CHAPTER 5

E-mail Technology

5.1   Local E-mail Architectures

5.2   Local and LAN E-mail Features

5.3   E-mail APIs

5.4   E-mail Gateways

5.5   E-mail Integration Servers

5.6   E-mail System Case Studies

5.7   Summary

In this chapter, we will discuss local messaging systems and e-mail integration servers. We define a local messaging system as an actually deployed (host or LAN-based) e-mail product. We define a LAN e-mail system as a system implemented for distributed LAN environments. These systems can include DOS/Windows LANs, Unix LANs, Apple LANs, or wherever client-server or file-sharing techniques are used to place e-mail intelligence in the user's front-end workstation rather than confining it to departmental or host systems. LAN and host e-mail architectures are discussed in Section 5.1.

A healthy market for e-mail has encouraged research and development. Although further progress is needed, an ongoing consolidation of the industry around a few popular interconnection standards and e-mail APIs has enabled vendors to begin mixing and matching their products. With this impetus, e-mail user interfaces, directories, message storage, message transfer, and system administration components are in the midst of a features explosion. Some of these features are advanced, others are basic. Some translate well when multiple systems are in use, others do not. We discuss e-mail features in Section 5.2, and APIs in Section 5.3.

Despite encouraging modularization trends, most existing local messaging products implement proprietary message transport, directory, or storage tech-

143

niques rather than building native, standards-based functionality. Users seem no more likely to converge on one brand of e-mail system than on one brand of automobile! Given this situation, standards that enable interworking between e-mail systems (and interworking between mail systems and mail-enabled applications) are essential. Where standards are not supported directly by products, gateways and e-mail integration servers can step in. We define a gateway as a product that can translate messages between the formats and protocols of two different messaging systems (see Section 5.4). We define an e-mail integration server as a dedicated system created specifically to enable communication between multiple local messaging systems (see Section 5.5).

In addition to discussing generic technologies and trends, we find it useful to present several short case studies (in Section 5.6) of actual major products, remembering that every e-mail product has unique features and too many products exist to be covered in exhaustive detail here.

5.1 LOCAL E-MAIL ARCHITECTURES

Picture the weekly departmental report winging its way across a messaging network, through gateways, and on to WAN links. It contains paragraphs assembled in an ad hoc cut-and-paste fashion from various staff reports, embedded spreadsheet figures, and an attached document pulled from a library server. A bit of workflow, a lot of mail-enabled applications, a few mouse clicks, several sips of coffee, and the job is done. Today, thousands of LAN e-mail users make casual use of this modern office automation miracle, now a routine capability that has changed our professional lives profoundly even as we begin to take its capabilities for granted.

Yet we live in a world of contradictions. While such a weekly report scenario is feasible with an advanced local e-mail system, not all systems are so advanced. The technologies described are only likely to work in a homogeneous environment. Where data must be shared between two or more local messaging systems connected through a gateway, the modern office automation miracle sometimes becomes the modern office automation nightmare.

Local messaging systems have progressed from humble beginnings—as just another application or utility inhabiting a single departmental host or a rustic LAN file server—to complex distributed environments overlaid on enterprise internetworks. Throughout, these systems (especially LAN e-mail systems) have retained an impressive ease-of-use, initially sporting colorful, character-based interfaces and later GUI interfaces with all the bells and whistles imaginable including toolbars, dialog boxes, and radio buttons.

The ease of use of these systems has been greatly improved. However, as e-mail evolves into an enterprise rather than a workgroup or departmental application, its architecture undergoes wrenching transitions to keep pace. Local messaging systems are rarely islands anymore. Generally they are connected through gateways to enterprise or public messaging backbone protocols. Their directories are rarely isolated. Server-to-server or host-to-host synchronization is maintained within the local messaging system, and often local directories are synchronized even with those of e-mail systems from different vendors. Thus they require increased management capabilities to route messages, monitor availability and performance, and synchronize the directories. But although physical interconnectivity between mail systems has improved in recent years, users within one local messaging system often find it difficult to address a message to users in a foreign system. Unless directories are synchronized and user-friendly names are presented, communication across local infrastructure boundaries may be sharply inhibited.

Even as local messaging has become more complex and functional from the server perspective, it has also become more complex from the client perspective. Once, a client was no more than a user interface for interpersonal mail. Today, client software often incorporates generic utilities to accommodate mail-enabled applications on the front end and drivers to diverse messaging systems on the back end.

5.1.1   Host E-mail Architecture

In host e-mail systems the e-mail software is based on a departmental mini-computer or mainframe host and is accessed by a user with a terminal. The terminal implements display capabilities and can communicate with the host via an asynchronous modem, IBM's SNA, X-Windows, or other protocols. However, all e-mail storage, directory, and transport capabilities are host-resident. This architecture is illustrated in Figure 5.1.

Host e-mail systems proliferated in the late 1970s and early 1980s. Some required the user to employ what were—by today's standards—relatively cumbersome command line interfaces. Others leveraged the highlighting and cursor positioning capability of most terminals, such as the venerable VT-100 or the 3270, to produce menu-driven user interfaces that were quite respectable, given adequate communications speeds. However, no host e-mail system can compete with LAN e-mail systems (where the user interface resides in the client) for responsiveness,

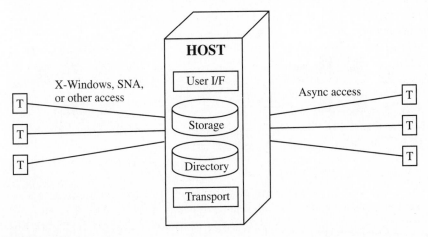

Figure 5.1   Host-based e-mail architectures.

graphics, or sound capabilities. For this reason, the late 1980s and early 1990s marked a slow transition from host-based to LAN-based e-mail.

One attribute of many host e-mail systems, which LAN systems are only now beginning to replace, is the (host-based) integration of e-mail with other office automation applications, such as conferencing, calendaring, and bulletin boards. For example, PROFS (IBM) and ALL-IN-1 (Digital) were sold based on their integration with such functions.

While downsizing is a megatrend in the industry, the advent of smarter, more sophisticated terminal standards, such as X-Windows, enables the modernization of host-based e-mail systems, particularly in the UNIX LAN environment. X-Windows can greatly improve the capabilities of terminal oriented e-mail client systems. With the modularization of LAN e-mail systems, a trend also exists toward implementing e-mail server functions on UNIX or NT-based hosts.

5.1.2   Basic LAN E-mail Architecture

Almost all LAN E-mail products are loosely based on the client-server paradigm, where the client resides in the user's desktop PC, Macintosh, or Unix workstation and provides the front-end interface, while the server provides mail storage, directory listings, and inter- and intra-LAN transport. These implementations were originally optimized for the low-end PC or Macintosh environments of the mid-1980s. That is, their disk, memory, and CPU demands are relatively low, and they take advantage of network operating system file sharing and asynchronous dial-up resources. Despite the general use of client-server terminology to describe basic LAN e-mail implementations, they are not true client-server systems because they use file-sharing access methods rather than client-server protocols.

The characteristic of the basic, or traditional, LAN e-mail architecture that the reader will immediately notice is its relative simplicity or lack of modularity (see Fig. 5.2). The client, often called a user agent, is simply a user interface that fetches mail from a message store (often called a post office) on the server. The

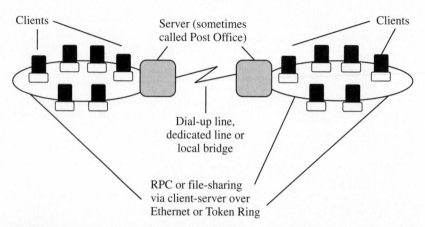

Figure 5.2   LAN-based e-mail architectures.

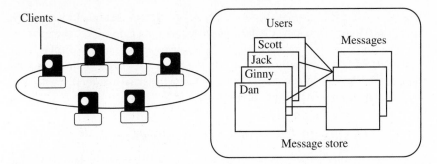

Figure 5.3   Single copy message concept.

message store is a file or file system that keeps track of mail messages that the user has received. A system of pointers is generally used to optimize the storage so that only a single copy of a message is retained when multiple users supported by the server are to receive the message. Only when the last user "deletes" the mail message does it actually disappear from the file system. Figure 5.3 illustrates the single copy message concept.

Clients typically communicate with their message store via LAN operating system file sharing facilities or remote procedure call mechanisms. File sharing over the NOS is often the only facility needed for client-to-message store communication. Where clients employ higher-level data communications protocols to access the message store, they are generally proprietary, for neither X.400's P3 and P7 standard access protocols nor Internet Mail's POP 3 are widely implemented in the LAN world.

The server message store and message transport functions are often placed on separate PCs because in many environments the local file server may be the least powerful machine in use. Such machines are fit for storage but are slow enough to become transport bottlenecks. Another more powerful machine can be used for transport instead. For example, in both the Microsoft Mail and cc:Mail filesharing architectures, the user's mailboxes are stored on a local file server, while software located on a separate dedicated machine performs the transport function of routing messages between post offices.

LAN e-mail servers from the same system typically employ a proprietary message transfer protocol, such as those for cc:Mail, Microsoft Mail, or Word-Perfect Office. Message transfer operates as an application over existing LAN bridges, dedicated X.25 lines, or dial-up lines. Basic routing and retransmission capabilities are provided. When two servers from the same vendor run on two different NOSs or when they are geographically remote, asynchronous modems, X.25 modems, or special gateways are needed between the two. Where access to standards-based backbones is required, a separate PC is usually needed to fill the role of a gateway.

Directories in the traditional LAN e-mail architecture are likewise simple, typically consisting of user-configurable address books on the client, shared directories on the server, or both. These directories are usually little more than text files stored in a fixed field format. The user can scroll through the directory or search on such fields as last name. A hotkey approach is often employed, where, as the user types the characters of a last name, the listing rapidly adjusts to display those entries matching the partially typed name. In early LAN e-mail architectures, directory synchronization (even between servers by the same vendors) was usually not available as an off-the-shelf offering.

5.1.3 Advanced LAN E-mail Architectures

The art of LAN messaging has grown more complex as unrelenting competition selects the best-of-breed in products and as large customers demand much larger and more manageable systems than previously required. As messaging grows more complex, LAN e-mail vendors distribute functions that formerly resided in a single server into multiple-server implementations. They are also gradually moving from simple file-sharing access techniques to more robust client-server techniques that will improve client control and signaling functionality, ramp up performance, reduce errors, and improve recoverability. Banyan has long incorporated client-server protocols in its architecture, and both Microsoft and Lotus are moving in that direction. LAN e-mail post office, server, and gateway products are becoming more robust thanks to the use of Windows, NT, UNIX, and OS/2 in place of DOS.

As noted in Chapter 3, all LAN e-mail functions—clients, servers, message stores, gateways, and directories—are becoming modular. This modularization is in response to customer demands for open architectures and the realization by vendors that their products must be able to interface to the products of their strategic partners (or even their competitors) in order to keep pace in the messaging technology race. The decoupling of messaging functionality into multivendor components is the mark of a maturing industry. One source observes that twenty-five years ago stereos came from a single vendor in an elaborate cabinet; today they are modular so that customers can buy speakers, CD players, and receivers from different manufacturers [SOFT93]. Clients are becoming decoupled from servers so that the same vendor may not provide both halves of the client-server equation. For example, Reach Software Corporation provides an "open client" that works with Banyan Vines or NetWare MHS transport. By making the industry more efficient, modularization is enabling a features explosion.

Vendors build libraries based on APIs, such as VIM and MAPI, which allow users or third party developers to plug and play. In some configurations, one can utilize Product X's user interface with Product Y's directory and Product Z's message store. By providing many such niches for third party offerings, modularization provides opportunities to small vendors in a Darwinian market that otherwise tends to coalesce around a few popular implementations.[1]

LAN e-mail architectures are advancing on the directories front as well. Although directories tend to remain simple in format, more advanced LAN e-mail

---

1. For the purposes of illustration, we note that Beyond, Inc., in addition to offering its own mail system, also lines its corporate wallet with the proceeds from a product called "Winrules," which is expressly designed to interwork with Microsoft Mail via MAPI.

architectures today are providing richer search capabilities, such as searching on the comments field as well as the last name field. Directory synchronization is now usually available between servers from the same vendor as exemplified by cc:Mail's Automatic Directory Exchange and Novell's NetWare Directory Services. Third party developers are building synchronization clients to popular mail systems, such as cc:Mail and Microsoft, using available server interfaces (such as the Import/Export API in the case of older cc:Mail versions). Synchronization clients download the updates from a master directory and apply them to the local directory. They compare the local directory with a snapshot they have kept from a previous synchronization run and upload the changes to the master. Local messaging system vendors are building interfaces that make it easier to import and export directory information for synchronization to third party implementations in the fashion described.

As enterprise LAN messaging networks become larger and more mission critical, many users will attempt to leverage cost savings by centralizing the management of distributed LAN sites. Multiple-server management capabilities then become much more important. (Greater integration of LAN e-mail management with the management of other LAN facilities such as files, printers, databases, and fax servers is also essential to support administrative cost cutting.) Vendors such as Banyan and Novell are laboring to satisfy the scalability and integration requirements by providing integrated, object-oriented directories whose information trees (like those of X.500 systems) span multiple LANs and departmental organizations. Other LAN e-mail vendors are struggling to provide utilities that can manage routing information in a unified fashion for a network of servers, rather than for just one server at a time.

5.1.4   Just Beyond the Leading Edge

Somewhat further out along the e-mail evolutionary timeline we can anticipate several key trends already discussed. These trends will include the convergence of e-mail and groupware systems and later the convergence of e-mail and artificial intelligence. These trends are already manifest in the integration of e-mail, calendaring systems, and electronic forms at the low end [DAWS93A]. They will eventually culminate in the integration of e-mail and workflow systems based on smart messaging techniques at the high end, and in the emergence of e-mail clients and message stores that are tightly integrated with enterprise applications and enterprise databases.

5.2   LOCAL AND LAN E-MAIL FEATURES

Because local messaging systems share some or all of the architectural characteristics just discussed, the most important gating factor in a user's decision to select one brand over another is not architecture but the given product's position in a never-ending features race. Two years ago, we developed an exhaustive list of e-mail features [BLUM92], only to discover that a significant number of new ones have since surfaced!

Multiple user interface or mail-enabled application features are available today. We have included the most important features in Table 5.1. The table identifies basic features present in most reasonably complete mail systems. Basic

Feature	Basic	Remarks
Basic User Interface Features (5.2.1)		
Send, read, delete, and scan	Yes	Basic
Forwarding and replying to messages	Yes	Basic
Editing capabilities	Yes	Basic
Request and receive *status* of message	No	Common, very important
Online help	No	Common
Basic Message Formats (5.2.2)		
Heading fields	Yes	Basic
Message body / text	Yes	Basic
Attachments	No	Common, interworking problematic
User Interface Features for Remote Access (5.2.3)		
Access and security	Yes	Basic
Upload / download	Yes	Basic
Commonality of interface	No	Emerging
Appropriateness of interface	No	Emerging
Single, or virtual, mailbox	No	Future
Other Client/User Interface Features (5.2.4)		
International character set display	No	Unusual, international requirement
API access	No	Common
Cross platform support / modularity	No	Emerging
Alerting	No	Common
Mailbox rules processing	No	Emerging
Bulletin board systems	No	Common
Accessories	No	Common
Extensibility	No	Emerging
Printing	No	Common
Terminate and stay resident (TSR)	No	Common (DOS products)
Message Formats and Fields (5.2.5)		
Electronic forms	No	Emerging, interworking problematic
Dynamic linking	No	Emerging, interworking problematic
Rubber stamps	No	Future
Privacy through encryption	No	Emerging, interworking problematic
Integrity through digital signatures	No	Emerging, interworking problematic
Voice and video annotation	No	Emerging, risk assessment needed
More general conversational capabilities	No	Unusual, interworking problematic

Table 5.1 Categorization of e-mail features.

Transport (5.2.6)

Basic Transport Capabilities

Submit / deliver message	Yes	Basic
Fax access and integration	No	Common
Deferred delivery	No	Unusual
Delete outgoing message	No	Unusual, interworking unlikely
Voice-mail integration	No	Future
Printing	No	Common
Redirection	No	Unusual

Transport Interconnection Issues

Underlying network connectivity	Yes	Basic
Routing	Yes	Basic
Gateways	No	Common (see Section 5.4)

Message Store or Container Features (5.2.7)

Online storage	Yes	Basic
Folders	No	Common
Infobases	No	Future
Archiving	No	Unusual

Directory Features (5.2.8)

User access / aliases	Yes	Basic
Update	Yes	Basic
Access control	No	Common (password prompt)
Hierarchy	No	Emerging
Flexible information content	No	Emerging
Integration with the NOS	No	Emerging
Distribution lists	No	Common
Workflow-related directory features	No	Future
Directory synchronization	No	Emerging

Management and Security Features (5.2.9)

Administration of user accounts	Yes	Basic
Administration of routing information	Yes	Basic
Administration of connections	Yes	Basic
Administration of directories	Yes	Basic
Administration of storage	No	Common, sometimes done manually
E-mail health monitoring	No	Emerging
Performance management	No	Unusual
Accounting and charge back	No	Unusual, sometimes done manually
Compatibility with other management systems	No	Unavailable pending standards
Access control	No	Common, at least password-based
Auditing	No	Unusual

Table 5.1   *continued*

features include fundamental user interface, storage, directory, and transport capabilities enabling the user to send, read, delete, and scan mail; to submit and receive delivery of messages with header fields and content information; to obtain remote access to a mailbox providing online storage of messages; and to query a directory of user names and addresses. In addition, administrators should have some tools or documented procedures for administering user accounts, mail system routing information, and mail system connections. Other (nonbasic) features in the table, though not yet in widespread use, are in many cases important.

Table 5.1 groups the entire gamut of features into nine categories, organized around aspects of user interface (client) operations followed by server features, including transport, directory, message store, and management. As indicated in the table, these categories are then covered in detail in Sections 5.2.1–5.2.9. We apologize in advance for the inevitable fact that dividing functionality into these categories sometimes appears oversimplified. For example, what we might call a message store or directory feature is often reflected in the user interface as well.

Comments in Table 5.1 indicate whether a given feature is in common use (but not yet universal), whether support for it seems to be emerging, whether it is not usually found (unusual) and, in some cases, whether the feature travels well when interworking across gateways between different mail systems. Those features which are still in the visionary stage are annotated as Future.

5.2.1   Basic User Interface Features for Client Access

A moderate quantity of e-mail activity should be a blessing for users, but too many messages can turn the medium into a curse. In heavy-usage environments attributes of a user's e-mail interface make the difference between whether the user is "mail-enabled" or "mail-enslaved." Ask the traveling professional trying to wield a user interface against the Sisyphean burden of an eternally crammed mailbox, and he or she will tell you that many factors—including the quality of that interface, the appropriate use of e-mail vis-à-vis bulletin boards and alternative groupware technology, and an arsenal of advanced capabilities such as rules-based filtering—make the difference between whether e-mail is viewed as a blessing or a curse.

The first line of defense against heavy e-mail traffic is the basic user interface seen at the time of local login or access through a mail-enabled application. Such user interfaces enable users to read messages, scan summaries of waiting messages, and compose messages to their correspondents. These user interfaces also provide our passport to the server-based directory, message store, and transport functions that will be discussed below. Figure 5.4 depicts a state of the art GUI[2] LAN e-mail client, replete with radio buttons, pull-down menus, and tool bars.

Any e-mail system must offer a main course of basic features, which consists of send, read, and scan capabilities, editing capabilities, and online help. In addi-

---

2. Note that while elaborate GUIs are de rigueur for desktop workstations, they do not always scale down to small devices such as palmtops or wireless personal communicators. Designers in the palmtop realm should look to offering pen-based technology and other innovations.

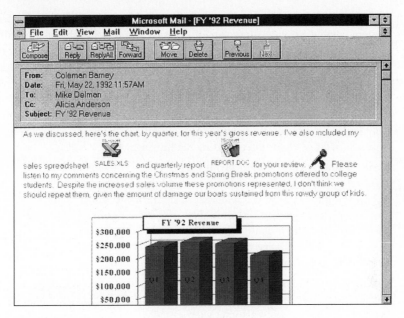

Figure 5.4   E-mail user interface example.

tion, it is desirable for mail systems to run on various platforms and to maintain an open door for mail-enabled applications.

- **Send, read, delete, and scan:** Send and read functions require little explanation, although special processing variations will be covered in our discussion of attachments and remote interfaces. User interfaces should allow the user to scan his or her mailbox for incoming messages as well as messages collected in various folders. (Each message item generally appears on a separate line with its date/time, originator name, and subject showing.) While examining scan lists, users should be able to delete unwanted messages or file messages in folders. The scanning process should enable the selecting or sorting of scan lists by name, date, subject, item read or unread status, text-search term, priority, and other criteria (or by any combination of these elements).

- **Forwarding and replying to messages:** Recall our message scenario in Chapter 2 that involved a message reply that had been forwarded among a dealership executive, parts supply manager, and engineering manager. This scenario was intended to illustrate the dynamic conversational nature of free-flowing e-mail. In fact, the user's ability to answer and forward messages during the process of reading and scanning enables the overall e-mail dynamic. The user should have the option of only replying to the originator or to the originator *and* all the other message recipients. When sending, a user should also be able to request a reply from the recipient(s). Often, much-forwarded messages become strings of information with long tails of previous replies and forwarded data.

- **Editing capabilities:** A message must be composed before it is sent. Mail systems should provide a number of compose-time options, including the ability to load information from previously created files or to launch the word processor of the user's choice. In addition, they should provide a built-in editor, either line-oriented or full-screen, with terminal emulation. More advanced note editing capabilities today include the ability to spell check, colorize, or highlight text.[3] In addition, the user must be able to store completed messages in a draft folder prior to sending, or to edit message envelope header or address fields after creating the message.

- **Request and receive status of message:** Has the recipient read the message yet? Has the purchase order been received? Users often wish to be informed automatically, via acknowledgment, of the status of important or business-related messages. Most LAN e-mail systems offer a "certified mail" capability. Also, high quality gateways are able to translate status notifications into X.400 delivery or nondelivery notifications and sometimes even into X.400 receipt or nonreceipt notifications.

- **Online help:** Online and written help, manuals, and screens should be provided. State-of-the-art e-mail systems come with interactive tutorials, video instruction, and 24-hour customer support.

5.2.2   Basic Message Formats

A basic message, sent from an originator to a recipient, consists of a routing envelope containing addressing information and a content. The nature of the routing envelope varies among systems and is highly dependent on the nature of the transport protocol. However, the envelope's content always contains a message header and a message body.

- **Heading fields:** Mail systems support different message header fields, the most common being "To," "From," "cc," "bc," and "Subject." A number of others are defined in X.400 and in RFC 822. The more standardized message header fields are supported, the better a mail system will interconnect with the rest of the world. In addition, some other X.400 fields (such as Priority), which pass through the X.400 envelope and into and out of user interfaces, should be supported.

- **Message body/attachments:** The system should be able to submit and receive attachments. It should be able to identify (usually as icons in a GUI) and launch the application (spreadsheets, word processors) in which the attachment was created. It should allow the user to configure new attachments and launch procedures. The client component, the server/backbone infrastructure, or both should be able to perform both horizontal (crossvendor) and vertical (crossplatform) format conversions, or they should at least be extensible enough to allow the user to plug in and launch third party conversion utilities.

---

3. Unfortunately, highlighted or colorized text in many e-mail user interfaces imposes interoperability problems.

5.2.3 User Interface Features for Remote Access

Woe to the traveling professional caught flatfooted without access to the mail system! Remote access, needed for personal computers, laptops, palmtops, and terminals, should be provided with the following features:

- **Access and security:** A remote access capability may allow the user to dial into a mailbox on a local e-mail system and make use of normal send, read, scan, and other basic functions from that point. However, such access raises user interface, cost, and security issues. Not every enterprise wishes to pay for a dedicated phone line (or lines) into a host or server; moreover, some companies consider the dial-up interface a security risk.

- **Upload/download:** A remote access capability should enable users to upload and download both text and binary files. The protocol used should be efficient. Incredible as it may seem, the authors have experienced upload/download times *for the same file on the same host* ranging from approximately four minutes to one hour (over a 9600 kb link) depending on the communications packages and protocols employed.

- **Commonality of interface:** Ideally, the remote user interface should look and feel the same as the local user interface to which the user is accustomed. However, some GUI features do not travel well even over the new (cheaper) crop of 14.4 Kbps V.42 bis modems.

- **Appropriateness of interface:** The remote user interface should be devised with sensitivity to response time issues. Before downloading messages, for example, a smart interface might display the size of the messages or allow the user to select which messages to download. While downloading or uploading messages, the users should be free to pursue other activities inside the mail program or outside of it in other applications—all this without any noticeable slowdown in system responsiveness. In addition, the smart interface would allow users to craft rules concerning the handling of messages while traveling (reply to all incoming messages with a notice of unavailability).

- **Single or virtual mailbox:** Surely every traveling professional's dream is to possess a single virtual mailbox. Before leaving the office, one could load the mailbox contents onto a laptop or notebook computer. While traveling, the desktop mailbox executes, adds, deletes, and changes its contents as new messages arrive and rules are executed. Certain classes of messages might be forwarded via a wireless e-mail service to the notebook mailbox, which is also undergoing changes as new mail arrives, rules execute, and the user reads and composes mail. But what is "virtual" about this? Simply that, during idle times, the user could run a utility to synchronize the desktop and notebook mailboxes over the phone line.

5.2.4 Other Client/User Interface Features

More sophisticated user interfaces go beyond the basic fare described above to offer capabilities such as international character set displays, enabling features for applications, mailbox rules processing, bulletin boards, an extensible user interface, and group scheduling or conference capabilities.

- **International character set display:** In providing environmental flexibility, vendors should bow to the desires of non-English speakers already suffering in an ASCII-dominated world. That is, the IA5 (ASCII) character set should be supported and configurable for different national character sets. European and other international users require support for their national characters, 305 of which are in the T.61 set. However, T.61 has met with disfavor in practical applications. The ISO 8859 character set standard is accepted in Western Europe as a stopgap until the more general ISO 10646 character set standard (which also supports Kanji and other Asian languages) is available.

- **API access:** Vendors should also salute our trusty digital assistants, the mail-enabled applications (word processors, calendaring systems, and spreadsheets). For these applications, API access of some kind, preferably compliant with the XAPIA's CMC [XAPI93] and VIM or MAPI, is desirable for maximum portability. Messaging capabilities in the OS often include optional dialog windows that pop up when the mail-enabled application calls on a send function. In addition, high-level scripting capabilities like those embodied in Microsoft's Visual Basic and made available through Dynamic Data Exchange (DDE) are useful for rapid mail enabling. (DDE is the Microsoft mechanism used to communicate between mail-enabled applications, such as a word processor or a spreadsheet, and an e-mail system when a user selects the "Mail" option.)

- **Cross platform support/modularity:** Major e-mail systems today operate on multiple client platforms (PC, Macintosh, UNIX, X terminals, and others), with similar functionality and look and feel in each environment. Ideally the mail system client should itself be decoupled from the server engine, obtaining access via a specified API. In this way, server vendors may build drivers to popular clients.

- **Alerting:** The system should alert users when new mail arrives at their mailbox. Alerts can be issued by beeping the terminal, flashing an onscreen message, or changing the color of a graphical icon.

- **Mailbox rules processing:** The UA should support alerting, filing or foldering, forwarding, deleting, and acknowledging messages using user-defined rules that examine message fields such as the Originator Name, Subject, Priority, or even keywords within the text. Rules-based mail capabilities were first pioneered in the LAN e-mail environment by BeyondMail [STRE92]. An industry joke has it that the BeyondMail user could go on vacation for six months, leave behind a set of mailbox rules linked to the Eliza package (an artificially intelligent computer program able to make conversation), and nobody would realize that he had left the company! Another quip gives rise to interesting questions about the social implications of e-mail: "Suppose you asked me why I didn't come to your party, and I told you that I never received the invitation. If the reason I never received the invitation was that it was filtered by my mailbox rules, did I just tell a lie?"[4]

- **Bulletin board systems (BBS):** BBSs are a somewhat neglected feature of e-mail. Mail glut problems can stem from the fact that users are on too many distribution lists and that they are receiving junk traffic that really should be posted on a BBS. Bulletin boards should act like shared e-mail folders and should also allow users to obtain summaries of items and new postings and alerts to new postings based on rules-based criteria. In addition to making bulletin boards available, enterprises concerned about mail glut should also institute appropriate training for administrators to ensure that they weed out junk distribution lists. Mail users should be trained to use the BBS when appropriate, to monitor their use of, or presence on, distribution lists continually, and to manage their e-mail online time wisely.[5]

- **Accessories:** Most LAN e-mail packages are currently shipped with accessories such as "chat" electronic conferencing programs and group scheduling (or calendaring) capabilities. Calendaring tools allow users to schedule meetings automatically. They mail invitations to prospective attendees whose calendars are then checked and appropriate responses mailed back automatically [DAWS93A]. In some cases, however, acquiring e-mail platform-dependent scheduling software can be a trap for unwary users who later discover they would have preferred a crossplatform scheduling utility. In this regard, availability of group scheduling in PROFS has often been cited as a disincentive for users to downsize to a LAN e-mail package.

- **Extensibility:** Some clients allow the front-end GUI to be extended by third party developers and end users. This approach permits the addition of menu items and iconic buttons that activate special procedures affecting message addresses, text, attachments, or other fields. Extensibility is sometimes offered at runtime, otherwise it is available only at install or compile time. One e-mail vendor representative boasts that his LAN e-mail user interface is so customizable that it can be put into what he calls "subliminal PROFS" mode, where it could be made to respond to function keys in much the same fashion as that venerable mainframe e-mail program.

- **Printing:** The user should be able to print a message, a folder of messages, or a group of messages by pressing a mouse button or function key.

- **Terminate and stay resident (TSR):** For the single tasking DOS operating system, "popup" Terminate and Stay Resident (TSR) capabilities should be offered. These capabilities can then be activated from deep within another

---

4. Esther Dyson, EDVenture Holdings, spoke at the 1992 San Francisco EMA conference regarding the social implications of e-mail filtering.

5. The author remembers missing a critical note amidst of forest of waiting messages on one hand and, on the other, missing a critical deadline while attempting to deal with piles of low-priority junk mail.

program by touching a function key. One such LAN e-mail program, Notework, can run in less than 5K of precious DOS main memory. Upon sending a Notework message, the user is presented with an animated sequence of a colorful envelope traveling across the screen, which is to say the least unique.

5.2.5   Message Formats and Fields

We are in the process of transitioning from decades of text-oriented interpersonal messaging to a more dynamic era of multimedia message formats used by both people and very active mail-enabled applications. A number of important features regarding message formats and fields include

- **Electronic forms:** E-mail systems today often come equipped with built-in, customizable forms for common office interactions such as phone messages. This feature should allow users/administrators to define their own forms for posting in personal/shared menus. It should allow a user to send a form to a recipient that the recipient will then fill out. Unfortunately, such forms are not standardized and therefore dissimilar across e-mail systems. However, third party form vendors (Jetforms, Delrina, and PerForm Pro) are active in the marketplace, and both the MHS Alliance and the XAPIA are developing standards for forms.

- **Dynamic linking:** Dynamic linking capabilities such as Object Linking and Embedding (OLE) under Microsoft Windows can be of assistance in generating ad hoc workflow or mail-enabled applications. For example, a weekly status report could consist of a short header added to an attachment which is linked to a spreadsheet file containing weekly sales figures. Such reports can be sent with a minimum of effort and always contain the most current available information.

- **Rubber stamps:** One way to make e-mail user interfaces and message displays more attractive is through the use of rubber stamps, which an originator can drag and drop into the message during message preparation. Examples of rubber stamps in General Magic's Magic Cap operating system (to our knowledge, the first to employ this feature) are "CONFIDENTIAL," "URGENT," a happy face, a sad face, and so forth. Some rubber stamps embody intelligence; for example, use of the "CONFIDENTIAL" stamp signals the system to encrypt the message.

- **Privacy using encryption:** Users often need to send sensitive messages in encrypted form. Some local mail systems encrypt messages before transferring them between hosts or servers. However, messages are usually not encrypted when stored and thus may fall into the wrong hands. Moreover, when messages leave the local messaging environment, they must first be decrypted at a gateway, unless a standard such as 1988 X.400 or the Internet's Privacy Enhanced Mail is utilized.

- **Integrity using digital signatures:** Users often need to send messages of legal or financial significance (value bearing) in a signed form that prevents them from being modified en route to the recipient(s). Signatures can also authenticate the originator of the message and can be applied to delivery reports to prove that the recipient received the message. Few local mail systems offer such capability. Moreover, when messages leave the local messaging environment, the digital signature becomes useless unless a standard such as 1988 X.400 or the Internet's Privacy Enhanced Mail is utilized in its formation.

- **Voice and video annotation:** The client should allow users to insert voice (and, in the future, video) annotations or to play voice annotations from correspondents. Other prospective features might include the display of a photograph of the sender or the capability for users to scan electronic photograph albums as a directory function. A point of warning, however: today's infrastructures (queues, disks, processors, gateways, backbone switches, and communications links) are not equipped to handle heavy use of true multimedia information. Users should conduct a risk assessment of their organizations' vulnerability to intentional or unintentional abuse of large attachments in conventional e-mail systems.

5.2.6   Transport Features

Transport features are essential to the movement of messages between users. Given the manner in which e-mail has evolved, one can think of the infrastructure of departmental hosts or local LAN e-mail servers as small streams flowing into larger rivers (enterprise backbones), which, in turn, flow into oceans (global messaging networks). If we consider all aspects of the passage of messages through these "waterways," then transport issues could be grouped in terms of basic transport capabilities apparent to the user, broader interconnectivity issues, and administrative issues related to transport.

Basic Transport Capabilities

The following basic transport capabilities should be available (and visible) to the user:

- **Submit/deliver message:** The user must be able to submit messages for transport and delivery. Messages must also be delivered to their mailbox.

- **Fax access and integration:** Users often wish to use their convenient e-mail interface to dispatch fax, telex, or postal missives. Such features have long been offered by public service providers, and fax gateways at least are almost de rigueur features of the LAN e-mail environment. Ideally, fax gateways should support inbound and outbound facsimile transmission, receipt, and display. On receipt, dial-in-direct (DID) lines should be configured in the PBX and supported by mail system routing to deliver facsimiles directly to the user's mailbox. (Alternatively, newly minted ITU standards for sub-addressing can be used.) Upon fax display, the user should be able to magnify or rotate the view. E-mail and fax integration may become even more compelling when Microsoft At Work-capable fax machines begin transmitting computer-generated messages containing Binary File Transfer (BFT) data as described in Chapter 2.

- **Deferred delivery:** This capability, an X.400 feature, enables originators to request that message delivery be deferred to a specific date and time.

- **Delete outgoing message:** In conversation, we sometimes say things we regret; as in conversation, so in e-mail. The seasoned user has probably often wished to retract a message once sent. Some systems allow outgoing messages to be deleted, even after they have been delivered on remote systems, provided they have not been read by the recipient.[6] Deletion of outgoing messages that have traveled to other servers (and foreign mail systems or foreign mail domains) requires a nonstandard protocol exchange between message switches. This feature is generally not available except when the originator and recipients utilize the same mail system.

- **Voice mail integration:** Constantly checking two mailboxes—e-mail and voice mail—is often inconvenient. Some farsighted vendors are focusing on the opportunity to integrate the media at least partially. Voice-mail systems could announce the number of waiting e-mail messages and other information requested through touchtone phone voice-response systems used as a means of access to the mailbox. Messages could then be read aloud by the computer. The e-mail system (given prodigious quantities of storage space) could download voice messages into files, play them, and allow them to be incorporated as attachments to messages.

- **Redirection:** The user (or administrator) should be able to designate a mailbox where incorrectly addressed messages can be processed. Also useful is a capability allowing users who are traveling or on vacation to redirect their messages to another mailbox.

Transport Interconnection Issues

There are also a number of interconnection issues associated with the transport of messages. Some of these, such as underlying network connectivity and routing, must be considered.

---

6. WordPerfect Office touted this featured in a 1993 release. Dialcom (a public e-mail service now merged with BT Tymnet) long offered deletion of outgoing messages, though only when the recipient and the sender were colocated on the same host.

- **Underlying network connectivity:** Message transport cannot occur without underlying network connectivity. LAN internetwork transport can be rendered fairly transparent to LAN e-mail servers with the use of routers and bridging equipment. LAN e-mail servers should and usually do support X.25 and asynchronous (dial-up) access. However, many well-conceived strategic plans foundered on network incompatibilities, such as the inability of a single LAN server to connect to clients residing on more than one NOS (for example, NetWare and LAN Manager). Plans have also foundered on network congestion, resulting (in one example) from the inability to add another Remote Job Entry (RJE) session to support a mail gateway via SNA to an IBM host. Because e-mail tends to expose any underlying weaknesses in a network, users should investigate the bandwidth limitations of servers over different network interfaces, since this will prove of critical importance when heavy volumes of remote message traffic are experienced or when users utilize the messaging network to transfer large objects such as engineering drawings, video, or voice attachments.

- **Routing:** All message switches, whether they are located in a lowly LAN e-mail server, in an enterprise backbone, or on a public messaging service, should provide the administrator with the ability to control the manner in which they route messages to other message switches. In general, there are several ways that routing can be handled including: (1) the extraction of the route directly from the address; (2) table lookup of an address components (such as the workgroup in a Novell MHS address); or (3) lookup of address components in a directory such as Banyan's StreetTalk or the Internet's DNS. Tables or directories may enable routing data aggregation, where all users in a workgroup or domain share a route, or they may facilitate routing down to the individual user level.

- **Gateways:** Section 5.4 discusses gateways in detail.

5.2.7   Message Store or Container Features

Local e-mail systems generally provide a message store capability where delivered messages can be held indefinitely on a host or a server, both before and after they are read. Some vendor product documentation refers to message stores as containers. The following are important message store features for LAN e-mail and other local messaging environments:

- **Online storage:** The system should furnish storage for unread mail, read mail, filed mail, and other user information. It should be possible to organize filed mail in folders. Even after the mail is filed, the user should be able to annotate it with useful information for later reference. System administrators should be able to impose quotas on how much storage a user is allowed to have.

- **Folders:** Mail-system defined folders (such as Draft, Trash, Desk, Out box, In box, Phone Messages, and File by Sender Name) should be provided.

These are personal folders belonging exclusively to one user. The system should also provide shared folders for a group. (In some cases, overlap between group or shared folders and bulletin board functionality may occur.) The system should allow users to define their own folders and types of folders. Some products offer hierarchical folders, online compression, associative links between messages, and database-style features such as keyword search. Message sorting on priority, sender, subject, date/time, and status can be provided within folders.

- **Infobases:** Because foldering systems have become more sophisticated, technologists have been inspired by the possibility that messages on bulletin boards and e-mail folders could become more than potentially useful junk. Filed messages could become an organizational information resource, where the history and thought processes underlying organizational decisions would be collected. The development of such capabilities, wherein e-mail becomes part of an enterprise database, represents a leading edge trend in the industry.

- **Archiving:** The user should be able to request the archiving of messages, groups of messages, or folders of filed messages. The user may wish to edit messages to remove extraneous parts prior to archiving. Archiving may occur in online document libraries or in offline tape or optical libraries.[7] The user should be able to scan the archives and request the retrieval of archived items. During cleanup operations where outdated mail is removed for storage reclamation by the client, the mail should be placed in short term (for example, 90 days) archives and a notification should be mailed to the user.

5.2.8   Directory Features

A local e-mail directory provides a list of user names and sufficient information to enable message addressing at minimum. These directories are sometimes called address books in product literature. While retaining their original ease-of-use, directories are gradually becoming more sophisticated as enterprises deploy larger LAN messaging networks and struggle to integrate them with other e-mail products. Important features are

- **User access:** Users should have very fast and flexible search capabilities on a variety of fields and should be able to view results on a variety of sorts. Many LAN e-mail directory user interfaces support an interfacing technique known as point and pick or hotkeying, where the user interface immediately adjusts the display (sometimes called a *picklist*) to show those names that match the characters as they are input by the user without waiting for a carriage return from the user.

---

7. In some cases, e-mail must be held indefinitely for public record or freedom of information purposes. For this reason, the White House was prevented by a judge from deleting the Reagan/Bush Administration's staff correspondence.

- **Update:** In some cases, users are allowed to update their own directory entries or to add information about external correspondents in other companies with whom they communicate regularly.

- **Access control:** Directory software should impose access controls over usage, especially for directory updates. Access controls should restrict access to certain directory operations against certain entries/fields according to the identity of the user.

- **Hierarchy:** Increasingly, local messaging directories are supporting hierarchical structures, wherein users are collected in groups (called *organizational units* or *localities* in X.500 and workgroups in Novell parlance).[8] Hierarchical LAN directories are advertised as X.500-like, meaning that the information structures are more or less compatible with X.500, but that X.500 protocols are not yet supported. A hierarchical directory organization is beneficial in limiting the number of entries users have to page through when addressing a message or finding a correspondent in another workgroup. If available, hierarchy should be employed when directories are very large (more than a few thousand names), but the structures defined should not be too elaborate or deep.

- **Information content:** Some local messaging directories only list first name, last name, a description field, and/or an address field. Address fields are generally capable of containing the local addresses belonging to users on the same server, the remote addresses of users on remote servers belonging to the same mail system, or the foreign addresses of users in other mail systems. In addition, as LAN e-mail directories become X.500-like, they will tend to support additional information fields, such as telephone numbers or photographs, and additional information types, such as organizational roles.

- **Integration with the NOS:** In some cases (Novell's NetWare 4.x and Banyan's StreetTalk) the e-mail directory and the directory of LAN users are one and the same, providing increased convenience for the administrator. Such combined NOS/e-mail directories may contain information about printers, databases, files, services, and other resources on the network. Even vendors such as Microsoft and cc:Mail who compete with Novell and use separate directories, continually work to facilitate NOS directory integration by providing users the option of populating their directory with NetWare NOS directory contents.

- **Distribution lists:** Many local messaging products support personal distribution lists, shared distribution lists, or both. Sometimes such lists can be nested; that is, the ALL-EMPLOYEES list points to the SALES, ENGINEERING, and other lists. Users should quantify their requirements for the number of names and the number of levels that must be supported. Access controls should be imposed on both the updating of, and submission to, shared distribution lists. Facilities should be available for cleaning up obsolete lists.

---

8. For an example of a hierarchical directory structure, see the discussion of Novell's Netware Directory Services (NDS) product in Section 5.6.

Lists should be able to contain a mixture of recipients from different e-mail systems, regardless of their address format.

- **Workflow related directory features:** Directories can contain role tables that associate individual employees with organizational roles that are focal points in workflow processes. Workflow routed mail could be addressed to roles rather than individuals, improving flexibility. Directories can contain electronic document authorization criteria describing an employee's organizational privileges, such as dollar spending limits. Authorization values could be checked automatically by workflow applications.

- **Directory synchronization:** Directory synchronization is a process that enables directory information from multiple servers within the same vendor enclave or between vendor enclaves to be exchanged automatically.

5.2.9   Management and Security Features

Inadequate management and security features are a major issue as local messaging systems become larger, mission-critical, distributed, highly interconnected, and increasingly complex. Some important features related to local and LAN e-mail administration include

- **Administration of user accounts:** Administrators need to be able to add and delete user accounts and to modify attributes, such as storage quotas, for those accounts. More advanced mail management systems allow the administrator to add an account on any server from a single screen. The system then takes care of creating the mailbox, sending the introductory message, updating the local mail directory, and replicating that directory update to the address books of remote servers.

- **Administration of routing information:** Message routing information must be configurable so that administrators can establish routes between servers or departmental hosts. Some e-mail management systems offer a global view of routing, allowing the administrator to define routes using a GUI where all the hosts or servers appear as nodes connected by lines. Other management systems require each server to be configured individually. Different models are used in performing and administering routing. For example, tables may reflect either a next hop or an end-to-end view. Routes may be direct (A to B) or indirect (A to B through C). Routing information may or may not be tightly coupled to the directory. All of the issues outlined here can have major implications for system functionality, maintainability, and performance. Administrators also appreciate the ability to define alternate routes in the event of failure or congestion. While useful support functions for routing can be easily defined within a single local messaging system, routing between different systems and domains can be very complex.

- **Administration of connections:** Each server or node in a local messaging network maintains a list (called an adjacency table or call list) of connected servers, message stores, gateways, and other components with which it communicates. Such a list contains information items such as the server's name, password, number of times to retry a connection, and other parameters. It may also indicate whether incoming calls should be accepted, outgoing calls initiated, or both.

- **Administration of directories:** Managers must be able to update user information and distribution lists or set access controls governing who is allowed to update such information. X.500-like directories are tending to support object typing, where administrators can change both the contents of entries and the very schema that controls which fields can be stored in user entries. If directory synchronization is employed for multiple directory environments, administrators must be able to control what data is synchronized, how often it is synchronized, and how the synchronization is paced; and the synchronized directories must have the ability to recover gracefully from error conditions.

- **Administration of storage:** Storage must be administered while it remains plentiful.[9] Administrators must have the means of monitoring storage availability, establishing quotas for user disk space, archiving aged messages, and billing storage back to the users if necessary. Management systems should generate alarms to attract an operator's attention when storage deficits become critical.

- **E-mail health monitoring:** Management utilities should provide a way to check on both the response and time availability of server components and to generate alarms when problems are detected.

- **Performance management:** E-mail performance must be continually tracked in order to ensure that user delivery expectations are being met. Administrators must have the means of monitoring performance statistics and of setting delay thresholds above which alarms will be generated.

- **Accounting and charge back:** In some environments, administrators wish to bill back mail usage charges to individual users or departments. To do this, administrators must be able to scan logged information, extract statistics regarding the number and size of messages sent and received, and generate reports.

- **Compatibility with other management systems:** Until recently, no e-mail management standards existed. However, management standards are now emerging from IFIP and from the IETF. Using an IETF-defined Simple Network Management Protocol (SNMP) Management Information Base (MIB) for message transfer agents, some level of interworking can be established between local messaging systems and management workstations.

---

9. In one instance, a corporate executive on a public e-mail system instructed a news tracking service to mail him all wire service stories containing the characters "IBM." The executive then failed to check his mailbox for six months! The problem was discovered when the disk for that executive (and several hundred other users) overflowed.

- **Access control:** Although e-mail's benefits are best obtained in an open environment where communication is encouraged at all levels, many enterprises have significant economic, security, or cultural reasons for wishing to put limits on the free flow of messages. System administrator-configured messaging access controls can restrict the ability of individuals or groups to send and receive messages to and from other groups or external enterprises. They may limit the privilege of assigning messages an "urgent" priority or the size or type of allowable attachments that a user can send or receive.[10] Access controls are particularly important at the enterprise boundary; that is, between companies or organizations. Often access control features are implemented in e-mail integration backbones, not in local messaging systems.

- **Auditing:** Either the user or the administrator (subject to local law or enterprise policy) should be able to request a detailed trace of all mail-related activity over some period (month, year, and so on). Such traces should indicate the originators and recipients of messages, the subjects and types of messages, and the location of archived copies of messages.

5.3   E-MAIL APIs

In Section 5.2.3, we held that the modularization of e-mail is the mark of a maturing industry. This modularization was anticipated in the 1988 X.400 and X.500 standards when open protocol interfaces were developed between UAs (clients) and MTAs (servers), and between UAs and Message Stores (servers). However, modularization has advanced in the platform environment (between mail-enabled applications and enabling UA software) as much as it has on the wire. Aiding that advance is a variety of e-mail APIs.

E-mail APIs break into two broad classes: those intended as a mechanism for clients to access a mail system (client or front-end APIs) and those intended as a mechanism for a mail system to access a client (service provider or back-end APIs). A third, less common variety of API serves as a gateway interface. This section will analyze the components of e-mail client infrastructure, differentiating client APIs from service provider APIs and messaging middleware[11] from driver functionality. Readers should note that these definitions serve as a model; vendors may use different terminology for the components of their client infrastructures.

These various types of APIs are described below. Figure 5.5 shows the common usage of the *client API*. It allows mail-user interfaces or mail-enabled applications to plug into workstation-resident program libraries that provide *middleware* functionality to process the API calls and *driver* functionality to connect to a server component. The driver and middleware functions (client infra-

---

10. Many users are concerned about the danger of receiving software viruses as e-mail attachments.

11. We appropriate the use of "middleware," more familiar in the realm of client-server architectures, to describe the layer of messaging software that exists between an e-mail client and the drivers that enable it to communicate with a server.

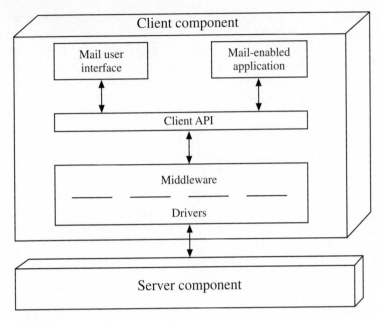

Figure 5.5 Client APIs.

structure) may be provided indistinguishably in a single program, or they may be implemented as separate libraries or modules. In cases where the infrastructure exposes only a client API, middleware and driver functionality are usually provided by the same vendor.

The middleware passes mail to and from users, formats directory (address book) requests from the API, and passes directory responses back through the subroutine calls of the API. It may provide useful functions for mail-enabled applications; for example, part of Microsoft's MAPI middleware includes a dialog box user interface component which word processors and other programs can call up when the user wants to send a message. It may provide such functions as directory picklist management to mail-user interfaces as well.

The driver function, on the other hand, interfaces to the server using one of three techniques: file sharing over the NOS, an RPC, or an access protocol.[12] Through such interfaces, messages are submitted and retrieved, and directory requests and responses are passed. The driver and server components collectively provide message transport, storage, and directory functionality.

Figure 5.6 displays a different API architecture that exposes a client API to mail-user interfaces or mail-enabled applications and a service provider API to drivers. The back-end *service provider API* enables drivers suited for a particular server component to plug into middleware that provides generic client infrastructure

---

12. Access protocols may be proprietary or standard. X.400 offers two possible access protocols: P3 and P7. Internet Mail offers several additional access protocols.

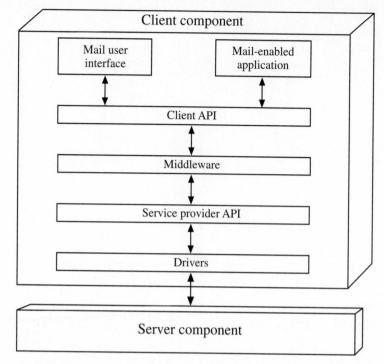

Figure 5.6 Service provider APIs.

functionality on the workstation. While the middleware and the driver collectively perform the same functions that we discussed above, they are now clearly architecturally separate from one another.

Both client APIs and service provider APIs allow users to mix and match client-server components. However, a subtle difference exists between using the two API approaches. Without a service provider API, the middleware that services the client API and the driver for the server component must come from the same vendor, or from two vendors sharing information that is not openly published about an interface. This means that a server vendor wishing to support a particular client API on a particular platform has to build both drivers and middleware for each platform where an API is to be supported.

To understand the importance of service provider APIs, consider the printer support situation in the Microsoft Windows environment, which has a service provider API for interfacing printer drivers. Not only does Windows transparently support applications wishing to print (via client printer APIs), but it also supports a choice of hundreds of different printers to print to. That would not have been possible without the use of a service provider API.

When service provider APIs are used, architectures can become highly modular. In Fig. 5.7, we see an example of e-mail driver functionality broken out into

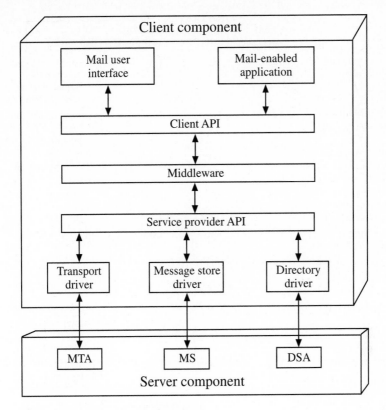

Figure 5.7   Service provider APIs.

transport, store, directory, and security functions. Such architectures are designed to allow these functional components to be provided by different vendors; that is, we can use a directory from one vendor and transport from another.

Table 5.2 classifies the major APIs in the message industry in terms of the above models. Some of these (VIM, MAPI, SMF) are discussed further in Section 5.6. In addition, a number of low-level APIs are defined for the X.400 protocol.

While APIs provide a level of modularization and while some of the promise of modularization has been realized, users wishing to mix and match clients and servers using any of the above APIs will not see the printer or stereo market degrees of modularity anytime soon. This is because of e-mail's many-to-many protocol interfaces. Thus, we can categorically state that APIs are not sufficient for full interoperability; two users of the same client product built to run over an e-mail API may not be able to interoperate unless both clients can access the same brand of server. This is because none of the APIs (other than those for X.400) say anything about the services and protocols that will be available on the wire between two servers supporting the same API. It would be possible, for instance, for a sending client to generate a message attachment, address, or message header field

API	Client interface	Service provider interface	Level of complexity	Remarks
CMC = Common Mail Calls	Yes	No	Low	Recently released by X.400 API Association as generic client API.
MAPI = Microsoft's Messaging API	Yes	Yes	Moderate	Similar in structure to Figure 5.7. See Section 5.6.2.
AOCE = Apple's Open Collaboration Environment	Yes	Yes	Moderate	Similar in architecture and intent to MAPI.
VIM = Vendor Independent messaging API	Yes	No	Moderate	From Apple, Lotus, Novell, IBM, and Borland.
SMF = Simple Message Format	Yes	Yes	Low	Interface to Novell/ Action Technologies MHS. Not really an API, but a file format for mail messages.
cc:Mail M&M API	No	Yes	Moderate	Recently released internal cc:Mail service provider API specifications.
X.400 application API	Yes	No	High	Native access to X.400 transport.

Table 5.2 Major APIs for local messaging systems in the industry

that was not supported by a receiving server or client even though the same APIs were used at both ends. Figure 5.8 diagrams the relationship between APIs, portability, and interoperability.

To improve interoperability prospects, client infrastructure components can be rendered capable of performing elementary gateway functions; for example,

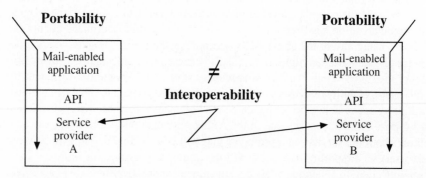

Figure 5.8 APIs, portability, and interoperability.

the API may treat the message recipient's address as an untyped string, but the infrastructure could massage the address into a more processable form before passing it to the server. It could examine the untyped address string and, depending upon whether it is a local, X.400, or Internet Mail address, assign it different processable forms through different transformations.

5.4   E-MAIL GATEWAYS

How many e-mail systems should you have? The easy answer is as few as possible because gateways between local messaging systems can be very problematic. However, many enterprises have a collection of incompatible mail systems left over from the past and must build a messaging network around those holdovers. In such cases, there may be no alternative to the use of gateways. Also, connectivity to the outside world usually requires gateways unless a standard protocol is used within the enterprise. Tomes could be written on the subject of gateways. We will provide a basic introduction here and raise the subject of gateways at various other points throughout the book.

5.4.1   Types of Gateways

A gateway is a component that translates (or maps) messages from one e-mail system (or protocol) to another. Architecturally, there are three types of gateways: point-to-point gateways, standards-based gateways, and multiway gateways. Figure 5.9 illustrates the three types of gateways with an example of a point-to-

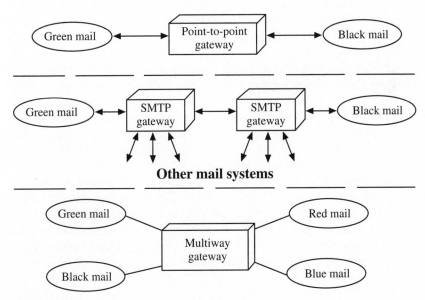

Figure 5.9   Point-to-point and standards-based gateway alternatives.

point gateway between "Green Mail" and "Black Mail," a pair of SMTP gateways to these (somewhat suspect) mail systems, and a multiway gateway between these and other mail systems. Real-world examples of such gateways would be Microsoft's IBM PROFS gateway (point-to-point), Microsoft Mail's X.400 Gateway (standards-based), and AlisaMail (multiway).

We can make some qualitative judgments about point-to-point and multiway gateways versus standards-based gateways. Architecturally, point-to-point or multiway gateways provide a *direct* translation between two local messaging protocols and offer a potentially superior mapping service[13] to that available via a pair of standards-based gateways. This is because standards-based gateways provide an *indirect* translation, first mapping into the standard form before mapping to the target form. Consider that if Green Mail supports feature X, which is similar to Black Mail's feature X', a pair of standards-based gateways linking the two systems could only supply the mapping if the standard protocol in question supports a feature X'' that is similar to X and X'.

On the other hand, standards-based gateways supply many-to-many mappings, since they exist for almost any product. A user deploying a new mail system with a standards-based gateway can be virtually assured of its ability to interoperate (at some level) with other mail systems. In this way, standards-based gateways protect the user's investment.

In most cases, a multiway gateway can double as a standards-based gateway, since virtually every e-mail integration product supports X.400, SMTP, or both. In fact, many e-mail integration servers base their internal format of messages and addresses on X.400. Vendors frequently choose X.400 as a gateway protocol because of its international mandate and because its extensive battery of features make it a superset of many mail systems. Other vendors choose SMTP as their gateway protocol because of its low cost of implementation and its native support in many UNIX-based environments. As SMTP is enhanced with MIME and other extensions, however, it will provide a wider and more attractive features pipe for gateway vendors.

For users with three or more local messaging systems, deploying a backbone e-mail integration server implementing standards-based or multiway gateway functionality can be less expensive and more manageable than maintaining groupings of point-to-point gateways. The backbone user's first concern should be connectivity to internal messaging systems and to standards-based environments. Another important concern may be the system's ability to *tunnel* features of a proprietary messaging protocol through the backbone.

Note that in all cases, gateway facilities can be private (owned and operated by the user) or public (owned and operated by a public service provider). Also, gateway functionality can be implemented in different physical configurations. In some cases, the gateway functionality is built directly onto the server or host that houses the e-mail system to which connectivity is being provided. An example of this is Digital's Message Router PROFS gateway, which shares a VAX with a

---

13. In practice, the quality of individual gateways depends more on their implementation than on the theoretical approach.

Message Router and, potentially, an ALL-IN-ONE Mail server. In other cases, such as Digital's PC-based Postmaster gateway to cc:Mail, the gateway must be on a separate dedicated system.

5.4.2   Gateway Functions

Gateway components translate messages from one e-mail system to another. What then are the functional elements of that translation? They can be broken down into seven elements:

- Header fields mapping
- Message Body Part (attachment) mapping
- Address mapping and reply capability
- Status indication mapping
- Security attribute mapping
- Tunneling
- Network connectivity

Figure 5.10 displays the basic elements of message mapping through gateways. We will discuss each of these gateway operation elements, with due attention to some of the problem cases (or horror stories).

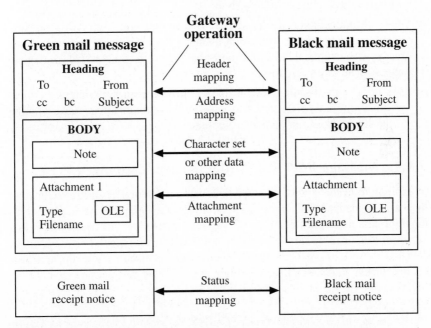

Figure 5.10.   Gateway mapping functions. *Note: X.400, MIME, and some other protocols support even more complex message structures than the one illustrated here.*

5.4.3   Header Fields Mapping

A message's content (as distinguished from its envelope) is generically composed of two parts: a *header* and a *body*. Messages are modeled this way in X.400, SMTP/RFC 822, and in many LAN e-mail systems. The header consists of a variety of fields; the body consists of one or more body parts or attachments. To the extent that message envelope fields are shown to recipients and thus acquire end-to-end significance, we will treat them as conceptually being part of the header.[14] The first body part is called a *note* in some mail systems.

As one might expect, it is generally the case that different e-mail systems based on different standards (or no standards) will implement different header fields. Beyond the obvious header fields that are almost universally implemented—*To, From, cc, Subject*—there is little commonality in the field. In mapping header fields between different e-mail systems, gateways often take the following actions:

- Perform an exact mapping; for example, between X.400's Subject field and RFC 822's Subject field.

- Perform an exact but flawed mapping between, for example, X.400's Subject field and the 80-character Subject field of a proprietary mail system, which can result in truncation. Also heading fields using international character sets do not map between many mail systems.

- Perform a partial mapping, such as between Microsoft Mail's Priority field with five levels and X.400's, with three.

- Take a heading field from the source e-mail system and insert it into the body of the message for the destination e-mail system. This can, however, wreak havoc with mail-enabled applications that expect the body of the message to appear in some precise format.

- Not convey the heading field to the destination mail system. Here critical information may be lost, such as when the X.400 Sensitivity field with the value "Company Confidential" is omitted.

5.4.4   Message Body Part (Attachment) Mapping

In addition to header fields, message body parts (sometimes called attachments) must also be mapped. This transformation involves mapping both attachment typing information and attachment data. Picture an attachment that began its life as a Word for Windows Version 2.0 file on the PC and was sent by a one user (whom we will call Bob) in a mail message to another user (Allison). Within the message, the attachment could contain an identifier, or tag, for the destination system to use in processing the file and its contents.

---

14. An example of a user-visible envelope field is X.400's Priority indication, which is part of the envelope but is also meant to be conveyed to the recipient and is often displayed by user interfaces to X.400 systems.

The following problems arise with attachment mapping and must be solved by gateways:

- E-mail systems use different forms of attachment identifiers or, in some cases, do not identify attachments. When present, attachment typing information must be either mapped or omitted. For example, a Microsoft Mail system would convey typing information about Bob's Word file internally. When Bob's file leaves for a 1984 X.400 system, it becomes an unidentified body part. When it leaves for a 1988 X.400 system, the file becomes an external body part with an X.400 Object Identifier corresponding to Word for Windows Version 2.0.

- Additional attachment typing information may consist of filenames or other file-heading information. This information can be difficult to map through point-to-point gateways; however, 1992 X.400 and Internet Mail's MIME now offer some useful capabilities.

- Attachment data may not be in the correct format for the destination system. Going from a system that supports binary attachments (X.400 and most LAN e-mail systems) to a system that does not (older SMTP systems), Bob's Microsoft Word file attachment may need to be uuencoded (a process of converting every three octets of binary data into four octets of seven-bit ASCII data) or amputated from the message. Indeed, the entire message may be rejected. Even textual data may suffer in translation because some systems use different international character sets or impose maximum line lengths. Outside English-speaking countries, these character set issues are critical.

- Two e-mail systems may both support binary data passage, but they may not support the conveyance of Object Linking and Embedding (OLE) in the same fashion. Thus, Bob's Word file may be ill fated if it has embedded spreadsheet or graphic information using OLE (or an equivalent mechanism such as the emerging Apple/IBM OpenDoc standard).

- Two e-mail systems may support the format of an attachment, but conversion of that data may be required between platforms. For instance, while Bob uses Microsoft Word, Allison may only accept WordPerfect files. Many gateways perform attachment format conversion, although there is much theoretical debate over whether this is an appropriate function for a gateway.

- Mail systems may support a limited number of attachments in a single message. SNADS, for example, supports only one. Thus, a message with 16 attachments going to a SNADS domain must be rejected or mapped to 16 separate messages.

Often e-mail systems earmark an area of the message content between the header and the attachments for conveying a Note from the originator to the recipient. In the past, the note object was usually textual in nature and therefore relatively easy to map. However, some LAN e-mail vendors are now adding allowing richer text in the note, with color, highlighting, bold, italic, and other font changes.

Since there is no widely accepted standard format for such embellishments, they are usually lost through gateways.

5.4.5   Address Mapping and Reply Capability

We have purposely omitted discussing address fields until now because they present unique problems in their own right. Addresses consist of the recipient's address, the originator's address, and the address of users to whom the message has been copied (the copy list). When a gateway processes a message, it must map the incoming addresses to outgoing addresses in such a manner that the message can be delivered by the destination e-mail system and so that the message recipient can reply to the message originator or copy recipients.

Gateways usually perform address mapping using one of three strategies: directory address substitution, algorithmic address substitution, or address encapsulation. With directory address substitution, the gateway simply looks in a directory and, for example, determines that the entry for recipient *Allison Smith* in Bob's cc:Mail directory corresponds to a RFC 822 user address *Allison.Smith@ plastics.sales.anycorp.com.* Directory substitution can offer complete flexibility where any address can map to any other, but it can be costly to administer.

With algorithmic address substitution, the gateway examines the incoming address and utilizes parts of the incoming address to compose an outgoing address. For example, suppose Allison uses a SNADS-based mail system. Her *Allison Smith* entry in Bob's cc:Mail directory must now correspond to the SNADS address *DGN=AS400 ; DEN=ASMITH.*[15] Alternatively, mapping might be done by a gateway, which could default her DGN to AS400 and create the DEN using the leading character of her cc:Mail first name and the first seven characters of her last name. Algorithmic substitution of this kind is easy to administer but is inflexible. Gateways are prone to bugs when dealing with users having unusual names. Also, algorithmic address mapping gone awry can lead to misdelivered mail—for example, where two different incoming addresses map to the same outgoing address.

With address encapsulation (sometimes called "two hop" addressing) part of the incoming address becomes the entire outgoing address. For example, the Internet Mail address *"C=US/A=MCI/P=ANYCORP/S=SMITH G=ALLISON"@ gateway.anycorp.com* could correspond to the X.400 address *C=US/A=MCI/P= ANYCORP/S=SMITH/G=ALLISON.*[16] This technique is flexible and requires no administration; but pity poor Bob who had to type in that convoluted address! (The X.400 standard refers to this form of the address as being the mnemonic form. When

---

15. SNADS addresses consist of two eight-character components: the Distribution Group Name (DGN) and the Distribution Entry Name (DEN). The DGN identifies the messaging node, or MTA, and the DEN the user.

16. X.400 addresses are covered in full in Chapter 6. The address subfields from our example denote, respectively, C: Country, A: Administration Domain, P: Private Domain, S: Surname, G: Given Name.

further combined with the Internet address, however, we might better term it the demonic form!)

Further measures related to address mapping in a gateway include *auto-registration*, which can enable a user to reply to a message from an originator in a foreign messaging system. For example, it is almost always impossible for a PROFS user, who is limited to two eight-character address fields, to create or receive an X.400 address. In such cases, gateways will often map a short PROFS alias address to a longer X.400 address. The alias may be created manually by an administrator and retained in a directory on the gateway or it may be auto-registered on the fly by the gateway when it receives an incoming X.400 message for the PROFS recipient.

Also some X.400 gateway products and some Internet Mail firewalls support an address rewriting feature when relaying messages. This feature allows use of a simple external address *john.doe@widgets.com* that can be printed on a business card and is unlikely to change, but a more complex internal address to support routing within an enterprise messaging network *john.doe@server6.east.chicago.widgets.com*. In some situations this duality can be confusing to users.

Other problems that may occur with address mapping include the loss of international character set data and the loss of addressing information in the case where a message is transferred from a mail system that supports two levels of address (an envelope-level address and a content-level address) in a message and a mail system that supports only one. Both Internet Mail and X.400 Mail support two levels of address. Microsoft Mail, cc:Mail, and other systems support only one. In the case where an Internet Mail distribution list is expanded, the envelope address, which is transmitted through SMTP, becomes different from the content address. That is, the content address continues to bear the name of the message originator, but the envelope address now bears the name of the list administrator (to whom error reports will be returned). The net effect of these machinations is that it may be impossible for the Microsoft Mail or cc:Mail recipient to determine who originally sent the mail to the list.[17]

5.4.6   Status Indication Mapping

When sending the Microsoft Word file to Allison, Bob might want to know whether or not it was delivered to her mailbox and whether she has read it. Most e-mail systems support some form of status indication regarding whether a message has been delivered to or read by the recipient.

Status indications are conveyed by some mail systems as an architected object (such as the X.400 Delivery Report), which contains special attributes, such as diagnostic codes, that are recognized and audited by the system. (In the case of

---

17. We must again gratefully acknowledge the assistance of Harald Alvestrand, who provided this and several other gateway horror stories.

positive status, summary information on the original message could be automatically updated. In the case of negative status the original message could automatically be placed in an undelivered folder.) Alternatively, status may be conveyed directly to the user within the format of an ordinary message that is not recognized by the originator's system or by management software, and therefore is not subject to any automated processing.

The following three problems arise in status handling by gateways. First, status reports come in different "flavors" depending on the standards and systems in question. X.400 supports four flavors: delivery notification, nondelivery notification, receipt notification, and nonreceipt notification. (The latter two deal with post-delivery processing or whether the recipient reads or rejects the message.) SMTP/RFC 822 support only a nonarchitected error report[18] (one that is not always generated). Many mail systems implement a "certified mail" euphemism; that is, the status indication that certifies the mail may be returned as a positive delivery notification when the message reaches the recipient's mailbox or it may be returned when the recipient reads the message. Some host-based mail systems acknowledge delivery with a beep at the sender's workstation.

Next, even status reports conveying the same intent (the nondelivery notification) contain different information payloads between systems. Architected nondelivery reports will generally contain special diagnostic codes; nonarchitected ones traveling as ordinary messages contain textual information at best. Gateways must make heroic efforts to map between two different architected status report types or from a textual report to an architected one.

Finally, the user must be helped in determining which message corresponds to a received status report. Suppose Bob sent multiple messages to Allison. Imagine his consternation if he receives status reports indicating that some of the messages were delivered and some were not, and the status reports identified the messages using a 20-character X.400 message identifier that has no relationship to any identifiers visible in his cc:Mail user interface. Effective gateways might use the X.400 message identifier to map to a corresponding proprietary message identifier that Bob understands or it might support the return of message content in delivery reports.

5.4.7   Security Attribute Mapping

Several security services can be supported in local messaging systems. These services include confidentiality through message encryption, message integrity protection through digital signatures, and nonrepudiation of delivery (using status reports to return a digitally signed parameter from the recipient to prove beyond a doubt that the message was received).

Because confidentiality and integrity services all require the use of a private cryptographic key, most of the work required to provide them must be done on the

---

18. However, positive and negative delivery (not receipt) status may be added as architected objects to Extended SMTP and MIME during 1994.

user's host system or on the end system. Servers, downstream transport nodes, and gateways can only convey certain parameters that need to be sent from end to end. Few local messaging systems implement security today beyond encrypting messages between servers using a single cryptographic key. Therefore, gateway vendors have had little incentive to progress in this area. This situation will begin to change as security-capable client infrastructures roll out with MAPI and AOCE and when security-capable native X.400 and native Internet Privacy Enhanced Mail (PEM) products acquire a large installed base.

Even as security capabilities become more prevalent, gateways remain severely limited in mapping security information. Combining message conversion and gatewaying services with security services is impossible unless the gateway holds the private keys of its users. In the typical case where the gateway is not trusted with the keys, it can at best encapsulate encrypted or signed information. But encapsulation only works when the originator and recipient are using the same protocol.

5.4.8   Tunneling

As enterprises begin consolidating their messaging networks using standard protocols and e-mail integration servers (or backbones), a tunneling problem arises, which may become a gateway issue in some cases. Consider what happens when local messaging systems at different geographic sites in an enterprise are connected to a standards-based gateway or a messaging backbone. Figure 5.11 poses an example where the local messaging systems at the New York, San Francisco, Chicago, Atlanta, and Cincinnati offices might all communicate with one another only through a backbone that they each access via a gateway.

Suppose the Chicago and the New York sites both use Microsoft Mail and each site is connected to the backbone. A message might be sent from an originator in Chicago to two recipients: one local and the other in New York. The local

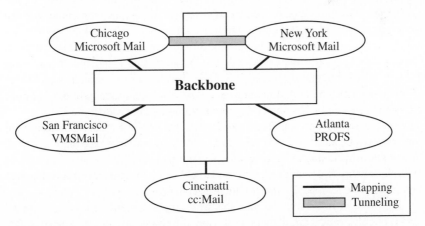

Figure 5.11   Mapping and tunneling through an e-mail backbone.

recipient in Chicago will receive the message intact. However, transmission through a gateway to the backbone may cause a loss of fidelity in the message copy to the New York recipient. Heading fields may disappear or be altered, highlighted information may no longer be highlighted in the cover note, and attachments may be altered. In such situations, the site e-mail managers for Chicago and New York are likely to complain with justification.

This loss of fidelity can be avoided if local messaging system features are somehow encapsulated, or tunneled, across the backbone. This can be accomplished by creating an extra body part in a message that is there only to carry the specific attributes of the local messaging system. Care must be taken to ensure that tunneled messages do not go astray; if a message were mistakenly tunneled by Microsoft Mail in Chicago to cc:Mail in Cincinnati, the recipient would not be able to read it. While tunneling is usually accomplished by local messaging systems themselves, the service is in some cases provided by gateways and e-mail integration servers.

5.4.9   Network Connectivity

Unless two local messaging systems are linked utilizing the same underlying network, the gateway must provide the network connectivity between them. For example, Retix's LAN e-mail gateways to its X.400 OpenServer product merely utilize shared file interfaces that operate transparently to the gateway. However, Soft*Switch's SNAPI gateways operate over TCP/IP or SNA; the choice of protocol is selected by the user. The Retix method offers transparency and simplicity for the customer, whereas the Soft*Switch method adds flexibility. What customers want to avoid is the requirement for special dedicated routers or other components needed solely for e-mail system-to-gateway interconnection.

5.5   E-MAIL INTEGRATION SERVERS

E-mail integration servers are dedicated switches housing or interconnecting the messaging, directory, and gateway facilities that collectively enable high-fidelity e-mail interconnection. E-mail integration servers also supply the means for users to interconnect local e-mail islands via standards-based protocols. When more than one e-mail integration server is deployed in an enterprise, that group of servers may be termed an e-mail integration backbone. E-mail integration backbones provide the glue between standards and local messaging products.

The basic concept of a backbone is diagrammed in Fig. 5.12. A backbone conveys certain administrative advantages to users of large, complex systems. Note that the backbone can consist of a single e-mail integration server (a hub) or multiple servers, and that it can be provided either by a privately owned and operated solution or by a public messaging service provider.

Figure 5.13 illustrates the internals of a single, generic, e-mail integration server. (Actual vendor implementations may differ and not all customer installations will include all components, especially when they are separately priced).

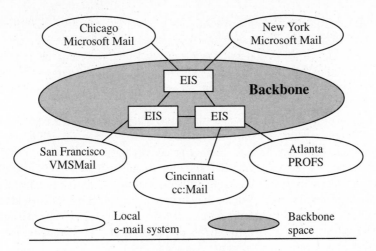

Figure 5.12   E-mail integration backbones.

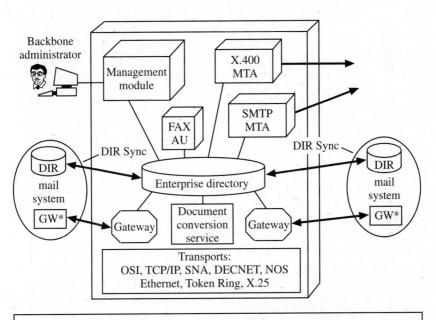

AU = Access Unit
MTA = Message Transfer Agent
NOS = Network Operating System
OSI = Open Systems Interconnection
SNA = System Network Architecture
TCP/IP = Transmission Control
             Protocol/Internet Protocol

* Some gateway implementations require
  code in both the local mail system and
  the switch; others require it just in
  the switch.

Figure 5.13   Internals of an e-mail integration server.

One can see from this example that the server actually solves the e-mail diversity problem through the use of gateways. These gateways will have the characteristics of those discussed in Section 5.4. The gateways, which represent the proprietary part of an e-mail integration solution, may be physically colocated with the e-mail integration server, the local messaging server, or on a separate dedicated piece of equipment.

E-mail integration servers and their attached gateways must provide some internal canonical representation of a message and its components, while mapping that message from one form to another or conveying it between two backbone switches. Some systems utilize X.400 as their canonical form. While X.400 is usually a superset of local messaging implementations, there are often features or formats in proprietary mail systems that do not map well to the standard and suffer in translation. Other systems are architected for multiway gateway translations. Soft*Switch's current SNAPI protocols are devised to preserve the proprietary attributes of attached e-mail systems. AlisaMail (from Alisa Systems) uses a relational database approach to accomplish the multiway mappings.

In Fig. 5.13, the standards-based part of the e-mail integration solution is provided by the components labeled "X.400 MTA" and "SMTP MTA." They enable the e-mail integration server to communicate with native standards-based e-mail systems within the enterprise, with Internet service providers, or with X.400 service providers. These standard MTAs provide the e-mail integration server with global reach. For the customer, they also take care of the unanticipated situation where a new mail system is added for which the server does not have a gateway. They are thus critical in protecting the customer's investment.

All arrows in Fig. 5.13 seem to converge on the Enterprise Directory. This directory is helpful in many ways. It can provide directory synchronization, allowing the names of all enterprise e-mail users to be propagated (either through incremental adds, deletes, and changes or through flat-file bulk import/export) to all local messaging systems. Gateways may participate in the directory synchronization process, or this function may be conducted through separate channels.

Once populated, the Enterprise Directory may perform other functions in addition to synchronization. It may assist the gateways and the MTAs in routing their messages to other entities and also in validating addresses on incoming messages. It may contain the names of external users in other messaging domains (these are not synchronized). The directory may also support names transformation, a process whereby naming/addressing irrationalities in the messaging network are papered over. For example, the directory may make it possible for users in two different local e-mail directories to contain duplicate names or for local messaging systems/gateways to contain complex addresses that are best hidden from the outside world. For compatibility with standards-based directories, the implementation may also support X.500.

Finally, our generic switch has some accessories. These include a document conversion service that could transparently convert Bob's Microsoft Word file into a WordPerfect format for Allison. In addition, there is a Fax Access Unit. Lastly, the switch includes a management module, enabling the administrator to control direc-

tory synchronization processes, names transformations, and gateway operation. It
may also support health monitoring of the attached local messaging systems.

5.6   E-MAIL SYSTEM CASE STUDIES

In this section, we present case studies for three of the major LAN e-mail products
on the market today: cc:Mail, Microsoft Mail, and Novel MHS. The intent is both
to brief the reader on these influential messaging products, and to illustrate by
example the concepts of this chapter. We also offer a brief overview of the host-
based SNADS protocol. Finally, we discuss a fully assembled multiprotocol
messaging network featuring an e-mail integration backbone and several local
messaging systems.

5.6.1   cc:Mail

cc:Mail is a family of approximately 20 products that provide high-end multimedia LAN e-mail capabilities. Figure 5.14 illustrates the basic elements of cc:Mail:
clients, Post Offices, and Routers.

The cc:Mail clients have long been available on DOS, OS/2, Windows,
Macintosh, and several varieties of UNIX. These clients provide the user interface
to cc:Mail transport, storage, and directory capabilities. With additional functionality released in late 1993, the clients offer almost all of the user interface features

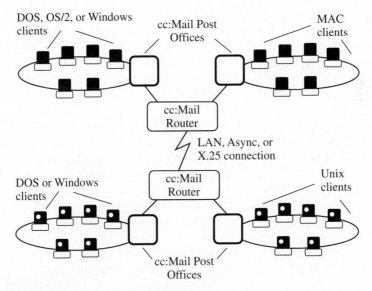

Figure 5.14   Basic cc:Mail architecture.

discussed in Section 5.3, notably a spell check capability in the editor, application launching, and color highlighting of text. The directory user interface features hotkey or automatic incremental entry access to a list of entries named by the user's full name. These entries hide the local or foreign address information from the user. cc:Mail addresses are of the form *name @ post office*; cc:Mail directory entries each contain the e-mail user's name, Post Office, a Comments field and optional (hidden) foreign system addressing information.

To obtain transport, storage, and directory capabilities, the clients access a shared composite mailbox, bulletin board, and directory database called the cc:Mail Post Office. Every file server in the company need not have a Post Office, but clients must have LAN access to a Post Office. The Post Office provides efficient storage, since it stores only a single copy of each message and because it is a database rather than a directory of files. No actual messaging program code runs on the Post Office, which is no more than a physical database. All message store type processing is accomplished by shared multiuser access to the Post Office database from the clients.

The strength of the cc:Mail Post Office architecture lies in the fact that the Post Office host's OS needs only support DOS file and record locking and its NOS must only be compatible with that of the clients. In many instances, enterprises employ a VAX (or some other superserver) as their Post Office host. The weakness of this implementation is that Post Offices must be shut down for periodic administrative maintenance and directories are simplistic flat files with nonextensible record structures. As of late 1993, Lotus/cc:Mail planned for newer Post Office releases (codenamed Sequoia) to support full (24×7) availability and for clients to support personal address books in addition to the shared directory.

Lotus/cc:Mail's evolutionary direction is to integrate cc:Mail more closely with Notes. Its strategic plan as of early 1994 was to support three client editions: cc:Mail Post Office Edition (which, like earlier offerings, will be based on file sharing), cc:Mail Client/Server Edition (which will access the Lotus Note Object Store, not a Post Office), and Public Mail Editions (which allows cc:Mail to provide clients to public mail systems). These client infrastructures will support VIM and MAPI access, rules-based filtering, and may be integrated with a forms package containing workflow functions.

As noted above, the cc:Mail Post Office has historically been a passive database that does not implement MTA functions. In many cases, clients send and receive messages through the database. Sometimes, however, users reside on incompatible or unconnected LANs and thus cannot share a Post Office, or file server capacity limitations may prevent all cc:Mail users in a given environment from sharing the same Post Office. In these instances, messages are transferred between Post Offices via the good offices of a product called the cc:Mail Router (formerly known as cc:Mail Gateway). We will first discuss the architecture of cc:Mail Router's product as it existed in 1993, then briefly describe the Lotus Communication Server slated to eventually replace the Router.

The cc:Mail Router contains the message routing software for cc:Mail. Diagrammed in Fig. 5.15, it generally runs on a dedicated DOS or OS/2 system and

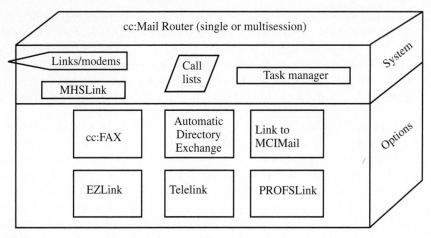

Figure 5.15   cc:Mail Router components in early 1993.

can support multiple Post Offices. The Router moves messages between cc:Mail Post Offices or to other routers over asynchronous TCP/IP or X.25 links. cc:Mail Routers communicate with one another over the various links using a proprietary protocol. A single session Router can only drive one link at a time; a multisession Router can drive up to eight links at up to 115.2 kbps each. Routing is controlled by the Task Manager according to the directives in administrator-configured call lists. A simplified version of the Router called Dialin, which supports only incoming calls, can also service Post Offices and cc:Mail Remote clients.

A number of unbundled options that require cc:Mail Router as a prerequisite can be included. These are the Automatic Directory Exchange, MHSLink, cc:FAX, EZlink, Link to MCI Mail, Telelink, and PROFSLink.

The Automatic Directory Exchange synchronization program enables directories to be shared, or propagated, between cc:Mail Post Offices. Thus, users in one Post Office will see the names of users in remote Post Offices and can address messages to remote users transparently (without having to specify which Post Office they are on). The MHSLink gateway product enables the router to communicate with a colocated MHS Hub program on the system to send and receive messages between cc:Mail and MHS users. The cc:FAX fax access unit product enables users to send and receive fax transmissions. Once received, faxes can be viewed using cc:Mail clients. The EZlink gateway product enables users to send and receive messages between cc:Mail and AT&T EasyLink. The Link to MCI Mail enables users to send and receive messages between cc:Mail and MCI Mail. Telelink enables users to send and receive messages between cc:Mail and Sprint Mail. PROFSLink enables users to send and receive messages between cc:Mail and PROFS.

In addition, a number of freestanding options to cc:Mail exist that do not require a router. The most important of these is cc:Mail Import/Export. Import/

Export is a file format specification allowing mail-enabled applications or gateway products to import messages or directory entries into and out of a cc:Mail Post Office. The software is designed to be invoked from a MS DOS batch file (".bat") and can be executed on a periodic basis through the Task Manager module of the cc:Mail Router. Traditionally, third party cc:Mail gateways and directory synchronization clients, such as those from Soft*Switch and Retix, have been built in this fashion. Other freestanding cc:Mail product options include Network Scheduler (a calendaring program), Link to SMTP, Link to Soft*Switch, Link to 3COM Mail, and the Lotus VIM Developers' Kit.

The cc:Mail Router will be replaced in 1994 with the Lotus Communications Server (LCS) and LCS/DOS. According to Lotus/cc:Mail, LCS is intended to combine the best elements of the Lotus Notes Object Store (with database capabilities, hierarchical directories, and client-server access) with the Router. LCS will also contain communications software enabling it to act as a hub for wireless (infrared) LANs. It will support native cc:Mail, native Notes, 1988 X.400 MTA functions, SMTP/MIME functions, several gateways, SNMP management, and in later releases, X.500.

5.6.2   Microsoft Messaging Capabilities

Microsoft messaging capabilities can be classed in three groups: the Microsoft Mail system, the MAPI middleware offering, and the Touchdown Server.

Microsoft Mail

There are actually two Microsoft Mail systems: Microsoft Mail for PC Networks and Microsoft Mail for Apple Networks. Both of these systems implement an architecture that is similar to that described for cc:Mail. Like Lotus/cc:Mail, Microsoft is migrating its legacy mail system toward a client-server implementation that facilitates e-mail/enterprise database integration and e-mail/workflow integration as well as native standards-based connectivity on the server side. MAPI and the Touchdown Server represent the key elements of Microsoft's future direction in messaging.

Microsoft Mail has historically supported, and continues to offer, a variety of clients, including Windows, DOS, OS/2, and Macintosh platforms. Post Office implementations are shipped on both the Macintosh and DOS platforms. Each Post Office supports a range of clients, allowing a user with mostly PCs to support a few Macintosh clients on the DOS Post Office, or vice versa.

Microsoft Mail clients communicate with Post Offices via the shared file system. To provide MTA functions for communicating between Post Offices, Microsoft Mail 3.2 (1993) and earlier versions utilize a program called External, which supports intra-LAN access as well as asynchronous modem and X.25 communication. A program called Dispatch is used for robust directory synchronization between Post Offices. To communicate between Microsoft Mail for PC Networks and Microsoft Mail for Apple Networks, a separate gateway product called Microsoft Mail Connection is required. Directory synchronization is avail-

able between Microsoft Mail Post Offices with a separate product required between PC and Apple networks.

Other Microsoft Mail products include Administrator Utility Programs,
Microsoft Mail Remote (remote client package), and Microsoft Mail gateways to
PROFS, OfficeVision, MCI Mail, AT&T Mail, X.400, SNADS, SMTP, FAX, and
MHS. Microsoft Mail offers a File Format API (FFAPI) Module that is often used
to create third party gateways. However, Microsoft's strategic direction lies with
MAPI.

Microsoft Messaging API Architecture

As we noted in Chapter 3, MAPI [MAPI93, MAPI93a] is a key element of
Microsoft's Workgroup Strategy. By exposing both Client and Service Provider
APIs (after the manner of the client infrastructure architecture shown in Figs. 5.6
and 5.7), MAPI furthers Microsoft's overall objective of promoting the sales of
both its workgroup applications and the Windows operating system.

Figure 5.16 depicts the MAPI architecture; the left-hand column relates back to
the client infrastructure model we described in Section 5.3. At its topmost layer,
MAPI supports three Client APIs: XAPIA's CMC, Microsoft's Simple MAPI, and
Microsoft's Extended MAPI. MAPI.DLL is a Dynamic Link Library that enables
applications to check addresses, interact with a message store, and send messages.
To send messages, MAPI.DLL utilizes the Message Spooler which, like the

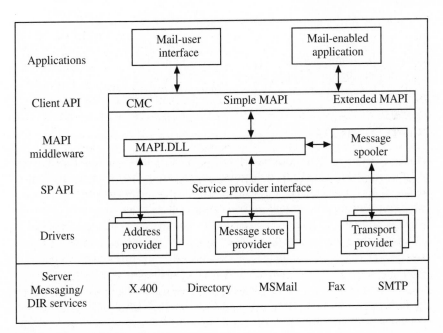

Figure 5.16   MAPI architecture.

Windows Print Manager, runs as a separate task in the background. At the Service Provider Interface (SPI), MAPI allows multiple address, message store, or transport providers to coexist and act as drivers to various messaging/directory systems.

Simple MAPI has 12 procedure calls, many of which give applications the option to call up a "dialog box" to interact with users. The Simple MAPI calls are

- MAPILogon and MAPILogoff begin and end MAPI sessions. MAPIFree releases the memory allocated by the messaging subsystem.

- MAPISendMail and MAPISendDocuments are used to send mail.

- MAPIFindNext, MAPIReadMail, MAPISaveMail, and MAPIDeleteMail enable the user to interact with the message store.

- MAPIAddress, MAPIDetails, and MAPIResolveName enable the user to interact with the directory system.

Extended MAPI offers a low-level, more comprehensive interface intended for full-featured e-mail clients and workflow systems.

Microsoft Touchdown Server

Microsoft's next generation architecture will implement Universal Client support through the MAPI API and middleware. Its pre-1994 Post Office and MTA will be replaced by an advanced Windows NT-based server (Touchdown Server) for advanced and a Shared File Server for basic, low-end environments. The Touchdown Server will support client-server–based access, 1988 X.400, SMTP/MIME, an X.500 directory service, and the extensive administrative and instrumentation capabilities of Windows NT. Existing Microsoft gateways will be ported to Windows NT so that they will work with the Touchdown Server; customers, however can continue using earlier gateway releases with the Touchdown Server as well. As noted in Chapter 3, sophisticated message database capabilities will also be provided to support advanced group collaboration applications.

5.6.3   NetWare Message Handling Service (MHS)

Novell's NetWare MHS (Message Handling Service) has become a de facto standard for many PC-based e-mail distributed applications. MHS handles the collection, routing, and delivery of messages and files to remote processes through a store-and-forward architecture on both local and wide area networks. NetWare MHS was originally developed by Action Technologies and marketed by Novell. Subsequently it was acquired by Novell. Although the predominant LAN server environment supported by MHS is DOS-based NetWare, MHS has been ported to other platforms such as UNIX, LAN Manager, and Portable NetWare.

MHS hubs typically operate on a dedicated PC. Even though the MHS hub is on a PC, it is still referred to as an MHS host. An MHS host has three major components: the Connectivity Manager, the Transport Server, and the Directory Manager. The Connectivity Manager performs MTA functions. In cooperation with the Transport Server, it provides the communication services for MHS, while the Directory Manager provides host name to address resolution and routing services. The way these services operate is as follows: (1) the Connectivity Manager queues a message and its routes based on tables set up by the Directory Manager; (2) the Connectivity Manager passes the message to a Transport Server, which establishes physical connections and sends the message; and (3) at the destination, a Transport Server stores the message in an MHS directory and the local Connectivity Manager moves the message to the recipient's directory.

Messages may optionally contain binary attachments and are submitted and delivered through a disk directory queue which is accessed through the shared network file system. Messages contain Destination Addresses and the Return Address. MHS addresses take the form of *username@hostname* or *username@workgroup*[19]. Additional addressing information for gateways can optionally be appended after the hostname between the special characters "{" and "}". Similarly to cc:Mail and Microsoft Mail addresses (but unlike X.400 and Internet Mail addresses), MHS addresses are not designed for global uniqueness and duplications could occur during corporate mergers and reorganizations. For example, it might become necessary to interconnect two different workgroups, both named "sales." Some e-mail integration servers facilitate such interconnection through address mapping such that no address information needs to be changed in the affected domains.

MHS is generally configured with users connected to a specific NetWare host. As illustrated in Fig. 5.17, hosts are logically grouped into workgroups and workgroups may be tied together by regional hubs. The regional hubs can then be

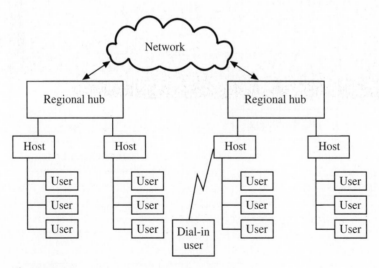

Figure 5.17 MHS network interconnectivity.

---

19. In earlier versions of the Novell Simple Message Format (SMF), the address components were limited to eight characters each. This restriction was later lifted, improving interoperability with Internet Mail and X.400.

connected via a public or private network. To support this hierarchy, MHS Connectivity Managers and Transport Servers relay messages utilizing the Directory Manager, which contains static routing tables from which they obtain the next hop.

NetWare MHS is only one component of a PC-based messaging network. It can be viewed as a building block. MHS is generally built upon the file structures, directories, and services of a LAN operating system (usually NetWare) and requires a client-mail application which uses its services. (The user, however, only sees the client-mail application, not MHS.) The client application accesses the MHS server via a shared file mechanism. The header and note portion of a message is placed in a file that conforms to a Novell-defined Simple Message Format (SMF) and stored in a transfer directory. If needed, attachments are placed in separate files.

The NetWare MHS Directory Manager maintained on an MHS host is integrated with the Novell Bindery (LAN users' directory) in the NetWare 3.x system and with Network Directory Services (NDS) in the NetWare 4.x systems. NDS takes a hierarchical view of directory information, associating users with workgroups (or organization units) and workgroups with organizations. Entire workgroups or organizations can be synchronized (or replicated) between MHS servers, allowing servers to share addressing information. E-mail systems such as a Da Vinci can extract a text file containing a copy of the NetWare directory information and display that file to its users.

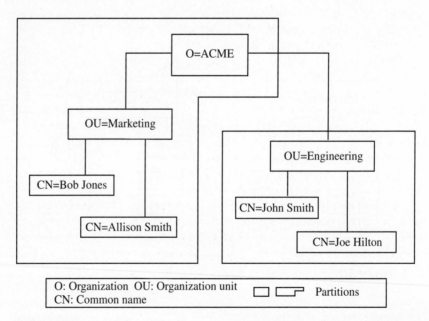

Figure 5.18 NetWare hierarchical directory example.

The NetWare addressing structure maps directly onto the hierarchy. Thus, Allison Smith's address would be *Allison Smith @ marketing.acme.* The hierarchical approach to directory organization now being adopted by the Novell Directory Service (NDS) and by the directories of other vendors conveys various advantages. Branches of the information tree can be replicated selectively to various server directories, and this approach permits a global view of synchronized directories without forcing the entire directory to be copied everywhere.

In 1992 and 1993, Novell expanded the connectivity and directory capabilities of NetWare MHS, renaming the product Global MHS [PETR93]. X.400, SMTP, and SNADS NetWare Loadable Modules (NLMs) were also made available,[20] (sometimes from third party vendors) allowing those standards-based protocols to run directly on MHS hosts. A version of MHS called "Personal MHS" was created to enable users of remote clients to communicate with other MHS users. With Novell's acquisition of WordPerfect, the WordPerfect Office product line and MHS will be integrated in a new architecture dubbed the Open Messaging Engine.

5.6.4   SNA Distribution Services (SNADS)

SNA Distribution Services (SNADS) is a messaging backbone protocol defined by IBM. At one time, it had the largest installed base of all the messaging backbone protocols. During the late 1980s in the United States, the SNA suite of protocols accounted for approximately 70 percent of network usage. Many vendors have built gateways between SNADS and their own messaging facilities. Thus SNADS can act as a messaging backbone for enterprises with an installed IBM base. Direct SNADS gateways are also a feature of many public e-mail services, such as AT&T EasyLink, Advantis, and SprintMail.

SNADS is a store-and-forward messaging service. It relays messages from originators to recipients over LU6.2, traversing the network via node-by-node hops. The connection to the initial adjacent node results in the establishment of a synchronous SNA session. A message may transit multiple intermediate nodes prior to being delivered to its intended destination. When the ultimate destination is not a point-to-point connection, the delivery is via store-and-forward with potential delays at each node. Revisable text and other binary formats can be exchanged between applications, although SNADS limits messages to only one attachment each.

As we noted above, SNADS addresses consist of two eight-character components: the Distribution Group Name (DGN) and the Distribution Entry Name (DEN). Routing Group Name (RGN) and Routing Entry Name (REN) are sometimes used. Like MHS addresses, SNADS addresses are not necessarily globally unique and are subject to the problems noted above.

---

20. The X.400 NLM was provided by Retix as a third party product.

5.6.5 An E-mail Network Using Soft*Switch Backbone Components

Figure 5.19 below features an actual case study of an enterprise messaging network involving the Soft*Switch EMX integration server and the following seven local messaging system offerings: All-In-One and VMS Mail from Digital, TAO from Fischer International, HP Desk and HP OpenMail from Hewlett-Packard, Microsoft Mail for PC Networks, and cc:Mail.

The Soft*Switch backbone for this scenario consists of three components: The EMX switch, offboard gateways, and the X.400 protocol. The EMX switch is implemented as a turnkey hardware/software solution aboard the Data General Aviion platform. Within the EMX lie X.400 and SMTP access units, a Names Directory (through which all the local messaging systems other than the HP ones are synchronized and which contains the information needed to enable name transformations between the local messaging domains), a SNAPI access unit that communicates via Soft*Switch's SNAPI[21] protocol to offboard Soft*Switch gate-

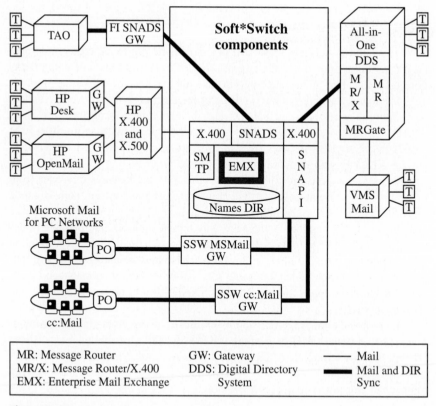

Figure 5.19. E-mail integration scenario.

---

21. SNAPI consists of a Soft*Switch defined API plus a Soft*Switch defined remote procedure call mechanism. It represents Soft*Switch's strategic direction for gateways.

ways, a SNADS access unit that communicates with a third party SNADS gate-way, and an Enterprise Mail Management (EMM) graphical mail network management application to run the EMX switch (not displayed in the figure).

Two dedicated, PC-based offboard gateways are required. They are the Soft*Switch Microsoft Mail Gateway and the Soft*Switch cc:Mail Gateway. Each gateway accesses EMX via SNAPI. In the case of cc:Mail, the Gateway communicates with a nearby cc:Mail Post Office via cc:Mail's Import/Export protocol. For directory synchronization with cc:Mail, a second dedicated PC-based product—DS/cc:Mail—is required. Soft*Switch's DS/cc:Mail client (not shown) interacts with the cc:Mail directory on the Post Office and communicates using e-mail (again passing through the Post Office) to the directory synchronization server (DS/EMX) on EMX. The connection to Microsoft Mail is similar; it employs Microsoft's FFAPI interface.

The X.400 protocol is used to communicate with the HP X.400 and the Digital Message Router/X.400 products. X.400 and SMTP on the EMX can also be used to communicate with external trading partners, customers, and suppliers either directly or via public messaging networks.

In this scenario, each local messaging system connected to EMX is responsible for routing its own local traffic internally (unless remote sites are designated to be reachable through EMX). Each local messaging system is also responsible for routing foreign traffic to the appropriate Soft*Switch or vendor-provided gateway/Post Office. In addition, each local e-mail environment is responsible for propagating directory information to and from a directory local to a Soft*Switch directory synchronization client. The local messaging systems, broken out by vendor, are

- **cc:Mail:** One cc:Mail Post Office is shown. Mail flows from this Post Office to other Post Offices via the cc:Mail Router. Section 5.6.1 describes the architecture of these components.

- **Microsoft Mail:** One Microsoft Mail Post Office is shown. Mail flows from this Post Office to other Post Offices via an MTA (the External program). Section 5.6.2 describes the architecture of these components.

- **Fischer International's EMC²/TAO Mail System:** TAO is an IBM host- and LAN-based mail system. It communicates with the SNADS access unit on the EMX via a Fischer-provided SNADS gateway system.

- **Hewlett-Packard's HP Desk and HP OpenMail:** These host-based HP mail systems communicate with HP X.400 via HP-provided X.400 gateways. HP X.400 then communicates with the EMX using X.400.

- **Digital ALL-IN-1 and VMS Mail:** These host-based mail systems communicate with Digital's Message Router product (in the case of VMSMail through the MRGATE facility). Message Router interfaces to Digital's MR/X product, sending and receiving X.400 messages to and from the EMX.

This scenario features a relatively high quality of interconnection. Messages can be sent, received, and replied to among and between any of the attached mail systems. They can contain binary attachments. Names transformations are effected in EMX to produce a reasonable enterprise addressing scheme that can be published to external trading partners, customers, and suppliers.[22] Directory synchronization is possible between all domains other than Hewlett-Packard; and, in HP's case, ASCII files of directory information can still be imported and exported with a little more effort. All this has been made possible by distributing gateway functions through both local messaging domains and the backbone and through adding value (such as names transformation and directory synchronization) to the e-mail integration server. However, if more of the e-mail systems in the scenario supported standard interfaces, much of this configuration could be simplified.

5.7   SUMMARY

We have now completed our tour of the local e-mail outposts on the e-mail frontier, that is, the established host e-mail, LAN e-mail, gateway, and e-mail integration server or backbone facilities. We have reviewed the architecture and features and we have examined case studies. Figure 5.20 summarizes some of the major trends in e-mail systems that we have highlighted throughout the chapter.

This figure shows that host-based systems are transitioning to LAN-based, distributed solutions as users downsize and as the price performance of desktop

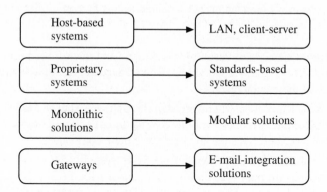

Figure 5.20   E-mail technology trends.

---

22. All users of the XYZ Corporation can put relatively straightforward X.400 addresses, such as *G=Bob;S=Jones;OU1=001;P=XYZ;A=;C=US,* on their business cards. The Organization Unit field in Bob's address contains a tie breaker number to be used in the event that there are duplicate names in the company. Bob's external Internet Mail address could be *bob.jones@xyz.com,* with the last name containing tie breakers if needed. Bob and all other XYZ users would have similar addresses for external viewing. Messages to these addresses can be delivered to these users, regardless of which attached local e-mail system they subscribe to and regardless of the local addressing form employed on that system.

workstation equipment inexorably improves. But while local e-mail systems remain largely proprietary fiefdoms, leading to incompatibility, outdated systems, and incomplete solutions, e-mail integration solutions are becoming more sophisticated and established standards are slowly taking over as well. Single vendor (monolithic) e-mail solutions are giving way to modularized solutions; and gateways are being replaced by e-mail integration servers.

In subsequent chapters, we will review electronic messaging and directory standards and provide ideas for how users can build cost-effective, modern message networks. We will also discuss opportunities for stretching the e-mail envelope in order to help local and global infrastructures become vehicles for true electronic commerce and workflow automation.

KEY POINTS

- Host-based e-mail systems house e-mail software on a departmental minicomputer or mainframe and the software is accessed by a user with a terminal or PC emulating a terminal.

- Traditional LAN e-mail architectures are built on simple file-sharing techniques optimized for low-end PCs. Advanced architectures break LAN e-mail into additional and more sophisticated components, such as multiple servers, message stores, gateways, and directories.

- An e-mail features explosion has resulted in a plethora of e-mail user interface, messaging, formatting, directory, storage, administration, and security capabilities in products available today.

- A variety of Application Program Interfaces (APIs) permit mail-enabled applications to access the infrastructure. APIs also facilitate the modularization of e-mail, allowing users to mix and match components from multiple vendors.

- Gateways, which translate or map messages from one mail system to another, must handle differing message headers, attachments, addresses, status indications, and security elements.

- E-mail integration servers are evolving from the (relatively simple) gateway model to the modern infrastructure model, and are aiming to provide comprehensive solutions for e-mail users' transport, storage, directory, and access requirements.

C H A P T E R 6

The X.400 Standard

First rolled out by the International Telegraph and Telephone Consultative Committee (ITU) in 1984, X.400 is a standard for both generic and interpersonal store-and-forward messaging [ITU84]. It was envisioned that enterprises would no longer need to fund the development, maintenance, and management of proprietary messaging protocols. Instead they would be able to install a standard messaging protocol designed to replace all existing messaging systems over the long run. Both the 1984 recommendations and the updated 1988 X.400 standard, reissued by ITU in collaboration with ISO, were advertised as providing global interoperability combined with the prospect of off-the-shelf product pricing, maintenance, and reliability.

X.400 has only partially lived up to these grand expectations. Despite its implementation in many products, its deployment as a backbone standard in the public messaging world, and its inclusion in the strategic migration or procurement plans of many multinational corporations, government agencies, and other institutions, X.400 has not achieved the crowning triumph of desktop dominance. Although for several years some large users have been interconnecting their proprietary e-mail systems using X.400 gateways (with mixed results), X.400 was never designed to be an integration tool. It is, rather, a standard specifying a messaging format and interfaces that were intended to displace existing technology. Some parts of the standard are successful, other parts are not. This chapter explains the technical attributes of X.400 and how the characteristics of its architecture have determined the nature of its progress to date.

We refine our analysis of the X.400 architecture by identifying the functional entities of X.400, the basic structure of messages, and the nature of X.400 addressing. We summarize the basic services offered in standard, and then deal with specific topics such as X.400 Application Program Interfaces (APIs) and X.400 synergy with X.500 directories. Throughout this chapter, we focus not only on the theoretical content of the standard, but also on its implementation and other issues surrounding its various functions.

This chapter also contains generic tutorial coverage of secure messaging and relevant security issues. The discussion of the means whereby local e-mail systems can protect their e-mail from disclosure or modification is also included here. Readers who do not already understand secure messaging concepts, such as digital signatures and public key Certificates, are advised to consult Section 6.13, which also provides the background for further security material in later chapters.

6.1   GENERAL ARCHITECTURE OF X.400

X.400 is designed for computer-to-computer electronic messaging including—but not limited to—interpersonal mail. It is also capable of importing or exporting messages from other messaging media, such as Telex, Teletex, fax, and postal mail. The architectural levels in X.400 are shown in Fig. 6.1. They are an interior Message Transfer Service (MTS) concerned with providing generic store-and-

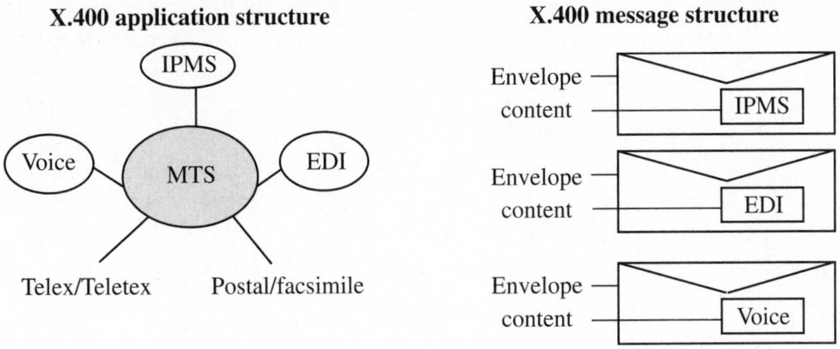

X.400 application structure   **X.400 message structure**

Figure 6.1   X.400 architecture and layers.   *Key: IPMS = Interpersonal Messaging System, EDI = Electronic Data Interchange, MTS = Message Transfer Service.*

forward services and an exterior layer where many messaging applications can be positioned. Such messaging applications include traditional (memo-like) interpersonal messages, EDI, and voice. Both the 1984 and 1988 versions of X.400 standardize the Interpersonal Messaging Service (IPMS); the ITU's X.435 recommendation standardizes Electronic Data Interchange (EDI) [EDI90/EDI91]; and the ITU's X.440 recommendation standardizes the use of X.400 for voice messaging.

This logical layering, or separation of the standard into a generic level and an application-specific level, allows virtually any messaging application the opportunity to make use of the backbone MTS. The layering of the X.400 application structure is also reflected in the structure of message formats standardized for use with X.400. Regardless of the messaging application, a message always consists of two parts: the *envelope* and the *content*. In this model, the envelope contains addressing and routing information associated with the transmittal of a message through the MTS, whereas the content contains application-specific information.

6.2   THE X.400 STANDARDS DOCUMENTS

The X.400 documents were initially published as the ITU 1984 X.400 recommendations (informally called the *Red Book*, because of its red covers). They were later revised in the ITU's 1988 X.400 recommendations (the *Blue Book*) and the 1988 ISO 10021 series. Their latest revision was issued in the 1992 X.400 suite of recommendations and the equivalent ISO 10021 standards series. The differences between 1988 X.400 and ISO 10021 are relatively minor and will be noted where important.

Detailed coverage of all three versions of the X.400 standards in their entirety cannot be provided in one single chapter. The 1988 *Blue Book* alone runs 628

ITU recommendation	Description	Year	1988 ISO number	Chapter 6 section number of relevant discussion	Remarks
X.400	System and service overview	1984 1988	10021–1	6.1–6.15	Overview material
X.402	Overall architecture	1988	10021–2	6.1–6.15	Overview material covering new 1988 X.400 features, such as security and use of directory.
X.403	Conformance testing	1988		6.14	Architecture for testing 1984 X.400 implementations.
X.407	Abstract service definition	1988	10021–3	6.3	Specification of a formal method for describing services/protocols.
X.408	Encoded information type conversion rules	1984		6.7	Not brought into ISO documents.
X.409	Presentation transfer syntax and notation	1984	8824 and 8825	6.12	In 1988, X.409 became a generic OSI standard, the Abstract Syntax Notation One (ASN.1) and Basic Encoding Rules (BER). It was relabeled as ITU X.208 and X.209.
X.410	Remote operations and reliable transfer service	1984	9066 and 9072	6.12	In 1988, X.410 became two generic OSI standards, the Remote Operations Service Element (ROSE) and the Reliable Transfer Service Element (RTSE). They were relabeled as ITU X.218 and X.219, X.228 and X.229, respectively.

Recommendation	Title	Year	ISO	Section	Description
X.411	Message transfer service: abstract service definition and procedures	1984 1988	10021–4	6.3–6.10	Describes the Message Transfer System (MTS) layer of X.400.
X.413	Message store: abstract service definition	1988	10021–5	6.3	Describes a Message Store (MS) capability standardized in 1988.
X.419	Protocol specifications	1988	10021–6	6.11	Describes the interaction of X.400 with the lower OSI layers.
X.420	Interpersonal messaging system	1984 1988	10021–7	6.3–6.10	Describes the Interpersonal Messaging System (IPMS) layer of X.400.
X.430	Access protocol for teletex terminals	1984	T.330		Describes the interaction between X.400 and Teletex. It was withdrawn to T.330 in 1988.
F.435, X.435	EDI message handling service	1992		6.15	Describes an X.400-based messaging service and protocol for use with EDI.
F.440, X.440	Voice message handling service	1992		6.15	Describes an X.400-based messaging service and protocol for use with voice messaging.

Table 6.1 The ITU and ISO X.400 documents.

pages on 8-1/2 × 14 inch paper with its text printed in 10-point font size. We shall seek instead to provide an overview and perspective. Table 6.1 lists the individual recommendations (and ISO parts) as they are structured by ITU and ISO, respectively. The table shows which parts were or were not carried over from the 1984 to the 1988 standard and in what sections of this chapter you can find material about a given standard.

The many features, functions, and options of X.400 are described as *elements of service* (EOS), several hundred of which appear in the complete set of standards. Because the ITU/ISO process produces standards with so many options, the implementation community felt the need to develop *functional standards* or *profiles* to describe functional subsets that users could reference for procurement purposes and as a means of gauging interoperability between the products of different vendors. These profiles classify the X.400 elements of service for implementation purposes so that, for two X.400 products from different vendors to interoperate, they must correctly support the same profile.

Relevant functional standards for X.400 are found in the U.S. National Institute of Standards (NIST) Open Systems Environment Implementors Workshop's (OIW) Stable Implementation Agreements [NIST93, NIST93A], similar European Workshop for Open Systems (EWOS) profiles, and joint International Standard Profiles (ISPs) that were still in the final stages of development as of 1993. While interoperability between implementations supporting different profiles was problematic during the early stages of X.400 implementation, the ISP harmonization process has minimized such problems. Henceforth in this chapter, we will refer to functional standards issues in terms of the OIW work; for more information on X.400 profiles and functional standardization in general, see Appendix A.

6.3 MESSAGE TRANSFER AGENTS, USER AGENTS, MESSAGE STORES, AND ACCESS UNITS

The basic processing entities of X.400 are the user (human or computer application), the User Agent (UA), the Message Transfer Agent (MTA), and the Access Unit (AU). In some 1988 systems, a Message Store (MS) may be present. Both 1988 and 1984 systems can use AUs to switch computer-based messages in and out of external media such as Telex or facsimile. These processing entities performing their functional roles are shown in Fig. 6.2. (Section 6.4 will explain how MTAs, UAs, and the other entities are related from an administrative, or management domain, perspective.)

6.3.1 The User Agent

The UA is the computer program or module that provides a messaging-user interface: it displays and encodes message contents and submits or receives messages. UAs often run directly on a PC or workstation, where they can take advantage of color or windowing features. UAs may provide storage for the user or produce reports on waiting messages. However, the term UA is not limited to mail-user interfaces. X.400-based EDI and other networked messaging applications also conceptually contain a UA. In such cases, the UA often provides an application program interface in place of an interactive user interface.

The UA is the X.400 processing entity that varies the most from application to application and from product to product. UAs often run on a client (desktop PC); alternatively, a single UA software program on a departmental system may be deployed to serve many logged-in users at once. In general, UAs offer many different user interfaces, ranging from simple prompt-and-response to graphical modes of presentation.

X.400 does not specify user interfaces but rather specifies only the services to be provided for users and the format of the message content used to convey the information required to realize those services. For example, "Subject Indication" is a service and "Subject" is a field in the message content. X.400-compliant IPMS UAs generate a content type known as "P2" (1984) or "P22" (1988). P2 and P22 contain fields such as Subject, Originator, Primary Recipient, and Copy Recipient. UAs create the P2 content for each X.400 message that MTAs will carry within an electronic envelope to its destination. Another example of a UA, the X.435 EDI UA, formats a message content known as P35 or P_{edi}.

Today, many UAs on the market are proprietary; that is, they do not support X.400 address and P2/P22 message formats directly. Such proprietary UAs can be mapped to X.400 solely via gateways. However, some native X.400 UAs are on the market as well. We define a native X.400 UA as one that more or less complies with the OIW's IPM Service functional group. Examples of these UAs are Enterprise Solutions' Enterprise Mail and ISOCOR's ISOPRO.

6.3.2   Message Transfer Agent

The Message Transfer Agent (MTA) is the key component of the Message Transfer System (MTS). The X.400 MTS consists of collections of MTAs that act as staging systems to relay and deliver messages in a store-and-forward fashion. These workhorses of X.400 read the envelope of the message, which contains whatever information is necessary to route it, deliver it, and perform associated functions. The format specification for the message envelope as encoded and decoded by MTAs is called P1. X.400 standardizes an Originator/Recipient (O/R) Address, which MTAs use to route messages. Individual MTAs usually run on servers or on departmental systems. In e-mail integration systems, they are often colocated with gateways to proprietary systems.

6.3.3   Message Store

The Message Store (MS) (available only in the 1988 and 1992 versions of X.400) provides a sophisticated message storage and retrieval facility. It is an optional component that can hold messages for pickup by a UA. It can also offload some of the UA's reporting, listing, and scanning responsibilities. An MS often runs on a server or departmental system that has ample disk storage facilities. It can be connected to various UA clients.

The MS supports a stored messages database. MTAs can deliver messages to the MS for indefinite periods, even when the receiving user is offline. UAs in turn access the MS via a standard protocol called P7. P7 allows users and service providers the flexibility of pairing UAs of one vendor with MS/MTAs from another vendor. The protocol offers various retrieval operations such as List, Summarize, Fetch, Delete, Alert, and Register-MS. These operations allow groups of messages to be flexibly manipulated with user-defined filters. New messages meeting certain criteria can trigger Alert operations or other automatic actions, such as dialing a beeper number. Not limited to servicing e-mail UAs, the Message Store can support multiple message content types like X.435 EDI as well.

The Message Store is useful as a high-capacity, mass-storage facility attached to a public messaging backbone or to the backbone of a large private messaging network. It has been implemented in some products. Presently, however, P7 is regarded as insufficient to serve as a "file cabinet" and rules-based mailbox/database for end users and groupware applications. Specifically, it has no concept of folders (directories) for filed mail. For this reason and because of its inherent complexity and the lack of a widely deployed dial-up X.400 protocol capable of working inexpensively over public telephone systems, relatively few P7-capable UA products appeared on the market as of late 1993.

6.3.4   Access Units

Access Units (AUs) are special types of UAs that serve as a bridge between X.400 and other messaging media, such as Telex. The 1984 standard described Telex and Teletex AUs; the 1988 standard added a Physical Delivery AU (PDAU) enabling X.400 messages to be output into postal systems or to printer devices. X.400 does not standardize the internal behavior of AUs other than Teletex, however. Facsimile AUs are also common features of public messaging services.

6.3.5   Entities, Protocols, and Configurations

Figure 6.2 shows the relationships among X.400 entities and the protocols that they use to interact with one another. At the innermost layer, the MTS provides a store-and-forward message transfer service using the P1 message transfer protocol between MTAs.

Outside the MTS, IPMS UAs exchange formatted messages on behalf of users. The IPMS UAs format the content of messages using the P2 or P22 message content format. Users access the IPMS UA via a user interface (UI), applications access the UA via an API. UIs and APIs are not standardized by X.400.

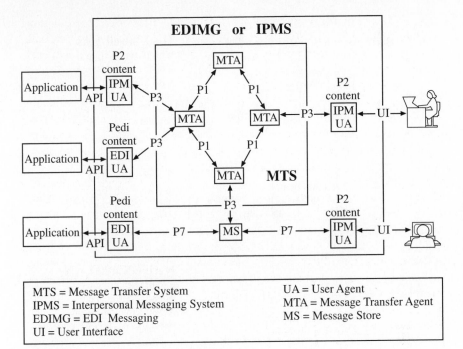

Figure 6.2 X.400 entities and protocols.

Figure 6.2 also shows EDI UAs, which support the P_{edi} protocol specified in ITU's X.435 standard. The P_{edi} protocol carries trade data such as quotes, invoices, or purchase orders encoded in either ANSI's X12 or the United Nations' EDIFACT. EDI applications must access the EDI UA via some API, though this interaction is not standardized in X.435. A Message Store can act as a clearing-house for EDI/X.400 transactions.

The standard covers the general case where each X.400 entity (except for the user) is on a separate processor, providing the P3 (a UA or MS to MTA) and P7 (a UA to MS) access protocols. However, X.400 systems have been implemented in a number of configurations, and P3 implementations are rare. Note that P7 and P3 support are not required by the OIW's IPM Service Functional Group. However, optional functional groups exist for Remote UAs of both the P3 and P7 variety.

Three X.400 configurations are shown in Fig. 6.3. The most common con-figuration features the UA and the MTA collocated on the same machine (top panel) or the MTA deployed aboard a server that is accessed through a gateway by a proprietary LAN e-mail system (middle panel). Behind the LAN gateways lie LAN e-mail systems. However, there are also a number of native X.400 LAN e-mail systems, and Message Store and X.500 Directory [ITU88A] components may become more common by the mid-1990s.

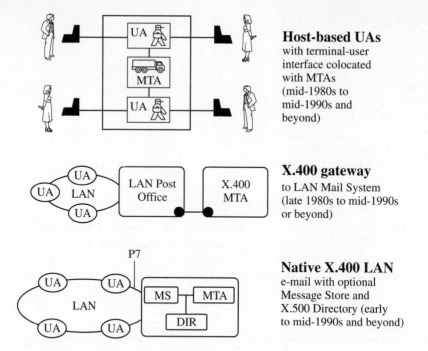

Host-based UAs
with terminal-user
interface colocated
with MTAs
(mid-1980s to
mid-1990s and
beyond)

X.400 gateway
to LAN Mail System
(late 1980s to mid-1990s
or beyond)

Native X.400 LAN
e-mail with optional
Message Store and
X.500 Directory (early
to mid-1990s and beyond)

Figure 6.3   Common X.400 configurations.

6.4   DOMAIN MODELING—ADMINISTRATION AND PRIVATE MANAGEMENT DOMAINS

A messaging standard's mail-domain modeling to a large extent determines the manner in which its processing components interact and its approach to naming, addressing, and routing. This section discusses the original CCITT/ITU management-domain model for X.400, ISO's "deregulated" model, and the scalability challenge facing X.400 practitioners today.

6.4.1   CCITT/ITU Management-domain Model

All X.400 messaging components are considered to exist within Management Domains (MDs). An MD is the X.400 term for an organizationally distinct messaging facility. Some MDs may consist of only a single MTA relaying messages; others may be full-blown services with collections of operators, equipment, and users. Multiple MDs can reside within a country and, in some cases, across national boundaries. X.400 models the global messaging environment as a collection of two basic classes of MDs: Administration Domains and Private Domains.

An X.400 Administration Management Domain (ADMD) is a public service licensed to handle international tariffed messages. ADMDs are operated by the

Postal, Telephone, and Telegraph (PTT) organizations, Recognized Public Operating Agencies (RPOAs), or other registered public information service providers. Some countries currently have only a single ADMD operated by the local PTT. Examples of ADMDs are MCIMail, SprintMail, AT&T Mail, and BT North America in the United States, Telecom Gold in the United Kingdom, ATLAS 400 in France, and Deutsche Bundespost in Germany.

A Private Management Domain (PRMD) is a privately operated messaging network owned by a company, government agency, or other institution. For example, the Hughes Aircraft Company in the U.S., British Petroleum in the U.K. and the Hoechst Company in Germany all operate private X.400 messaging networks with their own premise-based MTAs and UAs. Intra-enterprise messages between employees connected to X.400 can be routed by the domain's own MTAs and need never leave the PRMD.

In the original ITU view of ADMD–PRMD interaction (see Fig. 6.4), PRMDs were expected to route all their external message traffic through a single ADMD operated by the national PTT. They would not send messages directly to either each other or ADMDs in another country. Furthermore, PRMDs would reside entirely within a single country. Under this model, Hoechst and British Petroleum would have to exchange messages via their ADMD service providers. A message from the Hoechst PRMD might go through the Deutsche Bundespost ADMD in Germany to the BT Gold ADMD in the U.K. and, from there, into the British Petroleum PRMD. Hoechst and British Petroleum would not interconnect their MTAs directly, even if they had a great deal of bilateral traffic. A further restriction created the situation where a company such as BASF with offices in Germany, the U.S., and other nations would not operate as a single multinational PRMD; rather, it would have to send messages through the various national ADMDs.

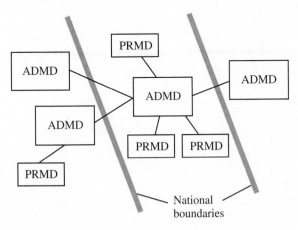

Figure 6.4   ITU view of management domains [ITU84].
Copyright CCITT Recommendation X.402,
"Message handling systems: Overall architecture"
(09/92), Figure 11 "The global MHS."

6.4.2   The "Deregulated" ISO Management-domain Model

The ITU definition of ADMD and PRMD roles reflects the influence of PTTs attempting to impose old-style telephone company/post office arrangements on the modern world of electronic messaging. But around the world, government-operated monopolies are on the wane. The ISO version of the 1988 X.400 standard actually relaxes most of the restrictions on PRMDs;[1] its X.400 document series (ISO 10021) contains a figure that differs from Fig. 6.3 in that it shows PRMDs both connecting to one another directly within and interconnecting across national borders. In terms of the actual international situation today, the ADMD/PRMD roles tend to vary between these ITU and ISO extremes from country to country.

The general acceptance of the deregulated ISO approach has brought competition to the ADMD public service provider market in many countries (see Chapter 4). Interconnection is generally well under control in the public messaging world. ADMDs have harmonized procedures for ADMD–ADMD interconnection through the International ADMD Operators' Group (IAOG). A May 1989 set of guidelines provides for the accounting, service, and operational aspects of Message Handling Services. The IAOG guidelines for settlement arrangements have been submitted to the ITU Study Group 3, where they have been relabeled as Recommendation D.36.

6.4.3   The Scalability Challenge

While ISO's intent was to deregulate X.400 messaging, the standard's addressing structure and infrastructure choices were already implicitly based on the ITU do-main model. The addressing structure reflects the ADMD/PRMD dichotomy and the infrastructure choice was *not* to build a routing/registration infrastructure, but to leave routing and registration in the hands of individual ADMDs (PTTs or oth-erwise), creating a scalability challenge for X.400. In a static routing environment[2] and without free international domain-name registration, it becomes difficult for PRMDs to operate independently of message-relaying ADMD services. It is too expensive for most PRMDs to manage numerous direct interconnections to other PRMDs. The general approach for X.400 PRMDs as of early 1994 was to sub-scribe to a single ADMD, through which they communicate with their trading partners (much as the ITU originally intended).

Nevertheless, PRMD operators continue to demand choices: the option of using none, one, or multiple ADMDs as their service provider. However, such flexibility requires that PRMDs wishing to use multiple ADMDs publish X.400 addresses that

---

1. Note that the ISO and ITU versions of 1988 X.400 are virtually identical technically; the divergent viewpoint on ADMD–PRMD interactions is one of the few differences.

2. In a static routing environment, MTAs route messages based on tables configured manu-ally by administrators rather than by dynamically exchanging routing information between domains. See Section 6.5.

do not contain an ADMD identifier. The use of addresses containing not only the PRMD information but ADMD identifier requires that a country's ADMDs be able to route messages (either directly or via a sister ADMD) to any PRMD in that country, even to PRMDs that are not their direct customers. This requirement effectively implies the existence of a national backbone infrastructure that, among other functions, can register PRMD names at a national level and publish the names and associated interconnection information to all participating ADMDs.

To create the infrastructure for national ADMD backbones that enable PRMD choice, many experts in the industry have pushed at national levels for acceptance of a 1988 X.400 addressing option whereby the "ADMD name" component of an X.400 address is set to the ASCII space character to indicate that any ADMD can be used to route the message. This "ADMD wildcarding" convention has been accepted in the United Kingdom and a handful of other countries. Established ADMD operators in the U.S. were initially cautious about ADMD wildcarding because they would need to reveal their PRMD customer list to competitors as a prerequisite for routing. However, as noted in Chapter 4, the U.S. National Message Transfer System (NMTS) consortium, which includes Advantis, AT&T, BT North America, GEIS, Infonet, MCI, Pacific Bell, and Sprint, is now moving to implement the necessary infrastructure for ADMD wildcarding.

Individual countries have solved ADMD and PRMD routing issues to the PRMD operators' satisfaction, but establishing multinational PRMDs and ADMD backbones is another matter. As yet no existing standards group or forum has stepped up to meet international PRMD name registration requirements. Thus, not only do multinational organizations wishing to operate PRMDs in multiple countries need to take into account the costs of regulatory approval for physical and electrical interconnection to ADMDs, but they also must be aware of the potential difficulties inherent in setting up relationships with multiple ADMD providers in the same country or with using the same ADMD across multiple countries.

PRMD interconnection issues are especially important because the general consensus in the industry today is that the future belongs to PRMDs. Increasingly, even small organizations are moving toward building internal messaging networks rather than utilizing public mailbox services.

6.5   ORIGINATOR/RECIPIENT (O/R) NAMES AND ADDRESSES

The handling of naming, addressing, and routing in a messaging system has important implications for its maintainability, flexibility, expandability, and user-friendliness. X.400 provides data structures to identify either the names or addresses of message originators and message recipients. These structures are called O/R Names and O/R Addresses. This section will begin by discussing generic naming, addressing, and routing considerations and proceed to define and evaluate the X.400 approach.

6.5.1   General Considerations

In the general sense, an e-mail *name* identifies a user, an *address* identifies the location of the user, and a *route* identifies the path to the user's location. In order to deliver mail, or relay it to an immediate destination, a mail system must minimally transform a name to an address and an address to a route. Figure 6.5 diagrams examples of an O/R Name, O/R Address, and a Route. The figure also indicates the name resolution and routing stages that an MTA must go through preparatory to relaying a message toward its destination. Note that MTAs perform name resolution using a directory and routing using either a dynamic routing directory or static routing tables.

Generally both names and addresses point to subscribers or other objects in the network. Addresses are the most primitive reference that can be used directly in message-routing processes. They often use a numeric or alphanumeric syntax that is difficult for users to remember. Whenever a subscriber moves, the address must change. By contrast, names are more descriptive than addresses and are also more stable. For example, a subscriber could move to another system, changing his or her address, but not need to change the name used by correspondents.

It is also important to distinguish between addresses and routes. As shown in Fig. 6.5, an MTA may have multiple routes to the same address, and these routes may change even when the address does not. Addresses or routes change when a user organization changes its ADMD (public service) carrier. Route changes also may arise from the need to scale or control congestion within an enterprise backbone network.

6.5.2   The X.400 Approach

With 1988 X.400, the O/R Name can be either an X.500 Directory Name or an X.400-routable O/R Address. With 1984 X.400, only the O/R Address is available. The O/R Address is a global addressing scheme that subdivides the world of X.400 users first into countries, then into management domains. To understand the next levels of the O/R address hierarchy, we must examine the construction of the O/R Address in greater detail.

An O/R Address consists of *attributes*, where an attribute is a field with a Type and a Value. The possible types of O/R attributes are standard attributes, domain-defined attributes, and extension attributes. The standard attributes are those defined in the 1984 version of the standard. They are

- ADMD name
- PRMD name
- Country name
- X.121 address
- Numeric user identifier
- Organization name
- Organizational unit name

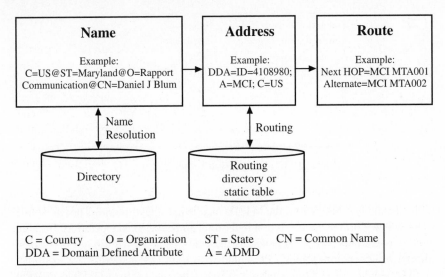

Figure 6.5   Names, addresses, and routes.

- Personal name (structured format)
- Terminal identifier
- Terminal type

The extension attributes include Common Name (unstructured format) and a number of attributes for postal interworking. Domain-defined attributes (DDAs) are specific to a single Management Domain and may not be understood by other domains except by special agreement. An example of a DDA is a mail identifier or login name for a proprietary mail system that connects via a gateway to X.400. Also, in the case of X.400 to SMTP Gateways, RFC 1327 specifies that the user's Internet Mail address can optionally be carried in a DDA.

There are four forms of O/R addresses: terminal-oriented, numeric, postal, and mnemonic. Terminal-oriented O/R addresses support the Telex and Teletex networks as well as telephone numbers for facsimile; the numeric O/R address could support users of numeric keypads or touchtone telephones; and postal O/R addresses support physical delivery. The mnemonic O/R Address is by far the most widely used form. Its elements include organization name, organizational unit name, and personal name attributes. This method allows the address space to be further subdivided into organizational hierarchies. Table 6.2 displays a sample mnemonic O/R Address.

A textual representation of the address in Table 6.2 is:

"G=John ; I=JH ; S=Doe ; OU=Sales ; O=ABC ; P=ABC ;
A=IBMX400 ; C=US"

When a UA submits a message to a 1988 X.400 MTA, it may provide an X.500 Directory Name, an O/R Address, or both. If a Directory Name is submitted

Country	US
Administration Domain	IBMX400
Private Domain	ABC
Organization	ABC
Organization Unit	Sales
Personal Name	Given Name = John
	Initials = JH
	Surname = Doe

Table 6.2 An example X.400 O/R address.

without an O/R Address, or if the MTA is unable to route the address provided, the MTA will perform name resolution by issuing an X.500 Read Operation. Once an address is available, the MTA generally uses the O/R address attributes to perform top-down incremental routing. Presented with John Doe's address, for example, an MTA would look at the "Country=US" term first, then at the ADMD, next at the PRMD, and so forth. If the MTA were located in France, it might well have no knowledge of the ABC MTA's name or network location. However, the French MTA could be set up to route all "US/IBMX400" messages to an IBMX400 MTA in the U.S. The IBMX400 MTA might in turn have no knowledge of the internal structure of the ABC PRMD; it would simply pass off the message to the ABC MTA for further incremental routing. In addition to this basic incremental routing, management domains can set up more sophisticated alternate routing algorithms to accommodate domain policies, load balancing, and redundancy concerns. Since the X.400 standard does not specify how routing should be done, products vary widely in their approaches.

6.5.3   Evaluating the X.400 Approach

One of the blocking factors to wider deployment of X.400 technology has been its approach to naming, addressing, registration, and routing. At the heart of the problem is the fact that both the X.400 O/R Name and Address can appear overly long and confusing to end users. User friendly implementations must beautify the O/R Name or Address, providing aliases that map gracefully between it and the first name/last name representation that users are accustomed to seeing.

Furthermore, the X.400 O/R Address offers numerous options, and the standards committees did not hand down guidelines on its use. It seems that no two PRMDs have implemented their internal addressing scheme in the same fashion. For example, one major PRMD uses addresses of the following form: *G=JOHN ; I=JHXXX ; S=DOE ; P=ABC ; A=" " ; C=US*. (The "XXX" in the Initials field is used as a tie breaker for name collisions. Name collisions occur frequently in this flat address space, because users are not subdivided into Organizational Units. If they were, however, addresses would have to be republished each time organizational changes occurred.)

Another PRMD also favors a flat address space but employs an Organizational Unit field to contain the tie-breaker numbers. Still another routinely includes each user's telephone number in a Domain-Defined attribute field. Other PRMDs populate Organizational Unit fields with the names of MTAs rather than with organizational structure, essentially embedding their routing scheme into an address.

Although the O/R Address succeeds in subdividing the global address space hierarchically, the price of its generality and its coded attribute structure is that the so-called mnemonic O/R Addresses are in fact difficult for users to guess or remember. They are also difficult to enter into a user interface, since every product presents them differently. For this reason, some UAs allow a user to enter an alias and then automatically fill in the rest of the O/R Address fields by consulting a directory. Most current X.400 products already feature proprietary directories of O/R addresses. X.500 directories can also be used to discover the O/R addresses of correspondents through online exploration. Flat address schemes absolutely require a directory underpinning, something that is not available in all products.

Unfortunately, the problems of the X.400 community do not end with complex addressing but are compounded by the community's lack of a dynamic routing directory and of any provision for free international PRMD name registration. The fact that static routing tables must be maintained everywhere forces PRMDs to rely heavily on ADMD message relaying services, driving up the costs of using this technology. The expense of registration in some countries (ANSI charges $1,500 in the U.S.) further deters usage.

Against this backdrop, a number of proposals to simplify X.400 addressing began circulating in 1993 and 1994. Some proposals entail standardizing the way users define their addresses. One proposal from ANSI advocated retrofitting Internet Mail addresses into X.400.

6.6   STRUCTURE OF MESSAGES, DELIVERY REPORTS, RECEIPT NOTIFICATIONS, AND PROBES

At the MTS level, X.400 information objects include Messages, Reports, and Probes. Message objects can be further subdivided based on the nature of their content. We will discuss Messages first, then Reports and Probes.

As shown in Fig. 6.6, an X.400 message is composed of an envelope plus a content object. The envelope contains all the X.400 addressing information necessary to transmit a message from one originator to one or more recipients, while offering X.400 service features such as Priority Indication, Content Type Indication, and numerous others. The content contains a Heading and a Body. The Body may consist of multiple Body Parts.

The division of a message into an envelope plus content mirrors the layered structure of the X.400 model, which separates the Interpersonal Messaging Service or other applications from the Message Transfer System (MTS). Apart from one exceptional case, where format conversion may be performed on Body Parts within the Content, the MTS layer does not concern itself with anything but the envelope.

Message = Envelope + Content

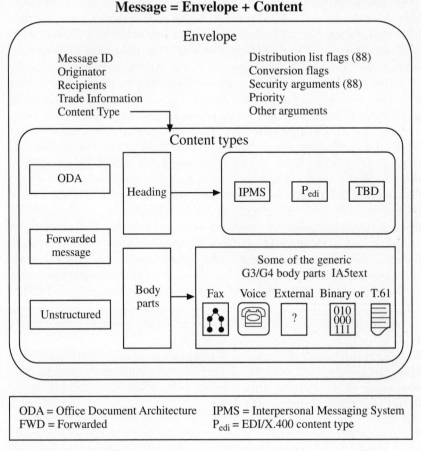

Figure 6.6   X.400 message structure.

On the other hand, the messaging application determines the content structure. Except in special cases, where the Content is a nested forwarded Message or is encrypted, the Content consists of a Heading and a Body. In the Interpersonal Messaging System (IPMS), the Content is an Interpersonal Message (IPM) with a heading rather like that of an office memorandum containing To, From, Subject, Reply Indication, and other fields. The Body of an IPM is composed of one or more Body Parts that are often generic and are known globally throughout the X.400 MTS, facilitating (in special circumstances) their MTA-level conversion from one format to another. The ability to embed so many different types of information in an X.400 message is one factor that gives the standard wide applicability, allowing it to be used with applications such as EDI.

The 1984 standard defined a number of built-in Body Parts including IA5Text (ASCII), G3 facsimile, G4 facsimile, Telex, Teletex, Videotex, Voice, and Encrypted data. However, the formats for voice and encrypted body parts were left for further study.[3] In some cases, MTAs will perform automatic conversion from one Body Part format to another (text-to-fax or telex-to-text). Note that MTA conversions mark the only exception to the rule that the MTA does not generally peek inside the message envelope. Most X.400 implementations support the IA5 Text Body Part. The others are optional and rarely implemented.

6.6.1   The Undefined Body Part

What the 1984 standard unfortunately omitted was a Body Part for unstructured binary data and a mechanism for two users to identify Body Parts to each other, even if their particular Body Part might be totally unknown to any of the MTAs transmitting the content. Thus, during the late 1980s, users were frustrated by an inability to transmit binary files (such as word processing files or spreadsheets) between MTAs of different vendor manufacture.

This problem was patched up in the OIW Agreements by reserving a Body Part type (Body Part 14) to carry undefined, or binary, data. Most vendors now support this agreement.

Although the Undefined Body Part allows users to carry any type of data (word processing files, spreadsheets, or drawings), it does not allow for automated end-to-end identification of the information type contained in the undefined package. Human users can deal with this option with relative ease by attaching explanatory notes in a text Body Part prefacing the message. For mail-enabled applications without human inferential powers, however, there must be an a priori bilateral agreement of some sort between the sender and receiver before the information can be interpreted. Even human users generally must unload a binary attachment manually into the file system, exit their UA, and run the word processor. If the Body Part had identified itself, however, the mail system might have enabled the user to launch the word processor for that document simply by clicking on a graphic icon that represents the body part.

6.6.2   The External Body Part (1988) and the File Transfer Body Part (1992)

1988 X.400 addresses the identification of Body Part types by adding a new type: the External Body Part. Each instance of an external Body Part contains an *object identifier* (OID) or an Integer *tag* to identify itself to UAs. The object identifier, which is the preferred mechanism, is a hierarchical number that can be registered by standards groups or identified organizations such that it is understood by all vendors, with little or no likelihood of duplicative interpretation. Thus, a Lotus spreadsheet might travel as an external Body Part using one object identifier value, and a Quattro spreadsheet using another.

---

3. The Voice Body Part was eventually defined in the 1992 X.440 recommendation.

Vendors today can register a branch of the Object Identifier number tree, and then populate it with an Object Identifier for each of their document types. In the U.S., this registration can be done under the auspices of the American National Standards Institute (ANSI) or with the Internet Assigned Numbers Authority (IANA). However, neither ISO, nor ITU, nor any other de facto standards organization has yet stepped up to the task of *publishing* all the external body part types to enable transparent interworking.[4] Thus, while some vendors outfitted early 1988 X.400 implementations with the capability to identify External Body Parts, these implementations initially found themselves with few defined types to carry.

Yet another option for Body Part identification is to use the 1992 X.400 File Transfer body part [ITU92]. X.400's File Transfer Body Part is a data structure designed to carry detailed information about files embedded in messages. While the File Transfer Body Part is part of the 1992 X.400 standard, the OIW and the EMA's Message Attachment Working Group are actively encouraging X.400 vendors to retrofit it into their 1988 X.400 implementations. Figure 6.7 displays an example of the File Transfer Body Part, where most of the fields are optional. They are, incidentally, compatible with the OSI File Transfer, Access, and Management (FTAM) standard [FTAM1–FTAM4].

Investigating vendor claims of 1988 X.400 support, users should find out how the Body Part type indication will be communicated to their mail-enabled applications (both those from the vendor and those provided by third parties) and how easy (or difficult) it will be to upgrade the products they have purchased once external body parts are officially registered. One question to ask is whether the implementation under consideration allows the object identifiers to be specified in configuration files at run time.

6.6.3   Delivery Reports, Receipt Notifications, and Probes

Other than messages, two additional objects can be transferred between either the 1984 or 1988 vintage X.400 MTAs. The additional objects are Reports and Probes. In addition, both the IPMS and the EDIMG standards define Notifications, but 1984 and 1988 X.400 MTAs handle these in the same fashion as ordinary messages.

A Report takes the form of either a Nondelivery Report or a Delivery Report. Reports are generated at the MTS level of X.400 by the delivering MTA. Either or both kinds of reports can be requested by a message-originating MTA for accounting purposes, or by an originating user. Delivery Reports do not indicate that the recipient user has actually read the message, but merely that the receiving MTA has dropped off the message in a mailbox or has delivered the message to a gateway.

To determine whether a recipient has actually read or at least scanned a message, originators must request an IPMS-level Receipt Notification or Nonreceipt

---

4. The EMA may take on the task of publishing object identifier values used for external Body Parts. A tutorial on the subject may be found in [BANA93].

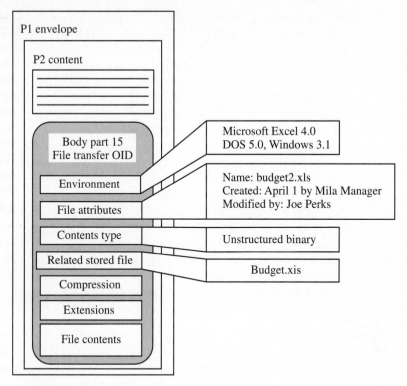

Figure 6.7   The X.400 file transfer body part.

Notification. These notifications travel as data structures within the content of an X.400 message. EDI notifications are similar.

X.400 users can generate probes to determine the deliverability of a particular kind of message to a particular recipient or recipients. A Probe contains many of the attributes of a message (but not the content), and it is never actually delivered to the recipient(s). It can be used to test X.400 recipient addresses for the first time, prior to sending a particularly lengthy or important message, or for management or monitoring purposes. A Nondelivery or Delivery Report returned in response to the Probe affirms the nondeliverability or deliverability of messages of the type denoted by the Probe.

6.7   A COMMON SET OF MESSAGING SERVICES

One of the most valuable aspects of X.400 is its definition of common messaging services. Services, in terms of X.400, are distinct from protocols, such as P1. Services reflect the end-user functionality, whereas protocols reflect the mechanics by which X.400 provides the service. Since the common X.400 services are so comprehensive (over 90 for the 1988 X.400 MTS alone), they are by and large a superset of services offered by proprietary mail systems. Thus X.400 provides a common denominator for mapping functionality between dissimilar mail systems and a common way of describing overlapping functionality.

Because X.400 has so many services, many attempts have been made to organize them into useful categorizations. For example, the OIW 1988 X.400 Agreements contain carefully crafted conformance requirements designed to ensure that products can interoperate without each having to implement every single service and protocol option of 1988 X.400. The OIW Agreements group functional aspects of the standards so that, rather than selecting from a bewildering menu of à la carte options, users can specify and vendors can build packages of options. These OIW packages (called functional groups) are shown in Table 6.3.

These functional groups represent the features of X.400 made available through UA, MTA, MS, and Physical Delivery AU (PDAU) processing entities. Each functional group categorizes service and protocol elements as mandatory or optional for compliance to that group. Some service elements affect only one processing entity; others affect multiple entities. For example, the Grade of Delivery element can be set by the user as part of the IPM Service, but the MTA actually provides the service. The basic elements of each functional group are described below.

- **Message Transfer Kernel:** This functional group classifies basic capabilities such as downgrading from 1988 X.400 P1 to 1984 X.400 P1, UA to MTA or UA to MS access management, content type indication, deferred delivery, disclosure of recipients, and multidestination delivery. It also includes various features for reliability and audit, such as message identification, nonde-

Functional group	Affected component
Message transfer kernel	MTA
IPM service	UA
EDI messaging service	EDI-UA
Security	MTA, UA, MS
Address support for Teletex (T.61) characters	MTA, UA, MS
Distribution lists	MTA, UA
Redirection	MTA, UA
Use of directory	MTA, UA
Conversion	MTA, UA
Message store	MS
Remote UA	UA
Physical delivery AU	UA, MTA

Table 6.3 OIW 1988 X.400 functional units and affected components. *Note: Other AUs, Redirection, and MHS Management are listed as functional groups in the OIW Agreements, but are left for further study elsewhere.*

livery notification, delivery notification, submission time-stamp indication, delivery time-stamp indication, and return of content.

- **Interpersonal Messaging (IPM) Service:** This functional group classifies elements of the X.400 P2/P22 content-based services for interpersonal messaging. These services include designation of message subject, primary recipient, copy recipient, blind copy recipient, indication that the current message is a reply, request for a reply, and many others.

- **EDI Messaging Service:** This functional group classifies X.435 services and protocols for EDI Messaging.

- **Security and Privacy:** Security and privacy-related services include message confidentiality and many others to be discussed in Section 6.13.

- **Address Support for T.61 Characters:** This functional group requires support for O/R address attributes that are represented in the T.61 character set.

- **Redirection and Distribution Lists:** These functional groups classify a 1988 X.400 MTA's ability to expand a recipient name that denotes a distribution list (DL) into the members of the DL or to redirect a message from one recipient to another. Available services enable an originator to prohibit redirection and/or DL operations. Also available are services enabling recipients (at the time of message delivery) and originators (by means of delivery reports) to be notified when redirection or DL expansion events have occurred.

- **Use of Directory:** MTAs and UAs supporting the functional group have the capability of using the X.500 directory and understanding its data types.

- **Conversion:** Some X.400 MTAs have the ability to convert message Body Parts from one format to another. This capability can be controlled through such service elements as prohibition of conversion by the originator, indication by the originating UA of the original encoded information types sent in the message content, indication by the MTA that it has converted the message, and registration by the UA of which information types its directory can receive so that the MTA can effect desirable conversions transparently. While this functional group defines requirements for how MTAs supporting conversion should manipulate the appropriate P1 protocol elements, it does not mandate that any specific types of conversions be supported.

- **Message Store:** A Message Store complying with this functional group supports the P7 protocol, including services such as stored message Fetch, List, Delete, and Summarize.

- **Remote UA:** A Remote UA complying with this functional group supports the X.400 P3 MTA access protocol or the P7 Message Store protocol.

- **Physical Delivery:** This functional group classifies services provided by the 1988 X.400 standard's physical delivery AU (PDAU), which is intended to handle interworking with postal services and controls the interaction between electronic mail and physical delivery devices, such as laser printers.

Users specifying their X.400 procurement requirements can pick and choose which groups to select; for example, an X.400 backbone procurement might demand the Message Transfer Kernel, Distribution Lists, Use of Directory, and Address Support for T.61 Characters. Almost universally in the U.S., vendors, consultants, and informed users recommend that the OIW Agreements be the basis for X.400 procurement. The current OIW Stable Agreements are mature and, in the case of X.400, are subject to enhancement only in regard to adding specifications for future content types. Moreover, they are now aligned with and reference the ISP, which is accepted worldwide.

6.8   GATEWAYS AND X.400 AS AN INTEGRATION TOOL

If users deployed only native X.400 mail systems, there would be no need for gateways. However, because native X.400 has not achieved desktop dominance and, despite its reservoir of political support and the emergence of implementations, is unlikely to do so in the future, multiple e-mail systems and multiple standards will remain in place. When multiple systems must coexist, gateways are required to link them together. Like death and taxes, it seems that gateways will always be with us. In this chapter on X.400, we limit ourselves to discussing the X.400 gateway phenomenon and to explaining the distinction between X.400 (standard) and e-mail backbones or integration tools (multiprotocol implementations).

Because X.400 offers a wide-ranging set of common services, many users in the industry labored under the misapprehension that it possesses some magic capacity to interconnect dissimilar e-mail systems. The fallacy of this belief was demonstrated in multiple gateways testing that attempted to accomplish interconnection solely through mapping proprietary e-mail protocols to X.400 without adding sufficient additional integration capabilities.[5] The fact that such problems occur in many X.400 gateways points to a need for users to calibrate their expectations of X.400 by understanding two key points: First, X.400 is a standard and not an e-mail integration tool, and secondly, users with heterogeneous e-mail environments require a first-rate e-mail integration tool (a backbone or collection of gateways) that supports X.400 and delivers high-quality end-to-end service within their domains.

A common set of messaging services or protocols is different from an e-mail integration tool. One crucial function performed by an integration tool is mapping between a proprietary mail system and some other system. In the case of a tool that

---

5. For example, [INFO92] explained the limitations of using the Retix OpenServer product as a LAN e-mail integration tool. As part of the research for the article, *InfoWorld* tested the ability of the X.400 OpenServer to interconnect six LAN e-mail systems (cc:Mail, BeyondMail, Microsoft Mail, Da Vinci Mail, Futurus Team, and WordPerfect Office) and found a number of problems, including the inability to reply to messages, and corrupted subject lines.

happens to be an X.400 gateway or X.400 backbone product, the mapping is between the proprietary mail system and X.400. Because X.400 itself is silent on the subject of how such a tool should work, such tools vary widely between vendors.

A relatively simple example should help to clarify the difference. Suppose that two users wish to engage in the basic activities of sending, receiving, and replying to messages. Suppose further that User A employs an X.400 mail system, and User B employs PROFS and has an X.400 gateway capable of mapping between X.400 and PROFS. Suppose that User A sends a message to User B and User B wishes to reply. Is this manipulation merely a case of simple message format mapping each way, or is a complex integration problem involved?

As it turns out, the latter is the case. Because X.400 uses long structured O/R addresses and PROFS uses eight-character addresses, it is impossible to pass the X.400 address of user A through PROFS to user B. Thus, with only straight mapping between X.400 and PROFS, it is impossible for a PROFS user to reply to an X.400 message using the originator's X.400 address.

The ability to resolve such dilemmas marks a genuine integration tool. Some products auto-register the address of the sender in their directory and create a PROFS name for use during the period that user A and user B will correspond. When user B replies through PROFS, the gateway automatically generates the correct X.400 address. User B, we hope, remains blissfully unaware of these contortions.

The role of e-mail integration tools is not limited to auto-registration and mapping. If it were, there would be no further need for such products, given mail systems which support native X.400. As we noted earlier, e-mail integration tools can also accomplish many other useful functions, such as directory synchronization, high performance message relay, message attachment format conversions, distribution list expansion, and mail-system monitoring.

6.9   THE X.400 APPLICATION PROGRAM INTERFACES

Software interfaces between X.400 UAs and MTAs are much more common in products than the P3 interface originally specified by the ITU for remote UA access. Although software programmatic interfaces are not addressed in X.400 itself, a need arose for a standard API for linking mail gateways and mail-enabled applications to X.400. Consequently a group of leading computer and communications vendors formed the X.400 Application Program Interface Association (XAPIA). The XAPIA undertook to speed the development of X.400 gateways (initially for LAN-based e-mail systems). The XAPIA was eventually joined by X/OPEN and IEEE in its endorsement of this API.

There are actually two variations of the X.400 API: an Application API and a Gateway API. Essentially, the difference between them lies in the way users are addressed. With the Application API, the client entity opposite the MTA acts like a UA or an MS, taking deliveries for a single user. With the Gateway API (which acts like a LAN e-mail post office), the client entity opposite the MTA acts like another MTA, taking messages for multiple users. This difference does not otherwise affect the data that can be transferred; it affects only the nature of the function calls and queuing mechanisms.

The X.400 API, which has since been implemented by a number of major vendors, specifies C programming language interfaces through which messages can be submitted and delivered to UAs or MTAs. It has been extended to incorporate OSI Object Management API Specifications and an X.500 Directory Services Specification. The XAPIA and X/OPEN have also standardized an EDI Messaging Package to provide X.435 (EDI) access and a Message Store API to provide UAs with programmatic access to the Message Store's P7 retrieval functions. Prior to the adoption of the Message Store API, only the services of the MTA were accessible using the XAPIA mechanisms.

The X.400 API's major limitation is that, in achieving a complete and faithful mapping to the richness of X.400, it created a programmatic mechanism appropriate for system developers but too complex for either independent software vendors (ISVs) of mail-enabled applications or corporate application programmers. For this reason, vendors often provide higher-level toolkits of subroutine interfaces layered over the XAPIA and, of course, their own proprietary APIs. As previously discussed, e-mail vendors such as Microsoft and Lotus have attempted to define messaging API standards, and the XAPIA itself is currently creating Common Mail Calls for generalized e-mail access. These APIs are different from the X.400 APIs in that they provide application access to local messaging software and do not presume that X.400 is the underlying protocol.

6.10   X.400 USE OF X.500 DIRECTORIES

One of the major problems for X.400 today is that presently deployed 1984 X.400 gateways do not provide a full enterprise messaging backbone solution. One of the gateway deficiencies is a lack of directory synchronization. There is a burning need in the marketplace for unified enterprise e-mail directory products enabling all enterprise users, regardless of their host e-mail system, to see one another's names and addresses in order to correspond readily. The 1984 X.400 standards were rolled out without directory facilities (although a need for them was anticipated and they were left for further study). The 1988 X.400 standards do include provisions for X.500 usage. Nevertheless, at this stage of the game, multivendor X.500 Directory Services standards have yet to achieve critical mass in terms of installed products and reference sites.

X.400 applications require a multivendor Directory Service because the community of users is large, widespread, and dispersed across multivendor computing platforms. X.500 will provide browsing capabilities, allowing users to identify intended correspondents and allowing both users and MTAs to perform directory name to O/R Address resolution. X.500 directories will also store shared distribution lists that can be expanded by MTAs, public encryption keys (or certificates), and information on user capabilities enabling MTAs to determine the deliverability of a particular message's content types and Body Parts to particular users.

The technical basis for using the directory stems from both Annex B of Recommendation X.402, where the format of the information to be stored on its behalf in the directory is defined, and from the OIW Agreements. Unfortunately, the existing Use of Directory provisions are inadequate at least in the following areas: (1) More directory fields (such as a list of undeliverable Body Part types) are needed to aid in assessing user capabilities; (2) since O/R Names can have components in arbitrary order and may be encoded in a number of variations, rules for matching an input X.400 O/R Name value with an O/R Name value stored in the directory are needed; and (3) obtaining the benefits of a standardized directory and still remaining backward compatible with 1984 X.400 systems requires that procedures for reverse mapping an O/R Address of a recipient into an X.500 name be defined as well.

At some point, MTAs will also publish routing information in X.500 directories, much as Internet Mail system components now store their routes in the Domain Name System (see Chapter 7 for how this is done in the Internet). The ITU and ISO have a work item for standardizing the management of routing information and its storage in the directory. Unfortunately they failed to complete it during the 1992 standards effort. However, X.400 users in the Internet community have experimented with storing MTA routing information in X.500 directories and have published an Internet Draft containing their recommendations [KILL93, ALVE93B].

6.11 MIGRATION BETWEEN 1984 AND 1988 IMPLEMENTATIONS

The original 1984 X.400 protocol was developed without hooks for future extensions. Therefore a 1988 implementation cannot interwork with a 1984 implementation except by resembling the behavior of the 1984 implementation. This process is called downgrading. Since MTAs cannot downgrade those 1988 messages that contain critical extensions over and above the 1984 protocol, some nondeliveries will result when a 1988 MTA transmits a message to a 1984 MTA or readies it for delivery to a recipient's 1984 UA or gateway.[6]

Once 1984 MTAs have been upgraded to understand the 1988 X.400 extension mechanism, they can accept 1988 messages. However, supporting the concept of extensions and actually supporting the extensions themselves are two entirely different matters. Recognizing that not all implementations will support all extensions, the 1988 X.400 standard defines different extensions as "critical for

---

6. Portions of this section are reprinted with permission from the Electronic Mail Association's "The 1988 X.400 Migration White Paper," prepared by Daniel J. Blum and published in 1993 [BLUM93A]. The EMA's support for that work is gratefully acknowledged.

delivery," "critical for submission," or "critical for transfer." MTAs can ignore noncritical extensions but must nondeliver a message or discard a report if they contain an unsupported "critical" extension. Two of the many possible examples are that neither a message with T.61 string elements in an O/R address nor a message with the "dl-expansion-prohibited" extension can be downgraded.

Other 1988 capabilities that show up in an X.400 message content or in the addressing of an X.400 message can also trigger nondelivery. Since the standard did not specify a P22-to-P2 downgrading procedure, the most serious concerns in this area have to do with exchanging or attempting to exchange self-identifying documents or other objects (such as External Body Parts) between 1988 and 1984 systems.

[BLUM93A] suggests that users chart their 1984-to-1988 X.400 migration in four stages as follows (also see Fig. 6.8):

1. Upgrade the underlying transport infrastructure (either public or premise-based) to support the OIW Agreements' MT Kernel functional group for 1988 X.400 MTAs. The MT Kernel includes a 1984 downgrading requirement and was carefully crafted to ensure that 1988 X.400 MTA products can interoperate without each having to implement every single option in the P1 protocol.

2. Upgrade all end-user or application facilities (UAs) to support some level of 1988 X.400 functionality.

3. Insert X.500-based enterprise directory functionality. Upgrade MTAs and UAs to access the enterprise directory.

4. Add advanced 1988 X.400 functional groups, such as document conversion, distribution lists, redirection, and security, as these capabilities become available from vendors and service providers.

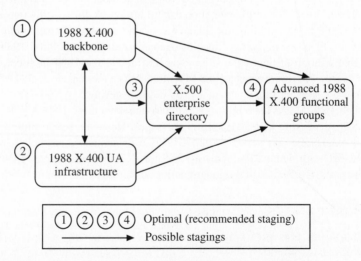

Figure 6.8   The four-stage 1988 X.400 migration model.

Like all models, the four-stage migration model in some cases oversimplifies reality. PRMDs using a single mail system may be able to accomplish steps 1 and 2 simultaneously. In more complex scenarios, PRMDs may be forced to undertake multiple iterations of the four basic stages as products become available. Finally, the desirable ordering of the insertion of functionality may vary on a regional or industry basis. For example, 1988 X.400 Message Stores are currently of greater importance in some parts of Europe than in the U.S., and the importance of robust security features varies by industry.

Nevertheless, the model is useful. By following it as closely as possible, X.400 networks will be able to migrate in a unified fashion and to minimize disruption to their users.

6.12   USE OF UNDERLYING COMMUNICATIONS LAYERS

To communicate with other X.400 components, an X.400 processing entity such as an MTA must have both upper and lower layer communications interfaces. This section discusses the position of X.400 in the OSI model, the X.400 application layer structure, Abstract Syntax Notation One (ASN.1), X.400 use of lower layers, X.400 operation over TCP/IP, and X.400 operation over dial-up connections.

6.12.1   The OSI Architecture and X.400

Figure 6.9 summarizes the role of all the OSI layers [ITU88B–P]. OSI provides a seven-layer model that was originally conceived by ISO in the late 1970s and was standardized by the ITU in 1984.

The X.400 processing entities that we have discussed—the MTA, the UA, and the MS—reside in the application layer and are shown in Figs. 6.10 and 6.11.

OSI standardizes a Transport-level protocol and several Network-level protocols. The popular TCP/IP protocols logically belong in layers 1–4 but are incompatible with OSI protocols. In addition, there are transport incompatibilities, even within the OSI world. For example, an application running over a LAN Ethernet-based transport stack cannot connect directly to an application running over an X.25-based transport stack. The benefit of the X.400 and the OSI layered architecture, however, is that the choice of transport service used is transparent to an MTA, MS, or UA. The disadvantage of the current transport incompatibilities is that two MTAs using different transport stacks can communicate only through an MTA relay that supports both stacks.

6.12.2   The Application Layer

Figure 6.10 shows the X.400 Application Layer architecture in the 1984 standard. Remote UAs communicate with MTAs using the P3 protocol supported by a Remote Operations Service (ROS), and MTAs communicate with one another using

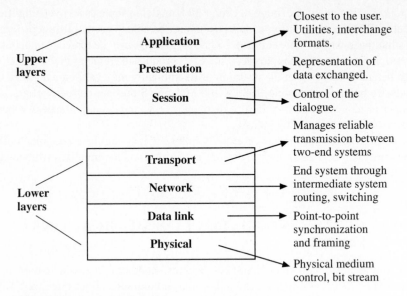

Figure 6.9   The OSI model.

the P1 protocol supported by the Reliable Transfer Service (RTS). Both ROS and RTS are defined in Recommendation X.410 and run directly over the OSI Session Layer [ITU84], since the Presentation Layer was in the process of parallel definition by another standards committee at the time of X.410 development.

The Application Layer architecture was refined considerably in 1988, as shown in Fig. 6.11. X.410 ROS was recast as the Remote Operations Service Element (ROSE) and moved to ITU Recommendation X.218/X.228 (ISO 9066) and X.410 RTS was recast as the Reliable Transfer Service Element (RTSE) and

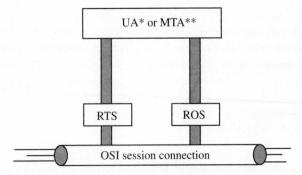

* ROS intended for UA to MTA (P3) interaction.

** RTS used for MTA to MTA (P1) interaction

Figure 6.10   1984 X.400 application architecture.

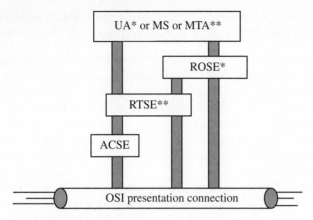

* ROSE used for all interactions except MTA to MTA
** RTSE optional except for MTA to MTA interaction

Figure 6.11   1988 X.400 application layer structure.

moved to ITU Recommendation X.219/X.229 (ISO 9072). Both are now intended for general use by other OSI applications in addition to X.400.[7]

The Association Control Service Element (ACSE) establishes and releases associations or application-level connections. The ROSE, used with P3 and P7, provides an OSI client-server protocol for reply/request interactions between OSI applications. The RTSE provides application entities with reliable transfer services that allow an MTA to resend only parts of messages (rather than entire ones) whose transfer was interrupted by errors such as line failures. An X.410 mode is used with RTSE and ACSE to retain backward compatibility with 1984 X.400 and RTS implementations.

Thus, when a user submits a message or a message enters through a gateway, the following activities occur:

- The local MTA performs its routing function to determine what to do with the message recipients. It executes local deliveries. If necessary, it relays one or more copies of the message to adjacent MTAs.

- For each remote MTA, the local MTA checks to see whether it has an active association. If not, it instructs its ACSE software to set one up. ACSE then drives the lower OSI communication layers to establish a seven-layer OSI connection.

- Assuming that an association existed or was established successfully, the MTA activates the RTSE. The RTSE drives the lower OSI communication layers to transfer the message.

---

7. The X.500 Directory Service, for example, makes use of ROSE.

6.12.3   Abstract Syntax Notation One (ASN.1) and Other Upper OSI Layer Functionality

OSI upper layer functionality used by X.400 includes Abstract Syntax Notation One (ASN.1), the Presentation Layer, and the Session Layer.

ASN.1 is a system of formal notation or language to express data structures in an abstract manner. The X.400 standards formally describe all P1 data structures, including messages, probes, and reports, as well as the P3 and P7 submission, delivery, retrieval, and other operations in the ASN.1 language. The P2 Interpersonal Messaging Content format and the P35 EDI Messaging Content format are also defined in ASN.1.

The *abstract syntax*, or formal ASN.1 representation of information can, with the aid of a set of encoding rules, become a *transfer syntax* capable of representing data in a canonical network form over the wire. For example, when an MTA actually sends a message, it encodes the envelope and content fields using the ASN.1 specification for message structure, and sends the resulting bits to an adjacent MTA.

Both the ASN.1 abstract and transfer syntaxes are complex. Software developers generally require ASN.1 compiler tools to develop the ASN.1 encoder/decoder modules for runtime activation.

The Presentation Layer allows applications to select, negotiate, and even modify bit representation of application information, used within an association. X.400 makes few demands on this layer. It makes rather more demands on the Session Layer, which essentially provides many of the underlying data communications functions needed to put the "reliable" into X.400's MTA/RTSE. Using the Session Layer's Activity Management functional unit, the MTA/RTSE structures messages as Session activities and can start, end, interrupt, and resume their transfer. It can also checkpoint the transfer of messages by interspersing data with synchronization points using the Session Layer's Minor Synchronization functional unit. Checkpointing and activity management together allow the MTA/RTSE to recover from network failures, even if the failures disrupt an association. In the case of disruption, the association is simply reestablished and the message (possibly large) is continued without retransmission.

6.12.4   Lower Layers

We should say a few words about the lower layers. The ITU originally intended X.400 to run primarily over PTT-operated, connection-oriented X.25 networks using an end-to-end protocol with minimal error checking called Transport Class 0 (TP0). When ISO joined ITU in the standardization process, it broadened transport conformance requirements for the underlying lower layers to encompass non-X.25 networks using a protocol with robust error checking called Transport Class 4 (TP4). This use of the lower layers remains a difference between the ISO and ITU 1988 X.400 versions of the standards.

In the area of network protocols, ISO also wished to address this more general *internetworking* problem: How can X.400 messages (or any OSI Application's data) be sent from a LAN running a broadcast protocol such as Ethernet [CSMD], across a wide area network (WAN) running X.25, to another LAN running perhaps yet a third protocol? ISO's answer was to develop the Connectionless Network Protocol (CLNP) in 1986 [CLNP86], as well as to support dynamic routing protocols for end system and intermediate system auto-configuration and discovery. CLNP is conceptually very similar to the Internet's IP. However, OSI/CLNP networks have been slow to spread, especially into the LAN world.

6.12.5   The Relationships Among X.400, Internet Mail, and TCP/IP

X.400 interworks with Internet Mail and TCP/IP in two ways. First, Internet Mail users can communicate with X.400 users via an application gateway. The Internet Engineering Task Force (IETF) has developed an Application Layer gateway mapping facility and codified it in Request for Comment (RFC) 1327. The more recent RFCs 1494 and 1495 have been provided for 1988 X.400 envelope/content to Internet RFC 822 message header mapping [ALVE93 and ALVE93D]. (X.400 to RFC 822 gateways are discussed further in Chapter 7.)

Second, since TCP/IP is a standard facility of UNIX releases and has penetrated proprietary vendor architectures as well, many enterprises are already operating TCP/IP networks. Some such enterprises desire the advanced functionality of X.400, but not at the cost of replacing their existing lower layer network with lower layer OSI protocol implementations. To satisfy such concerns, an OSI Transport to TCP/IP mapping facility (diagrammed in Fig. 6.12) was developed by the IETF and codified in RFC 1006 [ROSE87].

6.12.6   X.400 over Dial-up Lines

One of the advantages of the X.400/OSI layered architecture is that it permits application layer software (such as X.400 or X.500) to be developed without dependencies on what communications (network and transport) software is run beneath it. We have noted the current trend to run X.400 over TCP/IP as well as over OSI.

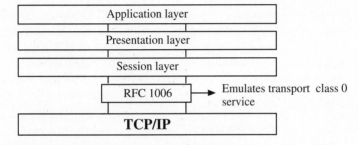

Figure 6.12   X.400 run over TCP/IP.

As presently profiled, OSI usually requires the use of X.25 over leased lines, and even TCP/IP is only beginning to be widely used over dial-up lines. However, there are millions of potential users in the field who have leased lines or who are equipped with low performance PCs. Many more users will come online in the near future with extremely lightweight portable computers. To date, such users have depended on dial-up access using such protocols as UNIX UUCP and NetWare MHS.

A Dial X.400 capability would present many advantages. Lightweight LAN-based MTAs could contact public or enterprise backbone MTAs without needing to have expensive dedicated lines extended to their premises. Lightweight or portable UA software could contact MTAs or Message Stores using "Dial P3" or "Dial P7," thus allowing inexpensive plug and play between multivendor products.

Some vendors have already experimented with Dial X.400 capabilities; for instance, a Canadian firm named OSIWare has long had a proprietary protocol it calls TTXP. To be truly useful, however, Dial X.400 capabilities must be profiled for broad implementation based on a common interpretation. One approach would be to run X.400 over TCP/IP with Serial Line Internet Protocol (SLIP) or the Point-to-Point Protocol (PPP) [SIMP93]. A group of vendors formed the Asynchronous Protocol Specification (APS) consortium in late 1992 with the express purpose of specifying OSI-based asynchronous transports for X.400 and X.500 [APS93] and completed their initial specifications in 1993 [APS93A]. These specifications were quickly incorporated in the ITU draft recommendation X.445. The availability of APS may someday increase X.400's usability, acceptance, and market share.

6.13 SECURITY

The 1984 X.400 recommendations contained no security provisions other than the ability to send a password in the clear (unencrypted) on establishment of an MTA-to-MTA association or connection. The 1988 recommendations added enhanced security capabilities supporting authentication of associations, message integrity, and message encryption. These capabilities are potentially very valuable in the electronic commerce environment, especially if they become legitimized in legal statutes. The 1988 X.400 security features are several years from widespread implementation, and numerous political issues remain to be resolved before X.400 security (even if implemented) could be effective.[8] This section first reviews the security threats present in most messaging environments and then discusses ge-

---

8. Early testing was performed in 1993 using research community implementations known as *OSISEC* and *SECUDE* from the University College of London and Gesellschaft für Mathematik und Datnenverarbeitung MBH respectively. Both implementations were based on the ISODE Consortium's PP X.400 software. These solutions, as well as X.500 software and Internet Privacy Enhanced Mail software, were employed in a PASSWORD pilot conducted in Europe. Secure X.400 implementations are also under development for the Defense Messaging System (DMS) in the U.S.

neric communications security techniques, 1988 X.400 security mechanisms, and additional related issues.

6.13.1 Security Threats

A number of security threats exist in e-mail environments. Nevertheless, users should be aware that e-mail is inherently fairly secure, and many of these threats are only realistic in the face of a very sophisticated adversary. We categorize the threats below based on whether or not they are addressed in X.400. Threats that are addressed in some way by 1988 X.400 include

- Unauthorized access to equipment
- Unauthorized reception of information through messaging
- Unauthorized disclosure of information through messaging
- One user masquerading as another
- Message modification attack
- Message sequence modification
- Message interception and resulting information disclosure
- Message replay
- Traffic analysis where an adversary collects critical intelligence by aggregating information spread over many messages over time
- Repudiation (denial of receipt) of messages
- Violation of security level (unauthorized usage or disclosure)
- Preplay of messages

    Threats beyond the scope of 1988 X.400 include

- Denial of service by flooding an MTA with spurious messages or other related techniques, which somehow disable connectivity to the MTA
- Modification of routing information in an MTA
- Modification of other data stores
- Introduction of software viruses in messages

6.13.2 Basic Concepts of Secure Messaging

The 1988 X.400 standard contains mechanisms to support secure messaging.[9] These mechanisms can be used to provide confidentiality, ensure correct delivery, ensure data integrity, protect against unauthorized use or disclosure of information in messages, and enforce security policy regarding the use of messaging. Confidentiality is

---

9. We are grateful to Richard Ankney for taking the time to clarify many of the security issues delineated here.

attained through the encryption of message data so that it cannot be viewed by third parties. Integrity involves protecting against modification, malicious or otherwise, of message data through the use of message authentication codes (MACs) or digital signatures. Ensuring correct delivery requires not only data integrity and possibly confidentiality, but also obtaining proof of delivery. Access control (protecting against unauthorized use and enforcing a security policy) involves ensuring that users cannot send messages to unauthorized recipients or receive messages from unauthorized originators.[10] (Access control could also be applied to routing by using labels to ensure that untrusted MTAs do not relay a message.) In a secure government environment, access control implies that users should not be able to receive messages whose security classification level is in excess of their clearance level or messages on subjects for which they do not have a need to know.

X.400 provides many security services through interlocking encryption, digital signature, and authentication mechanisms. Authentication guarantees that the identity (and possibly the clearance level) of the originator or recipient of a message is known. Digital signature mechanisms can ensure that not only the message content but also key envelope fields such as the message originator name, recipient list, and security label (classification) can be protected throughout transfer. Encryption can protect the content of a message directly or be used in a double-enveloping technique where the original envelope is encrypted and a dummy envelope is subsequently applied.

The following subsections discuss encryption, integrity, authentication, and digital signature mechanisms and their interrelationships. They also briefly overview encryption and digital signature algorithms, as well as key issues that must be resolved before secure messaging can become a reality.

Encryption

Contemporary cryptographic techniques can achieve confidentiality by encrypting either the entire message content or fields within the message. Encryption is also the basis for integrity and authentication.

There are two basic classes of encryption techniques or algorithms: symmetric and asymmetric. With symmetric key encryption, software scrambles or encrypts according to the instructions in a secret key and decrypts the data using the same key. This key is called a secret key, since it is a shared secret between the originator and recipient of the data.

With asymmetric encryption (usually called public key encryption), data are encrypted by a key so that they can be decrypted only by a dissimilar but matching key. Data are encrypted by the sender using the receiver's published public key. The receiver, who has the matching private key, is the only party able to decrypt the data. Figure 6.13 illustrates both symmetric and public key encryption.

When a message is sent from one originator to one recipient, either symmetric or asymmetric encryption can be used. When the message addresses multiple recipi-

---

10. Sender/receiver access lists are not subject to X.400 standardization but may be provided for added value.

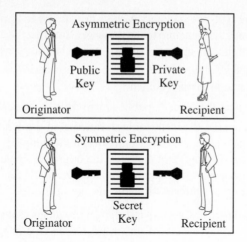

Figure 6.13   Symmetric and asymmetric encryption.

ents and those recipients do not share the same key, the preferred 1988 X.400 technique combines both symmetric and public key encryption. The content portion of the message must be encrypted using a single symmetric key, which is automatically generated for one-time use.[11] This content key is then replicated through the message envelope in successive per recipient slots and is itself protected through asymmetric encryption using the public key of each recipient.

Encryption key management and distribution issues are critical in both private key and public key implementations. Obviously if a secret key or a private key is compromised, there is no security. Key management is easier with public key encryption than with symmetric encryption. To see why, suppose you are a member of a group of users who wish to send messages back and forth securely. In a symmetric key environment, each possible user pairing must have a unique key. In a public key environment, however, only two keys are needed for each user. The disparity in the number of keys that must be issued, managed, and controlled increases geometrically with the size of the communicating user community.

Digital Signatures

Digital signatures can be used to guarantee the integrity of messages or of connection requests. They are created and processed in the following manner:

1.   The sender applies a *hash function* to create a *summary* of an entire message or of selected message fields. The summary is intended to be unique; hash algorithms are designed so that there is only a minuscule probability that any two messages will generate the same summary.

---

11. This use of a single symmetric key allows a message to be sent to multiple recipients with only one copy of the content. The other advantage to using symmetric key encryption for the content is that the processing is generally faster than when using asymmetric encryption.

2. The sender encrypts the summary with its private key to form a digital signature and attaches the signature to the message. Note that the asymmetric signing procedure is the opposite of that for encrypting, where the sender enciphers using the public key.

3. The message is sent to the recipient.

4. The recipient uses the sender's public key to decrypt the summary.

5. The recipient applies the identical hash function to the appropriate message fields and then compares the two summaries. If the summaries are equivalent, the recipient can be confident that only the originator could have generated the message, because any tampering with the data would cause the receiver to calculate a different summary from the one applied by the sender.

When enclosed in a message, digital signatures can guarantee the integrity of the message content, the identity of the originator, and the integrity of selected envelope fields. When used at connection establishment time, digital signatures provide peer-to-peer authentication capabilities. Digital signatures are particularly useful in conjunction with public key algorithms, because they convey authentication and nonrepudiation of origin services in addition to data integrity. (Note that MACs, similar in concept to signatures but encrypted with a symmetric key held by at least two parties, are not generally considered to provide authentication or nonrepudiation of origin.)

Authentication

Interactions or associations between X.400 processing entities can be authenticated using either a simple text password scheme known as *simple authentication* or a cryptographic scheme known as *strong authentication*. Strong authentication is intended to be computationally infeasible to defeat. However, either form of authentication is viable between any pairing of processing entities; that is, UA to MTA, UA to Message Store, Message Store to MTA, and MTA to MTA. Strong authentication achieves a higher degree of assurance regarding message transfer, submission, and delivery. Where a UA or MS requires authentication from an MTA, the MTA is authenticating an end user; that is, the UA or MS employs its current user's individual password or key. MTAs in turn authenticate themselves as a single application entity with a single password or key.

Strong authentication involves an exchange of information between two entities such that the user or the MTA irrefutably demonstrates that it possesses knowledge of its private key by digitally signing some information in a Bind (MTA Connect) request. Because random numbers and date/time stamps are included among these signed parameters, the exchange cannot be replayed successfully by an attacker.

Key Management and Certificates

We noted above that key management is critical in both the symmetric and asymmetric environments. The most basic issues of key management concern:

- **Generating, Distributing, and Protecting Secret or Public/Private Keys:** Keys can be held in software or in hardware. Hardware solutions generally involve holding the key on a device that emulates a removable disk or on a smart card. Smart cards can interface to DOS PCs via PC Memory Card Interface Adapters (PCMCIA). The cards and PCMCIA devices are expected to become commonplace in the 1995 time frame. The card may contain only the key, or it may contain the key and the software to execute signature and encryption processing. To utilize security functionality in a computer, users must possess their cards, know a password, and (optionally in more expensive systems) supply biometric proof of identity, such as a fingerprint or voice print.

- **Distributing Public Keys:** Unlike secret keys and private keys, public keys are intended to be distributed widely, even over nonsecure channels, such as postal mail, newspaper publication, public mail systems (including the Internet), and public directories or bulletin boards. The 1988 X.400 and X.500 standards address this part of the key management problem by recommending that public keys be encapsulated in nonforgeable *Certificates* and listed in the X.500 Directory.

- **Revoking Certificates/Public Keys:** A security authority issuing Certificates authorizing users to employ public keys for use within a community must also have a way of revoking that privilege.

Certificates are special data structures used to register and protectively encapsulate the public keys of users and prevent their forgery. Certificates are digitally signed by a *Certification Authority*. Certification Authorities are organizations that perform key management functions and issue Certificates.

Since Certificates identify not only the public key, but also the Directory Name of the user, the X.500 Directory can establish a link between the unique identity of a user (or application entity) and that entity's public key. It can also serve as a single repository which applications using secure messaging services can consult to obtain the key. However, neither X.400 nor X.500 specify the machinery to generate and distribute private keys, certificates, certificate revocation lists, and other facilities necessary to the operation of the public key infrastructure. Chapter 7 will describe certain Internet RFCs that take a first step toward defining the means by which certification infrastructures can be established. Without widespread Certification Authority infrastructures acknowledged by huge communities of users, it is clear that much of the secure messaging features touted in this chapter as well as the electronic commerce services to be discussed later will remain a pipe dream.

6.13.3 Attributes of X.400 Security

X.400 applies the basic security techniques that we have discussed, using protocol mechanisms that can be combined or manipulated to produce a broad spectrum of security services. Table 6.4 summarizes the 1988 X.400 security services.

The OIW Agreements define six security profiles for UAs and MTAs. These profiles begin with "S0," which provides security services such as Content Integrity,

Security service	Summary
Data origin authentication	Corroboration of origin using digital signatures; several services involving UA, MS, MTA, messages, reports, and probes
Proof or nonrepudiation of submission	Provision by MTA of signed proof to UA or MS that a message, report, or probe was submitted
Proof or nonrepudiation of delivery	Request by sending UA of proof of delivery in a message; return by receiving UA of signed proof via MTA in a report
Secure access management	See peer entity authentication and security context services
Peer entity authentication	Simple or strong authentication of UA-to-MTA, UA-to-MS, MS-to-MTA, or MTA-to-MTA
Security context	Agreement between UAs, MSs, or MTAs at connection time to limit the use of the connection to messages bearing specific security labels
Content confidentiality	Encryption of message content (UA-to-UA)
Message flow confidentiality	Maintaining complete secrecy through the use of double enveloping to encrypt both the original envelope and content
Content integrity	Signing the message content (UA-to-UA)
Message sequence integrity	Inclusion of signed sequence numbers in messages to prevent sequence alteration
Message security labeling	Labeling of a message with a Security Label, such as a classification mark
Change credentials	Change password or certificate (UA-to-MTA)
Register	Register allowed security labels (UA-to-MTA)
MS-Register	Register allowed security labels and change password or certificate (UA-to-MS)

Table 6.4 Summary of X.400 security mechanisms

Message Origin Authentication, and Proof of Delivery. S0a adds content confidentiality to S0. The S1, S1a, S2, and S2a profiles progressively implement the entire arsenal of 1988 X.400 security capabilities.

Whereas S0 and S0a services operate in an end-to-end (UA-to-UA) mode with the MTA taking a passive role, the higher OIW security classes require MTA support. Note that the use of X.400 confidentiality services generally precludes the use of other X.400 services, such as conversion, distribution list expansion, and redirection. Depending on how certain complex protocol mechanisms are deployed, X.400 nonrepudiation and integrity services may also preclude conversion, distribution list expansion, and redirection.

Figure 6.14 diagrams the potential use of various X.400 security services.

6.13.4   Security Algorithms

Security algorithms fall into the asymmetric and symmetric classes previously discussed. To obtain the full range of X.400 security services, both kinds of algorithms

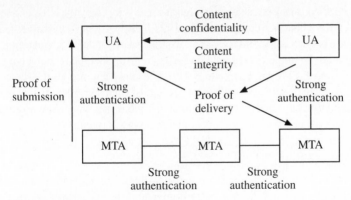

Figure 6.14 X.400 security scenario.

are used. Specifically, secret key (symmetric) algorithms are needed for encrypting a message content bound for multiple recipients, whereas public key algorithms produce the best results for authentication, integrity, and nonrepudiation services.

Although X.400 is algorithm independent, be aware that two implementations wishing to interoperate must support the same algorithm and that few implementations handling secure messaging will support more than one or two algorithms. Despite these limitations, the ability of a product to modularize its code so that new algorithms can be added in a more or less turnkey, object-oriented fashion by third party developers or even users could be an important feature in certain cases. Also some manufacturers will ship smart cards supporting multiple algorithms.

The development of secure messaging technology has been severely retarded by real and potential patent litigation and political impasses surrounding government acceptance of specific security algorithms. A conflict exists between industry's need for security and government's ability to perform wiretapping functions in the interests of law enforcement or intelligence gathering. The major actors in the ongoing security algorithm drama in the U.S. are the National Security Agency (NSA), an organization called Public Key Partners that holds a number of patents, and various national governments.

Secret Key Algorithms

The most commonly used secret key encryption algorithm is the Data Encryption Standard (DES). DES has been in operation for many years, and various attacks on it have been attempted. From time to time, sophisticated attacks have been devised that can break DES keys more efficiently than could be done by a brute force approach. Security experts fine tuning the algorithm are in a continually evolving contest with security experts devising new, ever more computationally feasible attacks. DES has been recertified for use by the federal government until 1998 but may not be certified again at that time.

DES therefore may need to be replaced. Two candidates to replace DES are Triple DES, where two or more DES keys are used in conjunction with each other, and Skipjack. Skipjack is a secret key algorithm developed by the NSA and released as part of the Clinton Administration's 1993 "Clipper Chip" initiative. Unfortunately, the Skipjack algorithm itself is a classified secret of the U.S. Government and must therefore be implemented only on hardware from specific manufacturers. Further, the Clipper Chip initiative came with an escrow key proposal, whereby two U.S. government agencies would each hold half of each secret key that was issued. With these limitations and provisos, Clipper Chip has met with disapproval in both the international and the U.S. commercial messaging community.

Public Key Algorithms

For digital signatures—required for message integrity, authentication, and non-repudiation—both a public key algorithm and a hash function algorithm are needed. The message digest is a summary of the signed contents. Three hash algorithms are currently touted as possible candidates for secure messaging: MD2, MD5, and SHA. Public key algorithms are also necessary to encrypt symmetric content keys to be enclosed in messages destined for multiple recipients.

There are currently two standards for digital signatures on the table for secure messaging in the 1990s: the Rivest/Shamir/Adelman (RSA) algorithm and the DSS algorithm. The RSA algorithm also supports public key encryption.

Of these two, RSA has the greatest longevity and has not been successfully attacked. It is used as the de facto standard public key encryption algorithm worldwide. However, in the U.S., RSA is controversial for several reasons, and U.S. vendors must therefore compete at a disadvantage. RSA is covered by a patent owned by the Public Key Partners (PKP), and vendors building RSA products must sign contracts with PKP as well as pay per user licensing fees in some cases for the use of the algorithm.

Moreover, the NSA has consistently opposed the inclusion of RSA encryption in standards and has placed RSA on the list of sensitive technologies that require special export approval.[12] Given export restrictions, not only are U.S. vendors unable to export RSA products overseas, but multinational firms operating in the U.S. may not be able to buy, install, and deploy consistent security infrastructures. We noted above that the NSA as well as other agencies such as the Federal Bureau of Investigation is motivated by intelligence gathering and law enforcement considerations. These considerations are not unique to the U.S.; many other countries have conflicting regulations governing the use and export of computer security technology.

El Gamal is another public key encryption algorithm that was recently proposed as the Digital Signature Standard (DSS) by NIST. This DSS provides the capability needed for all X.400 security services other than Content Confidentiality. However, it verifies digital signatures much slower computationally than RSA. If DSS is endorsed, it would be required for security interworking with civil-

---

12. Almost all algorithms used for encryption are subject to export controls. Even DES can be exported only for use in the financial industry. NSA and the U.S. Government sometimes allows exports of RSA products when they are used for signatures only.

ian federal agencies, a setback for the more than 70 vendors who have endorsed RSA. On the other hand, although NIST had originally hoped that DSS could be utilized patent free, litigation soon began over PKP's claim for patent rights to this algorithm as well.

In addition to holding patents through RSA Data Security, Inc. (RSADSI), the PKP is also an important industry supplier of enabling technology, such as RSA software for both key management and cryptographic operation. Now that PKP (which represents RSADSI, Cylink, Stanford, and MIT) may own the patent to DSS, RSADSI has been building DSS support into its products alongside RSA. Therefore, DSS support should become widely available if the U.S. Government persists in promoting it. However, DSS intentionally does not provide a public key encryption capability.

To solve the Content Confidentiality problem, part of the Clipper Chip initiative includes a mechanism called "Capstone." Capstone includes Skipjack, DSS, and a classified public key exchange algorithm that could be used to encrypt content-encrypting symmetric keys. Capstone is also used in a technology called "MOSAIC" that has been specified for use in the U.S. Defense Messaging System (DMS). Like the rest of the Clipper algorithms, however, Capstone is classified as secret and can only be used as part of a hardware solution. (The algorithm is purportedly based on a variation of a key exchange algorithm first developed by Diffie–Hellman.) In the future, similar public key exchange mechanisms may be developed by industry. For the time being, the RSA or Capstone hardware solution remains the only workable means of providing Content Confidentiality using public key technology.

6.14   TESTING X.400 IMPLEMENTATIONS

With the proliferating number of fielded X.400 implementations, how can users be sure that any one of these implementations conforms to the standard? Even if two implementations have passed conformance testing separately, will they be able to work together? These are important questions that should be examined by users procuring messaging systems and by vendors wishing to offer a credible product. Approaches to testing X.400 include conformance testing, interoperability testing, and performance testing.

In conformance testing, an implementation is tested against a tester product to see whether it implements a protocol correctly [ITU88Q]. When multiple implementations have been certified by the same conformance tester, the probability that they will interoperate with each other is increased. NIST has approved the Open System Testing Consortium (OSTC) test suite from Europe as suitable for GOSIP conformance/certification testing (1984 X.400). The test suite is based on an ITU suite of abstract test cases that derive from the X.403 ITU recommendations. The Joint Interoperability Test Center (JITC) manages the U.S. GOSIP register and database for conformance testers and tested products [JITC92]. Europe's Conformance Testing System 2 (CTS 2) organization is developing a 1988 X.400 and X.500 tester based on ITU-defined test scenarios.

Interoperability testing tests implementations directly against one another. NIST created a network testing service, called OSINET, now administered by the Corporation for Open Systems (COS), where vendors can test their products [HEAF92]. OSINET has developed X.400 interoperability test suites and also furnishes a database of published test results that users can query free of charge.

Performance testing involves more exhaustive tests of the implementations as products. This type of testing may involve benchmarking to ensure adequate performance of a product on one or several platforms. Performance testing is largely a local matter, left to the ingenuity of the vendors themselves or to large users.

These three approaches to testing are complementary; all can be specified and used during product development, procurement, and evaluation.

6.14.1   One-Stop Testing

Harmonized regional profiles (based on International Standard Profiles [ISPs]) are intended to lead to harmonized international conformance testing and international certification requirements. Both Europe's Open System Testing Consortium (OSTC) and the U.S.–based COS, have developed 1984 X.400 conformance test systems in accordance with a single set of abstract test cases standardized by the ITU. These testers were demonstrated to be largely equivalent. When they were each exercised against the same reference implementation, over 95 percent of the tests yielded the same verdict.

However, one-stop international certification for the seven-year-old 1984 X.400 standard as yet does not exist. Vendors may ultimately have to be certified in both Europe and the United States (at the minimum), and users should be careful in discerning whether their vendors have met the appropriate certification requirements. In this respect, conformance testing has the potential to become a barrier to trade between regions. However, most vendors undoubtedly will prefer one European Community certification process to twelve different national processes, as would have been the case prior to the development of the Common Market.

The outlook is brighter with interoperability testing, where products are tested against one another instead of against a test system. OSIone, an umbrella organization of international interoperability testing services, provides vendors with the opportunity to test against other implementations and to demonstrate interoperability to their customers. Users can access databases containing interoperability test results. OSIone offers about 70 X.400 tests harmonized internationally. As of 1993, OSIone had just put 1988 X.400 and X.500 testing interoperability programs in place.

6.14.2   Certification Requirements in Europe and the United States

In the U.S., the NIST and JITC certify 1984 X.400 Conformance Testers or Means of Testing (MOT) [BREI91]. Vendors must submit their products to these testers to certify an entire seven-layer communications stack. In Europe, an organization

called the CTS for Wide Area Networks (CTS–WAN) offers an accreditation program for a product's X.400 Application and Session Layers. Actual Tester software and test cases are based on ITU's Conformance Test System Manuals
(CTSMs), which contain an Abstract Test Suite based on the ITU X.403 and the
ISO 9646 standard for OSI conformance testing. The CTSMs for P1, P2, and RTS
describe what should be tested and what is expected from the product.

These certification capabilities are strictly for 1984 X.400 systems. However,
abstract test suites have been developed for 1988 X.400 and X.500, and Alcatel in
France and the U.S., Danet Gmbh in Germany, and the National Computer Center
(NCC) in the UK have independently developed test engine technology. Europe's
Conformance Testing System 2 (CTS 2) organization is developing a 1988 X.400
and X.500 tester based on ITU abstract test cases and Alcatel, Danet, and NCC
tester engines.

In the U.S., 1984 X.400 testing can be performed by the National Voluntary
Laboratory Accreditation Program (NVLAP)–validated laboratories operated by
organizations such as COS or by third parties who license tester software and
make a business out of testing [NIGH91]. Laboratories can also be operated as
first party test laboratories, where the vendor organization can test itself and submit the results to a registered agent who assigns the Pass/Fail verdict. Procedures
designed to ensure that first party testing is conducted legitimately are in place.
Organizations such as Hewlett-Packard, Honeywell Bull, and IBM have certified
test laboratories. Having such a laboratory is advantageous, because the vendor
can get faster turnaround on certifying new releases.

Obtaining certification is a bureaucratic process that can become expensive.
One large X.400 vendor held discussions with a test laboratory but delayed conformance testing because it would have cost approximately $50,000 for *each* at-
tempt to obtain NVLAP certification (based on estimated time to complete the
formal testing process at the laboratory's labor rates). In other words, returning to
retest after fixing one minor bug would cost an additional $50,000.

6.14.3 Protocol Implementation Conformance Statement (PICS)

All products that pass X.400 conformance testing are not created equal. Testing
and certification are based on the product vendor's Protocol Implementation Conformance Statement (PICS). The PICS classifies vendor support or nonsupport for
both the services specified in a standard and the standard's various protocol elements. Only those services that a vendor claims to support are tested (although all
mandatory services must be supported for a PASS verdict). The PICS used for
GOSIP-approved testing is derived from the OIW Stable Implementation Agreements for X.400.

Figure 6.15 shows an example of what part of an Interpersonal Messaging (IPM)
P2 PICS might look like. Support requirements for protocol elements are classified both in terms of the standard and in terms of a product's ability to originate or
receive a protocol element. For instance, the authorizing-users, blind-copy-recipients,

Protocol element	Support requirements					
	1884 X.400	OIW		Product		Notes
		O	R	O	R	
IPM heading						
this-IPM	M	M	M	✔	✔	
originator	O	M	M	✔	✔	
authorizing-users	O	O	M		✔	
primary-recipients	O	M	M	✔	✔	
copy-recipients	O	M	M	✔	✔	
blind-copy-recipients	O	O	M	✔	✔	
replied-to-IPM	O	M	M	✔	✔	
obsoleted-IPM	O	O	M		✔	
related-IPMs	O	O	M		✔	
subject	O	M	M	✔	✔	
....						

Figure 6.15 A sample PICS.

obsoleted-IPMs, and related-IPMs P2 fields are optional for origination. However, these elements are mandatory for reception. The implementor of a hypothetical product has filled out the PICS in Fig. 6.15, identifying the supported fields in columns four and five.

When a product is tested, no tests are run for optional or unsupported protocol elements or services. Thus, two products could both receive certification, but one may support more features than another. We recommend that buyers make a practice of requesting and reviewing their vendor's PICS to determine a product's breadth of feature support.

6.15 THE 1992 X.400 STANDARDS AND BEYOND

X.400 is now stable. The ITU 1992 X.400 recommendations [ITU92] do not make major overhauls to X.400. The most significant changes in the 1992 version are these:

- The X.435 standard was created, defining a new message content type with no effect on the baseline 1988 X.400 protocols. X.435 provides support for EDI communications.
- The 1992 versions of X.411 for MTAs, X.420 for IPM UAs, and so on, include resolutions to a large number of defect reports that were registered by

ITU and ISO after the publication of the 1988 standard. A few other minor enhancements were made to the X.411 and X.420 recommendations.

- The File Transfer Body Part was defined as an instance of an external Body Part usable with IPM UAs (or other types of UAs).

- The X.440 standard was created, defining a new message content type with no effect on the baseline 1988 X.400 protocols. X.440 provides support for voice-messaging communications. It defines a voice-message heading containing a spoken subject and other fields suitable for voice messaging.

Unfortunately, the 1992 recommendations left several important work items undone, the most pressing being multivendor X.400 management and MTA routing data exchange.

ITU's X.400 program for the 1992–1996 study period included work items such as these:

- Telephone network access to X.400

- Group communications (or messaging support for conferencing and bulletin boards)

- MHS testing

- MHS management

- Compression

- Facsimile communications

- Further use of directory provisions

- ISO 10646 character set support

- Multimedia heading fields

- Multiple EDI interchanges in messages

- Application program interfaces

- Message store enhancements

- Security enhancements

6.16 SUMMARY

X.400's greatest strength lies in the breadth of its services or features set. This flexibility has allowed X.400 to emerge as a backbone standard worldwide and could enable it to form the basis for industrial-strength messaging of financial or legal consequence in the future. However, X.400's greatest weakness has been the lack of a defined registration and routing infrastructure. Only now, as we enter the mid-1990s, is the standards community attending to such practical issues. Time will tell whether the shortage of X.400 implementations on the desktop and the long build-up process it has undergone will relegate the standard to a modest role in the world of messaging or whether X.400 will yet become ubiquitous as was once expected.

KEY POINTS

- X.400 defines e-mail Message Transfer Agent (MTA), User Agent (UA), Message Store (MS), and Access Unit (AU) components. It also defines Message, Delivery Report, Receipt Notification, and Probe formats.

- Gateways, APIs, and X.400 can work together to serve as tools to integrate all sorts of local and host-based e-mail systems. While X.400's success so far has been in the backbone (not desktop) infrastructure area, X.400 was not itself designed to act as an e-mail integration tool.

- X.400 defines organizationally distinct e-mail facilities as Administrative Management Domains (ADMDs), which are within the purview of carriers licensed to handle international tariffed traffic, and Private Management Domains (PRMDs), which are under the control of private organizations. This domain modeling was suited to an older PTT-dominated era, and its usage in practice is now being adapted (rather painfully) to a deregulated communications environment.

- X.400 defines an Originator/Recipient (O/R) Name consisting of a standardized list of attributes that collectively designate a single user. However, the O/R Name is difficult to use and particularly vulnerable to the Rolodex problem.

- The 1988 X.400 standard also defines an ambitious set of security mechanisms designed to work with an X.500-based Certification infrastructure. However, the difficulty of obtaining international industry/government consensus on how (or whether) sensitive encryption technologies should be regulated has thwarted progress toward secure messaging.

- To migrate from the 1984 version to the 1988 version of X.400, organizations should first convert their backbone MTA components, then work outwards toward converting user agents.

- X.400's success stems from its effectiveness in defining a comprehensive architecture and set of services, while its shortcomings stem from its complexity and a lack of attention by standards bodies to practical network issues such as domain and other technical object registration.

C H A P T E R 7

Internet Mail

The Internet Mail architecture was defined in the early to mid-1980s and was long dormant as the world awaited the ascendancy of X.400. However, X.400's long lag time to market and the inadequacy of X.400-to-Internet gateways as a means of interworking with the Internet installed base eventually stirred the Internet Mail standards community into action. The community has belatedly but rapidly moved to upgrade its infrastructure to handle multimedia messaging, security, and directories.

This chapter will detail both the traditional and emerging Internet Mail environment and their components. Internet Mail is complex, widespread, and defies easy definition. Section 7.1 provides a basic characterization of Internet Mail technology and distinguishes its functional and operational perspectives.

Traditional Internet Mail—discussed in Sections 7.2, 7.3, and 7.4—comprises support for text-based messages in the RFC 822 format carried over the Simple Mail Transfer Protocol or other facilities using a simple domain-based address form. The distributed DNS directory transforms domain addresses into IP addresses, enabling widespread connectivity.

Internet Mail has been enhanced with MIME (Section 7.5) to support the conveyance of binary, labeled binary, and/or multimedia information. It has been enhanced with PEM (Section 7.6) to support secure messaging capabilities. Enhancements to create an Extended SMTP protocol (Section 7.7) are in process. Many other Internet Mail enhancements are emerging from an active, productive IETF standards and implementors community. These enhancements will potentially include the convergence of MIME and PEM, the use of EDI over MIME, and delivery reports using Extended SMTP protocols and MIME formats.

While the great strength of the Internet (and Internet Mail) lies in its openness, not all organizations wish to expose themselves fully to the Internet. Such organizations can still interconnect with the Internet through firewall facilities that control and limit interaction between employees and the Internet. As we shall see in Section 7.8, there are two basic kinds of firewalls: one operating at the router level and one operating at the messaging level.

The other topics covered in this chapter are Internet directories (Section 7.9) and Internet Mail interworking with X.400 (Section 7.10). The chapter summary provides a table listing important Internet Mail RFCs and draft RFCs and also itemizes the strengths, weaknesses, and future prospects for the Internet Mail environment.

7.1 INTERNET MAIL PERSPECTIVES

Because Internet Mail is complex and widespread, it defies easy definition. This section provides a brief technical overview of both the traditional and emerging Internet Mail functional architectures. It then characterizes Internet Mail, first in terms of functional considerations or which protocols are used, and second in terms of operational considerations or how domains are interconnected.

7.1.1 Technical Perspective

Figure 7.1 describes the conceptual framework of the traditional RFC 822-centric Internet Mail architecture on which much of this chapter will focus [CROC82]. In this architecture, Internet Mail UAs support a basic RFC 822 content type for sending text messages. Messages encoded in the RFC 822 format are transported by MTAs using the Simple Mail Transfer Protocol (SMTP) specified in RFC 821 [POST82]. For the purposes of this chapter (unless otherwise indicated in the text), the term "UA" is used to refer to a program that can handle the RFC 822 content and "MTA" is used to refer to an SMTP program. SMTP implementations obtain routing information from a distributed directory of host names and ad-

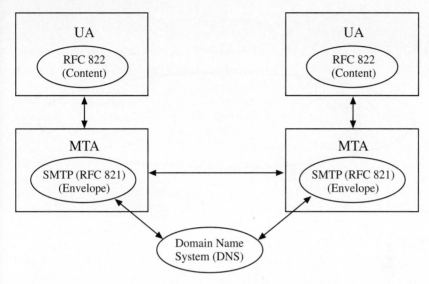

Figure 7.1 Traditional Internet Mail.

dresses—the Domain Name System (DNS)—and send messages on their way [MOCK87-87A, PART86, HARR85A].

RFC 1123 [BRAD89] collects host requirements for RFC 822, SMTP, and DNS support into a single document, advises users and implementors on common errors, and details which functional elements of these standards are mandatory or optional. RFC 1123 is conceptually similar to the functional profiles described earlier for X.400. It is, in fact, viewed as the final authority on various inconsistencies and changes in the RFC 821/822 specifications.

While very widely deployed, traditional Internet Mail has its limitations. Until recently, RFC 822 messages were largely restricted to seven-bit ASCII text.[1] Moreover, many SMTP implementations will only pass messages of 64K or less. They often perform character set conversions or line folding, behavior that cannot be disabled by a protocol flag (such as X.400's "Conversion Prohibited") because no such flag exists in SMTP. This nontransparent, non-eight-bit clean environment poses difficulties in enhancing Internet Mail independent of upgrading its SMTP backbone. Nevertheless, beginning in the early 1990s, as X.400, mail-enabled applications, and other drivers toward multimedia messaging emerged, Internet Mail began to evolve.

Figure 7.2 diagrams the shape of things to come. RFC 822 has been augmented by the MIME and PEM formats. MIME allows for identified binary object conveyance (otherwise known as multimedia mail) whereas PEM allows for

---

1. While a technique known as UUENCODE/UUDECODE is often used as a workaround to convert eight-bit binary into a seven-bit text encoded form, it is not consistently implemented and generally relies on manual handling by end users.

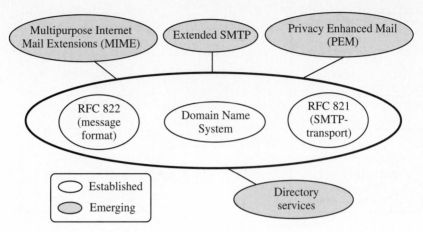

Figure 7.2   Emerging Internet architecture.

secure messaging with encryption and digital signatures. SMTP remains in operation, but implementations will be upgraded in accordance with various extension
mechanisms, including the ability to handle eight-bit binary data in messages and,
increasingly, messages of arbitrary sizes. In the meantime, MIME, PEM, and standards to come will struggle to live within the constraints of the existing ASCII-
oriented (SMTP) Internet. The DNS also remains in operation as a vital
component, but additional directory functionality (directories of users, not just
hosts) will eventually be provided.

As of early 1994 none of the new elements of Internet Mail functionality have
fully stabilized or been incorporated into the host requirements document. Internet
Mail today consists of a rich blend of old and new technologies. To understand
both the old and the new Internet Mail better, we will cover RFC 822, SMTP,
DNS, MIME, PEM, and directories for Internet Mail in the following pages.

7.1.2   Functional and Operational Perspectives

We noted earlier that the Internet is not a single network, organization, service, or
protocol. Internet Mail is any mail carried over the Internet and includes SMTP/
RFC 822, UUCP/RFC 822, BITNET, and even X.400 among others. However,
RFC 822 is the common denominator message format and SMTP is the usual
message transport. The Internet itself is a huge global internetwork loosely characterized as comprising all networks reachable via TCP/IP. In Chapter 4, we also
noted the importance of the Internet's domain-based address space (called "The
Matrix" by John Quartermain in his book by the same name), which ultimately
makes the Internet the core of a global mail relaying service and which extends
even into X.400 and proprietary LAN e-mail networks.

From a *functional perspective*, one can think of Internet Mail in terms of increasing rings of inclusive concentric circles, with functionality being greatest at

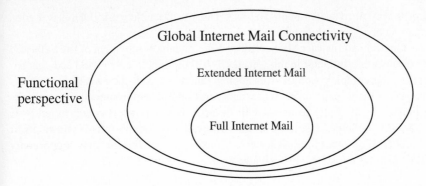

Figure 7.3   Functional Internet Mail perspectives.

the inner level, where pure Internet Mail SMTP/RFC 822/MIME technology is supported, and least at the outer level where connectivity is achieved only through low-function Internet gateways. This concept is diagrammed in Fig. 7.3.

However, we pose Fig. 7.4 as an alternative operational perspective[2] on Internet Mail. It distinguishes between the two types of Internet environments: Fully Connected IP Internet and Private Internet. The *Fully Connected IP Internet* environment uses underlying IP services end-to-end. It is a pure, full-stack RFC 822/SMTP/TCP/IP service. Internet Mail MTAs on the Connected IP Internet connect directly without intervening relays. A *Private Internet* environment may use IP and/or SMTP but, even so, it is not administered as part of the global Internet. Mail connectivity may occur only over a relay. Moreover, a Private Internet may be selectively isolated from the Fully Connected IP Internet by security firewalls, and it may limit

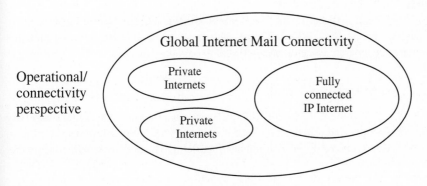

Figure 7.4   Operational Internet Mail perspectives.

2. We again acknowledge Dave Crocker, who also suggested a perspective somewhat similar to this one.

access only to relayed e-mail. The U.S. Defense Data Network (DDN) is a good example of a Private Internet.

Operational Internet Mail considerations and the deployment of firewalls will be discussed in full later in this chapter. It is important to understand and conceptualize the complex web of overlapping functional and operational capabilities that exists between domains in the real-world Internet environment. For example, a domain in the Fully Connected IP Internet may only support text-based RFC 822; a Private Internet isolated behind a firewall may support full MIME and PEM (but not FTP or other Internet services); another Private Internet may support only RFC 822 text translated through a gateway.

7.2 RFC 822 AND INTERNET USER AGENTS

The User Agent component of Internet Mail can be any program that supports the RFC 822 message content format.[3] The most common examples of such programs include traditional e-mail User Agents and a very widely used Internet bulletin board service (called USENET). RFC 822 is currently limited to handling text messages of a single Body Part (with no attachments), but MIME has been developed to extend the protocol to support multiple body parts. The Internet is also moving to provide secure messaging within PEM or a combined MIME-PEM.

Popular Internet UAs in the Unix host environment include programs named mail, rmail, xmail, elm, MH, and XMH. Some of these UAs are distributed by system vendors as part of their operating system and its utilities; others are public domain. In the PC environment, several popular UAs are Eudora, POPMail, and Techmail. Host-based UAs tend to interwork with a collocated SMTP MTA; PC-based UAs often employ the Internet Post Office Protocol (POP) or Interactive Mail Access Protocol (IMAP), both of which perform access functions analogous to X.400's P3 or P7 access protocols.

This section discusses the key elements of RFC 822 and Internet User Agents, specifically the basic RFC 822 message format, the Internet address, and the somewhat separate issue of Internet Mail access protocols.

7.2.1   Message Format

Like the P2 protocol in X.400, RFC 822 separates the message content into two areas: a header and a body. The header contains trace information (inserted as a message and relayed by MTAs) and heading fields. The body is separated from the

---

3. RFC 1123 [BRAD89] notes that the UA/MTA distinction is not always exactly reflected in the structure of typical host-based Internet Mail implementations. Often a program known as the "mailer" implements SMTP and also some of the User Agent functions; the rest of the User Agent functions are included in a user interface used for entering and reading mail.

headers by a null line. The header is a sequence of unordered fields, each consisting of a field name and a field value. An example heading field would be

To: don_delong@abc.com.

Generally heading fields reside on a single line of text, although the field value can be folded onto multiple lines. While heading fields are generally freeform strings, RFC 822 gives a great deal of space to defining various rules for ways in which structured text heading fields containing parentheses or quoted strings should be parsed. Figure 7.5 illustrates an RFC 822 formatted message.

RFC 822 heading fields include *To, From, Sender, cc, bcc, Message-ID, In-Reply-To, References, Keywords, Subject, Comments, Reply-to,* and *Encrypted.* In addition, extension fields can be defined in a standards document approved as a formal extension to RFC 822, and user- or implementation-defined fields can be added to any message. To ensure that implementation-defined header fields will never be confused with standardized headers, implementation-defined field names sometimes begin with the prefix "X-."

```
Received: by blue2.anon.navy.mil; Thu, 18 Feb 93 08:09:02 EST
Received: from wnyose.anon.navy.mil by dns.anon.navy.mil
(4.1/SMI-4.0)
        id AA04279; Thu, 18 Feb 93 08:00:25 EST
Received: from argos.anon.disa.mil by wnyose.anon.navy.mil
(5.59/25-eef)
        id AA00297; Thu, 18 Feb 93 08:08:14 EST
Received: from funnel.anon.disa.mil by argos.anon.disa.mil
with SMTP ;
        Thu, 18 Feb 93 08:03:33 EST
Received: from cc.ANON.DISA.MIL ([137.130.32.73]) by
funnel.anon.disa.mil (4.1/RB&BK-4.1.5)
        id AA21762; Thu, 18 Feb 93 08:02:59 EST
Received: from cc:Mail by CC.ANON.DISA.MIL (1.30/SMTPLink)
        id A27600; Thu, 18 Feb 93 07:59:40 EDT
Date: Thu, 18 Feb 93 07:59:40 EDT
From: John Doe <jdoe@CC.anon.disa.mil>
Message-Id: <9302180759.A27600@CC.ANON.DISA.MIL>
To: jsmith@wnyose.anon.navy.mil, bcoors@wnyose.anon.navy.mil,
        fhodgkins@CC.anon.disa.mil, jfisher@CC.anon.disa.mil
Subject: Comments

The text of the message appears after the header area ends
with a blank line.
```

Figure 7.5 Sample RFC 822 message.

Two final RFC 822 headers are used for trace information. These are *Received* and *Return-path*. Each time a message is relayed from one MTA to another, a Received-by is prefixed to the message content; the final MTA adds a Return-path. Received-by provides information about the mail relays, including their address and (optionally) local transport protocols used and local identifiers assigned to the message.

7.2.2   Addressing

Of particular interest in our study of RFC 822 is the addressing information. An Internet address takes the form

local-part@domain-part

Domain-part is a globally unique reference to a machine; local part is the address of a user's (person or application) mailbox on the machine specified by domain-part or accessible to it. Thus, local part is the address of a user's (person or application) mailbox on a local machine.[4] For example, *c.smith@widgets.com* would be a valid construct with *c.smith* as the local-part and *widgets.com* as the domain-part. One mailbox name, Postmaster, is reserved for administrative use. Section 7.4 on the DNS describes the purpose and structure of the domain-part in detail.

Internet addresses are relatively simple and compact. However, addressing becomes more complex in special cases such as source routing (where the user explicitly specifies the relay path), message tunneling by another protocol through the Internet, or Internet message tunneling through a gateway. Because of the availability of DNS, source routing is now discouraged in the Internet. In the case of Internet Mail tunneling through a gateway, the address can become complex. For example, in the address *c.smith%widgets.com@gateway.com* the entity denoted by *gateway* removes the domain-name reference to itself and passes the message on to *widgets.com*.

7.2.3   Internet Mail Access Protocols

An Internet draft for the IMAP2bis access protocol [CRIS93] posits three fundamental models of client/server access to e-mail: offline, online, and disconnected use. These models describe how Internet UAs access mailboxes on Internet mail servers to receive their mail.

The offline model is used by POP3 as defined in RFC 1460 [ROSE93]. In this model, the client application connects to a server periodically and downloads all pending messages; in effect, deleting those downloaded messages from the server. Thereafter the message processing takes place local to the client. POP3 was devel-

---

4. In the case where the user is not served by an RFC 822 mail system, local-part acts like an X.400 Domain-Defined Attribute and may contain a complex internal structure, possibly even a textual representation of an X.400 O/R Address.

oped for workstations lacking sufficient resources to run an SMTP server and an associated local mail-delivery system or to maintain connectivity for long periods of time. Such a client can, however, support a User Agent (such as Eudora over a SLIP or PPP dialup connection) and interact with a server which offers it a mail-drop service. RFC 1460 defines how this client workstation can open and close a session with—and retrieve mail from—a POP3 server. (All messages transmitted during a POP3 session are assumed to conform to RFC 822.) RFC 1460 also defines a security mechanism that reduces the danger of password capture during the session.

The online model is used with remote file-system protocols where the client application manipulates mailbox data on a server machine that, in effect, acts like a Post Office or Message Store. (No mailbox data is kept at the client, who only retrieves data from the server as needed.) A connection to the server is maintained throughout the session. IMAP2bis implements such an online model using considerably less bandwidth than a remote file-system protocol. It can minimize bandwidth use because there is often no need to do a wholesale transfer of an entire mailbox or even of the complete text of a message. Thus, IMAP2bis describes a protocol that is designed to transmit message data on demand and to provide the facilities to enable a client to decide what data it needs at a particular time. It allows more complex operations than POP3, including the search for specific messages and the selective fetching of messages, attributes, and parts. It also provides for the creation, deletion, and renaming of mailbox folders and the permanent removal of messages. Furthermore, IMAP2bis claims the capability of supporting the offline and disconnected models. This capability would be interesting to a user who wishes to switch between online and disconnected models on a regular basis, perhaps because of travel demands.

The disconnected model is an offline and online combination whereby a client downloads a set of messages from the server, manipulates them offline, and then uploads the changes. The protocol PCMAIL described in RFC 1056 [LAMB88] supports this model where the server remains the authoritative repository of the messages. The synchronization problems between multiple users are dealt with through the use of unique message identifiers.

The strengths and weaknesses of these models, as described in [CRIS93], are shown in Table 7.1.

Feature	Online	Offline	Disconnected
Can use multiple clients	No	Yes	Yes
Minimum use of server connect time	Yes	No	Yes
Minimum use of server resources	Yes	No	No
Minimum use of client disk resources	No	Yes	No
Multiple remote mailboxes	No	Yes	Yes
Fast startup	No	Yes	No
Mail processing when not online	n/a	No	Yes

Table 7.1 Strengths and weaknesses of e-mail access models.

It is important to note that neither the IMAP nor the POP3 protocols specify a means of submitting mail. This function is expected to be handled by the UA through SMTP.

7.3 INTERNET MTAs

The MTA component of Internet mail can be provided by any transport component that can carry the RFC 822 content type. Such MTAs are often host-based and communicate directly with collocated RFC 822 UAs. Less frequently, Internet MTAs communicate with UAs via a remote access protocol, or are implemented as relays or gateways. In practice, the most commonly used transports are SMTP, UUCP, and BITNET. The SMTP and UUCP protocols are discussed below.

7.3.1 SMTP

SMTP is described in the Internet RFC 821. RFC 821 limits the information that might be conveyed in a mail message to ASCII text, the number of recipients to 100, and the line length to 1000 characters. Often, implementations limit aggregate message size to 64K. SMTP extension work will facilitate a gradual Internet migration away from these limitations toward more industrial strength capabilities in the 1990s.

SMTP's design is based on a connection-oriented, lock-step model of communication that includes support for store-and-forward operation. As the result of a user mail request, the sending MTA establishes a connection to a receiving MTA. The receiver may be the end system or relay. The sender generally makes its choice of receiver by consulting the DNS. The sending MTA then generates commands for the receiving MTA, which generates replies. Thus, as a result of a user mail request, the following events take place:

1. The sending SMTP MTA establishes a TCP connection to a receiving MTA. The receiving MTA may be either the ultimate destination or an intermediate one. The sender greets the receiver with its domain name information using the HELO command.

2. The sending MTA sends a *MAIL FROM* command indicating the sending domain where the mail originated. If the receiving MTA can accept the mail, it responds with an OK reply.

3. The sending MTA then sends an *RCPT TO* command identifying a recipient of the mail. If the receiving MTA can accept mail for that recipient, it responds with an *OK* reply. If not, it responds with a reply rejecting that recipient (but not the whole mail transaction). The sending MTA and receiving MTA may negotiate several recipients; these are termed the "envelope" of an Internet Mail message. Whether to verify each recipient at the time of the *RCPT TO* command is an implementation decision; verification may re-

quire a DNS lookup. RFC 1123 requires that MTAs *not* reject a recipient on the basis of a DNS timeout (called a soft error). Thus, recipients may be rejected either at the time of the *RCPT TO* command or in an error report sent later.

4. When the recipients have been negotiated, the sending MTA sends the mail data preceded by the *DATA* command terminating with a special character sequence. If the receiving MTA has succeded in safely storing the mail data, it responds with an OK reply.

5. Multiple mail messages can be sent in this fashion. They terminate with a *QUIT* command.

In the case where an SMTP MTA is relaying, the argument to the MAIL FROM command is a reverse path, which specifies who the mail is from. As it relays a message, the MTA must augment the *Return Path* information in the RFC 822 content, and add its *Received* trace information to it. If a sending MTA relaying a message finds that mail cannot be delivered for whatever reason, it must construct an undeliverable mail notification as a separate mail message (sometimes also called an error report) and send it along the reverse path to the originator of the undeliverable message. Unlike the X.400 Delivery Report, the format of the traditional SMTP error report information is not architected and cannot necessarily be parsed by mail-enabled applications. Also, traditional SMTP provides no automated mechanism for the positive acknowledgment of delivery. However, Internet Drafts were under development as of early 1994 to support delivery status notification.

Some of the remaining SMTP functions/commands include TURN, VRFY, EXPN. TURN allows the sender and receiver to reverse roles. VRFY allows the sender to verify an address or an alias. Support for the VRFY command is required in RFC 1123, and support for EXPN is strongly recommended. Use of the TURN command is no longer recommended.

The EXPN command, which allows the sender to request the expansion of a distribution list or the use of an alias held in the receiving MTA, is used to support mailing lists (sometimes called mail exploders) on the Internet. When an SMTP MTA expands a distribution list, the RFC 822 Content is often sent without change to all recipients on the list. However, some implementations rewrite the RFC 822 header to include all actual recipients or modify the Message ID field. For mailing lists, error reports are supposed to go back to the list owner, rather than the message originator, but this often is not handled correctly.

Many SMTP implementations are variations of a program called Sendmail, which has been distributed along with the Unix kernel from various vendors. Vendors often enhance Sendmail. Control Data Corporation, for example, has created a version dubbed Turbo Sendmail that can be managed via the Internet's Simple Network Management Protocol (SNMP) and utilizes the X.500 directory to minimize reliance on Sendmail's traditional (and notoriously cryptic) configuration file. Some Sendmail implementations offer User Agent features, including the ability to save a message in a file, read saved messages, sort or screen messages in a mail file, and edit, forward, print, or reply to messages.

RFC 1123 specifies numerous additional requirements and implementation recommendations for SMTP MTAs. Some of these include

- Mandatory and recommended policies, algorithms, and configurable parameters for retrying messages to unreachable receiver MTAs. Given the dispersed Internet environment with its wide quality of service variations, an SMTP MTA following these recommendations may hold a message for as long as four or five days before returning an error report.

- Recommended timeout values for entire messages and for individual SMTP commands, such as *DATA*. These timeouts take into account the operation of SMTP over the connectionless Internet environment, with its wide variations in quality of service.

- Definitions of distinctions between mail "forwarders," "relayers," and "gateways," with slightly varying functional requirements for each.

7.3.2   UUCP

The Unix-to-Unix Copy Program (UUCP) is used as a transport mechanism for Internet hosts acting as MTAs connected via asynchronous dial-up links rather than over IP. UUCP nodes are identified by eight-character names. The sending UUCP entity creates a simple envelope around the RFC 822 message and executes a remote command on the receiving system to transfer the message.

7.4   DOMAIN NAME SYSTEM

The DNS is a distributed directory system containing information about addressing and services provided on Internet hosts. Though some SMTP MTAs rely on static host tables for routing, most use the DNS for address-to-route resolution and only rely on host tables when all or part of the DNS is unavailable to them. Unlike X.500 and other directory systems, the DNS is not designed for user name-to-address lookup. It is used primarily for mapping between host names and host addresses.

Recall from Section 7.2 that Internet addressing uses a *local-part@domain-part* format. The domain part of an address identifies the administrative authority responsible for the mailbox; the local part is a name identifying the mailbox. The form of the local part will vary from domain to domain. In some cases the local part may contain an embedded address for use by a gateway; this address may be either an Internet address or a foreign address.

The domain part is structured as a logical domain path. This path identifies a sequence or hierarchy of administrative subdomains. These administrative divisions need not have any relationship to physical networks and subnetworks. Consider, for example, the name *research.east.widgets.us*. *Research* is a subdomain of *east.widgets.us*, *east* is a subdomain of *widgets.us*, and *widgets* is a subdomain of *us*. This hierarchy is convenient and scalable for administrative purposes. The East Coast branch of the Widgets organization can register subdomains and local mailboxes independently of other locations. Arbitrary numbers of subdomain lev-

Domain name	Remarks
com	commercial domains
edu	educational domains
gov	government domains
int	international organization domains
mil	military domains
net	network provider domains
org	not for profit organization domains

Table 7.2 Traditional Internet root domains.

els may be specified in an address. However, the overall domain name must weigh in at less than 255 characters and implementations are supposed to support at least 63 characters.

In the example, "*US*" is the root of the domain name. Internationally, each country (using its two-letter country code from ISO 3166) can act as a root. However, because of the Internet's U.S. origins, a number of other domain name functional roots are in common usage and are shown in Table 7.2. The greatest number of hosts are registered under the *.edu* branch, but the *.com* population is growing rapidly as well. Most (though not quite all) of the entries registered under the functional roots refer to U.S.-based entities.

Using a DNS client component (called a resolver), SMTP MTAs contact the DNS, offering the domain part of each message recipient as a lookup parameter. The result of the query (or queries) may be the 32-bit IP address of the host directly serving the recipient, or it may be a set of mail relaying (MX) records for intermediate SMTP MTAs acting as relays. In the latter case, the MX record contains the domain name of the relay and a cost. Multiple relays can be defined for a domain, and the one with the lowest cost will be selected. However, should transfer to the lowest cost relay fail, the SMTP MTA can try another. There are two kinds of DNS resolvers: a full resolver, which is able to directly contact multiple DNS servers and to cache results, and a stub resolver which is able to contact one or more full resolvers that will pass their query to a server if it cannot be satisfied from a cache. Stub resolvers are often used in PC-based implementations. Figure 7.6 shows how the DNS can be used.

Internally, the DNS is a distributed directory service with its own TCP/IP-based client-server protocol. DNS servers each control a nonoverlapping portion, or zone, of the Internet domain name space. For example, in the *research.east.widgets.us* space, a different DNS server might be responsible for the research space than for the east space. Despite the fact that one and only one server may ever be authoritative for a given zone, servers may replicate information from other zones to improve performance.

The DNS has other features, including the ability to pursue queries from resolvers recursively (where one server contacts another on behalf of the resolver) or by referring the resolver to the distant server. The DNS is capable of resolving aliases. Also, replication is a formal and required part of the DNS, and a secondary

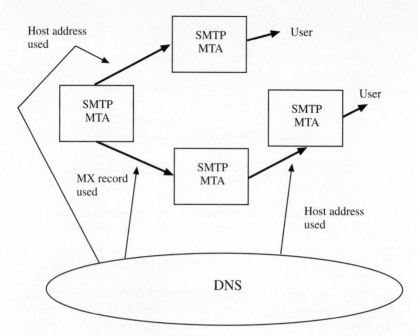

Figure 7.6   Using the DNS.

server that keeps a formal replicated copy of a zone may assert that the information it offers is as authoritative as the primary. Replication in the DNS not only improves performance but, perhaps more importantly, improves reliability.

7.5   MIME

The most important area of Internet Mail enhancement is the Multipurpose Internet Mail Extensions (MIME) codified in RFCs 1521 and 1522 [MIME93, MIME93A]. MIME extensions include support for structured, multipart message bodies and binary attachments. There are also features allowing non-ASCII character sets to be used. The MIME developers displayed considerable engineering creativity in crafting a solution that would allow Internet UAs to participate fully in the era of multimedia messaging while coexisting with an installed base of ASCII-only systems. Although earlier incarnations of MIME appeared as RFCs 1341 and 1342, the protocol has been stable since mid-1992 and has already attracted substantial support on the Internet.

7.5.1   Basic MIME Concepts and Enhancements to the RFC 822 Header

MIME essentially builds upon the RFC 822 and SMTP framework that we discussed earlier. By defining mechanisms for transferring binary messages using a special ASCII encoding, MIME provides for messages that are transparent to those old SMTP implementations which cannot carry "eight-bit clean" information. MIME also does not contravene RFC 822; it simply adds several new message header fields and incorporates some specifications for the format of message bodies.

The new header fields created by MIME include MIME-Version, Content-Type, Content-Transfer-Encoding, Content-ID, and Content-Description. Of these, MIME-Version, Content-ID and Content-Description are essentially self-explanatory. *Content-Type* is critical in that it determines the structure of the message body (or bodies). *Content-transfer-encoding* enables MIME to handle binary data in eight-bit clean mode or, for compatibility with old SMTP implementations, with one of several seven-bit transparent modes. Content-type and content-transfer-encoding header fields are used to define the initial structure of the Body. They are also used within the Body itself to demarcate nested Body Parts.

Besides enabling the transfer of arbitrary multipart data, the MIME standards support use of non-ASCII character data in the RFC 822 header fields.[5] This capability enables Europeans and other users to use their correct names (which may contain non-ASCII characters) in their Internet Mail addresses. A special header encoding mechanism enables non-ASCII header fields, such as addresses, to tunnel through ASCII-only SMTP relays and UAs. Essentially, each non-ASCII header field begins with a special character sequence that alerts UAs to the character set and encoding method used in the address data to follow. UAs capable of handling the character set used can then display the information to users in the correct local form. To users of ASCII-only UAs, the non-ASCII information may appear meaningless or garbled, but at least should not cause nondeliveries, keyboard lockup, program crashes, or other undesired side effects.

7.5.2 MIME Body and Body Part Constructs

The MIME Content-Type header contains a *type* specification followed by a *subtype* specification and zero or more parameters relevant to the subtype. Implementations thus embed type/subtype text strings, such as *application/postscript* or *image/g3fax*, in messages to tag MIME body parts. Implementors can interchange information tagged with private subtype values (beginning with the usual string "X-") or they can register new subtype values with the Internet Assigned Numbers Authority (IANA). Since all MIME UAs will recognize each of MIME's short and broadly known list of types, a MIME UA always starts out with some information about an unknown body part. This knowledge could assist the MIME UA in making intelligent decisions. For example, it may be appropriate to attempt to display an unknown type of text but not audio!

A Content-Type field will appear in the header of a MIME message and in Body Parts that are nested within other body parts. Table 7.3 summarizes the various MIME Content-Types or Body Parts and provides a brief explanation of each.

---

5. This capability is described in the second separate MIME RFC 1522 [MOOR93].

MIME content types	MIME subtypes	Remarks
Multipart	mixed	Body Parts are processed by the user agent sequentially; for example, word processed files.
	parallel	Body Parts are processed by the user agent in parallel; for example, video and audio clips.
	digest	Each Body Part contains a mail message.
	alternative	The Body Parts are alternatives to one another. Only one should be processed or displayed.
	header-set	As of early 1994, the header-set subtype was defined in an Internet Draft [CROC93]. It is intended for cases where a Body Part requires an internal header/data structure.
	delivery-status-notification	As of early 1994, the delivery-status-notification subtype was defined in an Internet Draft. See Section 7.7.5 for details.
Message	rfc822	The Body Part is a complete RFC 822 message.
	partial	The Body Part is a partial message that has been fragmented to tunnel through size-limited MTAs.
	external-body	The Body Part contains instructions to access its actual contents through FTP, a mail server, or other methods. It may denote a local or remote file that is rather large.
Text	plain	The usual seven-bit ASCII or an optional identified international character set.
	richtext	Simple text formatting language[1] supporting line breaks, page breaks, and optional additional text formatting languages.
Audio	basic	Uses eight-bit ISDN u-law format with a single channel, sampled at 8KHz.
Image	gif	Uses CompuServe's Graphics Interchange Format (GIF).
	jpeg	Uses ISO/IEC 10918's compressed rendering of full color and gray scale images.
Video	mpeg	Uses the ISO/IEC 11172 specification.
Application	octet stream	The Body Part contains binary data. Name, type, and conversions parameter can be standardized and registered.
	oda	Uses the ISO/IEC 8613 Open Document Interchange Format.
	postscript	Uses Adobe Systems' nonrevisable document rendition format. This format is already popular today as an interchange format for documents that one intends to print. Postscript tends to create large text files.

1. Attempts to standardize this language ran into difficulties, and the specification for richtext was removed from the main MIME document and placed in RFC 1523 [MIME93B].

Table 7.3 MIME Body Part types and subtypes.

We suggest that you review the table and then read on for examples of how some of the MIME machinery can be applied.[6]

Three examples of the MIME Body Part usage are as follows:

- A Microsoft Word file could be transferred as an *application/octet stream* using an IANA-registered string as its type. It seems likely that the use of registered Body Parts for different file types, essentially similar in concept to what could be done with the X.400 External Body Part, will become a common industry practice. Definition of formats for files for specific platforms, such as DOS/Windows and Apple Macintosh, is already underway.

- Notification of a new document posting in a document storage area (such as the Internet RFC repository) could be sent as a *multipart/mixed* or *multipart/ alternative* type where the first *text/plain* Body Part contains instructions for manual retrieval and the second *message/external* Body Part contains instructions for the document's automated retrieval using a file or mail server.[7]

- A multipart/mixed Body Part could contain a note in a text/plain Body Part and a nested multipart/parallel Body Part could contain nested audio and video body parts to be rendered simultaneously.

Figure 7.7 illustrates yet another example, the multipart/mixed conveyance of text, image, and audio data.

In addition to defining very sophisticated means of transferring multimedia data, MIME solves the problem of retrofitting multimedia into the Internet's traditional ASCII-only environment. To accomplish the retrofit, MIME defines several content-transfer-encodings. These are seven-bit, quoted-printable, eight-bit, and binary. Of these, the *seven-bit* encoding method constitutes an ASCII representation of the information. Using this strategy, the sender informs the receiving MIME UA that the original Body Part payload requires no encoding transformation. *Quoted-printable* is optimized for Body Parts containing mostly ASCII text. It encodes all binary characters (those with the eighth bit set), the "=" characters, and trailing spaces or tabs at the end of a line as an "=" followed by the two character hexadecimal value for the character. The *base64* encoding method expands each three octets of binary data in an input stream into four octets of coded ASCII data. The *eight-bit* and *binary* encodings are used to transmit binary

---

6. Many aspects of MIME design are extensible. The set of content type/subtype pairs and their associated parameters is expected to grow significantly with time. Several other MIME fields, notably character set names, access-type parameters for the message/external-body type, and possibly even Content-Transfer-Encoding values, are likely to have new values defined over time. In order to ensure that the set of such values is developed in an orderly, well-specified, and public manner, MIME defines a registration process using the IANA as a central registry for such values. New content types can be registered by filling out an e-mail form and sending it to an IANA mail box. Before being registered with IANA, a content type must be published in an RFC.

7. Messages of this type are already being used on the Internet to announce the publication of new RFCs.

From: vjk@relevantum.fi
Subject: Testing...
To: rdunbar@tni.com
Mime-Version: 1.0
Content-Type: text/plain; charset=ISO-8859-1
Content-Transfer-Encoding: 8bit
Content-Length: 26
Status: RO

This is plain text...

VK

Simple message
Text character set
ISO 8859-1 (ANSI)

Multipart message
• simple text
• picture (gif)
• voice

From: vjk@relevantum.fi
Subject: MIME test
To: rdunbar@tni.com
Mime-Version: 1.0
Content-Type: multipart/mixed; boundary=%#%record%#%
Content-Length: 1461

--%#%record%#%
Content-Type: text/plain; charset=US-ASCII
Content-Transfer-Encoding: 7bit
Content-Length: 54

Test message with GIF-picture and voice included.

VK

Text part
No transfer encoding

--%#%record%#%
Content-Type: image/gif
Content-Name: test.gif
Content-Length: 236
Content-Transfer-Encoding: base64

R0lGODdhCQAJAPQAAAAAAHdOPBsbG2ZmZhsAADAAAEMWFlUVFWYUKXcoKIcnJ5cAOqc4OLY3
SsU2SdRHWuJGWId0dJeXl6enp+KcRrZtAKdcAGYpAP//7uLi0cXFxVVVVUNDQzAwMAAAAAA
ACwAAAAACQAJAAAFMqAwbEJFVYFgCWxVrR1ldRqmsZ07cQAnsawIYBgxsXhDjksguwAuwJNl
aFkpp4DcaxMCADs=

GIF-picture
Original size 173 bytes
Base-64 transfer encoding

--%#%record%#%
Content-Type: audio/basic
Content-Name: test.au
Content-Length: 787
Content-Transfer-Encoding: base64

LnNuZAAAACAAAAImAAAAAQAAH0AAAAABAAAAAAAAADR+cZrTl5bzE/WYMvlVGBOzk7Pa9Li
U+RNzUzUadvbS95NyU3Z9+TWSNdOzFDf8/LSR9hQx1Xi6nPQQdtMyl3i22TLQNZMzFz+01zJ
QNhRz3dnz1nMQd9Y13lrzlvOROFi1Plf1F3PQuxv1OJo0VvXRXFv291j1WPdSWzr5dds12Hy
TGLk7dp12BvTmHb+8pc0lZnUF7YbcRbzUxqU2zh7chWzkTuTufv0Mxf40LkTuX3x9n5WUzm
XnDazNldSmjub/3K2+VGWGvi/tPW2lFKZWPN1dT2TlVOfNXF2upLUk1gzcvHZ1BOTXLQzczr
TIJH7dTOOf5yTkx03dTZYt5WWOv83eNV2Vvn119vW3jxZ9HLa1Nlb+lgw8veTT18XdblxttL
PVtXy77S0T9LSVDEwcRmSEtMVcLJxVtGWETX0cnQV1dJXdHQ3PBTakvhy9zgS/1Pe8/X1lVT
W1jVyOnoTF5N+MTY3VFaU0/lzd9jU/dH3sbbdEr/VlvDzutJV+tKysbVT0TvUe7AyHM+allZ
ysfNQkv6VNDNx1FBfVbXzcn3PV5d3sjO1D9LYnrDz8tEQV5hv9LHUz1cS7/LxXg5WETCxMfO
OE9B1rvNvzpEQ1y21LtDPkxDudW9aTxQPrrPx9w8YTy/ytbPPmM9xMDa2z5bQMq71fE+WkXY
u8vkP0xH77vG3kBLSXe/w9FGSUhuxMTNRkxKcMfKzUdNTvPL0dNOTFvl

Voice (0.1 sec)
Original size 582 bytes
Base-64 transfer encoding

--%#%record%#%
--%#%record%#%--

Figure 7.7 Example MIME message.

information in eight-bit clean form, omitting the overhead that inevitably results from encoding binary as ASCII using one of the other techniques. However, given the prevalence of ASCII-only implementations on the Internet, it may be many years before eight-bit clean data transfer becomes the norm.

Any content-transfer-encoding may be used with any MIME Body Part with the exception of multipart and message content types that are restricted to seven-bit.

7.5.3 Additional MIME Considerations

A great deal of innovation and change surrounds the ongoing development of MIME-based technology. Not only is MIME likely to bring vast areas of Internet Mail up to state-of-the-art multimedia operation, but the protocol will enable improved Internet Mail gateway operation and enhanced mail-enabling capabilities for Internet applications. At the E-mail World Conference in November 1993, one speaker lauded MIME's backward compatibility features, hailing the protocol as "the one good mole we need to run through all these tunnels and gateways."

The following list is a sampling of MIME-related activity and information sources as of the beginning of 1994:

- **RFC 1344, Implications of MIME for Internet Mail Gateways [BORE92]:** This RFC distinguishes between mail relays that do not modify message content and mail gateways that do perform transformations. (Gateways are needed within the Internet Mail environment due to its wide variations in functionality.) RFC 1344 highlights the use of the MIME message/partial feature as a means of splitting up large MIME messages to accommodate size limitations in destination systems as well as the possible use of message conversion capabilities. It also suggests that the access pointer in the message/external-body could be rewritten in cases where it is desirable to move the external data closer to the destination prior to delivering the message referencing it.

- **Interworking with Non-Internet Mail Systems:** MIME also has implications for gateways to other e-mail protocols. In general, its ability to label attachment information will much improve interworking between Internet Mail and both X.400 and LAN e-mail systems.

- **Facilitating the Interworking of MIME and Mail-enabled Applications:** RFC 1524 [BORE93A] suggests that MIME-capable UAs could use a standardized configuration file format, called *mailcap* (for mail capabilities), to determine how to process MIME Body Parts. It remains to be seen whether this will become an industry practice.

- **MIME as an Internet Information Service Delivery Mechanism:** In Chapter 4, we alluded to the use of MIME as a way of transferring hypertext information for the World Wide Web application. Other applications could use MIME's multimedia capabilities in this manner.

- **MIME and Multiple Language Support:** A recent Internet Draft proposed a new header field, *Content-language*, to be used with MIME [ALVE93A]. This Content-language header field could identify any of the languages listed in the ISO 636 standard. This information could be used with the multipart/alternative Body Part construct to enable electronic document distribution systems to be used in multilingual communities.

- **MIME and Multiple Character Set Support:** As of early 1994, a significant outpouring of research and effort has gone into developing specifications for the use of MIME with non-ASCII character sets. These include Korean and Hebrew character sets, for which RFCs were published in late 1993.

- **Minimal MIME Conformance:** Appendix A of the MIME RFC 1521 contains minimal conformance guidelines to which all MIME implementations should adhere. Some of these guidelines suggest that implementations should be able to set the MIME Version field to "Version 1.0," support at least the base64 and quoted-printable encodings, recognize at least the text/plain, message, multipart/mixed, and multipart/alternative Body Parts, treat unrecognized subtypes as raw binary data that can be made available to the user, support the U.S. ASCII character set, support the U.S. ASCII characters within the ISO 8859 character sets, and handle unsupported character sets as gracefully as possible.

7.6 PEM

The rapid expansion of Internet Mail into the commercial messaging environment magnifies the importance of dealing with pre-existing security risks. Indeed, secure messaging may well be the most important remaining area requiring enhancement to Internet Mail standards.

Like MIME, the Internet's existing PEM standard, RFC 1421 [PEM93A], builds on the RFC 822 message format, allowing users to encrypt messages or sign them to prevent their modification. Public key distribution in PEM is supported by sending Certificates in messages or by listing Certificates in directories, such as X.500. While PEM was originally defined before MIME, mechanisms are being developed to allow both PEM and MIME services to be combined in a single message. The use of these mechanisms may ultimately replace parts of the existing PEM technology. However, PEM has a slow adoption record, possibly due to the general complexity and controversy surrounding digital cryptography. It faces additional competition on the Internet from a standard called Pretty Good Privacy (PGP). Another variant of PEM, called RIPEM, has seen some use. Like PGP, RIPEM supports message confidentiality using ad hoc key exchange methods instead of certificates.

7.6.1 PEM Overview

PEM is defined in four related RFCs that provide secure messaging[8] for use with e-mail transfer in the Internet Mail environment. These four RFCs are RFC 1421:

---

8. Refer to Chapter 6, Section 6.13, for a generic definition of the terms "encryption," "authentication," and "integrity" in the electronic mail environment. The following text assumes that readers understand the material in Section 6.13, including the method by which digital signatures are computed.

Privacy Enhancement for Internet Electronic Mail: Part I: Message Encryption and Authentication Procedures [PEM93A]; RFC 1422: Privacy Enhancement for Internet Electronic Mail: Part II: Certificate-Based Key Management [PEM93B]; RFC 1423: Privacy Enhancement for Internet Electronic Mail: Part III: Algorithms, Modes, and Identifiers [PEM93C]; and RFC 1424: Privacy Enhancement for Internet Electronic Mail: Part IV: Key Certification and Related Services [PEM93D].

PEM provides four security capabilities: confidentiality (via the encryption of a message), originator authentication, content integrity (via a signed or encrypted Message Identification Code [MIC]), and nonrepudiation of origin (if public key mechanisms are used). PEM supports the use of either symmetric or asymmetric approaches for providing these services. All PEM capabilities are implemented in an end-to-end fashion by UA software and require no modification to SMTP servers. The PEM format (defined in RFC 1421) is compatible with RFC 822, and non-PEM compliant UAs in many cases allow their users to read PEM messages. (Of course, in the case where the message has been encrypted, ordinary mortals can make little sense of it.) PEM is algorithm-independent; however, most or all public key-based PEM messaging that has been practiced to date has utilized the RSA algorithm. The Internet Society has obtained the assurance from Public Key Partners (the RSA patent holder) that parties will be able to obtain the right to use RSA technology under reasonable, nondiscriminatory terms.

Unlike MIME, which superimposes heading fields in the RFC 822 header, PEM works by encapsulating its own information formats within the RFC 822 message body. PEM implementations look for the string "—BEGIN PRIVACY-ENHANCED MESSAGE—" to demarcate the beginning of a PEM message and the string "—END PRIVACY-ENHANCED MESSAGE—" to mark the end. As depicted in Fig. 7.8, a PEM heading and body occur within these boundaries. Forwarded messages can be nested within PEM encapsulations.

Encapsulated PEM messages are carefully engineered to live in a text-oriented SMTP jungle. In this environment, a UA can expect that MTAs or gateways may insert carriage return/line feed (CR/LF) pairs between lines that are longer than 1000 characters, that character set conversions may be undertaken, or that CR/LF layouts may be modified to suit the whim of the local system. The PEM UA (or any other type of UA) has no way of preventing such behavior by SMTP MTAs. But if a PEM UA signs a message and an SMTP MTA later inserts line breaks, the signature becomes invalid! And, in the case of encryption, the information later deciphered by the receiving UA would be corrupted by any MTA changes, however well intentioned.

To protect messages from accidental inter-SMTP corruption, PEM UAs first transform the data into an ASCII form and ensure that lines are separated by <CR><LF> delimiters. This transformation is called canonicalization. Next, encryption and/or signatures are applied; signing is done using a header field called MIC-info. Finally, the encrypted or signed message is encoded in a printable character set (using the same transformation known as base64 for MIME), with lines of 64 characters (guaranteed to be acceptable at all Internet sites). The receiving PEM UA reverses these steps by first decoding, then decrypting, then decanonicalizing the message.

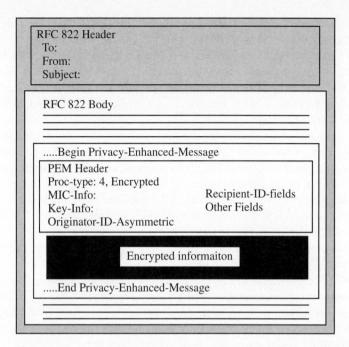

Figure 7.8   An RFC 822 message containing a PEM message.

Encryption and signing are performed with the aid of a Data Encrypting Key (DEK),[9] which is itself transmitted to each recipient in the key-info heading field. The DEK is protected by encryption using an Interchange Key (IK). Different combinations of additional heading fields are used depending on which services are employed and on whether asymmetric (public key) or symmetric (private key) algorithms are in effect. Note that different algorithms may be used to prepare the key-info for different recipients. Recipients supporting public key algorithms can either obtain the originator's public key (needed to check signatures) from a directory service or receive the key as part of an originator-certificate sent by the originator in the PEM message itself.

The first PEM header field, proc-type, identifies one of three combinations of PEM services used on the encapsulated body. The following combinations of services are available with PEM:

- "ENCRYPTED"—this flag signifies that the confidentiality, authentication, integrity, and (given use of asymmetric key management) nonrepudiation of origin security services have been applied to a PEM message's encapsulated text.

- "MIC-ONLY"—authentication, integrity, and (given use of asymmetric key management) nonrepudiation of origin security services have been applied to

---

9. DEKs may be generated by the PEM UA or obtained from a key distribution server.

PEM message data. MIC-ONLY messages are subjected to printable encoding prior to signing in order to protect against modification by SMTP MTAs. Users with non-PEM compliant RFC 822 UAs cannot read MIC-ONLY messages.

*   "MIC-CLEAR"—authentication, integrity, and (given use of asymmetric key management) nonrepudiation of origin security services have been applied to the PEM message text. However, printable encoding is not applied. Users with non-PEM–compliant RFC 822 UAs are able to read the message, but, of course, they cannot avail themselves of the security services. PEM-compliant UAs can make use of the security services provided that the message has not been corrupted by an MTA during its passage through the Internet.

In a public key environment, PEM key management is provided using Certificates and certification infrastructures. These mechanisms are discussed below.

7.6.2   PEM Certificates and Certification Infrastructure

Recall from Chapter 6 that Certificates are special data structures used to register and protectively encapsulate the public keys of users and prevent their forgery. A Certificate contains the name of a user, its public key, and other information. It also contains the name of the issuer, a Certification Authority (CA), which vouches that the public key in a Certificate belongs to the named user. This data, along with a time interval specifying the Certificate's validity, is cryptographically signed by the issuer using the issuer's private key. The subject and issuer names in certificates are Distinguished Names (DNs) as defined in the Directory System (X.500). Such Certificates are commonly called X.509 Certificates after the recommendation in X.500 where they were defined [ITU88A].

Certificates are used in PEM to provide the originator of a message with the authenticated public key of each recipient and to provide each recipient with the authenticated public key of the originator. Once protected by the issuer's signature, Certificates can be stored in generally accessible directory servers or transmitted openly in one of the PEM message header fields.

Prior to sending an encrypted PEM message, the originator acquires a Certificate for each recipient who is using a public key algorithm. The originator should validate each Certificate by checking its validity time interval, verifying that it is not on a Certificate Revocation List (CRL), and using the issuing CA's public key to check the issuer's signature. This certificate checking may need to be done recursively if the originator and recipient do not use the same CA.[10] That is, they may use a pair of CAs that are linked together in a Certification Path as described below. Once a Certificate for a recipient is validated, the public key contained in the certificate is used to encrypt the data encryption key (DEK) which, as noted above, is used to encrypt the message itself.

---

10. Checking CA signatures is a CPU-intensive process that should nonetheless be performed by a UA at least once during the lifetime of each Certificate it handles.

To ensure message integrity, a PEM UA employing public key algorithms computes a MIC, signs it with the originator's private key, and includes the resulting value in the MIC-Info message header field. Optionally, the originator may include its Certificate in another PEM message header field. The recipient checks the originator's Certificate, extracts the public key, and checks the MIC against a locally generated MIC.

As we can see, the certification mechanism forms a central component of PEM processing. To facilitate the management of a CA infrastructure, RFC 1422 defines an architecture with four entities: the user/UA, the Internet Policy Registration Authority (IPRA), Policy Certification Authorities (PCA), and other Certification Authorities. Essentially, the IPRA registers/certifies PCAs, PCAs register/certify CAs, and CAs register/certify users.

Since the Internet is acting as the world's first large-scale laboratory for the testing of public key technology, it is instructive to consider the RFC 1422 architecture in more detail. Therefore, the roles of the four entities as described in RFC 1422 are discussed here.

The PEM UA component must be able to compose and receive PEM messages, protect the private key of the user, check Certificates, and process CRL information held in the directory or sent to the UA in a message.

The IPRA component acts as the root of the Internet certification hierarchy and it is managed by the Internet Society. It registers and certifies the next level of PCAs, based on differences in their own registration policies, and ensures that they abide by established policies. The IPRA will make available to all requesters a digitally signed copy of the security policy on file for each PCA it registers, a PCA CRL list to be updated monthly, and a database (to prevent duplication) of the names of all PCAs, CAs, and user certificate subject names registered under its authority. The IPRA will license and support multiple public key algorithms as needed to sign certificates for PCAs. Work to date has been based on the RSA algorithm.

The PCA acts as the middle level of the Internet certification hierarchy. The intent is that there should be one PCA for each formally defined policy. Potential policies might include academic/light assurance, commercial/medium assurance, and strong assurance. The PCA certifies CAs. A PCA must specify its distinguished name, the type of CAs it will certify, its certification policy, its CRL management policy, and the nature of any naming conventions, business agreements, or other constraints it imposes on lower-level CAs.

CAs register and certify users. They are responsible for protecting their private key and for not allocating duplicate distinguished names (to which certificates are bound). There are three types of CAs: organizational CAs, residential CAs, and PERSONA CAs. Organizational CAs register/certify organizational user and residential CAs register/certify residential users. PERSONA CAs register users whose identity will remain anonymous. That is, the distinguished names in their Certificates do not represent the users' true identities, nor does the CA vouch for their identity. CAs must provide their CRLs to their PCAs and may send CRLs to PEM UAs by e-mail.

Thus, a private corporation, ABC, for example, might utilize an Organizational CA. This CA would in turn be certified by a PCA for medium assurance

CAs. The PCA would in turn be certified by the IPRA root CA. Individual ABC users would contain Certificates issued by the ABC Organizational CA.

Under the X.509 standard for Certificate structures, the Certificates for ABC users could be created as a Certification Path that shows the chain of certification from IPRA to the user. The important benefit of Certification Paths is that users in different organizations, with different CAs and different Certification Paths can still communicate securely. This is possible because Certificate checking software can trace the intersection of the Certification Paths at the IPRA or at a PCA and thus establish trust transitively. For example, if the ABC Corporation and the XYZ corporation trust the same PCA, then ABC and XYZ users can trust one another's Certificates.

We noted that the Internet is acting as the world's first large-scale laboratory for public key technology. The architecture discussed here is currently operating at a preliminary stage and could, in principle, be used by forms of messaging other than PEM (such as X.400). However, modifications to the architecture could come about through full integration with MIME.

7.6.3 MIME/PEM Compatibility

As of early 1994, two Internet Draft proposals were on the table for integrating MIME and PEM. These were [CROK93] and [SCHI93]. [CROK93] proposes breaking up PEM functionality and reengineering it into MIME; [SCHI93] would allow the two protocols to work together essentially without change. It is too early to determine which method will prevail, whether both methods will be practiced, or whether further changes await us downstream. With this health warning as a caveat, we will briefly describe the two proposals.

The first proposal [CROK93] involves creating six new MIME Body Part definitions: *application/pem-keys*, *application/pem-signature*, *application/pem-encrypted*, *application/quoted-mime-entity*, *application/pem-request*, and *application/certdata*. The first four of these would be combined within a multipart/header-set construct to provide the basic PEM services as follows:

1. Integrity and authentication are achieved by combining an *application/pem-signature* and an *application/quoted-mime-entity* in a multipart/headerset. The first Body Part contains the digital signature and parameters and the second contains the signed data.

2. Confidentiality is achieved by combining an *application/pem-keys* and an *application/pem-encrypted* Body Part in a multipart/headerset. The first Body Part contains keying information and the second encapsulates the encrypted data.

3. Confidentiality, integrity, and authentication services could be simultaneously utilized by first performing the signing procedure in (1) immediately above to produce a signed headerset, and then encrypting and encapsulating that headerset as in (2).

This "PEM breakup" proposal has several implications. First, confidentiality and authentication/integrity services are nicely separated (in the original PEM, encrypted data was also always signed). Second, the Certificate exchange mechanisms are separated from the other security mechanisms and enhanced. Thus, Certificate-related information (including revocation lists) can be requested using an *application/pem-request* Body Part and is returned in an *application/certdata* Body Part.

On the other hand, the second proposal [SCHI93] remains fully backward compatible with current PEM. It defines a means for a PEM message to be encapsulated as an application/pem-1421 Body Part within MIME. Alternatively, a PEM message could encapsulate a privacy-enhanced MIME message.

It is unfortunate that the MIME and PEM standards were developed on separate tracks, which will possibly result in the proliferation of at least four types of Internet Mail UAs: RFC 822 only, MIME-capable, PEM capable, and MIME-PEM capable. The interoperability possibilities among them are illustrated in Table 7.4.

Sender/Receiver	RFC-822	MIME	PEM	PEM-MIME
RFC 822	—	Yes	Yes	Yes
MIME	Partial	—	Partial	Yes
PEM	Partial	Partial	—	Partial
MIME-PEM	Partial	Partial	Partial	—

Table 7.4 Internet Mail User Agent interworking. *Note: MIME messages are in some cases readable (though ugly) by RFC-822 UAs and PEM UAs, provided that seven-bit or quoted-printable encoding is used. None of the potentially automated MIME mechanisms (such as reassembling partial messages or fetching messages with external Body Parts) are available with RFC-822 or PEM UAs. Also, PEM messages or MIME-PEM messages are in some cases readable (though ugly) by RFC-822 or MIME UAs provided that encryption is not employed.*

7.7 EXTENDED SMTP

We have seen that the designers of PEM and MIME bent over backwards to accommodate an installed base of legacy SMTP servers that are only capable of supporting ASCII text. On another front, however, SMTP itself is in the process of being extended to move into the world of multimedia messaging. While much can be done to work around the ASCII-only limitation, MIME's base64 encoding entails a 33 percent increase in message size—an expensive proposition over some links. Also, if Internet Mail is to continue evolving as a dynamic protocol suite, extension mechanisms must be developed to enable SMTP servers to support new services in the future.

For these basic reasons, four RFCs were developed in 1993 to provide an SMTP extension mechanism and to define several initial extensions for eight-bit clean message transfer and message size support declaration. These RFCs are

RFC 1425: SMTP Service Extension [ROSE93A], RFC 1426: SMTP Service Extension for eight-bit-MIME transport [ROSE93B], RFC 1427: SMTP Service Extension for Message Size Declaration [MOOR93A], and RFC 1428: Transition of Internet Mail from Just-Send-8 to eight-bit-SMTP/MIME [VAUD93].

This section discusses these various SMTP enhancements and introduces draft work on SMTP/MIME Delivery Reports.

7.7.1   SMTP Extension Mechanisms

RFC 1425 lays the foundation for the extensions in RFC 1426 and 1427 as well as for future work by defining a means whereby two extended SMTP MTAs may recognize and inform one another about the service extensions that they support. Three mechanisms provide the extensions capability: a new command (*EHLO*), a registry of SMTP service extensions (using the IANA), and a means of applying additional parameters to the SMTP *MAIL FROM* and *RCPT TO* commands.

An extended SMTP MTA uses the *EHLO* command instead of the traditional *HELO*. Upon opening a TCP connection, the initiating SMTP MTA issues an *EHLO*. The responding MTA replies with the list of service extension keywords (and, optionally, accompanying parameters) that it supports. An MTA that has not been updated to support service extensions will react to the *EHLO* command by generating an error. *EHLO* keywords must be registered in a standards track RFC or, if prefixed by "X-", may be recognized local extensions. Figure 7.9 displays an Extended SMTP (ESMTP) interaction scenario.

7.7.2   Service Extension for Eight-bit-MIME Transport

The service extension for eight-bit data utilizes an "8BITMIME" keyword with the associated *MAIL FROM* extension shown in Figure 7.9. When a sending SMTP MTA wishes to submit a content body (using the MAIL command) consisting of a MIME message containing octet aligned binary data, it issues the *EHLO* command to the receiving SMTP MTA.[11] This *EHLO* command queries the receiver about the extensions it supports. If the receiving MTA responds with code 250 to the *EHLO* command and if the response includes the *EHLO* keyword value 8BITMIME, then the *MAIL FROM* extension to ship binary MIME messages can be used. Otherwise, if the receiving MTA reacts to the *EHLO* with an error or does not cite support for the 8BITMIME extensions, the sending MTA must return an error report to the originator's MIME UA. Note that until Internet Mail implementations support a standardized error report format, the MIME UA cannot determine whether it is possible to resubmit the message automatically using one of the other content-transfer-encodings. However, an SMTP MTA that is collocated with the UA may reencode the message as a gatewaying feature.

---

11. This data must not contain line lengths greater than 1K bytes. Thus the MIME UA must still perform carriage return/line feed "stuffing" as part of encoding binary data.

```
S: <wait for connection on TCP port 25>
C: <open connection to server>
S: 220 college.nyc.edu SMTP service ready
C: EHLO college.ucla.edu
S: 250-college.nyc.edu says hello
S: 250 8BITMIME
C: MAIL FROM:<john.delaney@college.ucla.edu>
   BODY=8BITMIME
S: 250 <john.delaney@college.ucla.edu>... Sender and
   8BITMIME ok
C: RCPT TO:<deborah.egan@college.nyc.edu>
S: 250 <deborah.egan@college.nyc.edu>... Recipient ok
C: DATA
S: 354 Send 8BITMIME message, ending in CRLF.CRLF.
...
C: .
S: 250 OK
C: QUIT
S: 250 Goodbye
```

Figure 7.9 SMTP interaction scenario.

7.7.3   Service Extension for Size Declaration

One expected result of the use of MIME to carry revisable files or binary information for mail-enabled applications is that messages will become much larger and
SMTP MTAs will be expected to carry a much wider range of message sizes than
at any previous time in the history of Internet Mail. RFC 1427 therefore defines a
mechanism whereby a sending SMTP MTA may declare the size of a particular
message to a receiving SMTP MTA, after which the recipient may indicate to the
sender that it is or is not able to accept the message based on the declared size.
RFC 1427 also defines a mechanism whereby the receiving SMTP MTA may inform the sending MTA of the maximum message size it is willing to accept.

Message transfer may fail because of size constraints in a receiving SMTP
MTA, either because the MTA has a fixed upper limit[12] constituting the maximum-
size message it can accept or because the MTA is operating under temporary resource limitations, such as lack of sufficient storage. In the former case, failure
because of size is permanent; in the latter case, it is transient.

---

12. It is possible that a hard upper limit on a given SMTP MTA's acceptable message size
exists. Alternatively, such upper limits might be configurable by an administrator on a case-
by-case basis depending upon the domain of the sending MTA.

With this in mind, consider the following effects of the size declaration extension mechanisms:

- Permanent size constraints can be detected when the receiving MTA responds to the *EHLO* greeting with a SIZE keyword optionally followed by a number (the number zero is used to claim that no size limit whatsoever is in effect).

- Temporary size constraints can be detected when the sending MTA specifies the (estimated) size of a message as an extension to the MAIL FROM command.

- Without the size extensions, the sending MTA does not learn of permanent or temporary constraints until it has begun transmitting message data.

As in the case of eight-bit-MIME transport, a sending SMTP MTA finds (either through the size extension mechanism or trial and error) that its outgoing message is too large, and it must return an error report to the MIME UA of the originator. Note that until Internet Mail implementations support standardized error report format, the MIME UA cannot determine the necessity to resubmit the message automatically as multiple message/partial Body Parts; this would be up to the user. However, an SMTP MTA that is collocated with the UA might fragment a too-large message as a gatewaying feature.

7.7.4   Transition to Eight-bit Operation

Protocols for extending SMTP to pass eight-bit characters require the use of MIME encoding. Prior to the development of ESMTP, however, several SMTP implementations adopted ad hoc mechanisms for sending eight-bit data. Since it is desirable for the extended SMTP environment and these mechanisms to interoperate, RFC 1428 outlines compatibility problems in this environment and an approach to minimizing the cost of transitioning from the current usage of non-MIME eight-bit messages to MIME.

RFC 1424 describes what it terms "several interesting interoperability cases" and discusses the limits of interworking between traditional ASCII-only MTAs, MTAs that have been upgraded to support binary data transfer prior to the ESMTP specifications, and MIME/ESMTP compliant MTAs. These conclusions are summarized in Table 7.5.

Many of the problems occurring where mail becomes unusable or corrupted because of the use of different transport paradigms can be ameliorated with the aid of gateway transformations. RFC 1428 contains various recommendations and suggestions in regard to gateways. One possibility is for an Internet Mail site with some or all MTAs supporting non-ESMTP eight-bit transport to construct a gateway that converts all messages to MIME format, labeling the Body Part as text/plain or as text/unknown eight-bit if no information is available in a proprietary directory regarding the sender's character set. The RFC further recommends that MTAs indicate to the recipient user in the Received trace information fields of the RFC 822 header that such a transformation occurred.

Sender/Receiver	Seven-bit only	Eight-bit transparent	MIME/ESMTP
Seven-bit only	OK	OK provided sender uses ASCII or sender and receiver bilaterally agree on a common character set	OK
Eight-bit transparent	Mail is unusable, or corrupted	OK provided sender and receiver bilaterally agree on means of interpreting contents	Mail is unusable or corrupted
MIME/ESMTP	Mail is unusable or corrupted if binary, base64, or quoted-printable encoding is applied.	Mail is corrupted or unusable.	OK

Table 7.5 Internet Mail transport interoperability matrix.

7.7.5 SMTP/MIME Delivery Reports

In addition to the SMTP extensions that we have discussed, two Internet Drafts were in place by early 1994 for handling delivery status notifications (DSNs) through ESMTP and MIME. We provide a brief summary of the functionality in the drafts with the following health warning: Internet Drafts are subject to change!

The first of the drafts specifies a MIME content type that SMTP MTAs can use to generate DSNs; the second specifies an extension mechanism for SMTP where MTAs can request DSNs from one another on a per-recipient basis. Note that these DSNs are conceptually similar to X.400 Delivery Reports but are different from X.400 Receipt Notifications (which provide a post-delivery indication as to whether or not the user has actually read the message).

The MIME DSN is tentatively registered in [MOOR93B] as the *multipart/ delivery-status-notification* content type. The DSN contains two mandatory internal Body Parts and an optional additional Body Part in which it may return the content of the message in question (or a fragment of the content). The two mandatory Body Parts are:

1. A text/plain Body Part containing human-readable text explaining the problem

2. A special *message/delivery-report* Body Part containing an ESMTP-level message identifier, an optional Content Identifier, and a set of per-recipient delivery records containing a variety of parameters such as recipient addressing data, the name of the domain and the MTA generating the report, the nature of the delivery or nondelivery event, and the date and time of the event.

To support the DSN [MOOR93C] extends ESMTP to enable the sending MTA to request per recipient DSNs via an optional parameter to the *RCPT TO* command. It also enables the sending MTA to specify an envelope-level message identifier in the *MAIL FROM* command. These functions can only be used by the sending MTA if the receiving MTA supports the delivery report extension. The receiving MTA will indicate such support by responding positively to the sending MTA's session-initiating *EHLO* command and returning the *DRPT* keyword in its response to the *EHLO*. MTAs can request that DSNs not be returned, that they be returned in the case of delivery failure only, or that they be returned in the event of delivery success or failure. In the absence of a specific request from the sending MTA, the receiving MTA's default behavior should be to return only nondelivery reports.

7.8 OPERATIONAL USAGE WITH FIREWALLS

Up to this point, we have been primarily dealing with Internet Mail from the perspective of the environment in which the standards were intended to exist—a vast, open matrix of workstations and hosts linked by the web of IP connectivity. Yet as Internet Mail expands by leaps and bounds into commercial messaging realms, that openness must be restricted through firewalls in many cases. This section will briefly cover Internet Mail security concerns and then discuss firewall technology.

Within the expanses of the open Internet, there is a subculture of hackers[13] who are prone to attacking host computers and subnetworks. Many security penetrations are reported and still more go undetected or unreported. Once a host computer has been penetrated, the hacker may read, modify, or destroy information. He or she may also attempt to steal passwords [STOL89]. While the Internet has an Emergency Response Team (a sort of network posse intended to pursue and track down malefactors), hackers are rarely caught because little security protection is afforded by the underlying Internet infrastructure and network protocols.

As a result, many enterprises limit Internet access to one or several hosts or firewalls. These firewalls are equipped with special code to control access between the Internet and the enterprise's internal network. For the purposes of Internet Mail we can distinguish two general categories of firewalls: ones operating at the router level and ones operating at the mail level.

Firewalls operating at the router level may restrict access based on the point of origin of the outside user or on the type of application or resource being accessed by an outside user. For example, a router firewall configuration might allow internal users to set up FTP or TELNET sessions with outside hosts but prohibit outside users to FTP or TELNET into the enterprise. The only type of unsolicited traffic allowed into the enterprise might be e-mail, traveling over an SMTP connection. The firewall can differentiate SMTP, FTP, or other applications' connection establishment attempts by examining the "well-known" port addressed in the TCP connection establishment packet.

---

13. The word "hacker" also has (or once had) the more favorable connotation of expert programmer.

In this example, external SMTP hosts are still setting up direct connections with internal SMTP hosts. However, merely restricting external access to e-mail may be insufficient to satisfy the security concerns of some enterprises. Recall the notorious 1988 "Internet Worm" attack, where a self-replicating software program invaded computers across the U.S., slowing their processing to a crawl. This attack paralyzed the Internet for several days. One of the means by which the worm software could enter unsuspecting hosts was via the Sendmail "debug" port. While this hole has since been plugged, direct connection via SMTP to outside hosts poses some risk that additional problems could arise. Even in cases where incremental security risks posed by direct SMTP interconnection to the internal network are not considered significant, some organizations see a benefit in funneling all e-mail entering the enterprise through a single MTA that acts as a control point and thereby allows a single group to centrally manage mail connectivity and support issues.

These kinds of management and security concerns lead some enterprises to deploy the second type of firewall, one that operates at the mail level. A mail-level firewall acts as an SMTP relay or gateway to the internal environment. By deploying mail-level firewalls, enterprises have the opportunity to implement advanced (and still relatively uncommon) functions, such as:

- Selectively restricting mail access to and from the Internet by controlling which remote MTAs are allowed connection privileges and which external users or domains are allowed to communicate with which users in the enterprise.

- Implementing a "split DNS," wherein the enterprise's internal domain structure is not shown to the outside world. Thus *don_delong@srvr1.east.sales.abc.com* might be known to the external world by the more stable, less revealing *don_delong@abc.com*. The firewall would act as a gateway performing an address translation function.

- Monitoring and controlling incoming e-mail information. For instance, some external users might not be privileged to send binary information objects into the enterprise. The firewall software could conceivably check incoming messages for viruses. Although such functionality is problematical in many respects, it could become especially important as mail-enabled applications that launch attachments become more common and as smart messaging comes into general use.

- Encrypting/decrypting and signing/validating messages from external correspondents at the enterprise boundary.[14]

---

14. Enterprise gateway encryption functionality could employ a public/private key pair owned by the firewall and the Certificates of correspondents. Alternatively, it could make use of secret keys exchanged with correspondents on a bilateral basis.

7.9   INTERNET DIRECTORIES AND X.500

Historically, Internet Mail has not had a user directory service that provides global listings that users composing mail could employ to look up the names and addresses of their correspondents. The closest thing to an Internet user directory is a centralized database known as WHOIS. But this directory is usually out of date, not distributed, not comprehensive, and rarely consulted directly by Internet Mail UAs. Today, however, there are several possible solutions for a fully distributed, client-server protocol-based directory, including X.500 and WHOIS++.

7.9.1   X.500 on the Internet

For several years after the development of the standard in 1988, it was generally assumed that the Internet would gravitate to X.500. The PARADISE pilot and the Internet White Pages pilot were deployed on the Internet, free software was made generally available, and X.500 DSAs were installed at many Internet sites, such as universities and the research departments of commercial and government organizations. A number of RFCs were written to extend or adapt X.500 for Internet usage. These RFCs, which included specifications for a lightweight directory access protocol, a directory information replication protocol, and an SNMP MIB for monitoring X.500 servers, are listed in the summary table of Internet Mail RFCs and Drafts appearing at the end of this chapter. Some of the topics addressed in these RFCs are covered in more detail in the next chapter.

However, while many seeds were planted, X.500 has not yet fully taken root in the Internet community. This limited success appears to have three main reasons apparently related to the standard's complexity. First, until Internet Mail began to penetrate the LAN arena, most Internet Mail products were distributed free of cost or at low cost by system vendors and "shareware" providers. Such vendors had little incentive to pour substantial development resources into upgrading their UA or mailer products to support complex X.500 functionality. Second, while X.500 has been deployed at numerous Internet sites, it has proven difficult for the UNIX system administrators, who generally double as Internet Mail support personnel, to learn foreign X.500/OSI concepts.

Knowledge discovery and information indexing/retrieval would appear to be natural X.500 applications. However, specialized Internet applications such as World Wide Web, WAIS, Archie, and Gopher have been developed using custom databases as their data repository rather than X.500. Such systems are moving toward using Universal Resource Names and Locators that could be stored in X.500,[15] but they may also use Internet-developed distributed directory services as well.

As a result of X.500's limited success, the enthusiasm of some (but not all) former IETF X.500 advocates is on the wane. While X.500 may yet prosper in

---

15. Worldwide Web to X.500 gateways were developed and released in late 1993.

other environments and its usage on the Internet may continue to grow, some of the Internet-based research and energy that heretofore had been focused on X.500 has been diverted into a different channel. RFC 1588, "The White Pages Meeting Report," [POST94] documents the community's desire to leverage X.500's progress, but also move forward with alternatives for sites desiring simpler solutions. In that regard, an alternative to X.500—WHOIS++—has emerged.

7.9.2   WHOIS++

WHOIS++, an Internet directory service first broached at a July 1992 IETF meeting and (as of early 1994) in an Internet Draft, is intended as an extension to the Internet WHOIS service described in RFC 954 [HARR85]. The WHOIS service was originally developed for a small number of users registered with the Defense Data Network (DDN) Network Information Center (NIC). Over time its service was expanded and similar services were set up on other servers, all done in an ad hoc manner.

WHOIS++ is intended to permit distributed WHOIS-like servers to make more structured information available to Internet users in a standard manner. It is designed for simplicity, speed, global searching, and backward compatibility with WHOIS. The authors of the Internet Draft have also attempted to minimize extensions in order to create an application especially useful where the high cost of configuring and operating an X.500 White Pages service would not be justifiable.

7.10   X.400 AND INTERNET MAIL INTERWORKING

The de facto standard for interworking between X.400 and the basic RFC 822/ SMTP elements of Internet Mail is codified in RFCs 1327 (which obsoletes a number of earlier RFCs on the same subject). More recently RFCs 1494 and 1495, focusing on how to map between X.400 and MIME [ALVE93D and ALVE93], and RFC 1496 [ALVE93C], focusing on the means of mapping between 1988 and 1984 X.400 when MIME content types are present in the message, have appeared.

RFC 1327 defines mechanisms for translating service elements between X.400 and RFC 822. In particular, RFC 822 messages, X.400 interpersonal messages, delivery reports, and interpersonal notifications can be mapped. The mapping of X.400 Probes and X.400 messages employing content types other than IPM is not covered in the RFC.

Table 7.6 displays a sample diagram of an Internet Mail to X.400 mapping. It contrasts the X.400 P22 (1988) message heading with the RFC 822 message header. The header/heading fields shown in adjacent columns sometimes have a straightforward mapping. Where mapping services from X.400 to RFC 822 cannot be supported by RFC 822 (as indicated in the table by a "—"), new RFC 822 headers are defined.

The most difficult part of Internet Mail-to-X.400 translation involves RFC 822 to X.400 address mapping. While both address spaces are hierarchical and

X.400 fields	RFC 822 fields
this-IPM	message id, resent message id
originator	from, resent-from
authorizing-users	—
primary-recipients	to, resent-to
copy-recipients	cc, resent-cc
blind-copy-recipients	bcc
replied-to-IPM	in-reply-to
obsoleted-IPMs	—
related-IPMs	references
subject	subject
expiry-time	—
reply-time	—
reply-recipients	reply-to
importance	—
sensitivity	—
auto-forwarded	—
extensions	extension-field, user-defined-field
incomplete-copy	—
language	—
—	orig-date, resent-date
—	keywords
—	comments

Table 7.6 Mapping of X.400 to RFC 822 fields.

similar enough that the same user, addressed in both environments, might use the same top-level country and domain names as well as the same local part and personal name information, there are also many differences. These differences include discrepancies in some of the fields used (RFC 822 addresses do not contain an ADMD name, for example) and discrepancies in the printable character set syntax used for address fields (X.400 does not allow the "@" and the "_" characters in address fields). For these reasons, address translations are often problematic, especially when messages go through multiple gateways along their path to the destination.

The default method of RFC 822-to-X.400 mapping is to encapsulate the X.400 address in the RFC 822 address as follows:

"C=US/ADMD= PRMD=ABC/O=SALES/S=JJONES"@gateway.abc.com

The X.400 address is then simply extracted by the gateway. Going in reverse, from X.400 to RFC 822, an Internet address can be encapsulated as

DDA=RFC882=pyork@east.sales.xyz.com ; O=SMTPGATE ; P=XYZ ; A= ; C=US

These addresses are not attractive to end users. Therefore RFC 1327 defines a number of other strategies, wherein a gateway may attempt complex algorithmic mappings of parts of the RFC 822 address into X.400 address attributes and vice versa. Further work has since focused on configuring such mapping algorithms on a domain-by-domain basis in the X.500 directory. In addition, "brute force" directory-based address substitution is always possible.

RFC 1495 provides for mapping between X.400 message formats and RFC 822 messages containing a MIME-formatted Body. The RFC's approach is to map built-in MIME Body Parts to their X.400 counterparts. In cases where the MIME Body Part must be translated to X.400 and where there is no X.400 counterpart to a MIME Body Part, the RFC calls for encapsulating the entire MIME Body Part as an X.400 Body Part. In the other direction, where there is no MIME counterpart to an X.400 body part, the RFC calls for encapsulating the X.400 attachment in MIME. RFC 1496—once called HARPOON (Holistic Approach to Reliable Provision of Open Networking)—deals with the transfer of Body Parts between 1984 and 1988 X.400 when MIME Body Parts are present in the message. The RFC notes that MIME encapsulation is one way to solve part of the X.400 content downgrading problem, since 1988 X.400 external body parts could be encapsulated in MIME and tunneled through 1984 X.400.

There is no RFC for PEM-to-X.400 interworking. The solution recommended in the OIW X.400 agreements involves encapsulating PEM messages in X.400.

7.11   SUMMARY

The traditional RFC 822/SMTP Internet Mail architecture is being enhanced with a flurry of RFCs covering multimedia messaging (MIME and ESMTP), secure messaging (PEM), and directories. The transition from the traditional to emerging Internet Mail protocols will be long, but it will be rendered somewhat less painful than it might otherwise have been thanks to careful attention to backward compatibility by standards developers. Table 7.7 contains a summary of the RFCs and Internet Drafts mentioned in this chapter.

The Internet Mail enhancement process is building from a base that is at once strong in some respects but weak in others. The strengths of Internet Mail today are its user-friendly addressing scheme, entrenched worldwide registration structure, scalable DNS implementation, and the substantial experience base of thousands of engineers. In addition, the IETF has put in place a workable standards process that is peopled with a seasoned cadre of expert, dedicated, and highly energetic standards developers. (See Appendix A for additional information on the Internet/IETF standards making process.)

The weaknesses of Internet Mail stem mainly from the antiquity of its very widespread installed base and the incremental nature of the standards development process. For many years to come, Internet Mail's installed base will include ASCII-only SMTP implementations that enforce unreasonable size and

RFC number or draft: UA level	Title	Remarks
RFC 822	Standard for the format of ARPA Internet text messages	The basic single-text Body Part Internet Mail content type
RFC 1344	Implications of MIME for Internet Mail Gateways	Addresses the way in which MIME might deal with size limitations and message conversion
RFC 1460	Post Office Protocol— Version 3	Maildrop service for low resource nodes
RFC 1521	MIME (Multipurpose Internet Mail Extensions) Part One: Mechanisms for Specifying and Describing the Format of Internet Message Bodies	MIME extensions include support for structured, multipart message bodies and binary attachments. Obsoletes RFC 1341
RFC 1522	MIME (Multipurpose Internet Mail Extensions) Part Two: Message Header Extensions for Non-ASCII Text	Defines MIME header extensions for non-ASCII text. Obsoletes RFC 1342
RFC 1524	A User Agent Configuration Mechanism for Multimedia Mail Format Information	MIME-capable UAs could use standardized configuration file format—*mailcap*—to determine how to process MIME Body Parts
RFC 1563	The text/enriched MIME Content Type	A "richtext" specification for MIME

RFC number or draft: MTA level	Title	Remarks
RFC 821	Simple Mail Transfer Protocol	Core transport protocol for Internet Mail
RFC 976	UUCP mail interchange format standard	Transport mechanism for Internet hosts that are connected via asynchronous dial-up links
RFC 1137	Mapping between full RFC 822 and RFC 822 with restricted encoding	Updates RFC 976

RFC number or draft: directory	Title	Remarks
RFC 952	DoD Internet Host Table Specification	Pre-DNS, static routing
RFC 954	NICNAME/WHOIS	Directory service at NIC running a "trivial" protocol
RFC 974	Mail Routing and Domain System	Initial DNS definition

Table 7.7 Summary table of Internet Mail RFCs and drafts.

continued

RFC number or draft: directory	Title	Remarks
RFC 1034	Domain Names—Implementation and Specification	Further DNS refinements
RFC 1035	Domain Names—Concepts and Facilities	Further DNS refinements
RFC 1487	Lightweight Directory Access Protocol	A simpler, lightweight access protocol to X.500 directories
RFC 1276	Replication and Distributed Operations Extensions to Provide an Internet Directory Using X.500	Extension to 1988 X.500 based on technology pioneered in the QUIPU X.500 directory product
RFC 1567	X.50 Directory Monitoring MIB	SNMP MIB for monitoring an X.500 directory server
Internet Draft	Architecture of the WHOIS++ service	Architecture for a nonhierarchical mesh directory service
Internet Draft	Architecture of the WHOIS++ Index Service	Explanation of the index server feature
Internet Draft	WHOIS and Network Information Lookup Service WHOIS++	Explanation of client and server behavior and data records

RFC number or draft: PEM	Title	Remarks
1421	Privacy Enhancement for Internet Electronic Mail: Part I: Message Encryption and Authentication Procedures	Defines PEM format compatible with RFC 822
1422	RFC 1422: Privacy Enhancement for Internet Electronic Mail: Part II: Certificate-Based Key Management	Defines architecture for managing a Certification Authority infrastructure
1423	RFC 1423: Privacy Enhancement for Internet Electronic Mail: Part III: Algorithms, Modes, and Identifiers	Specifies message encryption algorithms, message integrity check algorithms, symmetric key management algorithms, and asymmetric key management algorithms (including both asymmetric encryption and asymmetric signature algorithms)
1424	RFC 1424: Privacy Enhancement for Internet Electronic Mail: Part IV: Key Certification and Related Services	Describes key certification, certificate revocation list (CRL) storage, and CRL retrieval
Internet Draft	MIME-PEM Interaction	Framework for interaction between MIME and PEM

Table 7.7 *continuing*

RFC number or draft: SMTP extensions	Title	Remarks
RFC 1425	SMTP Service Extension	Lays foundation for extensions in 1426 and 1427
RFC 1426	RFC 1426: SMTP Service Extension for eight-bit-MIME transport	Defines mechanism for transmitting eight-bit data over SMTP
RFC 1427	RFC 1427: SMTP Service Extension for Message Size Declaration	How a sending SMTP MTA declares the size of a message to a receiving SMTP MTA or receiving SMTP MTA tells sending SMTP MTA of its acceptable size limitations
RFC 1428	RFC 1428: Transition of Internet Mail from Just-Send-8 to eight-bit-SMTP/MIME	Compatibility issues between ASCII-only MTAs, ESMTP MTAs, and pre-ESMTP MTAs that support binary data transfer

Other RFCs and Internet drafts		
RFC 1123	Requirements for Internet Hosts Applications and Support	Host requirements for RFC 822, SMTP, DNS support into single document with advice to users and implementors on mandatory/optional functions and common errors
RFC 1327	Mapping between X.400 (1988) / ISO 10021 and RFC 822	Most recent RFC on basic 1988 X.400 to RFC 822 mapping
RFC 1506	A Tutorial on Gatewaying between X.400 and Internet Mail	Explains RFC 822 to X.400 gateways based on RFC 1327 mappings
RFC 1494	Equivalencies between 1988 X.400	Focuses on translation of message body between MIME and X.400
RFC 1495	Mapping between X.400 and RFC-822 Message Bodies	Focuses on translation of message body between MIME and X.400
RFC 1496	Rules for downgrading messages from X.400/88 to X.400/84 when MIME content-types are present in the messages	Originally known as "HARPOON." MIME can be used to tunnel 1988 body parts through 1984 X.400 systems
Internet Draft	MIME Content-Types for Delivery Status Notifications	Defines *multipart/delivery-status-notification* content type
Internet Draft	SMTP Service Extension for Delivery Reports	Enables sending MTA to request per-recipient delivery status notifications

Table 7.7 *continuing*

continued

**Other RFCs and
Internet drafts**

Internet Draft	Language tags for MIME content portions	Describes content-language header for use with MIME Body Parts
Internet Draft	MIME Multipart / Header-Set	Mechanism to enable MIME processors to encapsulate content types that require their own unique header information, and to enable UAs to process user data even when they do not understand the specific header which begins the set

Table 7.7 *continuing*

line length restrictions and do not support appropriate delivery status notification mechanisms. In addition, the present Internet Mail infrastructure does not implement sufficient security and audit capabilities to ensure reduced-risk operation.

It is a credit to the ingenuity of the IETF standards developers that MIME and PEM have been engineered to coexist in the pre-multimedia environment. We suspect that they have made the best tradeoffs between functionality, efficiency, simplicity, and backward compatibility possible under the circumstances. It appears that users of these protocols will be able to have the best of both worlds—multimedia functionality for those who are ready and connectivity to the user base for those who have not caught up—with the attendant frustration (for users) of sometimes needing to prepare different kinds of messages for multimedia-capable and multimedia-incapable recipients.

On the other hand, there is some risk (as of early 1994) that the separate origins of MIME and PEM could lead to further frustrating incompatibilities. Moreover, the continuing stream of SMTP and MIME enhancements (occurring in parallel with the rollout of multiple implementations) suggests that the capabilities of these implementations will vary widely. We project that after several years of rapid change and instability, common practice in the Internet Mail environment will coalesce around a new set of host requirement specifications tailored for multimedia usage.

Security is the most important gap remaining for a community aspiring to tap the vast, still largely undeveloped electronic commerce market. There is a good chance that the old PEM will die out peacefully, and its experienced implementors will develop and widely deploy new and improved MIME-PEM standards. If this happens, the new and improved Internet Mail will, at the very least, take the Internet community into the next century and, at best, be in position to become the global messaging network of our e-mail vision.

KEY POINTS

- Key Internet Mail standards include RFC 822 for the message format (header, body, and addresses), the Simple Mail Transfer Protocol (SMTP), and the Domain Name System (DNS).

- Enhanced Multipurpose Internet Mail Extensions (MIME) and Extended SMTP standards were written to support multipart message bodies and binary attachments, and to allow non-ASCII character sets to be used.

- The Internet community has also developed Privacy Enhanced Mail (PEM) to provide secure messaging in the Internet Mail environment.

- Private organizations often deploy Internet Mail behind firewalls in the interests of security.

- De facto standards that allow X.400 and Internet Mail to interwork have been developed.

- Internet Mail will evolve to use directory standards, such as X.500 and WHOIS++.

CHAPTER 8

E-mail and Directories

8.1 Directory Models

8.2 Directory Synchronization

8.3 The X.500 Directory Architecture

8.4 WHOIS++

8.5 Summary

It is a broadly accepted tenet in the messaging industry that large-scale distributed directories will play a central role in enabling integrated enterprise messaging to realize its full potential. In addition, directories serve as the centerpiece for more than messaging. In the LAN world, directories underpin print, database, file, and other network services. In the public carrier world, current directory databases are essential to the operation of telephone networks, and the intelligent networks of the future will depend on directories to provide ever more sophisticated dynamic configuration capabilities to their customers. In Chapter 2 we summarized both basic and advanced directory infrastructure requirements. To underscore their importance, these requirements are itemized again in Table 8.1.

Exaggerating the importance of directories to both local and global messaging infrastructures is difficult. For in the absence of directory functionality, local infrastructures cannot provide user-friendly addressing, enterprise backbones cannot furnish manageable e-mail integration with high quality mappings between proprietary mail systems, and public service providers cannot maintain an information-rich environment or provide facilities-managed, virtual private backbone solutions.

To meet user's requirements, to be able to perform the basic functions well, and to begin taking on advanced functions, local and global directory infrastructures must exhibit six characteristics: distributed global configuration; enterprise,

Basic functions
Easy name to address lookups (for users)
Address to route lookup (for infrastructure)
Advanced functions
Address translation (for gateways and firewalls)
Certificate listing for secure messaging services
Electronic commerce capability profiling
Organizational role and authority determination
A variety of other functions that extend beyond messaging to provide an information-rich environment

Table 8.1 Directory infrastructure requirements.

national, and international "views"; ubiquitous deployment and standardization; robust performance, reliability, and availability; levels of security appropriate to different environments; and a flexible information model.

Today's directory implementations—proprietary e-mail directories, Internet directories, and X.500—do not yet scale to provide both basic and advanced directory functions, nor do they exhibit all the necessary infrastructure characteristics. Yet signs of progress are visible on all fronts.

Existing Proprietary Directory Systems

Most pre-1994 LAN, host, midrange, and public mail directory systems were developed as islands and do not support the means of interworking with one another. They generally lack flexible information models and special security provisions, and they are not always scalable to distributed configurations even within a single mail system. Often local e-mail directories have served as little more than tools to browse flat text files. However, local directories are beginning to interwork through directory synchronization technology and some key LAN directory products are becoming more modularized and more extensible. Section 8.2 will discuss directory synchronization, while Section 8.3.10 discusses coexistence and transition between local directory infrastructures and X.500.

X.500 Directory Services

The 1988 and 1993 ITU/ISO X.500 Directory Services standards were crafted with the intent of meeting both the basic and advanced requirements noted in Table 8.1, but as of early 1994 X.500 proponents have yet to put in place a ubiquitous, high performance directory infrastructure. Large challenges loom for the standard in the areas of security, performance, and infrastructure construction. Section 8.3 will delve into X.500 standards, technology, issues, and implementation prospects.

Internet Directories

Finger and WHOIS are limited-purpose services with a highly bounded functional makeup. While enormously useful in its role as a Internet Mail host name resolver, the DNS is not readily extensible and was not designed with the flexibility needed to fulfill all the advanced functions of a general purpose messaging directory infrastructure. However, X.500 has now been deployed at many Internet sites. While Internet research into X.500 continues, research is also ongoing to create yet another distributed directory system: WHOIS++. We will explore the WHOIS++ architecture in Section 8.4. (There are also a number of Internet information services, such as World Wide Web and Gopher that at times exhibit directory-like functions. Increasingly such services will be integrated with genuine directories as they emerge.)

8.1 DIRECTORY MODELS

Before plunging into the weighty topic of directory infrastructures, it is useful to posit some helpful generic models which apply regardless of whether one is discussing local directory systems, directory synchronization, X.500, or WHOIS++. These models concern directory topology, directory access, and directory update methods (see Fig. 8.1).

Directory topologies may be centralized, distributed, or replicated (a hybrid of the first two). *Centralized directory topologies* collect all directory information at a single location. They are easy to secure, easy to administer, and easy to maintain in a consistent state. They are appropriate in host-based local messaging infrastructures (where most users are locally attached and can obtain excellent

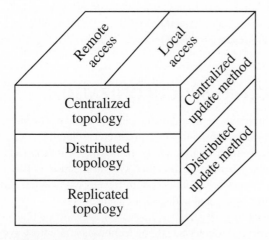

Figure 8.1   Directory models.

performance) but are not usually found in LAN e-mail configurations other than the single Post Office environment. Centralized topologies are not scalable to global infrastructures. Some e-mail integration backbones include a centralized directory, but e-mail users greatly prefer being able to access directory information from the (local) mail client while in the process of addressing a message.

Distributed directory topologies consist of cooperating directory facilities located at different sites. They are difficult to administer and maintain in a consistent state. Complex technology is needed to ensure security. Users obtain good performance when making local queries, but remote queries can be slow. However, distributed topologies are essential to the objective of building scalable global directory infrastructures. Multiple Post Office LAN directory implementations, the DNS, directory synchronization systems, X.500, and WHOIS++ all utilize distributed models.

Replicated topologies usually entail the use of either a distributed/replicated topology or a centralized/replicated topology. In either case, multiple copies of the directory are made available on the network. Hybrid directories with replication are even more difficult to administer than distributed directories, but the performance improvements they bring are attractive enough to encourage their use in most complex scenarios.

Independent of the directory topology, the mode of access and the mode of update can vary from one operational environment to another. Remote access is often required to a centralized directory and sometimes even to a distributed or replicated directory. Remote access is usually slower than local access, although the disparity need not be great if the client and server have sufficient bandwidth and processing resources. A distributed directory can be updated by administrators at each site or a central administration group can handle all updates to all sites.

Directory infrastructures in general must be able to support all of these models, depending upon the user's needs. Remote access, remote update, data distribution, and replication tend to be more appropriate for global infrastructures, whereas some mix of centralized topologies, local and remote access, and local or distributed updating is appropriate in many local messaging infrastructures.

8.2   DIRECTORY SYNCHRONIZATION

Directory synchronization, introduced earlier as a means for interchanging directory information between distributed proprietary directory systems, is now regarded as critical to managing large messaging networks with incompatible directories. The key benefit of directory synchronization is that it enables users attached to one proprietary e-mail system to see (within their familiar directory user interface) the names and addresses of users attached to other mail systems in the same organization.

As an enterprise directory backbone technology, directory synchronization is one of several technologies for directory integration. We will approach this discussion by focusing initially on the relationship of directory integration to directory synchronization from the large enterprise user's point of view. Then we will describe generic directory synchronization functional considerations. In our directory synchronization discussion, we assume the use of a distributed directory model with either distributed or centralized update methods.

8.2.1   Directory Integration Alternatives

The first consideration for enterprises with multiple proprietary local messaging systems is whether they wish to explore the possibility of integrating their directories. In most cases, this should be a fairly easy decision because directory integration is highly desirable to support messaging interconnection. The only inhibiting factors to directory integration for an enterprise might be the cost or the difficulty of putting a solution into place. However, note that there is a full range of alternatives for the enterprise, including:

- **No integration:** Each local messaging system maintains its own directory and does not share directory information with other domains. Users in Mail System X cannot see the names of users outside their domain, and users in other mail domains cannot see the names of users in Mail System X. In an extreme case, mail interconnection may be rendered impossible (such as in the case of some PROFS-X.400 gateways). In other cases, an e-mail backbone could compensate for the lack of directory integration by performing the algorithmic mapping of addresses and the auto-registration of directory information.

- **Partial integration:** Mail systems share directory information to a sufficient degree that, at a minimum, full mail interconnection is possible if a sender knows the recipient's address. However, not all mail domains keep a full copy of all enterprise directory information, and some directory information may be outdated.

- **Full integration:** Each mail domain retains a full copy of the integrated enterprise directory at each of its sites. Directory information is refreshed at known, acceptable intervals.

8.2.2   Directory Integration Technologies

Assuming that an enterprise has decided to implement full or partial directory integration, several techniques may be used. The technique employed directly affects the quality of the integration. These techniques, which are discussed here in terms of a distributed or decentralized directory approach are manual update, flat file exchange, and incremental update.

With manual update, operators key in updates to the same information for each system. Not viable outside of environments of a few hundred users or less, this "warm body" approach is also costly in terms of staff resources and is prone to error.

With flat file exchange, ASCII files containing directory information can be periodically exchanged (exported from one system and imported to another) between mail system directories. This process may be performed in an automated or semi-automated fashion. Flat files cannot be moved directly from one system to another but must first be massaged so that information is in the correct format for the destination system. During the import stage, the local directory is completely replaced with the contents of the file.

Finally, using directory synchronization, or incremental update, local directories are updated only with the adds, deletes, and changes that have taken place since the directory was updated. This update is usually performed in an automated fashion. There are three basic approaches:

1. **Fully incremental.** Updates are performed in a distributed manner by local e-mail system administrators. Updates are sent from a local e-mail directory to a directory synchronization server as they occur. The server passes them on to the other interconnected directories.

2. **Compare, merge, distribute.** Updates are performed in a distributed manner by local e-mail system administrators. The server periodically obtains a full copy of each local directory, compares each directory with its previous contents, and generates updates to the other interconnected directories. This approach is taken with Digital's Directory Synchronizer product.

3. **Centralized update.** Updates are performed against a central database by the e-mail system administrator. The server passes these updates on to the remaining directories. Although this approach is often preferred by large organizations who want to integrate security validation, e-mail directory management, and human resources databases, it is not always available in off-the-shelf directory synchronization products. A number of large enterprises have homegrown directory synchronization solutions based on centralized updating. (A variation on this approach would be to maintain some information via centralized update and other information via distributed update.)

Note that there are also hybrid approaches where flat file import/export and incremental synchronization are combined. This is common since many enterprise messaging networks contain legacy mail systems that are not supported by off-the-shelf directory synchronization products.

8.2.3 Directory Synchronization Implementation and Scenario

Directory synchronization software consists of components implemented as part of a dedicated e-mail integration (or directory integration) server and components implemented within, or close to, the local directory environments. Figure 8.2 displays the essential elements of an implementation (in this case, the Soft*Switch DS/Central or DS/EMX) that is representative of some, though not all, directory synchronization products on the market.

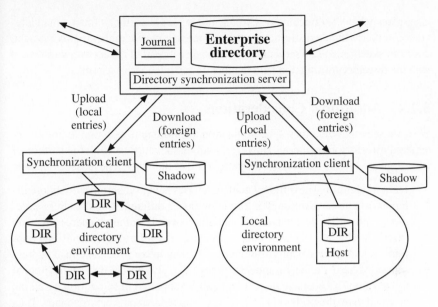

Figure 8.2 Directory synchronization.

A software program called the synchronization client resides within the local directory environment. This program may be coresident with a local e-mail host or Post Office, or it may be housed on a dedicated PC or workstation. The local directory component adjacent to the synchronization client must contain a full copy of all directory information for the local environment. Thus if the local directory environment is distributed, it must then possess internal (single vendor) directory propagation capabilities.

At periodic intervals (configured by the e-mail administrator), the synchronization client extracts a copy of the local directory (via flat file exchange, API calls, or some other method) and compares the copy with a shadow directory containing a snapshot of the local directory as it existed at the time of the last synchronization upload/download cycle. From that comparison, the synchronization client generates a list of updates and mails the list to the directory synchronization server. This part of the process is called the upload.

When the client uploads the changes to the server, the server updates the enterprise directory. The enterprise directory thus retains the updated contents of all the local directories and is also used to support messaging backbone functions, such as routing and address translation.

The client then requests a download from the server of changes to foreign directory entries from other systems. The server consults a journal to determine the time of its last download to the client and then downloads to the client any additions, deletions, or changes to foreign entries that have taken place since that time.

The directory synchronization server carries out the download-upload cycle on a continuing basis at the client's request. The only additional interaction involved takes place when the directory synchronization server is itself part of an e-mail integration server within a distributed enterprise messaging backbone. In this case, the directory synchronization server must synchronize its part of the enterprise directory with the directory information held in other e-mail integration servers.

8.2.4   Additional Considerations

We have seen that directory synchronization technology is essential to highly automated directory integration. However, many issues lurk beneath the surface of what appears to be a relatively straightforward technology. These issues include

*   **Data modeling:** The different mail directories being synchronized support different data models, different information fields, different e-mail address structures, and different methods of handling overall naming, addressing, and routing problems. Planners must ensure that the information fields and subfields selected for synchronization are sufficient to construct an e-mail address supported across all environments.[1] They must also ensure that any additional information (such as telephone numbers) is supported in some form by all the attached mail directories or can safely be dropped for some environments. Thus the enterprise naming, addressing, routing, and interconnection plan will dictate certain directory maintenance conventions and practices to local administrators and will also affect the way directory synchronization is handled.

*   **Flexibility:** Shuffling and generating the correct fields (or combinations of fields) to implement a given enterprise directory design may require considerable flexibility from the directory synchronization software, including an ability to generate field values based on user-defined rules.

*   **Performance and Recoverability:** Directory synchronization updates often carried in messages can generate many messages or large messages. Administrators should have the ability to configure the *schedule* and *pace* of directory synchronization activities.

*   **Scalability:** The scalability of directory synchronization is limited. It is not a public directory solution (other than as part of a facilities-managed virtual private messaging network offering). It is not always viable for very large enterprises because the directory synchronization product may not have good enough performance to handle very large databases. Also, many LAN e-mail directories are no more than flat lists that do not perform well when they contain thousands of entries; or, even if they do perform well, they are not attractive to users. For large directory synchronization implementations, a

---

1. For example, HP OpenMail requires the use of X.400-like Organization Unit attributes in order to name and address a user. A cc:Mail user appearing in an OpenMail directory must contain those fields. cc:Mail does not support Organization Unit fields, but this information can still be embedded in the cc:Mail directory Comments field, where it is available for pickup by the synchronization utility.

product must enable the administrator to configure filters controlling what information is synchronized to different environments.

- **Standards:** As with other aspects of e-mail and directory, users would find it desirable to have one recognized directory synchronization standard. Such a standard would greatly enhance users' ability to mix and match synchronization clients and servers. In this regard, the X.400 API Association (after earlier creating a standard API for X.500, called XDS) formed a working group in 1993 to develop standardized directory synchronization.

8.3   THE X.500 DIRECTORY ARCHITECTURE

Unlike other directory technologies, the 1988 and 1993 ITU/ISO X.500 Directory Services standards were crafted from their inception with the intent of providing global infrastructures. However, large challenges must be overcome before X.500 can live up to its promise. In the following subsections, we will explore the X.500 standard architecture, protocols, information model, distributed operations, security, and other related topics. We will also discuss related or complementary technologies and initiatives intended to build the X.500 directory infrastructure.

The 1988 X.500 [ITU88A] standard supports remote directory access, centralized and distributed topologies, and centralized or distributed update methods, as well as peer-entity authentication, digital signatures, and certificates. The 1993 version of the X.500 standard [ITU93] builds on top of the 1988 standard to support replicated topologies, access control, and other enhancements. For the most part, we will limit our discussion of the basic directory models to the 1988 functionality, since 1993 enhancements cannot be expected from most X.500 products before the 1996 to 1998 time frame. However, we will subsequently summarize the 1993 X.500 extensions.

8.3.1   Technical Overview

The "X.500 Directory" is the name for a standards-based information structure called the Global Directory Information Tree (DIT) and directory processing entities that access and maintain the DIT. Users, Directory User Agents (DUAs), and Directory System Agents (DSAs) make up the processing elements of X.500 Directory Service. The DIT is a hierarchical model spanning countries, organizations, and localities. As of early 1994, the DIT existed primarily in a research mode.

Users of the directory may be people or applications. A DUA is that part of a program interacting as a Directory client on the user's behalf. It may feature a human user interface or it may be merely a collection of software services acting as a module of another application. User interfaces are not standardized and will vary widely between products. APIs were not standardized by the ITU/ISO, but an X.500 Directory Services API (XDS) became a de facto standard and was also adopted by the IEEE on a standards track into POSIX [IEEE92].

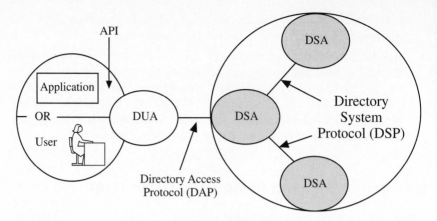

Figure 8.3 The X.500 directory processing model.

The DUA issues inquiry and update operations via a Directory Access Protocol (DAP) to the Directory. The Directory responds to the DUA's requests, providing a service that is independent of the location of both the DUA and the DSA(s) containing the target information. Figure 8.3 diagrams the basic X.500 processing architecture.

Inquiries and updates are actually resolved by groups of cooperating DSAs or servers. A DSA is a computer program controling a portion of the DIT. An individual DSA may satisfy the DUA's request from a local data store, refer the DUA to a remote DSA, or interact directly with peer DSAs to resolve the query. DSA-to-DSA interaction is accomplished using the Directory System Protocol (DSP). Like the X.400 protocols, both the DAP and DSP protocols make use of the underlying OSI communications standards, but the Reliable Transfer Service Element is not used except in the 1993 replication protocol.

8.3.2   Basic X.500 Information Model and DIT Structure

The 1988 X.500 information model defines a *logical* directory structure or schema. (The DSAs actually holding directory information may use any physical database that allows them to comply with this schema.) The model is designed for a global directory. On the one hand, it describes a DIT broad enough to encompass all countries and organizations; and, on the other, it provides an open-ended methodology for defining new information for many different purposes.

In line with X.500's hierarchical model, entries consist of objects related to one another in a tree structure. Entries at the bottom of the tree (usually representing people, applications, or resources) are called *leaf* entries. Entries in the middle of the tree are called *nonleaf* entries. By definition, this tree structure allows only one parent or superior node and multiple subordinates for each object. (The availability of an *alias object*, or pointer, relaxes the rigidity of this tree structure somewhat by allowing some nonhierarchical relationships between objects.)

Every entry in the DIT consists of a collection of attributes. An attribute has a type element and one or more value elements. Each entry has one or more attribute values termed *distinguished,* that is, guaranteed to be unique under their immediately superior entry. Figure 8.4 provides a model of X.500 entry construction, together with examples of how that model relates to familiar database terminology.

The X.500 information schema describes rules for the DIT structure, entries, attributes, and the attribute values. Four sets of rules exist:

- DIT structure rules constrain the hierarchical relationships in which objects may find themselves. For example, an Organization object will never be the superior of a Country object.

- Object class rules specify what attribute information an entry of a given object class (that is, object type) can contain in terms of attribute information. Every X.500 entry belongs to an Object Class or record type.

- Attribute type rules control whether particular kinds of attributes can contain a single value or multiple values and what syntax those values must follow. For example, a *Common Name* may contain multiple values following the *printable string* syntax.

- Attribute value rules control the defined syntax of attribute values. For example, the value of an *Integer* syntax must be an integer number.

The subsections below describe the basic X.500 information structures and structural rules.

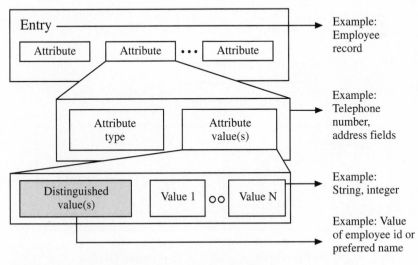

Figure 8.4   Entries (records) and Attributes (fields). *Copyright CCITT Recommendation X.501 "The Directory—Models," updated version 1993, Figure 3 "Structure of an entry." Reprinted with permission from ITU.*

The DIT Structure

Figure 8.5 illustrates what part of the DIT might look like through a scenario.

At the top of the DIT resides a purely conceptual Root immediately beneath which lie other objects, most commonly Countries. Beneath Countries, we will find Organization or Locality entries and so on down to the leaf entries.

Individual DSAs are responsible for portions of the DIT. In Fig. 8.6, the DIT is partitioned among several DSAs. DSAs A and C are long haul carriers, each maintaining a Country object. DSAs B and D are responsible for Organization subtrees and Locality subtrees respectively. Of course, there will be many more than one DSA at the U.S. level, providing more than one path into the U.S. directory.

At the Organization level, DSA B may in fact control the entire O=ABC single-handedly, or DSA B may devolve administrative authority of portions of O=ABC to subordinate DSAs. DSA B and its subordinates may or may not be considered as part of a single Directory Management Domain.

Of course, the DIT will be much larger and more varied than is indicated in this scenario. In an informative annex, X.500 recommends a set of structure rules that describe how instances of object classes may be organized in the DIT hierarchy. These rules are diagrammed in Fig. 8.6.

Root is at the top of the hierarchy and may be succeeded by Country, Locality, or Organization Objects. Locality is the most flexible object class appearing be-

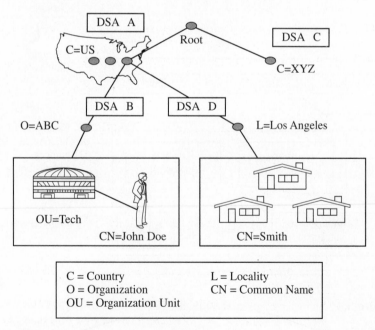

C = Country	L = Locality
O = Organization	CN = Common Name
OU = Organization Unit	

Figure 8.5   Global directory information tree.

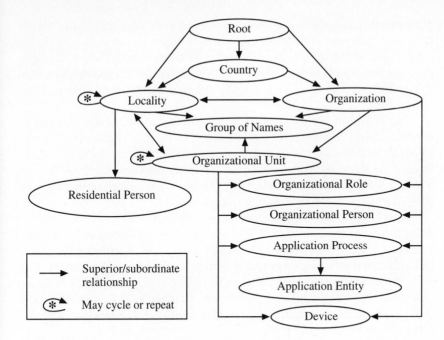

Figure 8.6   DIT structure rules (suggested in X.500).

neath the Country, Organization, or Organization Unit. Locality may also appear above Organization or Organizational Unit.

Organization objects are nonrepeating. Organization Units may appear beneath Organization entries and may repeat in sequence or be interleaved with Locality entries. Also, there are a number of objects associated with Organizational subtrees, such as Organizational Person and Organizational Role. Other objects appear in non-Organizational subtrees such as Residential Person.

One additional object which may appear, but is not shown in the structure diagram above, is the alias. An alias is a special type of X.500 object that can be employed to allow an entry to have more than one name. For instance, if an X.500 user moves to a new job, he or she could arrange to have an Alias entry left behind as a place holder for an old Directory entry. This allows queries to be redirected to the new Directory entry, thus providing a function conceptually similar to the Post Office's forwarding address or the phone company's number change recorded message.

The alias can also be used to provide multiple views of the directory information, thus leading to sophisticated capabilities. For example, the X.500 standard refers to the possible use of aliases to allow the same directory information to be viewed in a White Pages or Yellow Pages framework. The use of aliases is recommended in the X.400/EDI standard (X.435) to associate old alphanumeric EDI trading partner designators with more current X.500 distinguished names. Finally, aliases could be used in a complex organizational directory to allow users to find entries using either organizational structure or location-based search strategies. However, one drawback to the alias is that X.500 contains no procedures for managing alias information once it is created; that is, alias information can easily become inconsistent.

The DIT structure rules are very flexible and, consequently, difficult for implementations to support. Some products may therefore further constrain the allowable DIT structure. Some functional standardization profiles have also constrained the hierarchy. For example, the European Workshop for Open Systems (EWOS) X.500 profile at one time limited the placement of the Locality entry and allowed no more than four repeating Organizational Units.

X.500 implementors (who could be providers designing a service, vendors defining the way an X.500 product will work, or users configuring an X.500-based enterprise directory) are faced with the DIT design task of applying the generic DIT structure rules in a manner that is appropriate for a given directory environment. For example, a large corporation's DIT could deploy many levels of organizational unit or locality hierarchy. However, deep hierarchies invariably lead to cumbersome database search procedures for users. For directory lookups, shallower trees work more efficiently.

Distinguished Names and Registration Considerations

The DIT structure rules and the DIT design in a given X.500 environment determine the structure of X.500 directory names. In order for the X.500 naming model to function correctly, every entry in the DIT must have a unique or distinguished name (DN). This means that some of the distinguished attribute values of each entry must be different from the corresponding values of all of its siblings (children of the same superior). The attribute values that distinguish an entry from its siblings combine to form its *relative distinguished name* (RDN).

In Fig. 8.7, @C=GB (Country = Great Britain) is both the relative and the full distinguished name of the country object so denoted, and @O=WIDGETS has @O=WIDGETS for its RDN and {@C=GB@O=WIDGETS} for its DN.

The Organization Unit entry @OU=SALES@L=LONDON differs from the others in using two attribute values for its RDN. This indicates that @OU=SALES is not unique at that level of the tree.

Finally, among the leaf-level people entries, the entry denoted by RDN CN=WATSON has as its DN all the distinguished attributes in the path from the root, through the tree, to itself: @C=GB@O=WIDGETS@OU=SALES@L=LONDON @CN=WATSON.

Naming considerations inevitably lead to the question of RDN registration. That is, how are RDNs kept unique, and how are they allocated to users? Unless all the DSAs in the DIT agree on and register appropriate values for Country Names, chaos ensues. Chaos can also result at lower levels if Organization Names are not universally agreed upon.

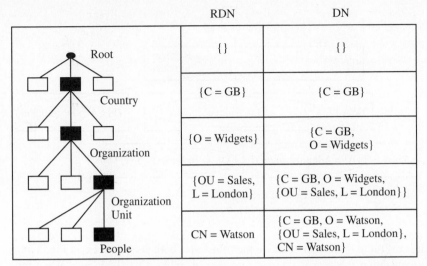

	RDN	DN
Root	{}	{}
Country	{C = GB}	{C = GB}
Organization	{O = Widgets}	{C = GB, O = Widgets}
Organization Unit	{OU = Sales, L = London}	{C = GB, O = Widgets, {OU = Sales, L = London}}
People	CN = Watson	{C = GB, O = Watson, {OU = Sales, L = London}, CN = Watson}

Figure 8.7 Distinguished names. *Copyright CCITT Recommendation X.501 "The Directory—Models," updated version 1993, Figure 4 "Determination of distinguished names." Reprinted with permission from ITU.*

Countries are registered by the ISO. Organization Names are registered by national ISO member bodies such as ANSI, designees of the member bodies, or civil registration authorities concerned with trade names. For instance, ANSI delegated U.S. Government registration authority to NIST which in turn delegated it to the General Services Administration. Within Organizations, the registration of Organization Unit names, locations, and proper names becomes a matter local to that organization.

In the United States, registration of organization names is not new and organizations registered at the state or country level should be able to list themselves in a directory at those levels. Organizations wishing to list themselves at the U.S. level must register with ANSI.

Unfortunately, having defined the DIT as a model, the CCITT/ISO standards committees were not chartered to establish the infrastructure to bring it into being. An X.500 infrastructure requires not only products, implementations, and users, but also agreement among the public services providers on registration and other issues. X.500 must be built from the top down, a process that is only now slowly getting underway through the work of organizations such as the North American Directory Forum (NADF).

Relating Logical (Information) and Physical (Topology) Directory Considerations

Now that we have discussed both the Directory's physical distribution (with DUAs and DSAs) and also its logical distribution (along the topology of the DIT),

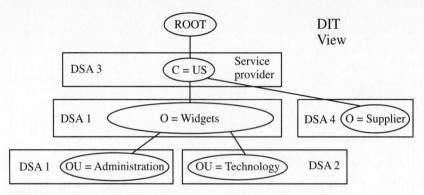

Figure 8.8 Logical view of the DIT.

it is useful to review an example that illustrates both perspectives. In Fig. 8.8, the organization Widgets is divided into two branches: OU=Tech and OU=Admin. Each is served by a different DSA. At the C=US level, there is at least one service provider-operated DSA. A supplier to Widgets in turn contains its own DSA.

Figure 8.8 represents the X.500 logical or *information* view that can be juxtaposed with the *connectivity* and *administrative* views shown in Figure 8.9.

OU=Tech and OU=Admin are controlled by different DSAs because they use incompatible hardware/software equipment types (LANs and mainframes). Together these two linked DSAs provide transparent directory service across the do-

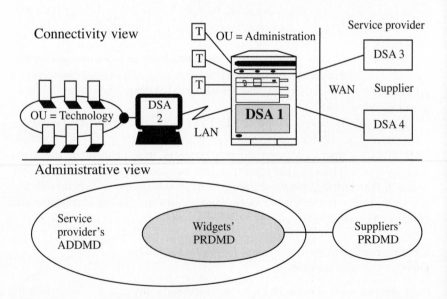

Figure 8.9 Connectivity and administrative views.

main. In addition, Widgets' connection to a supplier organization results in external directory interworking: full access to the outside world as provided by the directory connection to the service provider.

In administrative terms, Widgets and the Supplier are both Private Directory Management Domains (PRDMDs) and the service provider is an Administration Directory Management Domain (ADDMD).

8.3.3 Object Classes, Entries, and Attributes

Below the DIT structure definitions level in the X.500 schema, we find the rules for defining the entries that will exist in the DIT. The X.500 Information Framework employs object-oriented design concepts in order to allow for the reusability and extensibility of standard data type definitions. This object-oriented approach also makes the directory open ended, allowing new applications to be generated with each able to accommodate its own unique information requirements. Every user community can potentially customize the directory to fit its needs.

The first key point to understanding this approach is to distinguish between an *object class* and an *object instance*. An object class is a type of generalization that describes a category of things. In common database parlance, the object class is closely related to a record format or template; that is, it creates a template of the mandatory and optional attributes that instances of that object class will contain. For example, "Person" is an X.500 object class. David Litwack's entry in the X.500 directory, as an instance of Person, might contain a Common Name, Surname, and Telephone Number.

Every X.500 Directory entry (instance of an object class) contains an *object class attribute* that identifies its class. The value of the object class attribute is an *object identifier*—a number that uniquely identifies the object class.[2] When information about entries is transmitted in the X.500 DAP or DSP protocol, this object identifier is the key semantic linking factor allowing DUAs and DSAs to mutually identify the expected format of the entry.

When DSAs create entries at the DUA's request, they are required to maintain the semantics of the object class. This includes ensuring that all mandatory attributes are present. It is also possible for users to employ the object class attribute in queries such as "Select all the objects of type Application Entity within a portion of the DIT."

Object Class Definitions

An object class definition consists of object class name, object class identifier, mandatory attribute list (these attributes *must* be present in each instance of a

---

2. Object Identifiers were also discussed in Chapter 6. In X.500, Object Identifiers are used to label object class types. The Object Class ID for Object Class Person (see Fig. 8.10) is {2.5.6.6}, a "2" for joint-CCITT-ISO registration, a "5" for the directory services standard, a "6" for object classes, and a "6" for Person.

class), and optional attribute list (these attributes *may* be present in *some* instances of a class). Figure 8.10 displays an example of the X.500 Person object class.

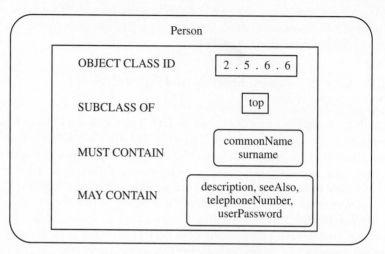

Figure 8.10 Person object class template.

In X.521 and elsewhere in the standard, Object Classes are formally defined using OSI's ASN.1. The Object Classes in the X.521 list, which include Country, Organization, Organizational Unit, Person, Locality, Application Entity, and others, should be viewed as a starter set, providing the ingredients for basic applications to run and a point from which other more complex applications can define additional types.

Object Class Inheritance

One attractive feature of using object-oriented techniques for defining X.500 information types is that the definitions can be reused. Once one Object Class is defined, a specialized version of the same class can be derived as a *subclass* of the original (which then becomes known as the *superclass* of the specialized subordinate class).

A subclass specialization is said to inherit all of the characteristics, or attributes, of its superclasses. It may then add additional mandatory or optional attributes, and it may specify different structure rules than the superclass. This approach allows for economy in specification and means that much of the software designed and built to support the superclass type can be reused to support the subclass. Figure 8.11 displays a partial map of the object class inheritance hierarchy defined in X.500.

The example in Fig. 8.11 shows TOP, the top-level object class (with no inherent characteristics of its own) and the Person and Application Entity object classes beneath it. Residential Person and Organizational Person are subclasses of Person

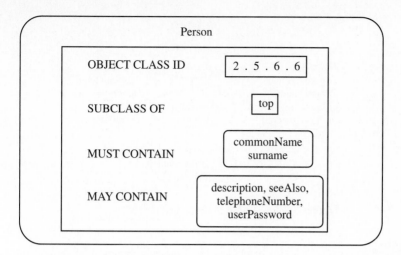

Figure 8.11   Example of object class hierarchy.

and specify different structure rules as well as attribute contents. DSA is a subclass of Application Entity.

Organizational Person, as shown in Fig. 8.12, is a subclass of Person that specifies additional optional attributes. The localAttributeSet provides a convenient way of grouping multiple attributes that serve similar purposes. Organizational Person may contain attributes beyond what the superclass Person contains, such as Job Title.

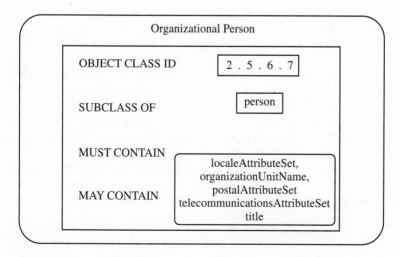

Figure 8.12   Organizational person subclass.

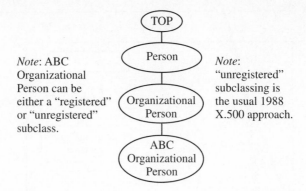

Note: ABC Organizational Person can be either a "registered" or "unregistered" subclass.

Note: "unregistered" subclassing is the usual 1988 X.500 approach.

Figure 8.13 Simple inheritance.

An example of simple object class inheritance is shown in Fig. 8.13. Note that ABC Organizational Person (a corporate employee record type based on X.500's Organizational Person) can be created either as a registered or unregistered subclass. If it is unregistered, it will use the same object class identifier (OID) as Organizational Person but contain additional locally defined attributes. DUAs or DSAs from other organizations (or DUAs/DSAs that have not yet been configured to understand ABC Organizational Person) will thus understand at least the X.500-defined attributes of Organizational Person that compose part of the ABC Organizational Person. This makes interoperability easier for 1988 X.500 implementations.

With the 1993 X.500 standard, however, DSAs may *publish* their local schemas in the directory itself, allowing foreign DSAs or DUAs to learn the local schema.

Multiple Inheritance

Object classes are not limited to only one superclass; multiple inheritance is allowed in the standard as long as the structure rules and other characteristics of the superclasses are not in conflict.

In the Fig. 8.14 example, an object class, MHS-USER, has been created. MHS-USER contains a package of attributes pertinent to X.400 Message Handling Systems. These attributes may be combined with the attributes and characteristics of a pre-existing object class to customize it for MHS usage. Thus from MHS-USER and residential person we can create MHS ResidentialPerson. MHS OrganizationalPerson could be created similarly. These entries could then contain O/R addresses and other X.400-related attributes.

In this example, MHS-USER is used as what has come to be called an *auxiliary object class*. There will never be an instance of MHS-USER, and it has no place in the structure of the DIT. However, it is used as a package to augment the contents of structural object classes such as organizational and residential persons when new subclasses, such as mhs-organizational-person or mhs-residential-person, are created.

Again, subclasses defined in this way can be either registered or unregistered. For 1993 X.500 implementations, it is recommended that the structural/auxiliary

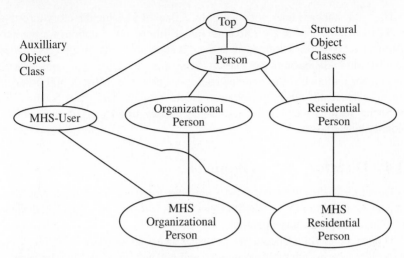

Figure 8.14   Multiple inheritance.

approach be used and then registered and published (as the schema) when these implementations are commercially available and have attained critical mass.

X.500 Attribute Types and Syntax

Once object classes are defined in the schema, their attributes can be specified. An X.500 Attribute Type defines the characteristics of the attribute. Its definition consists of its name, its identifier, an indication of whether it can be single or multivalued, an indication of the syntax its values may take on, and any (optional) size or range constraints. As with object classes, X.500 defines a starter set of attributes, including Country Name, Common Name, Organization Name, and others.

X.500 itself registers some attributes and assigns them identifiers. Standards for applications using X.500 can create attribute types and assign them identifiers. If an X.500 product supports extensibility, database administrators or product implementors may create additional attributes.

Also, every attribute is made up of one or more attribute values, and every attribute value is defined in terms of an *attribute syntax*. Attribute syntaxes contain the following elements: a name, an identifier, matching criteria, and a structure or template that values follow. Attribute value matching criteria enable exact matches or wildcard matching. Attribute syntax structures can be simple (string, integer) or complex (arbitrary ASN.1 structure). X.500 registers a starter set of attribute syntaxes.

Directory Customization

While X.500 is not a general purpose database, it is a general purpose communications directory. Moreover, it is international in scope, so that even such a basic information item as a U.S. Social Security number is not specified in the base standard.

Thus, the standard does not attempt to define all possible directory information components exhaustively. (Note the rather limited set of options for the Person object class above.) Rather, it defines a starter set and an object-oriented model by which the basic object classes (person, organization, and so on) can be extended for national, local, or organization-specific use. Most X.500 products build in mechanisms whereby users can create new attribute types (such as the U.S. Social Security number) and new object classes, usually as subclasses of the standard object classes.

8.3.4   Directory Access Protocol

The Directory Access Protocol (DAP) provides for Bind, Read, List, Abandon, Compare, Search, Add Entry, Modify Entry, Modify Relative Distinguished Name (RDN), and Remove Entry operations.

The Directory Bind Operation establishes an association between a DUA and a DSA over which such multiple inquiry and update operations may be carried. Figure 8.15 shows a brief example. The Bind Operation consists of a Bind Argument (request to Bind) and a Bind Result or a Bind Error. Each component of the operation carries a version identifier that is set by default to 1988.

One of the most important purposes of the Bind Operation is security checking. The *Credentials* element of the Bind operation facilitates bi-directional iden-

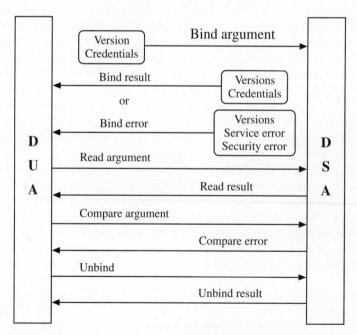

Figure 8.15   Scenario: Directory Bind and other operations.

tity authentication. Credentials may take a simple or strong form. Simple credentials and strong (cryptographic) credentials are discussed later.

Read, Compare, and Abandon Operations

The Directory Read Operation allows a directory application (possibly representing a human user) that has knowledge of the Distinguished Name of a target object in the Directory to retrieve additional information from the contents of the corresponding object entry. It might be used, for example, by an X.400 UA or MTA to retrieve an O/R address from the directory or by an MTA to expand a distribution list.

The Read Operation consists of a Read Argument (request to Read) and a Read Result or a Read Error. The Read Argument *object* is the Distinguished Name to Read, and *Selection*, is the list of attributes to retrieve. The DUA may specify only those attributes it is interested in; otherwise, all attribute values will be returned in a parameter called *Entry Information*. *Common arguments* and *Common results* may be specified by the Read operation components (as well as in other operations). These common elements perform the following functions:

- Allow the requester to fine tune the handling of the given operation by setting some general controls such as *time limit* and *size limit*. Other controls include the ability to disable chaining (remote inquiry between DSAs) or to prevent the use of copies of directory entries.

- Provide a place holder for digital signatures over directory requests or results.

- Provide a place holder for protocol extensions.

Similar to the Read Operation, the Compare operation offers an exact match on the distinguished name supplied by the requester. The Directory system will indicate whether the DUA's assertion of some attribute value (such as a user-supplied password) is true or false (matched or not).

The Abandon operation allows a directory user or application to cancel a previously submitted operation.

List and Search Operations

While the Read and Compare operations require that the requester have advance knowledge of the Distinguished Name of a directory object, the List and Search Operations enable requesters to explore the directory. The list operation may be used during exploration to view all the subordinates of an entry or to produce reports or listings intended for hard copy printout. In the Fig. 8.16 example, that base object is . . . @O=ABC@OU=ENGINEERING. This List operation example requests all the direct reports of Engineering.

The base object (entry) for the list is specified in the List argument along with Common arguments. The List Result (or, alternatively, a List Error) is returned. The List Result contains the Relative Distinguished Name (RDN) of each subordinate entry, an indication of whether the subordinate is an alias, and an indication of whether the information was obtained from the master entry or from a copy.

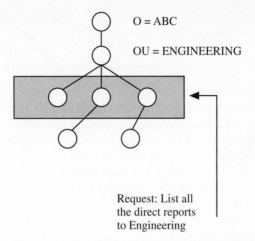

Request: List all
the direct reports
to Engineering

Figure 8.16   Directory list operation example.

Unlike the List operation, which retrieves only the RDNs of the first-level sub-ordinates of a base object, the Search operation allows an entire subtree to be ex-plored. The requester can specify which attributes are to be returned. In the example in Fig. 8.17, a search was applied to OU=MARKETING for all senior account ex-ecutives. Three hits were found in the subtree, denoted by the white circles.

In the Search Argument, the requester first specifies the distinguished name of the *base object*, that is, the starting point of the subtree where the search is to start. A *subset* parameter may be used to limit the search to exploring the base object only, the base object and first-level subordinates, or the entire subtree. (You could theoretically begin your search at the Root of the DIT with a subset of "en-tire subtree," but might find the wait, or the bill, not to your liking. More likely,

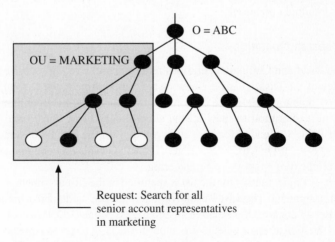

Request: Search for all
senior account representatives
in marketing

Figure 8.17   Example of search operation.

neither the DUA nor the DSA service provider would be foolish enough to allow such searches to proceed.)

Within the scope of a search, a *filter* can be applied to the contents of entries under the base object of the Search. The filter can consist of multiple filter sets combined using conjunction (AND), disjunction (OR), or negation (NOT) terms. This recursive definition allows the requester access to the full power of boolean algebra with precedence. An example filter might be: *OBJECT CLASS ID= Organizational Person AND Organizational Unit=Sales.*

Ultimately, successful X.500 directory user interfaces will be those which make directory navigation via the List and Search as easy and intuitive to the user as graphical file system interfaces (such as Macintosh folders or the Microsoft Windows File Manager).

Modify Operations

Modify operations include Add Entry, Remove Entry, Modify DN, and Modify Entry.

The Add Entry operation can be used to add a leaf-level entry to the Directory only. (Restricting additions to leaf entries ensures that the DSA responsible for that portion of the DIT is the DSA that performs the addition, otherwise X.500 protocols would need to be more complex than they are.) Likewise, the Remove Entry operation enables users to remove leaf entries. The Modify DN operation enables them to rename leaf entries.[3] Of the directory operations, only Modify Entry (which allows attributes and values to be added, removed or changed) is free of the nonleaf restriction.

The leaf update limitation is destined to create administrative headaches when enterprises reorganize a previously created reporting structure or consolidate their geographic locations. It is important for users to ask directory vendors how they handle such contingencies, especially when the enterprise database is held in multiple DSAs. Even with the best management software in individual products, multivendor distributed directories will be difficult to reorganize.

8.3.5   DSA Distributed Operations

DSAs communicate among themselves[4] to resolve requests on behalf of the user, giving that user a location-independent view of the Directory. Whether the information requested is on a LAN, at the computer center down the street, or across the ocean, the user should still be able (subject to access control) to retrieve or modify it. By the same token, two users accessing the same object in the Directory

---

3. The 1993 version of X.500 enables Modify DN to operate on nonleaf entries provided that the entry, its superior, and all its subordinates are held in the same DSA.

4. DSAs communicate among themselves . . . with one exception. The standard defines a "Centralized DSA" conformance class for a DSA that supports the DAP, but not the DSP.

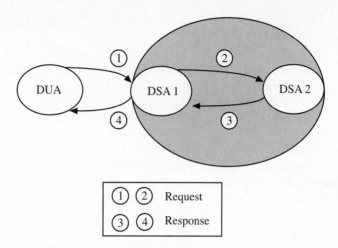

Figure 8.18   Chained DSA interaction.

should obtain the same information even if those users initiate operations from different offices, states, or countries.

DSAs provide a location-independent Directory service by interacting with one another using three mechanisms: chaining, multicasting, or referral. During the course of one request, more than one of these mechanisms may be called upon.

With *chaining*, one DSA forwards a request to another DSA. In Fig. 8.18, the DUA issues a request to DSA 1 (1). Next, DSA 1 chains the request to DSA 2 (2). DSA 2 responds (3), and the response is returned to the DUA (4). The data structures used—Chaining Arguments, Chaining Results, and Chaining Errors—are defined in the DSP protocol and contain various parameters. These parameters include trace information elements, which are added at each hop to suppress loops. Loop detection is a complex algorithm that must take the use of aliases and other intricacies of X.500 processing into account.

Multicasting is similar to chaining except that more than one DSA is contacted by the originating DSA.

In the *referral* mode, DSAs do not interact directly. Rather, one DSA informs the DUA (or a DSA) of the Presentation Address and Name of another DSA that may be able to handle the request. Referral is used when the originating DUA has indicated it does not want the DSA to chain or when the referring DSA does not have a bilateral interworking agreement with the referenced DSA. DSAs may pass back referrals for security reasons as well. DSA 2 in Fig. 8.18 above might trust and be able to authenticate the DUA, but it might not trust DSA 1 with the information it was willing to disclose to the DUA.[5] In yet another scenario (not shown here), DSAs may pass referrals to one another.

---

5. DSA implementations must always assume the worst: untrusted DSAs could cache information returned in directory results and distribute it freely, without regard for access controls.

When DAP operations are chained or multicasted from one DSA to another, the need arises for a DSA-to-DSA protocol for administrative bookkeeping and loop suppression purposes. This protocol—DSP—is expressed as an envelope around the original DAP operations. These envelopes are called chained argument and chained result.

DSA Knowledge and Information Distribution Models

Each DSA holds a portion of the DIT, formally called a *naming context*. A large organization (ABC) may begin with a single DSA controlling the O=ABC naming context which is linked to the DIT Root via the @C=US@O=ABC context prefix. As directories grow over time, the ABC enterprise may decide to add more DSAs to distribute the directory. Since it can be difficult to configure and administer the knowledge of arbitrary groups of entries, this is usually done by creating a new branch (OU or Locality) and delegating the entire branch to a new DSA.

Within the DIT, each entry is generally held by only one DSA except for Root, which is conceptually held by all first-level (country level) DSAs. One common practice among DSAs will be caching—that is, maintaining local (unsynchronized) copies of information logically residing in neighboring or distant branches of the DIT. In 1988 X.500, each entry is held by a single DSA. The standard lacks a specification for synchronized replication (sometimes called shadowing), and caching could introduce further consistency problems. In 1993 X.500, however, the model is upgraded to allow *replication*; DSAs may hold shadow copies of entries. Unlike cache copies, shadow copies may be updated automatically or on demand. Replication is very desirable for performance and reliability.

The philosophy of the X.500 Directory is one of transparent distribution. The user is supposed to view the Directory as a single distributed information base. The knowledge model ties everything together, making the transparent distribution and cooperative fulfillment of requests by DSAs possible. Every DSA holds both Directory Information (entry data) and knowledge information (where entries are). Altogether DSAs maintain five different types of knowledge references: superior, internal, cross, subordinate, and nonspecific subordinate.

Lower-level DSAs hold a *superior* reference to an *"uptown"* DSA controlling higher levels of the DIT. This type of reference consists of nothing more than the DSA Access Point (AE-Title and Presentation Address) of the superior DSA for a given naming context. By the same token, DSAs must retain information about subordinate, or *"downtown,"* naming contexts. These can take the form of either a *specific subordinate* reference where the RDN of the subordinate and the access point of the DSA are known, or a *non-specific subordinate reference* where the subordinate DSA is known but the specific RDNs identifying nested naming contexts are unknown. Optional *cross references* may be used to speed access to particular context prefixes. *Internal* references are the nonstandard pointers by which a DSA keeps track of locally controlled RDNs.

Using just the superior and subordinate knowledge references, DSAs can navigate from any point in the DIT to any other point, traveling up or down the hierarchy as necessary. In large, distributed DITs, no DSA can navigate based on full knowledge. However, DSAs with minimal knowledge will always be able to progress name resolution by passing operations to a superior or subordinate DSA. This request chaining process could culminate at a first-level DSA, which can reach first-level DSAs in other countries.

Figure 8.19 shows all of the knowledge references needed to provide cohesion among the four DSAs within a fictitious O=ABC naming context. DSA 1 holds the O=ABC naming context. DSA 2 holds the OU=R&D naming context for which the context prefix is ". . .@O=ABC@OU=R&D" and DSA 3 holds the OU=TECH naming context for which the context prefix is ". . .@O=ABC@OU=TECH." DSA 4 holds a number of naming contexts that are not specifically configured with other DSAs.

DSAs 2, 3, and 4 each maintain a superior reference to their superior neighbor DSA 1. Thus, unless DSAs 2, 3, and 4 maintain optional cross references for specific (frequently accessed) external DSAs, DSA 1 will always act as a gateway into the enterprise for directory inquiries.

DSA 1 contains specific subordinate references to the OU=R&D and OU=TECH naming contexts held by DSAs 2 and 3, respectively. It has a non-specific subordinate reference (NSSR) to DSA 4. The effect of the NSSR is that DSA 1 will have to chain list or search requests to DSA 4 rather more often than it would to DSA 2 and 3 (who are known to control specific naming contexts and can sometimes be eliminated from consideration by consulting DSA 1's knowledge information alone). Also, all directory operations to unknown (and possibly invalid) names in O=ABC would have to be chained to DSA 4.

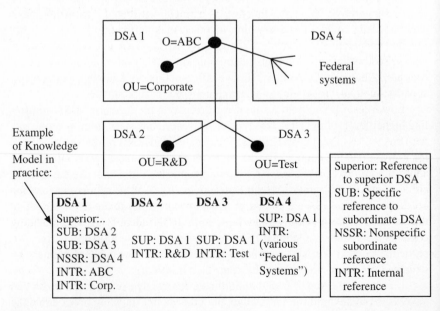

Figure 8.19   Knowledge distribution example.

Limitations of the Knowledge Model

The basic 1988 X.500 knowledge model has two significant limitations. One concerns the standard's assumption that an entry is held in one and only one DSA. But in reality, if one X.500 service provider furnishes the ABC Corporation's internal electronic mail user listings and another its telephone directory listings, the providers might list some entries twice with only partial (and possibly conflicting) information in each copy. External users querying for information about their ABC Corporation correspondents would not always get the same answer. This is commonly referred to in the directory standards trade as the *distributed entry* problem. The North American Directory Forum (NADF) has worked around this problem by creating a *naming link* attribute that can optionally be used by the requester's DUA to collect information from all directory manifestations of a real-world object.

The other limitation concerns X.500's assumption that there will be one and only one first-level DSA per country. This model is not viable in countries with deregulated communications environments and multiple public service providers. The NADF has also addressed this problem in terms of "virtual country DSA" functionality for the U.S. and Canada.

Management Considerations

Finally, there are management operations that involve DSAs or distributed directories in general. In addition to the usual fault, configuration, accounting, performance, and security management functions, users must wrestle with the following issues:

- Loading the Directory across multiple DSAs (bulk loading entries, setting up knowledge);

- Using shadows (proprietary or 1993 X.500) to improve performance and provide redundancy;

- Setting up access controls supporting organizational policies (using proprietary access control, or eventually, the 1993 X.500 standards); and

- Modifying information distribution and tree structure after initial directory establishment.

Many of these management functions pertain to information administration. They are needed because X.500's built-in operations such as Add Entry are not sufficient for wholesale buildup or modification of the tree structure. In current working situations, such as the North American Directory Forum, this conclusion has led to the specification of formats for the bulk loading of entry and knowledge data into a DSA.

In fact, a major weakness of the existing X.500 standard is its lack of certain distributed operation functions. When the DIT is set up or, more precisely, when a new DSA supporting DSP is added to the network, there are no protocols by which it can acquire immediate knowledge of the DIT topology. When an existing DSA reconfigures its portion of the DIT (when a Country, Organization, or

Organization Unit is renamed), there is no protocol for distributing this knowledge to peer DSAs. Also the Directory update operations are themselves limited, having no capability to add or remove nonleaf objects and no facility for delegating administrative authority over a portion of the DIT from one DSA to another.

Finally, it would be useful to be able to monitor and control a DSA from an integrated network management system, even if the management system had been developed by a different vendor than the DSA. ITU/ISO are working to develop directory MIBs that would enable management system interoperation using ITU/ISO's Common Management Information Protocol (CMIP). In addition, the IETF has published a Directory Monitoring MIB [MANS93] for interoperation via SNMP.

8.3.6   Security in 1988 X.500

The 1988 X.509 recommendation provides the following security capabilities:

- Peer entity (DUA–DSA) or (DSA–DSA) authentication using Simple Authentication (passwords), Protected Simple Authentication (encrypted passwords), or Strong Authentication (using digital signatures);

- DAP and DSP request integrity and authentication/nonrepudiation of the DUA or DSA requester (using digital signatures);

- DAP or DSP result integrity and authentication/non-repudiation of the DSA responder (using digital signatures); and

- Certificate storage for directory and other applications.

  Security features for access control are part of the 1993 Recommendation.

Certification Infrastructure

Future secure applications based on public key technology will require directory support to store the public key material to be used for verifying digital signatures and for encrypting message contents among large communities of users. Scalable public key infrastructures will become the basis for secure electronic commerce. Recall from Chapter 6 that public keys can be protectively encapsulated in a signed Certificate structure that can then be widely distributed. X.500 plays a key role in Certification infrastructures: first, in that X.509 provides the broadly accepted data structure and definition of a Certificate and, second, in that the global X.500 directory, once in place, would provide a potential repository for Certification Authority, Certificate, and Certificate Revocation List information.

The Directory DIT forms a viable repository for Certificates because every entry is represented by a unique distinguished name. Entries represent real-world people or objects, and they can contain a Certificate as one of their attributes. In secure messaging environments, user entries such as Organizational Units, Persons, and Roles as well as entries for application entities such as MTAs and DSAs will contain Certificates. Each secure messaging user will also hold a private key, perhaps embedded on a smartcard.

Any public key signature algorithm can be used with X.509, and multiple Certification Authorities (CAs), or key issuing authorities, can exist in the DIT. These CAs can cross-certify one another as a way of ensuring that users in disparate security domains can communicate securely. CAs can also publish lists of revoked (compromised) keys. Since the definition of public key certificates in the Directory is independent of both specific public key algorithms and CA relationships, the Directory can be used as a general purpose repository for public key information.

CAs themselves will be represented as entries in the DIT and possess accessible public keys of their own so that their signatures (affixed atop the user's public keys) can in turn be checked. CA entries also contain Certificate Revocation List and Certification Authority Revocation List information to warn directory users of canceled or compromised certificates that have been signed by the CA in the past.

For administrative purposes, X.500 allows CAs to be logically related to one another. Thus the management functions associated with maintaining Certificates, public keys, secret keys, and smartcards can be handled at a local level (corporation, university, government agency), but users served by different local CAs can still exchange secure messages. X.500 accomplishes this sleight of hand by allowing Certificates the option to be represented as *Certification Paths*, a data structure that links CAs to mutually trusted CAs represented at a higher level of the DIT. For example, with the Internet CA structure defined for PEM, two CAs registered under the same PCA might establish a Certification Path.

While the certification infrastructure role of the Directory is limited to publishing Certificates and Certificate Revocation Information in user and CA entries, the full management of the infrastructure involves the generation, distribution, and publication of smartcards, private key material, public key material, Certificates, and Certificate Revocation Lists belonging to users or Certification Authorities. Also, with regard to its own design, each secure directory application should specify a policy for utilizing the Certificate information published in the Directory. Such a policy must, at a minimum, address the performance/security tradeoffs between caching Certificate or CRL information and looking it up in the Directory as well as the validation of Certificate information either once, periodically, or on every instance of communication.

8.3.7   The 1993 Recommendation

The 1993 X.500 standard extends the basic 1988 model to add access control, replication, and schema management/publication functionality. To understand 1993 X.500, we must focus on what has been done to extend X.500's Information Framework. Essentially directory experts extended the concept of a Directory entry. In the new model, some entries denote Administrative Points (APs) within the DIT. Such entries are called Administrative Entries. APs, which often occur at the

Organization/Organization Unit level, will be able to set policies for the control of information residing in all or part of the subtree.

Both entries and administrative entries can contain Operational Attributes. Examples of operational attributes are access control lists, replication agreements between DSAs, directory knowledge, and schema rules. By publishing this kind of information in the Directory, the standard enables both the extension of existing Directory software and the creation of new Directory management software. Figure 8.20 displays the relationship of APs, subentries, entries, and operational attributes. When present in an administrative entry, operational attributes can affect multiple entries within the naming context below that AP. Subentries, subordinate to APs, allow collections of entries (or administrative areas) to be defined that are not strictly subtrees.

The extended information model is key to enabling 1993 X.500 access control, replication, and schema management and publication. These major new additions to X.500 are discussed next.

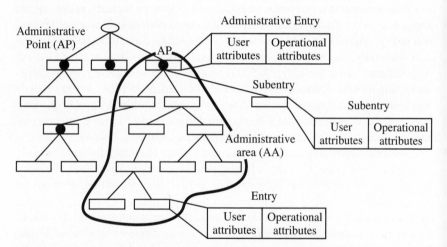

Figure 8.20   Extended 1993 information model. *Copyright CCITT Recommendation X.501 "The Directory—Models," Blue Book Fasc. VIII.8 (1988), Figure 7 "Model of directory administration and operational information." Reprinted with permission from ITU.*

Access Control

While most directory products implement some kind of access control functionality, DSAs from multiple vendors cannot share access control criteria without standards. This forces administrators and the DSAs they control to be much more restrictive regarding the use of replication. Even if two Directory management domains trust one another, they cannot replicate controlled information unless the access controls are also replicated. Thus, there were two principal motives for adding access control. The first was to enable users to buy products from multiple vendors and not have to learn new access control systems or be concerned whether X.500-compliant products will satisfy their security policy. The second was to support standardized chaining and replication to DSAs that could be trusted to enforce the access controls defined by the owners of the information.

Two schemes were defined for access control: basic and simplified. In the basic access control scheme, one or more access control information (ACI) elements may be held within access control related operational attributes. ACI can grant or deny a set of users permission to perform certain types of operations against particular directory information elements. An ACI element's scope of coverage may extend over a single directory entry or over an entire administrative area (called an access control domain).

The simplified access control scheme is a subset of the basic scheme. It operates within the context of a single access control domain. That is, it precludes the use of entry-level ACIs and of nested or overlapping access control domains. Since processing multiple overlapping ACI can be quite complex for a DSA, the simplified access control scheme is beneficial for developers; however, basic access control support would be beneficial for users, who could then use overlapping ACIs and entry ACIs to define multiple security policies flexibly over a region of the DIT.

Access control permissions include Compare, Read, Add, Remove, Modify, Export, and Import. These permissions can apply at the entry level, attribute level, or at the attribute value level. The permissions are interrelated in that, for example, Compare requires read permission at the entry level and the attribute level. Since entry and domain access control information is held in the form of an attribute, the ability to Add, Read, Compare, or Remove the ACIs themselves is controlled by the same means as other attributes.

Replication

Replication, whereby multiple copies of directory information are updated automatically or on demand, is critical to maintaining performance and reliability in a distributed directory environment. Cached information, which is not updated automatically, is a poor substitute.

The replication of information has several service objectives. Performance can be improved by bringing information closer to the user. Costs of inquiry are reduced. Redundancy or fault tolerance are improved: if two DSAs on separate processors each have a copy of a DIT fragment, one can serve as a backup for the other. Replication is not very useful, however, if the replicated data and the master copy are not kept consistent on a relatively short or well-defined update cycle.

Three types of replication (also called shadowing) may be requested. The *full shadow* embraces all the attributes, values, entries, and knowledge information that comprise the given fragment of the DIT. Such a fragment would become a naming context in the shadowing DSA, and it might be used when that DSA is acting as a warm standby ready to assume complete operational responsibility, or it might be used by an administration wishing to offer a broad variety of services incorporating the shadowed data. Alternatively, a DSA could request a *partial shadow*. It could pick up, for example, the RDNs of entries and a few (but not all of) the attribute types. It might or might not need the knowledge information as well. Finally, the *spot shadow* is a shadow of only a single entry.

Single (direct) or multistage (indirect) shadowing is supported in the replication model. Thus a DSA may serve as a shadow provider while in turn shadowing the data from the master DSA. The 1993 extensions define an Operational Binding Protocol by which Master and Shadow DSAs can negotiate a shadow agreement and then, using the Directory Shadowing Protocol, transfer the shadowed information. The areas of agreement that would have to be reached include not only the type of shadow and specification of the DIT fragment to be shadowed, but also how the shadow would be synchronously updated by the master. Synchronous updates can be issued automatically by the master or only on demand. Updates can consist of a complete replacement, a string of journaled updates, or single updates that mimic updates to the master copy as they occur.

Schema Management/Publication

Improved schema management and publication is needed because users can and will extend the directory by adding local object classes. Without a standard way of understanding these extensions, users with different schemas will not always be able to find software that lets them interchange directory information. The 1993 standard provides a set of operational attributes that can be used to publish the Directory Structure Rules (structural restrictions) and Directory Content Rules (object class definitions) in effect for an administrative area at an administrative point.

8.3.8   North American Directory Forum Initiatives

As noted in Chapter 4, North American telecommunications providers have formed a North American Directory Forum (NADF) in order to expedite the development of universally acceptable directories. The NADF's principal goal is to create the agreements and infrastructure needed for public directory interconnection in support of X.400 messaging. For the sake of consistency, public service providers serving a community or organization must acknowledge common naming and registration procedures for directory entries representing states, cities, or organizations. They must also acknowledge a common knowledge (or directory routing information) base, especially since it is not practical to implement a single first-level DSA in countries with multiple service providers such as the United States.

The NADF has focused on developing infrastructure agreements regarding the registration of directory information and knowledge sharing between providers. Their proposed solution calls for a pool of shared references called the *Central Administration and Naming (CAN)* information repository to be exchanged periodically between DSAs. This shared reference pool, a copy of which would be held by each of the interconnected public directory services, acts as a public namespace or common knowledge base. It accomplishes two purposes: first, it contains all the knowledge information needed for behind-the-scenes interworking between the DSAs operated by the public service providers; second, it acts as a public, user-friendly namespace wherein users can query for naming links or pointers to information without knowing which provider(s) holds the information. The NADF has developed directory synchronization-style technology that propagates the CAN information among DSAs.

Once the CAN and NADF services are in production, the following operational scenario could take place. To pursue a remote query into unknown namespace, an X.500 DSA could contact any of the public directory services first to obtain a reference to the target DSA in which the desired information is stored. This target DSA might be operated by another public service provider or it might be part of a privately operated network. Subject to bilateral arrangements authorizing access, the inquiring DSA could then chain queries to the target DSA.

The NADF intends for public directory services to follow existing federal and state registration mechanisms when naming organization and locality (State or County) entries in the United States.[6] These proposals are attractive because they require no changes to the 1988 X.500 protocol or additional registration authorities. Organizational data or references to organizational data will be listed in a provider's directory at the national, state, or place level of the DIT which, for the purposes of the CAN, will be structured as shown in Fig. 8.21. Residential users

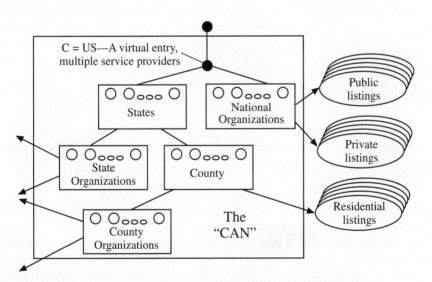

Figure 8.21 The NADF proposed top-level DIT (CAN) structure for the U.S.

---

6. This agreement represents something of a breakthrough for users, who had originally faced the prospect of having to pay ANSI $1500 for the use of their organization name(s). Instead, organizations to be listed at state and county levels can use existing registration procedures. Only organizations wishing to be listed at the national level may be required to register their organization name with ANSI.

will be listed at the place level only. As an optimization for fast lookup, the names of state-level organizations may be listed as state/organization pairs at the national level, and place/organization pairs may likewise be listed for fast lookup at the state level.

8.3.9   Complementary Technologies

The need for directory services has given rise to a number of initiatives. These include the Quipu directory implementation and a number of "X.500-like" solutions.

QUIPU

As we noted in Chapter 3, X.500 products have been slow to emerge but are now making their debut. Given the scarcity of such products, for the last several years a bright spot has been the publicly available, portable Directory implementation called Quipu.[7] Quipu is part of ISODE (the ISO Development Environment), which offers a suite of OSI reference implementations, including X.400 and FTAM. ISODE was originally available as free software, but has come under the stewardship of an ISODE Consortium that now makes it available on a paying basis to consortium members.

Quipu was developed beginning in 1987 at the University College London as a way to facilitate experimentation with Directory prior to the provision of large-scale services. The result of making the software freely available has been to provide seed code for projects and derivative products and to serve as the basis for most of the PARADISE pilot implementations.

Quipu includes the following features:

- The local component of the X.500 database is mapped onto UNIX text files so that the text database can be created and managed easily using standard UNIX text processing tools.

- The database can be accessed, searched, and modified using DAP and DSP.

- New object classes and attribute type definitions are configurable in a text file.

- Each nonleaf directory entry has an attribute identifying its Master DSA.

- Attribute inheritance is used to propagate commonly used attribute values to some or all entries in the local database.

- Chaining and referrals are used to resolve problems with regard to heterogeneous network communities.

- A simple replication model and function has been codified in RFC 1276 [KILL91A].

---

7. Quipu is the ancient Peruvian INCA word for strings with specially knotted colored threads that were used by the INCA in lieu of writing. This is a play on words; QUIPU development was originally funded by the European Integrated Network Communications Architecture initiative.

Although it is an early product with nonstandard access control and replication and only an in-memory database, Quipu has also served as seed code for a number of X.500 vendor products. Indeed, the Quipu replication technique may even prove to be a rival to 1993 X.500 simply because its usage is so widespread.

Lightweight Directory Access Protocol

One of X.500's weaknesses has been its complexity, which has made it difficult for vendors to implement the standard in local messaging environments.

The Lightweight Directory Access Protocol (LDAP) [YEON93] represents a considerable simplification over the DAP. It reduces the number of directory operations that a DUA must support by eliminating Read and List, relieves the DUA of the need to process referrals, and simplifies the structure of DAP operations to reduce protocol encoding/decoding complexity in the LDAP client (usually a PC or workstation). It can also run directly over TCP/IP.

OSF Paradigm

The Open Software Foundation (OSF) developed a creative approach toward obtaining distributed directories and global directory standardization via X.500, all without unduly compromising performance.

The OSF Distributed Computing Environment (DCE) provides an operating system and vendor independent integrated service set supporting the development, use, and maintenance of distributed applications that can communicate with one another and with network services, using a DCE-defined RPC mechanism. At the heart of DCE and its services lies a directory service that allows applications to identify by name resources such as files, disks, print queues, and servers.

This directory service consists of two parts: a Cell Directory and a Global Directory. The Cell Directory is Digital Domain Name System (DEC DNS, not to be confused with the Internet DNS) and the Global Directory is an X.500 implementation developed by Siemens-Nixdorf. The Global Directory claims the following characteristics:

- Open access using the X.500 API from X/OPEN and the X.400 API Association;
- Full protocol support for X.500;
- Caching for fast response;
- Integration with the DCE Security service, which provides Kerberos authentication and sophisticated access control capabilities; and
- Transport independence operating over the RPC that accommodates OSI, TCP/IP, and other protocols.

The OSF paradigm approach suggests an interesting possibility for migration from today's polyglot directory island environment to an environment that will be better suited for interconnection to X.500 via directory synchronization or gateway methods. In fact, with a number of X.500-like directories emerging (such as Novell's NDS and Banyan StreetTalk), an OSF-like paradigm for directory imple-

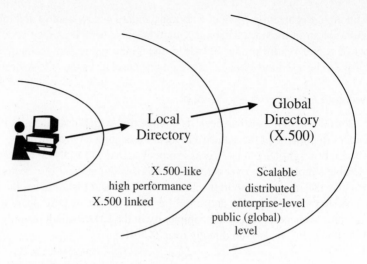

Figure 8.22   The OSF paradigm.

mentation could become commonplace. In more and more implementations, local directories may come to be provided by high-performance proprietary implementations, and global directories by X.500 products, as illustrated in Fig. 8.22.

Modularization represents yet another promising sign for X.500. The major LAN e-mail vendors are beginning to open their architectures. Figure 8.23 shows how it may be practical to move from directory synchronization to directory interworking via X.500 by the 1995 time frame. Emerging service provider APIs allow the mixing of the directory component of an e-mail client with other components. Thus, even if Microsoft Mail, cc:Mail, and other products do not support X.500 directly, third party X.500 DUAs can be tied in. Moreover, even products

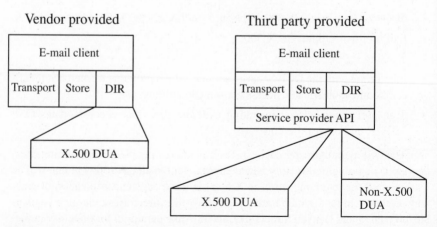

Figure 8.23   Inserting X.500 client functionality.

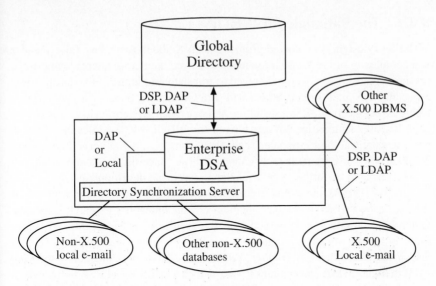

Figure 8.24   Enterprise directory coexistence.

that do not support X.500 fully will become more X.500-like—a factor that will at least improve the results of directory synchronization solutions.

With directory synchronization solutions becoming prevalent and the first X.500 DAP or LDAP client functionality emerging, the time may soon arrive when coexistence between X.500, directory synchronization, and local directory infra-structures is feasible. Figure 8.24 displays a generic integrated directory architecture offering full coexistence between X.500 and legacy proprietary local e-mail and human resources databases. The non-X.500 environment is serviced through a di-rectory synchronization server, while the X.500 environment supports global direc-tory interconnection and DSP, DAP, or LDAP access to the enterprise X.500 directory for X.500-capable enterprise messaging systems and applications.

However, while some ponder hybrid X.500 approaches, others argue that X.500 does not provide the technology and performance needed for global direc-tory solution.

8.4   WHOIS++

X.500 has received considerable attention from Internet devotees who, in their zest for experimentation, uncovered a number of problems with the protocol. Some of these problems resulted from bug-ridden early software and initial re-leases of the Quipu freeware; others were perceived to be problems inherent to the particular architecture of X.500. The proponents of an alternative to X.500 deter-mined that a global directory, particularly the component subset for small organi-zations and locations, merited a more performant technical solution. Thus was born WHOIS++.

8.4.1   The Rationale for WHOIS++

WHOIS++ designers perceived problems with X.500 in two areas. First, the size and complexity of the X.500 implementations and their consequent slowness and resource intensiveness were perceived to translate into high X.500 startup costs, especially for small organizations with limited staff resources. Second, from a technical perspective, X.500 searching and extensibility were seen as excessively complex. (We summarize the concerns of the WHOIS++ designers here both in order to establish their rationale for the development of a directory alternative to X.500 and because we believe that some of these concerns, once understood, can also be resolved by further X.500-related research and development.)

In [WEID93B], the author argues that searching in X.500 works well only if the user knows where in the naming hierarchy the object of the search is located. Otherwise, the query is processed globally, even in branches of the DIT where there is no possibility of a positive result. To retrieve and display *@C=US @O=DML Associates@CN=David Litwack*, an X.500 query must go to the *Root DSA*[8] to find the DSA that contains *@C=US*, then to a U.S.-level DSA to find which DSA holds the entry for *@C=US@O=DML Associates*, and finally to the third DSA for *CN=David Litwack*. While the hierarchy makes the administration and delegation of subtrees easy, it seems to severely hamper search abilities. Users have to know quite a bit about the layout of the DIT (which bits of the information the user has about the target reside at which levels of the DIT) to be able to focus a query.

[WEID93B] thus argues that chaining and referral can cause severe problems. In chaining, the initially queried DSA takes responsibility for forwarding the query to the DSAs which hold lower parts of the subtree, and for collating the results before presenting them to the client. Referral causes the client to propagate the query. In both cases, the query must be presented to every DSA holding part of the subtree, and both cases result in slow response times for searches and heavy DSA loading as well as problems connected with the issuing of the queries themselves, network transit times, error detection and correction, collation of responses, and additional queries based on responses.

Also, because of its naming hierarchy, X.500 is not considered easily extensible to the yellow pages requirement of providing directory services for nonperson objects. [WEID93B] gives the example of finding "all the computer scientists in the U.K.," which requires that some of the appropriate information be encoded in the namespace or requires a global search. He argues that X.500's hierarchical namespace and query propagation facilities are ill-suited for either of these operations.

The author describes several proposed solutions to these problems. First, a special index DSA, containing aliases or replicated entries for all the entries in the

---

8. In the PARADISE pilot environment a U.K.-based Root DSA known as "Giant Tortoise" disseminates sufficient knowledge among country-level DSAs to enable X.500 DIT operation. No Root DSA is called for in the X.500 standard, which said only that first-level DSAs must hold the Root Context. Thus, in effect, Giant Tortoise provides the Root Context.

DIB that match the indexing criteria, could be placed at a specific location in the DIT *(@C=UK@O=Computer Scientists)*. This approach, however, has the problem of quickly becoming out of date as directory updates are made. Also, the term "Computer Scientists" might not yield all the relevant entries. Finally, since the search term must be encoded into the namespace to help focus searches and since the search term must appear at all DIT levels (so that global searches can be avoided), the namespace may itself grow out of control.

Another approach proposes user-friendly naming through a method of specifying search attributes to alleviate the need for searches that might be required because of ignorance of the name space. The proposal essentially establishes a set of rules formalizing the formation of stylized queries such as *"David Litwack, DML Associates, U.S."* However, the author notes that while this technique reduces the complexities of the DN for the user, it does not reduce the knowledge required to traverse the DIT.

Lastly, the author proposes a solution to X.500 search problems equivalent to the Index Server solution proposed for WHOIS++. The technique creates indexes at each level of the DIT, which can then be used to cut down search time—in essence "pruning" the search tree so that a query will be sent only to servers who have indicated that they may have entries that satisfy the query. Since the indexing is not constrained by the namespace (although it may be anchored at specific places in the DIT), queries for information not encoded in the namespace become easier. This also allows the rapid creation of new indexes using new search terms.

We (the authors of this book) further note that the NADF's "CAN" approach and technology could be used in private environments and other countries. CAN would widely propagate knowledge, shortening chaining and referrals paths, and enabling public directory systems to act like gigantic, virtual index DSAs. Thus, it can be argued that these legitimate problems raised by the WHOIS++ proponents can be solved if the X.500 community is willing and aggressive.

In fact, [WEID93B] states that the work to build the index mesh structure for WHOIS++ may also be used to support X.500 and contribute to the integration of the two protocols, but the hearts of WHOIS++ proponents seem to be set on developing a wholly new directory technology.

8.4.2 The WHOIS++ Technology

As noted in Chapter 7, the WHOIS++ initiative is intended to permit WHOIS-like servers to make more structured information available to Internet users in a more standardized way.[9] The specification was designed for simplicity, speed, global searching, and backward compatibility with WHOIS. The authors of the Internet Draft [DEUT93] minimized the extensibility of WHOIS++ in order to create a

---

9. A significant portion of the information on WHOIS++ was derived from Peter Deutsch and the IETF Whois and Network Information Lookup Service Working Group's (WNILS) [DEUT93] paper.

useful application, especially when the high cost of configuring and operating an X.500 White Pages service is not justifiable. Furthermore, they separated WHOIS++ from any particular search and retrieval mechanisms so that dedicated database formats and fast indexing software can be used.

The original WHOIS model represents each individual record in the database as a Rolodex-like collection of text. Each record has a unique identifier and one or more lines of information. While each record contains information about a single user or service, there is no structure or specific ordering of this information. Users can issue searches for records as well as for individual text strings within individual records by using a simple query-response protocol. However, the current WHOIS service does not have sufficient response capability and reliability to handle the anticipated volumes of traffic required of a full-fledged White Pages directory service for the entire Internet.

WHOIS++ is based on a set of extensions to the original WHOIS information model and query protocol. These extensions were designed to be backward-compatible with existing WHOIS servers such that a new (WHOIS++) server receiving any of the older commands specified in RFC 954 [HARR85] will behave in the same manner as the original NIC WHOIS server. The WHOIS++ specification describes extensions to the WHOIS data model and query protocol as well as a companion extensible, distributed indexing service to facilitate searches. It also includes options permitting the addition or updating of information records, the use of multiple languages and character sets, and multiple views of a single set of data, and an optional authentication mechanism to protect all or part of the WHOIS++ database from unauthorized access.

WHOIS++ Information Models

The WHOIS service extensions are centered on the recommendation to structure user information around a series of standardized information templates. These templates will consist of ordered sets of data elements or attribute-value pairs. Each directory record will contain a specified ordered set of these data elements. The IETF is currently standardizing the format and content of these attribute-value pairs. Initially three types of data record have been proposed [GARG93]: people, hosts, and domains. (As of early 1994, hosts and domains were using the same template.) Tables 8.2 and 8.3 outline the contents of these proposed templates.

Thus each record is based on one of the specified templates (each containing a specified number of attribute-value pairs). Each value associated with an attribute can be any ASCII string up to a specified length. The intent is to simplify the user's ability to identify and search such templates because a given search is limited to a specific collection of information. While the creation of customized templates has been provided for, the WHOIS++ authors suggest discouraging their use where the appropriate standardized templates are available.

WHOIS++ records are identified by permanent "handles" rather than by their place in a specific naming hierarchy (as in X.500). It has been proposed that each WHOIS++ database on the Internet be assigned a unique handle similar to the handle associated with each database record. This handle would be registered with

Handle	A unique identifier for this record on the local server	Required
Name	Name of the individual	Required
Organization	Name of the organization	Required
Organization-type	Type of organization (university, commercial)	Optional
Work-telephone	Work telephone number	Optional
Fax-telephone	Fax telephone number	Optional
Work-address	Work postal address	Optional
Title	Working title or position within an organization	Optional
Department	Department	Optional
E-mail-address	E-mail address in RFC 822 format for this individual	Optional
Home-telephone	Home telephone number	Optional
Home-address	Home postal address	Optional
Last-update	Date this record was last updated	Required

Table 8.2 Proposed WHOIS++ PEOPLE record type.

the Internet Assigned Numbers Authority (IANA) to avoid duplication of server names and enable the identification of each entry as a unique record handle/server handle pair. Therefore each record's handle would be a unique combination of the record unique identifier plus the server unique identifier (*cweider@red*).

WHOIS++ Search Queries and Responses

In WHOIS++, users can issue search commands consisting of one or more search terms with an optional set of constraints. The Search terms allow the user to

Domain-name	Domain name registered with the Network Information Center (NIC)	Required
Network-address	Network address associated with this domain name	Required
Admin-name	Name of the Administrative Contact for this domain	Required
Admin-address	Postal address of the Administrative Contact for this domain	Required
Admin-telephone	Telephone number of the Administrative Contact for this domain	Required
Admin-e-mail	Electronic mail address in RFC 822 format for the Administrative Contact for this domain	Required
Tech-name	Name of the Technical Contact for this domain	Required
Tech-address	Postal address of the Technical Contact for this domain	Required
Tech-telephone	Telephone number of the Technical Contact for this domain	Required
Tech-e-mail	Electronic mail address in RFC 822 format for the Technical Contact for this domain	Required
Nameservers	Primary domain nameservers for this domain	Optional
Last-update	Last date this record was updated	Required

Table 8.3 Proposed WHOIS++ HOST or DOMAIN record type.

specify the template type, attribute, value, or handle. Each search term can have an optional set of local constraints to override any defaults or global constraints. Also, if a user were to specify more than one template type, no matches would occur (a record can have only one template type associated with it) and a warning message would be returned.

The authors have specified six different response modes for WHOIS++ servers. These include: *full*, when there is a single record matching the specified query; *abridged*, when there are between two and ten records matching the query; *handle*, returning a list of handles that match the query; *summary*, when there are more than ten records matching the query; *pointer*, indicating another WHOIS++ server who might be able to answer the query; and *MIME*, indicating that the body of the response has been encoded in MIME message format. The contents of responses are specified in terms of introductory and closing text and system messages (of recommended lengths) and a formatted response message with standardized lines, line lengths, and contents for each of the six responses.

WHOIS++ Distributed Operation

The WHOIS++ architecture provides for the distributed maintenance of the directory contents and the use of an indexing service for locating additional servers [WEID93].[10] Index servers would hold forward knowledge—indices of attribute values—for a set of other servers that can also be index servers. These servers would serve as the glue that ties the WHOIS++ world together. This capability is deemed the essential distinction between WHOIS++ and X.500. X.500 works well when the inquirer knows the desired object's location in the hierarchy; otherwise the query is processed globally, even in branches of the tree where there is no chance of a positive result. However, WHOIS++ index servers would provide advance knowledge of what is in a branch so that branches with objects not yielding a match will not be searched.

Figure 8.25 shows how indexing might work. In the figure, each index server contains enough indexing information to prune the search tree. For example, Server Z could be the U.S. server, Server A, the California server, Server C, the New York server, and Server E, the San Francisco server. The U.S. server would know that only the California and New York servers mention a "Weider." The California server would know that only the San Francisco server mentions a Weider. Thus the query can be rapidly routed to where it might be answered. If many types of forward information were exchanged, such pruning of the directory tree would become very efficient.

While many of the WHOIS++ capabilities resemble those contained in X.500, it should be noted that WHOIS++ operates as a "mesh" rather than a tree-oriented directory. Its architecture is designed more for speed and ease of implementation and use rather than as the all-encompassing, hierarchical, global

10. We are grateful to Chris Weider of Bunyip Information Systems for his help on WHOIS++ and especially for his expertise on how index servers are proposed to work in a WHOIS++ directory service.

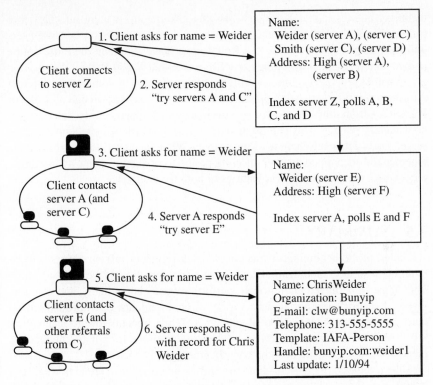

Figure 8.25   Using index servers. *Reprinted with permission of Chris Weider, Bunyip Information Systems.*

directory that the developers of X.500 envisioned. In this respect, the mesh is intended to allow a base or index server to participate in multiple virtual hierarchies, so that new views of the WHOIS++ space can be added by anyone at any time. Hierarchies can be traced for each server, and most servers will belong to many hierarchies. For example, a University of Virginia server might belong to a hierarchy for the state of Virginia and a hierarchy for universities on the east coast.

Lastly, the WHOIS++ initiative provides a framework for indicating that a particular transaction is to be authenticated and which mechanism to use. The actual mechanism is left up to individual implementors. Such authentication mechanisms include simple password authentication, KERBEROS-based authentication, and TICKET, which is based on a simple private key encryption scheme.

WHOIS++ Coexistence with X.500

There is considerable interest in WHOIS++ coexistence with X.500.[11] Such coexistence could be achieved through gateways residing on servers that intercept

---

11. We are grateful to Karen Petraska-Veum for this description of potential solutions to X.500-WHOIS++ coexistence.

incoming queries, either X.500 or WHOIS++, and convert them into the other format.[12] Initially, however, such approaches will not be seamless because users will have to pose their queries to a well-known entry point and therefore not be able to take full advantage of the capabilities of either X.500 or WHOIS++.

Another proposed solution involves using graphical or menu-based Internet information services such as Gopher or Mosaic to hide any knowledge of X.500 or WHOIS++ from users. While this approach does not require users to know a well-known entry point, it does require them to access the particular site's information server. Other proposals include a kind of meta-White Pages service to glue servers together and accommodate their differing protocols or to build a new hybrid directory service embracing the best features of both technologies.

8.5 SUMMARY

We noted at the beginning of this chapter that directory infrastructures will be required to support organizational, national, and international levels of operation. They must be deployed ubiquitously, perform robustly and reliably, and maintain levels of security appropriate to a variety of environments. Such infrastructures must be based on widely adopted standards. While impetus toward a directory infrastructure has lagged somewhat behind similar efforts for e-mail, the requirements remain set and are in some ways beginning to be met.

Nevertheless, the current directory infrastructure clearly remains weak and X.500 as well as such alternatives as WHOIS++ are still clearly immature. While directory synchronization usage is proceeding apace, it is still difficult, costly, and limited in functionality.

However, there are a number of positive trends. First, local directory infrastructures are becoming more modular and interconnectable. Emerging APIs will allow the mixing of the directory component of an e-mail client with other components so that third party X.500 DUAs will be able to tie into major directory products, and products that do not fully support X.500 are becoming more X.500-like. Directory synchronization solutions are becoming common, and directory synchronization standards are under consideration.

Global directory infrastructures are also advancing. X.500 offers a flexible information model with options for local solutions. As X.500 becomes deployed in a variety of environments, we will better understand all its possibilities. X.500 has already known some successes, including the PARADISE directory with its widespread database, the substantial research and creative solutions developed by NADF, the development of LDAP, and the emergence of products with X.500-like directories. In addition, a variety of agreements are still being executed by industry groups. These agreements are essential to ensure interoperability and stabilize the standard. While the requirement for further rounds of agreement is frustrating

---

12. A WHOIS++ front end to X.500 has been implemented at the University of Adelaide in Australia.

to some, such activity may serve to ensure that X.500 will take its place as a central player in the worldwide global e-mail infrastructure.

Furthermore, X.500 can still succeed in becoming the global directory it was intended to be if certain trends continue to manifest themselves. Such trends include the pursuit of current carrier efforts to establish a global directory infrastructure, the development of applications to use the existing and imminent infrastructure, and the evolution of local messaging systems either to become X.500 or X.500-like with the capability of easily interworking with the global infrastructure.

While the WHOIS++ initiative has had a late start (vis-a-vis X.500), it may yet make rapid inroads in the Internet world. It poses the intriguing possibility of serving as the Internet solution to a standardized directory while also fitting into the worldwide, X.500-based infrastructure. The fact that the IETF and others are investigating solutions to directory coexistence provides hope that there is impetus for a lasting, if hybrid, worldwide solution.

KEY POINTS

- E-mail directory needs are many and diverse. Many other computer applications also need integrated enterprise directories. Most needs can be satisfied through the use of high performance local directories, global X.500 directories, and directory synchronization technologies.

- Directory synchronization techniques are important in today's directory environment for integrating directory information between incompatible local e-mail systems, so that all users can address mail to all other users in an enterprise.

- The international X.500 1988 and 1993 directory services standards define Directory User Agents (DUAs), or client entities, and Directory System Agents (DSAs), or server components. The 1993 X.500 standards add support for replication and access control.

- The X.500 information model is designed for a directory that is global in scope. The hierarchically organized international directory information tree (DIT) is general enough to include all countries, organizations, and locations. X.500's information structure is sufficiently open ended to define new information for many different purposes.

- X.500 also provides the standard lookup and update operations and Certificate storage for secure applications.

- Directories are likely to evolve towards an OSF Paradigm, where high performance, X.500-like products serve local applications, and X.500 global directories attempt to link the world's directory information into a logical whole.

- WHOIS++ may become an important directory standard, coexisting with X.500 in the Internet environment.

C H A P T E R   9

Electronic Commerce and Messaging

Enterprises are coming to the realization that their disparate processes for doing business have resulted in the duplication of business information systems and an inundation of work. They are also realizing that computers should be engaged to do what they do best—process routine information 24 hours a day—thus freeing people to do what they do best—deal with exceptions and make critical decisions. The convergence of advances in electronic technology with these realizations has created a trend, still in its early stages, toward integrating office technologies under the umbrella of electronic commerce.

We use the term "electronic commerce" to describe multiple technologies. As illustrated in Fig. 9.1, electronic commerce is broader than messaging, and messaging is broader than electronic commerce.

Although some electronic commerce applications require real-time response from the network and are more suited to transaction processing, others are quite

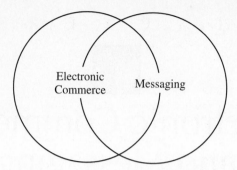

Figure 9.1   Electronic commerce and
messaging.

amenable to store-and-forward processing. Once primarily thought of as a mechanism for interpersonal messaging, e-mail is now recognized as a bearer service for
electronic commerce applications. Electronic commerce applications that are candidates for message-based solutions fall into two main categories:

- **Public commerce:** Via EDI, e-mail, and other technologies, separate enterprises can engage in electronic trading.
- **Private commerce:** Through e-mail, mail-enabled applications, or workflow, enterprises can automate their internal workflow technologies and enhance group communication.[1]

Many message-based private and public commerce applications[2] are at the
forefront of the e-mail frontier and are beginning to make an impact in the marketplace. They have the potential to revolutionize the workplace if coherent standards
in key areas such as EDI communications, security, and smart messaging can be
developed.

This chapter describes electronic commerce technologies and trends. In addition, it will suggest ways in which the global messaging infrastructures will be
used to support electronic commerce in the near future and ways in which the
various electronic commerce technologies can be used together to revolutionize
the workings of the modern office. Our coverage of different topics ranges from
nuts and bolts to the visionary—a necessary variance given the different stages at
which we find electronic commerce/messaging technologies. In particular, EDI
formats are well established and can be described in terms of concrete examples,
and mail-enabled applications are proliferating rapidly. But the workflow market
is still quite fluid, and both smart messaging and electronic document authorization technologies remain at the proverbial bleeding edge.

---

1. In 1994, these public/private commerce boundaries began to blur. AT&T introduced a
public Lotus Notes server for "virtual private workflow" usage.

2. The use of the terms "private commerce" and "public commerce" was suggested to us in
[WHIT94], the General Magic Telescript White Paper.

9.1   PROCESS REENGINEERING AND WORKFLOW AUTOMATION: REVOLUTIONIZING THE WAY WE WORK

Before beginning our coverage of electronic commerce messaging technologies, we must clarify the relationship between electronic commerce technologies and process reengineering. This clarification is important because, in many cases, neither reengineering nor technology upgrading should take place independently of one another.

A business person would define reengineering as the ability to take a business process that has some degree of irrationality to it and rationalize it [MCCR93]. In essence, this means formalizing process knowledge and rules in order to eliminate errors and omissions and to increase the speed and throughput of processes. A technologist would define electronic commerce technologies as ways of formalizing and computerizing the business process. Workflow automation can involve electronic routing of forms and other business documents through a sequence of users in order to complete a business task. It embraces such functionality as e-mail, database access, computer conferencing, and modeling tools.

Through process reengineering and workflow automation, we are told that Bell Atlantic reduced the time it takes to install a new circuit from two weeks to three hours; Ford trimmed its accounts receivable process by 80 percent; and IBM absorbed a 100-fold increase in transactions without adding a single new employee [HAMM93]. As shown in Fig. 9.2, process reengineering and workflow automation can be pursued independently or simultaneously. If technology changes but business models remain the same, *downsizing* results, whereas if business application models change but technology remains the same, *reengineering* results.

Automating a bad process only perpetuates the problem which the automation was intended to solve. Changing a business application while employing yesterday's model is still not enough. Only if both technology and business application models change can users obtain the double win—a true breakthrough. The payback potential lies in rationalizing the process and then enabling applications to perform certain filtering and triage on messages, forms, and documents in order to free humans to deal with complex issues and decisions. Today's enterprises have no alternative but to engage in process reengineering and electronic commerce. The need for a high performance business team moving with maximum speed, efficiency, and flexibility is paramount to the virtual enterprises of the Information Age.

The relationship between risk and return is clearly evident here: The reengineering and electronic commerce enabling of the production environment (loan applications, insurance claims, mortgage processing, and other complex applications using databases) might yield the greatest return but incur the greatest risk. Alternatively, administrative tasks (expense reports, sales proposals, purchase requests) carry the least return but suggest the most fertile area to provide a testing ground for workflow, both because of the minimal risk and

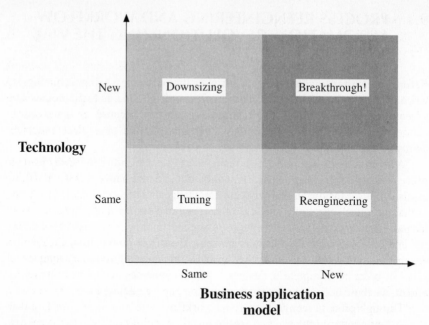

Figure 9.2   Changes in technology and business models—the double win.

because of the opportunity to use the e-mail infrastructure for these highly distributed processes [MCCR93]. However, an organization intending to use workflow or EDI should begin by determining which applications will yield a strategic advantage in terms of increasing the number of customers, of providing better service to current customers, and of engendering a technological lead over competitors.[3]

9.1.1   Top-Down and Bottom-Up Approaches

It has been suggested that there are basically two contrasting alternatives to automating business processes [SPIES93].[4] One approach can be characterized as top-down (which can also be referred to as burn-and-replace), whereby the business

---

3. Some processes that lend themselves to workflow automation, such as purchase approval and travel reimbursement, are perceived as slow and cumbersome in their present manual mode. Ad hoc processes, such as planning, coding, design, and marketing, are more difficult to automate, although they are still appropriate for knowledge sharing.

4. The authors are grateful to Michael Spies, Vice President of Marketing, Reach Software Corporation, for the ideas in this section, many of which were derived from "Business Process Automation: Automation and Evolution vs. 'Re-Engineering'" presented at the Electronic Mail Association Conference of June 1993.

undertakes to reengineer its processes completely in order to meet such requirements as speed, efficiency, and the reduction of errors. This approach requires that the entire suite of processes be reengineered before workflow automation and EDI are installed so that automation becomes the tool to implement, rather than the driver of change. The second alternative, which can be characterized as bottom-up (also referred to as automate-and-evolve) provides for installing an automated electronic commerce infrastructure based on messaging and database access as well as applications that use these services, and then evolving business processes to fit the installed infrastructure.

The *top-down approach* must begin with an analysis to determine the cycle time of subprocesses and of an overall process as measured against a desired cycle time, which becomes the overall objective. For example, a process could involve the authorization of a purchase order (PO) and consist of subprocesses beginning with the submission of a requisition form; proceeding to the checking of databases for parts numbers and costs, the conversion of the requisition into a purchase order, and the requisite approvals; and culminating in the shipping of the PO to the trading partner. The goal could be to reduce the time required for the entire process from one week to one day. The analysis requires understanding the role that current computing and communications capabilities should continue to play in the process. This analytical approach also requires agreements among those most affected by the processes in terms of their respective roles, authorities, and responsibilities.

The *bottom-up approach* calls for automating an existing process, observing the results, and then refining the given process based on the observed results. One could start with the automation of budget updates to reflect a purchase, with the acquisition of the appropriate circulation list to launch the PO approval process, with the automatic circulation of purchasing requisitions for multiple authorizations using a forms program, or with the automatic updating of an inventory database to reflect a received purchase. This more discrete approach results in an evolutionary change characterized by an initial analysis and mapping of existing processes, by the building and implementation of various workflow applications (using rapid development tools such as compilers, routing definers, and role tables), by integrating new processes with legacy systems that may exist in isolation, by auditing and recording the performance (tracking messages and database queries), and by improving the process as a result of the reports received. The bottom-up approach also suggests that candidate processes can be divided into and analyzed in three categories: those that exist but are not yet automated (candidates for automation), those new processes that may be automated (candidates for engineering), and those processes that are not working properly and may be ripe for change as well as automation (candidates for reengineering).

With either the bottom-up or top-down approach, it is essential that users work in conjunction with systems professionals to define the current processes and reengineer them. Workflow experts urge that participants in the design process include those who understand business processes as well as those who understand the application of technology. Furthermore, the human factor must be considered by creating role-based process automation to achieve maximum flexibility. For example, processes should be described in terms of roles such as requester, approver, and purchasing agent, and these roles would be mapped through the network directory.

9.2   A UNIFYING SCENARIO FOR ELECTRONIC COMMERCE

When electronic commerce technologies and process reengineering are combined in a synergistic manner, breakthroughs result. This section introduces a unifying scenario to demonstrate the potential of electronic commerce. This scenario embodies a Purchasing Application. It involves automated trading through EDI and automated processing using an Epicurean blend of e-mail, workflow, mail-enabled applications, electronic forms, business applications, databases, and spreadsheet technologies. This hypothetical scenario, which could only be achieved after a substantial reengineering effort and technology insertion, will be a centerpiece for the rest of the chapter.

It begins with an employee filling out a Purchase Request form for redesigned engine parts and sending it to a Purchasing Application. The Purchasing Application automatically extracts the relevant corporate budget information from online spreadsheet databases and attaches it to a Purchase Approval form. It consults a Purchasing database—joining the identity of the requester with the type of product being purchased and the dollar amount of the request—to obtain a circulation list of managers who must approve the request. It also fills in blank fields on the form using such values as part numbers generated from the database. It then manages the circulation of the messages, requesting approvals from those in the authorization chain.

Once all the requisite approvals have been obtained, the Purchasing Application notifies the requester and generates an EDI purchase order (PO), which is dispatched via a public messaging network to the appropriate engineering vendor. On receiving the PO, the supplier ships the item and sends messages containing an EDI shipping notice and an EDI invoice. The Purchasing Application then closes the internal loop on the PO by notifying the requester and updating the departmental budget and purchasing databases. Again via EDI, the Purchasing Applications (or other business systems) request electronic payment for the item. At any point along the process, interpersonal messages could be sent between employees to resolve exceptions.

Figure 9.3 diagrams the process described. (In the interest of space we stopped the event numbering before the electronic payment and did not consider the interaction that must have taken place between the Purchasing Application, Accounts Payables, and other business systems.)

In this scenario (hereafter referred to as the Purchasing Application scenario), mail-enabled applications, workflow, and EDI are combined to enable

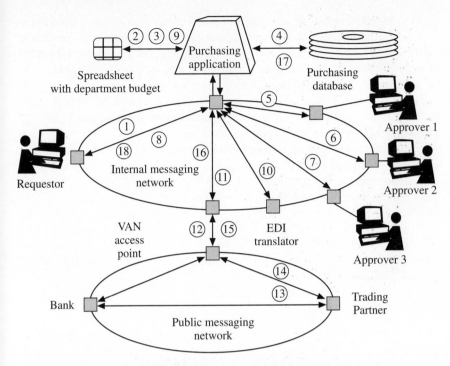

Electronic Purchase Order Scenario
1. Requester submits Requisition form to Purchasing Application
2. Purchasing Application checks departmental budget (spreadsheet)
3. Purchasing Application updates departmental budget to reflect Pending Purchase
4. Purchasing Application obtains Circulation List from Purchasing database
5. Purchasing Application submits approval form with attached Requisition form to Approver 1
6. Purchasing Application submits Approval form with attached Requisition and (optional) approver comment forms to Approver 2
7. Purchasing Application submits Approval form with attached Requisition and (optional) approver comment forms to Approver 3
8. Purchasing Application notifies Requester of approvals
9. Purchasing Application posts Open Purchase Requisition on spreadsheet and database
10. Purchasing Application requests EDI Purchase Order translation
11. Purchasing Application sends message to EDI gateway
12. EDI gateway forwards message to VAN over X.400, X.435, or other available protocols
13. VAN forwards message to trading partner
14. Trading partner sends Shipping Notice and Invoice
15. VAN forwards message to EDI gateway
16. EDI gateway forwards message to Purchasing Application
17. Purchasing Application updates spreadsheet and purchasing database with Closed Purchase
18. Purchasing Application notifies the requester of fulfillment

Figure 9.3   Electronic commerce Purchase Order scenario with routing and approval.

the development, approval, and expediting of a corporate purchase. Both internal and external processes are fully automated. The requester can launch the entire suite of processes from one workstation, and the requester need not be directly involved in the process of acquiring approvals, processing paper work, or sending out the PO. The document is never rekeyed, which significantly reduces the chances for introducing errors. The time required for overall order fulfillment is reduced by the electronic transfer from buyer to seller, and the possibility of lost orders is minimized.

The opportunities for reinventing business processes suggested by this scenario challenge our imaginations. This approach is a far cry from the costly and time-consuming manual alternative with its requirement for numerous information load-bearing middle managers, its opportunities for loss and error, and the consequent costs of such interventions and errors. These applications are true information management solutions that allow companies to link their departments and trading communities electronically, improving productivity and customer satisfaction. Also, when multiplied by the number of transactions throughout our economy, these processes will have saved significant time and human energy, savings which must result in significant financial economies. (Ecologically, large numbers of trees will also have been saved from the paper mill.)

9.3   ELECTRONIC DATA INTERCHANGE

EDI is currently the most technically evolved element in our Purchasing Application scenario. Indeed, the economic attraction of EDI and the accompanying vision of a paperless enterprise have made it an attractive complement to electronic mail and mail-enabled applications. EDI and its financial counterpart Electronic Funds Transfer (EFT) reduce the costs of doing business for trading partners by ensuring the timely flow of proper parts or the more rapid payment of bills. EDI increases the efficiency of interenterprise commerce and decreases the number of times documents are processed by human beings. It also can improve internal operating procedures such as inventory control and shipment scheduling. Lastly, EDI can result in the creation of strong trading partner relationships. EDI transfers that were traditionally handled as batch data transfers (and thus do not require real-time, transaction processing response time) are suitable for conveyance over a messaging network.

EDI enables the exchange of routine business transactions between trading partners, in a computer-processable format. The EDIFACT and X12 standards define the structured data formats used to communicate data between such traditional EDI applications.

While the EDI data formats are widely supported and provide a stable basis for continued growth and enhancement, the arena of EDI communications (and security) is evolving rapidly. EDI communications protocols, including *conventional EDI communications* (typically using VANs in a nonmessaging fashion) and *store-and-forward EDI communications* (such as EDI over X.400, or X.435, and EDI over MIME), are discussed later along with trading partner agreements and security issues.

9.3.1 EDIFACT and X12

EDI is a set of data definitions or formats that permit business forms to be exchanged electronically, rather than by using paper as in the past. EDI format standards enable disparate systems to translate and understand the exchanged documents. They have evolved to enable the translation from internal to external formats and vice versa. [TRUS93] lists common business functions that have been standardized in such computer-processable transactions as invoices, purchase orders, health care and disability insurance claims, requests for student educational records, economic census reports, tax returns, warranty registrations, shipment information (air, rail, ship) automotive inspections, warehouse orders, and contract proposals.

There are two primary standards for EDI formats: The American National Standards Institute's X12 and the United Nations' Electronic Data Interchange for Administration, Commerce, and Trade (EDIFACT). (A third, less-used standard was developed by the United Nations and dubbed UN/TDI.) X12 dominates in the U.S. and EDIFACT dominates outside the U.S. U.S. companies that interact with overseas companies must translate between the two formats, but they are similar enough that some EDI systems can accommodate both standards. Efforts are underway to merge the two by 1997, with X12 being

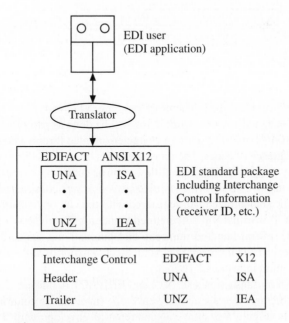

Figure 9.4 Two primary EDI interchange
packages: EDIFACT and X12.

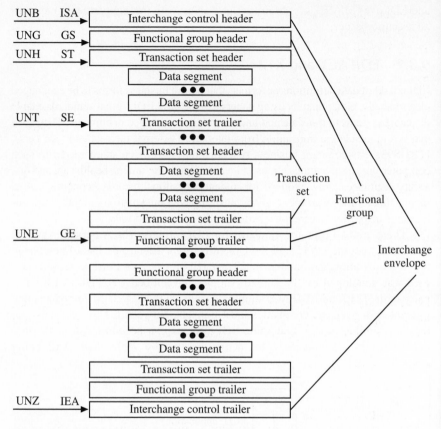

Figure 9.5   Elements of a complete interchange.

grandfathered into EDIFACT. Therefore ongoing X12 work items will be completed and closed, and any new work items will be done as part of EDIFACT.

Both EDIFACT and X12 define a character-oriented format where each interchange is a sequence of codes. The inner segments of an interchange contain data elements such as prices, dates, quantities, control numbers, and product codes. Generic or industry-unique forms called *transaction sets* constructed out of data elements can be standardized and registered with the UN organizations administering EDIFACT or with ANSI's Accredited Standards Committee (ASC) X12. As of early 1994, several hundred domestic and international standard transaction sets were approved and more are in development, a majority of them in the transportation and retail industries.[5]

In addition to transaction sets, X12 and EDIFACT define certain addressing and control structures that are actually envelope (interchange control header and trailer) formats. Figure 9.5 shows an interchange envelope with a header and

---

5. In 1987, there were only 16 X12 transaction sets. By 1991, there were 106 approved transaction sets and development projects for an additional 150.

trailer for transmission. The interchange envelope contains transaction sets including two that are contained in a *functional group* (a group of similar transaction sets such as purchase orders) bounded by a functional group header and trailer. Each of these transaction sets will be assigned a functional identifier code, which is the first data element of the header segment. Only those transaction sets with the same code are considered members of one functional group.

The information included in a transaction set is the same as that contained in a conventional printed document such as a purchase order or invoice. The function of each transaction set and its segments (its logically related data elements appearing in a defined sequence) is delineated in the standards. Figure 9.5 shows the UN. designations (UNB, UNG, UNE, UNZ, etc.) from EDIFACT and the equivalent X12 designations (ISA, GS, GE, etc.). These designations indicate the interchange envelope, functional group, and transaction set headers and trailers.

Figure 9.6 shows a typical paper Purchase Order, possibly the one generated by the requester of redesigned engine parts in the Purchasing Application scenario at the beginning of this chapter.

Figure 9.7 shows how this information is represented as a transaction set in EDI format. The information is divided into a header describing the detail to follow, the detailed information from the purchase order with the appropriate tag identifiers, and a summary area or trailer which totals the relevant Purchase Order information including the number of segments and prices [HAIS93].

** PURCHASE ORDER **

PO Number 3655167   Date 940617

** Buyer **	** Vendor **
MFG Company, Inc.	ABC Engines
Purchasing Dept.	2112 Comer Ln.
123 Wannapune	Harmony, VA 22222
St. Simone, MO 61616	Attn: CAD Eng.
Attn: A.J. Mittenmir	

Line No.	PO Qty	Unit of Measure	Purchaser Part No.	Vendor Part No.	Unit Price
1	100	EA	123	1234	290.50
		Special Assembly			
2	25		456	2568	100.00
		Complete Assembly			
3	5		789	7954	525.75
		Driver Mechanism			

Figure 9.6 Typical paper purchase order. *Larry J. Hastings, "EDI: A New Way of Doing Business." Reprinted with permission of St. Paul Software. Copyright © 1993.*

```
GS*PO*612410984*313434666*870617*1232*00223*X*002002
ST*850*000123
```

BEG*00*SA*3655167*00*00*870617*12341234*AC

N1*BY*MFG COMPANY INC.

N2*PURCHASING   *Header area*

N3*123Wannapune

N4*St. Simone*MO*61616

PER*BD*A.J. Mittenmir*TE*(813)444-3333

N1*SF*ABC ENGINES

N2*2112 Comer Ln.

Harmony*VA*22222

PO1*1*100.00*EA*290.50*CA*PI*123*VP*1234
PID*F****SPECIAL ASSEMBLY   *Detail area*

CTT*3*130

SE*28*00123   *Trailer area*

GE*1*00223

Figure 9.7   Primary components of an EDI Purchase Order transaction set. Larry
J. Hastings, "EDI: A New Way of Doing Business." Reprinted with
permission of St. Paul Software. Copyright © 1993.

The BEG data segment in Fig. 9.7 is highlighted to illustrate a typical
segment's content and structure. The segment identifier is "BEG" (for begin).
Both BEG and the remaining elements are defined in ANSI EDI documentation.
The other tags in this segment are as follows:

00:	Transaction Purpose
	00-Original
	06-Confirmation
SA:	Purchase Order Type
36551671:	PO Number
01:	Release Number
00:	Change Order Sequence
870617:	Purchase Order Date
1234:	Request Reference Number
1234:	Contract Number
AC:	Acknowledgment Type

Note that the header information serves as a lead into the detail that follows, and this information tracks in a fairly straightforward manner with the information on the paper Purchase Order. Also note that the information in the detail area may be represented in thousands of lines depending on the number and complexity of the items to be purchased [HAIS93].

Illustrated earlier in Fig. 9.5, all of these data segments are placed inside transaction sets, which are in turn grouped by function. The functional groups are then placed inside an interchange envelope in order to be conveyed in communications packets.

9.3.2 EDI Communications

EDI communications address the means of enveloping and transmitting EDI data. Closely related issues include the security of the interchange, the establishment of trading partner agreements, and the discovery of trading partner profile information. While the situation for EDI communications was much improved by the growth of an EDI VAN infrastructure during the 1980s, much progress is still needed and continued efforts are underway, including enhancements to conventional EDI communications themselves and the development of standards for carrying EDI data over store-and-forward messaging networks.

Conventional EDI Communications

Most EDI connections currently employ conventional EDI communications techniques (characterized earlier as dial, dump, and pray arrangements between trading partners). Therefore the sending network accumulates transactions for trading partners located on a second network. Then, at a scheduled time, the network dials out to a mailbox on the other network and dumps the transactions as messages which are subsequently distributed. Such interconnections are known to lack sufficient audit trails and result in finger pointing when problems occur on interconnected data links.

X12 has actually defined specifications for the use of common de facto standard link protocols. IBM Remote Job Entry (RJE) and 2780/3780 binary synchronous are the most common link protocols used in today's EDI environment. However, available value-added network services vary widely in terms of communications protocols, line speeds, reporting (audit) capabilities, data-handling charges, and data storage. X12 also supports EDI-level acknowledgment transaction sets, some operating at the syntax level (indicating that a transaction was successfully translated) and others at the application level (indicating that an EDI application has reviewed and accepted the transaction).

In 1991, ANSI also defined the Interconnect Mailbag standard, which delineates procedures for the exchange of EDI transactions between EDI VANs. This protocol is intended for batching EDI interchanges together, but it is not a true store-and-forward solution and it does not provide for multimedia integrated messaging, security, or basic needs such as receipt notifications, message tracing, and other features. At the time of its development, it was seen primarily as an interim solution to improve conventional EDI communications until the X.435 standard was in widespread use. As of early 1994, the major VAN carriers are supporting Mailbag and only just beginning to put X.435 EDI into place.

X12 communications-related developments have not stopped with Mailbag. Additional work is underway within X12 to support the conveyance of binary attachments in standard interchanges and the crossreferencing of linkages between documents attached to interchanges, as well as for integrity, authentication, and confidentiality security mechanisms [X1258] within interchanges, functional groups, or transaction sets. Security capabilities have also been developed within EDIFACT.

Many of the X12 security and other enhancements are similar to functions originally defined in the X.435 standard for carrying EDI over X.400. Implementing communications and security capabilities at the EDI data format level has the advantage of guaranteeing that they will be available to trading partners regardless of the underlying communications protocol. However, these conventional EDI communications enhancements arrive with the disadvantage of introducing a plethora of options that could make comprehensive EDI communications solutions difficult to implement. Such enhancements could delay the convergence of EDI and messaging, curtail the anticipated increase in EDI volume, and deny users their long-awaited price reductions. Time will tell whether or not the EDI standards community has made a strategic error in continuing to emphasize conventional EDI communications solutions.

Store-and-Forward EDI Solutions

EDI data can potentially be carried by any messaging infrastructure. If an enterprise built an integrated messaging networking for electronic mail, it should determine how to leverage that resource to carry EDI traffic as well. Furthermore, since public messaging services have now established worldwide links using X.400 and Internet Mail, these same network providers will court EDI traffic, sometimes by offering valued-added EDI services and sometimes simply by leveraging their widespread connectivity.

EDI Trading Partner Agreements

Before EDI trading and communication can occur, however, trading partner agreements and preauthorizations must be in place. Having the technical basis for EDI and (possibly) secure communications services does not convey legal (as opposed to technical) proof that a particular transaction occurred. Preauthorization agreements are still required before business arrangements entered into through EDI can be regarded as binding, and the requirement for these agreements has served as a barrier to EDI deployment on a wider scale. Today these agreements are maintained on paper forms and kept in long-term storage. Moreover, when many parties have bilateral agreements, the paper and time burden is greatly multiplied.

In the future, however, agreement information could be transferred electronically or stored in global directories. [ANSI93], a Certification Management standard for financial applications from ANSI's X9 committees, argues that the need for bilateral agreements could be greatly reduced if parties wishing to trade electronically could set up an agreement with a Certification Authority. Multilateral agreements through CAs would essentially create the infrastructure for *electronic trading communities*. Trading partners could then enter into bilateral agreements semi-automatically.

Suppose that two organizations wish to conduct electronic commerce. Both have registered Certificates with a Commercial CA and have signed a generic trading partner agreement, which—among other things—acknowledges the efficacy of selected EDI practices, digital signatures, certificates, and other cryptographic instruments. The responsible officer at Organization A can then contact his or her authorized counterpart at Organization B. The two organizations agree to trade and arrange for attribute certificates to be created. The attribute certificates are data structures that have been digitally signed by Organization A's Organizational Authority and Organization B's Organizational Authority, respectively.[6] They convey authorizations, such as the ability for Organization A to exchange EDI Purchase Orders, Invoices, or Remittances with Organization B. At the time of communication, the X.509 Certificates authenticate the parties to one another, and the attribute certificates authenticate their agreement.

The X9.30 Certificate Management standard defines draft specifications for attribute certificates. The document's authors believe that attribute certificates will become the basis for electronic commerce in the financial world, for the U.S. Government, and possibly for the European Commission. However, the draft also acknowledges that "to ensure interoperability and security, rules procedures and the functions of the parties and CAs must be agreed upon and worked out."

Attempts to confer greater legitimacy on electronic security mechanisms (such as digital signatures) are simultaneously underway in the legal and legislative communities. Indeed, the EDI development of mechanisms for security and mutual trust will prove essential to other applications as well. Note that attribute certificate functionality might be used even more broadly than for EDI. It could enable a broad range of services that today are only possible via subscriptions and bilateral agreement. For example, a user could conceivably publish a file for billed FTP retrieval on the Internet.

EDI Naming and Addressing

In order to communicate, EDI trading partners must also know one another's EDI address or identifier. Conventional EDI systems utilize simple alphanumeric strings, such as Dun & Bradstreet numbers. Since many EDI systems utilize even older styles of identifiers, some VANs will map identifiers to different values between trading partners.

---

6. Organizational Authorities are akin to Certification Authorities. Attribute Certificates can be stored in trading partner profiles (local directories) or, once available, in the global X.500 directory.

9.3.3   X.435—EDI over X.400

Early attempts at running EDI over 1984 X.400 essentially involved disguising the character-oriented EDIFACT or X12 interchange document as an e-mail message and sending it to a special mailbox monitored by a mail-enabled EDI application. Two approaches were used: (1) enclosing the EDI message in a P2 (X.400 IPM) content type; or (2) sending the EDI message as a special content type (defined at the OIW) known as P0.

To further standardize the method of carrying EDI over X.400 and to add more advanced features tailored specifically for EDI, the ITU began creating the X.435 recommendations in 1988. These recommendations were completed in 1990 under the first-ever use of the ITU's fast-track mechanism.

The ITU's F.435 (service) [EDI90] and X.435 (protocol) [EDI91] recommendations contain specifications for the use of X.400 transport and secure messaging services as well as X.500 Directory Services on behalf of an EDI User Agent (EDI UAs tailored to assist an EDI user in EDI messaging). Tailored Message Stores and Access Units may also be used (although there are no standards for how an EDI message should be translated into paper media).

Figure 9.8 shows the flow of information between EDI users and the X.400 Message Transfer System. These users are EDI applications that submit one of the recognized EDI standard packages to the EDI UA. The EDI UA then places the EDI heading and EDI package in a submit envelope for submission to the MTS. It maps the receiver ID in the EDI header into an X.400 O/R Name, and it forms the requisite content for submission to the MTS. Upon receipt of the content from the MTS or Message Store, the receiving EDI UA extracts the EDI package for delivery to the EDI application.

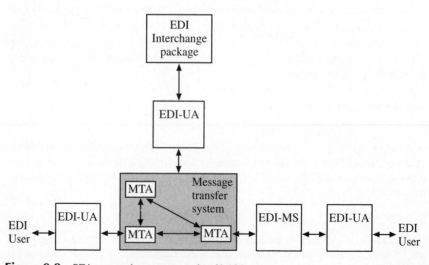

Figure 9.8   EDI messaging system using X.400.

EDI User Agents (EDI UAs) create messages containing content encoded in the P_{edi} (formerly known as P35) format shown in Fig. 9.9. An EDI/X.400 message consists of an MTS Envelope and P_{edi} Content. The first body part of the content is the EDIFACT Interchange. (P_{edi} supports ANSI's X12 as well, but leans toward EDIFACT in its terminology.) Selected fields of the interchange map into the P_{edi} Heading. The entire interchange, including the selected fields, is placed in the primary body part. While it may seem redundant to carry the same information in two places, the standards developers wanted to keep the interchange intact and in established EDI formats rather than in X.400's complex Abstract Syntax Notation One encoding. This approach also obviates the need for the EDI UA to construct an EDI interchange. Additional body parts in the message may consist of supporting documents, drawings, or interpersonal notes.

Thus the P_{edi} content type can be submitted by the EDI UA to the MTS in the same way that an Interpersonal Messaging UA submits messages. The receiving EDI UA decodes the P_{edi} content and makes it available to its user, which is a computer application. The Message Store supports P_{edi} in the same way that an IPMS P2 message is supported. It allows the user to search for particular P_{edi} fields to determine which messages to retrieve.

In large organizations, receiving EDI messages at a central EDI UA where such functions as logging and auditing on all EDI traffic can be performed may be desirable. Or a VAN-based EDI UA might perform value-added functions on the EDI content of a message before forwarding it to a recipient. The message is then relayed to the destination EDI UA for presentation to the EDI application. Should

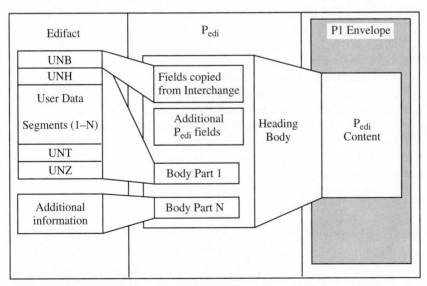

Figure 9.9 P_{edi} format. *Copyright CCITT Recommendation F.435 "Message handling: electronic data interchange messaging system" (03/91), Figure 6 "EDI message structure for typical EDI transaction."*

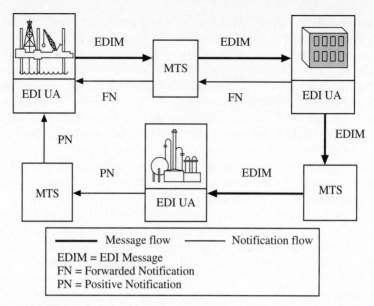

Figure 9.10   X.435 EDI notifications.

such relaying occur, X.435 introduces a concept of *responsibility,* which helps distinguish between an EDI UA responsible for that message or one receiving an informational copy.

To implement the responsibility concept, X.435 specifies its own EDI notification feature. (This is in addition to X.400 Delivery Reports, which can be used but do not convey responsibility semantics.) The originator of an EDI Message can request an EDI notification from the Recipient EDI UA entity. The Recipient EDI UA will return a *positive* notification indicating that the message was received and accepted, a *negative* notification that responsibility is rejected, or a notification that responsibility has been *forwarded.*[7] If the originator receives a forwarded notification, it may subsequently receive a positive or negative notification from the new recipient. Figure 9.10 illustrates this process.

If an EDI entity rejects responsibility, it must thereafter ignore the message. Also, if it has modified the message content, it must accept responsibility prior to forwarding the message.

X.435 Security

X.435 uses a mix of X.435-defined and pre-existing X.400 security mechanisms. The new X.435 security services added at the P_{edi} protocol level are called Proof

---

7. Acceptance of an EDI Message occurs at the X.435 level. The interchange could still be rejected later by an EDI translator or an EDI application. X12 or EDIFACT-level acknowledgments can be used in such cases. The EDI UA handles X12 or EDIFACT-level acknowledgments like any other interchange.

(or nonrepudiation) of Content and Proof (or nonrepudiation) of Notification. Also, some or all of the EDI body parts may be encrypted using the existing X.400 Content Confidentiality service, and X.435 can make use of X.400's nonrepudiation of delivery and nonrepudiation of submission services.

There are limits to the security that can be provided. In particular, X.400 does not provide for Proof of Retrieval from a Message Store or for Proof of Transfer between MTAs. Nor does it offer Proof of Nondelivery. Thus, EDI applications must put some degree of trust (although not total trust) in the underlying MTS.

X.435 and the Use of X.500

Subject to access control, EDI applications must be able to read, search, or modify information in messaging directories in order to obtain addressing or capabilities information about trading partners. More advanced usages, such as obtaining information about pre-authorization agreements, terms of contract, and translator capabilities may be considered in the future.

X.435 defines two X.500 object classes: the *EDI User* and the *EDI User Agent*. The EDI user will contain the edi-name and edi-capabilities attributes (also created for X.435). The EDI User Agent will contain only the edi-capabilities. The *edi-name* is an alphanumeric string. The *edi-capabilities* attribute is a complex field that indicates whether the user supports EDIFACT, X12, or UN/TDI, and also the Standard Version Number, Standard Syntax Identifier, Document Type, Document Version, Document Release, Controlling Agency, and Agency Assigned Code.

The X.500 Alias can be used to create multiple views of the Directory so that entries engaged in EDI Messaging may be accessed both by EDI applications using the conventional alphanumeric EDI identifier style of naming and by X.435 applications expecting the usual hierarchical X.500 information layout.

9.3.4 EDI over MIME

Whereas X.435 defines a number of security and notification options for an "industrial strength" EDI messaging capability, an early 1994 Internet Draft [CROC93A] written by Dave Crocker of Silicon Graphics takes a much simpler approach. In a still earlier version of this draft, Crocker argued that the test that most users would apply to EDI messaging is a simple comparison with the features available today from the post office. (However, later the statement is made that adding security to MIME is one of the most critical enhancements remaining to Internet Mail.)

Crocker builds a pre-standard for EDI over MIME by defining Application/ EDI-X12, Application/EDIFACT, and Application/EDI-consent (for all other EDI standards) body parts. Each body part can carry an EDI interchange with one optional parameter indicating the character set used. (This machinery is significantly simplified over that provided in an earlier version of the Internet Draft by Crocker.)

The author's initial motivation appears to be to position Internet Mail as a vehicle for EDI communications, particularly EDI that is more of the bulk mail variety than of the high-end, high-value electronic commerce variety (see the discussion in Chapter 4, Section 4.2.2). However, should Internet Mail delivery status notification and MIME-PEM secure messaging definition efforts (discussed in Chapter 7) be successfully completed, a case could someday be made for employing industrial strength MIME/EDI even for high-end or high-value electronic commerce.

9.3.5 A Case Study

The EDI case study illustrated in Fig. 9.11 shows the interface between an application and a translator and then between the translator and a messaging network.[8] St. Paul Software has developed an EDI translator called SPEDI*TRAN (pronounced "speedy tran"), which receives the EDI-bound file from an application and prepares the EDI transaction to be forwarded by a communications facility. (This illustration can be considered generic in that other vendors use a similar approach.)

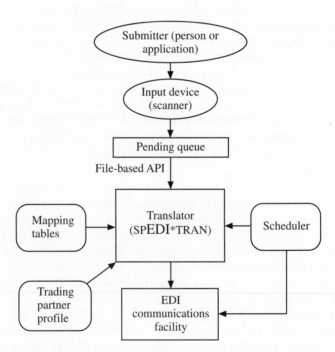

Figure 9.11   EDI message preparation through SPEDI*TRAN translator.

---

8. We are grateful to Larry Haisting, Director of Sales, St. Paul Software, for his assistance in preparing this case study.

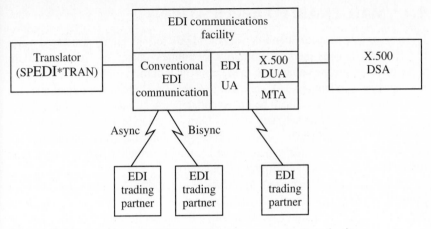

Figure 9.12 Interface of SPEDI*TRAN and communications facility.

In this example, the file is entered in a pre-existing state from an application via fax or optical scanner. In our Purchase Order scenario (Step 10), the file would have entered as an e-mail message.

In Fig. 9.11, the SPEDI*TRAN translator receives files from applications and maps their native format into an EDI format for forwarding. The sequence of events occurs as follows:

1. The data structure is mapped (broken out and reformatted) into EDI format (EDIFACT or X12).[9]

2. The data is parsed to the appropriate syntax (correct number of characters and data type).

3. The resulting data is then packaged in transaction set, functional group, and interchange envelopes as shown earlier in Fig. 9.5.

4. The result is then passed to the EDI communications facility via a script program.

Figure 9.12 shows the interface between SPEDI*TRAN and the communications facility.

The communications facility could be a multiprotocol EDI switch with the ability to send data via asynchronous, bisynchronous, or X.400. The latter could be via the X.400 P0 or P2 protocols or the mapping and protocol provided by an X.435-compliant EDI UA as shown in Fig. 9.9. Optionally, X.500 access could be used by the EDI UA and MTA for name resolution and other functions.

---

9. The mapping is done according to a mapping table. The major effort by users in implementing EDI involves creating the mapping tables that instruct the translation on the format of the application data structures. Computer-aided software engineering (CASE) tools are often used in this process.

9.4   MAIL-ENABLED APPLICATIONS

It is now time to turn our attention from the highly formal, highly structured world of EDI (a technology intended primarily for public commerce) to various and diverse forms of private commerce. In the remainder of this chapter, we will discuss mail-enabled applications and workflow technology. While these technologies are distinct from EDI, they can all be linked and they can all make use of the messaging infrastructure. They facilitate various forms of group interaction. Group interaction may be formalized in workflow processing. Informal group interaction may not strictly qualify as electronic commerce, but nevertheless plays an important role in increasing overall enterprise productivity.

Recall that the Purchasing Application scenario in Section 9.2 provides a prime illustration of linking mail-enabled application, workflow, and EDI. What began as an electronic Purchase Requisition from a mail-enabled application and was routed through a sophisticated workflow system, ultimately was transmitted out of the enterprise as an EDI Purchase Order.

In some sense EDI and workflow automation applications are mail-enabled applications. Many mail-enabling concepts and capabilities are not only intrinsically important and valuable in their own right, but are also vital stepping stones to powerful forms of workflow automation. This section will discuss various aspects of mail-enabled applications, including: linking mail-enabled applications to the infrastructure, electronic conferencing systems, and electronic forms.

9.4.1   Linking Mail-enabled Applications to the Infrastructure

Mail-enabled applications move data among users over messaging infrastructures. "Mail" is becoming a ubiquitous pulldown option from within an application, enabling users to send files or other objects to their correspondents with ease. Mail enabling is already employed in such well-known applications as group scheduling (calendaring), electronic forms processing, word processing, and electronic conferencing. Such popular uses only scratch the surface of mail enabling because powerful forms of automation can be achieved when intelligent distributed applications add store-and-forward messaging to their communications repertoire.

Mail-enabled applications generally communicate with mail systems in a manner virtually transparent to the user of the application. Thus a user might be working in the application (such as a word processor) when she determines the need to send the file contents in a mail message. She then clicks on the *Mail* option in the *File* menu, as shown in Fig. 9.13, and receives a dialog box that asks for the address of the recipient and for other pertinent information, such as the priority of the message and whether a receipt notice should be requested. This approach eliminates any unnatural transition between the user interface of the primary application and the user interface to the messaging network.

Various mail-enabling techniques are used in some UNIX and many DOS- or Microsoft Windows–based systems. Simple UNIX applications communicate with mail systems via shell scripts. More complex UNIX applications utilize oper-

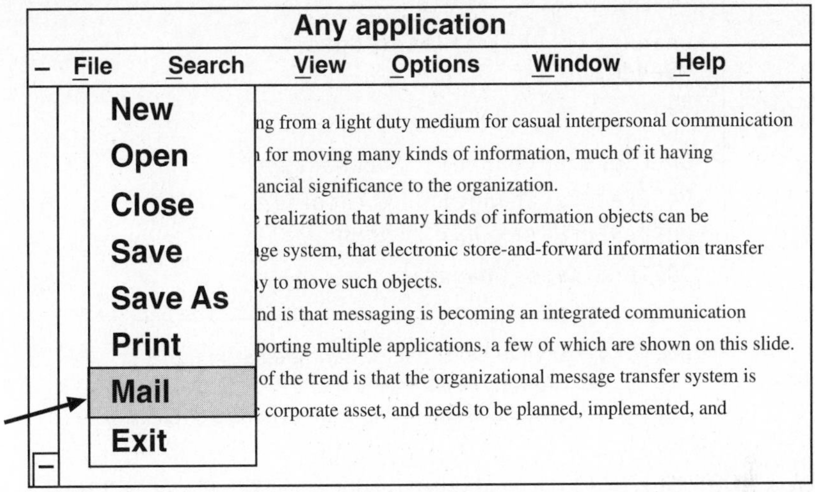

Figure 9.13   Mail-enabling from within an application.

ating systems sockets or streams facilities. In DOS or Windows environments, applications communicate with the mail system directly via the shared file system after the fashion of NetWare's Simple Message Format interface. Other DOS applications can exchange data with pop-up applications that run in a Terminate and Stay Resident (TSR) mode.

In Windows environments, mail-enabled applications also have the option of using a Microsoft intertask communication interface called Dynamic Data Exchange (DDE) or calling e-mail–related procedures in Dynamic Link Libraries (DLLs). The usual mechanism is via a *macro language* capability that ships with many Windows desktop applications. Application macro languages, such as Visual Basic or Word Basic, enable users or third party developers to extend the menus and commands of the application. The user or a vendor utilizes the macro facility to install a verb (mail or send) on one of the application's menus. When the user selects that option, the macro is invoked in order to send the current working document from within the application.

Interpreted or executed code is then invoked within the macro. In some cases, the macro will communicate directly with a messaging application that has been set up for DDE interaction. Figure 9.14 from [PCCO92] displays part of a macro called SendMail. This macro was written to enable Word Basic to send mail through Lotus Notes. Following a few commands to initialize the macro function and ensure that Notes is running, the main body of the macro appears.

The *DDEExecute* commands activate NotesMail's sending procedure. After NotesMail loads the file, a dialogue window appears prompting the user for message-addressing options.

In the Windows mail-enabling environment, another approach has the application's macro facility directly call globally accessible procedures available in Windows DLLs. These procedures can be provided by any vendor. Microsoft

```
Channel = DDEInitiate("Notes",
"SendMail")

If Channel > 0 Then

DDEExecute Channel, "NewMessage"

DDEExecute Channel, "AttachFile " + A$

DDEExecute Channel, "SEND"

DDETerminate Channel
```

Figure 9.14   Sample DDE macro. *Reprinted from PC/ COMPUTING, December 1992. Copyright © 1992, Ziff-Davis Publishing Company, L.P.*

offers MAPI.DLL and Lotus and other vendors already offer or will soon offer VIM-based or CMC-based DLLs.

9.4.2   Electronic Forms

Many mail-enabled applications are based on electronic forms. (Parts of the Purchase Order scenario described at the beginning of this chapter provide examples of the use of forms-based mail-enabled applications.) These range from simple text-based forms to elaborate graphical forms with input-edit capabilities, conditional logic, color, and sound.

Users can often develop custom electronic forms without necessarily having formal training in computer programming. Forms development environments often provide base templates that the designer can modify to fit an enterprise's unique application. They may also provide a richer forms development capability; for example, Microsoft's Electronic Forms Designer allows a user to define a form in Visual Basic.

Electronic forms may be manually inserted into or extracted from a message by a human user and loaded into or out of a forms application that is not integrated with the mail system. Alternatively, a forms distribution application may work directly with the mail system. It may have the ability to recognize that a form is embedded in a message and to extract it. Such applications are also typically able to import and export data to or from databases, spreadsheets, and text files.

Electronic forms products used with mail-enabled applications fall into two classes: those that are closely integrated with a local e-mail infrastructure, and those that are designed to be independent of the underlying e-mail system and can be used in an enterprise-wide environment. Which forms product to use can pose a difficult decision for users.

Forms products that are closely integrated with an e-mail product can offer many advanced features:

*   The mail-system user interface may display the form as an icon, enabling the user to launch the forms application.

- The mailbox may execute the form directly when the user reads a message. It may generate a form automatically when a user selects a special function, such as Take Phone Message. Sophisticated mail systems integrating forms in this way support some type of extensible forms registry system, so that the mail system can be configured to process a wide variety of user-defined forms.

- Smart foldering functionality may exhibit database-like features, enabling users to display different views of messages that contain forms—for example, to view by customer number, or to view by product type or any other form-embedded field.

- The mailbox rules engine may be able to read an incoming form and act on information in the form by (for example) forwarding the message, automatically filling in fields, alerting a user, or taking any number of automatic actions.

On the other hand, heavily integrated electronic forms functionality will only work in specific enclaves and not across a multivendor messaging network. Moreover, forms engines that have been developed by an e-mail vendor may not work at all once sent out of that vendor's mail system—or, at best, they might be converted into a text format by a gateway.

Ideally, the structure of forms should be agreed on by the widest number of users possible, again underscoring the attractiveness of standardization. With standardized forms, registries will become much easier to build, manage, and update. The MHS Alliance has undertaken to address electronic forms standardization.

9.4.3 Electronic Conferencing and Bulletin Boards

Another type of mail-enabled application, electronic conferencing and bulletin boards, employs techniques developed from a combination of document database and e-mail applications. Public mail systems (SprintMail) and host-based systems (EMC²/TAO for IBM mainframes) support such conferencing. Lotus Notes offers an advanced private knowledge-sharing solution with bulletin board capabilities. Many local messaging systems offer some type of shared folder or bulletin board functionality.

A variation on electronic conferencing is content-based dissemination where messages are routed to users based on interest profiles. Similar systems have been used for a number of years by U.S. intelligence agencies, and NewsEDGE from Desktop Data is an example of a recently available commercial system. Such an approach provides for filtering documents for dissemination to those users who meet pre-established profiles. Content-based dissemination can be combined with bulletin boards to achieve higher degrees of flexibility.

The USENET, the largest electronic news group/bulletin board system in the world today, employs content-based dissemination across the vast distributed Internet environment. [KROL92] describes USENET as a bulletin board system made up of seven major news categories (or *parents*) including *comp* (computer science), *news* (regarding the news network and news software with files providing information for new users), *rec* (recreation and the arts), *sci* (scientific research and applications), *soc* (social and political issues), *talk* (providing forums for debate on controversial topics), and *misc* (a catch-all for those things that don't fit in the other categories). A number of alternative news groups are also considered part of USENET, such as the *bionet* groups of interest to biologists and *gnu* which sponsors discussions relating to the Free Software Foundation. Several commercial information services are also available (including Clarinet, which provides United Press International articles and syndicated columns indexed for the news system). Altogether, there are over 1500 news groups.

The actual USENET news is usually organized hierarchically with the parents followed by subgroupings. The groups can be accessed with a notation that involves using a period to separate the parent and subgroupings. Thus, "rec.music.folk" would lead the user to a discussion of folk music via the parent heading "recreation," followed by its subgroup "music" and music's subgroup "folk" music.

However, the news groups available to a given user depend on what computer his or her news reader uses as a news server. That is, the news reader interrogates a news server to receive menus of articles and can receive the articles themselves upon request. USENET is essentially a set of voluntary rules for passing news and maintaining news groups including how to use, create, and delete groups. Server administrators make bilateral agreements with other administrators to transfer specific news groups over the Internet. An organization's server can thus set up its own local news groups according to what users require. In this way, a departmental server in an organization might provide employee announcements that it makes available to the other servers in the organization (but not to the outside world).

News servers communicate via an SMTP-like Network News Transfer Protocol (NNTP) defined in RFC 977. A news item is similar to an electronic mail message with a header that tells the news software how to send the item through the Internet and a body containing the message text. The header is also used to build an index on news servers and, in addition to the submitter and subject, includes a synopsis and keywords for indexing. Each item is part of a discussion *thread*, and follow-on postings in response to that item become part of the same thread and the resulting presentation grouping.

An interesting aspect of the USENET mail-enabled service is the way cultural attributes have sprouted with its usage. An ethic of courtesy and consideration has evolved regarding proper posting of articles and replying to postings, how to start a new discussion, how to maintain courtesy, and how to be selective in choosing groups and articles. A specific facility provides the e-mail address of each item's originator so that a reader might respond to that item privately (in effect, off-line) by e-mail. There is even a voluntary code called *rot13*, which is used to encrypt potentially offensive postings. Thus, USENET has served as a laboratory not only to test news distribution technology, but also to evolve a new sociology for how electronic bulletin boards and conferencing might work in our heavily mail-enabled (near) future.

9.5   WORKFLOW AUTOMATION AND THE MESSAGING DEVELOPMENT PLATFORM

White-collar assembly lines have existed for some time. One very elaborate system, which was recently still in use at Schiphol Airport in Amsterdam, involves the physical routing of paper in cylinders through pneumatic tubes that terminate at the white-collar worker's desktop. The French PTT offered a pneumatic tube mail system between post offices throughout Paris until the late 1970s. (Eugene Lee of Beyond, Inc., refers to such vacuum systems as Hoovernets.)[10] Such a system could be described as the plumbing that enables the transport of objects, provides almost unlimited bandwidth, is relatively secure, and uses existing forms. It lacks such niceties as directories, digital signatures, or other methods of authentication and still requires the rekeying of information. Thus, while the concept of a white-collar assembly line (or enterprise work process infrastructure) is not new, the automation tools available today to support such an infrastructure certainly are, and the very availability of these tools serves to suggest new, faster, and more efficient ways of doing business.

Like EDI, the workflow aspect of electronic commerce is broader than messaging. There has always been something of a paradigm disparity between the shared database approach and the store-and-forward approach to workflow.

The shared database approach is most effective when the updating of information can be done in a centralized fashion by a relatively small number of users. Shared database systems are often used in applications such as banking, where checks as scanned images become part of the records structure. When workflow applications become more diverse, involving loosely coupled, relatively unpredictable conjunctions of multiple users, multiple applications, and multiple databases, the use of messaging becomes critical.

Even database-oriented workflow systems can make good use of add-on messaging capabilities. E-mail can be used to request action from a user, to notify the user of database changes, and to transmit information to staff members who do not have access to the database. Workflow systems such as Lotus Notes are in fact hybrids between mail-enabled applications and shared database applications.

This section discusses workflow systems with messaging components. These systems can be based on any of several technical tools and approaches, including smart applications, where the intelligence is in the application and the messaging network provides simple transport; smart mailboxes, where the intelligence to route and process workflows through messaging is in the mailbox; and smart messages, where the intelligence is in the message.[11]

---

10. We are grateful to Eugene Lee, vice president of product planning at Beyond, Inc., for the conceptual framework he provided on mail-enabled applications and workflow automation.

11. Many of the concepts and terminology set forth in the remainder of this section owe a great deal to a presentation by Theodore Myer (Rapport Communication) at the 1991 EMA conference.

We will also cover two additional topics: object-oriented perspectives for advanced applications development and analysis, and electronic document authorization techniques intended to alleviate security concerns over the potential loss of human control and organizational checks and balances in the wider deployment of workflow automation.

9.5.1   Smart Applications

Intelligent, distributed messaging applications are not a new phenomenon, but linking these applications using interoperable messaging is new. Most of today's workflow automation or advanced groupware products fall into the smart application category. Such software solutions coordinate access to a range of services through mail enabling, database sharing, or a combination of the two.

In the sections below, we will model our Purchasing Application scenario from Section 9.2 as a smart application, provide a case study of a smart applications development platform, and consider some of the reasons why workflow applications will ultimately move beyond the smart application model to smart mailboxes and smart messaging.

The Purchasing Scenario as a Smart Application

The key feature of smart applications is their facile and transparent linkage to an embedded messaging utility through APIs or file-based interfaces. Another key feature is the integration of messaging and database resources, including directories.

Our Purchasing Application scenario receives a purchase requisition from an employee (or even another line of business application). It joins the requester name with the type of product and its actual or estimated cost. It opens an approval list and generates e-mail forms to each manager. The managers are thus prompted to review the requisition, fill out the form, and reply. If a manager delays too long, the application dispatches a reminder. The eventual reply (a completed form) does not go to another human user but back to the agent, who circulates it as further e-mail messages to a chain of co-signers prior to feeding the approved information back into the database and proceeding with the purchasing process. Accounts payable and budgetary systems are subsequently activated.

While integrated messaging networks are of critical importance to making our Purchasing Application scenario possible, much of the development effort in producing such an application would necessarily have gone into interfacing with the messaging system, directories, and mail folders. Since few organizations can afford to develop many Purchasing Applications at this level of sophistication from the ground up, a market has emerged for powerful tools to enable the rapid development of smart applications. A market has also emerged for smart (or workflow) application development platforms. High-end products include Beyond Corporation's BeyondMail, Digital Equipment Corporation's TeamLinks,

Hewlett-Packard's Workflow Manager, Lotus Development Corporation's Notes, and Reach Software's Workman.

Workflow Application Development Platforms—A Lotus Notes Case Study

Prominent among workflow application development platforms is Lotus Notes, a product designed to support both small and highly distributed, multisite organizations. Lotus Notes has become something of an industry standard groupware, or workflow application development platform, attracting widespread third party support. It employs a two-pronged approach to workgroup computing based on two fundamentally different models of information access. [LOTU92] refers to point-to-point communications between named individuals or groups as the *send* model, while the *share* model involves collecting information that can be shared and managed by groups. The emphasis in the send model is on getting information from one place to another where the recipient decides what to do with it; the emphasis in the share model is on collecting the information in one place and organizing it for group access.

Lotus Notes is a knowledge-sharing system that combines messaging, distributed document database, electronic conference, and various tools that enable the creation of applications customized to a group's requirements. The Notes Object Store database can store text, graphics, images, and editable objects in a single compound object. Also, Notes provides an integrated messaging layer for delivering documents between users or databases, and it supports gateways to other electronic mail systems. Notes clients run in the Windows, OS/2, Macintosh, and UNIX environments.

The Notes User Workspace or Desktop is a graphical environment that displays various user-configurable windows, the most important of which displays the icons representing Notes Document Databases (also called applications). The desktop of a customer service worker might feature Call Tracking, Customer Service Tracking, and Customer Sales/Account databases as well as an internal Support Conference database. When the user selects a database, a list of all the documents posted in the database is displayed according to a user-selected view. For example, the Customer Service Tracking database could be organized by Customer, by Support Person, or by Problem. The user can post new items, update the status of posted items, mail items to another user, or detach items into the file system.

Messaging services are available through the NotesMail facility. NotesMail is a Notes database that delivers mail by transferring Notes message documents from one user's database to another. An example of NotesMail's utility might be an application that tracks client requests in a shared database and also sends a message to the client representative when the request is acted on. Mail-enabled applications can make use of NotesMail through VIM. Lotus also offers a Mail Exchange Facility which allows message exchange and directory synchronization between Notes and cc:Mail.

Other mail systems, such as X.400 and SMTP/MIME are or will soon be accessible via other Notes gateways. In the more recent versions of Notes, users can access cc:Mail directly from the Notes menu. (Lotus also intends to develop a common user interface for the two products.) Directory synchronization combines the users of Notes and cc:Mail into a single hierarchical directory.

Developers can create new databases or applications by writing scripts in a Notes macro language or by selecting and customizing templates for commonly used database formats. In effect, the selection of templates creates forms and views that users see when they view an item or fill out when they post an item. Macros can act as workflow agents, monitoring the work process and taking automatic actions such as alerting management if problem tickets remain open past a designated time interval. Once created, an application can be locked so that users cannot change the design. A reseller or system integrator could then distribute the application as a commercial product.

In the Notes architecture, databases are stored on servers that sort and categorize the documents for shared access. The databases are distributed among multiple servers and use a replication technology to ensure the synchronization of updates to databases. Thus, the shared architecture of Notes brings all information on a given project together in a single place, while replication enables that information to be distributed to all the field offices that require it.

Notes also allows developers to assign different access controls to different sections of a single form. This allows a form to be routed so that one recipient can only read or sign the section pertaining to his or her role. Authors and readers also have access control designations. Roles can be combined with author and reader field types to provide additional access control. When these features are used in combination with selective replication, they offer a secure way to maintain only relevant, selected subsets of data at each site. Within the Notes environment, authentication of origin, integrity, and confidentiality services are also provided via RSA public key encryption and digital signatures.

Lotus has added a number of features to Notes which will support true forms of workflow automation through mail-enabling and database sharing. These features include a group calendar and scheduler, a group document library, and a workflow manager. In addition, Lotus applications such as 1-2-3, Ami Pro word processor, and Freelance graphics are currently mail enabled.

Integration with Notes goes beyond mail enabling to "Notes enabling." Detached applications can make use of Notes (importing and exporting documents) via the Notes API. With Notes/FX integrating technology released in early 1994, desktop applications such as word processors and spreadsheet programs will be directly able to save and load their output to or from a Notes database as well as exchange document fields with Notes databases.

Moving Beyond Smart Applications

As powerful and popular as workflow development platforms like Lotus Notes may be, they remain proprietary applications. Few vendors can or will afford to match the investment required to produce such high-end products. Products that compete with Lotus Notes and other industry leaders will find much of their intelligence and processing power absorbed in managing the communications burden. The application or application development platform still has to micromanage the operation of the mail system, sifting mailboxes for replies and generating notices. It still has to define rules and semantics for the routing and circulation of the message and for tracking the status of messages. Each intelligent, distributed application dealing with that same workgroup, department, or enterprise must duplicate these remaining redundant communications chores. But what if that were not the case?

Economies of scale can be achieved by pushing intelligence down into the messaging network. If intelligent routing and filtering services were available in the messaging platform itself, developers of smart applications and smart application development platforms could focus exclusively on applications, not communications issues. Given such support, automated workflow systems development will be streamlined, utility will increase, and prices will fall. Large numbers of tightly customized and customizable workflow applications would rapidly emerge to support the automation of intra-organizational transaction flows such as the movement of expense reports, timesheets, purchase requisitions, and human resource forms. Indeed, this process is well underway.

A messaging system can become a development platform by bringing to bear various kinds of smart messaging techniques. Smart messaging can be implemented at the mailbox level, at the message level, or at both levels. Smart mailboxes can filter messages, forward messages, and trigger events. Smart messages can embed procedures to be executed or interpreted before or after message delivery. With both smart mailboxes and smart messages, the messaging system becomes an intelligent, programmable instrument able to embody or distribute complex procedures.

9.5.2 Smart Mailboxes

Smart or programmable mailboxes add intelligence to the messaging system and offload communications chores from the application. Smart mailboxes can be used to filter messages, forwarding or deleting useless information; they can be used to trigger special procedures; and they can be used to implement complex rules associated with routing, approval, and forms construction. We will discuss smart mailboxes primarily in terms of private electronic commerce or workflow, since workflow is the environment where smart mailboxes are mostly found. However, smart mailbox functionality can also be built into public messaging networks.

Smart mailboxes may be used by people or applications. Some or all of the Purchasing Application's processing described in our scenario could have been implemented with the aid of a smart mailbox. People can use these mailboxes for filtering and forwarding. In this regard, the mailbox can alleviate a common complaint from e-mail users that they are inundated by a flood of junk mail. Filtering can

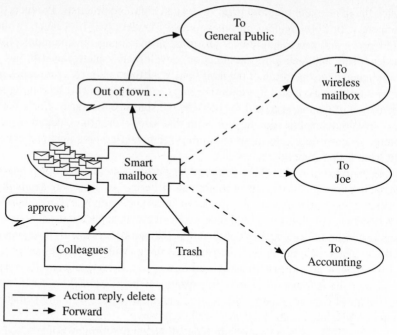

Figure 9.15   Smart mailbox functionality.

select the important messages, delete or forward the unimportant ones, respond automatically to routine requests, and organize information into folders. Some suggested examples of filters (and other processes triggered by the mailbox) include

- Forward messages from the boss to my wireless mailbox.
- Forward messages with Subject line containing the words "Customer Order" to Joe.
- File any messages with Subject line "Purchase Requisition Approval" in my approvals folder.
- Send spreadsheet file in reply to budget requests from Accounting.
- Reply to any other messages with a note explaining that "I will be out of town until Thursday."
- Put any other messages into the Trash folder if they haven't been read after a week.

Filtering criteria can be changed to become more restrictive when a user is out of town or very busy. While the concept of a programmable mailbox may sound intimidating (implying that one must be a rocket scientist to use the facility), relatively easy user interfaces can be set up. For example, the BeyondMail product from the Beyond Corporation is an early pioneer in the field of smart mailboxes. A screen from their user interface is shown in Fig. 9.16. This screen illustrates the definition of a rule called *move urgent messages*, which is part of the rule set *daily management*. Different rule sets can be enabled for different circumstances at different times, such as when the user is on travel, when the user is the Acting Director, while the Director is on travel, during normal times, or during busy times.

BeyondMail™ supports a smart mailbox paradigm with a rules language that can examine message field variables and evaluate conditional statements at execution time. Different actions can be taken for different types of messages. Applications can be launched and databases consulted. BeyondMail procedures can become quite complex and can be imported and exported between mailboxes or even developed by third parties.

In general, many products offered today are in fact mail-enabled applications that can be triggered or awakened by a certain message's arrival at a smart mailbox. Mail-enabled applications may also have the intelligence to manipulate their smart mailboxes through an API. Components of distributed applications can be set up on the messaging network as virtual users with smart mailboxes to perform various kinds of electronic routing-and-approval groupware processes. For example, company employees reporting a casual encounter with a potential

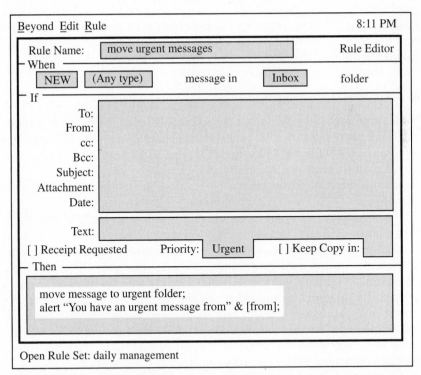

Figure 9.16   Defining rules for a smart mailbox. *"Rule Editor™ is a subset of BeyondMail™, a licensed product of Beyond Incorporated, a wholly owned subsidiary of Banyan Systems Incorporated."* *Reprinted by permission of Banyan Systems Inc.*

customer at a trade show might fill out a Sales Lead form and send it to the Sales Department mailbox. The mailbox would file the lead in a database, cross-reference it against previous customer leads, prioritize it, assign it to a free sales-person, track contacts with the lead, and maintain statistical records all the way to the point of order processing where inventory, production, and accounting logic would be triggered.

To the degree that smart mailbox functionality is self-contained and driven by recognized characteristics of a message (such as originator, recipients, subject, or priority, which are almost all universally supported), proprietary smart mailbox implementations could scale well to the multivendor department, enterprise, or vertical industry messaging environment. Forms of smart mailbox processing that are driven by more deeply embedded message information scale only by bilateral agreements and could become the subject of future standardization. Other likely topics for future standardization are electronic forms and APIs which applications could use to manipulate smart mailboxes dynamically from multiple vendors.

Smart folder functionality is a subset of some smart mailbox implementa-tions. Smart folders are aware of the internal attributes of message-borne objects like forms. They enable the user to take or define different views of stored mes-sages based on various fields. With a mixture of private folders and shared folders existing alongside many other objects and object collections in the distributed object-oriented operating systems of the late 1990s, e-mail, workflow, and groupware will merge seamlessly into an enterprise database.

9.5.3   Smart Messages

In the preceding section, we noted the potential of smart mailboxes to position intelligence at designated static points in the messaging network. However, this approach has a built-in scalability limitation. That is, distributing processes across too many smart mailboxes eventually creates excessive complexity even within the internal world of private commerce, let alone in the vast reaches of public commerce.

Another approach, which can be combined with smart mailbox technology, utilizes smart messages. This approach involves actually embedding instructions or intelligence in the message and sending that message to selected points in the network. With smart messaging, compiled object code, macros, or scripts are placed inside a message and executed automatically once the message reaches a mailbox. The message may propagate itself and visit multiple stops in support of a process involving loosely coupled network elements cooperating in a particular task. For example, the approvals segment of our Purchasing Application scenario could have been implemented using a smart message that propagated itself through a circulation list of approvers.

Many types of distributed processes can be supported in this fashion. In Fig. 9.17, a user mails a request for a report to his or her expert system. The expert system prepares a smart message and dispatches it to a mail user who is then interviewed using an electronic form. After several additional stops (perhaps to

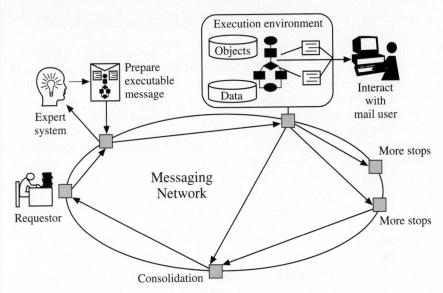

Figure 9.17   Smart messages.

query bulletin boards, news feeds, databases, or spreadsheets), the message comes home to the requester. Such smart messaging could be used for self-activating questionnaires, time card collection, expense report collection, or any procedure requiring remotely triggered program interaction with the user.

Security will be a major issue for smart messaging technology. Smart messages may require strong authentication of the generating user or application as well as digital signatures to guarantee the integrity of the embedded procedures. Both capabilities could be built on top of 1988 X.400 or the Internet PEM. In addition, access control authorization schemes will be needed, to control which data, devices, and other objects the smart message is allowed to use or see. The smart message execution environment will need constraints both to enforce the access controls and to limit the havoc that might be wreaked by a virus designed for this medium. These constraints might be imposed by execution or interpretive shells enforced in the operating system or by placing inherent limitations in the language used for executable messages.

The issue of standards is also important in the smart messaging medium, since one of its main attractions is its potential ability to deliver intelligence to any location reachable by the messaging system. But without standards for the language used, smart messaging will not scale well to the enterprise or vertical industry level. Therefore, we consider two possible standards: a public domain language called Tcl and General Magic's Telescript language.

Tcl Case Study

An indication of the viability of smart messaging is the creation of a powerful universal scripting language called Tcl (pronounced "tickle") and an attendant toolkit called Tk.[12] Tcl is the acronym for tool command language and Tk is a toolkit for the X Window System.

The intent of Tcl is to foster a single interpretive language that controls all aspects of a variety of interactive applications [OUST93A]. These aspects include the functions, interfaces, and composing pieces of a given application as well as the communication between applications. Tcl offers a syntax similar to sh, C, Lisp and generic facilities deriving from built-in commands. Tk extends the core Tcl facilities by providing commands for building user interfaces via Tcl scripts.

Tcl and Tk are touted as providing a number of benefits to users and application developers.[13] First, they speed up development vis-à-vis using a lower-level programming language (less to learn and less code than writing in C). Also, Tcl is an interpreted language, which means that the developer can generate and execute scripts on the fly (without recompiling or restarting the application). Tcl commands, which are linked to a Tcl library, can be coded within an application and executed at runtime.

Thus, an application for reading an electronic bulletin board might contain a Tcl command to query the bulletin board for new messages and another to retrieve a given message. Scripts can then be written to enable cycling through the new messages and displaying them (or a selected, topical subset) one at a time or recording which messages have been read and which have not in disk files.

Tcl scripts can be used to allow different applications to work together. Since any windowing application based on Tk can send a Tcl script to any other Tk application (to be executed by the recipient), Tcl can be used to make multimedia effects more accessible, to enable spreadsheets to update themselves from database applications, and to modify the behavior of live applications as they run. Its proponents also claim that once an application developer learns Tcl and Tk, he or she will be able to write scripts for any Tcl/Tk application by learning a few application specific commands.

Tcl and Tk can be used specifically for active messages as follows:

- An arriving e-mail message contains the program built using the scripting language.

- The recipient executes the program to read the message.

- The program can then interact with the user—for example, by performing a survey or providing a form template.

- The program can take such actions as sending a response or a filled-in form to an authorized recipient.

---

12. The information here is derived from presentation material and a work in progress, *Tcl and the Tk Toolkit* by John Ousterhout, to be published by Addison-Wesley (Reading, MA) in 1994.

13. In a presentation at the November 1993, Email World Conference, Nathaniel Borenstein noted, as a credibility check, that he had abandoned all his previous interactive mail languages (Ness, ATK, ATOMICMAIL) for Tcl—one he did not invent.

Tcl/Tk also comes with mechanisms to protect calls including access controls, a series of careful checks, encryption techniques, digital signing, and provisions for a certification authority. These mechanisms have become core to a subset of the Tcl environment called Safe-Tcl, which is intended to be safe for evaluating programs potentially written by an unknown or hostile party.

Tcl source, including the Tcl command language library, the Tk toolkit, and a few Tcl-based applications, is now publicly available. The fact that it has been in the (Internet) public domain and subject to experimentation since 1991 suggests that it has attained a modicum of stability. (Tcl is in version 7.2 and Tk is in version 3.5.) Meanwhile, a working group, inspired and led by Nathaniel Borenstein and populated by a number of Internet luminaries, was formed in 1993 to implement a prototype Safe-Tcl.

Telescript Case Study

Whereas Tcl and Safe-Tcl comprise a relatively well-established scripting language that has been extended for smart messaging use, Telescript is a new, object-oriented language designed from the beginning with the intent of creating a smart messaging (or more generally, distributed programming) infrastructure.[14]

Telescript has two essential concepts: *Agents* and *Places.* Agents are active Telescript programs, either residing within a Place to fulfill a custodial or network management role or on the move to visit places on behalf of a user. Places are those sites in the network capable of executing Telescript programs. In an electronic messaging environment, mailboxes can be places and smart messages can be agents. In the world of private commerce (as embodied in the internal portion of our Purchasing Application scenario), a purchasing agent could visit a database place to obtain the list of approvals and multiple mailbox places to obtain the approvals.

The General Magic Telescript White Paper [WHIT94] predicts that the electronic marketplace (see Chapter 4) will be full of Telescript places. For example, a user's home place might exist in a personal communicator, while other places might exist as shop places nested within a virtual electronic mall, housed on a public service provider's mainframe. Thus, a user might send an agent to the directory place in an electronic mall to obtain a list of shops and services; another agent might visit a ticketing place to purchase theater or sporting tickets.

Agent *travel* between Telescript *regions* (akin to domains) is initiated by means of the Telescript *go* instruction. Parameters to *go* include the destination, a *telename,* and the agent's *ticket.* The *telename* identifies the originating user, and the ticket indicates the level of resources the agent is allowed to consume. Once at the destination place, an agent may use the *meet* instruction to interact with another agent. The agent may also establish a connection to communicate

---

14. As of 1994, both the Telescript and Tcl languages were too new and untried for us to make any prediction as to which will "win" as a standard. Other smart messaging languages also exist and are under development.

with another agent back at the home place or another location. Agent transport and connections are accomplished via Telescript's Platform Interconnect Protocol (PIP), which is described as a thin veneer over a wide variety of communications media, including e-mail. PIP handles agent procedure, data, and execution state encoding as well as authentication exchanges.

Once in a place, Telescript agent programs are interpreted by a Telescript engine. The agent has no direct access to the operating system's resources. A number of security precautions are built into the engine, including the concept of a *permit*. The permit constrains the agent's lifetime, size, and use of resources. The permit is negotiated based on the agent's ticket and the place's policies. In some cases, access may be refused. Access may also be refused if the credentials in the agent's telename cannot be properly authenticated using RSA.

The engine interacts with the platform via three APIs: an External Applications API, a Storage API, and a Transport API. These APIs and the Telescript language are published by General Magic. The engine is designed for portability. General Magic will make available a Telescript Developer's Kit, which provides object code for the engine, as well as tools, documentation and sample programs, and a Telescript Porting Kit, which provides source code and documentation. The developer's kit is intended for application developers and the porting kit for system or platform manufacturers.

As of early 1994 there were two existing Telescript engine implementations: one within General Magic's Magic Cap operating system, and the other within AT&T's PersonaLink service.

9.5.4   Distributed Programming Object-oriented Perspectives

When considering software development problems in the complex world of networked applications, great economies of design and development can be achieved from studying the problem using an object-oriented approach. From the vendor perspective, object-oriented analysis should be applied to as many application scenarios as possible when designing smart messaging products. From the user perspective, applied object-oriented analysis could validate the vendor's design against the goals of enterprise development projects. When applied to smart messaging and workflow automation, this type of analysis is still in its infancy and no doubt constitutes a fertile area for academic theses and further research. Here we may find the proving ground where e-mail and artificial intelligence technologies will ultimately converge, where the infrastructure for electronic communities will be constructed, and where workflow automation breakthroughs will be forged.

Smart mailboxes may be viewed as stationary objects that interact with message objects and system objects. What these objects and their interfaces look like is very much a function of the smart mailbox implementation and the implementation of its attached applications. Interfaces may be elegant and flexible or cumbersome and complex. Rules fed into the smart mailboxes can be treated as objects as well.

The executable portion of smart messages may be viewed as *methods* (object-specific procedures) dispatched by local objects to manipulate remote objects. A smart message contains one or more embedded methods able to interact with the objects in its execution environment. These methods may be either standalone programs that interact with objects in the execution environment, or they may be subroutine components that mesh with larger programs prepositioned in the execution environment. A standalone method example would be a program sent to interview a user remotely as part of a survey.

In a more interesting case, the executable portion of a smart message may be part of a distributed method. In other words, the transferred executable element plugs itself in, as a user-defined extension component, to a prepositioned program in a remote environment. For example, a user might send a smart message containing a user-defined method for scanning a bulletin board to locate interesting items. The resulting specialized method would be executed in a highly integrated fashion by a bulletin board server for each bulletin board item available under a topic or list. In this case, the bulletin board is a generic object with a set of generic methods called a bulletin board scanning program and the smart message contains specialized extensions to those generic methods.

In another variation, the smart message may itself be a generic method which plugs into locally specialized methods at the execution scene. These local methods might know how to manipulate a user's printer, terminal, or other components of the local environment.

Smart messages may also extend their environment by defining new object classes or subclasses. Smart messages can extend themselves by discovering and using new classes of information.

9.6 ELECTRONIC DOCUMENT AUTHORIZATION AND SECURITY

As we have noted throughout this chapter, electronic commerce (the exchange of commercial papers, financial transactions, and a wide variety of value-bearing documents) demands various assurances for participants. Indeed, we believe that once the blocking factors to secure messaging (algorithm wars, legal roadblocks, high costs, unavailable technology, unavailable certification infrastructures) are removed it will be rare to find messages on the network that do not contain digital signatures. At that point, almost any two trading partners wishing to communicate will be able to

- Validate that an agreement exists
- Authenticate each other's identity at a moment in time
- Authenticate that what was sent was received without compromise
- Communicate confidentially if need be
- Determine each other's organizational authorization to perform a specific operation or transaction at a moment in time

So far we have focused primarily on public key encryption and signature-based services from the point of view of authentication, integrity, nonrepudiation, and confidentiality. Other than in the earlier discussion of attribute certificates, we have not focused on authorization or access control considerations. Yet these considerations are very important. In most organizational environments, employees carry identification badges and have specific roles and authorizations. They work together in a system of checks and balances to accomplish a business process with minimal risk of damage through fraud or malfeasance. To succeed in an automated environment, workflow automation systems must therefore provide means of identification, access control, audit, authorization, and the imposition of organizational checks and balances.

Ample precedent exists for such access control in the messaging environment. The long-term plan for the U.S. Defense Department's Defense Messaging System (DMS), is to use a Message Security Protocol (MSP) to encapsulate X.400 message data within a security envelope. This envelope will provide security labeling and other services. MSP will also provide end-to-end access control using access control certificates that describe the user's capabilities in terms of attributes. At message origination, the attributes in the originator and recipient certificates will be matched to determine if there is a common set of attributes to allow communication. In addition, disposition controls could prevent recipients from forwarding or printing a sensitive message or from extracting it into a file.

Access control can be applied to servers and databases. Products such as Lotus Notes provide various access control capabilities. These capabilities include authentication at login and access rights controls for such roles as author, manager, database designer, and document editor. Field-level access control is supported through encryption or using certificates to prove the identity of the requester on a remote system. In some systems such as DEC's Distributed System Security Architecture, a user may delegate authority to a node to act on behalf of the user by signing a short-term certificate that has a key used to prove to a remote system that it is the node identified in the certificate.

Electronic Documentation Authorization (EDA) is a concept embracing an architecture and digital signature protocol designed to provide authoritative assurance across organizational boundaries [WORK93B]. (The concept of EDA was developed by Fischer International and is under consideration as a standard by ANSI's X9F1 committee.) The goal of EDA is to provide a framework allowing the valid exercise of authority, such as spending authority, so that this authority can be verified electronically without requiring human intervention or decision. EDA's fundamental requirements are that no single user can suborn the system and that complete, provable accountability and responsibility are provided for all authorizations.

EDA could be used to control financial transactions, EDI transactions, CAD/CAM releases, human resource evaluations, and instructions to automated devices. Another example might derive from our Purchasing Application scenario. In that case, the Purchase Order connotes a contractual obligation and must be signed by the person in the organization authorized to permit the purchase. Currently EDI is conducted between trusting partners communicating across controlled networks and channels. In the future, EDI will become more widespread and will be conducted across a variety of networks and channels. Such a development will increase the opportunity for misuse and forgery and the attendant possibility of resulting major losses if mechanisms such as EDA are not put in place.

EDA technologies could be based on the PKCS.7 cryptographic message syntax, developed in 1991 by representatives from Apple, DEC, Fischer International, Lotus, Microsoft, Novell, RSA Data Security Inc., and Sun. The PKCS specifications are based on X.500 and ISO 9796. EDA uses an X.509 public key certificate for identification and PKCS structures for carrying the authorization and enforcement specification. It provides full authentication to all parties and full and accountable authorization as part of digital signatures.

EDA protects the issuing organization by ensuring that digital documents are subject to at least as many checks and balances as those applied to paper documents [ANKN92]. It protects the receiving organization by providing a machine-verifiable authority audit trail. This audit trail begins the association of every digital signature with an authorizing certificate. This certificate is one way of conceptualizing attribute certificates. It indicates that authorization has been granted by the signer's organization. A hierarchical chain of authority delegation up to a meta-certificate (or organizational root) is recognized as trustworthy. Additional data structures within EDA certificates define delegated co-signers who must ratify any use of authority by the delegated authority in order to minimize the risk of misuse and inhibit the illegal use of a compromised key. This means that a digital signature is not to be considered valid unless accompanied by other certified digital signatures. The use of co-signers can be stipulated at any (or all) levels.

The scenario presented in Fig. 9.18 shows how EDA can be used to designate purchasing or other kinds of authority in a corporate environment. Jane's Certificate authorizes her to engage in purchasing transactions of a monetary value up to $5,000 when cosigned by John and Jenny. Jane's purchasing authority is embodied in her Authorization Certificate. The authority was delegated to her via the digital signatures *X Bob* and *X Alison* that are present in her Certificate. Both *Bob's* and *Alison's* authorizations, as expressed in their Certificates, are in turn delegated from the organization meta-certificates ABC 1 and ABC 2.

To order an actual product or service using her authority, Jane would activate purchasing software programmed to generate an EDA proof packet along with the purchase request or order. Figure 9.19 displays a conceptual view of the resulting data structure.

The EDA mechanism is deemed trustworthy for the following purposes: (1) assuring the document or data is unchanged since it was digitally signed; (2) authenticating the user who signed the document or data and (3) ensuring that the document or data is authorized in conformance with the rules set forth by the organization for whom the individual is acting.

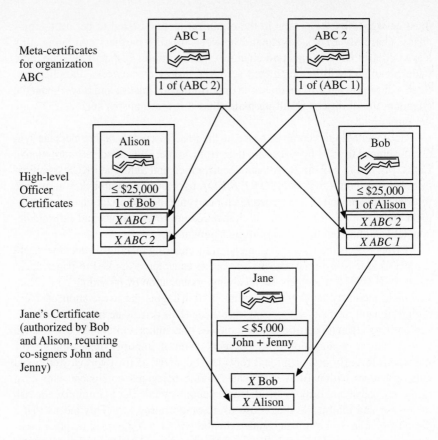

Figure 9.18   EDA Authorization Certificate scenario.

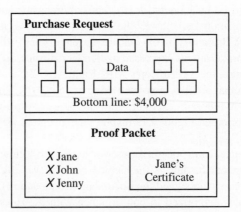

Figure 9.19   An example using EDA proof packet.

9.7 SUMMARY

When ultimately in place, the global messaging infrastructure will be positioned to provide a store-and-forward engine for all manner of electronic commerce applications in addition to interpersonal messaging and attached file transfer. These breakthrough applications will change the nature of how business is done, a change deemed essential for enterprises to remain competitive.

Breakthrough electronic applications will include those that support electronic commerce such as EDI as well as intelligent processes such as report and forms generation and distribution. Collaborative environments such as engineering design will coalesce around electronic conferencing and bulletin boards. Intelligent mailboxes and messages will automatically perform repetitive functions and provide for appropriate routing. All of these technologies will be available to enable workflow resulting in the automation of a variety of processes. Figure 9.20 diagrams the architectural hierarchy of the electronic applications and infrastructure components that we have discussed in this chapter. As the figure suggests, many levels of interfaces and platform functionality can and do coexist. Early mail-enabled and workflow applications interface directly to the

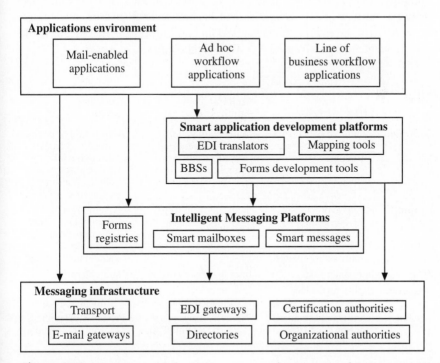

Figure 9.20 An integrated electronic commerce/messaging architecture framework.

messaging platform. Simultaneously, smart application development platforms such as Lotus Notes have been enormously successful. More recently, intelligence is being added to the messaging infrastructure itself. Figure 9.20 suggests that the highest degree of leverage can be obtained by combining technologies at all levels of the architecture.

While there are some differences (see Table 9.1) in the three major message-based electronic commerce technologies we have described, together they will provide a synergy that greatly increases the value of the ubiquitous messaging infrastructure now on the horizon.

Nevertheless, for such synergy to be achieved, some obstacles still need to be overcome. EDI will have to settle on a reduced set of communications standards as it has done with data format standards. Also, security issues will have to be resolved with a focus on the need to coalesce around a bounded set of options and to build the certification infrastructure that will enable widespread, safe, and legally sanctioned trading.

Many of the issues regarding mail-enabling technology have been resolved, particularly in local implementations. Applications are being developed and deployed at an impressive rate. Nevertheless, there are lingering problems when it comes to interoperating mail-enabled applications between disparate messaging infrastructures, and mail-enabled applications requiring multimedia attachments could overwhelm available bandwidth. This concern takes on some immediacy when we note that e-mail, groupware, and database technologies are converging to become part of the enterprise database. At the same time, mail-enabling technologies are blending into advanced workflow technologies.

	EDI	Mail-enabled Applications	Workflow Automation
Definition	Structured data formats used for electronic trading.	Mail-sending and mail-aware group productivity applications.	Automation of complex office processes through intelligent messaging applications or platforms.
Example	Purchase orders, invoices, shipping notices, remittances, waybills, quotes, requests for quotes.	Send file from word processor, electronic forms, bulletin boards, calendaring.	Expense tracking/ personnel actions, electronic routing and approval, automatic filtering.
Scope	Inter-enterprise	Inter or intra-enterprise	Intra-enterprise
Structure	Highly formatted/ highly structured data	Unformatted and formatted data	Unformatted and formatted data
Format	International standard forms (character-oriented)	Primarily proprietary forms (multimedia)	Primarily proprietary forms (multimedia)

Table 9.1 Comparison matrix: EDI, mail-enabled applications, and workflow automation.

Workflow automation brings with it its own unique set of technical and cultural challenges. Workflow must be seen from both a business model and technological perspective. Workflow automation technology offers the opportunity to reengineer business processes in a way that few other technological developments have done. Implementers have the choice of performing a wholesale replacement of an entire process or gradually trying out elements of workflow one subprocess at a time. While businesses are wrestling with such issues, even more intelligent technologies are on the horizon. Smart applications and mailboxes as well as the anticipated convergence of e-mail and artificial intelligence suggest a future replete with opportunities for workflow process reengineering.

These developments are exciting as new technology, but their true value will be in the way they assist in redefining the nature of our work and our economy. By providing speed and accuracy through the application of rules and intelligence, they will enhance business efficiency and reduce the drudgery and repetition that is often a part of blue- and white-collar work environments. Most significantly, they will lend new meaning to the challenge of what we call the e-mail frontier.

KEY POINTS

- When combined with organizational reengineering, EDI, workflow, and mail-enabled electronic commerce technologies have the potential to revolutionize the way we work.

- EDI EDIFACT and X12 formats for common business transactions are well established, but there are perhaps an overabundance of EDI communications options, including conventional EDI communications, enhanced X12 enveloping and security, X.400/EDI, X.435, and MIME/EDI.

- The process of establishing trading partner agreements needs to be streamlined through the use of Certification Authorities and devices such as attribute certificates.

- Simple mail-enabled applications and the use of electronic forms are proliferating; advanced workflow applications and workflow development platforms are beginning to make their mark.

- Smart mailboxes and smart messaging technologies promise major advances for both workflow and public electronic commerce.

C H A P T E R 10

The E-mail Vision

10.1 E-mail Issues for Users

10.2 Planning and Implementing Large Messaging Networks

10.3 Issues for Vendors

10.4 Issues for Public Service Providers

10.5 Issues for Public Policy Developers and Influencers

10.6 Conclusion

Now that you have read the previous nine chapters, we trust that you are convinced of both the opportunity and the challenge of implementing e-mail. There is no more fitting way to begin this, our final chapter, than to restate the E-mail Vision first postulated in Chapter 1.

> E-mail is a key communications application of the Information Age. It enables people or mail-enabled applications to exchange revisable multimedia information, workflow, and electronic data interchange transactions. This exchange can occur with anyone, anytime, anywhere with speed, ease-of-use, intelligence, security, and at a low cost.

Individuals in search of better communications and productivity tools, small organizations, and large organizations are users of e-mail and have a growing need for these technology tools. Vendors, service providers, and public policy influencers and developers should all be judged by their success in bringing this vision closer to all users. This chapter will address the concerns of these industry players by defining key e-mail issues and providing recommendations for users, vendors, and public policy developers; by providing specific recommendations to large users for planning and implementing messaging networks; and by assessing industry progress toward the vision and identifying remaining barriers and stumbling blocks.

381

10.1   E-MAIL ISSUES FOR USERS

Depending on the size of their installation and the diversity of their installed base, users need to consider different factors with regard to using or implementing messaging networks. In this section we discuss e-mail issues with this need in mind, and we make recommendations appropriate for individual users, small organizational users, and large organizational users. In section 10.2, we grapple with the dilemmas facing a typical large organizational user who wishes to build a coherent messaging network on top of an installed base of diverse, nonstandard local e-mail environments.

Before proceeding, we need to clarify our objective. The following recommendations and evaluation criteria are high level only. Even for the single user, there are many ways to use e-mail, and service provider selection can be a complex task. Supplying a complete cookbook, let alone a buyer's guide comparing current product or service offerings, is beyond the scope of this book. We trust, however, that users will find this material valuable as a starting point for more elaborate planning. Moreover, vendors and service providers can benefit from studying these sections, so as to better understand user requirements and to better structure their offerings.

10.1.1   Issues for Individual Users

Individual e-mail users include residential users as well as those in small businesses that do not own a LAN or host e-mail system. From the e-mail perspective, the latter operate as individuals. Individual users will increasingly use e-mail for their interpersonal correspondence with other individuals, for electronic commerce, and for access to electronic shopping and consumer information services. Your primary concern as an individual user is to obtain access to the right public service provider at a reasonable cost. You must therefore determine exactly how e-mail will be used and select a public service provider and a means of access to the service. Figure 10.1 diagrams the suggested planning process for the individual user.

As an individual you may choose *not* to treat the selection of an e-mail service as an elaborate investigation, any more than you would spend a solid week deciding which long distance telephone carrier to use. Nevertheless, selecting an e-mail carrier is much more complicated today than selecting a telephone carrier, and if acquiring just one or two ideas that will help make your decision more rational, your time will have been well spent. We also suggest taking a look at the *One Minute E-mail Service Provider Selection Guide* at the end of this section.

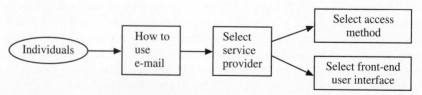

Figure 10.1   Implementation/evaluation process for individual users.

Determine How E-mail Will Be Used

There are many different public service offerings to choose from, each with its strong suit. The first step in the selection process should be to identify how you will be using e-mail. To assist in this process, we have posed a number of questions in the following checklist.

Checklist for Individual Use of E-mail

- Who will you be communicating with via e-mail and what types of mail services do your correspondents use?

- Do you have correspondents on any or all of the types of services described in Chapter 4?

- Do you need to send frequent short messages, infrequent large messages, or both?

- Do you sometimes require both "business-class" audit and message tracing capabilities?

- Do you need land line access, wireless access, or both?

- Will your messages contain sound or video?

- How important is it for e-mail to be integrated with voice mail and fax (universal mailbox functionality)?

- What mail-enabled applications must be supported?

- What other information services (besides e-mail) do you need on your information menu?

Select a Public Service Provider

Based on a determination of how you will be using e-mail, you can now select a service provider. Recall from Chapter 4 that possible choices include the international X.400 carriers, Internet service providers, a private consumer information provider, or a vertical industry service offering. You will almost certainly want to consider the following Service Provider Evaluation Checklist below.

Checklist for Service Provider Evaluation

- Cost of communicating with your correspondents[1]
- Convenience of communicating with your correspondents
- Convenience of accessing the service (local phone call, 800 number)

---

1. You will need to study the service provider's pricing model carefully. Is there a flat monthly charge? Are there usage-sensitive charges based on connect time or number and size of outbound or inbound messages? Are there charges for special information services, such as news clippings? Based on your anticipated usage of the service, try to estimate what your typical monthly bill would be.

- Convenience of the user interface
- Ability to transport binary or multimedia information
- Audit, tracing, and reliability capabilities
- Value-added services, such as enhanced fax, stock price quotations, news briefs, access to various Internet services, electronic shopping available from the service provider or accessible third parties

As of early 1994, individual subscribers can be found on consumer information services, the Internet, and public X.400 services. One way or another, mail can usually flow between all of these networks, enabling you to reach your correspondents.

In summary, our One Minute E-mail Service Selection Guide provides these rules of thumb:

One Minute E-mail Service Selection Guide

- **Birds of a feather flock together:** If most of your correspondents use a particular consumer information service, that service may have unique capabilities interwoven with messaging. You may want to share those capabilities, and this suggests choosing the same service as your correspondents. This rule of thumb applies whether your service is Internet-based, Telescript-based, X.400-based, or based on other technologies.

- **Don't price yourself into extinction:** Use a provider whose pricing model reflects your usage of e-mail. For instance, if you spend a lot of time reading mail over a 1200 baud modem, don't use a provider that charges by connect time. However, if you are given to sending large messages or many messages to many people, use a provider that charges you a usage-insensitive flat rate per month.

Select a Means of Access to the Service Provider

Service providers usually offer a range of choices with regard to how you, as an individual user, should access their offering. Physical access is available through either a leased line at variable speeds or asynchronous dial-in access at speeds up to 14.4 kilobits with compression. Some public service providers offer certain specialized means of access, including cellular or other kinds of wireless links. Generally you will find the asynchronous option more attractive unless extremely large files must be sent and received on a frequent basis or you travel frequently and need wireless connectivity.

Over these various physical media, you can either access a host e-mail system as a dumb terminal or employ special access protocols for use with e-mail client software. Service providers often support proprietary access protocols, but standardized access protocols will become increasingly available in the X.400, Internet, and wireless realms. Internet Mail access protocols in wide use include

POP-3, IMAPbis, UUCP, or SMTP over TCP/IP with the aid of SLIP or PPP. X.400 access protocols could include P7 or P1 with the aid of the APS specification. Using a standard means of access is especially important in cases where you plan to use the same front-end client with multiple service providers.

Select a User Interface (Client) Software Package

Front-end client software packages that work with public e-mail service offerings can enable individual users to use those offerings from within their native computing environment. These client packages are generally available both from the service provider itself, from third party vendors, and from major e-mail system vendors (a fairly recent trend). For example, Microsoft Mail now includes an ATTMail driver. Lotus/cc:Mail announced a plan to publish "Public Editions" of the cc:Mail client. For Internet Mail, the Eudora package has become popular. One might expect that remote user interfaces from vendors whose main business is e-mail client development will have superior functionality (and be more expensive) than service provider-offered front ends. Evaluate user interfaces in terms of which e-mail client features (discussed in Chapter 5) you find relevant to your planned use of e-mail.

Summary

Given the above selection factors, you might decide to try the Advantis service offering using 9600 kb dial-up access and the native IBM Mail Exchange interface. You might obtain a personal communicator and employ ATTMail's new Telescript-based PersonalLink service. Or you could try the Internet-based PSILink service using the Chameleon front-end product from NetManage. Of course, many other choices are also possible.

Based on the information in this section, we recommend that you draw up a list of five to ten key cost, quality of service, access speed, access type, and user interface-related requirements. Then contact at least three service providers, obtain the necessary information, and rate the offerings before selecting a service. Review your selection at least once every two years in order to ensure that you are still obtaining the best possible price/performance mix.

10.1.2   Issues for Small Organizational Users

A small organization can benefit from e-mail in many ways. It can communicate with external trading partners as well as harvest the benefits of improved communication through using the technology internally.

Like individuals, small organizations must determine how they will use e-mail and, in most cases, select a public service provider for external connectivity. A small organizational user differs from an individual user primarily in that the organization consists of a group of people sharing access to a privately owned facility, such as a host or a LAN. This group may be tiny (less than a dozen users) or moderately sized (tens or hundreds of users). However, small organizational

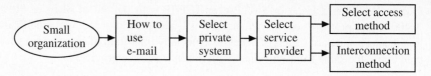

Figure 10.2   Implementation/evaluation process for small organizational users.

users differ qualitatively from large organizational users in that they generally operate only one or two local e-mail systems. Interworking, addressing, administrative, and other issues are therefore relatively trivial. Figure 10.2 diagrams the decision process for small organizational users.

In some cases, an organization may decide to rent public mailboxes and not own an internal mail system. In this case, it operates as a collection of individuals. However, the connect hour or volume charge costs of using public mailboxes often drive organizations to seek an internal mail system. (In the beginning of Chapter 3, we analyzed the basic public/private messaging tradeoff.) In the case where both an internal (private) and an external (public) offering are in place, the user must make a secondary decision regarding what kind of gateway (or other means of access) should be used to communicate between the two systems. These decisions are discussed in the following sections.

Determine How E-mail Will Be Used

Organizations (small and large) must answer the same questions as individuals concerning their use of e-mail. In addition, they should consult the following checklist for organizational use of e-mail.

Checklist for Organizational Use of E-mail

- What is the organizational mission and what are some of the ways that e-mail and electronic commerce can support it?
- To which employees will e-mail access be provided?
- What workgroup applications will be integrated with e-mail? Will full-blown workflow and store-and-forward EDI be used?
- What is the organization's policy regarding personal (as opposed to work-related) use of e-mail by employees?
- What expectations of privacy can employees have regarding personal or work-related use of e-mail?[2]

---

2. The EMA has recommended that organizations adopt a privacy policy and notify employees of that policy in order to ward off potential litigation stemming from misunderstandings. As of early 1994, however, legislation was pending in the U.S. Congress that might expand an employee's right to privacy.

Selecting an E-mail System for Internal Use

Those organizations deciding to own and operate their own private e-mail systems must select an e-mail vendor. In the first instance their choice will be narrowed by the type of computing platform(s) they employ. There are only a small number of choices for most host environments, and even in the DOS and UNIX environments choices are still limited. Users should review the local e-mail features described in Chapter 5 and draw up a list of ten or more key local e-mail system requirements before evaluating products and making a selection. In addition to features, users should evaluate vendor viability factors, such as size, support, and strategic direction, and—*this is absolutely vital*—they should check at least three references from other users.

Selecting a Public Service Offering

If the user is not deploying a private internal messaging system, the public service selection criteria are much the same as for an individual user. However, the picture changes somewhat when the user employs multiple (one public and one or more private) e-mail systems. In this case, the user has two choices: first, employees may maintain dual mailboxes (one public and one private), or message relay service from the carrier may be obtained.

The dual mailbox choice is only viable when a very small number of employees are using the public mailboxes infrequently. In other cases, instead of evaluating front-end user interfaces to public services, the user must evaluate the means of message level access or gateways. The small organizational user's public service selection is also complicated when the user's offices are located in a number of countries, particularly those in remote areas of the world. In such cases, the user must either find a service with access only a local phone call away in all the relevant countries, or use multiple services. Depending upon its level of message traffic (whether the user operates in one country or many), one or more dedicated lines (fractional T1, T1, or higher speeds) may also be justified and the pricing of dedicated access becomes a key evaluation factor.

Interconnecting to the Public Service

Interconnection to the selected public service(s) may be simple or complex depending on which protocol the user's internal mail system supports. In some organizations, the "interconnection device" between the internal and external mail systems is a secretary who manually loads, unloads, and forwards messages to/from the two systems. Fortunately for secretarial practitioners, such procedures are becoming increasingly passé as automated interconnection becomes more feasible than ever before. Native Internet or X.400 mail systems can access many public service providers without needing a gateway. Also, some public service providers offer direct support for popular protocols, such as NetWare MHS, internally in their networks. In other cases, users must procure a gateway certified to operate with their chosen e-mail system and public service provider.

Summary

Thus, a small organizational user might acquire a LAN e-mail facility with access to public services for all employees. Certain users might also be issued remote client software for use at home; others might be provided with wireless clients. The organization might tolerate personal use of e-mail (much as personal telephone use often is) as long as employee performance remained high and e-mail bills low. The employee's personal computer file system and mailbox (like her desk drawer) would be treated as strictly private. Intrusion by one employee into another employee's personal file system or mailbox would be cause for termination. On the other hand, an employee leaving documents needed by the workgroup in an inaccessible state during his absence would be subject to reprimand. In highly unusual cases, the organization might need to "drill the lock" into an employee's mailbox and obtain information. Employees would be advised of network monitoring that might lead to their messages being inadvertently read by network operations staff.[3]

Physically, a small organizational user's e-mail implementation might fit into one of many possible profiles—for example: Internet Mail or X.400 mail internally and externally, a Microsoft Mail system with an SMTP gateway to an Internet service provider, a DEC All-In-One system with an X.400 gateway to an X.400 service provider, or a cc:Mail system with native protocol support in the service provider's network. In general, the more transparent the interconnection, the more natural interenterprise messaging will seem to users. Most X.400 gateways require that the organization invest heavily in training, and SMTP gateways require some skill level as a UNIX system/network administrator. The prospect of such costs often leads small organizations to connect to a service provider offering a gateway to the organization's internal e-mail protocol, and multiprotocol support is increasingly available from service providers.

10.1.3   Issues for Large Organizational Users

As characterized here, a large organizational user differs from a small organizational user in terms of the diversity of its e-mail demographics as much as its absolute number of users. Where the small organizational user employs one or at most two e-mail systems, our typical large organization employs three or more e-mail systems and runs geographically dispersed facilities, each with a substantial user base.

Large organizations can include government institutions, universities, international organizations, multinational corporations, banks, and Fortune 2000 corporations. Often, these organizations are made up of multiple internal departments

---

3. This policy is along the lines of an approach described by Robert Denny, President of Alisa Systems. It does not necessarily comply with all regulations in readers' home countries.

or subsidiaries (which we will call business units) that currently make, or have in the past made, autonomous e-mail deployment decisions. Faced with the difficulty of coordinating between business units, some large organizations avoid the difficult issue of deploying an enterprise messaging network and function as if they were multiple small organizations with respect to e-mail. Increasingly, however, the imperatives of globalization and the demands of the information age are driving enterprises toward addressing organization-wide messaging issues. For example, at the June 1993 EMA conference, a U.S. General Services Administration (GSA) representative declared that the U.S. Government had a goal of becoming a "customer-driven electronic government" and requested industry assistance in developing a government-wide messaging network pilot.

While many issues related to the use of e-mail and to e-mail policies do not substantially change with the size of the organization, size adds a number of new dimensions that must be considered in planning and implementing a logical and physical messaging infrastructure. In particular, the size and diversity of large organizations often leads them to deploy one or more e-mail integration servers in a backbone configuration, especially when an unmanageable number of point-to-point gateways would otherwise be required to interconnect multiple local e-mail systems.

Moreover, the typical organization in this category is large enough that the central e-mail administration group (if there is one) does not enjoy complete control over the e-mail–related decisions of the business units. Even when such control exists, mergers or acquisitions can drastically alter a stable messaging environment. Thus, large organizations often mandate the internal use of standards to promote stability. Business units are often allowed to implement e-mail components on an independent basis provided they follow the agreed-upon standards. Organizations must also choose whether to administer messaging network components owned by different organizational divisions in a central, autonomous, or hybrid arrangement.

Large organizations have the opportunity to influence the e-mail industry substantially by communicating their requirements to vendors and by participating in standards bodies or industry associations. The influence of even a few large user organizations acting in concert can be significant and should be exercised at times to further an organization's strategic goals and prevent vendor turf battles from leading the industry down a blind alley. When backed by cash, such influence can assume monumental proportions. The Internet began as a DOD project. The U.S. Aerospace Industry Association orchestrated the interconnection of U.S. public services via X.400 in the late 1980s. More recently, in 1991 and 1992, the expressions of outrage by user after user at EMA meetings chilled the API wars and sparked the development of the X.400 API Association's CMC API.

Of all these issues, the most complex center around implementation of large, heterogeneous enterprise messaging networks. These are covered in more detail in the next section.

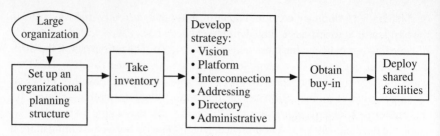

Figure 10.3   Implementation/evaluation process for large organizational users.

10.2   PLANNING AND IMPLEMENTING LARGE MESSAGING NETWORKS

Suppose you were hired to be the e-mail coordinator for a large Fortune 50 organization. The sun never sets on this global conglomerate's holdings, which comprise multiple independent-minded subsidiaries and a plethora of incompatible local e-mail platforms and other messaging components. Suppose your Chief Information Officer (CIO) makes the following demand: "I want you to evaluate our current e-mail network and give me specific recommendations for cutting costs and improving service." Where do you start?

Having ruled out a premature retirement, you must first ascertain whether or not your organization has a documented electronic messaging strategy or plan. If so, the strategy must be evaluated; if not, a strategy must be developed. Suppose there is no strategy or you determine to start from scratch. Consider following the methodology diagrammed in Fig. 10.3.

10.2.1   Set Up an Organizational Structure

You can set up an organizational structure to go through this methodology and have some chance of success. Or you can try to do it alone and risk being slaughtered when you reach the "Obtain buy-in" stage.

Your messaging strategy cannot be developed in a vacuum. Organizational politics is an inescapable component of planning, procuring, and deploying a messaging network. E-mail is multi-site and multi-organizational. It is probably the largest and most complex application your enterprise has ever deployed. Unless you have already developed truly Machiavellian skills in the realm of office politics, we would suggest consulting one of the many texts that deals exhaustively with project management strategies in a large organizational environment. As a brief overview, however, the following strategies have proven helpful to e-mail managers seeking to develop and carry through a messaging strategy:

- Obtain an executive sponsor who can provide critical support and organizational advice.

- Encourage the establishment of a management-level e-mail steering committee or council, where critical decisions can be reviewed with all the "stake-

holders" in your organization, including those belonging to user groups, subsidiary organizations, operations, or personnel operating networks and services (fax or EDI) that may be affected by the new integrated messaging
regime.

- Establish a smaller "tiger team" drawn from technical personnel reporting to
the e-mail steering committee to actually develop detailed strategies and
implementation designs and to handle vendor evaluations.

- Create a "win-win" environment, so that your success means the team's success, the steering committee's success, and thus the organization's success.

10.2.2   Take Inventory

How are you using e-mail today? To develop an appropriate e-mail strategy that
fits the enterprise, review the checklist for taking inventory of a large messaging
network.

Checklist for Taking Inventory of a Large Messaging Network

- What legacy local e-mail systems, mail-enabled applications, gateways,
backbone components, or public service provider offerings are in place and
which business units own them? What are the ongoing costs and cost centers?

- For what business purposes are employees using e-mail today? If possible,
divide your user base into categories: managers, knowledge workers, clerical
workers, and so on. Develop user profiles and gather statistics for each category, such as the average number and type of messages sent and received by
a user each day.

- Who are your trading partners and do they have adequate access to the network? If so, what are your security and cost exposures?

- What kind of expertise exists in the organization for administering different
kinds of internal messaging networks?

- How long does it take to send a message through the messaging network? Are
messages lost? What is your aggregate traffic level?

- How reliable are the existing components? Where are the scalability limits in
your network? Are the existing systems perceived to be adequate?

- Is EDI being used and are the existing EDI systems perceived to be adequate?

- What is the logical and physical design of your messaging network, and its
supporting management and directory subsystems? What naming and addressing conventions are used?

- Does the network include custom or internally developed applications, directories, or other facilities? What are the dependencies on such systems?

- Are e-mail usage and privacy policies clearly stated to employees?

10.2.3   Set a Future Vision

How will the enterprise be using e-mail tomorrow? In order to answer this question, you must first establish the planning context. That is, does the organization intend to plan a strategy for a five-year horizon? An 18-month horizon?

In addition, the following objectives might be "givens" in your planning equation, ranging from the relatively tactical:

"We want our e-mail capability to stay the same, but become cheaper,"

or

"We want to gradually move toward centralized administration of the network."

To the visionary:

"We want full standards-based integrated messaging, directories, and transparent interconnection of all nodes on our messaging network,"

or

"We want workflow technology that will help us carry out sweeping reengineering efforts."

Based on these high-level givens and on internal user surveys, you should next determine the answers to the questions in the following checklist. Note that this checklist builds on our earlier Checklist for Organizational Use of E-mail.

Checklist for Setting the Large Messaging Network's Future Direction

- For what business purposes will integrated, organization-wide messaging be employed in the future?
- How many sites/users should be connected to the network and what is the time frame for connecting them?
- Are major corporate acquisitions, expansions, or (conversely) selloffs planned that would affect long-term mailbox demographics?
- Do individual business units plan to install specific new local e-mail systems or other components, scrap components, or replace components, and what is their time frame?
- Does the organization want to own and operate its own messaging backbone or outsource the task to a service provider?
- Has the organization already committed itself to follow any industry standards?
- How fast should the messages flow from user to user?
- How much are the business units willing to pay for messaging?
- What value-added services are needed from both backbone and local e-mail components?

- Should the messaging and directory network be administered centrally, locally, or as a hybrid of the two? How much autonomy do business units require?

- Should e-mail be a "free" organizational resource or should its use be charged back to business units?

10.2.4 Develop a Strategy

The difference between how e-mail is being used and how it is perceived today and plans that have been made (or expectations established) over a given planning horizon will determines the gap which must be closed through your messaging strategy. As an e-mail planner, you will need to develop a strategy that breaks your future vision into specific goals and covers both strategic and implementation requirements for the system's evolution to those goals.

For example, an organization may set a *goal* of having multiple mail-enabled applications to raise workgroup productivity. It might decide that the *strategy* for fostering the deployment of these applications might be to standardize on a single API with which mail-enabled applications can access the messaging networks. Based on a desire to support standards, it may decide that CMC should be the *implementation* of that API. CMC then becomes part of the plan. But to use CMC, the organization may need to install the newest version of an internal mail system. This then will become a *stage* in implementation.

A sample messaging strategy might contain the following elements: platform strategy (local infrastructure), interconnection strategy (internal considerations), interconnection strategy (external considerations), naming and addressing strategy, directory strategy, and administrative strategy.

Platform Strategy

This strategy should determine which local infrastructures should be employed within the organization and which APIs should be used to support mail-enabled applications. Sample goals that might set the platform strategy could be

"All employees should use the same e-mail system."

At one regimented extreme, or at the other freeform extreme

"Each business unit can select the e-mail system that best suits its needs."

However, both of these visions have problems. This section will address the problems and conclude with an alternative strategy statement.

Regimented Platform Approach.   It may prove impossible to find a single platform that provides the best means of meeting the needs of all the business units. Moreover, using a single platform may create a dangerous dependence upon a single vendor and may even be politically impossible to achieve within the organization.

If an organization currently uses a multitude of local e-mail systems, converging on a single one will be difficult. Ask any network manager and he or she will tell you that the most intractable element in a network is not the hardware nor the software, but the user. Users acquire a keystroke memory that endears them to their current e-mail user interfaces; individual users have stored databases of filed mail that represent part of the organizational memory. Moreover, business units may have deployed mail-enabled applications and mail-related procedures that cannot be transplanted cost effectively from one mail system to another. Thus, a company with the goal of employing a single mail system will find the migration process brutal, if not impossible, over any three year period.

Freeform Platform Approach.   On the other hand, an organization planning to tolerate or encourage e-mail diversity should seriously consider the downside of that strategy. A regime of e-mail anarchy does not bode well for organization-wide e-mail communication or for cost effective operation. Interconnection will be poor, and an increasingly baroque assortment of gateway integration components may be needed.

An Alternative: Strategic Platform Approach.   Fortunately, today's modularization and standardization trend offers an alternative to both the regimented platform and the freeform platform approaches. A company could, for example, allow departments to select any of several e-mail systems that can be effectively interconnected to the organization's backbone infrastructure. Or it could standardize on a single LAN e-mail server implementation but allow business units to select any e-mail client able to work with that server over a standard API.

Organizations should therefore consider offering their business units a small but complete range of proven choices or the option of deploying a single platform whose provider supports standards and an open architecture between product components. A better goal statement might hold that

> "All employees should use a single e-mail system or one of a few systems that work well together; the systems used should each offer the architectural flexibility for change."

Based on this goal, the enterprise should set a plan for the attrition of unwanted sunset mail systems and migration toward those messaging systems that are considered strategic. An important factor in selecting strategic platforms should be their openness. But first one must resolve what defines an open architecture. Our proposed definition is this: An open architecture minimizes risk. It enables a system to interwork at various levels with other systems, protecting customer investment in the face of change. It enables customers to transfer their information assets easily to other systems.

How do you really tell if a platform is open in today's market environment where no vendor will admit that their architecture is anything *but* open? Evaluate the openness of a local infrastructure product carefully by examining its architecture using the following open systems evaluation checklist.

Checklist for Open Systems Evaluation

- What protocol standards does it offer? Does it support 1988 X.400/X.500 and/or Internet Mail standards?

- Does it offer client-level and service provider-level APIs? Do these follow industry standards, such as CMC, VIM, or Simple MAPI (high-level APIs), or Extended MAPI (low-level APIs)?

- Are the service provider APIs differentiated by function? What other kinds of interfaces does it expose?

- How easy is it to get data in and out of the management and directory systems or to add your own software procedures to augment these systems?

- Does it support emerging workflow standards for calendaring, electronic forms, and smart messaging languages?

After reviewing the architecture, check references to determine that the claimed open functionality is actually supported by the vendor and that customers have actually been able to succeed in interworking using the product in environments similar to your own.

Interconnection Strategy—Internal Considerations

Assuming that an enterprise messaging environment consists of more than one e-mail system and is likely to do so for some time, you must develop an interconnection strategy. The nature of the interconnection strategy depends largely on the installed base, the platform strategy, and the company's vendor preferences. It is also influenced by the company's set of external trading partners.

Organizations finding it in their business interest to support the long-term coexistence of host and LAN e-mail systems should rely on a backbone e-mail integration solution, such as the Control Data, DEC, HP, or Soft*Switch offerings, or a facilities-managed solution from a service provider. They should be aware, however, of a very rough rule of thumb: Establishing a high-quality e-mail integration solution comprising standards, gateways, enterprise directories, and directory synchronization generally requires capital costs for hardware, software, and vendor-provided consulting services that *start* at approximately a million dollars per 10,000 users served (exclusive of internal support costs).

Organizations wishing to pursue an expedited downsizing process from host to LAN e-mail may not need to deploy a high-quality e-mail integration backbone solution on a long-term basis. For example, Microsoft offers a migration strategy for Microsoft Mail that involves the use of transitional gateways and 3270 terminal emulation for interconnection to PROFS. However, users should be aware that gateways from vendors such as Microsoft or Lotus may sometimes be adequate but are rarely as rich in features as those from gateway specialists, such as Soft*Switch, Boston Software Works, or the Worldtalk Corporation.

Large organizations must also determine whether or not they need a dedicated backbone installation. As an additional set of components, a backbone adds to equipment and software costs but can reduce management and support costs because each dissimilar local infrastructure (or enclave) connects to the backbone rather than to other enclaves, thus reducing the need for tedious cross-system interconnection testing and other coordination activities. The following thresholds, although not absolute, are good indicators that a backbone should be considered:

- Three or more incompatible local e-mail systems that would otherwise need to be interconnected via point-to-point or protocol gateways
- 50 or more geographic sites for which routing tables must be configured
- Complex or incompatible addressing forms between enclaves.

Interconnection Strategy—External Considerations

The interconnection strategy must also encompass interconnection to external trading partners. Recall the "birds of a feather flock together" principle; if most trading partners are accessible via X.400, then an X.400 service provider should be selected or direct X.400 connections established. Likewise, if most trading partners are on the Internet, then an Internet service provider should be selected. Generally with X.400 the importance of using a service provider to relay messages increases with the number of trading partners, since numerous interconnects can be inconvenient and expensive to administer. An X.400 service provider may be accessed directly via X.400 or via local e-mail protocols supported by the service provider. This choice is usually determined by the presence or absence of X.400 gateway or backbone functionality in the internal enterprise messaging network. Similar considerations pertain to selecting a VAN and an interconnection policy for EDI communication services.

Of course, many enterprises will likely have trading partners on both the X.400 and the Internet global networks. In 1992 and 1993, many service providers offered connectivity to both networks, but few did both well. However, with time and convergence, it may become more feasible for users with heavy traffic on both networks to select a single X.400/Internet provider.

With an Internet service provider, the user is often connecting directly with the trading partner and merely using the provider for IP packet relay service. Costs tend to be low, but the relatively open and uncontrolled environment poses some incremental security risks that concern many commercial organizations. A common strategy for such organizations is to deploy a firewall (or SMTP gateway) capable of filtering message traffic. PEM or MIME-PEM could be used to enable encryption and digital signing of data between trading partners that have exchanged private encryption keys or use compatible public key infrastructures, and this would have the effect of neutralizing Internet security concerns. (Similar security mechanisms may be used over X.400 services, but might be regarded as less critical since the X.400 service providers operate relatively closed, controlled networks.)

Naming and Addressing Strategy

An effective naming, addressing, and directory strategy is an important adjunct to the enterprise interconnection strategy. Potential goals might be that

- Employees should be able to continue using the address form that they are accustomed to.
- The addressing strategy should simplify, not complicate, interconnection.
- Addresses should be very simple to use and remember.
- Addresses should be very stable, never changing.

Some of these goals will prove to be contradictory or intractable. While the small organization with a single messaging network is in the enviable position of being able to define simple internal addresses as friendly names ("John Smith") and global addresses of the form *"john_smith@tiny.com"* or *"G=John ; S=Smith ; P=Tiny ; A= ; C=US,"* larger organizations rarely enjoy this priviledge.

The difficulty of developing a reasonable addressing strategy in a large organization is due sometimes to its size, sometimes to the diversity of its installed base, and often to both. When an organization is very large, tie breaker fields must be used to disambiguate friendly names. Thus, instead of *"john_smith@massive.com,"* addresses such as *"john_smith001@massive.com"* must be defined. Another method of disambiguating addresses is to let the address reflect the topology of a distributed network environment—*"john_smith@ east.sales.massive.com"* for example.

In the X.400 environment, gateways without directories often require the use of one or more address fields—for example, *"G=JOHN ; S=SMITH ; I=A001 ; OU1=POSTOFFICE1 ; O=CCMAILGATE ; P=MASSIVE."* In multinode internal Internet environments, most SMTP/DNS implementations do not support routing on the local part of the address, but easily support greater elaboration (using subdomains) in the domain part. Also, even when gateways or switching components contain a routing directory with sufficient performance that it can be loaded with the addresses of all the users in a connected enclave, administrators may not wish to load that directory with a large number of addresses that change frequently. Messaging planners should become aware of such functional or administrative constraints before—not after—designing an enterprise naming and addressing strategy.

Very often, address stability and routing concerns clash. An address that reflects the network hierarchy (or the organizational hierarchy) is easier to administer from a routing perspective than a simple flat address like *john_smith001@massive.com.* But the hierarchical address is also more likely to change, creating inconvenience for users and their correspondents. The ultimate solution to this dilemma is eventually to employ ubiquitous directories for both user browsing and for routing on every component of the address. In the meantime, the Internet address and the DNS infrastructure have proven scalable, and X.400-based e-mail integration solutions are improving in quality.

The enterprise naming and addressing plan should take into consideration the fact that advanced local and global messaging infrastructure developers today are already focused on making e-mail addressing easier for users. Recently designed local e-mail systems tend to hide addresses as much as possible. Also, some implementations support address translation on messages, enabling users to design an addressing scheme with a complex internal address optimized for routing (*"G=JOHN ; S=SMITH ; I=001 ; OU1= POSTOFFICE1 ; O=CCMAILGATE ; P=MASSIVE"*) but a simple external address optimized for stability (*"G=JOHN ; S=SMITH ; I=A001 ; P=MASSIVE"*). Trading partners address messages to the company's employees using the simple external form. The address is then rewritten using the optimized internal form as the message passes through an e-mail integration server.

Directory Strategy

Hand in hand with developing a naming and addressing strategy, you must also formulate a directory strategy. Potential strategies range from the minimalist, to the middle of the road, to the visionary.

- **Minimalist:** "Only local e-mail directories will be maintained."
- **Middle of the road:** "E-mail address information will be synchronized across the enterprise so that employees will be able to see each other's addresses."
- **Visionary:** "We will construct an integrated corporate directory spanning all local e-mail systems, the human resources, and other MIS departments to enable integrated enterprise application development and process automation fully."

In this section, we will discuss the latter two approaches.

A first principle with regard to an e-mail directory is that users want directory access seamlessly integrated with their local e-mail client. Therefore multiple technologies must be used. Prior to the full implementation of integrated directories based in both local e-mail and human resources systems, directory synchronization technology of one kind or another is needed for both the middle of the road and the visionary approach. Those users forging ahead with directory synchronization may elect to employ manual rekeying, semi-automated bulk file exchange, or fully automated, product-assisted incremental synchronization.

While automated directory synchronization is difficult today, users or prospective users can take heart from the fact that this technology has enjoyed a great deal of attention. The X.400 API association is deliberating a synchronization standard, and numerous products are rolling out. No respectable e-mail integration solution arrives anymore without a directory synchronization architecture (or at least a "marketechture"). Even such unlikely players as Hitachi have entered the directory synchronization fray. Much more is known today about what users need to evaluate in such a product. Users should ask their vendors whether their directory synchronization solution can

- Support all the e-mail systems in the enterprise messaging network.
- Import and export (if necessary, in a rules-based manner) all the fields needed to make up the addresses for a given addressing scheme.
- Support both centralized and distributed directory update models.
- Provide good performance with large directories.
- Allow for filtering.
- Be sufficiently robust to automatically recover from network or disk failures.

Despite the promises and the hype, an inescapable dilemma underlies directory synchronization technology:

No amount of directory synchronization can compensate for a lack of commonality between the data structures of the underlying local e-mail directories; in other words, one cannot synchronize what is not there to begin with.

It is our opinion, therefore, that even middle of the road directory planners should keep their long-term focus on X.500 or X.500-like directory technology. Also, middle of the road planners may want to consider that a directory synchronization solution may be easier to cost justify if the resultant database is seen as a component of or a transition to a widely useful enterprise and global directory.

Around the 1995 time frame, it should be practical to move from directory synchronization to directory interworking. Local e-mail systems are becoming modularized by emerging service provider APIs. These APIs allow the mixing of the directory component of an e-mail client with other components. Thus, even if Microsoft Mail, cc:Mail, and other products do not support X.500 directly, third party X.500 DUAs can be tied in. Moreover, even products that do not support X.500 fully will become more X.500-like, a factor that will at least improve the results of directory synchronization solutions.

If your organization is one of the growing number of companies that has decided to plan for an integrated directory service, the checklist below poses some questions to consider. (While we use the international X.500 standard as the framework for the checklist, many items on the list will also be relevant for a wide range of X.500-like technologies likely to emerge in the mid-1990s.)

Checklist for Defining an X.500 Directory Strategy

- **Define your audience:** What users and resources will be listed in the directory? Who will use this information and in what manner? What types of human and programming interfaces are needed to the directory? What performance and security requirements must it meet?
- **Define your naming structure:** Information in X.500 is organized hierarchically using organization unit or locality hierarchies. How you choose to

represent your organizational/geographical structure determines how your directory entries will be named, with implications for both user friendliness and stability of names. How will you assign (register) organization unit or locality names?

- **Define your schema:** For the information listed, what existing X.500 object classes (records) and attribute types (fields) must be present? What custom subclasses or new attributes do you need to create for the information you intend to list and the use you intend to make of the directory?

- **Define your data management strategy:** Where will you obtain the data for your initial directory load? How will X.500 coexist with other directories (payroll, LAN NOS, proprietary e-mail)? Will X.500 or the legacy directory be the master? How and how often will information be exchanged between these environments? Will you be updating the directory centrally or at distributed points? Which department will be responsible for which fields of which entries? What access controls and other security policies should be established?

- **Define your topology:** Where, physically, will you be installing X.500 Directory System Agent(s)? If you implement a distributed directory, will data be replicated between DSAs? Will you interconnect your directory to external X.500 directory systems?

Administrative Strategy

Either an implicit or formally stated administrative strategy must be conceived in order to develop the platform, interconnection, and directory strategies that we discussed above. This strategy must define the organization's fundamental administrative model (or models), identify broad administrative responsibilities, and resolve numerous other issues.

Several basic administrative models present themselves including centralized (a central administrative group administers messaging network components[4]), distributed (autonomous business units administer messaging network components), and hybrid (some components are administered by business units, others by a central administrative group).

Organizations must consider whether parts of the enterprise messaging network administration should be insourced or outsourced. (In the outsourcing model, the provider becomes, in effect, part of the central administrative group.) The cube diagrammed in Fig. 10.4 provides a three-dimensional matrix showing the main physical elements of the network, the administrative model, and whether responsibilities are outsourced or internal.

We include the messaging administration matrix here to make the point that not all messaging components need to be treated uniformly. For example, a user

---

4. *Administration* is usually associated with *ownership,* though it need not be.

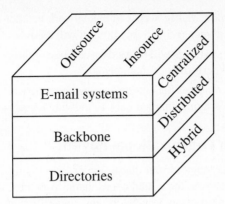

Figure 10.4   The cube of messaging administrative choices.

might employ centralized/outsourced administration for the backbone components, but distributed/internal administration for the local e-mail and directory components. Part of developing your administrative strategy could be to construct a table whose rows include all 18 permutations of the cube. Then evaluate which alternatives to incorporate in your administrative strategy.

The following checklist identifies a number of other subjects that should influence organizational management and administrative strategies.

Checklist for Messaging Management/Administrative Policies

- Is your objective to provide the messaging system on a 7 days a week by 24 hours basis?
- If the messaging network is insourced, what type of relationship do you maintain with your component vendors (strategic partnership, select best of breed, other)? Generally, an organization can obtain lower prices by handling procurements competitively, but Request for Procurement (RFP) processes often require significant internal resource commitments.
- Will custom components be used in the network? If so, who develops them and how will they be maintained?
- What are the interfaces and escalation processes between the consumers and suppliers in your network? For example, users might go to the business unit help desk, which then escalates unresolvable problems to central administration.
- What security policies will be put in place? Will all users have e-mail access to all other internal or external users or will access controls be placed on mail

flows? Will remote dial-in access to the network be allowed? Will operators have access to all management functions or will these be compartmentalized?

- What tools and strategies will be used for reactive or proactive network health monitoring and performance maintenance?

- Who owns and operates the enterprise messaging network? Who pays for it? Is the use of messaging charged back to individual users or departments?[5]

10.2.5   Obtain Organizational Buy-In

Recall that we set the stage for our discussion of large organization e-mail strategies with a request to you, the e-mail coordinator, from the CIO to evaluate your organization's current messaging network and suggest recommendations for the future. You (or rather, the organizational team that you established) have completed that task. The CIO likes the messaging strategy and recommendations and asks you to proceed.

Based on your messaging strategy, you have either decided to prepare an RFP for competitive procurement, or preselected a vendor with whom your organization will establish a partnership. Either way, there is no free lunch. Sooner or later, the cost of your messaging strategy will come into focus and budgetary outlays must be requested. Up until now, your job has been relatively easy!

Your CIO does not control the entire company. Your organization's business units operate in a relatively autonomous manner, and MIS cannot implement systems without their support. Moreover, the MIS budget is limited: large capital expenditures require executive and/or Board of Directors approval.

If you have followed the correct organizational as well as technical strategies, buy-in should be attainable. Buy-in at the funding stage is possible because you obtained buy-in at all stages of messaging network construction. You worked through the difficult issues during your planning phase; a too-easy planning phase for a complex messaging network may be a warning sign that important issues are being neglected.

The first critical checkpoint in actually deploying your messaging network may arrive when an appropriation request for funding reaches senior management. At this point, you may already have selected a vendor or vendors and completed much of the network's logical and physical design. But given that messaging networks for complex environments are rarely cheap, you may be asked for additional justification in the form of buy or lease analysis and cost/benefit assessments following submission of the appropriation request.

At this point, you must be prepared to make a strong case for building a messaging network. Be prepared for the challenging task of quantifying the benefits of

---

5. The cost of creating and maintaining the accounting and invoicing software for usage-sensitive chargeback can exceed the savings. A former e-mail manager, Paul Heller of Heller and Associates, noted that his organization calculated the break-even point for chargeback: if usage-sensitive chargeback induced users to modify their use of messaging by plus or minus five percent, it would be cost effective.

an infrastructure that must sometimes be put in ahead of the applications that will later be enabled or designed to use it.

10.2.6   Deploy Shared Facilities

Another critical checkpoint in building the messaging network is actually putting it into production on schedule. In this regard, we strongly advise that you conduct both reference checks and an extensive architecture/implementation design analysis of all product configurations in your target solution. If possible, make payouts to vendors contingent upon successful completion of pilot (preproduction or beta) messaging network operation. Once your service goes live with real users, you will never get a second chance to make a good first impression.

10.3   ISSUES FOR VENDORS

Vendors must understand current and near term user requirements, the competitive marketplace, and industry directions in order to develop profitable product families. Given the rapid rate of change in the industry, it has become increasingly difficult for vendors to understand and react to trends quickly enough to bring reliable features to market within a reasonable window for success.

As was documented in earlier chapters, the main private messaging market segments are LAN e-mail and workflow, host e-mail (IBM, UNIX, etc.), and e-mail integration (middleware, gateway, backbone).

Increasingly, large user organizations need products and services overlapping all of these segments. The temptation for private messaging vendors, particularly large vendors, is to try to cover them all. But this is no longer possible.

It is true that large vendors, such as IBM, Microsoft, Novell, and Lotus/cc:Mail, may for a time drive the marketplace before them, build huge infrastructures from their massive revenues (supporting large development staffs), and set de facto industry standards. But in so doing, they run the risk of turning off their echo suppressors, that is, believing their own sales force. Even small vendors are not immune to this tendency. But large ships on the ocean turn much more slowly than small ships; when large vendors lose their focus, they lose their dominance as well.

Vendors—both large and small—should consider the following prescription to remain on track in the rapidly shifting messaging marketplace:

- Conduct regular user surveys and make executives regularly accessible at user conferences to industry analysts and to all levels of management staff from user organizations.
- Foster internal consulting expertise and make use of external consultants.
- Follow successful industry standards and support the development of those standards; standards can protect vendor and user investments in the long term.

- Maintain product differentiation, where possible by being able to advertise honestly that your products interwork better than the competition's.

- Service and support are also critical differentiators. Provide automated management tools that minimize the need for support or expedite the support process. Build responsive support organizations using internal resources or distributor-provided resources.

- Work through partnerships with other vendors. Avoid monolithic product lines by leveraging the modularization trend.

The last piece of advice is perhaps the most important. Gateway vendors teaming with messaging backbone vendors have produced major advances in the functionality and number of e-mail integration products during 1992 and 1993. LAN e-mail vendors teaming with group productivity vendors or media vendors (for example, imaging and electronic forms) have greatly enhanced the quality of LAN e-mail offerings. General Magic wove a complex web of partnerships that is now culminating in a messaging-capable personal communicator linked through intelligent public networks, a feat that could not have been accomplished by any one company. Partnerships can be better for the customer as well, since each product component can receive complete focus (quality, reliability, and performance) from its vendor.

10.4 ISSUES FOR PUBLIC SERVICE PROVIDERS

Like messaging system vendors, public service providers confront an imperative to understand and leverage industry trends. They also face many of the same kinds of problems. Recall that the types of public service providers are commercial X.400 and EDI VAN, Internet access services, consumer information services, wireless services, and vertical industry-specific providers.

Of these, a few operate as global carriers and most operate as end carriers. Together, global and end carriers form most of the global messaging infrastructure, and, if they read the market correctly, they have the potential to win back a great deal of message traffic that now traverses private messaging networks. In order to leverage the main public messaging market trends to their individual advantage, all carriers should follow the general recommendations listed for vendors. In addition, global carriers must pay attention to all of the points highlighted in the bullet list below, and end carriers should review the bullets with an eye for what makes sense given their present market niche. Therefore, carriers should

- Form partnerships to provide internationalized integrated messaging services and universal mailboxes (video, voice, fax, and e-mail) accessible through both land line and wireless links.

- Support message relay for major messaging standards, multiprotocol access services for local e-mail clients, and alternate delivery services between both interpersonal messaging and EDI media (electronic commerce offerings).

- Form partnerships with e-mail integration vendors to provide virtual private messaging backbones.

- Form partnerships with LAN e-mail vendors to provide direct client access to public mailboxes, and develop POP 3 access for Internet Mail.

- Make intelligence via smart messaging languages, such as Telescript, ubiquitous in mailboxes and network services.

Further Recommendations

E-mail will not fully achieve its potential unless public service providers cooperate in an enlightened fashion. Without a single, simple address format and low-cost international registration of user domains, e-mail will continue to be harder to use than fax and may continue to lag that medium in market share.

As good citizens helping to grow the market, service providers should

- Support efforts to develop a single standard for a written e-mail address. (Our feeling is that the Internet Mail address has proven very successful, and represents a good tradeoff between flexibility and simplicity. Proposals have even been developed to use Internet Mail addresses in X.400.)

- Support efforts to develop an inexpensive, common means of X.400 and Internet user domain registration.

- Take measures to increase volume and reduce prices. Especially employ pricing models and policies that encourage rather than suppress message flow between the Internet and other messaging networks.

- Accelerate implementation of global X.500 directories and other knowledge discovery systems.

- Support both research and legislative efforts to develop a distributed worldwide certification infrastructure.

These policies are in the long-term interest of all public service providers who are interested in providing a worthwhile service in a free market. After all, is it not preferable to have a one percent share of a 50 billion dollar market rather than a five percent share of a two billion dollar market?

10.5   ISSUES FOR PUBLIC POLICY DEVELOPERS AND INFLUENCERS

Public policy developers include local governments, national governments (executive and legislative branches), judicial courts, standards bodies, and industry associations (such as the EMA, the Electronic Frontier Foundation, and the Corporation for National Research Initiatives) advocate positions on mail-related regulatory matters and are in a position to substantially influence government policy. These entities are sometimes themselves large users of e-mail and face the same kinds of issues that confront other large organizations.

In addition, however, public policy developers also must deal with the following enigmas:

- What privacy rights should employees enjoy over their e-mail, and how can these be reconciled with the legitimate need of organizations to control and manage their networks?

- What privacy rights should organizations have to encrypt their intra- or interorganizational traffic, and how can these be reconciled with law enforcement concerns?

- By what process should standards be developed? Should governments set standards, such as GOSIP, in advance of market dominance, or should they wait for open standards to achieve market dominance before ensconcing them in procurement regulations?

- What role should governments play in developing national and international electronic commerce infrastructures? The judicial and legislative communities are, to a considerable extent, the arbiters of how far and how fast a free market civilization can move into the Information Age. Someday—hopefully soon—digital signatures will be a legitimate instrument of commerce, even as paper postmarks are today. Someday national certification infrastructures will legitimize public cryptographic keys, removing one major blocking factor to electronic commerce. Trading partners will be able to enter into agreements electronically using attribute certificates. But progress in this arena has been painfully slow.

- Should e-mail, EDI, and other information services be taxed and, if so, would this have a chilling effect on the development of software and services by enterprising entrepreneurs? The State of Florida attempted to impose taxes on information services in 1993, but the effort was beaten back by concerned businesses and associations.

- Who should police information highways, and how? A special emergency response "posse" exists on the Internet today to track down hackers and prevent damage.

- How can the government encourage mass access to e-mail in order to ensure that we do not create a class of information "have nots"? Should e-mail be subsidized in order to encourage mass access for public good, or would such subsidies distort the commercial messaging market?[6]

We believe that individuals should enjoy reasonable expectations for e-mail privacy. Governments should continue to encourage messaging-related standards

---

6. In the U.S., the Clinton administration announced various proposals for a national information infrastructure in 1993. These proposals highlighted private industry's role in building an "information highway" and government's role in ensuring that the highway is universally accessible.

with some flexibility, provided that such standards emerge from an effective standards making process and reflect practical network experience. Efforts should be made to encourage the emergence of industrial strength messaging networks, including the legal recognition of digital signatures and the establishment of scalable certification infrastructures, infrastructures that we can then leverage to establish massive electronic commerce markets.

In general, information services should be neither subsidized nor taxed, but left to the free market; however, governments could encourage mass access by providing public terminals and group Internet accounts at such public locations as post offices and libraries. The explosive growth of the Internet and other information services signals that we have crossed a new threshold into the Information Age. It is vital that information networks (and the profound social and economic changes they will bring) strengthen rather than weaken the democratic and free market foundation of modern civilization.[7]

10.6 CONCLUSION

We are fast approaching the end of our adventure along the e-mail frontier. Though this part of our journey is finished, as a player in the industry you will undertake many such journeys, for the e-mail frontier is still advancing. Indeed, e-mail will continue to advance in the future until the vision is fully achieved, and then further as new paradigms are found.

Consider the elements of the vision: multimedia information transmitted at blinding speed over intermittent networks, a seamless convergence of messaging and groupware into an integrated enterprise database, electronic commerce conducted with unassailable security, and the beginnings of messaging and artificial intelligence convergence. It sounds like hype. *But is anything less than this worthy of being our ultimate destination?*

If not, then where are we along the event continuum to achieving that vision?

10.6.1 How Close Are We?

Paradoxically, we are both very close to and very far from achieving that vision. First, with respect to private messaging systems (privately operated local infrastructures and e-mail integration components), we can divide users into two classes: those with simple environments and those with complex environments. Users in workgroup environments with common means of client-server access reaching every desktop and high bandwidth private or virtual private networks connecting every site—environments that are either fairly small or are not saddled with too many incompatible legacy systems—are fortunate in being able to do a

---

7. Jonathan Gill of the U.S. White House staff articulated these points eloquently at the November 1993 E-mail World Conference.

great deal with e-mail. Less fortunate are the large organizational users with complex enterprise messaging environments. The problems facing global messaging and electronic commerce systems are even more serious.

Workgroup Environments

Users in such environments have many tools today to support the multimedia mail and groupware (or workflow) elements of the vision. While we expect that many of today's workgroup messaging infrastructures will break down under an enormous increase in message traffic, we are also aware that today's LAN e-mail Post Offices (based on file sharing paradigms) are blossoming into enterprise class messaging servers with robust client-server architectures. Multimedia and workflow technologies will continue their dramatic improvement trajectory. If users select today's best of breed messaging solutions from viable vendors with open architectures, they should be able to keep in step with advancing e-mail technology wavefronts at a reasonable cost.

Enterprise Messaging Environments

Less fortunate are the large user organizations with heterogeneous environments. They can still fully realize the vision within those enclaves that are relatively well positioned, but they must pay more and work harder to achieve the basic elements of the vision from an enterprise-wide perspective. Their major problem is achieving interoperability. A combination of messaging standards and e-mail integration solutions have made great strides in enabling basic internal connectivity with untyped binary file transfer, but directories, management, and document interchange remain problematic.

Global Messaging and Electronic Commerce

In general, with respect to external or inter-enterprise messaging, the tools that were adequate in the past are rapidly becoming inadequate as we move from closed enterprises to virtual enterprises. Directories and knowledge sharing systems are not sufficiently encompassing to enable easy acquisition of information about our trading partners' addressing, delivery method, and media or security capabilities.

In general, the conditions for secure messaging in support of ubiquitous electronic commerce just aren't here yet; today's local e-mail technology is very good at enabling communication for total information sharing within and between workgroups, but once security walls have been erected (of necessity) around the enterprise, the technology is less effective at opening panels in the walls to allow our customers, trading partners, and suppliers the appropriate access level. For example, an organization may wish to have very restrictive security policies against outside users in general, but to allow offsite contractors who are members of key workgroups access almost equivalent to that of an employee. Considerable further progress on global messaging and directory infrastructures, as well as gen-

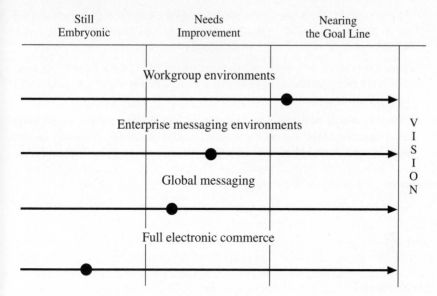

Figure 10.5 Progress to date toward approaching the vision.

eral security technologies for signing, encrypting, authenticating, and authorizing users or data are needed.

Figure 10.5 provides a rough visual measurement of our expected progress by the end of 1994 in reaching the vision.[8]

10.6.2 The Remaining Stumbling Blocks

A number of stumbling blocks remain in the path of achieving the vision. The most important barriers include lack of maturity of the physical infrastructure, lack of maturity of the messaging infrastructure, problems in manageability of local and global infrastructures, and lack of internationally legitimized security techniques and infrastructures.

Maturing of the Physical Infrastructure

The maturing of the physical infrastructure is necessary for e-mail to fulfill burgeoning demands for compound document distribution and multimedia information packaging, as well as increasingly heavier use of messaging as a medium. Fortunately, bandwidth and capacity advances are emerging on a number of fronts, which can be briefly summarized as follows:

- The convergence of bandwidth-voracious multimedia applications (such as video conferencing) and optical fiber–based technologies (such as SONET,

---

8. We are grateful to Mark Smith of the Intel Corporation for helping us refine this figure.

SMDS, and ATM) ensures that both the motivation and the means are at hand to produce a bandwidth explosion. Messaging will benefit from the bandwidth explosion in local area, wide area, and metropolitan area networks.

- The convergence of e-mail and the distributed file system features of mid-1990s operating systems suggests that a more efficient use of bandwidth will be made for local traffic.

- Wireless e-mail will enjoy an increase in bandwidth as data compression techniques improve and as the frequency allocations are increased by the FCC in the U.S. and by similar communications authorities in other countries.

Maturing of Messaging Infrastructures

We noted in earlier chapters that there are two global messaging networks and two global messaging infrastructures: one centered around the Internet and the other centered around the public commercial X.400 networks and attached commercial messaging backbones. In order to achieve vision and post-vision messaging/AI convergence, we must first see advances in connectivity between the two global messaging infrastructures, in their ability to connect to local messaging infrastructures, and also in the manageability and robustness of local messaging networks.

Global Messaging.   The X.400 and Internet Mail environments are still evolving. In broad terms, X.400 networks are rapidly migrating to support the 1988 X.400 standards and an increasingly wide array of services, while Internet Mail standards are climbing out of their text-oriented SMTP past (the "ASCII jail") and being upgraded to support advanced services, such as typed multipart binary attachments, confidentiality, and integrity.

In terms of infrastructure, Internet Mail is scalable and quite advanced, possessing international domain registration, a relatively friendly address form, and a dynamic routing (DNS) infrastructure that X.400 advocates are still struggling to construct. Thus, X.400 could aptly be described as an advanced standard/technology still searching for an infrastructure, while Internet Mail could be described as an infrastructure in search of more functionality. Future X.400 networks will probably have infrastructure attributes similar to the Internet, while post-SMTP/MIME/PEM standards will attain rough functional parity with the 1988 X.400 specifications.

Broadly speaking, the networks will converge, and the differences will be more in each network's customer base and implementation and less in their functionality and infrastructure characteristics. Again, in broad terms, X.400 implementations and services are likely to continue being more expensive and complex, but they will also continue to be marketed as more robust and more secure.

The ideal solution for users would be a pain-free migration to a single solution comprised of one or the other network, or a blend of both networks. A move to a single network is unlikely to occur or, if it does occur, is unlikely to occur painlessly, but users can still hope to move beyond today's uneasy coexistence toward genuine convergence as follows:

- A single standard for the written form of the e-mail address as it appears on a business card. (This is arguably the single most important event that could take place in the world of messaging.)

- One-stop shopping for international domain registration.

- Availability of both networks in every country and every city, worldwide.

- Transparent message flow between both global networks and all major local e-mail environments. This can be approached through a combination of gateway and tunneling technologies—*if* the semantics of e-mail systems continue to converge (loosely) around those originally described in the 1988 X.400 standard and since emulated and extended in MIME/PEM.

- Common or coexisting directory structures.

This convergence is likely to occur within several years. Just as we make do with pounds and kilograms, feet and meters, we may be able to accomplish the vision with X.400, Internet, and whatever comes after them. But we will also require the greatly improved local messaging, e-mail management, and e-mail security infrastructure characteristics described next.

Local Messaging.   Critical factors that will enable local messaging networks to play their part in achieving the vision include

- Support for a single written address.

- Support for 1988 X.400 or post-SMTP/MIME/PEM semantics.

- Support for global object registration mechanisms (Internet IANA or X.400's object identifiers) and global security (certification) infrastructures.

- The ability to leverage massive capacity increases and to support seamless dial-up, dedicated line, and wireless operation in an appropriate manner.

- The ability to participate fully in intelligent collaborative messaging via emerging workflow and smart messaging language standards.

Manageability of Local and Global Infrastructures

For e-mail to achieve its full potential, local and global infrastructure management must become as good as, or better than, the telephone system equivalent. This implies "lights out" management of large private messaging networks (or even virtual private messaging outsourced from a provider). Global messaging networks should be highly reliable, provide usage sensitive billing/settlement, enable automated message tracing when appropriate,[9] and be supported by interconnected global directories of addresses and routing information.

---

9. Usage sensitive billing and settlement as well as message tracing runs somewhat counter to the Internet Mail model, where messages are generally treated as one more rider over an IP packet bearer service. This model has proven very viable for vast volumes of casual messaging. However, formal electronic commerce can benefit significantly (as has been proven first by the EDI VANs and recently by X.400 service providers) from an intermediary message-level service amenable to audit, tracing, and usage sensitive billing, much along the lines of today's registered (paper) mail services.

Yet current local and global infrastructures are primitive and not very manageable. Nor are local and global infrastructures very robust or survivable. For messaging networks to become more manageable and more robust, they must not only be designed for multimedia traffic levels, but management capabilities must be modularized and standardized (in much the same way as transport and directories) in order to allow for best of breed selection. In the absence of multivendor management standards or conventions specifically tailored for messaging, visibility into heterogeneous local e-mail environments from a central management station is poor to nonexistent, configuring routing information and alternate routing information is laborious and error prone, message tracing is nearly impossible, and proactive fault detection and automatic correction are completely beyond us. Directory synchronization and integration is a nightmare. The problem is vast and in some respects it may worsen even as we chip away at it, for new e-mail technologies are continually being invented.

The following summarizes some developments that might move messaging management in a positive direction:

- **Overall management:** The International Federation for Information Processing (IFIP) has formed an E-mail Management Group, which is modeling all aspects of e-mail management. Both it and an IETF group for messaging/directory management are developing standards for managing messaging networks via SNMP or CMIP. An EMA committee has also come up with procedures for message tracing and interdomain directory query by mail.

- **Directory establishment/management:** The NADF is gradually fostering an X.500 directory infrastructure in the U.S. The X.400 API Association is deliberating a directory synchronization standard. An IETF group is sponsoring an X.400/X.500 pilot called GO-MHS that is testing the use of X.500 to store X.400 routing information.

- **Global messaging interconnection/management:** X.400 carriers in the U.S. have formed a National Message Transfer System (NMTS) consortium to tackle U.S.-level PRMD registration and routing issues. This consortium may move on to deal with other issues. Working through CCITT and other organizations, X.400 carriers may eventually establish international PRMD registration. On the Internet side, new national and supranational Internet backbone networks are being formed, taking over in some cases, from amateur networks operated by universities.

We applaud those volunteering their time and energy to these various activities, especially those who are approaching messaging and directory management from the broadest possible perspective for the benefit of all users. We only hope that their efforts are successful in producing usable standards and conventions that do not conflict and will see wide implementation. Achieving our e-mail management ideals may take years. We often lose sight of the fact that modern phone systems did not spring into being overnight but have had most of the twentieth century to evolve to their present level.

Internationally Legitimized Security Techniques and Infrastructures

Earlier we speculated that the X.400 and Internet global networks could peacefully coexist in somewhat different niches. We used the "pounds–kilograms" and "feet–meters" analogy to point out that Internet and X.400 interworking can potentially be perfected to the point where the network origin of a message is never an issue to the users involved. No such happy resolution exists for certain chasms in the landscape of security standards and policies, however. The situation with respect to security may be more aptly epitomized by the image of two railroad tracks of different gauge and width meeting incongruously at a national border. Like the train at that border, secure electronic commerce can in no way pass where security standards and policies diverge.

At the present time, we can be more effective at identifying the problems than the solutions. The problems are

- Messages between parties using different security features and algorithms cannot be successfully massaged into the correct semantics by gateways because gateways, in most cases, are not trusted with the private keys of users.

- X.500 only supports access control in its 1993 version, which is several years from widespread implementation. Standards for attribute certificates to facilitate organizational authorization are only just beginning to emerge. Both Internet and 1988 X.400 security markets are scarcely out of their infancy.

- In most countries, digital signatures are not legally recognized except by bilateral agreement, nor does the Certification Authority infrastructure yet exist to enable their use in a scalable fashion.

- The clash between privacy and law enforcement concerns has made data encryption problematic, especially encryption using the one well-known and widely respected public key standard (RSA). Numerous regulations in numerous countries, sometimes outdated, often prohibit or hobble the use of RSA and other encryption standards.

- The effects of the Cold War linger on export regulations, to the point where a multinational corporation, wishing to create a secure private e-mail global infrastructure, may be forbidden to install the products that it has bought in certain countries.

- While the recently released Defense Message System (DMS) RFP may spur some investment in secure messaging technology, DMS security is not based on internationally standardized algorithms, nor are these algorithms yet accepted in commercial circles.

We will probably see improvements in the current situation, but only slowly. The bureaucratic, legal, and regulatory morass surrounding security will never see resolution until a market develops and impatient users force the issue. Yet that market cannot develop until at least some of the roadblocks are cleared. We cannot predict at what time the industry will escape from this latest "chicken and egg" syndrome.

All the same, there are signs of hope. Unlike encryption, digital signatures are relatively non-threatening to governments and could be amenable to international agreements. On the standards/technology front, PEM implementations from various vendors and X.400/X.500 security implementations from vendors such as the ISODE Consortium are emerging. Various organizations are planning and piloting Certification Authority infrastructures. Security hardware is getting cheaper. The economic imperative for secure electronic commerce using ubiquitous messaging networks should eventually prevail over these many obstacles.

10.6.3   Closing Thoughts

Tremendous progress has already been made in the construction of e-mail technology and global messaging networks. At least within local enclaves, truly remarkable e-mail and groupware solutions are becoming available. The volume of electronic commerce conducted through messaging will build, though not as rapidly as it might if security and manageability concerns could be fully resolved. E-mail will continue its massive growth, perhaps heavily hybridized with enhanced facsimile.

We will approach the realization of the e-mail vision, though that vision will remain on a continually receding horizon. This is at once bad news and good news. The sensation of a receding horizon not only reflects new problems surfacing, but also a continual refinement in the vision itself.

Yes, a host of compatibility, manageability, and security problems have arisen since the 1980s when this basic vision began to be widely articulated. On the other hand, we have also recently updated the subtext of the vision to include e-mail, groupware, and AI convergence over object-oriented network information services and databases—a powerful brew of new and evolving applications that we have not yet begun to master and carrying the promise of applications as yet inconceivable today.

E-mail Standards, Bodies, and Consortia

A.1   OVERVIEW

We cannot overemphasize that standards are essential to truly integrated messaging. In this era of continuing diversification and of the proliferation of specialty applications, few enterprises can continue to manage with single vendor networks, and multivendor networks will not interoperate consistently without standards agreed to by the application suppliers.

Standards are needed to define the common (expected) services of a global messaging infrastructure, to specify message envelope formats, and to identify the formats of text, voice, fax, telex, EDI and other data that will be enclosed in a message. Standards are also needed for directories and for message acknowledgment procedures.

A goodly amount has been written about standards organizations and about the standardization process. This appendix will provide a summary of the mission and activities of those organizations that are key to the evolution of integrated messaging and to which we refer frequently throughout this book.

415

The organizations described in this appendix can be categorized into three groups—the accredited standards community, the Internet community, and industry consortia—which can be thought of as a triumvirate in an often uneasy relationship. In one respect, each group addresses a slightly different set of problems and so complements the other two. However, the three groups may also address a given problem in different ways, resulting in competition and in the potential for confusion in the marketplace.

A.2   TWO UNIVERSES IN THREE COMMUNITIES

Since the late 1970s, networking standardization has taken place in two parallel universes: (1) the Internet (originally started by DoD funding) represented by the Internet Engineering Task Force (IETF); and (2) internationally accredited standards represented by the International Organization for Standardization/ International Electrotechnical Committee (ISO/IEC or just ISO), as well as the International Telecommunications Union Telecommunications Sector (ITU-T or just ITU).[1]

These two communities today continue as two rivals in the triumvirate, with the internationally accredited one (represented by the ITU and ISO) having enjoyed ascendancy during the 1980s but having had some of its work somewhat discredited recently, whereas the Internet standards community has of late experienced a resurgence, including significant activity in the messaging arena.

However, despite competition between the Internet (SMTP and MIME) and ITU/ISO (X.400), there is also a significant degree of hybridization—RFC 1006 permitting OSI applications to run over TCP/IP, the Internet specification of SMTP-to-X.400 gateway features, and the Internet X.500 pilots—that could ultimately lead to the enrichment of the standards emanating from both communities. Also, in a very recent development, the Open Systems Environment Implementors Workshop has formed a Convergence Subcommittee with the express purpose of enabling the convergence and coexistence of OSI and TCP/IP protocol suites. This subcommittee, which has ambitions of becoming a full-fledged OIW Special Interest Group (SIG), is suggesting that TCP/IP and its companion protocols be recognized as co-equals with the OSI suite of protocols and be subject to the same rigors of documentation and conformance testing. The latter suggestion would constitute a dramatic paradigm shift for the Internet community, and it remains to be seen whether the two communities can work together to converge. However, we believe that stratification and tiering in the messaging marketplace, implying a need for "high end" TCP/IP and Internet Mail, may encourage the Internet community toward such a paradigm shift.

---

1. The ITU-T was formerly known as the International Telegraph and Telephone Consultative Committee (CCITT).

The third element of the standards triumvirate consists of industry consortia and associations of various kinds which are important in both setting and defining infrastructures that make the standards workable and usable. They also have the unenviable task of wrestling with the sometimes competing requirements emanating from the two standards communities.[2]

A.3   THE ISO AND ITU WORLDS

ISO and the ITU approach interoperability through what we call the "grand architecture," standards developed by committee and agreed to by worldwide ballot. While ISO represents vendors and users and the ITU represents providers of telecommunications services, the two organizations have developed a close working relationship. First, we will discuss their respective areas of focus and provide contact information for documentation (and participation), then we will describe how their processes work.

A.3.1   International Telecommunications Union Telecommunications Sector (ITU-T)

The ITU Telecommunications Sector is made up of postal, telephone, and telegraph (PTT) organizations and Registered Private Operating Agencies (RPOAs). (In some countries, PTTs now control or once controlled all in-country communications.) The ITU first became involved in data communications standardization with the release of the X.25 packet switching standards in 1976. In 1981, work began on defining the OSI and X.400 protocols, which were completed in 1984. Trade fairs demonstrated the interconnection of compliant products, and government and industry pilots or procurement specifications spurred the standards toward acceptance. Also, after 1984, ISO specified its Message-oriented Text Interchange Service (MOTIS) and joined forces with the ITU. In 1988, the ITU released a version of X.400 with major new features, the X.500 Directory standard, and the ability for X.400 to use X.500.

In the past, the ITU issued recommendations governing telephony, data character sets, and such protocols as X.25, on a four-year cycle. (The creation of a fast track mechanism has essentially liberated the organization from that requirement.) Each new version of a recommendation supersedes all earlier versions, although in general provisions are made for backward compatibility at least to the immediately preceding version.

---

2. For example, in a recent meeting of OSIone, the world-wide umbrella organization for regional interoperability testing consortia (set up to test ITU and ISO standards), a new emphasis was placed on hybridization or "convergence." In particular, this has taken the form of placing a new importance on the interoperability of such applications as X.400 and X.500 over TCP/IP as well as OSI.

To participate or to order recommendations, contact:

International Telecommunication Union
Place des Nations
1211 Geneva 20
Switzerland
Tel: (41) 22 730 5554/5338
Fax: (41) 22 730 5337

The ITU has sporadically flirted with using a free online service to make its documents available (via File Transfer Protocol). As of early 1994, it was possible to use the ITU's Teledoc Auto-Answering Mailbox (TAM) to access the ITU Document Store. It can be addressed by sending e-mail to the X.400 address

C=ch; A=arcom; P=itu; S=teledoc

or to the Internet address

ITUDOC@itu.ch

By embedding simple commands in the text of the message (first LIST, then GET), the user will receive a mail message reply from TAM with the requested information. We must warn readers in advance, however, that this and any modes of document access cited in this appendix are subject to change.

A.3.2 International Organization for Standardization/ International Electrotechnical Commission (ISO/IEC)

ISO membership consists of national bodies such as the American National Standards Institute (ANSI) in the U.S., which are in turn populated by representatives of the relevant user and vendor communities. Unlike the ITU, ISO does not issue standards on a four-year timetable; rather, it has a series of stages through which a standard is progressed upon presentation to the membership. For example, ISO began considering X.400 as soon as the standard was issued by the ITU, by commencing work on a series of extensions known as the Message-oriented Text Interchange Service (MOTIS). These extensions were eventually folded into the 1988 version of X.400.

Membership in the national body consists of corporations, companies, firms, partnerships, and other organizations that engage in industrial or commercial enterprises (or in education, research, and testing). Annual dues for ANSI are structured on a sliding scale, whereby companies with sales under $1 million pay $100, and those from $1 million to $200 million pay $125 plus $7 per $1 million of sales. The latter figure rises to $7.25 per $1 million for companies with sales above $200 million and to $7.50 per $1 million for those with sales above $800 million.

To participate or to order documents, contact:

American National Standards Institute
11 West 42nd Street
New York, NY 10036
United States of America
Tel: (212) 642-4900
Fax: (212) 398-0023
Sales fax: (212) 302-1286

A.3.3 International Federation for Information Processing (IFIP)

IFIP TC6 formed its electronic mail working group, WG 6.5, in 1978; and it began serious work in 1979. The working group completed its prestandards work (which became X.400) and received the question on the ITU work items list for the 1980–1984 work period. Then WG 6.5 turned its attention to Directory and handed over that prestandards work (which became X.500) to ITU/ISO for the 1984–1988 work period.

IFIP WG 6.5 has subsequently become more active in the Internet community than in the ISO/ITU community. It produced work on the X.400/RFC822 gateways and, more recently, on MIME and on messaging management.

A.3.4 Implementation Groups/Workshops

ISO and ITU standards tend to be generic, deadline-driven, and the result of compromise. National, regional, and industry needs tend to be more specific. For this reason and because there are no implementations during standards development, a number of organizations are engaged in *profiling* (the creation of subsets of the full specification). Such regional or industry organizations, attended by standards users or vendors, may issue profiles (also known as *functional standards*) clarifying an international standard, specifying conformance requirements, or restricting field values and thereby assuring a greater likelihood of interoperability. Occasionally they may set special requirements over and above those that the standard has specified.

Open Systems Environment Implementors Workshop and the GOSIP Mandate

The most important X.400 and X.500 functional standardization forum in North America is the Open Systems Environment Implementors Workshop (OIW) sponsored by the National Institute of Standards and Technology (NIST) and the IEEE Computer Society. Implementors and users gather quarterly at the NIST headquarters in Gaithersburg, Maryland. Participants are divided into such groups as the X.400 Special Interest Group (X.400 SIG or MHSSIG). Each meeting produces updates to the SIG's Stable Agreements (as long as the new text has spent at least one meeting cycle in the Working Agreements). Once each December, NIST issues Stable Implementation Agreements for all the SIGS. These Agreements form the basis for the U.S. Government's Open Systems Interconnection Profile (GOSIP) specifications.

GOSIP is the specification of the approach that the U.S. Federal Government adopted in the early 1990s with the intent of interconnecting its information systems. Promulgated by NIST, GOSIP is mandated in phases or versions to ensure that government procurement officers can specify existing open systems technology.

Versions 1 and 2 of GOSIP were mandated in August 1989 and October 1992, respectively. They were based on the OIW's Stable Implementation Agreements, which defined the 1984 version of X.400 and its underlying protocols. Originally scheduled for early 1994, Version 3 was expected to specify the 1988 version of X.400 and the 1992 version of X.500 as well as User Agents to support both interpersonal messaging and EDI. This version was to reference the technical specifications for X.400 and X.500 as found in the IGOSS.

GOSIP points to the Stable Implementation Agreements as well as procurement policies, procedures, and guidelines. In this regard, it provides government agencies with the specification, instruction, and evaluation (including conformance testing and certification) parts of the Request for Proposal.

The GOSIP specification could be important to vendors because the U.S. Government represents a huge market for Information Technology products. In addition, states and other governmental entities are likely to follow Federal guidelines. (It is also noteworthy that other governments, such as those of the UK [GOSIP] and Sweden [SOSIP], have mandated similar specifications for their purchase of computer network products and services.)

However, in late 1993, a panel on Federal Internetworking Requirements was convened to study and make recommendations regarding the place of Internet as well as OSI protocols in federal government deployments. The panel pointed out the strengths and weaknesses of both protocol suites and recommended that NIST provide advice to government agencies rather than create mandates such as GOSIP. As of this writing, NIST has not determined how to act on the panel's recommendation, and the future of GOSIP Version 3 is in doubt. On the other hand, the OIW Convergence Subcommittee is working to give the OSI and TCP/IP protocol suites equal billing, and this effort might serve to rescue the idea of specifying government profiles.

To participate in the OIW Workshops, contact:

NIST
Building 225, Rm B217
Gaithersburg, MD 20899
Tel: (301) 975-3664

To order documents, contact:

NIST
Tel: (301) 975-3664

To acquire GOSIP FIPS, contact:

National Technical Information Service
5285 Port Royal Road
Springfield, VA 22161
Tel: (703) 487-4600
Sales tel: (703) 487-4650
    or
NIST tel: (301) 975-2816

To acquire an online copy of GOSIP Version 2 via the Internet, it was possible as of early 1994 to perform an anonymous FTP (file transfer) from osi.ncsl.nist.gov (129.6.55.1) as *./pub/gosip/gosip_v2.txt* (or *.ps* for postscript, *.ps.z* for compressed postscript, and *.w51* for WordPerfect 5.1).

European Regional Workshop and Other European Standards Groups

Other important regional groups include Europe's Councils for Electronics Standardization (CEN/CENELEC), the Council of European PTTs (CEPT), the European Workshop for Open Systems (EWOS), the Conformance Testing Service (CTS), and the European Technical Standards Institute (ETSI). These organizations develop profiles and procedures in an effort to harmonize standards, testing, and administrative regulations throughout the European Community. EWOS evolves European norms or standards and then develops profiles on a par with the OIW. The other groups participate in the profiling process and/or provide conformance testing and certification rules for the OSI and ISDN worlds.

To participate in or order from EWOS, contact:

European Workshop for Open Systems
Rue de Stassart 36
B-1050 Brussels
Belgium
Tel: (+32 2) 511 74 55
Fax: (+32 2) 511 87 23

Asian Regional Workshop and Other Asian Standards Groups

In Asia, the OSI Asian and Oceanic Workshop (AOW) provides a regional equivalent to the OIW and EWOS. An important participating organization has been Japan's standards promulgation body, the Promotion Conference for OSI (POSI).

To participate in or order from AOW, contact:

AOW Council Secretariat
Interoperability Technology Association for Information Processing
Sumitomo Gaien Building 3F, 24 Daikyo-Cho
Shinjuku-Ku, Tokyo 160
Japan
Tel: (+81 3) 3358 2721 ext. 300
Fax: (+81 3) 3358 4753

Harmonization of Workshop Profiles

The ISO harmonization process is designed to help evolve the various functional
(regional) standards into a single standard profile. Members of the NIST OIW
MHS Special Interest Group (SIG) and its AOW and EWOS counterparts have
engaged in a liaison process to coordinate their work. They exchange liaison statements and draft copies of their documents to reduce the number of profile differences to the bare minimum made necessary by genuine national or cultural
differences.

Some of these groups may even now be deliberating matters of concern to
your enterprise. We will therefore describe the philosophy and approach of the
ISO/ITU communities, an approach whereby standards are first developed, workable subsets are then created from the standards, and implementation issues (testing and deployment) are addressed as a sequel to the stabilization of those
standards.

A.3.5   The International Standards Process

The international standardization process begins with the creation of *base standards* proposed by national bodies through a process that is often iterative and
fraught with compromise. The U.S. national bodies are the American National
Standards Institute, representing U.S. interests in ISO, and various committees
sponsored by the State Department to represent U.S. interests in the ITU. The
standards are eventually agreed to by consensus through a committee process involving international representation.

In the ITU, national interests are represented by PTTs or, in the case of the
United States where there are only Registered Private Operating Agencies
(RPOAs), by the State Department. Study Groups, such as Study Group D, address numbering plan and crossbilling issues. In the past, the ITU operated on a
four-year cycle, which meant that recommendations would be approved and published every four years. Recently the organization has introduced a fast-track
mechanism (used to produce X.435, the recommendation for running EDI over
X.400) to speed up this process.

ISO members are national (member) bodies. Unlike the ITU, ISO does not
issue standards on a four-year timetable, but implements a series of stages through
which a standard is progressed. A body of work originates as a Working Document

(WD), and then evolves into a Committee Draft (CD), a Draft International Standard (DIS), and an International Standard (IS). At the CD and DIS stages, the standard is issued for member ballot and comment. If it is rejected, the document regresses to its previous stage and may eventually be declared unworkable. Future updates to an international standard are known as addendums, which go through similar balloting and comment.

A.3.6 The Regional Workshop Process

The ITU and ISO work collaboratively on an ongoing basis to develop key international networking standards. Nevertheless, if the standardization process stopped altogether with these standards, the road to interoperable messaging solutions would be impassable. At their best, the internationally approved ITU/ISO X.400, X.500, and OSI standards offer a grand architecture and provide the sweeping breadth of vision and generality to revolutionize the electronic messaging world. At their worst, they tend to be vague and option laden. Products that are coded to the specifications of the base standards alone will not necessarily interoperate. Implementation agreements and profiles are needed that refine and clarify the standards.

Implementors of the standards therefore congregate in the special regional open systems workshops: the OIW, EWOS, and AOW. These workshops produce profiles that perform the vital work of clarifying vague areas of the standard, specifying maximum field lengths in a protocol, or declaring whether certain features of a standard are to be considered mandatory, optional, or prohibited.

In North America, some progress has also been made in reducing incompatibilities between profiles through publication of the Industry/Government Open Systems Specification (IGOSS). The IGOSS consolidates the procurement requirement of the U.S. and Canadian Governments as well as the Manufacturing Automation Protocol (MAP) and Technical and Office Protocol (TOP) groups and the electric power industry represented by the Electric Power Research Institute (EPRI). Each of these organizations had previously published its own profile.

Still, the regional profiles are currently incompatible with one another because each one presents an incompatible document structure and kernel subset for standards conformance. This incompatibility complicates the job of international product implementors. Because the regional profiles form the basis for government procurement specifications such as the U.S. Government Open Systems Interconnections Profile (U.S. GOSIP), the U.K. GOSIP, and the European Procurement Handbook for Open Systems (EPHOS), incompatibilities between the regional profiles raise costs to users and diminish the benefits of interoperability. Figure A.1 diagrams the present standards dilemma.

Fortunately standards writers have foreseen the danger of incompatible profiles and as early as 1986 began work on a mechanism for harmonizing the output of regional workshop into a single, internationally functional standard on which much smaller regional profiles could be built to reflect genuine regional differences. ISO's Technical Report 10000 (TR10000), *Framework and Taxonomy of*

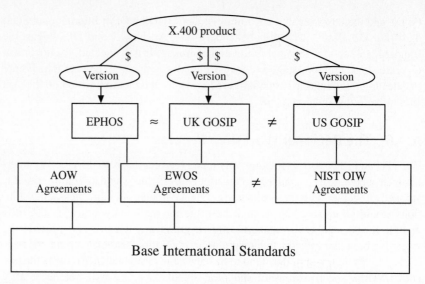

Figure A.1 The cost of incompatible profiles.

International Standardized Profiles (ISPs), offered a plan whereby regional profiles are coordinated through a Regional Workshop Coordinating Committee
(RWCC) populated by equal representation from the regional workshops. Figure
A.2 shows the revised concept of standardization using the ISP mechanism. Comparing this figure with Fig. A.1, we can see readily that the size of the regional
profiles will shrink along with the respective incompatibilities of profiles and
product costs.

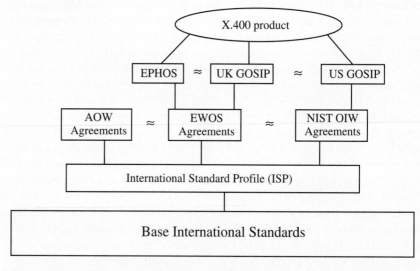

Figure A.2 Reduction of profile incompatibility through ISP harmonization.

European Profile Name	EWOS Profile Id	NIST Equivalent	ISP ID
MHS: Access to Public MHS (1984)	A/311	—	—
MHS: PRMD to PRMD (1984)	A/3211	Chapter 7	—
MHS: P1 (1988)	A/3311	Chapter 8	AMH 11
MHS: P7 (1988)	A/3312	Chapter 8	AMH 12
Directory Access Profile	A/711	Chapter 11	ADI 1
Directory System Profile	A/712	Chapter 11	—
Directory: Behavior of DSAs for Distributed Operation	A/713	Chapter 11	—
Directory: Dynamic Behavior of DUAs	A/714	—	—
Directory: Common Directory Usage	Q/511	Chapter 11	—
Directory Usage by MHS	Q/512	Chapter 8	—
Directory Usage by FTAM Q/513	—	—	—

Note: A/3211 is equivalent to ENV 41201. A/311 is equivalent to ENV 41202. ENVs are prestandards.

Table A.1   Regional profiles or working documents and ISP designations.

Various regional profiles for OSI standards, such as File Transfer, Access, and Management (FTAM), have already been reduced to Draft or Proposed Draft ISPs. Work is underway on the X.400 and X.500 profiles. Table A.1 cross-references some of the regional profiles with ISP documents.

Even with ISPs, differences reflecting truly unique regional, national, and cultural characteristics will remain. For instance, T.61 character sets are popular in Europe because they can display special European characters such as the umlaut. Extended character sets are popular in the Far East because they can represent nonLatin graphic characters. These characteristics suggest that support of those X.400 options associated with T.61 may be mandatory in Europe and Latin America, whereas options associated with extended character sets will be mandatory in Asian countries.

A.3.7   The Grand Architecture

The international standardization process does have problems. ISPs may serve vendors and users well in the end, but they add additional layers of bureaucracy and can slow down the standards development process. Some argue that the time taken to write ISPs reflects the time needed to do the job right. Other pundits hold that the ITU/ISO process is fatally flawed because standards are generally not subjected to implementation testing along their road to development. The Internet Engineering Task Force (IETF) follows a standards development methodology that requires implementation testing (the burden of proof lies with the developer). Perhaps as a result, the IETF has tended to develop *simpler* standards with a scope more limited than that of ITU/ISO standards.

We emphasize that there is a place in the world for simple standards and a place for grand architectures. The scope of some of the problems that we must solve to develop a grand architecture makes it impractical to perform implementation testing during the standards development process. In the case of X.400 and X.500, the benefits already gained, as well as much greater potential future benefits, may justify the risks and drawbacks associated with the ITU/ISO process.

A.4 THE INTERNET STANDARDS WORLD

Although the Internet community traces its origins to research begun in 1968, it is only in the last five or six years that the commercial world has fully recognized and supported its role in establishing open systems standards. While the Internet is not formally accredited, it has an extremely broad base of participation because of its open membership and its use of online information exchange and commentary. It is also international in scope.

A.4.1 The Roots of Internet Standardization

Chapter 4 traced the roots of the Internet to the early ARPANET project, begun in 1969 by the Defense Advanced Research Projects Agency (DARPA), which was originally founded to promote U.S. military technology innovation. The Internet working Protocol (IP) was developed to provide a common address space and routing across multiple lower-layer subnetworks. The Transmission Control Protocol (TCP) was developed to ensure the end-to-end integrity of data that crossed these subnetworks. Both were proposed around 1974 and implemented by 1976. The continued growth of the ARPANET and its transition to the modern Internet provided an early demonstration of the efficacy of standards in the world of networking.

Additional factors contributed to what has become the world's largest network and most widely adopted standards suite. The advent of the National Science Foundation Network (NSFNET) provided a high-bandwidth IP backbone, and seed money was allocated for consortia and regional networks. An inexpensive reference implementation of TCP/IP provided the interoperability model for emerging TCP/IP implementations. Standards documents were electronically available free of charge on the network, and the R&D community provided a bountiful supply of volunteer engineering labor free of charge. With the distribution of Berkeley Software Distribution (BSD) version 4.1, TCP/IP, and later Internet Mail, came to be shrink-wrapped in various vendor products.

The Internet, which had international involvement from its earliest days, has also spread to many countries and is now being offered in various guises to the general public. In Europe, two organizations employ, coordinate, and develop Internet technology and provide for crossmembership with the Internet Architecture Board (IAB, formerly known as the Internet Advisory Board). These two are the Réseaux Associés pour la Recherche Européenne (RARE) and the Réseaux IP Européens (RIPE). These organizations work with the IETF to ensure that international factors are considered in IETF work; in fact, MIME was initiated in part to permit Internet Mail messages to be in character sets other than ASCII in order to support languages other than English.

It is against this background that Internet Requests for Comments (RFCs), originally intended as working documents to be used within the relatively small Internet community, have become de facto standards in this ever-growing community.

A.4.2   The Internet Standards Process

In the Internet's early days, if a protocol described in a Request for Comment (RFC) seemed like a workable idea, someone would try to implement it; if the implementation proved successful, it was copied by other members of the Internet technical community. If the protocol was thus widely deployed, it would eventually be declared a standard. The Internet technical community has always been diverse and fluid, comprising research, academic, and engineering participants in an environment of open debate and the sharing of software and test results.[3] This "bottom-up" approach is the opposite of the ITU/ISO technique of creating grand architectures that are then mandated as international standards in advance of implementation.

The nature of the Internet standards orientation results in a quest for a simple, practical architecture that can be developed and deployed rapidly, rather than in the extended deliberation and search for an ultimate architectural solution that characterizes ISO and ITU proceedings. The intent is to build now, then test, deploy, and modify as required, providing for a lean architecture that has resulted in an installed base of thousands of networks and millions of users. An adjunct principle is that documentation and specifications be freely available to all interested parties.

Internet standards work is coordinated through the IAB which was organized from an earlier DARPA Internet Configuration Control Board. The IAB holds its authority by virtue of the technical credibility of its members and limited funding from the Federal Networking Council (a group of U.S. government agencies). When efforts to associate with an existing standards body did not prove useful, the Internet Society (ISOC) was formed and the IAB was placed under its aegis to be responsible for the "oversight of the architecture of the worldwide multiprotocol Internet." In this respect, the Internet community has slightly shifted its orientation and now embraces ISO and ITU, as well as popular proprietary protocols, along with its traditional TCP/IP suite.

The main engine of Internet standardization—the IETF—was added in 1986. Internet standards meetings are held in one-week sessions three times a year, including a plenary session for operations and technical reports, parallel working group meetings, and Birds of a Feather (BOF) exploratory meetings. During the late 1980s and early 1990s, the scope and agendas of these meetings grew to the point where a spin-off Internet Research Task Force (IRTF) was created to handle

---

3. We are grateful to David Crocker for his assistance and his chapter in [LYNC93] for most of this information on the Internet process.

long-term, exploratory activities, professional staff were hired (including an Executive Director for the IETF), an Internet Engineering Steering Group (IESG) was formed, and an "Area Director" sub-structure was instituted to assist the IETF Chair in administering technical topics and activities.

The IAB operates by the consent of the governed, meaning the IETF and the IRTF. It is expected to see that fairness and quality are maintained. Thus, it has instituted a more formal practice of reviewing and providing written feedback for specifications submitted to it as a way of improving the focus of the evaluation process as well as avoiding unproductive or redundant pursuits. It also reviews appeals to ensure that fairness is maintained.

The IRTF pursues long-term projects, such as the enhancement to Internet e-mail known as Privacy Enhanced Mail (PEM), that was recently submitted to the IETF for standardization. The IESG is made up of Area Directors and is responsible for overseeing working group activities. In a 1992 development, authority to approve or disapprove final standards was transferred from the IAB to the IESG. (The previous process had the IESG recommending standards to the IAB for their approval.) In addition, IAB members are now elected to two-year terms.

The IETF continues to develop specifications and provide a forum for ongoing discussions with emphasis on near-term solutions. Projects are selected based on a critical mass of workers willing to spend development time in working groups. Area Directors oversee working group activities that fall into one (or more) of such IETF areas as applications, user services, service applications, Internet services, routing and addressing, network management, operational requirements, and security. The Applications Area, for example, has oversight for electronic mail and standard application support infrastructures. The working group chair has responsibility for advancing the group's work in a consensus-based format (no formal votes are taken) and for utilizing diplomacy and negotiations in order to resolve differences while minimizing debate and time-to-market.

It is notable that the status of RFC documents has not always been well understood. Whereas all Internet standards are RFCs, not all RFCs have standards status. Work from other standards bodies are incorporated by reference (as an Informational RFC representing an easily accessible snapshot of current work). It is also notable that the first RFC to be called a standard, RFC 733, was the first formal specification for formatting ARPANET mail.

The RFC editor is a member of the IAB and is responsible for the style, format rules, and timely publication of these documents. The process is documented in RFC 1310: The Internet Standards Process [CHAP92].

A document positioned to become an Internet standard goes through three stages, each requiring the review and approval of the IESG, the IAB, and the entire IETF (via a Last Call electronic poll). A preliminary stage involves basic development, usually in the context of a group operating under charter from the IESG, where the specification has no formal status and may or may not be submitted to the next level. When the specification is deemed stable and is supported by a sufficient constituency attesting to its stability (preferably through implementation and testing, which the IESG has the option of requiring), it formally enters the standards track at the first stage as a *Proposed Standard.*

A specification can be elevated to *Draft Standard* status when there are at least two independent implementations that have interoperated to test all functions, and when it has been a proposed standard for six months or longer. If the testing results only in minor problems, the specification may progress; in the case of major changes introducing instability, it will be required to reenter the process as a Proposed Standard. (Major changes to the document's writing style should not affect progress along the standardization track, as long as the "bits sent over the wire" are not changed.)

A cornerstone of the Internet culture is the production of a reference implementation of the specification made available to the Internet community and perhaps placed in the public domain. A reference implementation is not a requirement for standardization, but it is considered to be an effective method for furthering the adoption of the specification.

When a Draft Standard holds this status for at least four additional months and gains field experience as well as demonstrates community interest in its use, it may be elevated to the status of *Internet Standard.* Its evaluation requires that it satisfy the following criteria (called the "4 C's" in [LYNC93]): competence, constituency, coherence, and consensus. The specification must also reflect an adequate consensus of the technical community.

Show stoppers to Internet standardization include claims of unfairness or technical inadequacy, which may eventually be addressed by the IESG. If a specification has not reached the Internet standard stage 24 months after becoming a proposed standard, the IESG reviews it and may determine that it has no further viability. Likewise, new versions of a given specification must go through the entire standards process. Finally, standards are assigned required, recommended, or elective status.

A good illustration of the Internet process for enhancing its specifications occurred when the IETF sought improvements to its Simple Mail Transfer Protocol (RFC 821) and the formats specified in RFC 822 (with a particular interest in supporting international character sets). A debate surfaced between those people who wished to modify the protocol to allow eight-bit traffic, and those who wished to modify the mail format specification to allow encoding of eight-bit data inside the message for transport over the current seven-bit paths. Two working groups were formed, and it is likely that the efforts of both groups will become standardized and used within the Internet.

Obtaining Copies of Internet RFCs and Drafts

The Internet has a number of sites at which interested parties can obtain copies of RFC or Internet draft documents. We describe the method of accessing one such site next; procedures to access other sites are similar.

To acquire RFCs or drafts through a mail server, send a message to:

NIS-INFO@NIS.NSF.NET

Use a blank subject line and, in the first line of the message, type *rfcxxxx.txt* where *xxxx* is the RFC number to be retrieved. (For three-digit RFCs, type *0xxx.*)

For Internet drafts, type the filename. To obtain the list of RFCs, type *index.rfc*; to obtain the list of drafts, type *1id-abstracts.txt*. When using anonymous FTP, direct inquiries to NIS.NSF.NET with user name as *anonymous* and password as *guest*. There are two directories: documents/rfc and documents/internet-drafts. Be aware, however, that server and file names are subject to change.

A.5 THE MAJOR ORGANIZATIONS AND CONSORTIA

Users in industry have had to grapple with the incompatibilities in electronic messaging standards that are created by the two parallel universes. In response to this challenge and with the aim of implementing standards through the further refinement of profiles or, more recently, through a drive toward convergence, industry consortia and associations have become increasingly important in the world of messaging and directories.

This section will describe briefly the missions and successes of those organizations, including:

- Aerospace Industries Association (AIA)
- Asynchronous Protocol Specification (APS) Alliance
- Corporation for Open System (COS)
- European Electronic Mail Association (EEMA)
- (North American) Electronic Mail Association (EMA)
- Institute of Electrical and Electronics Engineers (IEEE)
- ISODE Consortium
- Manufacturing Automation Protocol/Technical and Office Protocol (MAP/TOP)
- North American Directory Forum (NADF)
- Open Software Foundation (OSF)
- Utilities Communication Architecture (UCA)
- Vendor Independent Messaging (VIM) Consortium
- API Association (XAPIA)

A.5.1 Aerospace Industry Association

Aerospace contracts are typically too large for a single firm to handle; also, they are often bid to more than one firm to foster competition and to avail the government of more than one source. Aerospace firms found that their employees had a need to communicate via electronic mail with employees of related firms.

Thus, the Aerospace Industries Association's (AIA) Committee on Information Technology became the prime driver in fostering the X.400 interconnection of major carriers (ADMDs). Consisting of 54 member companies, the AIA was the first user organization forcibly to urge U.S.-based carriers to interconnect their electronic messaging capabilities. It was thus that AT&T, Dialcom, GEIS, IBM, MCI, Tymnet, Sprint, and Western Union undertook efforts to connect their X.400 services in the interest of global electronic messaging access. This effort was led by Boeing, General Dynamics, Grumman Corporation, Hughes, LTV Corporation, McDonnell Douglas, Northrop Corporation, and Westinghouse Electric Corporation.

Having accomplished the first phase, the AIA committee began running experimental messages across and among these networks to measure their effectiveness. The committee produces regular reports, or scorecards, which measure delays, lost messages, and recorded errors, all of which are then delivered to the VANs. The committee has also tested PRMD to ADMD connections as well as EDI data exchanges with an eye to implementing X.435 when feasible.

A.5.2 Asynchronous Protocol Specification Alliance

The Asynchronous Protocol Specification (APS) Alliance is made up of international vendors who have set about developing a standard that supports the transmission of X.400 traffic over dial-up telephone lines. The APS specification will allow Remote User Agents to dial into X.400 servers. It will also allow X.400 servers to dial other X.400 servers. The Alliance is led by Isocor and Norwegian Telecom/maXware along with 23 other vendors.

The APS Alliance developed a specification finalized in early 1993 to enable the dial-up transfer of X.400-based traffic, including EDI, interpersonal mail, voice, images, and facsimile. The specification will allow remote PC users to dial into their local-area networks or to send e-mail abroad without leased or dial-up X.25 connections. It will also be devised to allow X.400 over TCP/IP and will support low-speed and very high-speed modems. The APS is currently before the ITU as draft recommendation X.445 and will soon be submitted as a draft RFC.

For more information, contact:

The APS Alliance
Tel: 1 (800) 267-7737

A.5.3 The Corporation for Open Systems International

The Corporation for Open Systems International (COS) was established in 1986 to accelerate the deployment of interoperable OSI and ISDN technology. Founded primarily by vendors intent on stimulating the open systems market, COS initially focused on developing test systems to measure the conformance of OSI products to the standards or, more precisely, to the profiles or subsets of those standards. COS has issued stack specifications to describe the tests that products will undergo, and provides testing services through the administration of testing centers and the certification of first-party testing facilities.

For a time, COS awarded a certification, the COS Mark, for conformant products. The Mark required a commitment on the part of the vendor to intervene in cases where interoperability between COS marked products is not achieved.

Hewlett-Packard's OpenMail was the first X.400 product (1984) to pass conformance testing.

For more information, contact:

COS
8260 Willow Oaks Corporate Drive, Suite 700
Fairfax, VA 22031
TEL: USA (703) 205-2700
FAX: USA (703) 846-8590

A.5.4   OSINET

OSINET, an organization formed to foster the development and use of OSI products, now operates under the management of COS. It includes over 30 user and vendor member companies and operates with the assistance of volunteers from the membership.

Foremost among OSINET's accomplishments is the development of interoperability tests intended to provide a measure of confidence in OSI products beyond conformance testing. These tests are often used as qualifiers for participation in network demonstrations. They include tests for X.400 and X.500 that have been applied to a significant number of products in the marketplace or under development. More recently OSINET has begun to focus on testing the convergence of international standards, especially running such applications as X.400 and X.500 over TCP/IP.

OSINET also offers an on-line database containing entries for products that have been interoperability tested. Interested parties can dial into the OSINET database at USA (703) 846-8586 (2400 baud modem set at 8-N-1), via X.25 at 31342023004570, or via the Internet's telnet protocol to osinet@ coinrs6000.cos.com.

Sister companies around the world—including OSINET, Brisa (Brazil), EurOSInet (Europe), HOSIC (Hong Kong), INTAPnet (Japan), OSIcom (Australia), and OSnet (Singapore)—have joined together in an umbrella group, called OSI^{one}, to facilitate their interaction. They have agreed on a common set of interoperability tests and a common mechanism to report tests results, the latter in order to provide a measure of confidence to multinational companies who sell or purchase X.400 and X.500 products around the world. OSI^{one} is also building a database of known "Success Stories" of open systems implementations as gathered by member organizations.

For more information, contact OSINET using the address information for COS above.

A.5.5   Electronic Messaging Association

The Electronic Messaging Association (EMA) is an industry trade association dedicated to the promotion of electronic mail and more recently of integrated messaging. Founded in 1983, it had 261 member companies by 1993 and enjoys healthy attendance from the user, vendor, and public service provider communities. The individuals who attend have an interest in promoting electronic messaging and standards to increase the overall market share or the availability of products and services. From time to time, the EMA publishes handbooks designed to facilitate the job of those who must make the case to their management for investing in messaging components.

The EMA meets several times a year. Its primary meeting takes the form of a conference that may also be attended by nonmembers. In addition, committees addressing industry issues—such as the PRMD Operators and Interconnection Committee, the Directory Committee, the Privacy and Security Committee, the Market Awareness Committee, the LAN E-mail Committee, and the Standards Committee—may meet more often throughout the year.

For more information, contact:

Electronic Messaging Association
1655 N. Fort Myer Drive, Suite 850
Arlington, VA 22209
Tel. (703) 524-5550
Fax. (703) 524-5558
E-mail: EasyLink, Envoy 100, GEnie, MCI, Pacific Bell
SprintMail: EMA
AT&T Mail: !EMA
CompuServe: 70007,2377
Dialcom: 52:PRDOO3
IBM Mail Exchange: USEMA001 at IBMMail

A.5.6   The European Electronic Mail Association

The European Electronic Mail Association (EEMA) was established in 1987 to create an electronic mail forum for users, vendors, suppliers, policy makers, and consultants. It serves a purpose in Europe similar to that served by the EMA in the U.S. with a special focus on the interconnection of European ADMDs and the development of a continent-wide infrastructure. Like the EMA, the EEMA does its work through task groups and committees, and it also meets in conference annually.

For more information, contact:

EEMA
Pastoral House, Ramble Close
Inkberrow, Worcs, WR7 4EL
United Kingdom
Tel: +44 386 793028
Fax: +44 386 793268
SprintMail: EEMA
AT&T Mail: !EEMA
Mercury: 19043155
X.400: C=GB;ADMD=TMAILUK;O=EEMA;S=Dean;
   G=ROGER;DDA=ID;EEMA

A.5.7 Electronic Mail Management Working Group

A joint IFIP WG 6.5 and 6.6 Electronic Mail Management Working Group was formed in mid-1992 to examine the overall problem of e-mail network management (including X.400/X.500, SMTP, and LAN e-mail). Its objective has been to produce a requirements document, a model, and managed object definitions for multivendor end-to-end e-mail network management.

The mail management group deliberates in two ways. First, there is a mailing list—*ifip-e-mailmgt@ics.uci.edu*–upon which open discussions are posted and through which documents are disseminated. Second, the group seeks to hold breakout meetings at any industry assembly where messaging and/or network management expertise gathers. For example, meetings have been held at the NIST OIW and at the IETF. There tends to be high turnover between such meetings; however, all binding decisions and approvals are made via the mailing list rather than at physical meetings.

A.5.8 Institute of Electrical and Electronics Engineers (IEEE)

The IEEE is a professional association dedicated to the development and advancement of electrical and electronics engineering technology. It also sponsors various working groups to advance standards in a wide range of fields. As part of the Open Systems Environment work conducted by the Technical Committee on Operating Systems (TCOS), the IEEE P1224 working group has standardized X.400, X.500, and Object Management API Specifications based on the X.400 API Association and X/Open API documents. These standards will be submitted to the Joint Technical Committee 1 (JTC1) for fast-track approval as international standards. The X.400 API Association and X/Open EDI and Message Store APIs, as well as the "simple set" of e-mail APIs, are being considered for standardization by the IEEE P1224 group beginning in late 1993.

For more information, contact:

IEEE
345 East 47th Street
New York, NY 10017-2394
Tel: (212) 705-7018

A.5.9 ISODE Consortium

The ISODE Consortium is a not-for-profit organization established to promote and develop the ISODE package of OSI applications. The intent of the consortium is to stimulate the marketplace by developing software more rapidly than would be possible for any single member. The major goal of the Consortium is to evolve OSI-based applications with high functionality that can be used directly or as the basis (seed code) for products. Development work is done either directly by the consortium, through subcontracts, or through contributions from the membership.

ISODE developments have been used extensively in the research community. The X.400 (PP) and X.500 (QUIPU) products, which represent the major focus of the Consortium, have been particularly successful. Also, support for use of applications over TCP/IP have been promoted in parallel with use over the OSI lower layers. Consortium releases are made available exclusively to its membership; and academic, not-for-profit, and government organizations with research as their primary purpose are given access to ISODE releases at minimal cost.

For more information, contact:

ISODE Consortium
P.O. Box 200195
Austin, TX 78720
Tel: (512) 338-3340
Fax: (512) 338-3600

or

P.O. Box 505
London SW11 1DX UK
Tel: (+44) 71-223-4062
Fax: (+44) 71-223-3846
E-mail: RFC 822: ic-info@isode.com
X.400: C=GB; A=0; P=ISODE;
    O=ISODE Consortium; S=ic-info

A.5.10 Manufacturing Automation Protocol/Technical and Office Protocol

Since March 1984 (following the GM task force selection of OSI as a basis for manufacturing automation), the Manufacturing Automation Protocol/Technical and Office Protocol (MAP/TOP) Users Group has chartered regional (North American, Asian, European, Eastern Bloc) Users Groups and a World Federation. These organizations develop specifications and work with standards-setting organizations to ensure that the needs of the factory floor and office automation are considered in standards development.

The TOP Users Group was formed in December 1985, following the participation of such companies as Boeing Aircraft in the National Bureau of Standards demonstration of the first OSI LAN (TOP Version 1.0). Its principal goal has been to accelerate the availability of multivendor, economical, interoperable, off-the-shelf computing systems, devices, and components.

TOP soon became allied with MAP, where it has focused on office automation and engineering OSI application profiles (hence, the reference now is always to the MAP/TOP Users Group). User applications supported by the TOP Specification include electronic mail, word processing, text and graphics merge, database access, file transfer and access, distributed CAD/CAM, spreadsheet exchange, banking transactions, and resource sharing. In this regard, X.400 plays a major role as the electronic messaging application and as a carrier for EDI and ODA applications.

The TOP Specification is built on international standards and, where no international standards exist, on national standards. In defining the TOP Specification, the MAP/TOP Users Group draws on the work of standards-making bodies including ISO, the ITU, and ANSI, as well as of standards-related bodies such as the IEEE and ECMA. In addition, TOP will be consistent with and complementary to GOSIP via the Industry/Government Open Systems Specification (IGOSS).

A.5.11   North American Directory Forum

The North American Directory Forum (NADF) is an organization of telecommunications carriers and information service providers that has reached consensus on the fundamental shape of X.500 interconnections among directories in North America. As of early 1994, NADF was still in the process of conducting an experimental pilot involving both public service providers and users. Formed in 1990, the NADF is discussed in detail in Chapters 4 and 8. NADF documents can be obtained by following the instructions in RFC 1417.

A.5.12   Open Software Foundation (OSF)

OSF is a consortium of unlikely bedfellows (IBM, DEC, and many others) originally founded during the "UNIX wars," pitting them against AT&T, Sun Microsystems, and their fellow travelers. The OSF has forged ahead with de facto standards for the network computing environment, including the Distributed Computing Environment (DCE). DCE, which is being licensed to OSF members, is intended to provide a comprehensive, integrated service set supporting the development, use, and maintenance of distributed applications.

A feature of DCE and its services is the X.500-compliant name service that allows users to identify by name resources such as files, disks, print queues, and servers. OSF's directory service is described [OSF91] as seamlessly integrating the X.500 global naming system with a fast-replicated local naming system. It provides full protocol support for X.500 and open access using the X.500 API from X/Open and the X.400 API Association (and accommodating OSI, TCP/IP, and other protocols).

Major vendors expect to implement DCE in their software. Also, DCE may end up having a place in NIST's Application Portability Profile (APP).

A.5.13   Utilities Communication Architecture (UCA)

The utilities industry has acquired a plethora of networks for corporate data communications (engineering, customer information, general business), supervisory control (modeling, simulation, work and records management), data acquisition (energy management and accounting, data exchange, metering), and real-time monitoring and control (protection, equipment configuration and diagnostics, load control). These implementations are complicated by multiple network management systems and a dispersal of telecommunications responsibility throughout utility organizations.

In response to these developments and under the auspices of the Application Portability Profile (APP), the industry has developed a Utility Communication Architecture "to specify OSI standards that meet the specific communication needs of the electric utility industry and are practical to specify in procurements at this time." This architecture, directed to utility MIS and procurement personnel as well as vendors and systems integrators, includes the implementation of X.400 and X.500 standards.

The thrust of the UCA specification is to assist utilities in deploying the recommended protocols, and it will also become part of the IGOSS concurrent with GOSIP Version 3. It is noteworthy that Digital Equipment Corporation announced the first UCA-compliant products. Although these products are not new, Digital worked with EPRI during 1991 and 1992 to ensure that they conform to UCA specifications, and X.400 1984 and 1988, as well as X.500, are included. (DEC also claims that its products are certified for OSI conformance by the COS.) According to EPRI, 33 other companies are working on UCA-compliant products.

For more information, contact:

Electric Power Research Institute
3412 Hillview Ave.
Palo Alto, CA 94304

A.5.14   Vendor Independent Messaging Consortium

The Vendor Independent Messaging (VIM) consortium was formed in February 1992, with impetus from Lotus Development Corporation in collaboration with Apple Computer, Novell, and Borland International. The consortium released a nonproprietary programming interface, dubbed VIM and designed to help software and corporate developers write mail-enabled applications. VIM was a competitive response to the Microsoft API (MAPI); however, the consortium has promised MAPI integration that allows VIM applications to run even if the programs to which they are interfaced were developed according to MAPI specifications.

A.5.15   X.400 Application Program Interface Association

The X.400 Application Program Interface (API) Association has developed a standardized API for X.400 and X.400 gateways as well as an X.500 API in cooperation with X/OPEN. The X.500 API is intended to foster the spread of the standard by allowing developers to code their directory applications to a normalized set of specifications.

APIA founders are Retix and Sprint. Additional (1993) APIA members include American Express, AT&T Bell Labs, Boeing Computer Services, British Telecom, BULL HN Information Systems, cc:Mail/Lotus, Data Connection, Ltd., Digital Equipment Corporation, Hewlett-Packard, Hitachi, GM Hughes Electronics, IBM, Isocor, Microsoft Corporation, Monsanto, Novell, OSIware, RAM Mobile Data, Soft*Switch, and Tandem Computers.

During the API wars between Microsoft and the VIM Consortium, Microsoft approached the XAPIA and requested that it develop a simple send API for the industry. The XAPIA agreed and has developed a Common Messaging Call (CMC) API with simple send, fetch, and get address functions. The intent of CMC is to replace existing proprietary API calls with equivalent functionality, thus sharply reducing the necessary effort to develop mail-enabled desktop applications across platforms.

CMC can be used over X.400, SMTP, and proprietary mail systems. It provides the means for application programs to accomplish such functions as simple send, fetch, and get, even when the underlying message system is not known. Also, for developers who want to accommodate features specific to a given message system, XAPIA has specified extensions; these can be registered with XAPIA as a way of encouraging consistent implementations across the industry. The XAPIA is also working to develop a calendar/scheduling enabling API.

For more information, contact:

XAPIA Public Relations and Marketing
10151 Western Drive
Cupertino, CA 95014
Tel. (408) 446-9158
Fax. (408) 257-1478

A.6   SUMMARY

Standards are now recognized as essential to building an enterprise messaging network. However, as more than one pundit has remarked, "The wonderful thing about standards is that there are so many of them!" In the case of open systems electronic messaging standards, there are really only two major sets, which is still more than enough to challenge the strategic planning prowess of the most courageous of users. Nevertheless, the very fact that consortia organized to make standards workable are proliferating confirms that the marketplace has accepted this premise as given: electronic messaging products and consequent enterprise messaging networks will be standards-based—whether de jure or de facto—and thus will be increasingly amenable to achieving the goal of worldwide interoperability.

A P P E N D I X B

Bibliographic References

ALMQ92   Almquist, P. "Type of Service in the Internet Protocol Suite: RFC 1349." (Updates RFCs 1248, 1247, 1195, 1123, 1122, 1060, 791), 1992.

ALVE93   Alvestrand, H., S. Kille, R. Miles, M. Rose, and S. Thompson. "Mapping between X.400 and RFC-822 Message Bodies: RFC 1495." (Obsoletes RFC 1327), 1993.

ALVE93A   Alvestrand, H. "Language Tags for MIME Content Portions." Internet Draft <draft-alvestrand-language-tag-00.txt>, 1993.

ALVE93B   Alvestrand, H., K. Jordan, and S. Langlois. "Introducing Project Long Bud Internet Pilot Project for the Deployment of X.500 Directory Information in Support of X.400 Routing." <Internet Draft <draft-ietf-mhsds-long-bud-intro-00.txt>.

ALVE93C   Alvestrand, H., J. Romaguera, and K. Jordan. "Rules for Downgrading Messages from X.400/88 to X.400/84 When MIME Content-Types Are Present in the Messages: RFC 1496." (Updates RFC 1328), 1993.

ALVE93D   Alvestrand, H., and S. Thompson. "Equivalences Between 1988 X.400 and RFC-822 Message Bodies: RFC 1494, 1993.

ANKN92   Ankney, Richard. "Security for Groupware Applications." Fischer International Systems Corporation, 1992.

ANSI93   "Public Key Cryptography Using Irreversible Algorithms for the Financial Services Industry: Draft ANSI X9.30." 1993.

APS93   "Asynchronous Protocol Specification (APS) Alliance: Program Description and Meeting Plan." Cupertino, CA: Asynchronous Protocol Specification Alliance, 1993.

APS93A   "Asynchronous Protocol Specification: Message Handling Sys-
                tems—Asynchronous Protocol for OSI Network Service over
                the Telephone Network: Draft Recommendation X.APS."
                Geneva: International Telecommunication Union/Telecommu-
                nication Standardization Sector, 1993.

BANA93   Banan, Mohsen. "Body Part 15 White Paper." Arlington, VA:
                Electronic Mail Association, 1993.

BLUM92   Blum, Daniel J., and DML Associates. *The Messaging Connec-
                tion: Integrated Messaging and Directories Based on X.400/
                X.500 Standards in the 1990s.* Fairfax, VA: DML Associates
                and Bethesda, MD: Phillips Publishing, 1992.

BLUM93   Blum, Daniel, and Gary Rowe. "E-mail Switches Emerge as
                Enterprising Idea." *Network World*, February 15, 1993, pp. 82–
                88.

BLUM93A   Blum, Daniel. "The 1988 X.400 Migration White Paper." Ar-
                lington, VA: Electronic Mail Association, 1993.

BORE93   Borenstein, Nathaniel. "Infrastructure for Personal Liberation."
                Conference Presentation: E-mail World, November 3, 1993.

BORE93A   Borenstein, Nathaniel. "A User Agent Configuration Mecha-
                nism for Multimedia Mail Format Information: RFC 1524,"
                1993.

BORE92   Borenstein, Nathaniel. "Implications of MIME for Internet Mail
                Gateways: RFC 1344," 1992.

BRAD89   Branden, R., ed. "Requirements for Internet Hosts—Applica-
                tion and Support: RFC 1123." (Updated by RFC 1349), 1989.

BREI91   Breitenberg, Maureen A. *Laboratory Accreditation in the
                United States.* Gaithersburg, MD: National Institute of Stan-
                dards and Technology Standards Code and Information Pro-
                gram, 1991.

BROW93A   Brown, Bob. "Directory Sync Plans Under Way." *Network
                World*, Volume 10, Number 25, June 21, 1993, pp. 1 and 63.

BROW93B   Brown, Bob. "Call Is Sounded for Calendar Standards." *Net-
                work World*, Volume 10, Number 28, July 12, 1993, pp. 7 and
                46.

BURN93   Burns, Christine. "Banyan Details StreetTalk Net Control En-
                hancements." *Network World*, Volume 10, Number 40, October
                4, 1993, p. 7.

CARL92   Carl-Mitchell, Smoot, and John S. Quarterman. "Growth of the
                Internet." *RS Magazine*, November, 1992, pp. 28–32.

CARL93   Carl-Mitchell, Smoot, and John S. Quarterman. *Practical
                Internetworking with TCP/IP and UNIX.* Reading, MA: Addison-
                Wesley, 1993.

CASI93   "EMS—The MetaMail System for CICS." Irvine, CA: Computer Application Services, Inc., 1993.

CHAP92   Chapin, Lyman. "The Internet Standards Process: RFC 1310," 1992.

CHOI93   Choi. "Korean Character Encoding for Internet Messages: RFC 1557," 1993.

CLNP86   Information Processing Systems—Protocol for Providing the Connectionless Network Service, ISO 8473, 1986.

CNRI91   "Announcing the Internet Society." Reston, VA: Corporation for National Research Initiatives, 1991.

CNRI92   "Charter of the Internet Society." Reston, VA: Corporation for National Research Initiatives, 1992.

COME88   Comer, Douglas, and David L. Stevens. *Internetworking with TCP/IP: Principles, Protocols, and Architecture*. Englewood Cliffs, NJ: Prentice–Hall, 1988.

COME92   Comer, Douglas. *Internetworking with TCP/IP, Volume II: Design, Implementation, and Internals*. Englewood Cliffs, NJ: Prentice-Hall, 1992.

CRIS93   Crispin, Mark. "Interactive Mail Access Protocol—Version 2bis." Internet Draft <draft-ietf-imap-imap2bis-02.txt>, 1993.

CROC82   Crocker, David H. "Standard for the Format of ARPA Internet Text Messages: RFC 822," 1982.

CROC93   Crocker, D. "MIME Multipart/Header-Set." Internet Draft <draft-crocker-headerset-00.txt, .ps>, 1993.

CROC93A   Crocker, D. "MIME Application/EDI-X12." Internet Draft <draft-crocker-edi-00.txt>, 1993.

CROK93   Crocker, S., N. Freed, and J. Galvin. "MIME–PEM Interaction." Internet Draft <draft-ietf-pem-mime-03.txt>, 1993.

DAVI92   Davidow, William H., and Michael S. Malone. *The Virtual Corporation: Structuring and Revitalizing the Corporation for the 21st Century*. New York: Edward Burlingame Books/ HarperBusiness, 1992.

DAWS93   Dawson, Frank. "XAPIA X.400 Association CMC 2.0 Project." EMA 1993 Fall Membership Meeting, 1993.

DAWS93A   Dawson, Frank. "XAPIA X.400 Association Calendaring and Scheduling Project." Conference Presentation: EMA 1993 Fall Membership Meeting, 1993.

DENN92   "E-mail: Now Come the API Wars." *LAN Times*, November 23, 1992, pp. 60–62.

DEUT93   Deutsch, Peter. "Architecture of the WHOIS++ service." Not quite an Internet Draft, 1993.

EDI90   "Message Handling: EDI Messaging Service: Draft Recommendation F.435." Lausanne: CCITT, 1990.

EDI91   "Message Handling Systems, EDI Messaging System: Recommendation X.435." Lausanne: CCITT, 1991.

EDI91A   *FIPS PUB 161: Electronic Data Interchange (EDI)*. Federal Information Processing Standards Publication, 1991.

EDI93   Van Kirk, Doug. "EDI Is Coming Soon to a PC Near You." *InfoWorld*, August 16, 1993, pp. 51–52.

EDI93A   "E-mail and EDI Under Electronic Commerce." *Electronic Messaging News*, Volume 5, Number 14, July 7, 1993, pp. 5–6.

EDIFACT   *Electronic Data Interchange for Administration, Commerce, and Transport (EDIFACT)—Application Level Syntax Rules: ISO 9375*, 1988.

EEMA93A   Sleeman, Bob. "Banks Request EU Code." *EEMA Briefing*, Volume 5, Number 1, July 1992, p. 13.

EEMA93B   Arnum, Eric. "The Internet Goes Commercial." *EEMA Briefing*, Volume 5, Number 4, December 1992, p. 16.

EEMA93D   "Internet Goes Commercial in Finland." *EEMA Briefing*, Volume 5, Number 6, April 1993, p. 3.

EEMA93E   Romaguera, Jim. "X.400 Meets Internet—Special Project Making Good Progress." *EEMA Briefing*, Volume 6, Number 2, August 1993, pp. 3 and 12.

EEMA93F   Romaguera, Jim. "E-mail in Internet: A Commercial Viewpoint." *EEMA Briefing*, Volume 6, Number 3, October 1993, pp. 11–13.

EEMA93G   "European ADMD Interconnection Status: October 15, 1993." *EEMA Briefing*, Volume 6, Number 3, October 1993, pp. 8–10.

EEMA93H   Romaguera, James A. "Can I Reach the Internet, RARE, BITNET, EARN...?" *EEMA Briefing*, Volume 5, Number 4, December 1992, p. 12.

EMGT93   "Electronic Mail Management Group Charter." IFIP, March 1, 1993.

EMMS93   "AT&T EasyLink Interconnects with EMBARC and Six Other ADMDs." *Electronic Mail & Micro Systems*, Volume 17, Number 5, March 1, 1993, pp. 11–13.

EMMS93A   "E-Mail and Fax in Europe and North America Compared." *Electronic Mail & Micro Systems*, Volume 17, Number 11, June 1993, pp. 6–10.

EMMS93B   "How Huge Is 'Microsoft At Work' for Fax?" *Electronic Mail & Micro Systems*, Volume 17, Number 13, July 1, 1993.

EMMS93C "Corrections to AT&T Easylink Interconnection Chart." *Electronic Mail & Micro Systems*, Volume 17, Number 7, April 15, 1993, pp. 12–13.

EMMS93D "How Huge Will 'Microsoft At Work' Be for Computer-based Fax?" *Electronic Mail & Micro Systems*, Volume 17, Number 14, July 15, 1993.

EMMS93E "What Are the Pitfalls of 'Microsoft At Work for Fax?' for Computer-based Fax?" *Electronic Mail & Micro Systems*, Volume 17, Number 15, August 1, 1993.

EMMS93F "X.400 Pulls Even with the Internet as Four More Countries Join EEMA X.400 List." *Electronic Mail & Micro Systems*, Volume 17, Number 18, September 1, 1993, pp. 5–6.

EMMS93G "Lotus Merges Messaging Products and Multiplies the Platforms They Run On." *Electronic Mail & Micro Systems*, Volume 17, Number 20, October 15, 1993, pp. 1–6.

EMMS93H "Year-end 1992 E-mailbox Installed Base Report." *Electronic Mail & Micro Systems*, Volume 17, Number 1, January 1, 1993, pp. 1–5.

EMMS93I "Just How Big Is the Internet, Anyway?" *Electronic Mail & Micro Systems*, Volume 17, Number 1, January 1, 1993, pp. 1–5.

EMMS93J "Just How Big Is the Internet, Anyway?" *Electronic Mail & Micro Systems*, Volume 17, Number 10, May 15, 1993, pp. 3–5.

EMMS93K "Consumer E-mail Services Grow; America Online's Stocks Skyrockets." *Electronic Mail & Micro Systems*, Volume 17, Number 19, October 1, 1993, pp. 1–5.

EMMS94 "U.S. E-Mail Installed Base Soars Past 31 Million Mark." *Electronic Mail & Micro Systems*, Volume 18, Number 1, January 1, 1994, pp. 1–10.

EMN93A "ISODE Launches New Version of QUIPU." *Electronic Messaging News*, Volume 5, Number 7, March 31, 1993, pp. 5–6.

EMN93B "Company Size Plays Significant Role in E-mail Use." *Electronic Messaging News*, Volume 5, Number 11, May 26, 1993, pp. 1–2.

EMN93C "API Wars May Be Coming to an End." *Electronic Messaging News*, Volume 5, Number 13, June 23, 1993, pp. 1–2.

EMN93D "European E-mail Market Revenues on the Rise." *Electronic Messaging News*, Volume 5, Number 21, October 13, 1993, pp. 1–2.

EWOS91 "EWOS Guide to Profiles for the Open Systems Environment: Issue 1, Draft 5." Brussels: EWOS, 1991.

EXEC93 "Streamlining Procurement Through Electronic Commerce." *Federal Register*, Volume 58, Number 207.

FAVR92   Favreau, Jean-Phillipe. "The Five Q's (Cues) of the U.S. GOSIP
                Testing Program." Gaithersburg, MD: NIST Computer Systems
                Laboratory, 1992.

FERR93   *Annual Corporate Survey.* Ferris Networks, 2993.

FTAM1   Information Processing Systems—Open Systems Interconnec-
                tion—File Transfer, Access and Management Part I: General
                Introduction, ISO 8571–1 (ISO T97/SC21 N2331).

FTAM2   Information Processing Systems—Open Systems Interconnec-
                tion—File Transfer, Access and Management Part 2: The Vir-
                tual Filestore Definition, ISO 8571–2 (ISO T97/SC21 N2332).

FTAM3   Information Processing Systems—Open Systems Intercon-
                nection—File Transfer, Access and Management Part 3: File
                Service Definition, ISO 8571–3 (ISO T97/SC21 N2333).

FTAM4   Information Processing Systems—Open Systems Intercon-
                nection—File Transfer, Access and Management Part 4: File
                Protocol Specification, ISO 8571–4 (ISO T97/SC21 N2334).

GARG93   Gargano, Joan, and Ken Weiss. "Whois and Network Informa-
                tion Lookup Service Whois++." Internet Draft, 1993.

GOSI88   FIPS PUB 146: Government Open Systems Interconnection
                Profile (GOSIP), Version 1.0. Federal Information Processing
                Standards Publication, 1988.

GOSI91   FIPS PUB 146-1: Government Open Systems Interconnection
                Profile (GOSIP), Version 2.0. Federal Information Processing
                Standards Publication, 1991.

GUPT93   Gupta, Upenda. "X.400 and the Internet." Sprint International.

HAIS93   Haisting, Larry J. "EDI: A New Way of Doing Business." St.
                Paul, MN: St. Paul Software, 1993.

HAMM93   Hammer, Michael. "Re-engineering Work: Don't Automate,
                Obliterate." *Harvard Business Review*, July–August, 1990.

HARR85   Harrenstien, K., M. Stahl, and E. Feinler. "NICNAME/WHOIS:
                RFC 954." (Obsoletes RFC 811), 1985.

HARR85A   Harrenstien, K., M. Stahl, and E. Feinler. "DoD Internet host
                table specification: RFC 952." (Obsoletes RFC 810), 1985.

HEAF92   Heafner, John. "What OSINET Has Done for You Lately?"
                Fairfax, VA: OSINET, 1992.

HORT86   Horton, M. "UUCP Mail Interchange Format Standard: RFC
                976." (Updated by RFC 1137), 1986.

IEEE92   "Standard for Information Technology—Directory Services
                Application Program Interface (API)—Language Independent
                Specification: P1224.2." IEEE Open Systems Environment:
                Technical Committee on Operating Systems (TCOS), 1992.

INFO92   "What We Have Here Is a Failure to Communicate." *Infoworld*, October 12, 1992.

ISO92   "ISO Open Systems Interconnection—Basic Reference Model, Second Edition." ISO/TC 97/SC 16 [ISO CD 7498-1], 1992.

ITU84   *CCITT Recommendations X.400 to X.430 (1984): Data Communication Networks, Message Handling Systems.* Red Book.

ITU84A   *CCITT Recommendation X.25 (1984): Interface Between Data Terminal Equipment (DTE) and Data Circuit-Terminating Equipment (DCE) for Terminals Operating in the Packet Mode on Public Data Networks.* Red Book.

ITU88   *CCITT Recommendations X.400 to X.420 (1988): Data Communication Networks, Message Handling Systems.* Blue Book. Also ISO/IEC Standards ISO 10021-1 to ISO 10021-7.

ITU88A   *CCITT Recommendations X.500 to X.521 (1988): Data Communication Networks, Directory.* Blue Book. Also ISO/IEC Standards ISO 9594-1 to ISO 9594-7.

ITU88B   *CCITT Recommendation X.200 (1988): Reference Model of Open Systems Interconnection for CCITT Applications.* Blue Book. Also ISO/IEC Standard ISO 7498 (1984).

ITU88C   *CCITT Recommendation X.208 (1988): Specification of Abstract Syntax Notation One (ASN.1).* Blue Book. Also ISO/IEC Standards ISO 8824 and ISO 8824/ADI (1987).

ITU88D   *CCITT Recommendation X.209 (1988): Specification of Basic Encoding Rules for Abstract Syntax Notation One (ASN.1).* Blue Book. Also ISO/IEC Standards ISO 8825 and ISO 8825/ ADI (1987).

ITU88E   *CCITT Recommendation X.214 (1988): Transport Service Definition for Open Systems Interconnection for CCITT Applications.* Blue Book. Also ISO/IEC Standard ISO 8072 (1986).

ITU88F   *CCITT Recommendation X.224 (1988): Transport Protocol Specification for Open Systems Interconnection for CCITT Applications.* Blue Book. Also ISO/IEC Standard ISO 8072 (1986).

ITU88G   *CCITT Recommendation X.215 (1988): Session Service Definition for Open Systems Interconnection for CCITT Applications.* Blue Book. Also ISO/IEC Standards ISO 8326 and 8326/AD2 (1987).

ITU88H   *CCITT Recommendation X.225 (1988): Session Protocol Specification for Open Systems Interconnection for CCITT Applications.* Blue Book. Also ISO/IEC Standards ISO 8327 and 8327/ AD2 (1987).

ITU88I   *CCITT Recommendation X.216 (1988): Presentation Service Definition for Open Systems Interconnection for CCITT Applications.* Blue Book. Also ISO/IEC Standard ISO 8822 (1988).

ITU88J   *CCITT Recommendation X.226 (1988): Presentation Protocol Specification for Open Systems Interconnection for CCITT Applications.* Blue Book. Also ISO/IEC Standard ISO 8823 (1988).

ITU88K   *CCITT Recommendation X.217 (1988): Association Control Service Definition for Open Systems Interconnection for CCITT Applications.* Blue Book. Also ISO/IEC Standard ISO 8649.

ITU88L   *CCITT Recommendation X.227 (1988): Association Control Protocol Specification for Open Systems Interconnection for CCITT Applications.* Blue Book. Also ISO/IEC Standard ISO 8650.

ITU88M   *CCITT Recommendation X.218 (1988): Reliable Transfer: Model and Service Definition.* Blue Book. Also ISO/IEC Standard ISO 9066-1.

ITU88N   *CCITT Recommendation X.228 (1988): Reliable Transfer Protocol Specification.* Blue Book. Also ISO/IEC Standard ISO 9066-2.

ITU88O   *CCITT Recommendation X.219 (1988): Remote Operations: Model, Notation and Service Definition.* Blue Book. Also ISO/IEC Standard ISO 9072-1.

ITU88P   *CCITT Recommendation X.229 (1988): Remote Operations: Protocol Specification.* Blue Book. Also ISO/IEC Standard ISO 9072-2.

ITU88Q   *CCITT Recommendation X.290 (1988): OSI Conformance Testing Methodology and Framework for Protocol Recommendations for CCITT Applications.* Blue Book. Also ISO/IEC Standards ISO 9646-1 and 9646-2.

ITU92   *CCITT Recommendations X.400 Series (1992): Data Communication Networks, Message Handling Systems.* Blue Book.

JITC92   "U.S. GOSIP Testing Program Registers." Fort Huachuca, AZ: Defense Information Systems Agency Joint Interoperability and Engineering Organization, 1992.

KABA93   Kabay, Michael. "ITAR Sticks Users with Unfair Encryption Restrictions." *Network World*, November 8, 1993, p. 42.

KILL86   Kille, S. "Mapping Between X.400 and RFC 822: RFC 987." (Obsoleted by RFC 1327), 1986.

KILL89   Kille, S. "Mapping Between Full RFC 822 and RFC 822 with Restricted Encoding: RFC 1137." (Updates RFC 976), 1989.

KILL91   Kille, S. "Replication Requirements to Provide an Internet Directory Using X.500: RFC 1275," 1991.

KILL91A   Kille, S. "Replication and Distributed Operations Extensions to Provide an Internet Directory Using X.500: RFC 1276," 1991.

KILL92   Hardcastle-Kille, S. "Mapping Between X.400(1988)/ISO 10021 and RFC 822. RFC 1327." (Obsoletes RFCs 987, 1026, 1138, 1148; Obsoleted by RFC 1495; Updates RFC 822), 1992.

KILL93   Kille, Steve. "MHS Use of Directory to Support MHS Routing." Internet Draft <draft-ietf-mhsds-routdirectory-03.txt>.

KOBI93   Kobielus, James. "Directory Synchronization: Too Vital to Leave to Vendors." *Network World*, October 25, 1993, p. 40.

KROL92   Krol, Ed. *The Whole Internet: User's Guide & Catalog.* Sebastopol, CA: O'Reilly & Associates, 1992.

LAMB88   Lambert, M. "PCMAIL: A Distributed Mail System for Personal Computers: RFC 1056." (Obsoletes RFC 993), 1988.

LEE93   Lee, Eugene. "Mail-enabled Applications." Presented at the Electronic Mail Association Membership Meeting, January 26, 1993.

LOTU92   *Lotus Backgrounder.* Cambridge, MA: Lotus Development Corporation, 1992.

LOTU93   *The Lotus Notes Guide.* Cambridge, MA: Lotus Development Corporation, 1993.

LOTU93A   *Lotus Messaging Strategy.* Cambridge, MA: Lotus Development Corporation, 1993.

LYNC93   Lynch, Daniel C., and Marshall T. Rose. *Internet System Handbook.* Reading, MA: Addison-Wesley, 1993.

MANS93   Mansfield. "X.500 Directory Monitoring MIB: RFC 1567," 1994.

MAPI93   "Microsoft Client Developer's Guide." Microsoft Messaging API (MAPI), Beta Version 1.08. Redmond, WA: Microsoft Corporation, 1993.

MAPI93A   "Microsoft Service Provider Developer's Guide." Microsoft Messaging API (MAPI), Beta Version 1.08. Redmond, WA: Microsoft Corporation, 1993.

MARI93   Marine, April. "X.500 Pilot Projects." Internet Draft <draft-ietf-ids-pilots-00.txt>, 1993.

MICR93   "Microsoft Workgroup Computing Strategy." Redmond, WA: Microsoft Corporation, 1993.

MCCR93   McCready, Scott. "Workflow Specialist Speaks Out." *Network World*, July 5, 1993, pp. 27–30.

MICR93A   "Microsoft At Work Architecture Backgrounder." Redmond, WA: Microsoft Corporation, 1993.

MIME93   Borenstein, N., and N. Freed. "MIME (Multipurpose Internet Mail Extensions) Part One: Mechanisms for Specifying and Describing the Format of Internet Bodies: RFC 1521." (Obsoletes RFC 1341), 1993.

MIME93A   Moore, K. "MIME (Multipurpose Internet Mail Extensions), Part Two: Message Header Extensions for Non-ASCII Text: RFC 1522." (Obsoletes RFC 1342), 1993.

MIME93B   Borenstein, N. "The Text/Enriched MIME Content-type: RFC 1563," 1993.

MOCK87   Mockapetris, Paul V. "Domain Names—Concepts and Facilities: RFC 1034." (Obsoletes RFCs 973, 882, 883; updated by RFCs 1348, 1183, 1101), 1987.

MOCK87A   Mockapetris, Paul V. "Domain Names—Implementation and Specification: RFC 1035." (Obsoletes RFCs 973, 882, 883; updated by RFCs 1348, 1183, 1101), 1987.

MOOR93   Moore, K. "MIME (Multipurpose Internet Mail Extensions), Part Two: Message Header Extensions for Non-Ascii Text: RFC 1522." (Obsoletes RFC 1342), 1993.

MOOR93A   Moore, K. "SMTP Service Extension for Message Size Declaration: RFC 1427," 1993.

MOOR93B   Moore, K. "MIME Content-Types for Delivery Status Notifications." Internet Draft <draft-moore-mime-delivery-00.txt>, 1993.

MOOR93C   Moore, K. "SMTP Service Extension for Delivery Reports." Internet Draft <draft-moore-smtp-drpt-00.txt>, 1993.

MYER93   Myer, Theodore H. "Electronic Directories: A Speculative Look Ahead." Conference Presentation: Electronic Mail Association, June, 1993.

NETW93   "Exploding Growth in Options Makes It Harder to Get a Grip on Internet Access." *Network World Buyer's Guide*, July 19, 1993, pp. 31–36.

NIGH91   Nightingale, J. Stephen. *GOSIP Conformance and Interoperation Testing and Registration.* Gaithersburg, MD: National Institute of Standards and Technology GOSIP Testing Program, 1991.

NIST89   OSI Implementors Workshop, Stable Implementation Agreements, Version 3, Edition 1. Gaithersburg, MD: National Institute of Standards and Technology Special Publication 500-177, 1989.

NIST90   Trus, Steve, Curtis Royster, and Paul Markovitz. *Guidelines for the Evaluation of Message Handling Systems Implementations.* Gaithersburg, MD: National Institute of Standards and Technology Special Publication 500-182, 1990.

NIST91A   *Government Open Systems Interconnection User's Guide.* Gaithersburg, MD: National Computer and Telecommunications Laboratory, National Institute of Standards and Technology, 1991.

NIST91B   *Government Open Systems Interconnection Profile: Version 2.* Gaithersburg, MD: National Computer and Telecommunications Laboratory, National Institute of Standards and Technology, 1991.

NIST93   *Stable Implementation Agreements for Open Systems Environment Protocols: Part 7—1984 Message Handling Systems.* Gaithersburg, MD: National Computer and Telecommunications Laboratory, National Institute of Standards and Technology, 1993.

NIST93A   *Stable Implementation Agreements for Open Systems Environment Protocols: Part 8—1988 Message Handling Systems.* Gaithersburg, MD: National Computer and Telecommunications Laboratory, National Institute of Standards and Technology, 1993.

NIST93B   *Stable Implementation Agreements for Open Systems Environment Protocols: Part II—Directory Services Protocols.* Gaithersburg, MD: National Computer and Telecommunications Laboratory, National Institute of Standards and Technology, 1993.

NUSS93   "Handling of Bi-directional Texts in MIME: RFC 1556." 1993.

NUSS93A   "Hebrew Character Encoding for Internet Messages: RFC 1555." 1993.

ODA88   *CCITT Recommendations T.411 to T.418: Open Document Architecture and Interchange Format.* Blue Book. Also ISO/IEC Standards ISO 8613-1 to 8613-8 (1988).

OPEN93   "Europe Tackles X.400/Internet Integration." *OPEN: The International Newsletter of Multivendor Networking, Technologies, Trends, and Products,* Volume 6, Number 11, June 1993, pp. 1–3.

OSF91   "Distributed Computing Environment: Overview." Cambridge, MA: Open Software Foundation, 1991.

OSF91A   "Directory Services for a Distributed Computing Environment: A White Paper." Cambridge, MA: Open Software Foundation, 1991.

OSF92	"The Value of the Open Software Foundation for Users: A White Paper." Cambridge, MA: Open Software Foundation, 1991.
OUST93	Ousterhout, John. "Using Tcl and Tk for Active Messages." Conference Presentation: E-mail World, November 1993.
OVUM88	"OSI: The Commercial Benefits." London: OVUM Consultancy, 1988.
OVUM91	"The X.500 Electronic Directory: The Business Opportunity." London: OVUM Consultancy, 1991.
PART86	Partridge, C. "Mail Routing and the Domain System: RFC 974," 1986.
PCCO92	Bonner, Paul. "A Tale of Six Windows Macros." *PC Computing*, December 1992.
PEAR93	"A Rage to Reengineer." *The Washington Post*, July 25, 1993, pp. H1–H4.
PEM93A	Linn, J. "Privacy Enhancement for Internet Electronic Mail: Part I: Message Encryption and Authentication Procedures: RFC 1421." (Obsoletes RFC 1113), 1993.
PEM93B	Kent, S. "Privacy Enhancement for Internet Electronic Mail: Part II: Certificate-Based Key Management: RFC 1422." (Obsoletes RFC 1114), 1993.
PEM93C	Balenson, D. "Privacy Enhancement for Internet Electronic Mail: Part III: Algorithms, Modes, and Identifiers: RFC 1423." (Obsoletes RFC 1115), 1993.
PEM93D	Kaliski, B. "Privacy Enhancement for Internet Electronic Mail: Part IV: Key Certification and Related Services: RFC 1424," 1993.
POST82	Postel, J. "Simple Mail Transfer Protocol: RFC 821." (Obsoletes RFC 788), 1982.
POST93	Postel, J., ed. "Internet Official Protocol Standards: RFC 1540." (Obsoletes RFC 1500), 1993.
RAPP93A	Myer, Theodore H., Daniel J. Blum, and Gary J. Rowe. *The Rapport Messaging Review*, Volume 1, Number 1, October 1993.
RAPP93B	Myer, Theodore H., Daniel J. Blum, and Gary J. Rowe. *The Rapport Messaging Review*, Volume 1, Number 2, December 1993.
REAC93	"What Happened to the Promise?" Sunnyvale, CA: Reach Software Corporation, 1993.
ROSE87	Rose, Marshall, and Dwight E. Cass. "ISO Transport Service on Top of the TCP/IP: RFC 1006, Version 3: RFC 1006." (Obsoletes RFC 983), 1987.

ROSE88   Rose, M. "Post Office Protocol: Version 3: Extended Service Offerings: RFC 1082," 1988.

ROSE90   Rose, Marshall. *The Simple Book: An Introduction to Management of TCP/IP-based Internets.* Englewood Cliffs, NJ: Prentice-Hall, 1990.

ROSE91   Rose, Marshall. *The Little Black Book: Mail-bonding with OSI Directory Services.* Englewood Cliffs, NJ: Prentice-Hall, 1991.

ROSE93   Rose, M. "Post Office Protocol–Version 3: RFC 1460," 1993.

ROSE93A   Rose, M., E. Stefferud, and D. Crocker. "SMTP Service Extensions: RFC 1425," 1993.

ROSE93B   Rose, M., E. Stefferud, and D. Crocker. "SMTP Service Extensions for 8bit-MIMEtransport: RFC 1426," 1993.

ROSE93C   Rose, M. "The Content-MD5 Header Field: RFC 1544," 1993.

ROSE93D   Rose, Marshall T. *The Internet Message: Closing the Book with Electronic Mail.* New York: Prentice-Hall, 1993.

RUSK93   Rusk, Harriet J., and David J. Taylor. "EDI Integration." Conference Presentation: Electronic Mail Association, June 1993.

SCHI93   Schiller, J. "An Alternative PEM MIME Integration." Internet Draft <draft-ietf-pem-mime-alternative-00.txt, .ps>, 1993.

SEYB93   Seybold, Andrew M. "The Hype, the Reality, and the Opportunities." *E-Mail World Conference Proceedings*, November 1993.

SGFS90   *Information Technology—Framework and Taxonomy of International Standardized Profiles—Part 1: Framework.* Geneva: ISO/IEC JTC 1, 1990.

SGFS91   *Information Technology—Framework and Taxonomy of International Standardized Profiles—Part 2: Taxonomy.* Geneva: ISO/IEC JTC 1, 1991.

SIMP93   Simpson, W. "The Point-to-Point Protocol (PPP): RFC 1548" (Obsoletes RFC 1331).

SOFT89   "Electronic Mail: Technology, Applications, and Infrastructure." Soft*Switch, 1989.

SOFT93   "Electronic Mail and Knowledge Sharing Systems." A Soft*Switch White Paper.

SPIES93   Spies, Michael. "Business Process Automation: Automation and Evolution vs. 'Re-Engineering.'" Conference Presentation: Electronic Mail Association, 1993.

STOL89   Stoll, Clifford. *The Cuckoo's Egg.* New York: Doubleday, 1989.

STRE92   Strehlo, Kevin. "BeyondMail Can Help You Stamp Out E-mail Overload." *InfoWorld*, Volume 14, Issue 24, August 24, 1992.

TAPS93   Tapscott, Don, and Art Caston. *Paradigm Shift: The New Prom-
                ise of Information Technology.* New York: McGraw-Hill, Inc.,
                1993.

TRUS93   Trus, Steve, and Len Gebase. *Electronic Commerce.* Gaithers-
                burg, MD: National Institute of Standards and Technology,
                1993.

VAUD93   Vaudreuil, G. "Transition of Internet Mail from Just-Send-8 to
                8bit-SMTP/MIME: RFC 1428," 1993.

WEID93   Weider, Chris, Jim Fulton, and Simon Spero. "Architecture of
                the WHOIS++ Index Service." Internet Draft <draft-ietf-wnils-
                whois-02.txt>, 1993.

WEID93A   Weider, Chris and Peter Deutsch. "A Vision of an Integrated
                Internet Information Service." Internet Draft <draft-ietf-iiir-
                vision-01.txt>, 1993.

WEID93B   Weider, Chris. "Search Deficiencies in the X.500 Protocol and
                Its Implementations." Draft Paper, 1993.

WHEA93A   Wheatman, Victor. Inter-Enterprise Systems Research Notes:
                "1992 EDI VAN Market Shares." Stamford, CT: Gartner
                Group, 1993.

WHEA93B   Wheatman, Victor. Conference Presentation: "Strategic Plan-
                ning Assumptions." Stamford, CT: Gartner Group, 1993.

WHEA93C   Wheatman, Victor. Electronic Commerce Strategies Research
                Notes: "Evaluating the Internet for Electronic Commerce."
                Stamford, CT: Gartner Group, 1993.

WHEA93D   Wheatman, Victor. Electronic Commerce Strategies Research
                Notes: "Cautions on Using the Internet for Electronic Com-
                merce." Stamford, CT: Gartner Group, 1993.

WHIT94   White, James E. "Telescript Technology: The Foundation for
                the Electronic Marketplace." Mountainview, CA: General
                Magic, 1994.

WILS93   Wilson, Tim. "X.500 Global Directories See Progress." *Com-
                munications Week*, March 22, 1993, pp. 1 and 71–72.

WORK93   "Workflow Specialist Speaks Out." *Network World*, July 5,
                1993, pp. 27 and 31.

WORK93A   Lee, Eugene, Denis O'Neil, Thomas E. White, and Michael
                Spies. "Workflow: Process Re-engineering." Conference Pre-
                sentation: Electronic Mail Association, June, 1993.

WORK93B   Fischer, Addison M. *Workflow.2000—Electronic Documenta-
                tion Authorization in Practice.* Naples, FL: Third Millennium
                Corporation, 1993.

X1258   "Security Structures (for Managing Electronic Data Interchange): X12.58." Alexandria, VA: Data Interchange Standards Association, Version 3, Release 4, 1993.

XAPI93   "XAPIA Common Messaging Call API Available to Vendors, Companies Building Mail-Enabled Applications." Cupertino, CA: XAPIA, 1993.

XAPI93A   "Common Messaging Call Questions and Answers: 6/93." Cupertino, CA: XAPIA, 1993.

YEON93   Yeong, W., T. Howes, S. Hardcastle-Kille. "X.500 Lightweight Directory Access Protocol: RFC 1487," 1993.

List of the Frequently Used Acronyms

ACI	Access Control Information (X.500)
ACSE	Association Control Service Element (OSI)
ADDMD	Administration Directory Management Domain
ADMD	Administrative Domain (X.400)
AI	Artificial Intelligence
AIA	Aerospace Industries Association
ANSI	American National Standards Institute
AOW	Asia Oceania Workshop
AP	Administrative Point (1993 X.500)
API	American Petroleum Industry Association
API	Application Program Interface
APP	Application Portability Profile
APS	Asynchronous Protocol Specification Alliance
ARPA	Advanced Research Projects Agency
ASCII	American Standard Code for Information Interchange (IA5)
ASN.1	Abstract Syntax Notation One
AU	Access Unit (X.400)
BBS	Bulletin Board System
bcc	Blind courtesy copy

BER	Basic Encoding Rules (CCITT/ISO)
BFT	Binary File Transfer
CA	Certification Authority
CAD/CAM	Computer-aided Design/Computer-aided Manufacturing
CALS	Computer-aided Acquisition and Logistics System (U.S.), recently changed to Continuous Acquisition and Life-cycle Support
CAN	Central Administration and Naming (NADF)
cc	Courtesy copy
CCITT	International Consultative Committee on Telephony and Telegraphy (now known as the Telecommunications Standardization Sector of the ITU)
CD	Committee Draft (ISO)
CEN/CENE-LEC	Councils for Electronics Standardization (Europe)
CEPT	Council of European PTTs
CLNP	Connectionless Network Protocol (OSI)
CMC	Common Mail Calls (XAPIA)
COS	Corporation for Open Systems International
COTS	Commercial-off-the-shelf
CRL	Certificate Revocation List
CR/LF	Carriage Return/Line Feed
CTS	Conformance Testing Service (Europe)
DAP	Directory Access Protocol (X.500)
DARPA	Defense Advanced Research Projects Agency (U.S.)
DCE	Distributed Computing Environment (OSF)
DDA	Domain Defined Attribute (Internet/X.400)
DDE	Dynamic Data Exchange (Microsoft)
DDN	Defense Data Network (U.S. DoD)
DDS	Digital Directory System (DEC)
DEK	Data Encrypting Key (PEM)
DES	Data Encryption Standard
DIB	Directory Information Base (X.500)
DIS	Draft International Standard (ISO)
DISA	Defense Information Systems Agency (U.S. DoD)
DISOSS	DIStributed Office Support System (IBM)

DIT   Directory Information Tree (X.500)

DL   Distribution List (X.400)

DLL   Dynamic Link Libraries (Microsoft)

DMS   Defense Messaging System (U.S.)

DN   Distinguished Name (X.500)

DNS   Domain Name System

DoD   Department of Defense (U.S.)

DSA   Directory System Agent (X.500)

DSN   Delivery Status Notification (Internet)

DSP   Directory System Protocol (X.500)

DSS   Digital Signature Standard

DUA   Directory User Agent (X.500)

DX   Directory Exchange Protocol (Retix)

EAOG   European ADMD Operators Group

EDA   Electronic Document Authorization

EDI   Electronic Data Interchange (Electronic Commerce)

EDIFACT   Electronic Data Interchange for Administration, Commerce, and Transport

EDIUA   EDI User Agent

EEMA   European Electronic Mail Association

EFT   Electronic Funds Transfer

EMA   (North American) Electronic Mail Association

EMC   Electronic Medical Claims

EMX   Enterprise Mail Exchange (Soft*Switch)

EPHOS   European Procurement Handbook for Open Systems

EPRI   Electric Power Research Institute

ESMTP   Extended Simple Mail Transfer Protocol (Internet)

ETSI   European Technical Standards Institute

EWOS   European Workshop on Open Systems

FIPS   Federal Information Processing Standard (U.S.)

FTAM   File Transfer, Access, and Management

FTP   File Transfer Protocol (Internet)

GOSIP   Government Open Systems Interconnection Profiles (U.K. and U.S.)

GUI   Graphical User Interface

IA5	International Alphabet Number 5 (ASCII)
IAB	Internet Architecture Board
IANA	Internet Assigned Numbers Authority
IAOG	International ADMD Operators Group
IEC	International Electrotechnical Commission
IEEE	Institute of Electrical and Electronics Engineers (IEEE)
IESG	Internet Engineering Steering Group
IETF	Internet Engineering Task Force
IGOSS	Industry Government Open Systems Specification (U.S.)
IK	Interchange Key (PEM)
IMAP	Interactive Mail Access Protocol (Internet)
IP	Internet Protocol
IPM	Interpersonal Messaging
IPRA	Internet Policy Registration Authority
IRTF	Internet Research Task Force
IS	International Standard (ISO)
ISO	International Organization for Standardization
ISOC	Internet Society
ISP	International Standardized Profile (OSI)
ISV	Independent Software Vendor
ITU	International Telecommunication Union
JITC	Joint Interoperability Test Center (U.S. DoD)
LAN	Local Area Network
LDAP	Lightweight Directory Access Protocol
MAC	Message Authentication Code (security)
MAP	Manufacturing Automation Protocol
MAPI	Messaging API (Microsoft)
MAW	Microsoft At Work
MEA	Mail-enabled Application
MHS	Message Handling System (X.400); also Novell e-mail product
MIB	Management Information Base
MIC	Message Identification Code (PEM)
MIME	Multipurpose Internet Mail Extensions (Internet Mail)
MOT	Means of Testing (OSI/GOSIP conformance)

MOTIS	Message-oriented Text Interchange Service (ISO)
MS	Message Store (X.400)
MSP	Message Security Protocol (U.S. DoD)
MTA	Message Transfer Agent (X.400)
MTS	Message Transfer System
NADF	North American Directory Forum (NADF)
NDS	Network Directory Services (Novell)
NIC	Network Information Center (Internet)
NIST	National Institute of Standards and Technology (U.S.)
NLM	Network Loadable Module (Novell)
NMTS	National Message Transfer System (U.S. consortium)
Normes	European standards
NOS	Network Operating System
NSA	National Security Agency (U.S.)
NSAP	Network Service Access Point (OSI)
NVLAP	National Voluntary Accreditation Laboratory (U.S.)
OCE	Open Collaboration Environment (Apple)
ODA	Open Document Architecture (OSI)
OEM	Original Equipment Manufacturer
OID	Object Identifier (OSI, X.400, X.500)
OIW	Open Systems Environment Implementors Workshop (North America)
OLE	Object Linking and Embedding (Microsoft)
O/R	Originator/Recipient name/address (X.400)
OS	Operating System
OSF	Open Software Foundation
OSI	Open Systems Interconnection
OSTC	Open System Testing Consortium (Europe)
P1	1984 and 1988 X.400 message transfer protocol (X.400 envelope)
P2	1984 X.400 interpersonal message content type (X.400)
P22	1988 X.400 interpersonal message content type (X.400)
P3	MTA access protocol (X.400)
P7	Message Store access protocol (X.400)
PCA	Policy Certification Authority (Internet)

PCMCIA	PC Memory Card Interface Adapter (security)
PDAU	Physical Delivery Access Unit
Pedi	EDI content type (X.435)
PEM	Privacy Enhanced Mail (Internet)
PGP	Pretty Good Privacy (Internet)
PICS	Protocol Implementation Conformance Statement (OSI)
PKP	Public Key Partners
POP	Post Office Protocol (Internet)
POSI	Promotion Conference for OSI (Japan)
POSIX	Portable Operating System Interface
PPP	Point-to-Point Protocol (Internet)
PRMD	Private Management Domain (X.400)
PROFS	Professional Office System (IBM)
PTT	Post, Telephone, and Telegraph
RBOC	Regional Bell Operating Company (U.S.)
RDN	Relative Distinguished Name (X.500)
RFC	Request for Comment (Internet)
RFP	Request for Proposal
RIPE	Reseau IP Europeen (Internet)
RISC	Reduced Instruction Set Computing
RJE	Remote Job Entry (IBM)
ROS	Remote Operations Service (CCITT/ISO)
RPC	Remote Procedure Call
RPOA	Recognized Public Operating Agency
RSA	Rivest, Shamir, Adelman (digital signature algorithm)
RTS	Reliable Transfer Service (OSI)
RWCC	Regional Workshop Coordinating Committee
S0, S1, S1a, S2, S2a	OIW security profiles
SGML	Standard Graphics Markup Language
SLIP	Serial Line Internet Protocol (Internet)
SMF	Simple Message Format (Novell)
SMTP	Simple Mail Transfer Protocol
SNA	Systems Network Architecture (IBM)

SNADS	SNA Distribution Services (IBM)
SNMP	Simple Network Management Protocol
SWIFT	Society for Worldwide Interbank Financial Transactions
Tcl	Tool Command Language
TCP/IP	Transmission Control Protocol/Internet Protocol
TLI	Transport Layer Interface (UNIX)
TOP	Technical and Office Protocol
TP4	Transport Class 4 (OSI)
TSR	Terminate and Stay Resident
UA	User Agent (X.400)
UCA	Utilities Communication Architecture
UN/GTDI	United Nations Electronic Data Interchange standard
UUCP	Unix-to-Unix Copy Program (Internet)
VAN	Value-added Network
VIM	Vendor Independent Messaging (Lotus-led consortium)
WAIS	Wide Area Information Service (Internet)
WAN	Wide Area Network
WD	Working Document (ISO)
WWW	World Wide Web
X12	ANSI Electronic Data Interchange standard
X.121	Addressing standard (CCITT)
X.25	CCITT packet switching interface
X.400	CCITT Message Handling System recommendation
X.435	CCITT EDI over X.400 recommendation
X.500	CCITT Directory Services recommendation
XAPIA	X.400 Application Program Interface Association
XDS	X.500 API (XAPIA and X/OPEN)

I N D E X

463